'A warm, generous, profound book about the complications of modern humanity. Haig is one of the most important writers of our time'

'Explores how to stay sane ... orld'

'Mixing anecdotes with a ... with advice throughout, this is ... ment, and appreciate modern life without letting it overwhelm you'
Stylist

'Warm and wise. If the modern world is making you anxious, this is the perfect book for you'
CLAUDIA HAMMOND

'Matt Haig has written movingly of his struggle with depression in *Reasons to Stay Alive*, and here he tackles the anxiety that threatens to scupper his equilibrium'
Psychologies

'Look at how the world impacts on our mental health . . . Haig's approach is warm, personal and practical; the book is reassuring and inspiring'
Women & Home

'Matt Haig writes books that feel like friendships you want to keep'
JORDAN STEPHENS

'Many readers will find this book helpful. Haig's tone is kind and encouraging'
iNews

ALSO BY MATT HAIG

NOTES ON A NERVOUS PLANET

Matt Haig

CANONGATE

This paperback edition published in 2019 by Canongate Books

First published in Great Britain in 2018 by Canongate Books Ltd,
14 High Street, Edinburgh EH1 1TE

canongate.co.uk

1

British Library Cataloguing-in-Publication Data
A catalogue record for this book is available
on request from the British Library

ISBN 978 1 78689 269 0

Typeset in Granjon by Biblichor Ltd, Edinburgh

Printed and bound in Great Britain by Clays, Elcograf S.p.A.

For Andrea

Contents

'Toto, I've a feeling we're not in Kansas anymore.'

—Dorothy in *The Wizard of Oz*

I

A STRESSED-OUT MIND
IN A STRESSED-OUT WORLD

A conversation, about a year ago

I WAS STRESSED OUT.

I was walking around in circles, trying to win an argument on the internet. And Andrea was looking at me. Or I *think* Andrea was looking at me. It was hard to tell, as I was looking at my phone.

'Matt? Matt?'

'Uh. Yeah?'

'What's up?' she asked, in the kind of despairing voice that develops with marriage. Or marriage to me.

'Nothing.'

'You haven't looked up from your phone in over an hour. You're just walking around, banging into furniture.'

My heart was racing. There was a tightness in my chest. Fight or flight. I felt cornered and threatened by someone on the internet who lived over 8,000 miles away from me and who I would never meet, but who was still managing to ruin my weekend. 'I'm just getting back to something.'

'Matt, get off there.'

'I just—'

2

The thing with mental turmoil is that so many things that make you feel better in the short term make you feel worse in the long term. You distract yourself, when what you really need is to *know* yourself.

'Matt!'

An hour later, in the car, Andrea glanced at me in the passenger seat. I wasn't on my phone, but I had a tight hold of it, for security, like a nun clutching her rosary.

'Matt, are you okay?'

'Yeah. Why?'

'You look lost. You look like you used to look, when . . .'

She stopped herself saying 'when you had depression' but I knew what she meant. And besides, I could feel anxiety and depression around me. Not actually *there* but close. The memory of it something I could almost touch in the stifling air of the car.

'I'm fine,' I lied. 'I'm fine, I'm fine . . .'

Within a week I was lying on my sofa, falling into my eleventh bout of anxiety.

A life edit

I WAS SCARED. I couldn't not be. Being scared is what anxiety is all about.

The bouts were becoming closer and closer. I was worried where I was heading. It seemed there was no upper limit to despair.

I tried to distract myself out of it. However, I knew from past experience alcohol was off limits. So I did the things that had helped before to climb out of a hole. The things I forget to do in day-to-day life. I was careful about what I ate. I did yoga. I tried to meditate. I lay on the floor and placed my hand on my stomach and inhaled deeply – in, out, in, out – and noticed the stuttery rhythm of my breath.

But everything was difficult. Even choosing what to wear in the morning could make me cry. It didn't matter that I had felt like this before. A sore throat doesn't become less sore simply because you've felt it before.

I tried to read, but found it hard to concentrate.

I listened to podcasts.

I watched new Netflix shows.

I went on social media.

I tried to get on top of my work by replying to all my emails.

I woke up and clasped my phone, and prayed that whatever I could find there could take me out of myself.

But – spoiler alert – it didn't work.

I began to feel worse. And many of the 'distractions' were doing nothing but driving me further to distraction. In T.S. Eliot's phrase from his *Four Quartets*, I was 'distracted from distraction by distraction'.

I would stare at an unanswered email, with a feeling of dread, and not be able to answer it. Then, on Twitter, my go-to digital distraction of choice, I noticed my anxiety intensify. Even just passively scrolling my timeline felt like an exposure of a wound.

I read news websites – another distraction – and my mind couldn't take it. The knowledge of so much suffering in the world didn't help put my pain in perspective. It just made me feel powerless. And pathetic that my invisible woes were so paralysing when there were so many *visible* woes in the world. My despair intensified.

So I decided to do something.

I disconnected.

I chose not to look at social media for a few days. I put an auto-response on my emails, too. I stopped watching or reading the news. I didn't watch TV. I didn't watch any music videos. Even magazines I avoided. (During my initial breakdown, years before, the bright imagery of magazines always used to linger and clog my mind with feverish racing images as I tried to sleep.)

I left my phone downstairs when I went to bed. I tried to get outside more. My bedside table was cluttered with a chaos of wires and technology and books I wasn't really reading. So I tidied up and took them away, too.

In the house, I tried to lie in darkness as much as possible, the way you might deal with a migraine. I had always, since I was first suicidally ill in my twenties, understood that getting better involved a kind of life edit.

A *taking away*.

As the minimalism advocate Fumio Sasaki puts it: 'there's a happiness in having less'. In the early days of my first experience of panic the only things I had taken away were booze and cigarettes and strong coffees. Now, though, years later, I realised that a more general overload was the problem.

A life overload.

And certainly a technology overload. The only real

technology I interacted with during this present recovery – aside from the car and the cooker – were yoga videos on YouTube, which I watched with the brightness turned low.

The anxiety didn't miraculously disappear. Of course not.

Unlike my smartphone, there is no 'slide to power off' function for anxiety.

But I stopped *feeling worse*. I plateaued. And after a few days, things began to calm.

The familiar path of recovery arrived sooner rather than later. And abstaining from stimulants – not just alcohol and caffeine, but these other things – was part of the process.

I began, in short, to feel free again.

How this book came about

MOST PEOPLE KNOW the modern world can have physical effects. That, despite advances, aspects of modern life are dangerous for our bodies. Car accidents, smoking, air pollution, a sofa-dwelling lifestyle, takeaway pizza, radiation, that fourth glass of Merlot.

Even being at a laptop can pose physical dangers. Sitting down all day, getting an RSI. Once I was even told by an optician that my eye infection and blocked tear ducts were caused by staring at a screen. We blink less, apparently, when working on a computer.

So, as physical health and mental health are intertwined, couldn't the same be said about the modern world and our mental states? Couldn't aspects of how we live in the modern world be responsible for how we *feel* in the modern world?

Not just in terms of the *stuff* of modern life, but its values, too. The values that cause us to want more than we have. To worship work above play. To compare the worst bits of ourselves with the best bits of other people. To feel like we always *lack* something.

And as I grew better, by the day, I began to have an idea about a book – this book right here.

I had already written about my mental health in *Reasons to Stay Alive*. But the question now was not: *why should I stay alive?* The question this time was a broader one: *how can we live in a mad world without ourselves going mad?*

News from a nervous planet

AS I BEGAN researching I quickly found some attention-grabbing headlines for an attention-grabbing age. Of course, news is almost *designed* to stress us out. If it was designed to keep us calm it wouldn't be news. It would be yoga. Or a puppy. So there is an irony about news companies reporting on anxiety while also making us anxious.

Anyway, here are some of those headlines:

STRESS AND SOCIAL MEDIA FUEL MENTAL HEALTH CRISIS AMONG GIRLS (*The Guardian*)

CHRONIC LONELINESS IS A MODERN-DAY EPIDEMIC (*Forbes*)

FACEBOOK 'MAY MAKE YOU MISERABLE', SAYS FACEBOOK (*Sky News*)

'STEEP RISE' IN SELF-HARM AMONG TEENAGERS (BBC)

WORKPLACE STRESS AFFECTS 73 PER CENT OF EMPLOYEES (*The Australian*)

STARK RISE IN EATING DISORDERS BLAMED ON OVER-EXPOSURE TO CELEBRITIES' BODIES *(The Guardian)*

SUICIDE ON CAMPUS AND THE PRESSURE OF PERFECTION *(The New York Times)*

WORKPLACE STRESS RISING SHARPLY *(Radio New Zealand)*

WILL ROBOTS TAKE OUR CHILDREN'S JOBS? *(The New York Times)*

STRESS, HOSTILITY RISING IN AMERICAN HIGH SCHOOLS IN TRUMP ERA *(The Washington Post)*

CHILDREN IN HONG KONG ARE RAISED TO EXCEL, NOT TO BE HAPPY *(South China Morning Post)*

HIGH ANXIETY: MORE AND MORE PEOPLE ARE TODAY TURNING TO DRUGS TO DEAL WITH STRESS *(El País)*

ARMY OF THERAPISTS TO BE SENT INTO SCHOOLS TO TACKLE ANXIETY EPIDEMIC *(The Telegraph)*

IS THE INTERNET GIVING US ALL ADHD? *(The Washington Post)*

'OUR MINDS CAN BE HIJACKED': THE TECH INSIDERS WHO FEAR A SMARTPHONE DYSTOPIA *(The Guardian)*

TEENAGERS ARE GROWING MORE ANXIOUS AND DEPRESSED
(The Economist)

INSTAGRAM WORST SOCIAL MEDIA APP FOR YOUNG PEOPLE'S
MENTAL HEALTH (CNN)

WHY ARE RATES OF SUICIDE SOARING ACROSS THE PLANET?
(Alternet)

As I said, it is ironic that reading the news about how things are making us anxious and depressed actually can make us anxious, and that tells us as much as the headlines themselves.

The aim in this book isn't to say that everything is a disaster and we're all screwed, because we already have Twitter for that. No. The aim isn't even to say that the modern world has uniformly worse problems than before. In some specific ways it is getting measurably better. In figures from the World Bank, the number of people worldwide living in severe economic hardship is falling radically, with over one billion people moving out of extreme poverty in the last thirty years. And think of all the millions of children's lives around the globe saved by vaccinations. As Nicholas Kristof pointed out in a 2017 *New York Times* article, 'if just about the worst thing that can happen is for a parent to lose a child, that's about half as likely as it was in 1990.' So for all the ongoing violence and intolerance and economic injustice prevalent in our species, there are – on the most global of scales – also reasons for pride and hope.

The problem is that each age poses a unique and complex set of challenges. And while many things have improved, not all things have. Inequalities still remain. And some new problems have arisen. People often live in fear, or feel inadequate, or even suicidal, when they have – materially – more than ever.

And I am keenly aware that the oft-used approach of pointing out a list of advantages of modern life, such as health and education and average income, does not help. It is like a wagging finger telling a depressed person to count her blessings because no one has died. This book seeks to recognise that what we feel is just as important as what we have. That mental wellbeing counts as much as physical wellbeing – indeed, that it is part of physical wellbeing. And that, on these terms, something is going wrong.

If the modern world is making us feel bad, then it doesn't matter what else we have going for us, because feeling bad sucks. And feeling bad when we are told there is no reason to, well, that sucks even more.

I want this book to put these stressed-out headlines in context, and to look at how to protect ourselves in a world of potential panic. Because, whatever else we have going for ourselves, our minds are still vulnerable. Many mental health problems are quantifiably rising, and – if we believe our mental wellbeing is important – we need, quite desperately, to look at what might be behind these changes.

Mental health problems are not:

A bandwagon.
Fashionable.
A fad.
A celebrity trend.
A result of a growing awareness of mental health problems.
Always easy to talk about.
The same as they always were.

Yin to the yang

SO, IT IS a tale of two realities.

Many of us, it is true, have a lot to be grateful for in the developed world. The rise in life expectancy, the decline in infant mortality, the availability of food and shelter, the absence of major all-encompassing world wars. We have addressed many of our basic physical needs. So many of us live in relative day-to-day safety, with roofs over our heads and food on the table. But after solving some problems, are we left with others? Have some social advances brought new problems? Of course.

It sometimes feels as if we have temporarily solved the problem of scarcity and replaced it with the problem of excess.

Everywhere we look, people are seeking ways to change their lifestyles, by taking things away. Diets are the obvious example of this passion for restriction, but think also of the trend for dedicating whole months in the calendar to veganism or sobriety, and the growing desire for 'digital detoxes'. The growth in mindfulness, meditation and minimal living is a visible response to an overloaded culture. A yin to the frantic yang of 21st-century life.

Breakdown

AS I LEFT my most recent bout of anxiety behind me, I began to waver.

Maybe this was all a stupid idea.

I began to wonder if it was a bad thing to dwell on *problems*. But then I remembered that it is precisely *not* talking about problems that is itself a problem. It's what causes people to break down in their office or classroom. It's what fills up addiction units and hospitals and raises suicide figures. And in the end I decided that, for me, knowing this stuff is essential. I want to find reasons to be positive, and ways to be happy, but first you need to know the reality of the situation.

For instance, personally I need to know why I have a fear of *slowing down*, like I am the bus in *Speed* that would explode if it dropped below 50 miles per hour. I want to work out if the speed of me relates to the speed of the world.

The reason is simple, and partly selfish. I am petrified of where my mind can go, because I know where it has already been. And I also know that part of the reason I became ill in my twenties was to do with the way I was living. Hard drinking, bad sleeping, aspiring to be something I wasn't, and the pressures of society at large. I never want to fall back into that place, and so I need to be alert not only to where stress can take people, but also where it comes from. I want to know if one of the reasons I sometimes feel like I am on the brink of a breakdown is partly because the world sometimes seems on the brink of a breakdown.

Breakdown is an unspecific word, which might explain why medical professionals shy away from it these days, but at its root we understand what it conveys. The dictionary defines it as '1. A mechanical failure' and '2. A failure of a relationship or system'.

And it doesn't take too much looking to see the warning signs of a breakdown not just inside our selves, but in the wider world. It might sound dramatic to say the planet could be heading for a breakdown. But we do know beyond doubt that in all kinds of ways – technologically, environmentally, politically – the world is changing. And fast. So we need, more than ever, to know how to edit the world, so it can never break us down.

Life is beautiful (but)

LIFE IS BEAUTIFUL.

Even modern life. Maybe even *especially* modern life. We are saturated with a billion kinds of transient magic. We can pick up a device and contact people a whole hemisphere away. We can, when choosing a holiday, look at the reviews of people who stayed in our desired hotel last week. We can look at satellite images of every road in Timbuktu. When we are ill, we can go to the doctor and get antibiotics for illnesses that could once have killed us. We can go to a supermarket and buy dragon fruit from Vietnam and wine from Chile. If a politician says or does something we disagree with, it has never been easier to voice that disagreement. We can access more information, more films, more books, more *everything*, than ever before.

When, back in the 1990s, Microsoft's slogan asked, 'Where do you want to go today?' it was a rhetorical question. In the digital age, the answer is *everywhere*. Anxiety, to quote the philosopher Søren Kierkegaard, may be the 'dizziness of freedom', but all this freedom of choice really is a miracle.

But while choice is infinite, our lives have time spans. We can't live every life. We can't watch every film or read every book or visit every single place on this sweet earth. Rather than being blocked by it, we need to edit the choice in front of us. We need to find out what is good for us, and leave the rest. We don't need another world. Everything we need is here, if we give up thinking we need everything.

Invisible sharks

ONE FRUSTRATION WITH anxiety is that it is often hard to find a reason behind it. There may be no visible threat and yet you can feel utterly terrified. It's all intense suspense, no action. It's like *Jaws* without the shark.

But often there are sharks. Metaphorical, invisible sharks. Because even when we sometimes feel we are worried for no reason, the reasons are there.

'You're gonna need a bigger boat,' said Chief Brody, in *Jaws* itself.

And maybe that's the problem for us, too. Not the metaphorical sharks but our metaphorical boats. Maybe we would cope with the world better if we knew where those sharks were, and what we need to navigate the waters of life unscathed.

Crash

I SOMETIMES FEEL like my head is a computer with too many windows open. Too much clutter on the desktop. There is a metaphorical spinning rainbow wheel inside me. Disabling me. And if only I could find a way to switch off some of the frames, if only I could drag some of the clutter into the trash, then I would be fine. But which frame would I choose, when they all seem so essential? How can I stop my mind being overloaded when the world is overloaded? We can think about *anything*. And so it makes sense that we end up sometimes thinking about *everything*. We might have to, sometimes, be brave enough to switch the screens off in order to switch ourselves back on. To disconnect in order to reconnect.

Things that are faster than they used to be

Mail.
Cars.
Olympic sprinters.
News.
Processing power.
Photographs.
Scenes in movies.
Financial transactions.
Journeys.
World population growth.
The deforestation of the Amazon rainforest.
Navigation.
Technological progress.
Relationships.
Political events.
The thoughts in your head.

24/7 catastrophe

WORRY IS A small, sweet word that sounds like you could keep an eye on it. Yet worry about the future – the next ten minutes, the next ten years – is the chief obstacle I have to being able to live in and appreciate the present moment.

I am a catastrophiser. I don't simply *worry*. No. My worry has real ambition. My worry is limitless. My anxiety – even when I don't have capital-A *Anxiety* – is big enough to go anywhere. I have always found it easy to think of the worst-case scenario and dwell on it.

And I've been like this for as long as I can remember. I have gone to the doctor many times, convinced of my imminent demise because of an illness I've googled myself into having. As a child, if my mum was late picking me up from primary school it would only take about a minute for me to convince myself she had probably died in a hideous car accident. That never happened, but it's continual not-happening-ness never stopped the possibility that it *could* happen. Every moment my mother wasn't there was a moment in which she might *never* be there again.

The ability to imagine catastrophe in horrific detail, to picture the mangled metal and the spray of white-blue glass glittering on the road, occupied my mind far more than the rational idea that such a catastrophe was unlikely. If Andrea doesn't pick up her phone I can't help but think a likely scenario is that she has fallen down the stairs or maybe even spontaneously combusted. I worry that I upset people without meaning to. I worry that I don't check my privilege enough. I worry about people being in prison for crimes they didn't do. I worry about human rights abuses. I worry about prejudice and politics and pollution and the world my children and their entire generation are inheriting from us. I worry about all the species going extinct because of humans. I worry about my carbon footprint. I worry about all the pain in the world that I am not actively able to stop. I worry about how much I'm wrapped up in myself, which makes me even more wrapped up in myself.

Years before I ever had actual sex I found it easy to imagine I had AIDS, so powerful were the British Government's terrifying public awareness TV slots in the 1980s. If I eat food that tastes a little funny, I immediately imagine I will be hospitalised from food poisoning, even though I have only had food poisoning once in my life.

I can't be at an airport and not feel – and therefore *act* – suspicious.

Every new lump or ulcer or mole is a potential cancer. Every memory lapse is early-onset Alzheimer's. On and on and on. And all this is when I am feeling relatively okay. When I'm ill the catastrophising goes into overdrive.

In fact, now I think about it, that is the chief characteristic of anxiety for me. The continual imagining of how *things could get so much worse*. And it is only recently that I have been understanding how much the world feeds into this. How our mental states – whether we are actually ill or just *stressed out* – are to a degree products of social states. *And vice versa*. I want to understand what it is about this nervous planet that *gets in*.

There is a world of difference between feeling a bit stressed and being properly ill, but as with, say, hunger and starvation, the two are related in that what is bad for one (lack of food) is also bad for the other. And so, when I am well – but stressed – the things that make me feel a little bit worse are often the things that make me feel *much* worse when I am ill. What you learn when you are ill, about what hurts, can then be applied to the better times, too. Pain is one hell of a teacher.

Some more worries on top of those mentioned in the last chapter (because there are always more worries)

— *The news*.

— *Underground trains*. When I am on the tube, I imagine all the things that could go wrong. The train could get trapped in the tunnel. There could be a fire. There could be a terrorist incident. I could have a heart attack. To be fair, I once did have a legitimately terrifying experience on an underground train. I stepped off the Paris Métro and into wispy mouth-burning clouds of tear gas. There was a battle going on above ground between union workers and police, and the police had set off some tear gas a bit too close to the Métro station. I didn't know this at the time. At the time, covering my face with a scarf just to breathe, I thought it was a terrorist attack. It wasn't. But simply thinking it was one was a kind of trauma. As Montaigne put it, 'He who fears he shall suffer, already suffers what he fears.'

— *Suicide*. Although I was suicidal when I was younger, and very nearly threw myself off a cliff, in more recent times my obsession with suicide became more a fear of doing it, rather than a will to do it.

– *Other health worries*. Such as: sudden and total heart failure from a panic attack (a ludicrously improbable occurrence); a depression so annihilating I wouldn't be able to move ever again and would be stuck there for ever, as though I had gazed on the face of Medusa; cancer; heart disease (I have high cholesterol, for hereditary reasons); dying too young; dying too old; mortality in general.

– *Looks*. It is an outdated myth that men don't worry about their looks. I have worried about my looks. I used to buy *Men's Health* magazine religiously and follow the workouts in an attempt to look like the cover model. I have worried about my hair – the substance of it, the potential loss of it. I used to worry about the moles on my face. I used to stare for long periods in the mirror, as if I could convince it to change its mind. I still worry about the lines on my face, but I am getting better. It might be a strange irony that the cure for worrying about ageing is sometimes, well, *ageing*.

– *Guilt*. At times I have felt the guilt of being a less than perfect son, and husband, and citizen, and human organism. I feel guilt when I work too hard – and neglect my family – and guilt when I don't work hard enough. The guilt doesn't always have a cause, though. Sometimes it is just a feeling.

– *Inadequacy*. I worry about a lack and I worry about how I can fill it. I often sense a metaphorical void inside me that I have at various times in my life tried to fill with all kinds of stuff – alcohol, partying, tweets, prescription drugs, recreational drugs, exercise, food, work, popularity, travel, spending money, earning more money, getting published – that of course haven't fully worked. The things I have thrown in the hole have often just deepened the hole.

– *Nuclear weapons*. If nuclear weapons have been on the news – which seems to happen on increasing amount these days – I can visualise mushroom clouds through every window. The words of former US general Omar Nelson Bradley offer a chilly echo today: 'Ours is a world of nuclear giants and ethical infants. We know more about killing than we know about living.'

– *Robots*. I am only half joking. Our robotic future is a legitimate source of worry. I boycott self-service checkouts in a continual act of pro-human defiance. But the flip side is that thinking about robots sometimes makes me value the tantalising mystery of being alive.

Five reasons to be happy you are a human and not a sentient robot

1. William Shakespeare was not a robot. Emily Dickinson was not a robot. Neither was Aristotle. Or Euclid. Or Picasso. Or Mary Shelley (though she would be writing about them). Everyone you have ever loved and cared for was not a robot. Humans are amazing to other humans. And we are humans.

2. We are mysterious. We don't know why we are here. We have to craft our own meaning. A robot is designed for tasks or a set of tasks. We have been here for thousands of generations and we are still seeking answers. The mystery is tantalising.

3. Your not-so-distant ancestors wrote poems and acted courageously in wars and fell in love and danced and gazed wistfully at sunsets. A future sentient robot's ancestors will be a self-service checkout and a faulty vacuum cleaner.

4. This list actually has only four things. Just to confuse the robots. Though I did ask some online friends why

humans are better than robots, and they said all kinds of stuff: 'self-deprecating humour', 'love', 'soft skin and orgasms', 'wonder', 'empathy'. And maybe a robot could one day develop these things, but right now it is a good reminder that humans are pretty special.

Where does anxiety end and news begin?

ALL THAT CATASTROPHISING is irrational, but it has an emotional power. And it isn't just folk with anxiety who know this.

Advertisers know it.

Insurance sales people know it.

Politicians know it.

News editors know it.

Political agitators know it.

Terrorists know it.

Sex isn't really what sells. What sells is fear.

And now we don't just have to *imagine* the worst catastrophes. We can see them. Literally. The camera phone has made us all telejournalists. When something truly awful happens – a terrorist incident, a forest fire, a tsunami – people are always there to film it.

We have more food for our nightmares. We don't get our information, as people used to, from one carefully considered newspaper or TV news report. We get it from news sites and social media and email alerts. And besides,

TV news itself isn't what it used to be. Breaking news is continuous. And the more terrifying the news, the higher the ratings.

That doesn't mean all news people *want* bad news. Some do, judging from the divisive way they present it. But even the best news channels want high ratings, and over the years they work out what works and what doesn't, and compete ever harder for attention, which is why watching news can feel like watching a continuous metaphor for generalised anxiety disorder. The various split screens and talking heads and rolling banners of incessant information are a visual representation of how anxiety feels. All that conflicting chatter and noise and sensationalist drama. We can feel stressed watching the news, even on a slow news day. Because, really, there is no longer such a thing as a slow news day.

And when something truly terrible has happened the endless stream of eyewitness accounts and speculation and phone footage does not help anything. It is all sensation and no information. If you find the news severely exacerbates your state of mind, the thing to do is SWITCH IT OFF. Don't let the terror into your mind. No good is done by being paralysed and powerless in front of non-stop rolling news.

The news unconsciously mimics the way fear operates – focusing on the worst things, catastrophising, listening to an endless, repetitive stream of information on the same worrying topic. So, it can be hard to tell these days where your anxiety disorder ends and where actual news begins.

So we have to remember:

There is no shame in *not watching news*.

There is no shame in *not going on Twitter*.

There is no shame in *disconnecting*.

2

THE BIG PICTURE

'We seldom realise, for example, that our most private thoughts and emotions are not actually our own. For we think in terms of languages and images which we did not invent, but which were given to us by our society.'

—Alan Watts, *The Culture of Counter Culture: Edited Transcripts*

Life moves pretty fast

OF COURSE, IN the cosmic perspective, the whole of human history has been *fast*.

We haven't been here long. The planet is around 4.6 billion years old. Our specific and wonderful and problematic species – Homo sapiens – has only been here for 200,000 years. And it was only in the last 50,000 years that things picked up a gear. When we started wearing clothes from animal skins. When we began burying our dead as a matter of practice. When our hunting methods became more advanced.

The oldest known cave art is probably Indonesian and over 40,000 years old. In world terms that was a blink of an eye ago. But art is older than agriculture. Agriculture arrived basically yesterday.

We've only had farms for 10,000 years. And writing has only been around, as far as we know, for a minuscule 5,000 years.

Civilisation, which began in Mesopotamia (roughly Iraq and Syria on today's map), is under 4,000 years old. And once civilisation began, things *really* began to speed up. It was time to fasten our collective seat belts. Money. The first alphabet. The first musical notation system. The pyramids. Buddhism and Hinduism and Christianity and Islam and Sikhism. Socratic philosophy. The concept of democracy. Glass. Swords. Warships. Canals. Roads. Bridges. Schools. Toilet paper. Clocks. Compasses. Bombs. Eyeglasses. Mines. Guns. Better guns. Newspapers. Telescopes. The first piano. Sewing machines. Morphine. Refrigerators. Transatlantic telegraph cables. Rechargeable batteries. Telephones. Cars. Aeroplanes. Ballpoint pens. Jazz. Quiz shows. Coca-Cola. Polyester. Thermonuclear weapons. Rockets to the moon. Personal computers. Video games. Bloody *email*. The world wide web. Nanotechnology.

Whoosh.

But this change – even within the last four millennia – is not a smooth, straight upward line. It is the kind of steepening curve that would intimidate a professional skateboarder. Change may be a constant, but the rate of change is not.

How do you stay human in a world of change?

WHEN LOOKING AT triggers for mental health problems, therapists often identify an intense change in someone's life as a major factor. Change is frequently related to fear. Moving house, losing a job, getting married, an increase or decrease in income, a death in the family, a diagnosis of a health problem, turning 40, whatever. Sometimes, it doesn't even matter too much if the change is outwardly a 'good' one – having a baby, getting a promotion. The intensity of the change can be a shock to the system.

What, though, when the change isn't just a personal one?

What about when change affects everyone?

What happens when whole societies – or a whole human population – undergo a period of profound change?

What *then*?

These questions are, of course, making an assumption. The assumption is that the world is changing. How is the world changing?

Chiefly, and most measurably, the change is technological.

Yes, there are other social and political and economic and environmental changes, but technology is related to all of them, and underlies them, so let's start with that.

Of course, as a species, we humans have always been shaped by technology. It underpins everything.

Technology, in its baggiest sense, just means tools or methods. It could mean language. It could mean flints or dry sticks used to make fire. According to many anthropologists, technological progress is the most important factor driving human society.

Inventions such as man-made fire, the wheel, the plough or the printing press weren't just important for their immediate purpose but in terms of their overall impact on how societies developed.

In the 19th century, the American anthropologist Lewis H. Morgan announced that technological inventions can lead to whole new eras of humanity. He saw three phases of social evolution – savagery, barbarism and civilisation – with each one leading to the next due to technological leaps forward. This seems a bit dodgy now, I think, because it implies an increasingly questionable moral advancement from 'savages' to the 'civilised'.

Other experts have had different takes.

In the 1960s a Russian alien-hunting astrophysicist named Nikolai Kardashev thought the best way to measure progress was in terms of *information*. In the beginning there was little more than the information contained in our genes. After that came things like language and writing and books and, ultimately, *information technology*.

Nowadays, contemporary sociologists and anthropologists pretty much agree that we are heading deep into a post-industrial society, and that change is happening faster than ever.

But how fast?

According to Moore's Law – named after the co-founder of Intel, Gordon Moore, who forecast it – processing power for computers doubles every few years. This exponential doubling is the reason the small smartphone in your pocket packs way more power than the giant room-sized computers of the 1960s.

But this rapid power growth isn't just confined to computer chips. It occurs across all kinds of technological things, from bits of stored data to internet bandwidth. It all suggests that technology doesn't simply progress – its progress *speeds up*. Progress breeds progress.

Computers now help to build new computers with

increasingly small amounts of human involvement. Which means lots of people have started worrying about – or hoping for – the 'singularity'. This is the stuff of fever dreams and nightmares. The singularity is the point at which artificial intelligence becomes more intelligent than the brainiest human being. And then – depending on your inner optimism-to-pessimism ratio – either we will merge with and advance with this technology, and become immortal and happy cyborgs, *or* our sentient robots and laptops and toasters will take us over and we will be their pets or slaves or three-course meal.

Who knows?

But we are heading in one of those directions. According to world-renowned computer scientist and futurist Ray Kurzweil the singularity is near. To emphasise this point, he even wrote a bestselling book called, well, *The Singularity Is Near*.

At the dawn of this century he claimed that 'we won't experience 100 years of progress in the 21st century – it will be more like 20,000 years of progress (at today's rate)'. And Kurzweil isn't some stoned eccentric, overdosing on sci-fi movies. His predictions have a habit of coming true. For instance, back in 1990 he predicted a computer would beat a chess champion by 1998. People laughed. But then, in

1997, the greatest chess player in the world – Garry Kasparov – lost to IBM's Deep Blue computer.

And just think what has happened in the first two decades of this century. Think how fast normality has shifted.

The internet has taken over our lives. We have become increasingly attached to ever-cleverer smartphones. Human genomes can be sequenced in their thousands by machines.

Self-service checkouts are the new norm. Self-drive cars have gone from far-out prophecy to such an actual real-world business model that taxi drivers fear for their jobs.

Just think. In the year 2000, no one knew what a selfie was. Google did just about exist but it was a long way from becoming a verb. There was no YouTube, no vlogging, no Wikipedia, no WhatsApp, no Snapchat, no Skype, no Spotify, no Siri, no Facebook, no bitcoin, no tweeted gifs, no Netflix, no iPads, no 'lol' or 'ICYMI', no crying-with-laughter emoji, almost no one had sat nav, you generally looked at photographs in *albums*, and the cloud was only ever a thing which produced rain. Even writing this paragraph I sense how quickly it will date. How in a few years there will be so many embarrassing omissions from that list – so many technological brands and inventions which haven't quite arrived. Indeed, think about that. Think how shamefully dated technology becomes in a mere matter of years. Think of fax machines, and old mobile phones, and compact discs, and dial-up modems, and Betamax and VHS, and the first e-readers, and GeoCities and the AltaVista search engine.

So, regardless of what you or I think of the prospect of the singularity, there is no doubt that: a) our lives are becoming ever more technological; and b) our technology is changing at ever increasing speeds.

And, just as technology has always been the deepest root of social change, so this dizzying pace of technological change is triggering other changes. We are heading towards many alternate singularities. Many other points of no return. Maybe we have passed some without even noticing.

Ways the world is changing
that aren't entirely good

THE WORLD MAY have progressed fast in some ways, but the speed of change has not made us all very calm. And some changes, particularly those fuelled by technology, have been faster than others. For instance:

– *Politics*. The polarisation of the political right and left, fuelled in part by our social media echo chambers and gladiatorial combat zones, where compromise and common ground and objective truth seem like ever more outdated concepts. A world where, in the words of American sociologist Sherry Turkle, 'we expect more from technology and less from each other'. Where we need to share ourselves, simply to be ourselves. There have been good aspects to this change. A lot of good causes – including mental health awareness – have had their profile raised thanks to the viral nature of the internet. But, of course, not everything has been so good. The rise of fake news on social media, of politically malicious Twitter bots, and of massive online privacy breaches, has already shaped and steered our politics in strange and irreversible directions.

– *Work*. Robots and computers are taking people's jobs. Employers are taking people's weekends. Employment is becoming a dehumanising process, as if humans existed to serve work, rather than work to serve humans.

– *Social media*. The socialisation of media has rapidly taken over our lives. For those of us using it, our pages on Facebook, Twitter and Instagram are magazines of us. How healthy can that be? We are seeing ever more frequent ethical breaches, such as Cambridge Analytica's illicit harvesting of millions of psychological profiles through Facebook and the company's use of these to influence electoral results. Then there are other serious psychological concerns. To be constantly presenting ourselves, and packaging ourselves, like potatoes pretending to be crisps. To be constantly seeing everyone else looking their best, doing fun things that we are not doing.

– *Language*. The English language is changing faster than at any time in history, according to research carried out by University College London. The growth in text speak and initialisms and acronyms and emojis and gifs as communication aids shows how technological advancements influence language (think also of how, many centuries ago, the printing press led to standardisations of spelling and grammar). So, it's not just what people are saying but how they're saying it. Many millions of people now have more text message conversations than face-to-face ones. This is an unprecedented shift that has taken place within a single generation. It isn't a *bad* thing in itself, but it is definitely a *thing*.

– *Environment*. Some changes, though, are clearly bad. Straightforwardly, horrendously *bad*. The changes to our planet's environment are so grave that some scientists have put forward the idea that we – or our planet – have entered a fundamentally new phase. In 2016, at the International Geological Congress in Cape Town, leading scientists decided that we were leaving the Holocene epoch – one marked by 12,000 years of stable climate since the last Ice Age – and entering something else: the Anthropocene age, or 'new age of man'. The massive acceleration of carbon dioxide emissions, sea-level rises, the pollution of our oceans, the increase in plastic (plastic production has multiplied 20 times since the 1960s, according to the World Economic Forum), the rapid extinction of species, deforestation, industrialised farming and fishing, and urban development mean for those scientists that we have arrived at a new interval of Earth time. So, modern life is, basically, slowly killing the planet. Small wonder that such toxic societies can damage us, too.

Future tense

WHEN PROGRESS HAPPENS fast it can make the present feel like a continual future. When watching a viral clip of a human-sized back-flipping robot, it feels like reality has become science fiction.

And we are encouraged to desire this state of affairs. 'Embrace' the future and 'let go' of the past. The whole of consumerism is based on us wanting the *next thing* rather than the *present thing we already have*. This is an almost perfect recipe for unhappiness.

We are not encouraged to live in the present. We are trained to live somewhere else: the future. We are sent to kindergarten or *pre*-school, which by its very nature reminds us of what is about to hit us. *School* school. And once there, from an increasingly early age, we are encouraged to work hard so we pass tests. Eventually, these tests evolve into actual exams, which we know will dictate important future things like whether we pursue further education or decide to get a job at the age of sixteen or eighteen. Even if we go to university, it doesn't stop there. There will be more tests, more exams, more looming decisions. More *where do you see yourself in a few years' time?* More *what career path would you like to pursue?* More *think very carefully about your future.* More *it will all pay off in the long run.*

All through our education we are being taught a kind of reverse mindfulness. A kind of Future Studies where – via the guise of mathematics, or literature, or history, or computer programming, or French – we are being taught to think of a time different to the time we are in. Exam time. Job time. When-we-are-grown-up time.

To see the act of learning as something not for its own sake but because of what it will *get* you reduces the wonder of humanity. We are thinking, feeling, art-making, knowledge-hungry, marvellous animals, who understand ourselves and our world through the act of learning. It is an end in itself. It has far more to offer than the things it lets us write on application forms. It is a way to love living right now.

I am coming to realise how wrong many of my aspirations have been. How locked out of the present I have found myself. How I have always wanted *more* of whatever was in front of me. I need to find a way to stay still, in the present, and, as my nan used to say, *be happy with what you have.*

Goalposts

YOU WILL BE happy when you get good grades.

You will be happy when you go to university. You will be happy when you go to the *right* university. You will be happy when you get a job. You will be happy when you get a pay rise. You will be happy when you get a promotion. You will be happy when you can work for yourself. You will be happy when you are rich. You will be happy when you own an olive grove in Sardinia.

You will be happy when someone looks at you *that way*. You will be happy when you are in a relationship. You will be happy when you get married. You will be happy when you have children. You will be happy when your children are exactly the kind of children you want them to be.

You will be happy when you leave home. You will be happy when you buy a house. You will be happy when you pay off the mortgage. You will be happy when you have a bigger garden. In the countryside. With nice neighbours who invite you to barbecues on sunny Saturdays in July, with your children playing together in the warm breeze.

You will be happy to sing. You will be happy to sing in front of a crowd. You will be happy when your Grammy-winning debut album is number one in 32 countries, including Latvia.

You will be happy to write. You will be happy to be published. You will be happy to be published *again*. You will be happy to have a bestseller. You will be happy to have a number *one* bestseller. You will be happy when they turn your book into a movie. You will be happy when they turn it into a *great* movie. You will be happy when you are J.K. Rowling.

You will be happy when people like you. You will be happy when *more* people like you. You will be happy when *everyone* likes you. You will be happy when people *dream* of you.

You will be happy to look okay. You will be happy to turn heads. You will be happy with smoother skin. You will be happy with a flat stomach. You will be happy with a six-pack. You will be happy with an eight-pack. You will be happy when every photo of yourself gets 10,000 likes on Instagram.

You will be happy when you have transcended earthly woes. You will be happy when you are at one with the universe. You will be happy when you are the universe.

You will be happy when you are a god. You will be happy when you are the god to rule all gods. You will be happy when you are Zeus. In the clouds above Mount Olympus, commanding the sky.

Maybe. Maybe.

Maybe.

Maybe

MAYBE HAPPINESS IS not about us, as individuals. Maybe it is not something that arrives *into* us. Maybe happiness is felt heading out, not in. Maybe happiness is not about what we deserve *because we're worth it*. Maybe happiness is not about what we can *get*. Maybe happiness is about what we already *have*. Maybe happiness is about what we can *give*. Maybe happiness is not a butterfly we can catch with a net. Maybe there is no certain way to be happy. Maybe there are only maybes. If (as Emily Dickinson said) 'Forever – is composed of Nows –', maybe the nows are made of maybes. Maybe the point of life is to give up certainty and to embrace life's beautiful uncertainty.

3

A FEELING IS
NOT YOUR FACE

*'It's such a weird thing for young people to look at distorted
images of things they should be.'*

—Daisy Ridley, on why she quit Instagram

Unhappy beauties

NEVER IN HUMAN history have so many products and services been available to make ourselves achieve the goal of looking more young and attractive.

Day creams, night creams, neck creams, hand creams, exfoliators, spray tans, mascaras, anti-age serums, cellulite creams, face masks, concealers, shaving creams, beard trimmers, foundations, lipsticks, home waxing kits, recovery oils, pore correctors, eyeliners, Botox, manicures, pedicures, microdermabrasion (a strange cross between modern exfoliation and medieval torture, by the sound of it), mud baths, seaweed wraps and full-blown plastic surgery. There are facial-hair trimmers and nose-hair trimmers and pubic-hair trimmers (or 'body groomers'). You can even bleach your anus if the mood so takes you. ('Intimate bleaching' is a thriving sub-market.)

In this age of the beauty blog and make-up vlogger and online workout instructor, there has never been such a plethora of advice on looking good. We are bombarded with diet books, and gym memberships, and 'dream abs' workouts and 'action hero' workouts and 'face yoga' videos we can access via YouTube. And there are ever more digital apps and filters to enhance what the products can't. If we so desire we can make ourselves into our own unrealistic aspirations and create an ever wider gap between what we can see in a mirror and what we can digitally enhance. Women – and increasingly men – are doing more than ever to improve their appearance.

Yet, despite all our new methods and tricks to look better, a lot of us remain unhappy with our looks. The largest global study of its kind, conducted by research group GfK and published in *Time* magazine back in 2015, suggested that millions of people were not satisfied with how they look. In Japan, for instance, 38 per cent of people were found to be seriously unhappy about their appearance. The interesting thing about the survey was that it showed that how you feel about your looks is surprisingly far more determined by the nation in which you live than by, say, your gender. In fact, all over the world, levels of anxiety about how you look are moving towards being as high in men as they are in women.

If you are Mexican or Turkish, you are likely to be fine about what you see in the mirror, as over 70 per cent of people there are 'completely satisfied' or 'fairly satisfied' with their looks. People in Japan, Britain, Russia and South Korea were much more likely to be miserable.

So why are so many people – with the exception of Mexicans and Turkish people – unhappy with their looks? A few reasons, it seems:

1. While we have an increased ability to look better than ever before, we also have much higher standards of what we want to look like.

2. We are bombarded with more images of conventionally beautiful people than ever before. Not just via TV and cinema screens and billboards, but via social media, where everyone presents their best, most filtered selves to show the world.

3. As people become more neurotic generally, worries about appearance increase. According to the authors of another survey (for the American National Center for Biotechnology Information in 2017), people who were unhappy with their looks had 'higher neuroticism, more preoccupied and fearful attachment styles and spent more hours watching television'.

4. Our looks are presented as one of the problems that can be fixed by spending money (on cosmetics, fitness magazines, the right food, gym membership, whatever).

But this is not true. And besides, looking convention-ally attractive does not make you stop worrying about your looks. There are as many good-looking people in Japan and Russia as Mexico and Turkey. And, of course, many very good-looking people – models, for instance – are more worried about their looks than people who don't walk down catwalks for a living.

5. We still aren't immortal. All these products aiming to make us look younger and glowing and less death-like are not addressing the root problem. They can't actually make us younger. Clarins and Clinique have produced a ton of anti-ageing creams and yet the people who use them are still going to age. They are just – thanks in part to the billion-dollar marketing campaigns aimed at making us ashamed of wrinkles and lines and ageing – a bit more worried about it. The pursuit of looking young accentuates the fear of growing old. So maybe if we embraced growing old, embraced our wrinkles and other people's wrinkles, maybe marketers would have less fear to work with and magnify.

Insecurity is not about your face

I USED TO be the tallest boy in my school and skinny as a rake. I binge-ate and drank beer just to get bigger. I probably had a bit of body dysmorphia, I now realise. I was unhappy in my own skin. And *with* my own skin. I used to do sets of 50 press-ups, wincing through the pain, trying to look like Jean-Claude Van Damme. Not just disliking my body, actively *hating* it. A real intense physical shame that sometimes people imagine only girls and women can feel. I wish I could go back through time and tell myself, *Stop this. None of this matters. Chill out.*

I once hated a mole on my face so much that, as a teenager, I took a toothbrush to it and tried to scrub it off. But the problem was never the mole. The problem was that I was viewing my own face through the prism of my insecurity. I like that mole now. I have no idea why it used to trouble me so much, why I would stare at it in the mirror, wishing it into non-existence.

As Hamlet said to Rosencrantz, 'there is nothing either good or bad, but thinking makes it so'. He was talking about Denmark. But it applies to our looks, too. People might be encouraged to feel inadequate, but they don't have to, as soon as they realise that the *feeling* is separate from the *thing* they are worried about. So, while there is a lot of awareness about the dangers of obesity, there seems to be less awareness of the other kind of problems with our physical appearance. If we are feeling bad about our looks, sometimes the thing we need to address is the feeling, not our actual physical appearance.

Professor Pamela Keel of Florida State University has spent her career studying eating disorders and issues around female and male body image, and concludes that changing the way you look is never going to solve unhappiness about your looks. 'What is really going to make you happier and healthier?' she wondered at the start of 2018, presenting her latest research findings. 'Losing ten pounds or losing harmful attitudes about your body?' And when people feel less pressure about how their bodies look, it's not just minds that benefit, but bodies too. 'When people feel good about their bodies, they are more likely to take better care of themselves rather than treating their bodies like an enemy, or even worse, an object. That's a powerful reason to rethink the kind of New Year's resolutions we make.'

This might explain why rates of obesity are themselves dangerously rising. If we were happier with our bodies, we'd be kinder to them.

Just as being overly anxious about money can paradoxically result in compulsive spending, so worrying about our bodies is no guarantee we'll have better bodies.

The pressure on people to worry about how they look, to eat 'clean', to consider things like thigh gaps, to have 'beach ready' bodies, has been traditionally very gender-focused, with advertisers putting much more pressure on women. And even now, as increasing numbers of men feel the pressure to look a way that is not how most men naturally look, to have gym-defined bodies, to be ashamed of their physical flaws, to look good in selfies, to worry about their hair going grey or falling out, the pressure on women to fret about their appearance has never been greater. Instead of trying to reduce women's appearance-related anxiety, we are raising men's appearance-related anxiety. In some areas, in some kind of distorted idea of equality, we seem to be trying to make everyone equally anxious, rather than equally free.

Just a moment ago, as I looked at Twitter, I saw someone retweet an article from the *New York Post* captioned 'Male sex dolls with bionic penises will be here before

2019'. There is a picture of these sex dolls – hairless and impossibly toned bodies, complete with hair that will never fall out and penises that will never fail to be erect. Of course, inevitably, bionic female sex robots are being advanced, too, with even greater zeal. Now, wanting to look like a photoshopped model on the cover of a magazine is one thing. But will the next stage be wanting to look as blandly perfect as an android or robot? We might as well try to catch rainbows.

'In nature,' wrote Alice Walker, 'nothing is perfect and everything is perfect. Trees can be contorted, bent in weird ways, and they're still beautiful.' Our bodies will never be as firm and symmetrical and ageless as those of bionic sex robots, so we need quite quickly to learn how to be happy with not having society's unrealistic version of the 'best' body, and a bit happier with having *our* body, as it is, not least because being unhappy with our body doesn't make us look any better. It just makes us feel a lot worse. We are infinitely better than the most perfect-looking bionic sex robots. We are humans. Let's not be ashamed to look like them.

A note from the beach

Hello.

I am the beach.

I am created by waves and currents.

I am made of eroded rocks.

I exist next to the sea.

I have been around for millions of years.

I was around at the dawn of life itself.

And I have to tell you something.

I don't care about your body.

I am a beach.

I literally don't give a fuck.

I am entirely indifferent to your body mass index.

I am not impressed that your abdominal muscles are visible to the naked eye.

I am oblivious.

You are one of 200,000 generations of human beings.

I have seen them all.

I will see all the generations that come after you, too.

It won't be as many. I'm sorry.

I hear the whispers the sea tells me.

(The sea hates you. The *poisoners*. That's what it calls you. A bit melodramatic, I know. But that's the sea for you. All drama.)

And I have to tell you something else.

Even the other people on the beach don't care about your body.

They don't.

They are staring at the sea, or they are obsessed with *their own* appearance.

And if they *are* thinking about you, why do you care? Why do you humans worry so much about a stranger's opinion?

Why don't you do what I do? Let it wash all over you. Allow yourself just to be *as you are*.

Just be.

Just beach.

How to stop worrying about ageing

1. Understand that old people aren't actually that worried about old age, according to numerous surveys. The most recent one I can find was undertaken by American research firm NORC in 2016. It polled over 3,000 adults and found that old people are more optimistic about growing old than younger adults: 46 per cent of thirty-somethings said they were optimistic about ageing, compared to 66 per cent for the seventy pluses. It seems that worrying about growing old is a sign you are young. And the main reason to be optimistic about old age is that old people themselves are. Resilience seems to grow.

2. It happens. Ageing is something we can't do much about. We can eat healthily, exercise and live sensibly but we will still *age*. Our 80th birthday will still be on the same date. Sure, we can make it more likely we will reach 80, but we can't stop the wheels of time. And the certainty is actually quite reassuring. When there is nothing we can do about something, the point of worry begins to diminish. 'Everybody dies,' wrote Nora

Ephron. 'There's nothing you can do about it. Whether or not you eat six almonds a day.'

3. The problems you associate with old age might not be the problems you have. You aren't Nostradamus. You don't know what you will be like when you are old. You don't know, for instance, if your mind will decline or if it will shine ever brighter, like Matisse, who produced some of his best works of art in his eighties.

4. The future isn't real. The future is abstract. The now is all we know. One now after another now. The now is where we must live. There are billions of different versions of an older you. There is one version of the present you. Focus on that.

5. You will regret the fear. In *The Top Five Regrets of the Dying,* Bronnie Ware – a nurse who worked in palliative care – shared her experience of talking to those near the end of their lives. Far and away the biggest regret they had was *fear.* Many of Bronnie's patients were in deep anguish that they had spent their whole lives worrying. Lives consumed by fear. Worrying what other people thought of them. A worry that had stopped them being true to themselves.

6. Embrace, don't resist. The way to get rid of age anxiety might be the way you get rid of all anxiety. By

acceptance, not *denial*. Don't fight it, feel it. Maybe don't inject yourself with Botox. Do some knifeless mental surgery instead. Reframe your idea of beauty. Be a rebel against marketing. Look forward to being the wise elder. Be the complex elegance of a melting candle. Be a map with 10,000 roads. Be the orange at sunset that outclasses the pink of sunrise. Be the self that dares to be true.

4
NOTES ON TIME

Fear and time

'THE ONLY THING we have to fear is fear itself.' That phrase, first uttered by Franklin D. Roosevelt in 1932 during his inaugural speech as president, is probably the one I have thought about most in my life. It used to taunt me, during my first bout of panic disorder. Fear is enough, I used to think. The words have also been in my mind while writing this book. Like 'time heals' and all the best clichés, it has become a cliché for good reason – it has the power of truth.

When I think about my own fears, most of them are to do with time itself. I worry about ageing. I worry about our children ageing. I worry about the future. I worry about losing people. I worry I am late with my work. Even writing this book I worry I will fall behind dead-line. I worry about the time I have spent unwisely. The time I have spent ill. And, while researching, I began to wonder about whether our concept of time is itself temporal. Has our attitude to time changed? Is the way to be free from fear to come to a new relationship with the tick-tock of minutes and hours and years? I feel if I can begin to understand the way my mind – and maybe your mind – reacts to the modern world, I need to look at time itself.

Stop the clocks

WE DIDN'T ALWAYS have clocks. For most of human history the concept of, say, 'a quarter to five' or 'four forty-five' would have been meaningless.

No one has ever found a Neolithic cave painting of someone waking up stressed because they slept through their alarm and missed their nine o'clock management meeting. Once upon a time, there were really just two times. Day and night. Light and dark. Awake and asleep. Of course, there were other times, too. There were meal times and hunting times and times to fight and times to relax and times to play and times to kiss, but these times weren't dictated artificially by clocks and their numbers and endless partitions.

When time-keeping methods were first used they typically still kept this dual structure sacred. After all, when the Ancient Egyptians looked at the shadows from their time-telling obelisks, or when the Romans looked at their sundials, they could only do so in daylight. Even when mechanical clocks first appeared in Europe in the early

14th century, on things like churches, they were quite casual affairs. They generally didn't have minute hands, for instance, and couldn't be seen from most bedroom windows.

Pocket watches first came about during the 16th century and, like so many consumer desirables, were exclusive status symbols to begin with – novelties for the nobility. A fancy pocket watch in the middle of that century cost in the region of £15, which was more than a farm labourer earned in a year. All that for a watch that didn't even have a minute hand. It was, however, the pocket watch that seemed to make people become a bit antsier about time. Or, at least, antsier about *checking* the time.

When the diarist Samuel Pepys first treated himself to a pocket watch – 'a very fine [one] it is' – in London in 1665 he quickly realised – like so many modern internet users – that having access to information gives you one kind of freedom at the expense of another. He wrote in his diary on 13 May:

But, Lord! to see how much of my old folly and childishness hangs upon me still that I cannot forbear carrying my watch in my hand in the coach all this afternoon, and seeing what o'clock it is one hundred times; and am apt to think with

myself, how could I be so long without one; though I remember since, I had one, and found it a trouble, and resolved to
carry one no more about me while I lived.

Surely anyone who has ever had a smartphone or a Twitter
account can relate to such compulsive behaviour. Check,
check, check, and once more, just to see. When the ability
to check something turns into the compulsion to do so, we
often find ourselves craving the time before, when there
was no ability to check in the first place.

The thing is, Pepys' pocket watch wasn't even very
good. It wasn't even *quite* good. It was a very crap piece of
tech for a year's salary. But no pocket watch in 1665 was
good, at least not at telling the time. It wasn't until a
decade later with the invention of the hairspring, which
controlled the speed of the watch's balance wheel, that
even vaguely accurate pocket watches were possible.

Since then, of course, our ways of measuring time have
become ever more advanced. We are now in the age of
atomic clocks. These are incredibly, intimidatingly accurate clocks. For instance, in 2016, physicists in Germany
built a clock so accurate that it won't lose or gain a second
for 15 billion years. German physicists now have no excuse
for being late for anything ever again.

We are too aware of numerical time and not aware enough of natural time. People for thousands of years may have woken up at seven in the morning. The difference with these last few centuries is that now we are waking up *because* it is seven in the morning. We go to school or college or work at a certain time of day, not because that feels the most natural time to do so, but because that is the time that has been given to us. We have handed over our instincts to the hands of a clock. Increasingly, we serve time rather than time serving us. We fret about time. We wonder where time has gone. We are obsessed with time.

A phone call

'MATTHEW?' IT'S MY mum. She is the only one who ever calls me Matthew.

'Yeah.'

'Were you listening to what I was saying?'

'Um. Yeah. Something about going to the doctor . . .'

Shamefully, I hadn't been listening. I was staring at an email I was halfway through writing. So, I change strategy. I tell her the truth.

'I'm sorry. I'm just on the laptop. I'm very busy. I seem to have no time at all at the moment . . .'

Mum sighs, and I hear the sigh instantaneously, even though she is 200 miles away. 'I know the feeling.'

We need the time we already have

THE THING IS, we should have more time than ever. I mean, think about it. Life expectancy has more than doubled for people living in the developed world during the last century. And not only that, we have more time-saving devices and technologies than ever before existed.

Emails are faster than letters. Electric heaters are faster than fires. Washing machines are speedier than hand-washing over a sink or a river. Once laborious processes like waiting for your hair to dry or travelling ten miles or boiling water or searching through data now take next to no time at all. We have time- and effort-saving things like tractors and cars and washing machines and production lines and microwave ovens.

And yet, for a lot of our lives we feel rushed off our feet. We say things like 'I'd love to read more/learn a musical instrument/go to the gym/do some charity work/cook my own meals/grow strawberries/see my old school friends/train for a marathon . . . *if only I had the time*.'

We often find ourselves wishing for more hours in the day, but that wouldn't help anything. The problem, clearly, isn't that we have a shortage of time. It's more that we have an overload of *everything else*.

Remember

Feeling you have no time doesn't mean you have no time.

Feeling you are ugly doesn't mean you are ugly.

Feeling anxious doesn't mean you need to be anxious.

Feeling you haven't achieved enough doesn't mean you haven't achieved enough.

Feeling you lack things doesn't make you less complete.

5

LIFE OVERLOAD

An excess of everything

THERE IS, IN the current world, an excess of *everything*.

Think of just one single category of thing.

Think, say, of the thing you are holding – a book.

There are *a lot* of books. You have, for whatever reason, chosen to read this one, for which I sincerely thank you. But while you are reading this book you might also be painfully aware that you aren't reading other books. And I don't want to stress you out too much but there are *a lot* of other books. The website Mental Floss, relying heavily on data from Google, calculated there were – at a conservative estimate – 134,021,533 books in existence, but that was halfway through 2016. There are many millions more now. And anyway, 134,021,533 is still, technically, *a lot*.

It wasn't always like this.

We didn't always have so many books, and there was an obvious reason. Before printing presses books had to be made by hand, written on surfaces of clay, papyrus, wax or parchment.

Even after the printing press was invented there wasn't that much stuff to read. A book club in England in the early 16th century would have struggled as there were only around 40 different books published a year, according to figures from the British Library. An avid reader could therefore quite easily keep up with every book that was published.

'So, what are ye all reading?' a hypothetical member of the hypothetical book club would ask.

'Whatever there is, Cedric,' would be the reply.

However, the situation changed quite quickly. By the year 1600 there were around 400 different titles being published per year in England – a tenfold increase on the previous century.

Although it is said that the poet Samuel Taylor Coleridge was the last person who read everything, this is a technical impossibility as he died in 1834, when there were already millions of books in existence. However, what is interesting is that people of the time could *believe* it was possible to read everything. No one could believe such a thing now.

We all know that, even if we break the world record for speed reading, the number of books we read will only ever be a minuscule fraction of the books in existence. We are drowning in books just as we are drowning in TV shows. And yet we can only read one book – and watch one TV show – at a time. We have multiplied everything, but we are still individual selves. There is only one of us. And we are all smaller than an internet. To enjoy life, we might have to stop thinking about what we will never be able to read and watch and say and do, and start to think of how to enjoy the world within our boundaries. To live on a human scale. To focus on the few things we can do, rather than the millions of things we can't. To not crave parallel lives. To find a smaller mathematics. To be a proud and singular one. An indivisible prime.

The world is having a panic attack

PANIC IS A kind of overload.

That is how my panic attacks used to feel. An excess of thought and fear. An overloaded mind reaches a breaking point and the panic floods in. Because that overload makes you feel trapped. Psychologically boxed in. That is why panic attacks often happen in over-stimulating environments. Supermarkets and nightclubs and theatres and overcrowded trains.

But what happens when overload becomes a central characteristic of modern life? Consumer overload. Work overload. Environmental overload. News overload. Information overload.

The challenge today, then, is not that life is necessarily worse than it once was. In many ways, human lives have the potential to be better and healthier and even happier than in eras past. The trouble is our lives are also cluttered. The challenge is to find who we are amid the crowd of ourselves.

Places I have had
panic attacks

Supermarkets.

The windowless basement floor of a department store.

A packed music festival.

At a nightclub.

On an aeroplane.

On the London underground.

In a tapas bar in Seville.

In the *BBC News* green room.

On a train from London to York (it lasted most of the journey).

In a cinema.

In a theatre.

At a corner shop.

On a stage, feeling unnatural, with a thousand faces staring at me.

Walking through Covent Garden.

Watching the TV.

At home, very late at night, after a busy day, with a

streetlight glowing an ominous orange through the curtains.

In a bank.

In front of a computer screen.

A nervous planet

'IMAGINE IF THE world didn't simply make people mad,' a friend said to me recently, after I'd told him about the book I was trying to write. 'Imagine if the world was itself mad. Or, you know, the bits of the world to do with us. Humans. I mean, what if it is *literally mad*. I think that's what is happening. I think human society is breaking down.'

'Yes. Like a patient having a nervous breakdown.'

'Yeah. I mean, obviously the world isn't a person. But it is increasingly connected, like you say – like a nervous system. Been like that a while, in fact. There was a guy I was reading about, in the 19th century. He said that all the telegraph cables were like a nervous system.'

On further research, I found the man was called Charles Tilston Bright – the man in charge of the first transatlantic telegraph cable. He referred to the global telegraph network as 'the world's system of electrical nerves'.

We no longer have telegraphs as such, as they didn't prove too good at posting ninja cat videos and emojis.

But the world's nervous system has not gone away. It has evolved in scale and complexity to the extent that, since June 2017, over half the world's population is connected to the internet, according to figures from the United Nations International Telecommunications Union (which, incidentally, used to be the International *Telegraph* Union).

The number of internet users has been growing rapidly, year by year. It's wild to think that back in 1995 comparatively no one was on the internet: 16 million people, just 0.4 per cent of the world population. A decade later, in 2005, it was up to a billion people, which meant 15 per cent of the world's population was online. And by 2017 those digits flipped to 51 per cent.

In that same year the number of active Facebook users – people who use Facebook at least once a month – reached *2.07 billion*. At the start of this decade, back in 2010, there weren't even that many people on the entire internet. This is a *rapid* amount of change. It has happened because many parts of the world have 'modernised' and have changed their infrastructure quickly to make way for broadband internet. The other factor is the rise of the smartphone, which has made accessing the internet far easier than it used to be.

And it's not just the amount of people who use the internet that is rising, the amount of time we spend online is rising too.

Human beings are more connected via technology than ever before, and this radical change has happened in little over a decade. And, if nothing else, it's leading to a lot of arguments online. As Tolstoy wrote, back in 1894, in *The Kingdom of God Is Within You*:

> The more men are freed from privation; the more telegraphs, telephones, books, papers, and journals there are; the more means there will be of diffusing inconsistent lies and hypocrisies, and the more disunited and consequently miserable will men become, which indeed is what we see actually taking place.

And things are happening too quickly for us to take stock of it all. Certainly quicker than in Tolstoy's time. All this falling out. All this information. All this technological connection. The world's brain is a common but fitting metaphor. We are the nerve cells of the world's brain, transmitting ourselves to all the other nerve cells. Sending the overload back and forth. Overloaded neurons on a nervous planet. Ready to crash.

6

INTERNET ANXIETIES

'The Internet is the first thing that humanity has built that humanity doesn't understand, the largest experiment in anarchy that we have ever had.'

—Eric Schmidt, former CEO of Google

'A handful of people, working at a handful of technology companies, through their choices will steer what a billion people are thinking today . . . I don't know a more urgent problem than this . . . It's changing our democracy, and it's changing our ability to have the conversations and relationships that we want with each other.'

—Tristan Harris, former Google employee

Things I love about
the internet

Collective action against social injustice.

Watching old pop videos I had forgotten about.

Watching movie trailers without having to be in a cinema.

Wikipedia, Spotify, BBC Good Food recipes.

The process of researching a trip away.

Goodreads.

Finding people who understand what you feel like when you are low.

Talking to readers I would otherwise never talk to.

Friendliness, which does happen quite a lot.

Watching videos of animals doing incredible things (a gorilla dancing in a pool, an octopus opening a jar).

Being able to go up to people via email or a message in a way I wouldn't be able to in real life.

Funny tweets.

Staying in touch with old friends.

The ability to test out ideas with people.

Really good yoga instructors from Austin, Texas, whose practices I can follow without living in Austin, Texas.

Equally good cool-down stretch running videos.

Researching the downsides of the internet, via the internet.

Things I should do less
of on the internet

Post about a meaningful experience, when I could be having
an actual meaningful experience.

Write tweets containing opinions that will win nobody
over.

Click on articles I don't really want to read.

Browse my Twitter feed when I should be eating breakfast.

Read my Amazon reviews.

Compare my life to the lives of other people.

Stare at emails without answering them.

Answer emails while I should be listening to my mum talk
about her trip to see a doctor.

Feel the empty joy of likes and favourites.

Search my own name.

Click off videos for songs I like on YouTube without waiting until the end, because I have seen another video
I like.

Google symptoms and self-diagnose (just because you are a
hypochondriac it doesn't mean you aren't actually dying).

Google things – *any* things ('number of atoms in a human body', 'turmeric health benefits', 'cast of *West Side Story*', 'how to download photos from iCloud') – after midnight.

Check how a tweet/photo/status update is going down (and keep checking).

Want to go offline, without going offline.

The world is shrinking

LIFE OVERLOAD IS a feeling that partly stems from how contracted and concentrated the world seems to have become. The human world has sped up and has effectively shrunk, too. It is becoming more connected, and as it becomes more connected, so are we. The 'hive mind' – first coined in a science fiction short story, 'Second Night of Summer' by James H. Schmitz, in 1950 – is now a reality. Our lives, information and emotions are connected in ways they have never been before. The internet is unifying even as it seems to divide.

This shrinking of the world hasn't been an overnight process. Humans have been communicating further than their voices allow for centuries. Using everything from smoke signals to drums to pigeons. A chain of signal beacons from Plymouth to London announced the arrival of the Spanish Armada.

In the 19th century the electrical telegraph connected continents.

Then the global nervous system evolved with the telephone, radio, television and, of course, the internet.

These connections are, in many ways, making us ever closer. We can email or text or Skype or Facetime or play multiplayer online games in real time with people 10,000 miles away. Physical distance is increasingly irrelevant. Social media has enabled collective action like never before, from riots to revolutions to shock election results. The internet has enabled us to join together and make change happen. For better and for worse.

The trouble is that if we are plugged in to a vast nervous system, our happiness – and misery – is more collective than ever. The group's emotions become our own.

Mass hysterics

THERE ARE THOUSANDS of examples in history of individuals getting their emotions influenced by the crowd, from the Salem witch trials to Beatlemania.

One of the most amusing/frightening examples is the case of the French convent in the 15th century where a nun began to miaow like a cat. Pretty soon, other nuns started to miaow, too. And within a few months the nearby villagers were startled to hear *all* the nuns miaowing for several hours a day in a loud cat chorus. They only stopped miaowing when the local authorities threatened to whip them.

There are other odd examples. Such as the Dancing Plague of 1518, where, over the course of a month, 400 people in Strasbourg danced themselves to the point of collapse – and in some cases death – for no understandable reason. No music was even playing.

Or during the Napoleonic Wars when, legend has it, the inhabitants of Hartlepool, England, collectively convinced themselves that a shipwrecked monkey was a French spy and hanged the poor, confused primate. Fake news has been around for a while.

And now, of course, we have a technology – the internet – that makes collective group behaviour more possible and more likely. Different things – songs, tweets, cat videos – go viral on a daily, or hourly, basis. The word 'viral' is perfect at describing the contagious effect caused by the combination of human nature and technology. And, of course, it isn't just videos and products and tweets that can be contagious. Emotions can be, too.

A completely connected world has the potential to go mad, all at once.

Baby steps

IT WAS THE same again. 'Matt, get off the internet.'

Andrea was right, and she was only looking after me, but I didn't want to hear it.

'It's fine.'

'It's not fine. You're having an argument with someone. You're writing a book about how to cope with the stress of the internet and you're getting stressed on the internet.'

'That's not really what it's about. I'm trying to understand how our minds are affected by modernity. I'm writing about the world *as a nervous planet*. How our psychology is connected. I'm writing about all aspects of a—'

She held up her palm. 'Okay. I don't want the TED talk.'

I sighed. 'I'm just getting back to an email.'

'No. No, you aren't.'

'Okay. I'm on Twitter. But there's one point I've just got to get across—'

'Matt, it's up to you. But I thought the whole idea was that you were doing all this to try to work out how not to get like this.'

'Like what?'

'So wrapped up in stuff you shouldn't be wrapped up in. I just don't want you ill. This is how you get ill. That's all.'

She left the room. I stared at the tweet I was about to post. It wasn't going to add anything to my life. Or anyone else's life. It was just going to lead to more checking of my phone, like Pepys with his pocket watch. I pressed delete, and felt a strange relief as I watched each letter disappear.

An ode to social media

When anger trawls the internet,
Looking for a hook;
It's time to disconnect,
And go and read a book.

Mirrors

NEUROBIOLOGISTS HAVE IDENTIFIED 'mirroring' as one of the neural routes activated in the brains of primates – including us – during interaction with others.

In a connected age, the mirrors get bigger.

When people feel scared after a horrific event, that fear spreads like a digital wildfire.

When people feel angry, that anger breeds.

Even when people with contradictory opinions to us exhibit an emotion, we can feel a similar one. For instance, if someone is furious at you online for something, you are unlikely to adopt their opinion but it is quite likely you will catch their fury. You see it every day on social media: people arguing with each other, entrenching each other's opposing view, yet also mirroring each other's emotional state.

I have done this many times, which is why Andrea was frustrated with me. I have become embroiled in some argument with someone who has called me a 'snowflake' or 'libtard' or who has tweet-shouted 'LIBERALISM IS A MENTAL DISORDER' at me. I kind of know that arguing with people online is not the most fulfilling way to spend our limited days on this earth and yet I have done it, without much control. I recognise this now. And I need to stop it.

Anyway, my point is that while I am politically very different to the people I argue with, psychologically we are fuelling each other with the same feelings of anger. Political opposition but emotional mirroring.

I once tweeted something silly in a state of anxiety.

'Anxiety is my superpower,' I said.

I didn't mean anxiety was a *good thing*. I meant that anxiety was ridiculously intense, that we people who have an excess of it walk through life like an anxious Clark Kent or a tormented Bruce Wayne knowing the secret of who we are. And that it can be a burden of racing uncontrollable thoughts and despair but one, just occasionally, that we can convince ourselves has a silver lining.

For instance, personally I am thankful that it forced me to stop smoking, to get physically healthy, that it made me work out what was good for me, and who cared for me and who didn't. I am thankful that it led me to trying to help some other people who experience it, and I am thankful that it led me – during good patches – to feel life more intensely.

It was essentially what I had written in *Reasons to Stay Alive*. But I hadn't expressed it very well in this tweet. And then, suddenly, I was getting a lot of attention on Twitter.

I decided to delete my tweet, but people had screen-grabbed it and were rallying the ranks of the Twitter angry to direct their ire in my direction. 'SUPERPOWER???? WTF!!!' '@matthaig1 IS TOXIC' 'Delete your account' 'What a fucking idiot' and so on. And you stay on, scared, watching this car crash of your own making, as your timeline fills with tens then hundreds of angry people, convinced that as they were touching a raw nerve they had a point. By the way, 'touched a raw nerve' is an irrelevant phrase if you have anxiety. Every nerve feels raw.

The anger became contagious and I could feel it almost like a physical force radiating from the screen. My heart started to beat twice as fast. Everything felt like it was closing in. The air got thinner. I was backed into a corner. I began to feel a bit like reality was melting away. 'Oh shit, oh shit, oh shit.' I lost myself in a brief panic attack. I felt an unhealthy fusion of guilt and fear and defensive anger, and became determined never to live-tweet my way out of anxiety again.

Some things are best kept to yourself.

But also – more importantly – I wanted to find a way to stop other people's view of me becoming *my* view of me. I wanted to create some emotional immunity. Social media, when you get too wrapped up in it, can make you feel like you are inside a stock exchange where you – or your online personality – is the stock. And when people start piling on, you feel your personal share price plummet. I wanted free of that. I wanted to psychologically disconnect myself. To be a self-sustaining market, psychologically speaking. To be comfortable with my own mistakes, knowing that every human is more than them. To allow myself to realise I know my inner workings better than a stranger does. To be able for other people to think I was a wanker, without me feeling I was one. To care about other people, but not about their misreadings of me within the opinion matrix of the internet.

How to stay sane on the internet: a list of utopian commandments I rarely follow, because they are so damn difficult

1. Practise abstinence. Social media abstinence, especially. Resist whatever unhealthy excesses you feel drawn towards. Strengthen those muscles of restraint.

2. Don't type symptoms into Google unless you want to spend seven hours convinced you will be dead before dinner.

3. Remember no one really cares what you look like. They care what *they* look like. You are the only person in the world to have worried about your face.

4. Understand that what seems real might not be. When the novelist William Gibson first imagined the idea of what he coined 'cyberspace' in 1982's 'Burning Chrome', he pictured it as a 'consensual hallucination'. I find this description useful when I am getting too caught up in technology. When it is affecting my non-digital life. The whole internet is one step removed from the physical world. The most powerful

aspects of the internet are mirrors of the offline world, but replications of the external world aren't the actual external world. It is the real internet, but that's all it can be. Yes, you can make real friends on there. But non-digital reality is still a useful test for that friendship. As soon as you step away from the internet – for a minute, an hour, a day, a week – it is surprising how quickly it disappears from your mind.

5. Understand people are more than a social media post. Think how many conflicting thoughts you have in a day. Think of the different contradictory positions you have held in your life. Respond to online opinions but never let one rushed opinion define a whole human being. 'Every one of us,' said the physicist Carl Sagan, 'is, in the cosmic perspective, precious. If a human disagrees with you, let him live. In a hundred billion galaxies, you will not find another.'

6. Don't hate-follow people. This has been my promise to myself since New Year's Day, 2018, and so far it is working. Hate-following doesn't give your righteous anger a focus. It fuels it. In a weird way, it also reinforces your echo chamber by making you feel like the only other opinions are extreme ones. Do not seek out stuff that makes you unhappy. Do not measure your own worth

against other people. Do not seek to define yourself *against*. Define what you are *for*. And browse accordingly.

7. Don't play the ratings game. The internet loves ratings, whether it is reviews on Amazon and TripAdvisor and Rotten Tomatoes, or the ratings of photos and updates and tweets. Likes, favourites, retweets. Ignore it. Ratings are no sign of worth. Never judge yourself on them. To be liked by everyone you would have to be the blandest person ever. William Shakespeare is arguably the greatest writer of all time. He has a mediocre 3.7 average on Goodreads.

8. Don't spend your life worrying about what you are missing out on. Not to be Buddhist about it – okay, to be a little Buddhist about it – life isn't about being pleased with what you are doing, but about what you are being.

9. Never delay a meal, or sleep, for the sake of the internet.

10. Stay human. Resist the algorithms. Don't be steered towards being a caricature of yourself. Switch off the pop-up ads. Step out of your echo chamber. Don't let anonymity turn you into someone you would be ashamed to be offline. Be a mystery, not a demographic. Be someone a computer could never quite know. Keep empathy alive. Break patterns. Resist robotic tendencies. Stay human.

Never let go

OF THE CHALLENGES we face over the next century, as we begin to merge in more and more complex ways with technology, one of the most interesting might be this: how do we stay human in a digital landscape? How do we keep hold of ourselves and never let go?

Be careful who you pretend to be

KURT VONNEGUT SAID, decades before anyone had an Instagram account, that 'we are what we pretend to be, so we must be careful who we pretend to be'. This seems especially true for the social media age. We have always presented ourselves to the world – chosen which band T-shirt to wear and which words to say and which body parts to shave – but on social media the act of presenting is heightened a stage further. We are eternally one step removed from our online selves. We become walking merchandise. Our profiles are *Star Wars* figures of ourselves.

A picture of a pipe is not a pipe, as Magritte told us. There is a permanent gap between the signifier and the thing signified. An online profile of your best friend is not your best friend. A status update about a day in the park is not a day in the park. And the desire to tell the world about how happy you are, is not how happy you are.

How to be happy

1. Do not compare yourself to other people.
2. Do not compare yourself to other people.
3. Do not compare yourself to other people.
4. Do not compare yourself to other people.
5. Do not compare yourself to other people.
6. Do not compare yourself to other people.
7. Do not compare yourself to other people.

One more click

IF A RAT presses a lever and gets a treat every time, it will keep pressing. But not as often as the rat who presses the lever and gets mixed results – sometimes a treat, sometimes nothing at all.

I used to think social media was harmless. I used to think I was on it because I enjoyed it. But then I was still on it even when I wasn't enjoying it. I remembered that feeling. It was the feeling you get at three in the morning in a bar after your friends have gone home.

Algorithms eat empathy

NOW, THANKS TO clever algorithms, when we do our shopping we are presented with lots of other things that we might like. Things that *people like us* would buy.

If we are on Spotify or YouTube listening to music, they present us with a list of music that is almost exactly like the music we are already listening to.

If we are on Amazon, we are shown the books that people who bought this book also bought.

If we are on social media, we are told to follow more people like the people we already follow. More like us.

We are encouraged to stay in our zone and play it safe, because the internet companies know that on average most people generally like to listen and read and watch and eat and wear the kind of stuff they have already listened to and read and watched and eaten and worn. But all through history we weren't able to do that. We had to go out and compromise and deal with people who weren't like us. With things that weren't like the things we liked. And it was *horrid*.

But now it might be *even worse*.

Now we might end up utterly hating anyone who doesn't think like us. Politicians might end up never trying to reach out to the other side. Difference becomes something to fear, and sneer at, not celebrate. People with similar views end up falling out, unable to stomach even the slightest difference of opinion, until they are trapped in a little echo chamber of one, reading a million versions of the same book, listening to the same song, and retweeting their own opinions until the end of time.

But we are humans. We can resist this. We can resist being confined to a little digital tribe. We can embrace life at its full bandwidth. We are finding ways to do so all the time. Yes, we might be a mess. But our strength *is* our messiness. We don't do things simply because they make sense. The internet can be our ally, not our enemy, in this. The internet contains a whole world. The internet can be what we want it to be. The internet can lead us anywhere we choose. We just have to make sure that we – not the technology, not the designers and engineers able to manipulate our every mood – are the ones doing the choosing.

What people on social media think of social media

IN MY QUEST to insulate my mind from the nervous planet I began to imagine what I would feel like if I abandoned social media altogether. So, while imagining what life would be like without social media I, um, went to social media to try to find out. I decided to ask some of my Twitter followers a big, simple question: 'Is social media good or bad for your mental wellbeing?' The question hit a nerve. I received over 2,000 answers. They offer, of course, a complicated picture. Although, considering that these are people who are active and regular users of social media, the picture is quite negative. I mean, if you imagine asking regular book readers or cinemagoers or horse riders or hill walkers the same thing, it would be unlikely you would get such a mixed response. Anyway, here is a representative selection:

April Joy @AprilWaterson
It's both a coping mechanism and a cause for anxiety. When I've been anxious it's nice to mindlessly scroll and

read for distraction. But at the same time, the incessant need to post things that are 100% guaranteed to be judged by people isn't exactly a calming thought.

Dean Smith @deansmith7
Bad. I can find myself comparing my behind-the-scenes footage (loneliness, anxiety etc) to people's highlights reel (socialising, success etc). I know it's not a true reflection of their lives but it can still get to me.

Miss R! @Fabteachertips
I find when I'm feeling at my lowest, I can easily lose hours to scrolling through my social media feeds in bed alone. I really don't know why I do it, there are so many more productive things I could be doing. It doesn't make me feel better, that's for sure!

Immi Wright @immi_wright
I quit Facebook after I reached v suicidal levels . . . and found I started to feel more confident in myself. I guess FB often presents people's ideal self. On Twitter I just follow rock stars and @dog_rates, so there's far less of that to worry about.

Kieran Sangha @kieran_sangha
It's good in the sense you can connect with others that understand what you're going through. The downside is that it feeds an addiction, like substance abuse, and it can have the power to take over your life.

Hayley Murphy @hayleym_swvegan
Good. There's no one, and I mean NO ONE who understands me in 'real life'. It's literally life-saving to know I'm not alone. Any tool used in the wrong way can be dangerous, but used in the right way it can be incredible.

Bonnie Burton @bonniegrrl
Mixed. Good because I can connect easily with people who inspire me & whom I admire. Bad because social media ends up being a platform for harassment because there are no consequences for horrible behaviour.

Shylah Ellis @MsEels
As a kid, without social media, I basically assumed I was the only person out there suffering from depression. I felt isolated all the time and the only people I had contact with were toxic. Social media has allowed me to interact with incredible people from all over the world.

Kyle Murray @TheKyleMurray

I work in social media and while I think it has some positives, I think if I could keep up with distant friends in other ways, I'd probably just avoid it altogether. It's been weaponized by awful people. I've had FB since 2004 and mostly for nostalgia factor I keep it live.

James @james____s

A quote I heard recently: 'Facebook is where everyone lies to their friends. Twitter is where they tell the truth to strangers.'

Abigail Rieley @abigailrieley

Both. I've made real friends online & the support if you reach out can be very real BUT if you're down & feeling useless it can be a window into a world you're locked out of, isolating.

Kate Leaver @kateileaver

Mixed, but better than its reputation would suggest. Believe legit friendship can be conducted via social media, which is helpful if you can't leave the house. Getting to glimpse other lives when you're lonely/depressed is helpful at times.

Jayne Hardy @JayneHardy_
Both, I have to have good boundaries around it but when I manage and assert those boundaries, social media is a positive for me.

Gareth L Powell @garethlpowell
As a self-employed writer, Twitter is like my office water cooler. It's where I go to talk to friends and colleagues. Without it, I would feel very isolated.

Claire Allan @ClaireAllan
Mixed. As a writer working alone it gives me social interaction which is sanity saving. But I think it spotlights the best & more frequently the worst of humanity so that increases my anxiety.

Yassmin Abdel-Magied @yassmin_a
It's like anything. It can be great, but needs to be managed well in order for the good to outweigh the bad. Some of my best new friends I've connected with on Twitter.

Hollie Newton @HollieNuisance
I like the ideas and the news and the colourful pictures. I like seeing what my friends are up to. Interacting. But

spend more than a few minutes . . . And I start to feel, increasingly, like an inadequate nobody.

Cole Moreton @colemoreton
Not good. It agitates me, draws me into its angry argument, then I get repulsed and want to shut it all down. Then the cycle starts again.

Rachel Hawkins @ourrachblogs
Mixed. Instagram can leave me feeling jealous. Facebook makes me feel the rage and Twitter sometimes stresses me out.

Kat Brown @katbrown
Both. I get a lot from it (work, laughter, friends, contacts) but I know that my attention span has totally shifted. My focus is very often online. What's about to happen? What COULD have happened? News and dopamine = argh.

Nigel Jay Cooper @nijay
There are times when it feels like being in a room full of people shouting at one another and not listening, so I have to step away from it . . . but there's also the way it connects people, its supportive side and the sense of community. (1/2)

I think the smartphone 'always on' part of the equation is the bigger thing for me. I have to create time when I put the phone down and focus on the real world around me instead of the virtual one. For me, managing that is the key to not being overwhelmed by social. (2/2)

How to be happy (2)

DON'T COMPARE YOUR actual self to a hypothetical self. Don't drown in a sea of 'what if's. Don't clutter your mind by imagining other versions of you, in parallel universes, where you made different decisions. The internet age encourages choice and comparison, but don't do this to yourself. 'Comparison is the thief of joy,' said Theodore Roosevelt. You are you. The past is the past. The only way to make a better life is from inside the present. To focus on regret does nothing but turn that very present into another thing you will wish you did differently. Accept your own reality. Be human enough to make mistakes. Be human enough not to dread the future. Be human enough to be, well, *enough*. Accepting where you are in life makes it so much easier to be happy for other people without feeling terrible about yourself.

7
SHOCK OF THE NEWS

The multiplier effect

IT'S A NERVOUS planet with good reason. The world can be terrifying. Political polarisation, nationalism, the rise of actual Hitler-inspired Nazis, plutocratic elites, terrorism, climate change, governmental upheavals, racism, misogyny, the loss of privacy, ever-cleverer algorithms harvesting our personal data to gain our money or our votes, the rise of artificial intelligence and its implications, the renewed threat of nuclear war, human rights violations, the devastation of the planet. And it's not just *what happens*. After all, the world has always had terrible things happening somewhere. The difference now is that – thanks to camera phones and breaking news and social media and our constant connection to the internet – we *experience* what is happening elsewhere in a more direct and visceral and intimate way than ever before. The experience is multiplied, and leaks out, from a thousand different angles.

Imagine, for instance, if there had been social media and camera phones during the Second World War. If people had seen, in full colour, on smartphones, the consequences of every bomb, or the reality of every concentration camp, or the bloodied and mutilated bodies of soldiers, then the collective psychological experience would have expanded the horror far beyond those who were experiencing it first-hand.

We would do well to remember that this feeling we have these days – that each year is worse than the one previously – is partly just that: a feeling. We are increasingly plugged in to the ongoing travesties and horrors of world news and so the effect is depressing. It's a global sinking feeling. And the real worry is that all the increased fears we feel in themselves risk making the world worse.

If we see footage of a terrorist attack happening it becomes far easier to imagine another one happening, at any time, wherever we live. It doesn't matter if, rationally, we know that we are far more likely to die from cancer or suicide or a traffic accident, the sensational terror we have seen on the news becomes the one that dominates our thoughts. And politicians exploit this, and ramp up the fears and create more division. Which leads to more instability and more opportunities for terrorists to do what they set out to do: cause terror. And then the politicians or political agitators ramp up the fear even higher.

It is like someone who is ill with a compulsive disorder continually underlining their fears – staying indoors, or washing their hands 200 times a day. They are actually doing more to hurt themselves, in the name of protecting themselves. But this time the disorder isn't individual. It is social. It is global.

Shocks to the system

THE WORD 'SHOCK' crops up increasingly among political commentators on TV. You watch/read/scroll the news in the 21st century and it feels like a continual barrage of it. Of shock.

'Oh crap, what now?' That becomes the general reaction.

You click on your favourite news site in the morning and flinch.

Shock may be an unpleasant thing for an individual or a society to experience, but it can be a useful political tool. Ask anyone who has ever had a full-blown panic attack and they will tell you that it makes you think about nothing else but the fear. If you are shocked you are confused. You aren't thinking straight. You become passive. You go where the people tell you to go.

Naomi Klein coined the term the 'shock doctrine' to describe the cynical tactic of systematically using 'the public's disorientation following a collective shock' for corporate or political gain. Oil companies exploiting the shock of war to make inroads into a new country, for instance, or an American president exploiting terrorism to push hard-line anti-immigration measures.

'We don't go into a state of shock when something big and bad happens,' she says. 'It has to be something big and bad *that we do not yet understand*.'

And the trouble is that now we have 24-hour news coverage, where events are continuously breaking but rarely absorbed. We are in a world of news, which by its very nature skims the new moment, garnished with head-lines and sound bites, rarely giving us a calmer, more reflective understanding of the big picture.

Shock results in negative but understandable emotions. Fear, sadness, impotence, anger. The temptation to spend our lives tweeting rage at the injustices of the world is a human one, but it isn't enough. Ultimately, it may simply be adding more wails to the collective wails of shock which aid those in power, or on the political extremes, who might want us distracted.

When an individual goes through panic disorder, the main response – amid the terror – is to feel cross and utterly fed up. But there comes a point where, in the process of recovery, you have to reach some kind of under-standing and acceptance. Not because it isn't that bad. But precisely because it is *that bad*.

I remember once, during depression, staring up at a clear sky of stars. The wonder of the universe.

At the bottom of the pit, I always had to force myself to find the beauty, the goodness, the love, however hard it was. It was hard to do. But I had to try. Change doesn't just happen by focusing on the place you want to escape. It happens by focusing on where you want to reach. Boost the good guys, don't just knock the bad guys. Find the hope that is already here and help it grow.

Imagine

IMAGINE IF WE had a day where we called human beings human beings. Not nationalities first. Not the religion they follow. Not British. Not American. Not French. Not German. Not Iranian. Not Chinese. Not Muslim. Not Sikh. Not Christian. Not Asian. Not black. Not white. Not man. Not woman. Not CEO of Coca-Cola. Not gang member. Not mother-of-three. Not historian. Not economist. Not BBC journalist. Not Twitter user. Not consumer. Not *Star Trek* fan. Not author. Not aged 17. Or 39. Or 83. Not conservative. Not liberal. Change it all to human. The way we see all turtles as turtles. Human, human, human. Make ourselves see what we pretend to know. Remind ourselves that we are an animal united as a species existing on this tender blue speck in space, the only planet that we know of containing life. Bathe in the corny sentimental miracle of that. Define ourselves by the freakish luck of not only being alive, but being aware of that. That we are here, right now, on the most beautiful planet we'll ever know. A planet where we can breathe and live and fall in love and eat peanut butter on toast and say hello to dogs and dance to music and read *Bonjour Tristesse* and binge-watch TV dramas and notice the sunlight accentuated by hard shadow on a building and feel the wind and the rain on our tender skin and look after each other and lose ourselves in daydreams and night dreams and dissolve into the sweet mystery of ourselves. A day where we are, essentially, precisely as human as each other.

Six ways to keep up with the news and not lose your mind

1. Remember that how you react to the news isn't just about what the news is, but how you get it. The internet and breaking news channels report news in ways that make us feel disorientated. It is easy to believe things are getting worse, when they might just make us *feel* worse. The medium isn't just the message, it's the emotional intensity of that message.

2. Limit the amount of times you look at the news. As my Facebook friend Debra Morse recently commented: 'Remember that in 1973 we typically got our news twice a day: morning paper and evening TV broadcast. And we still got rid of Nixon.'

3. Realise the world is not as violent as it feels. Many writers on this subject – such as the famed cognitive psychologist Steven Pinker – have pointed out that, despite all its horrors, society is less violent than it used to be. 'There is definitely still violence,' says the historian Yuval Noah Harari. 'I live in the Middle

East so I know this perfectly well. But, comparatively, there is less violence than ever before in history. Today more people die from eating too much than from human violence, which is really an amazing achievement.'

4. Be near animals. Non-human animals are therapeutic for all kinds of reasons. One reason is that they don't have news. Dogs and cats and goldfish and antelope literally don't care. The things that are important to us – politics and economics and all of those fluctuating things – are not important to them. And their lives, like ours, still go on. As A.A. Milne wrote in *Winnie-the-Pooh*: 'Some people talk to animals. Not many listen though. That's the problem.'

5. Don't worry about things you can't control. The news is full of things you can't do anything about. Do the things you can do stuff about – raise awareness of issues that concern you, give whatever you can to whichever cause you feel passionate about, and also accept the things you *can't do*.

6. Remember, looking at bad news doesn't mean good news isn't happening. It's happening everywhere. It's happening right now. Around the world. In hospitals, at weddings, in schools and offices and maternity wards,

at airport arrival gates, in bedrooms, in inboxes, out in the street, in the kind smile of a stranger. A billion unseen wonders of everyday life.

In praise of positivity

THE OLD ME, before I ever became ill, was cynical about positivity, about happy songs and pink sunsets and optimistic words of hope. But when I was ill – when I was in the thick of it – my life depended on abandoning that pessimistic side of myself. Cynicism was a luxury for the non-suicidal. I had to find hope. *The thing with feathers*. My life depended on it.

It might seem a stretch to tie psychological healing with social and political healing, but if the personal is political, the psychological is, too. The current political climate seems to be one of division – a division partly fuelled by the internet.

We need to rediscover our commonality as human beings. How does that happen? Well, an alien invasion would be one way, but we can't rely on that.

The problem of politics is the problem of tribes. 'When you separate yourself by belief, by nationality, by tradition, it breeds violence,' taught the philosopher Jiddu Krishnamurti.

One thing mental illness taught me is that progress is a matter of acceptance. Only by accepting a situation can you change it. You have to learn not to be shocked by the shock. Not to be in a state of panic about the panic. To change what you can change and not get frustrated by what you can't.

There is no panacea, or utopia, there is just love and kindness and trying, amid the chaos, to make things better where we can. And to keep our minds wide, wide open in a world that often wants to close them.

8

A SMALL SECTION ON SLEEP

The war on sleep

BEFORE 1879, WHEN Thomas Edison came up with the first practical incandescent light bulb, all lighting had been fuelled by gas and oil. The light bulb, heavily promoted via the Edison & Swan United Electric Light Company, literally set the world alight. The bulbs were practical – small and cheap and safe – and emitted just the right amount of light, and began to take off in homes and businesses throughout the world.

Human beings had, finally, conquered the night. The dark – the source of so many of our primal fears – could now be negated at the flick of a switch. And now, as our evenings could stay lighter for longer, people increasingly started going to bed later. This didn't worry Edison at all. Indeed, he saw it as an unequivocally good thing. In 1914, Edison, by now a living global icon, declared that 'there is really no reason why men should go to bed at all'. He went further: he actually believed sleep was bad for you, and too much was likely to make you lazy. He believed the light bulb was a kind of medicine, and that artificial light could cure 'unhealthy and inefficient' people.

Of course, he was wrong. Without sleep we don't function properly.

Humans, like birds and sea turtles, have body clocks. They – we – have circadian rhythms. That is to say, our bodies react differently at different times of the day. They have evolved to function differently at daytime and night-time. In another 150,000 generations humans might evolve and adapt to unnatural light, but right now our bodies and minds are still the same bodies and minds of those humans who existed before Edison patented his light bulb. In other words: we need our sleep.

And yet we aren't really getting what we need. The World Health Organization – which has declared a sleep loss epidemic in industrialised nations – recommends we sleep between seven and nine hours a night. But not that many of us do. According to research from the American National Sleep Foundation average American, British and Japanese people all sleep well under seven hours a night while other countries – such as Germany and Canada – hover precariously at the seven-hour mark. And according to more research – this time from Gallup – the average person sleeps for an hour less than they did in 1942.

However, artificial light isn't the only contributing factor here. Sleep experts point to things like the way we work nowadays as well as a growth in loneliness and anxiety that increases our desire to stay up chatting or distract ourselves with entertainment in a frantic 24/7 world.

There are so many incentives to stay awake. So many emails to answer. So many more episodes of our favourite TV show to sit through. So much online shopping to do. Or eBay auctions to monitor. So much news to catch up on. So many social media accounts to update, or concerts to go to, or books to read, or potential dates to chat to, or ambitions to fulfil. So many people – unknown disciples of Edison – wanting us to stay awake.

We all know we tend to be more sad and worried and irritable and lethargic when we haven't slept. Sleep is essential for our wellbeing. When we don't sleep well, it can have serious consequences on our physical and mental state. While some effects of sleeping badly are debatable, there are some on which the medical community have a broad consensus. For instance, according to numerous overlapping studies and sources, not sleeping well:

– Runs down your immune system
– Increases your risk of coronary heart disease

- Increases your risk of stroke
- Increases your risk of diabetes
- Increases your risk of having a car accident
- Is associated with higher rates of breast cancer, colorectal cancer and prostate cancer
- Impairs your ability to concentrate
- Interferes with your memory
- Increases your risk of getting Alzheimer's
- Makes weight gain more likely
- Reduces sex drive
- Increases levels of the stress hormone cortisol
- Increases the likelihood of depression

As University of California 'sleep scientist' Matthew Walker writes in his book *Why We Sleep*: 'there does not seem to be one major organ within the body, or process within the brain, that isn't optimally enhanced by sleep . . . The physical and mental impairments caused by one night of bad sleep dwarf those caused by an equivalent absence of food or exercise.'

Sleep is essential, and amazing. And yet, sleep has traditionally been an enemy of consumerism. We can't shop in our sleep. We can't work or earn or post to Instagram in our sleep. Very few companies – beyond bed manufacturers and duvet sellers and makers of black-out blinds – have actually made money from our sleep. No one has found a way to build a shopping mall that we can enter via our slumber, where advertisers can pay for space in our dreams, where we can spend money while we are unconscious.

Slowly, sleep is becoming a little more commercialised. Now, there are private sleep clinics and sleep centres where people pay for advice on getting a better sleep routine. There are 'sleep trackers', which monitor movement and have been criticised (for instance in a 2018 *Guardian* article on 'clean sleeping') for being unreliable and counter-productive, as they only serve to make people more anxious about sleep.

But largely, sleep remains a sacred space, away from distraction. Which is why seemingly no one can go to bed early.

And now, at this later stage of capitalism, sleep has become seen not just as something that slows work down, but as an actual business rival.

The chief executive of Netflix, Reed Hastings, believes that sleep – not HBO, not Amazon, not any other streaming service – is his company's main competitor. 'You know, think about it,' he said at an industry summit in Los Angeles back in November 2017, cited in *Fast Company*.

'When you watch a show from Netflix and you get addicted to it, you stay up late at night . . . we're competing with sleep, on the margin. And so, it's a very large pool of time.'

So this is the attitude to sleep: something to be suspicious of because it is a time when we are not plugged in, consuming, paying. And this is also our attitude to time: something that mustn't be wasted simply by resting, being, sleeping. We are ruled by the clock. By the light bulb. By the glowing smartphone. By the insatiable feeling we are encouraged to have. The feeling of *this is never enough*. Our happiness is just around the corner. A single purchase, or interaction, or click, away. Waiting, glowing, like the light at the end of a tunnel we can never quite reach.

The trouble is that we simply aren't made to live our lives in artificial light. We aren't made for waking to alarm clocks and falling asleep bathed in the blue light of our smartphone. We live in 24-hour societies but not 24-hour bodies.

Something has to give.

How to sleep on a nervous planet

THERE ARE ALL kinds of pay-for or technological solutions out there. From those sleep-tracking devices to light bulbs free of blue light to hypnotherapy to sleep masks. But many of these consumer products seek to increase our anxiety around sleep.

In fact, the best ways are simple. The most consistent expert advice includes getting into a routine, avoiding caffeine and nicotine and too much late night alcohol (I can vouch for all this), exercising early in the day, avoiding late large meals, relaxing before bed, and getting some natural daylight.

Doing ten minutes of (very) light yoga and slow breathing has worked well for me during anxiety patches where sleep has been problematic.

But one of the most effective solutions, if a little boring, is breathtakingly simple. According to Professor Daniel Forger of the University of Michigan, who led a team of researchers looking at sleeping patterns around the world, we are in the midst of a 'global sleep crisis' as society pushes us to stay up later. The answer, as he told the BBC, is not having more lie-ins. It's going to bed a little earlier, as the later people go to bed, the less sleep they get. Whereas what time we wake up in the morning makes surprisingly little difference. But even the act of going to bed a little earlier might require cultural change. 'If you look at countries that are really getting less sleep then I'd spend less time worrying about alarm clocks and more about what people are doing at night – are they having big dinners at 22:00 or expected to go back to the office?'

Another solution is to be disciplined about your phone and laptop use, and try not to be on them in bed, as the blue light negatively affects the sleep hormone melatonin.

Anyway, I've just realised it's now after midnight as I type these words. I better close my laptop. And I'm going to try to fall asleep without even checking my phone.

9
PRIORITIES

A trip to a homeless shelter

EVEN WHEN THE world is not overtly terrifying us, the speed and pace and distraction of modern existence can be a kind of mental assault that is hard to identify. Sometimes life just seems too complicated, too dehumanising, and we lose sight of what matters.

A few months ago I went to a homeless shelter. It was in Kingston upon Thames, an affluent London suburb which many might imagine would be unlikely to have a homeless problem.

I had been invited there to talk about books and mental health. The place – the award-winning Joel Centre – is based around more than just the idea of giving people a bed for the night. Its ethos is 'Helping People to Believe in Themselves'. A volunteer there told me the idea is that 'the people here are lacking more than somewhere to sleep, they are lacking *belonging*. We aim to give them that. The problem is homelessness not houselessness. And when you are homeless you are missing more than just a bedroom.' He added that working there had made him realise what people 'really need in life – away from all the crap'.

So, the people there, alongside a bed and a lockable wardrobe and access to a washing machine and bathroom, also get to sit around a table with other guests and eat a wholesome meal every day. Often the guests help to cook the meal themselves, and they also play an active part in cleaning the shelter and tending the garden and helping in the local community.

The shelter is *theirs*. They are a part of it.

After I spoke about my experience of mental health problems with them I got talking to the man sitting next to me. He was about my age. He looked like he'd been through a lot, mentally and physically, but he was smiling. He said he'd become homeless after his relationship had broken down and he'd fallen into a depression that he'd tried to deny and had then become an alcoholic. He told me that the centre had saved his life. He pointed vaguely to the door and told me that 'out there' life didn't make sense. He got lost in it.

He found the world dehumanising. Here, though, it was the simple things. 'Just talking to people, sitting around the table with people, working for stuff you can see.'

That was the feeling I had of the place. It was like a distillation of the things people need in life. And it strictly edited out the stuff that harmed the guests – the place was very strict about drink and drugs and so on. It had thought hard about what to let in and what to – literally – shut out.

Although most of us are in a better place in life than the guests at the Joel Centre, its ethos is a good one to adopt. And deceptively simple. Accentuating the things that make you feel good, cutting back the things that make you feel bad, and letting people feel truly connected to the world around them.

That is the biggest paradox, I think, about the modern world. We are all connected to each other but we often feel shut out. The increasing overload and complexity of modern life can be isolating.

Added to that is the fact that we don't always know precisely what makes us feel lonely or isolated. It can make it hard to see what the problems are. It's like trying to open an iPhone to fix it yourself. It sometimes feels like society operates like Apple, as if it doesn't want us to get a screwdriver and look inside to see what the problems are for ourselves. But that's what we need to do. Because often identifying a problem, being mindful of it, becomes the solution itself.

Lonely crowds

THE PARADOX OF modern life is this: we have never been more connected and we have never been more alone. The car has replaced the bus. Working from home (or unemployment) has replaced the factory floor and, increasingly, the group office. TV has replaced the music hall. Netflix is becoming the new cinema. Social media the new meeting friends in the pub. Twitter has replaced the water cooler. And individualism has replaced collectivism and community. We have face-to-face conversations less and less, and more interactions with avatars.

Human beings are social creatures. We are, in George Monbiot's words, 'the mammalian bee'. But our hives have fundamentally changed.

I have noticed as the years pass that the number of my virtual friends is rising while the number of friends I see in real life is shrinking.

I have decided to change this. I am making an effort to get out and socialise with friends at least once a week and I am feeling better for it.

I'm not nostalgic about vinyl and compact discs but I am nostalgic about face-to-face contact. Not Facetime contact. Not Skype contact. But actually talking to someone, out in the elements, with nothing but air between you. At home, I am trying to put my laptop down and speak to my kids so they don't grow up feeling they were behind a MacBook Pro in importance. I am trying not to cancel seeing friends out of sheer can't-be-bothered-ness.

And it is an effort. It's so bloody hard. There are days when I'd find it easier to talk North Korea out of its nuclear weapons programme than to talk myself out of checking social media seventeen times before breakfast.

Online socialising is *easy*. It is *weather-proof*. It never requires a taxi or an ironed shirt. And it's sometimes wonderful. It's often wonderful.

But deep, deep down in the subterranean depths of my soul, I realise that the scent-free, artificially illuminated, digitised, divisive, corporate-owned environment can't fulfil all my needs, any more than takeaway meals can replace the sheer pleasure of eating in a lovely restaurant. And I – someone whose anxiety once tipped into agoraphobia – am increasingly forcing myself to spend longer in that messy, windswept thing we sometimes still romantically call the *real world*.

How to be lonely

HAVE YOU EVER heard a parent moan about their kids' need for constant entertainment?

You know. 'When I was young I could sit in the back of the car and stare out the window at clouds and grass for 17 hours and be perfectly happy. Now our little Misha can't go five seconds in the car without watching *Alvin and the Chipmunks 17* or playing game apps or taking selfies of herself as a unicorn . . .'

That sort of thing.

Well, there is an obvious truth to it. The more stimulation we have, the easier it is to feel bored.

And this is another paradox.

In theory, it has never been easier not to be lonely. There is always someone we can talk to online. If we are away from loved ones then we can Skype them. But loneliness is a feeling as much as anything. When I have had depression, I have been lucky enough to have people who love me all around me. But I had never felt more alone.

I think the American writer Edith Wharton was the wisest person ever on loneliness. She believed the cure for it wasn't always to have company, but to find a way to be happy with your *own* company. Not to be antisocial, but not to be scared of your own unaccompanied presence.

She thought the cure to misery was to 'decorate one's inner house so richly that one is content there, glad to welcome anyone who wants to come and stay, but happy all the same when one is inevitably alone'.

10

PHONE FEARS

A therapy session in the year 2049

ROBOT THERAPIST: So, what is the problem?

MY SON: Well, I think it goes back to my parents.

ROBOT THERAPIST: Really?

MY SON: My dad, specifically.

ROBOT THERAPIST: What was the matter with him?

MY SON: He used to be on his phone all the time. I used to feel like he cared about his phone more than me.

ROBOT THERAPIST: I'm sure that's not true. A lot of people from that generation didn't know all the consequences of their phone use. They didn't know how addictive they were. You have to remember, it was all relatively new back then. And everyone else was doing it, too.

MY SON: Well, it gave me issues. I used to think, Why aren't I as interesting to him as his Twitter feed? Why wasn't I as good to look at as the screen of his phone? If only I didn't feel like I had to distract him to get attention. This was in the days before the 2030 revolution, of course.

ROBOT THERAPIST: Hmmm. Where's your father now?

MY SON: Oh, he died in 2027. He was run over by a driverless car while trying to find a funny gif.

ROBOT THERAPIST: How sad. And what have you been doing since then?

MY SON: I invested in a robot dad. I looked into all the hologram options but I wanted a dad I could hug. And I have programmed him never to check his notifications. He's there when I want him.

ROBOT THERAPIST: That is so wonderful to hear.

How to own a smartphone and still be a functioning human being

1. Don't feel you always have to be there. In the not-so-olden days of letters and landlines, contacting someone was slow and unreliable and an effort. In the age of WhatsApp and Messenger it's free and easy and instant. The flipside of this ease is that we are expected to be there. To pick up the phone. To get back to the text. To answer the email. To update our social media. But we can choose not to feel that obligation. We can sometimes just *let them wait*. We can risk our social media getting stale. And if our friends are friends they will understand when we need some headspace. And if they aren't friends, why bother getting back anyway?

2. Turn off notifications. This is essential. This keeps me (just about) sane. All of them. All notifications. You don't need any of them. Take back control.

3. Have times of the day where you're not beside your phone. Okay, I'm bad at this one. But I'm getting better. No one needs their phone all the time. We

don't need it by the bed. We don't need it while we're eating meals at home. We don't need it when we go out for a run. Here's something I do now: I go for a walk without my phone. I know it sounds ridiculous to present that as some big achievement, but for me it was. It's like exercise. It takes effort.

4. Don't press the home button to check the screen every two minutes for texts. Practise feeling the urge to check and don't.

5. Don't tie your anxiety levels to how much power you have left on your phone.

6. Don't swear at your phone. Don't plead with your phone. Don't bargain with your phone. Don't throw your phone across the room. It is indifferent to your feelings. If the phone has no signal, or no power, it is not because it hates you. It is because it is an inanimate object. It is, in short, a phone.

7. Don't put your phone by the bed. I'm not judging, by the way. Most people sleep with their phone by the bed because they've replaced alarm clocks. Most nights I have the phone by the bed. My parents have their phones by the bed. Everyone I know has their phones by their beds. Maybe one day our beds will *be* our phones. But I do seem to sleep better when my phone

isn't by my bed. You know, if it's in another room, or even just another part of the room. I know it might be unrealistic. But it's good to have an aspiration. A dream to work towards. To fantasise about the day when we're strong enough never to need to have the phone by our beds. Like the olden days. The 1800s. The 1900s. 2006.

8. Practise app minimalism. An overload of apps and options adds to the choice but also stress of phone use. We are given an almost infinite array of things we can add to our phones. But more choice leads to more decisions and more stress. You were born without any apps on your phone. Hey! Guess what? You were born without any phone at all. And life was still beautiful.

9. Don't try to multitask. We have phones that can do everything from map read to tune our guitars, and it's tempting to imagine that we can do as many things, and all at once. For instance, while writing this one point alone I have had to consciously stop myself from checking my emails, checking my text messages, checking my social media. It took effort. According to neuroscientist Daniel Levitin, we aren't really made for the kind of multitasking the internet age

encourages us to do. 'Even though we think we're getting a lot done, ironically, multitasking makes us demonstrably less efficient,' he writes, in *The Organized Mind: Thinking Straight in the Age of Information Overload*. Multitasking creates a dopamine-addiction cycle, rewarding the brain for losing focus. It can also increase stress and lower IQ. 'Instead of reaping the big rewards that come from sustained, focused effort, we instead reap empty rewards from completing a thousand little sugar-coated tasks,' concludes Levitin.

10. Accept uncertainty. The temptation to check your phone is down to uncertainty. That's what makes it so addictive. You want someone to get back to your text but you don't know if they have. You want to check. You want to see the promise and mystery of the three little circles, dancing with hope. You want to know how your photo or status update is going down. But why do we need to know right now? Why can't it all wait till after your lie-in/meeting/walk/TV show/meal/daydream? Do people really need to check their phones during meetings, or while attending funerals? Maybe if we understood that the checking is never fully satisfying we wouldn't. Because there is no end to the uncertainty. There is no final checking of your

phone. Think of all the times you checked your phone yesterday. Did you *really* need to so often? I certainly didn't. I have definitely cut down, but still have a way to go. How many times do you touch your phone a day? Or look at it? It might be hard to keep count. The answer might be well in the hundreds. Imagine, I say to myself, if you just looked at your phone, say, five times a day. What catastrophe would occur?

Glow

I USED TO be obsessed with glowing windows and street-lamps when I was a kid. From the back of the car I would stare out and look at windows glowing pink through red curtains, like ET's chest, and wonder about the life going on inside. There is something about the glow of artificial light that I find mesmerising. When I was eight years old – in 1983 – my parents had an old AA travel guide called *Discover America* and it had a double image of the Las Vegas Strip as seen at night. 'I want to go *there*,' I announced to my mum, to her distaste. She never took me.

'It's late,' I say to Andrea.

We read a little, then switch the lights off, always later than we should. Every time, I imagine the square light of our window turning black, to anyone walking by outside.

'Night,' Andrea says.

'Night.'

It will be some time after midnight and the room will be dark except for the glow of a phone.

'Matt, are you going to go to sleep?'

'I tried. My mind's racing.'

'You should put the phone down.'

'It's just my tinnitus is bad. This distracts me.'

'Well, it's stopping me going to sleep.'

'Okay, sorry. I'm putting the phone down.'

'You know what'll happen if you have too many bad nights.'

'I know. Night . . .'

And I close my eyes, and my mind still races with a thousand worries, attracting attention like illuminated signs in Vegas, tainting my dreams and waiting to dissolve in daylight.

How to get out of bed

1. Wake up.
2. Pick up phone.
3. Stare at phone for 72 minutes.
4. Sigh.
5. Get out of bed.

Alternatively, once in a while, try skipping stages two to four.

A problem in your pocket

WHILE WRITING THIS book, early in 2018, I was asked by *The Observer* to contribute to an article where lots of writers asked the novelist and essayist Zadie Smith questions. I took the opportunity, not least because I had seen Zadie Smith at a couple of literary parties when I was newly published and had been crippled and mute with anxiety and hadn't dared to go over and talk to her.

I had read about her social media scepticism and how she values her 'right to be wrong', and so I asked her, 'Do you worry about what social media is doing to society?'

She didn't mince her words, and started with a critique of smartphones.

'I can't stand the phones and don't want them in my life in any form. They make me feel anxious, depressed, dead inside, unhinged. But I fully support anyone who finds them delightful and a profound asset to their existence.'

Although a self-described 'Luddite abstainer', Smith does think the time is right to look at how we're using this technology. 'What is this little device in your pocket doing to your intimate relationships with others?' she asked. 'To your behaviour as a citizen within a society? Maybe nothing! Maybe it's all totally cool. But maybe not? . . . Do we need it resting by our pillows at night? Do our seven-year-olds need phones? Do we wish to pass down our own dependency and obsession? It all has to be thought through. We can't just let the tech companies decide for us.'

I use my phone a lot more than Smith does but despite that – or maybe because of it – I share a lot of her anxieties. And there are signs that even those working for the tech companies are concerned, which means we should be even more worried about where those stupendously powerful companies are leading us. For instance, it's been known – at least since *The New York Times* reported it in 2011 – that many Apple and Yahoo! employees choose to send their kids to schools which shun technology, such as the Waldorf School of the Peninsula in Los Altos.

There are also many tech insiders who have come out to warn against the things they have had a hand in creating. There was the guy who invented the 'Like' button on Facebook, Justin Rosenstein, who has said that technology is so addictive his phone has a parent-control feature to stop him downloading apps and restrict his use of social media. And, as a side point, it is worth mentioning that the Facebook 'like' function is also what helps the data miners understand who we are. Our online likes reveal everything from our sexual orientation to our politics, and can be harvested to better influence us, as seen in the Cambridge Analytica scandal in 2018, where reports suggested 50 million Facebook members had their data improperly accessed by the British firm that helps businesses and political groups 'change audience behaviour'.

'It is very common,' Rosenstein told *The Guardian* in 2017, like a latter-day Dr Frankenstein, 'for humans to develop things with the best of intentions and for them to have unintended, negative consequences . . . Everyone is distracted, all the time.'

And two of Twitter's founders have expressed similar regrets. Ev Williams – who stepped down as CEO in 2010 – told *The New York Times* in 2017 that he was unhappy with the way Twitter had helped Donald Trump become president. 'It's a very bad thing, Twitter's role in that.'

Another Twitter co-founder Biz Stone has other regrets. He stated in an interview with Inc. that he thought the big wrong turn Twitter made was when it allowed strangers to tag people in their posts, as it created an environment rife for bullying. Another employee, according to Buzzfeed, has called Twitter a 'honeypot for assholes'.

And, in early 2018, Tim Cook – CEO of Apple – declared to a group of students in Essex, England, that he doesn't think children (such as his nephew) should use a social network, or overuse technology at all, which shows that these aren't simply 'Luddite' concerns.

Indeed, a group of former tech employees have gone further, and set up the Center for Humane Technology, aimed at 'realigning technology with humanity's best interests' and reversing the 'digital attention crisis'.

Now, at long last, there are many instances of tech people getting together to discuss concerns. For instance, at a 2018 conference in Washington called Truth About Tech, speakers included Google's former 'ethicist' and now prominent tech whistleblower Tristan Harris and early investor of Facebook Roger McNamee, along with politicians and members of lobby groups such as Common Sense Media, who are trying to combat tech addiction in young people. A variety of concerns were raised, such as the way Google's Gmail 'hijacks' minds, or how Snapchat exploits teenage friendships to fuel tech addiction via functions like 'Snapchat streaks' where users can see how many interactions they've had with friends per day. According to *The Guardian*, Harris compared the tech world to the Wild West in that the ethos is 'build a casino wherever you want' and McNamee compared it to the tobacco and food industries in the past, where cigarettes were promoted as healthy, or where manufacturers of ready meals failed to mention their products were loaded with salt. The difference being that with, say, an addiction to cigarettes, is that the cigarettes had no information about us. They didn't collect our data. They couldn't know us better than our own families. The internet, of course, can know everything about us. It can know who our friends are, it can know our taste in music, it can know our health concerns, our love life, and our politics – and internet companies can keep using this information to make their products ever more addictive. And at the moment, warn the tech insiders, there isn't much regulation to stop them.

An increasing amount of research reinforces their concerns. For example, studies that show how technology contributes to a state of 'continual partial attention' and how it can be addictive. One 2017 study from the McCombs School of Business at the University of Texas concluded that the mere presence of your smartphone can reduce 'cognitive capacity'.

At the time of writing, there is still no official recognition that 'smartphone addiction' or 'social media addiction' are psychological disorders, although the fact that the World Health Organization now classifies video game addiction as an official mental disorder suggests that there is a growing understanding of how seriously technology can affect our mental health. But that understanding still has a long way to go, and clearly lags behind the disorientating speed of technological change.

Though pressure is rising. In 2018, for instance, CNN reported that the mighty Unilever threatened to pull its advertising from Facebook and Google unless they combat toxic problems – including privacy concerns, objectionable content and a lack of protections for children – which are 'eroding social trust, harming users and undermining democracies'. There is a growing awareness that the great power of internet companies must come, Spiderman-style, with a great sense of responsibility. However, it is debatable as to how much responsibility they will develop without real social and financial pressure of the kind we are only beginning to see. As with fast food or cigarettes or the gun industry, the companies making a profit from something might be the most reluctant to see the potential problems. So when the people on the inside are among those raising the alarm, we should really listen.

THE DETECTIVE
OF DESPAIR

'These fragments I have shored against my ruins'

—T.S. Eliot, *The Waste Land*

Awareness

WHEN I FIRST became ill, at the age of 24 – when I 'broke down' – the world became sharper. Painfully so. Shadows had sudden weight, clouds became greyer, music became louder. I became more alert to everything I had been numb to. I noticed the things that made me feel worse about the modern world. Things that probably make many of us feel worse. I felt the wearying pressure of advertising, the frantic madness of crowds and traffic, the suffocating nature of social expectation.

Illness has a lot to teach wellness.

But when I am well I forget these things. The trick is to keep hold of that knowledge. To turn recovery into prevention. To live how I live when I am ill, without being ill.

Hope

THERE ARE SOME factors affecting our mental health that are genetic, and down to an individual's wiring or brain chemistry. But we can't do much about the things handed down to us in our genetic code. What is more interesting are the transient aspects, the triggers that change with time and societies. These are the things we can do stuff about.

Other eras have had their own particular mental health crises of course. But the fact that every age has struggled with its own particular problems should not make us complacent about our own culture.

And the great thing about this – the liberating thing – is that if our anxiety is in part a product of culture, it can also be *something we can change by changing our reaction to that culture*. In fact, we don't even need to consciously change at all. The change can happen simply by being aware.

When it comes to our minds, awareness is very often the solution itself.

The detective of despair

I THINK THE world is always going to be a mess. And I am always going to be a mess. Maybe you're a mess, too. But – and this bit is everything for me – I believe it's possible to be a happy mess. Or, at least, a less miserable mess. A mess who can *cope*.

'In all chaos there is a cosmos,' said Carl Jung, 'in all disorder a secret order.'

Mess is actually okay. As you will be aware by now, I am trying to write about the messiness of the world and the messiness of minds by writing a deliberately messy book. That's my excuse, anyway. Fragments that I hope together make a kind of whole. I hope it all *makes sense*. Or if it doesn't make sense, I hope it makes nonsense in ways that might get you thinking.

The problem is not that the world is a mess, but that we expect it to be otherwise. We are given the idea that we have control. That we can go anywhere and be anything. That, because of free will in a world of choice, we should be able to choose not just where to go online or what to watch on TV or which recipe to follow of the billion online recipes, but also what to feel. And so when we don't feel what we want or expect to feel, it becomes confusing and disheartening. Why can't I be happy when I have so much choice? And why do I feel sad and worried when I don't really have anything to be sad and worried about?

And the truth is that when I first became ill, at the very beginning, I didn't even know what I had, let alone what might be triggering it. I had no understanding of the hell I wanted to escape, I just wanted to escape it. If your leg is on fire you don't know the temperature of the flames. You just know that you're in pain.

Later, doctors would offer labels. 'Panic disorder', 'generalised anxiety disorder' and 'depression'. These labels were worrying, but also important, because they gave me something to work with. They stopped me feeling like an alien. I was a human being with human illnesses, which other humans have had – millions and millions of humans – and most of them had either overcome their illnesses or had somehow managed to live with them.

Even after I knew the names of the illnesses I had, I believed they were all stemming from inside me. They were just *there*, the way the Grand Canyon was just there, a fixed feature of my psychic geography which I could do nothing about.

I would never be able to enjoy music again. Or food. Or books. Or conversation. Or sunlight. Or cinema. Or a holiday. Or anything. I was rotten now, to my core, like a, like a, like a (there are never enough metaphors for depression), like a diseased tree. A diseased tree whose girlfriend and parents say, over and over, 'You'll get better. We'll find a way and we will get you better.'

And, of course, there were different remedies. I tried the diazepam a doctor gave me. I tried the various tinctures a homeopath gave me. I tried the recommendations of friends and family. I tried St John's Wort and lavender oil. I tried sleeping pills. I tried talking to telephone helplines. Then I stopped trying. I had a nightmarish time on diazepam and an even more nightmarish time coming off diazepam. I should probably have tried taking different pills, but – judge me if you will – I didn't. I wasn't thinking rationally. Complicating the situation was the fact that I was scared – I mean, terrified beyond anything I'd ever known – of trying more pills, or of seeking more help now that nothing had worked.

When I mentioned this in *Reasons to Stay Alive* a couple of people thought I was making a statement against pills, so I will say here, as clearly as possible: I am not against pills. Yes, there are all kinds of issues with the pharmaceutical industry and the scientific research is still a work in progress (as scientific research, by its nature, tends to be), but I also know that pills have saved many people's lives. I know of people who say they could not survive without them. I also believe there would be medication out there that could probably have helped me, but I didn't find it. I don't believe pills are a *total* solution. I also believe certain misprescribed pills can make some people feel worse, but that is the same with anything. You could get the wrong pills for arthritis or your heart condition. And to say that pills aren't the only answer is common sense. They rarely are. If you have arthritis, yoga and swimming and hot sunshine might be helpful and pills might also be helpful. It's not an either/or situation. We have to find what works for us. Also, in my case, I was traumatised, and wasn't even close to thinking straight.

At that time, trying things that didn't work only made life worse. As I said, there may well have been the right treatment out there for me – talk or medication – but I wasn't lucky enough to find it. I wasn't brave enough to seek it out. The pain was as much as I could bear to *just about* stay alive. I couldn't risk a gram of difference, that was my logic. Every day felt like life or death. Not because the pain wasn't bad enough to keep going back to the doctor, but because it was too bad. Writing that down, I realise how ridiculous that sounds, but that was my reality then. Everything I had tried to combat the turmoil inside my head had failed. And, to be honest, the doctors I had encountered hadn't been that understanding. I sincerely believe that things have moved on in lots of ways since the turn of this century.

So, anyway, I was there, in this pit, desperately trying to find a way out as every escape route seemed to be closing.

And, as many people in this situation discover, you acquire evidence like a detective trying to solve a murder. At first there were no clues, or none I could see. Every day in that pit was hell. Every day, in those first few weeks and months, contained moments of such heavy emotional pain that they stopped any hope breaking through. But the pain, I started to realise, although internal, often had external triggers. There was nothing I had found that made me feel better. Then I realised that certain things could make me feel worse: drinking alcohol, smoking, loud music, crowds. The world *gets in*. It always gets in, however we are doing. But until I became ill, I never knew how.

Note to self

KEEP CALM. KEEP going. Keep human. Keep pushing. Keep yearning. Keep perfecting. Keep looking out the window. Keep focus. Keep free. Keep ignoring the trolls. Keep ignoring pop-up ads and pop-up thoughts. Keep risking ridicule. Keep curious. Keep hold of the truth. Keep loving. Keep allowing yourself the human privilege of mistakes. Keep a space that is you and put a fence around it. Keep reading. Keep writing. Keep your phone at arm's length. Keep your head when all about you are losing theirs. Keep breathing. Keep inhaling life itself.

Keep remembering where stress can lead.

(Keep remembering that day in the shopping centre.)

Fear and shopping

I WAS IN a shopping centre, crying.

Me, aged 24, surrounded by crowds of people and shops and illuminated signs, unable to cope.

'No,' I whispered, as my breathing lost its rhythm. 'I can't do this.'

'Matt?'

It had been a test. To go with Andrea, then my girl-friend, to this city near her parents' home – Newcastle, in the north of England – and do some shopping. I had no idea what we were shopping *for*. My focus was simply on making it through without having a panic attack.

To be like any other normal person.

'I'm sorry, I just can't, I . . .'

There I was. Pathetic. A young man. In a world that had told me – everywhere from TV shows to the school sports field – that being a man means being *strong* and *tough* and *silent* in the face of pain, a world that showed us that being young was about having fun and being free in the bright, shining land of youth. And here I was, in the supposed prime of my life, *crying about nothing in a shopping centre*. Well, it wasn't really about nothing. It was about pain. And terror. A pain and terror I had never known until a little over a month before, while working in Spain, when I had a panic attack that started and didn't stop and then became fused with a terrible, indescribable sense of dread and malaise and hopelessness which seeped into my flesh and bones.

The despair had been so strong that it had very nearly taken my life. There had seemed no way out. However scary death was, this living terror had seemed worse. Everyone has a limit – a point at which they can't take any more – and, almost out of nowhere, I had reached mine.

'It's all right,' Andrea was saying, holding my hand. More mother or nurse than girlfriend in that moment.

'No, it isn't. I'm sorry. I'm sorry.'

'Did you take the diazepam this morning?'

'Yes, but it's not working.'

'It's going to be all right. It's just panic.'

Just panic.

Her concerned eyes made it worse. I'd already put her through so much. All I had to do was walk. Walk and talk and breathe like a normal human being. It wasn't rocket science. But right then, it might as well have been.

'I can't.'

Andrea's face hardened now. Her jaw clenched and mouth tightened. Even she had limits. She was cross *at* me and *for* me. 'You can do it.'

'No, Andi, I really fucking can't. You don't understand.'

People were looking at us, casting sideways glances in our direction as they walked along weighed down with carrier bags.

'Just breathe. Just breathe slowly.'

I tried to breathe deep, but the air could hardly make it beyond my throat.

'I . . . I . . . I . . . There's no air.'

Earlier in the day, I hadn't been feeling as bad as this. Just a low-level unshiftable despair. On the bus into the city, the fear had crept over me, like being slowly wrapped in an itchy blanket.

Now my whole body was alive with terror.

I was frozen right there, standing outside Vision Express, surrounded by life yet alone. I began to swallow. To try to direct myself. Compulsive swallowing had been one of a few mild OCD symptoms I had developed. This time I was actually wanting that symptom just to distract me from a worse one. But it didn't work.

There was no hope. There was no way out. Life was for other people.

I had held back the world, and now it was caving in. And Andrea's voice became something far away, the last hope, trying to reach the person I no longer was.

You only have one mind

WHEN I LOOK back on the shopping centre experience – one experience among many similar ones that sometimes burst into my brain like a Vietnam flashback without the violence – I try to dissect it. I relive the past in order to accept it and learn from it. Not just to learn how not to have panic attacks, but to learn how my mind intersects with the world and work out how to be less stressed generally.

The first problem was that it took place within my earliest experience of anxiety and depression. When you have a bout of mental illness for the first time, you imagine this is how your life is going to be for ever. You will have depression punctuated by panic attacks and that is how things will stay. And that was terrifying. The claustrophobia of it. There seemed no way out.

The second problem was that I still had no idea how to deal with panic attacks. That lesson was going to take years to learn.

And the third problem was that I didn't understand how the external and the internal were connected. I didn't know how related 'what you feel' is to 'where you are'. I didn't know that the world of shops and sales and marketing is not always good for minds. A lot of research has been done in recent years about the effect of external environments on our health. For instance, a 2013 study commissioned by the mental health charity Mind and run by the University of Essex compared the experience of walking in a shopping centre with a 'green walk' around Belhus Woods Country Park in Essex. Although walking is known to be good for a mind – indoors or outdoors – 44 per cent of the people who walked in a shopping centre said they felt a decrease in self-esteem. Whereas nearly all (90 per cent) of the people who went for the forest walk felt their self-esteem increase. There is an increasing amount of research like this, as I'll mention later, about how nature is good for our minds. But at the time I knew none of that. Indeed, most of the research hadn't been done.

It makes sense that shopping centres aren't easy places to be in. A shopping centre is a deliberately stimulating environment, designed not to calm or comfort, but merely to get us to spend money. And as anxiety is often a trigger for consumption, feeling calm and satisfied would proba-bly work against the shopping centre's best interests.

Calmness and satisfaction – in the agenda of the shopping centre – are destinations we reach by *purchasing*. Not places already *there*.

The fourth problem was guilt. I felt guilty about symptoms I didn't really see as symptoms of an illness. I saw them as symptoms of me-ness.

Another lesson I am still coming to understand – and writing this book is helping me – is that distraction didn't and doesn't work. For one thing, shopping centres are deliberately very distracting environments, but they didn't take me out of myself, only into myself. The bustling crowds of other people didn't help connect me to humanity. I felt more alone among masses of people than I did when it was just me and one other person, or even just myself.

This was an already familiar tactic of mine: trying to distract myself from one torment by finding another. Years before Twitter, and the mind-numbing compulsive checking of social media, I had the desperate need for distraction. But it was no good. You develop symptoms more by fighting them than inviting them. Distraction is an attempt to escape that rarely works. You don't put out a fire by ignoring the fire. You have to acknowledge the fire. You can't compulsively swallow or tweet or drink your way out of pain. There comes a point at which you have to face it. To face yourself. In a world of a million distractions you are still left with only one mind.

The mannequins who
inflict pain

WHEN I NOW think of that particular panic attack I think of how the world got in. Even at the time I had an instinctive – if not totally conscious – idea of the triggers around me. Even a shop's mannequins added to it.

There I was. In that enclosed and busy and artificial commercial space. Past the point of no return. My own personal singularity. The rational knowledge, as I looked at Andrea, that I was in the all too familiar process of ruining our day.

I closed my eyes to escape the stimulation of the shopping centre and saw nothing but monsters and demons, a mental bank of creatures and images worse than any hydra or cyclops – my own personal underworld that was now only ever a blink or a thought away.

'Come on, you can do it. Breathe slowly.'

I tried to do what she said: to breathe slowly, but the air didn't feel like air. It didn't feel like anything. My *self* didn't feel like anything.

I wiped my eyes.

Opposite Vision Express was a clothes shop. I can't remember which one. But what I can remember, printed with the weight of trauma in my memory, is that there were mannequins in dresses in the window. The kind of mannequins with heads. Heads which were grey and hairless and with features that hinted abstractly at a nose and eyes, but no mouth. The mannequins stood in unnatural angular poses.

They seemed deeply malevolent. As if they were sentient beings who not only knew my pain, but were part of it. Were partly *responsible* for it.

Indeed, this would be a key feature of my anxiety *and* depression over the following months and years. The sense that parts of the world contained a secret external malevolence that could press a despairing weight and pain into you. It could be found in a smiling face on a glossy magazine. It could be found in the devilish red stare of rear tail-lights. Or the too-bright blue glow of a computer screen.

And yes, it could be found in the sinister echo of humanity in a shop mannequin.

One day, when I was ready to face my pain, this feeling of extreme sensitivity would actually help me. It would help me understand that if external things could have a negative impact, then other external things might have a positive impact. But right then I was worried I was losing my mind.

I was convinced I wasn't made for the reality of the world. And in a way, I was right. I wasn't made *for* the world. I was, like everyone, made *by* the world. I was made by parents and culture and TV and books and politics and school and maybe even shopping centres.

So, I either needed a new me. Or a new planet. And I didn't yet know how to find either. Which is why I felt suicidal.

'I've got to get out of here,' I said at the time, wiping my eyes like a toddler lost in a supermarket.

The 'here' was broad enough to mean anything from 'my head' to 'the planet'. More immediately, of course, the 'here' was the shopping centre.

'Okay, okay, okay,' Andrea said. She was right next to me. She was also thousands of miles away. She scanned around for the nearest exit. 'This way.'

We got outside, into natural light. And we went back to Andrea's parents', and I lay on Andrea's childhood bed and told her parents I had a bit of a headache, because a headache was easier for them to understand than this invisible cyclone. Anyway, I felt varying degrees of bad for many weeks and months, but eventually I began to recover. And, even better, to understand.

A wish

I SO WISH I could explain something to my younger self. I wish I could tell myself that it wasn't all *me*. I wish I could say that there were things I could do. Because my anxiety, my depression, wasn't just *there*. Illness, like injury, often has context.

When I fall into a frantic or despairing state of mind, full of unwelcome thoughts that can't slow down, it is often the result of a series, a sequence of things. When I do too much, think too much, absorb too much, eat too badly, sleep too little, work too hard, get too frazzled by life, there it is.

A repetitive strain injury of the mind.

How to exist in the 21st century and not have a panic attack

1. Keep an eye on yourself. Be your own friend. Be your own parent. Be kind to yourself. Check on what you are doing. Do you need to watch the last episode of the series when it is after midnight? Do you need that third or fourth glass of wine? Is that *really* in your best interests?

2. Declutter your mind. Panic is the product of overload. In an overloaded world we need to have a filter. We need to simplify things. We need to disconnect sometimes. We need to stop staring at our phones. To have moments of not thinking about work. A kind of mental feng shui.

3. Listen to calm noise. Things that aren't as stimulating as music. Waves, your own breath, a breeze through the leaves, the purr of a cat, and best of all: *rain*.

4. Let it happen. If you feel panic rising the instinctive reaction is to panic some more. To panic *about* the panic. To meta-panic. The trick is to try to feel panic

without panicking *about* it. This is nearly – but not quite – impossible. I had panic disorder – a condition defined not by the occasional panic attack but by frequent panic attacks and the continuous hellish fear of the next one. By the time I'd had hundreds of panic attacks I began to tell myself I wanted it. I didn't, obviously. But I used to work hard at trying to invite the panic – as a test, to see how I could cope. The more I invited it, the less it wanted to stay around.

5. Accept feelings. And accept that they are just that: feelings.

6. Don't grab life by the throat. 'Life should be touched, not strangled,' said the writer Ray Bradbury.

7. It is okay to release fear. The fear tries to tell you it is necessary, and that it is protecting you. Try to accept it as a feeling, rather than valid information. Bradbury also said: 'Learning to let go should be learned before learning to get.'

8. Be aware of where you are. Are your surroundings over-stimulating? Is there somewhere you can go that is calmer? Is there some nature you can look at? Look up. In city centres, the tops of buildings are less intense than the shop fronts you see at head level. The sky helps, too.

9. Stretch and exercise. Panic is physical as well as mental. For me, running and yoga help more than anything. Yoga, especially. My body tightens, from hours of being hunched over a laptop, and yoga stretches it out again.

10. Breathe. Breathe deep and pure and smooth. Concentrate on it. Breathing is the pace you set your life at. It's the rhythm of the song of you. It's how to get back to the centre of things. The centre of yourself. When the world wants to take you in every other direction. It was the first thing you learned to do. The most essential and simple thing you do. To be aware of breath is to remember you are alive.

12
THE THINKING BODY

Four humours

ONCE UPON A time, in Ancient Greece, doctors explained the human body with reference to the 'four humours'. Every health complaint could be assessed as an excess or deficiency of one of four distinct bodily fluids: black bile, yellow bile, phlegm and blood.

In Roman times, the four humours evolved to correspond with four temperaments. For instance, if you had anger issues, you would be told you had too much yellow bile, the fire humour. Which means when you tell someone to 'chill' you are echoing official health advice from Ancient Rome.

If you were feeling depressed, or melancholic, that was down to an overload of black bile. In fact, the very word 'melancholia' stems via Latin from the ancient Greek words *melas* and *kholé*, which literally meant 'black bile'.

This system seems ludicrously unscientific. But in one way, at least, it was advanced. Namely, it did not make a division between physical and mental health.

The philosopher René Descartes is largely to blame for this distinction. He believed minds and bodies were entirely separate. Back in the 1640s he suggested that the body works like an unthinking machine and that the mind, in contrast, is non-material.

People liked the idea. It was a hit. And it still impacts society.

But this split makes little sense.

Mental health is intricately related to the whole body. And the whole body is intricately related to mental health. You can't draw a line between a body and a mind any more than you can draw a line between oceans.

They are entwined.

Physical exercise is known to have a positive impact on all kinds of mental things, from depression to ADHD. And physical illnesses have mental effects. We can hallucinate with flu. A cancer diagnosis can make us depressed. Asthma can cause us to panic. A heart attack can cause mental trauma. If you have a bad lower back – or tinnitus, or chest pain, or a lowered immune system, or a painful stomach – because of stress, is that a mental or a physical problem?

I feel we need to stop seeing mental and physical health as either/or and more as a both/and situation. There is no difference. We are mental. We are physical. We are not split up into unrelated sections. We are not an existential department store. We are everything at once.

Guts

BRAINS ARE PHYSICAL.

And besides, thoughts aren't just the products of brains. As cognitive scientist Guy Claxton writes in *Intelligence in the Flesh*, 'the body, the gut, the senses, the immune system, the lymphatic system, are so instantaneously and so complicatedly interacting with the brain that we can't draw a line across the neck and say, "above the line it's smart and below the line it's menial". We do not have bodies. We *are* bodies.'

Then there is the issue of the 'little brain' – a network of 100 million neurons (nerve cells) in our stomach and gut. Okay, so it is nowhere near the 85 billion neurons that our 'first brain' has, but it is not to be sniffed at. One hundred million neurons are the amount a cat has in her head.

When we get 'butterflies' in the stomach before a job interview, or when we get hungry before a late lunch, that is our 'second brain' talking to our first brain.

So, in other words, this suggests that the idea of 'mental health' being separate to our physical self is as outdated as Descartes' dodgy wig.

And yet we still suffer from the divide. We separate the world of work into mind jobs and body jobs. 'Skilled' jobs, which need what we generally see as intelligence and a 'good education', and lower-valued 'unskilled' jobs which often tend to be manual labour. White collar and blue collar.

There is an intelligence to movement. An intelligence to dance. An intelligence to playing sport. And yet we casually section people off, from school age, deciding if someone is sporty or academic or – in *Breakfast Club* speak – a 'jock' or a 'brain'. This then determines their career path, whether it will result in a lower-paid manual job or a higher-paid job staring at an Excel spreadsheet. And we divide culture into high and low. Books that make us laugh or give us heart palpitations are seen as less worthy than books that make you 'think'.

The line we draw between minds and bodies makes no sense the more we stare at it, and yet we base our entire system of healthcare on that line. And not just healthcare. Our selves and societies, too. It's time to change this. It's time to rejoin the two parts. It's time to accept our whole human self.

A side note on stigma

WE AREN'T ENCOURAGED to talk about our mental health until we are mentally ill, as if we have to fake being in 100 per cent full health. Stress simply isn't taken seriously enough. Or it is taken so seriously that people are ashamed of talking about their bad mental health days. Either way, this leads to more people becoming not just stressed, but ill.

And when we become ill, and might talk about it, we encounter a new stigma.

Too often, we view mental illness as a product of the person in a way we don't with other illnesses. Because mental illness is seen as intrinsically different, we talk of it in different, more scandalised terms. Think of the words used about mental illness.

Newspapers and magazines sometimes talk about celebrities 'confessing' to depression and anxiety and eating disorders and addictions, as if those things are crimes. And *actual* crimes are too often explained as the product of an illness – mass shootings and sexual abuse are often given the media context of 'mental health problems' or 'addiction' rather than terrorism and sex crimes. In reality, people with mental illness are far more likely to be *victims* of crimes.

We also don't really know how to talk about suicide. When we do talk about it we tend to use that verb – commit – which carries connotations of taboo and criminality, an echo of the days when it *was* criminal. (I have recently been trying to say 'death by suicide' but it still feels a bit forced and false on my tongue.) Many people struggle to deal with the very idea of taking your own life, as it seems a kind of insult to us all, if you see suicide as a choice, because someone has chosen to give up on living, this sacred precious thing, as fragile as a bird's egg. But personally I know that suicide isn't such a clear-cut choice. It can be something you dread and fear but feel compelled towards because of the new pain of living. So, it's uncomfortable, talking about it. But talk we must, because an atmosphere of shame and silence prevents people getting the right help and can make them feel more freakishly lonely. It can, in short, be fatal.

Suicide is the biggest killer of women and men between the ages of 20 and 34. It is also the biggest killer of men under the age of 50 (at least in the country where I live, the UK. Other European countries have similarly bleak statistics. In the US, where firearms contribute to the depressing statistics, suicide is the tenth leading cause of death overall, across all ages and genders, though as with Europe, Canada and Australia, men are over three times more likely to kill themselves than women). These deaths are so often preventable. This is why we must ignore the pleas to 'man up' and find true strength instead. The strength for men and women to speak out.

The echoes of historical shame are everywhere in our words. For another example, when we talk about someone 'battling their demons' we are conjuring up those Dark Age superstitious ideas of madness as the work of the devil.

And all this talk, over and over, of bravery: it would be nice one day if a public figure could talk about having depression without the media using words like 'incredible courage' and 'coming out'. Sure, it is well intentioned. But you shouldn't need to *confess* to having, say, anxiety. You should just be able to tell people. It's an illness. Like asthma or measles or meningitis. It's not a guilty secret. The shame people feel exacerbates symptoms. Yes, absolutely, people are often brave. But the bravery is in living with it, it shouldn't be in *talking about* it. Every time someone tells me I am brave I feel like I should be scared.

Imagine if you were heading for a quiet walk in the forest and someone came up to you.

'Where are you going?' she asks.

'I'm going to the forest,' you tell her.

'Wow,' she gasps, stepping back.

'Wow what?'

And then a tear forms in her eye. She places a hand on your shoulder. 'You're so brave.'

'Am I?'

'So *incredibly* brave. An inspiration, in fact.'

And you would gulp, and go pale, and be permanently put off going into the forest.

Additionally, there is still a lingering toxic idea that people share mental health issues for 'attention'.

That attention people seek can save lives.

But, as C.S. Lewis once put it, 'The frequent attempt to conceal mental pain increases the burden: it is easier to say "My tooth is aching" than to say "My heart is broken".'

We should work towards making this a world where it is easier to talk about our troubles. Talking isn't just about raising awareness. As the various successful types of talk therapy have shown over the last century, talk can have medicinal benefits. It can actually ease symptoms. It heals the teller and the listener through the externalising of internal pain and the knowledge that others feel like we do.

Never stop talking.

Never let other people make you feel it is a weakness or flaw inside you, if you have a mental health problem.

If you have a condition like anxiety, you know that it isn't a weakness. Living with anxiety, turning up and doing stuff with anxiety takes a strength most will never know. We must stop equating the condition with the patient. There needs to be a more nuanced understanding of the different pressures people feel. Walking to a shop can be a show of strength if you are carrying a ton of invisible weight.

Psychogram chart

(pg = psychograms)

Imagine if we could come up with a way to measure psychological weight as we each feel it. Wouldn't that be helpful in bridging the mental and the physical? Wouldn't that help people realise the reality of stress? Wouldn't that help us cope with the stresses of modern life? Humour me. Let's call this imaginary unit a *psychogram*.

'Oh no, I can't check my emails. I've had my limit of psychograms today.'

Walking through a shopping centre	1,298pg
Phone call from the bank	182pg
Job interview	458pg
Watching the news	222pg
A full inbox of unanswered emails	321pg
Your tweet that no one likes	98pg
Guilt from not going to the gym	50pg
Guilt from neglecting to phone close relatives	295pg

Observing how old/overweight/tired you look	177pg
Fear of missing out on a party you see on social media	62pg
Realising you posted a tweet with a spelling mistake	82pg
A worrying symptom you have googled	672pg
Having to do a speech	1,328pg
Looking at images of perfect bodies you'll never have	488pg
Arguing with an online troll	632pg
An awkward date	317pg
Paying utility bills on credit cards	815pg
The realisation that it is Monday and you have to work	701pg
Having your job replaced by a robot	2,156pg
The things you haven't done but wish you had	1,293pg

Note: psychological weight fluctuates greatly. Psychograms are a subjective measurement.

13
THE END OF REALITY

'. . . this collision between one's image of oneself and what one actually is is always very painful and there are two things you can do about it, you can meet the collision head-on and try and become what you really are or you can retreat and try to remain what you thought you were, which is a fantasy, in which you will certainly perish.'

—James Baldwin, *Nobody Knows My Name*

I am what I am what I am

YOU SOMETIMES NEED to go back to move forward. You need to face the pain. The deepest pain. And I've recently felt ready.

I need to go back.

To before the shopping centre.

To a room of surgical whiteness.

'Who am I?' I asked, in the Spanish medical centre, during the beginning phase of my first mental collapse.

Of course, when I am well and calm, the question isn't that scary. Who am I? There is no I. There is no you. Or rather, there are a million Is. A million yous. 'I' is the largest word in the English language.

Behind every you there is another you, and another you and another you, like a Russian doll. Is there a base you? A base me? Or are our identities not Russian dolls but just spirals with no end? Is identity a universe you can never reach the end of but which might lead you back to where you started?

Being relatively well, I enjoy the pointless philosophising

of such questions. Because there is, I suppose, a clear *self* doing the asking. But when I was ill these weren't simply abstract concerns. These were desperate mysteries to solve, as though my life depended on it. Because my life *did* depend on it. The feeling of me-ness had gone – it had been crowded out – and I felt like *I* could become trapped in the *infinite I*, silently floating in panic, with nowhere to land.

Reality versus supermarkets

PANIC ATTACKS OFTEN happen in supermarkets.

I know someone who has had only one panic attack in her life. It happened in a supermarket.

When I used to trawl early noughties message boards for tips on dealing with anxiety, the panic-attack-in-the-supermarket concept came up more than almost any other. I am looking at one thread now that starts: 'WHY DO PANIC ATTACKS STRIKE YOU WHILE SHOPPING IN A SUPERMARKET?'

Panic is there to help us. As it is for many other animals, panic is our mind and body telling us to do something. Fight or flight. Run from the predator or fight the predator. But a supermarket is not a bear or a wolf or a cave-dwelling warrior. You can't fight a supermarket. You can definitely run from one, but that will only increase your chance of having a panic attack the next time you have to go there. It might not just be that supermarket either. If you start playing the avoidance game, it might soon be all supermarkets that become triggers. Then all shops. Then the outside world.

People who have never had a period of living with anxiety and panic don't understand that the *realness* of you is an actual feeling that you can lose. People take it for granted. You don't get up in the morning and think, as you spread peanut butter onto your toast, 'Ah, good, my sense of self is still intact, and the world is still real, I can now get on with my day.' It's just *there*. Until it isn't. Until you are in the cereal aisle, feeling inexplicable terror.

When trying to express what a panic attack feels like it's easy to talk about the obvious symptoms: the racing thoughts, the palpitations, the tightness of the chest, the breathlessness, the nausea, the tingling sensations inside your skull or your arms and legs. But there is another more complicated symptom I used to get. One which I have come to realise is at the heart of what my panic attacks have always been about. It is the one called, tellingly, *derealisation*.

Within a feeling of derealisation, I still *knew* I was me. I just didn't *feel* I was me. It is a feeling of disintegration. Like a sand sculpture crumbling away.

And there is a paradox about this sensation. Because it feels like both an extreme intensity of self and a nothingness of self. A feeling of no return, as if you have suddenly lost something that you didn't know you had to look after, and that the thing you had to look after was you.

And I think the reason supermarkets are such triggers for this is because they are already *derealised*. Supermarkets, like shopping centres, are wholly unnatural places. They might seem old-fashioned now, almost quaint, in this era of online shopping, but they are far more modern than our biology.

The light is not natural light. The humming noise of refrigerators sounds like the ominous soundtrack of an artsy horror movie. The abundance of choice is more than we are naturally built to cope with. The crowds and the shelves are hyperstimulating. And so many of the products themselves aren't natural. I don't just mean because most of them have chemical additives, though that as well. I mean, they have been tampered with. The tins of fish, the bags of salad, the boxes of sweetened puffed rice, the breaded chicken goujons, the processed meat, the vitamin pills, the jars of pre-chopped garlic, the packets of chilli-flavoured sweet potato crisps. They are not natural. And in unnatural settings, when your anxiety is raw enough, you can feel unnatural, too. You can feel as removed from yourself as a packet of toilet roll is removed from a tree. To me, during my panic attacks in supermarkets, the objects on the shelves took on a sinister quality. They seemed alien. And, in a way, they were and *are* alien. They have been taken from where they belong. I related to that. And that is the root of it, I suppose. I didn't feel like *I* belonged. I found it impossible to find peace in such an unnatural and overloaded place. The only thing I knew about myself was the fear. And all the repeated objects in the supermarket were making me worse.

'Objects should not touch because they are not alive,' said Sartre, in *Nausea*, while clearly having a bit of a bad week. 'But they touch me, it is unbearable. I am afraid of being in contact with them as though they were living beasts.'

Objects in a supermarket aren't normal objects either. They are *branded* objects. While products live in a world of physical space, brands seek out mental space. They seek to get into our heads. In many cases companies employ marketing psychologists to do just that. To manipulate us into buying. To toy with our minds.

Caveperson

IMAGINE A CAVEPERSON was frozen for 50,000 years.

Let's call her Su.

Imagine the block of ice she was frozen in suddenly melting in front of your local supermarket.

The caveperson – Su – steps inside. The automatic doors magically close behind her. The light and colours and crowds frighten her. Shopping trolleys appear like strange metallic beasts, domesticated by the humans that push them along. The shining shelves of plastic packaged goods bewilder her. The self-service checkouts are mystifying. The carrier bags look like sacks of strange white skin.

'Unexpected item in bagging area,' the robotic voice says. 'Unexpected item in bagging area . . . Unexpected item in bagging area . . .'

Su begins to panic. She runs towards the window and bangs into the glass.

Su begins to wail. 'Owagh! Agh! Ug-aggh!'

More noises.

The twist at the end of the story arrives.

(Drumroll.)

Su is effectively *Us*.

(Ironic gasp.)

Su is all of us. It's just that we are a bit more used to supermarkets.

We haven't biologically changed for 50,000 years.

But society has, massively. And we are expected to be grateful for all this change. After all, if she hadn't been frozen Su would probably have been killed by a stampede of wild boars at the age of 22 or by a sacrificial ritual at the age of 16. And we *are* lucky. Nothing is luckier than being a living 21st-century human compared to being a Neolithic dead one.

But because of that luck, we need to cherish this life we have. And if we can not only feel *lucky* but also other things – *calm*, *happy*, *healthy* – then why not? Why not know what the world can do to us? Because that knowledge can help us.

It helps me, now, in a supermarket. In shopping centres. In IKEA. On the computer. On a crowded street. In an empty hotel room. Wherever. It helps to know I am just a caveman in a world that has arrived faster than our minds and bodies expected.

Blur

TWO DAYS AGO, I wobbled. I felt the strange psychological pain of grey skies. Picking up my daughter from her dance class, I felt as if I was sinking into the pavement. I began compulsively swallowing, and started to feel the old agoraphobia pitch for an unwanted sequel.

But now I have a little more awareness than I used to have. I could see I hadn't been sleeping well. I'd been working too hard. I'd been worrying too hard about this book. I'd been worried about a million stupid little things. So, I stopped obsessing about emails and stepped away from this Word document and did a moderate 'Yoga for Sleep' video and ate healthily and tried to disconnect. I took the dog for a long walk by the sea.

And I realised: *it doesn't matter*. *Stop being neurotic*.

Nothing I was worried about would fundamentally change anything. I would still be able to walk the dog. I would still be able to look at the sea. I would still be able to spend time with the people I love.

The anxiety retreated, like a criminal under the spotlight of an investigation.

14
WANTING

'Perhaps when we find ourselves wanting everything it is because we are dangerously near to wanting nothing.'

—Sylvia Plath

Wishing well

TYPING 'HOW CAN I become' into Google, as I write this, the top five consequent autofill suggestions are:

— rich
— famous
— a model
— a pilot
— an actor

Transcendence

WE ARE BEING sold unhappiness, because unhappiness is where the money is.

Much of what is sold to us is the idea that *we could be better than who we are if we tried to become something else*.

Think about fashion magazines.

Lucinda Chambers served as fashion director of British *Vogue* for 25 years. Shortly after leaving her job, she gave a damning verdict on the industry she had left behind. She declared that, despite their talk of empowerment, few fashion magazines actually make anyone feel empowered. 'Most leave you totally anxiety ridden,' she said in an interview with the fashion journal *Vestoj* that soon went viral, 'for not having the right kind of dinner party, setting the table in the right kind of way or meeting the right kind of people.' In addition, the way fashion magazines focus on unattainably expensive (for most readers) clothes just exacerbates the misery, by making people feel poor.

'In fashion we are always trying to make people buy something they don't need,' said Chambers. 'We don't *need* any more bags, shirts or shoes. So we cajole, bully or encourage people into continuing to buy.'

Fashion magazines and websites and social media accounts sell a kind of transcendence. A way out. A way to escape. But it is often unhealthy, because to make people want to transcend themselves you first have to make them unhappy with themselves.

Yes, people might end up buying a diet book to get the body of a model who endorses it, or a perfume to be more like the image of a celebrity whose name is on the bottle, but that all comes at a cost that is more than financial. People might feel better in the instant hit of the purchase, but in the long term it just feeds a craving to be someone else: someone more glamorous, more attractive, more famous. We are encouraged out of ourselves, to want to have other lives. Lives that are no more real than pots of gold at the end of rainbows.

Maybe the beauty secret no magazine wants to tell us is that the best way to be happy with our looks is to accept the way *we already look*. We are in an age of Photoshop and cosmetic surgery and soon to be in an age of designer robots. It is probably the perfect time to accept our human quirks rather than trying to aim for the blank perfection of an android.

We might think: oh, I need to look a certain way to attract people. Or we could think: actually, there is no better way of filtering out the people who will be no good for me than by looking and being myself.

Being unhappy about your looks is not about your looks: when fashion models develop eating disorders it isn't because they are ugly or overweight. Of course not.

There are various indicators worldwide that eating disorders are on the rise. The non-profit group Eating Disorder Hope reported in 2017 that eating disorders around the world have tended to rise in line with western-isation and industrialisation, and looked at a comprehensive overview of international research. In Asia, for instance, places like Japan, Hong Kong and Singapore have far higher rates than the Philippines, Malaysia and Vietnam, though those latter countries have rapidly rising rates as these countries 'advance' and 'westernise'.

Another telling case is Fiji. Research there has found that eating disorders began to rise in the mid-nineties, just as TV was introduced to the South Pacific island state for the first time. *The New York Times* first reported back in 1999 how eating disorders in Fiji had been virtually unheard of, before TV gave them the slender role models of global hits such as *Melrose Place* and *Beverly Hills 90210*.

Indeed, 'you've gained weight' used to be a common flattering compliment in Fiji, before American television gave girls and young women other body ideals.

In the UK, figures from NHS Digital in 2018 showed that hospital admissions from eating disorders had almost doubled within less than a decade, with girls and twenty-something women most at risk. Caroline Price, from the UK's leading eating disorder charity Beat, told *The Guardian* at the time the figures were published that although eating disorders are 'complex' and down to 'many factors', modern culture has a lot to answer for.

'Eating disorders are on the rise partly because of the challenges of today's society,' she said. 'This includes social media and exam pressure.'

Although these things don't entirely cause the problem, as experts like Price acknowledge, they compound it for those personalities predisposed to eating disorders. According to the UK's National Centre for Eating Disorders (NCED), causal factors include genetics, parents with food issues, fat-teasing, childhood abuse or neglect, childhood trauma, family relationships, having a friend with an eating disorder, and, last but not least, the 'culture'. Particularly problematic is a culture where there is always a new diet to try, and where, according to the NCED website, 'a vulnerable individual internalises the impossibly ideal images they see on TV or in magazines, and continually compares herself unfavourably to those images'.

The website also adds that 'people who can admire a beautiful model but say "I could never look like her but it doesn't bother me too much" are the people who are least likely to fall victim to problems with food'. Maybe there is a lesson for all of us here: in that disconnect between the images we see and the selves we are. We need to build a kind of immune system of the mind, where we can *absorb* but not get *infected by* the world around us.

How to be kinder to yourself about yourself

1. Think of people you have loved. Think of the deepest relationships you have ever had. Think of the joy you felt when seeing those people. Think of how that joy had nothing to do with their looks except that they looked like themselves and you were pleased to see them. Be your own friend. Be pleased to recognise the person behind your face.

2. Change your perspective of how you view photos of yourself. Every photo you look at and think, Oh, I look old, will one day be a photo you look back on and think, Oh, I looked young. Instead of feeling old from the perspective of your younger self, try feeling young from the perspective of your older self.

3. Love imperfections. Accentuate them. They are what will make you different from androids and robots. 'If you look for perfection, you will never be content,' says Lvov's wife, Natalie, in *Anna Karenina*.

4. Don't try to be like someone who already exists. Enjoy your difference.

5. Don't worry when people don't like you. Not everyone will like you. Better to be disliked for being you, than being liked for being someone else. Life isn't a play. Don't rehearse yourself. *Be* yourself.

6. Project your thoughts outwards. Think of nature. Google pictures of Amazonian glass frogs. Place yourself in the natural order. There are 9 million known species and that is estimated as 20 per cent of the animals out there. Appreciate that life is beautiful. And you are quite literally alive. Ignore idiots with narrow definitions of beauty. They are blind to life's imperfect wonder.

7. Never let a stranger's negative opinion of you become your own negative opinion of you.

8. If you're feeling bad about yourself, stay away from Instagram.

9. Remember no one else is ever worried about what your face looks like.

10. Do something somewhere in the day that isn't work or duty or the internet. Dance. Kick a ball. Make burritos. Play some music. Play Pac-Man. Stroke a dog. Learn an instrument. Call a friend. Get into a child's pose. Get outside. Go for a walk. Feel the wind on your face. Or lie on the floor and put your feet up against a wall and just breathe.

A note on wanting

IT IS ALL right to want something – fame, the semblance of youth, 10,000 likes, hard abs, doughnuts – but wanting is also lacking. That is what 'want' means. So we have to be careful of our wants and watch that they don't cause too many holes inside us, otherwise happiness will drip through us like water through a leaky bucket. The moment we want is the moment we are dissatisfied. The more we want, the more we will drip ourselves away.

If you were already good enough
what on earth would you
spend your money on?

HAPPINESS IS NOT good for the economy.

We are encouraged, continually, to be a little bit dissatisfied with ourselves.

Our bodies are too fat, or too thin, or too saggy.

Our skin is expected to have the right 'sun-kissed glow', or the right shade of lightness. Depressingly, the global skin lightening industry is a multi-billion-dollar one that is growing year by year.

This is a particularly troubling example, but this central idea of *not feeling good enough* is one that businesses try to exploit almost everywhere. Indeed, it can sometimes seem as though the whole purpose of marketing itself is to make us feel bad about ourselves.

For instance, listen to Robert Rosenthal, author of *Optimarketing: Marketing Optimization to Electrify Your Business*. Back in 2014 he wrote in *Fast Company* magazine that to be successful marketers need to think in terms of the *benefits* of the product, rather than the product's *features*. Sounds innocent, enough, right?

But he adds that benefits often have a 'psychological component'. 'Fear, uncertainty, and doubt, or FUD, is often used legitimately by businesses and organizations to make consumers stop, think, and change their behaviour. FUD is so powerful that it's capable of nuking the competition.'

The success of the campaign is all, for the marketing gurus. The ends justify the means. Let's not think about the wider consequences of making millions of human beings more anxious than they need to be.

But even when an advertising campaign isn't overtly trying to conjure fear, it can still be bad for our psychology. If we are being sold the idea of cool via a pair of trousers, we subconsciously feel a pressure to obtain and maintain that coolness. And all too often, when we have spent a lot of money on a desired item, we have a sinking feeling. The craving for the thing is rarely met by the satisfaction of getting it. And so we crave more. And the cycle repeats. We are encouraged to want what will only make us want more.

We are, in short, encouraged to be addicts.

Never enough

NOTHING IS EVER enough.

I have always been addicted to something. That something changes but the sense of need doesn't.

Drink used to be my thing. I could drink and drink and drink.

When I used to work in an office block, doing a media sales job under the bleak skies of Croydon, I just dreamed of escape. The three pints I drank each night, followed by a vodka Coke, softened the blow of the evening only to harden it again when I woke up the next morning.

Some years after I broke down, I found it suddenly easy to stop drinking. And smoking. And everything. I stopped all stimulants. Even coffee and tea and Coca-Cola. I was in a state of continual panic and pain and would have done anything to take my mind off my mind but by now I knew alcohol wouldn't work. And I thought drugs wouldn't work. I was convinced, by then, that though they clearly worked for other people I was one of the unlucky ones for whom they wouldn't. I was also convinced that I had once had addictive tendencies. It was more difficult to realise I still had them, but that I was now finding 'positive' addictions. Running, for instance, like my dad advised. Yoga. Meditation. Work. Success.

Then, years later, when I felt comparatively better I started drinking again. I wouldn't drink every day, or even every week, but when I did drink I drank irresponsibly. The difference was that this time I could see how alcohol affected my mind. I could see the cycle that happened. I would feel a bit bad – not panic disorder bad, just a general low-level depression – and drink and feel better. Then I would feel hungover and guilty. And this feeling would linger and lower my self-esteem, which would then create more need for distraction. For drink. For eight pints and a gin cocktail. But it was dangerous. It was impossible to be a good husband or father or a good writer when you were that hungover, and the irony was that the feeling of inadequacy and self-loathing made future hangovers more likely. I have learned that however strong the craving gets the guilt afterwards will be stronger. But it's hard. And I have immense sympathy for those who have sought to drown their relentless despair in a sea of booze. And get judged for it in the process by those who have never had that painful yearning to escape themselves.

When people talk about mental health stigma getting better they may be right about an improvement in conditions for people suffering from depression or panic attacks. They probably aren't talking about alcoholism, or self-harm, or psychosis, or Borderline Personality Disorder, or eating disorders, or compulsive behaviours, or drug addiction. Those things can test the open minds of even the best of us. That's the problem with mental illness. It's easy not to judge people for having an *illness*; it's a lot harder not to judge people for how the illness occasionally causes them to *behave*. Because people can't see the reasons.

I can remember going to see the unique, rare genius that was Amy Winehouse in concert and having tears in my eyes at how the crowd – largely drunk themselves – laughed and jeered as she slurred her words between songs and desperately struggled, inebriated, to compose herself. It made me burn with a kind of anger and shame. I tried – ludicrously, embarrassingly – to send silent telepathic messages to her. *It's okay. You'll be okay. They just don't understand.*

Right now, writing this, with the sun outside the window, I am fantasising about a Caipirinha. Brazil's national cocktail. Cachaça, lime, sugar. Heaven in a glass. I have memories of drinking it in shady Spanish squares, and the craving is in part a craving to return back to being carefree and 21 again. But I know that would be a bad idea. I have to remind myself why I want it and what might happen. I have to remember that there wouldn't just be one glass. I have to remember a craving for an innocent drink has previously – after a perfectly respectable afternoon work meeting – ended up with a phone call home from Victoria station at six in the morning after losing my wallet. I have to remember the subsequent spiral into a furious relapse of depression and anxiety – the kind where you end up crying as you stare at your sock drawer and where the sight of grey clouds or a magazine cover prompts feelings of infinite despair. Doing all that remembering, being *mindful* of causes and consequences, makes it a lot easier to resist. An evening of heaven in a glass doesn't outweigh a month of hell in a cage.

My point here isn't specifically about alcohol. It's about how the pattern of addiction – dissatisfaction to temporary solution to increased dissatisfaction – is the model for most of consumer culture. It is also the model for a lot of our relationships with technology. The dangers of excessive technological use are becoming clearer than ever. In 2018,

Apple's CEO, Tim Cook, began to talk about the overuse of technology.

'I don't believe in overuse. I'm not a person that says we've achieved success if you're using it all the time. I don't subscribe to that at all.'

The trouble is, not overusing technology is sometimes easier said than done.

'Make no mistake,' writes neuroscientist Daniel Levitin in his book *The Organized Mind: Thinking Straight in the Age of Information Overload*: 'Email, Facebook, and Twitter checking constitute a neural addiction.' Each time we check social media 'we encounter something novel and feel more connected socially (in a kind of weird impersonal cyber way) and get another dollop of reward hormones' telling us we have 'accomplished something'. But as with all addiction, this feeling of reward is unreliable. As Levitin puts it: 'it is the dumb, novelty-seeking portion of the brain driving the limbic system that induces this feeling of pleasure, not the planning, scheduling, higher-level thought centres in the prefrontal cortex.'

As with living in Ibiza, or in a religious cult, it is hard to see the things we may have problems with if everyone has the same problems. If everyone is spending hour after hour on their phones, scrolling through texts and timelines, then that becomes normal behaviour. If everyone is getting out of bed too early to work 12-hour days in jobs they hate, then why question it? If everyone is worrying about their looks, then worrying about our looks is what we should be doing. If everyone is maxing out their credit cards to pay for things they don't really need, then it can't be a problem. If the whole planet is having a kind of collective breakdown, then unhealthy behaviour fits right in. When normality becomes madness, the only way to find sanity is by daring to be different. Or daring to be the you that exists beyond all the physical clutter and mind debris of modern existence.

A paradox

THERE'S A PARADOX about modern hi-tech consumer societies. They seem to encourage *individualism* while not encouraging us – actually forbidding us – to think *as individuals*. They discourage us from standing back from their distractions, like serious addicts have to if they want their life back, and asking: what am I doing? And why do I keep doing it if it doesn't make me happy? In a weird way, this is easier if you choose a socially unacceptable compulsion like heroin addiction than if you have a socially acceptable one like compulsive dieting or tweeting or shopping or working. If the madness is collective and the illness is cultural it can be hard to diagnose, let alone treat.

Even when the tide of society is pulling us in one direction it has to be possible – if that direction makes and keeps us unhappy – to learn how to swim another way. To swim towards the truth of ourselves, a truth our distractions might be hiding. Our very lives might depend on it.

You are more than a consumer

DON'T LET ANYONE or anything make you feel you aren't enough. Don't feel you have to achieve more just to be accepted. Be happy with your own self, minus upgrades. Stop dreaming of imaginary goals and finishing lines. Accept what marketing doesn't want you to: you are fine. You lack nothing.

15
TWO LISTS ABOUT WORK

'How many young college graduates have taken demanding jobs in high-powered firms, vowing that they will work hard to earn money that will enable them to retire and pursue their real interests when they are thirty-five? But by the time they reach that age, they have large mortgages, children to school, houses in the suburbs that necessitate at least two cars per family, and a sense that life is not worth living without really good wine and expensive holidays abroad. What are they supposed to do, go back to digging up roots? No, they double their efforts and keep slaving away.'

—Yuval Noah Harari, *Sapiens: A Brief History of Humankind* (2011)

'I want to say, in all seriousness, that a great deal of harm is being done in the modern world by belief in the virtuousness of work, and that the road to happiness and prosperity lies in an organised diminution of work.'

—Bertrand Russell, *In Praise of Idleness* (1932)

Work is toxic

1. We have become detached from the historic way of working. We, as individuals, rarely consume what we make. People often can't get the work for which they are qualified. Slowly, human work is being taken on by machines. Self-service checkouts. Assembly-line robots. Automated phone operators.

2. Also, the world economy is unfair. Yes, some progress is being made. The numbers of people in extreme poverty is falling year by year, according to figures from the World Bank. But other inequalitites are rising. The world's eight richest billionaires own the same wealth as the 3.6 billion people who make up the poorest half of the world, according to a 2017 report from Oxfam. The Western middle classes are shrinking, according to research from Credit Suisse, while the extremes of rich and poor are getting greater. Meritocracy is a hard myth to cling on to.

3. Workplace bullying is rife. The competitive nature of many work environments fuels aggressive rivalry that

can easily tip over into manipulation and bullying. According to research conducted by the University of Phoenix, 75 per cent of workers in America have been affected by workplace bullying, either as a target or a witness. But the targets aren't always who you think. According to the Workplace Bullying Institute, rather than the targets being weaker members of a team, they can often be more skilled and proficient than the bullies – workplace veterans who might be a threat. And research from the TUC in collaboration with the Everyday Sexism Project found that 52 per cent of women said that they had been sexually harassed at work.

4. In extreme cases, workplace stress can be fatal. For instance, between 2008 and 2009 and again in 2014 the French telecoms company Orange reported waves of employee suicides. After the first wave, where 35 employees killed themselves in a matter of months, the boss dismissed it as a 'fashion' although an official report quoted in *The Guardian* blamed a climate of 'management harassment' that had 'psychologically weakened staff and attacked their physical and mental health'.

5. Assessment culture is toxic. The Belgian professor of psychoanalysis, Paul Verhaeghe, believes that the way

work is now set up in our societies, with supervisors supervising supervisors and everyone being watched and marked and continually assessed, is toxic. Even people who aren't in work suffer the same equivalent endless rounds of tests and monitoring. As our school-children are also discovering, all this testing and evaluating makes us stress about the future rather than be comfortable with the present.

6. Work culture can lead to low self-esteem. We are encouraged to believe that success is the result of hard work, that it is down to the individual. So, it is no surprise that when we feel as if we are failing – which is almost continually in an aspirational culture that thrives on raising the bar of our happiness – we take it personally. And think it is down to ourselves. We aren't encouraged to see the context.

7. We like to work. It gives us purpose. But work can also be bad for physical health. In 2015, the Finnish Institute of Occupational Health published a study – the largest ever of its kind – looking at the link between overwork and alcohol. They compiled a dataset of over 333,000 workers across 14 different countries and found, conclusively, that the longer our working hours, the more alcohol we drink.

8. It is hard to challenge our cultural obsession with work. Politicians and business leaders keep up the idea of relentless work as a moral virtue. They talk with misty-eyed sentiment and a dose of sycophancy about 'decent ordinary working people' and 'hard-working families'. We accept the five-day working week as if it was a law of nature. We are often made to feel guilty when we aren't working. We say to ourselves, like Benjamin Franklin did, that 'time is money', forgetting that money is also luck. A lot of people who work very long hours have far less money than people who have never worked in their life.

9. People work ever longer hours, but these extra hours do not guarantee extra productivity. When a Swedish trial experimented with a six-hour working day for nurses in Gothenburg, the results showed that the nurses felt happier and more energised than when they worked for eight hours. They ended up taking fewer sick days, had less physical complaints like back and neck pain, and had an increase of productivity during the hours worked.

10. Our working culture is often dehumanising. We need to assess whether our work is making us ill, or unhappy, and if it is what we can do about it. How

much pressure are we actually putting on ourselves, simply because the way we work makes us feel continually behind? Like life is a race that we are losing? And in our struggle to keep up we don't dare to stop and think what might be good for us.

Ten ways to work without breaking down

1. Try to do something you enjoy. If you enjoy work you will be better at it. If you enjoy work it won't feel like work. Try to think of work as productive play.

2. Aim not *to get more stuff done*. Aim to have *less stuff to do*. Be a work minimalist. Minimalism is about doing more with less. So much of working life seems to be about doing less with more. Activity isn't always the same as achievement.

3. Set boundaries. Have times of the day and week that are work-free, email-free, hassle-free.

4. Don't stress about deadlines. This book is already behind deadline, but you're still reading it.

5. Know that your inbox will never be empty. Accept that.

6. Try to work, where possible, in a way that makes the world a little better. The world shapes us. Making the world better makes us better.

7. Be kind to yourself. If the negatives of the work outweigh the positives of the money, don't do it. If

someone is using their power to bully or harass you, don't stand for it. If you hate your job, and can get away with walking out on your lunch break, walk out on your lunch break. And never go back.

8. Don't think your work matters more than it does. As Bertrand Russell put it: 'One of the symptoms of an approaching nervous breakdown is the belief that one's work is terribly important.'

9. Don't do the work people expect you to do. Do the work you want to do. You only get one life. It's always best to live it as yourself.

10. Don't be a perfectionist. Humans are imperfect. Human work is imperfect. Be less robot, more human. Be more imperfect. Evolution happens through mistakes.

16

SHAPING THE FUTURE

Progress

IT WOULD BE seen as crazily reactionary and conservative to say that technological progress is a uniformly bad thing.

Almost none of us would trade the technology we have now, to live a hundred years ago. Who would give up a world of cars and sat nav and smartphones and laptops and washing machines and Skype and social media and video games and Spotify and X-rays and artificial hearts and cash machines and online shopping? Not me, for sure.

In writing this book I have tried to look at the human psychological cost of the world by looking at the only psychology I truly know – my own. I have written about how we *as individuals* can try to stay sane within a maddening world. The fact that I have had mental illness, though a nightmare in reality, has educated me on the various triggers and torments of the modern world.

The thing I really struggle with, though, is what we can do *as a society*. We can't reverse the clock. We can't suddenly become non-technological, and wouldn't want to. So how do we – the collective we – make a better world for ourselves?

One of the best people to answer this is Yuval Noah Harari, the history professor at the Hebrew University of Jerusalem whose ground-breaking books *Sapiens* and *Homo Deus* question what makes us human, and how technology is not only reshaping our world but also redefining humanity itself. He has written about the nightmarish scenario of a future world where humans could be surpassed by the machines they create and concludes, bleakly, that 'Homo sapiens as we know them will disappear in a century or so'.

After reading Harari's work I wondered why humans are so wilfully ushering in a future that will slowly make themselves redundant. It made me think of another work that had inspired me when I was younger – *Straw Dogs* by the philosopher John Gray – which quite brutally explored the idea that human societal progress is a dangerous myth. After all, we are the only animals that are – as far as we know – obsessed with the idea of progress. If there are turtle historians congratulating previous turtles on their creation of a more enlightened turtle society we don't know about them.

In a piece for *The Observer*, I asked Harari if we should try to resist the idea of the future as one of inevitable technological advancement. Should we try to create a different kind of futurism?

'You can't just *stop* technological progress,' he said. 'Even if one country stops researching artificial intelligence, some other countries will continue to do it. The real question is what to do with the technology. You can use exactly the same technology for very different social and political purposes.'

The internet, of course, would be the obvious case in point in the present. But it is also an example – in the case of what used to be known as the 'world wide web' – of things which started with utopian ideals soon becoming dystopian.

'If you look at the 20th century,' Yuval continued, 'we see that with the same technology of electricity and trains you could create a communist dictatorship or a liberal democracy. And it's the same with artificial intelligence and bioengineering. So, I think people shouldn't be focused on the question of how to stop technological progress because this is impossible. Instead the question should be what kind of usage to make of the new technology. And here we still have quite a lot of power to influence the direction it's taking.'

So, like many things, the answer to fixi[...]
seems first to be *aware* of the problem. In ot[...]
answer to making our minds and our planet h[...]
happier is essentially the same one. When Hara[...] [...]at
you can use the same technology for very different
purposes, that is of course as true on the micro level of the
individual as it is on the macro level of society. Being
mindful of how our own use of technology affects us is
indirectly being mindful of how technology affects the
planet. The planet doesn't simply shape us. We shape the
planet by how we choose to live our lives.

And sometimes, when we – and our societies – are
heading in unhealthy directions we have to do the bravest
and most difficult thing of all. We have to *change*.

That change can take different forms. It can mean using
technology to help our minds, by getting an app that limits
our social media use, or getting a dimmer switch, or walking more, or being more considerate to people online, or
choosing a car less likely to contaminate the air. Being kind
to ourselves and being kind to the planet is, ultimately, the
same thing.

'Progress,' wrote C.S. Lewis, 'means getting nearer to
the place you want to be. And if you have taken a wrong
turning, then to go forward does not get you any nearer.'

This is a phenomenally good way of looking at it, I think. Forward momentum, on an individual or social level, is *not automatically good* simply because it is forward momentum. Sometimes we push *our lives in the wrong* direction. Sometimes societies push themselves in the wrong direction. If we feel it is making ourselves unhappy, progress might mean doing an about-turn and walking back to the right road. But we must never feel – personally or as a culture – that only one version of the future is inevitable.

The future is ours to shape.

Space

IN TERMS OF shaping our own future, spaces are key. We need to make sure there are spaces to be free. To be ourselves. Literal spaces, psychological spaces.

Increasingly, our towns and cities are places which want us there primarily as consumers, rather than people. Which makes it all the more important that we value those threatened spaces where economically irrelevant *being* is still allowed. Forests, parks, state-funded museums and galleries, libraries.

Libraries, for instance, are wonderful places currently at risk. Many people in power dismiss them as irrelevant in the age of the internet. This really misses the point. Many libraries are using the internet in innovative ways, enabling access to books and the internet itself. And besides, libraries aren't just about books. They are one of the few public spaces we have left which don't like our wallets more than us.

But there are other spaces which are threatened, too.

Non-physical spaces. Spaces of time. Digital spaces. Some online companies increasingly want to infringe on our selfhood, seeing us as less of a human being and more as an organism full of data to be mined, or sold on.

There are spaces in the day and week that are being continually devoured in the name of work or other responsibilities.

There are even spaces of the mind that are under threat. The space to think freely, or at least calmly, seems to be harder to find. Which might explain the rise not only in anxiety disorders but also of counterbalancing habits such as yoga and meditation.

People are craving not just physical space but the space to be mentally free. A space from unwanted distracted thoughts that clutter our heads like pop-up advertising of the mind in an already frantic world. And that space is still there to be found. It's just that we can't *rely* on it. We have to consciously seek it out. We might have to set time to read or do some yoga or have a long bath or cook a favourite meal or go for a walk. We might have to switch our phone off. We might have to close the laptop. We might have to unplug ourselves, to find a kind of stripped-back acoustic version of us.

Fiction is freedom

BOOKS MIGHT BE one way to recover some space. Stories. Fiction.

When I was eleven, friendless, struggling to fit in at school, I read *The Outsiders* and *Rumble Fish* and *Tex* by S.E. Hinton, and I suddenly had friends again. Her books were friends. The characters were friends. And real ones, too, because they helped me out. Just as at other times Winnie-the-Pooh and Scout Finch and Pip and *Bonjour Tristesse*'s Cécile were friends. And the stories they inhabited could be places I could hide inside. And feel safe.

In a world that can get too much, a world where we are running out of mind space, fictional worlds are essential. They can be an escape from reality, yes, but not an escape from truth. Quite the opposite. In the 'real' world, I used to struggle with fitting in. The codes you had to follow. The lies you had to tell. The laughs you had to fake. Fiction felt not like an escape from truth but a release into it. Even if it was a truth with monsters or talking bears, there was always some kind of truth there. A truth that could keep you sane, or at least keep you *you*.

For me, reading was never an antisocial activity. It was deeply social. It was the most profound kind of socialising there was. A deep connection to the imagination of another human being. A way to connect without the many filters society normally demands.

So often, reading is seen as important because of its social value. It is tied to education and the economy and so on. But that misses the whole point of reading.

Reading isn't important because it helps to get you a job. It's important because it gives you room to exist beyond the reality you're given. It is how humans merge. How minds connect. Dreams. Empathy. Understanding. Escape.

Reading is love in action.

It doesn't need to be books. But we do need to find that space.

We are frequently encouraged to want the most extreme and exciting experiences. To act on a heady impulse for action. To 'Just Do It' as Nike always used to bark at us, like a self-help drill instructor. As if the very point of life is found via winning a gold medal or climbing Mount Everest or headlining Glastonbury or having a full-body orgasm while sky-diving over the Niagara Falls. And I used to feel the same. I used to want to lose myself in the most intense experiences, as if life was simply a tequila to be slammed. But most of life can't be lived like this. To have a chance of lasting happiness, you have to calm down. You have to just be it as well as just do it.

We crowd our lives with activity because in the West we often feel happiness and satisfaction are achieved by acquisition, by 'seizing' the day, or by going out and 'grabbing' life by the horns. We might sometimes do better to replace life as something to be grabbed at, or reached for, with something we already have. If we clear out the mental clutter we can surely enjoy it more.

The Buddhist monk Thích Nhất Hạnh writes in *The Art of Power* that while 'many people think excitement is happiness', actually 'when you are excited you are not peaceful. True happiness is based on peace.'

Personally, I wouldn't want a life of total neutral inner peace. I'd want to occasionally experience some wild intensity and exhilaration. That is part of me. But I crave that peace and acceptance more than ever.

To be comfortable with yourself, to know yourself, requires creating some inner space where you can *find* yourself, away from a world that often encourages you to lose yourself.

We need to carve out a place in time for ourselves, whether it is via books or meditation or appreciating the view out of a window. A place where we are not craving, or yearning, or working, or worrying, or over-thinking. A place where we might not even be hoping. A place where we are set to neutral. Where we can just breathe, just be, just bathe in the simple animal contentment of being, and not crave anything except what we already have: life itself.

Aim

TO FEEL EVERY moment, to ignore tomorrow, to unlearn all the worries and regrets and fear caused by the concept of time. To be able to walk around and think of nothing but the walking. To lie in bed, not asleep, and not worry about sleep. But just be there, in sweet horizontal happiness, unflustered by past and future concerns.

17
THE SONG OF YOU

Sycamore trees

DURING THE WRITING of this book, my mum had to have a major operation. She had open heart surgery to remove and replace a damaged aortic valve. The operation went well, and she recovered, but her week in intensive care was a bit of a rollercoaster, with doctors and nurses needing to keep a close eye on the levels of oxygen in her blood. They reached worrying lows.

Andrea and I went up and stayed in a hotel near the hospital. I sat by her bedside with my dad as Mum slid in and out of sleep. I helped spoon-feed her hospital meals and brought in carrier bags full of shop-bought smoothies, and the occasional newspaper for Dad. My worry about Mum stripped everything else away. I felt incredible guilt about having hardly listened when she had told me about her initial visits to the doctor.

Now, I didn't care about any urgent emails I hadn't got back to. I didn't have any temptation to check social media. Even world news seemed like a background irrelevance when you were sitting in an intensive care unit hearing the wails of grief coming from beyond a thin hospital curtain as the patient in the next bed passes away.

Intensive care units are bleak places, sometimes, but those sterile rooms full of people perched between life and death can also be hopeful ones. And the nurses and doctors were an inspiration.

It's just a shame, I suppose, that it takes such major events in our lives, or in the lives of the people we love, for perspective to arrive. Imagine if we could keep hold of that perspective. If we could *always* have our priorities right, even during the good and healthy times. Imagine if we could always think of our loved ones the way we think of them when they are in a critical condition. If we could always keep that love – love that is always there – so close to the surface. Imagine if we could keep the kindness and soft gratitude towards life itself.

I am trying now, when my life gets too packed with unnecessary stressful junk, to remember that room in the hospital. Where patients were thankful just to look at the view out of a window. Some sunshine and sycamore trees.

And where life, on its own, was everything.

Love

Only love will save us.

Minus psychograms
(things that make you feel lighter)

Imagine that, as well as psychograms, there could be things that make your mind feel lighter. We could call these minus psychograms, or -pg.

The sun appearing unexpectedly from behind
   a cloud   57-pg
The all-clear from a doctor   320-pg
Being on holiday somewhere with no wi-fi
   (after the initial panic)   638-pg
Walking the dog   125-pg
A yoga session   487-pg
Being lost in a good book   732-pg
Arriving home after a terrible train journey   398-pg
Being surrounded by nature   1,291-pg
Dancing   1,350-pg
A close relative recovering from an operation   3,982-pg

And so on.

Sri Lanka

I HAD BEEN asked to visit the beautiful fort city of Galle, on the southwest coast of Sri Lanka, to attend the literature festival there and give a talk on mental health. The event was quite special, as Sri Lanka is still a place where talking about mental illness can be taboo. And it was emotional, hearing stories of anxiety and depression and OCD and suicidal tendencies and bipolar disorder and schizophrenia in a context where they aren't normally publicly aired. It was like you could *feel* stigma evaporating in real time.

But it wasn't the event I remember, it was the day after. On Hikkiduwa beach, alongside locals and backpackers, feeding giant sea turtles seaweed straight from my hand. Andrea and the children were there. It was the kind of moment I never believed I would have when I was an agoraphobic twentysomething convinced I wouldn't live to reach 30, having pushed everyone I loved away. Then, at 40, in the Southern Hemisphere, there I was with people I loved, on an idyllic beach, close up to these large ancient reptiles. They seemed so calm and wise in their longevity. I wondered what secret wisdom they had. And wished there was a way for a human to ask a turtle questions.

So, when depression slugs over me I close my eyes and enter the bank of good days and think of sunshine and laughter and turtles. And I try to remember how possible the impossible can sometimes be.

An amphibious approach to life

'Hello, turtle.'

'Oh. Hi there.'

'Any advice on life?'

'Why are you asking me?'

'Because you're a turtle.'

'And?'

'Turtles have survived for millions of years. You've been around for 157 million years. That's more than 700 hundred times as long as Homo sapiens have been around. You must know some things, as a species.'

'You're conflating length of existence with breadth of knowledge.'

'It's just humans who have made a mess of the world. Turtles don't seem to.'

'I know. We are near extinction because of you.'

'I'm sorry.'

'I was using "you" in the plural sense. But also, yes, you.'

'I know. I'm a human. I share the blame.'

'Yes. You do.'

'Yes.'

'Anyway, if you really want to know, the advice I would give is stop it.'

'Stop *what*?'

'It. The rushing after nothing. Humans seem in such a rush to escape where they are. Why? Is it the air? Does it not hold you up well enough? Maybe you need more time in the sea. I would say: stop it. Don't just take your time, *be your time*. Move fast or slow, but be aware you will always take yourself with you. Be happy to paddle in the water of existence.'

'Right.'

'Look at my head. It's tiny. My brain-to-body-mass ratio is embarrassing. But it doesn't matter, you see. If you take life carefully, you can focus. You can be how you need to be. You can have an amphibious approach to life. You can be at one with the rhythms of the whole earth. The wet and the dry. You can tune in to the wind and the water. You can tune in to yourself. It's rather wonderful, you know, being a turtle.'

'I bet. Thanks, turtle.'

'Now, may I have some more seaweed?'

Reversing the loop

ANXIETY IS SELF-PERPETUATING. When you have it in its illness form it is a feedback loop of despair. The only way out is to stop the meta-worry, to stop worrying *about* the worrying, which is near impossible. Sometimes the trick is to find a reverse kind of loop. I do this by accepting that I am in this state of non-acceptance. By being comfortable with being uncomfortable. By accepting I don't have control.

A cliché but true: you can't get to where you want to be without first accepting where you are. The world tries to tell us not to accept ourselves. It makes us want to be richer, prettier, thinner, happier. To want more. When we are ill, this becomes doubly true, and yet this is when we most need to accept ourselves, accept the moment of pain, in order to release it. Slowly release it, into the world from which it came.

The sky is always the sky

JUST NOW I looked out of the window and felt calmer. The moon is a real flirt tonight behind a veil of bruise-blue cloud. This sky is sensational. No photo would catch it.

And this reminded me of something. When I had a long episode of depression about a decade ago, the worst depression I have had since my breakdown in my twenties, one of the few comforts I used to get was looking at the sky. We lived in Yorkshire, and there wasn't that much light pollution, and so the sky was vast and clear. I'd take the bins out and just look at the night sky and feel myself and my pain getting smaller. I'd stand there for a while breathing the cool air, staring at stars and planets and constellations. I would breathe deeply, as if the cosmos was something you could inhale. I'd sometimes place my hand on my stomach and feel the stuttery flutter of my nervous breathing begin to settle.

I often wondered, and still wonder, why the sky, especially the night sky, had such an effect. I used to think it was to do with the scale. When you look up at the cosmos you can't help but feel minuscule. You feel the smallness of yourself not only in space but also in time. Because, of course, when you stare into space you are staring up at ancient history. You are staring at stars as they *were*, not as they *are*. Light travels. It doesn't just instantaneously appear. It moves at 186,000 miles per second. Which sounds fast, but also means that light from the closest star to Earth (after the sun) took over four years to get here.

But some of the stars visible to the naked eye are over 15,000 light years away. Which means the light reaching your eye began its journey at the end of the Ice Age. Before humans knew how to farm land. Contrary to popular belief, most of the stars that we see with our eyes are not dead. Stars, unlike us, exist for a very long time. But that adds to, rather than takes away from, the therapeutic majesty of the night sky. Our beautiful but tiny brief role within the cosmos is as that rarest of galactic things: a living, breathing, conscious organism.

When looking at the sky, all our 21st-century worries can be placed in their cosmic context. The sky is bigger than emails and deadlines and mortgages and internet trolls. It is bigger than our minds, and their illnesses. It is bigger than names and nations and dates and clocks. All of our earthly concerns are quite transient when compared to the sky. Through our lives, throughout every chapter of human history, the sky has always been the sky.

And, of course, when we are looking at the sky we aren't looking at something outside ourselves. We are looking, really, at where we came from. As physicist Carl Sagan wrote in his masterpiece *Cosmos*: 'The nitrogen in our DNA, the calcium in our teeth, the iron in our blood, the carbon in our apple pies were made in the interiors of collapsing stars. We are made of starstuff.'

The sky, like the sea, can anchor us. It says: hey, it's okay, there is something bigger than your life that you are part of, and it's – literally – cosmic. It's the most wonderful thing. And you need to make like a tree or a bird and just feel a part of the great natural order now and again. You are incredible. You are nothing and everything. You are a single moment and all eternity. You are the universe in motion.

Well done.

Nature

THE SKY HAS been shown to soothe us.

In 2018 a research study conducted by King's College London found that being able to see the sky helps our mental health. And not just the sky. Seeing trees, hearing birdsong, being outside, and feeling in contact with nature.

Participants in the study went out into the world, and were instructed to record their mental states at different locations. Interestingly, the study was quite nuanced as it factored in each individual's risk of developing poor mental health by doing some early tests on each participant to assess impulsive behaviours.

The study, catchily titled 'Urban Mind: Using Smartphone Technologies to Investigate the Impact of Nature on Mental Wellbeing in Real Time', found that while being out in the natural world is good for everyone, it is of particular benefit for those who are more predisposed to mental health problems like addiction, ADHD, antisocial personality disorder and bipolar disorder.

'Short-term exposure to nature has a measurable beneficial impact on mental wellbeing,' concluded Dr Andrea Mechelli, who had helped to lead the research.

Ecotherapy or 'green care' projects are on the rise. Many city farms and community gardens are now used for mental health work to lower stress, anxiety and depression. Of course, in many ways this is all acting on old advice: 'Get yourself some fresh air.' In 1859, in her *Notes on Nursing*, Florence Nightingale wrote that 'after a closed room, what hurts them [patients] most is a dark room' and advised that 'it is not only light but direct sunlight they want'. Finally, evidence is catching up.

The trouble is, over half the world's population now live in big cities. In 1950 more than two-thirds of the world's population lived in rural settlements. Now, worldwide, most people live in urban areas. And, as people spend more time indoors than ever before, it's clear that we aren't existing much amid forests and under natural skies.

It's time we started being more aware that the blues and greens of nature can help us. And the lives of children, too. More fresh air, more direct sunlight, maybe even if we are lucky the odd walk across fields and through forests. And perhaps also, armed with evidence, we can help to make the communal urban spaces we inhabit a bit more green and pleasant, too, so that everyone can benefit from nature, not just the lucky few.

The world inside

SO, YES, THE beauty of nature can heal. But in Ibiza, in 1999, I stood on top of a cliff near the villa where I was living, tucked into one of the quieter corners on the east of the island, and urged myself to jump.

I literally had no way of coping – or none that I could see – with the mental pain and confusion I was going through, and wished I had no one who cared about me, so I could just leave and disappear with minimal impact.

I sometimes think of that cliff edge. Of the scrubby grass I stood on, of the glittering sea I stared out at, and the limestone coastline stretching out. None of that, at the time, consoled me. Nature is shown to be good for us, but in the moment of crisis nothing helps. No view in the world could have made me feel any better in that moment of extreme invisible pain. That view won't have changed much over two decades. And yet I could stand there now and feel its beauty, and feel so different to the terrified young man I had been.

The world affects us, but it isn't quite *us*. There is a space inside us that is independent to what we see and where we are. This means we can feel pain amid external beauty and peace. But the flipside is that we can feel calm in a world of fear. We can cultivate a calmness inside us, one that lives and grows, and gets us through.

There is a cliché about reading. That there are as many books as there are readers. Meaning every reader has their own take on a book. Five people could sit down and read, say, *The Left Hand of Darkness* by Ursula K. Le Guin and have five totally different legitimate responses. It isn't really about what you read, but how you read it. The writer might start a story but they need a reader for it to come alive, and it never comes alive the same way twice. The story is never just the words. It is also the reading of them. And that is the variable. That is where the magic lives. All a writer can do is provide a match, and hopefully a dry one. The reader has to strike the flame into being.

The world is like that, too. There are as many worlds as there are inhabitants. The world exists in you. Your experience of the world isn't this objective unchangeable thing called 'The World'. No. Your experience of the world is your interaction with it, your interpretation of it. To a certain degree we all make our own worlds. We read it in our own way. But also: we can, to a degree, choose what to read. We have to work out what about the world makes us feel sad or scared or confused or ill or calm or happy.

We have to find, within all those billions of human worlds, the one we want to live on. The one that, without us imagining it, would never arrive.

And, likewise, we have to understand that however it might influence them, the world is not our feelings. We can feel calm in a hospital, or in pain on a Spanish clifftop.

We can contradict ourselves. We can contradict the world. We can sometimes even do the impossible. We can live when death seems inevitable. And we can hope after we knew hope had gone.

You, unplugged

LIFE CAN SOMETIMES feel like an overproduced song, with a cacophony of a hundred instruments playing all at once. Sometimes the song sounds better stripped back to just a guitar and a voice. Sometimes, when a song has too much happening, it's hard to hear the song at all.

And like that overcrowded song we, too, can feel a bit lost.

Our natural selves haven't changed in tens of thousands of years, and we should remember that, with every new app or smartphone or social media platform or nuclear weapon we design. We should remember the song of being human. To think of the air when we feel stuck underwater. To find some calm amid an age of saturated marketing and breaking news and the million daily jolts of the internet. To be unafraid of being afraid. To be our own brilliant, true, beautiful, fragile, flawed, imperfect, animal, ageing, wonderful selves, trapped in time and space, made free by our ability to stop, at any moment, and find something – a song, a sunbeam, a conversation, a piece of pretty graffiti – and feel the sheer improbable wonder of being alive.

18
EVERYTHING
YOU ARE IS ENOUGH

'There is only one corner of the universe you can be certain of improving, and that's your own self.'

—Aldous Huxley

Things that have almost always been

CLIFFS. TREE FERNS. Companionship. Sky. The man in the moon. The sentimentality of sunrises and sunsets. Eternal love. Dizzy lust. Abandoned plans. Regret. Cloudless night skies. Full moons. Morning kisses. Fresh fruit. Oceans. Seas. Tides. Rivers. Lakes as still as mirrors. Faces full of friendship. Comedy. Laughter. Stories. Myths. Songs. Hunger. Pleasure. Sex. Death. Faith. Fire. The deep silent goodness of the observing self. The light made brighter by the dark around it. Eye contact. Dancing. Meaningless conversation. Meaningful silence. Sleep. Dreams. Nightmares. Monsters made of shadows. Turtles. Sawfish. The fresh green of wet grass. The bruised purple of clouds at dusk. The wet crash of waves on slow-eroding rocks. The dark slick shine of wet sand. The gasping relief of a thirst quenched. The terrible, tantalising awareness of being alive. The now that for ever is made of. The possibility of hope. The promise of home.

What I tell myself when
things get too much

1. It's okay.

2. Even if it isn't okay, if it's a thing you can't control, don't try to control it.

3. You feel misunderstood. Everyone is misunderstood. Don't worry about other people understanding you. Aim to understand yourself. Nothing else will matter after that.

4. Accept yourself. If you can't be happy as yourself, at least accept yourself as you are right now. You can't change yourself if you don't know yourself.

5. Never be cool. Never try to be cool. Never worry what the cool people think. Head for the warm people. Life is warmth. You'll be cool when you're dead.

6. Find a good book. And sit down and read it. There will be times in your life when you'll feel lost and confused. The way back to yourself is through reading. I want you to remember that. The more you read,

the more you will know how to find your way through those difficult times.

7. Don't fix yourself down. Don't be blinded by the connotations of your name, gender, nationality, sexuality or Facebook profile. Be more than data to be harvested. 'When I let go of what I am,' said the Chinese philosopher Lao Tzu, 'I become what I might be.'

8. Slow down. Also Lao Tzu: 'Nature does not hurry, yet everything is accomplished.'

9. Enjoy the internet. Don't use it when you aren't enjoying it. (Nothing has sounded so easy and been so hard.)

10. Remember that many people feel like you. You can even go online and find them. This is one of the most therapeutic aspects of the social media age. You can find an echo of your pain. You can find someone who will understand.

11. As Yoda nearly put it, you can't *try* to be. Trying is the opposite of being.

12. The things that make you unique are flaws. Imperfections. Embrace them. Don't seek to filter out your human nature.

13. Don't let marketing convince you that happiness is a

commercial transaction. As the Cherokee-American cowboy Will Rogers once put it, 'Too many people spend money they haven't earned, to buy things they don't want, to impress people they don't like.'

14. Never miss breakfast.

15. Go to bed before midnight most days.

16. Even during manic times – Christmas, family occasions, hectic work patches, city holidays – find some moments of peace. Retreat to a bedroom now and then. Add a comma to your day.

17. Shop less.

18. Do some yoga. It's harder to be stressed out if your body and your breath isn't.

19. When times get rocky, keep a routine.

20. Do not compare the worst bits of your life with the best bits of other people's.

21. Value the things most that you'd miss the most if they weren't there.

22. Don't try to pin yourself down. Don't try to understand, once and for all, who you are. As the philosopher Alan Watts said, 'trying to define yourself is like trying to bite your own teeth'.

23. Go for a walk. Go for a run. Dance. Eat peanut butter on toast.

24. Don't try to feel something you don't feel. Don't try to be something you can't be. That energy will exhaust you.

25. Connecting with the world has nothing to do with wi-fi.

26. There is no future. Planning for the future is just planning for another present in which you will be planning for the future.

27. Breathe.

28. Love now. Love right now. If you have someone or something to love, do it this instant. Love fearlessly. As Dave Eggers wrote: 'It is no way to live, to wait to love.' Throw love out there selflessly.

29. Don't feel guilty. It is almost impossible, unless you are a sociopath, not to feel some guilt these days. We are cluttered with guilt. There is the guilt we learned at childhood mealtimes, the guilt of eating while knowing there are starving people in the world. The guilt of privilege. The eco-guilt of driving a car or flying in a plane or using plastic. The guilt of buying stuff that may be unethical in some way we can't quite see. The guilt of unspoken or unfaithful desires. The guilt of not being the things other people wanted you to be. The guilt of taking up space. The guilt of not

being able to do things other people can do. The guilt of being ill. The guilt of living. It's useless, this guilt. It doesn't help anyone. Try to do good right now, without drowning in whatever bad you might once have done.

30. See yourself outside market forces. Don't compete in the game. Resist the guilt of non-doing. Find the uncommodified space inside us. The true space. The human space. The space that could never be measured in terms of numbers or money or productivity. The space that the market economy can't see.

31. Look at the sky. (It's amazing. It's always amazing.)

32. Spend some time with a non-human animal.

33. Be unashamedly boring. Boring can be healthy. When life gets tough, aim for those beige emotions.

34. Don't value yourself in line with other people's valuation of yourself. As Eleanor Roosevelt said, 'No one can make you feel inferior without your consent.'

35. The world can be sad. But remember a million unsung acts of kindness happened today. A million acts of love. Quiet human goodness lives on.

36. Don't beat yourself up for being a mess. It's fine. The universe is a mess. Galaxies are drifting all over the place. You're just in tune with the cosmos.

37. If you're feeling mentally unwell, treat yourself as you would any physical problem. Asthma, flu, whatever. Do what you need to do to get better. And have no shame about it. Don't keep walking around on a broken leg.

38. It's okay to cry. People cry. Women cry. And *men* cry. They have tear ducts and lachrymal glands just like other human beings. A man crying is no different from a woman crying. It's natural. Social roles are toxic when they don't allow an outlet for pain. Or sentimental emotion. Cry, human. Cry your heart out.

39. Allow yourself to fail. Allow yourself to doubt. Allow yourself to feel vulnerable. Allow yourself to change your mind. Allow yourself to be imperfect. Allow yourself to resist dynamism. Allow yourself not to shoot through life like an arrow speeding with purpose.

40. Try to want less. A want is a hole. A want is a lack. That is part of the definition. When the poet Byron wrote 'I want a hero' he meant that he didn't have one. The act of wanting things we don't need makes us feel a lack we didn't have. Everything you need is here. A human being is complete just being human. We are our own destination.

Diminishing returns

PLANET EARTH IS unique. It is the only place we know of where life exists in the vast cosmic arena of the universe. It is an incredible place. On its own, it gives us everything humans need to survive.

And you are also incredible. Equally so. You were incredible from the day you were born. You were *everything* from the day you were born. No one looks at a newborn baby and thinks, oh dear, look at all that *absence of stuff*. They look at a baby and they feel like they are looking at perfection, untainted by the complexities and baggage of life yet to come.

We come complete. Give us some food and drink and shelter, sing us a song, tell us a story, give us people to talk to and care for and fall in love with and there you go. A *life*.

But somewhere along the way we have raised the threshold of what we need, or feel we need, to be happy.

We are encouraged to buy stuff to make ourselves happy because companies are encouraged to make more money to make themselves more successful. It is also addictive. It isn't addictive because it makes us happy. It is addictive because it *doesn't* make us happy. We buy something and we enjoy it – we enjoy the *newness* of it – for a little while but then we get used to having it, we acclimatise, and so we need something else. We need to feel that sense of change, of variety. Something newer, something better, something upgraded. And the same thing happens again.

And over time we get used to more and more stuff.

And this applies to everything.

The Instagrammer who enjoys getting a lot of likes for their selfie will soon seek more likes, and be disappointed if the number stays the same. The grade A student will come to feel like a failure if they get a single B. The entrepreneur who becomes rich will seek to earn more money. The gym-goer who likes their new sculpted body will want to train harder, and harder. The worker who gets the promotion they wanted will soon want another one. With every achievement, acquisition or purchase the bar is raised.

I once thought I'd be happy for ever if I got articles published. Then a book published. Then if I could get *another* book published. Then if a book became a bestseller. And then if another one could. Then if it became a *number one* bestseller. Then if the film rights were sold. And so on. And I did, like lots of people, get happy, fleetingly, at each career goal I set myself, but my mind quickly got used to the previous achievement and found a new goal. So, the more I got, the more I needed to get in order to stay level.

The more 'success' you get, the easier it is to be disappointed by not getting things. The only difference is that now no one feels sorry for you.

No matter what we buy or achieve, the feelings don't last. A sports champion always wants another win. The millionaire always wants another million. The spotlight-hungry star wants more fame. Just as the alcoholic wants another drink and the gambler wants another bet.

But there are always going to be diminishing returns.

The child with a hundred toys is going to play with each new one less and less.

And think about it. If you could afford a holiday ten times more expensive than your last holiday, would you feel ten times more relaxed? I doubt it. If you could spend ten times longer looking at your Twitter feed, would you be ten times more informed? Of course not. If you spent twice as long at work would you get twice as much done?

Research suggests you wouldn't. If you could buy a car ten times more expensive than your current one would it get you from A to B ten times quicker? Nope. If you bought more anti-ageing creams would you age less with each extra purchase? Also nope.

You are conditioned to want more. Often this conditioning comes from companies who themselves are conditioned, collectively, to want more. Wanting more is the default setting.

But just as there is only one planet – a planet with finite resources – there is also only one you. And you also have a finite resource – time. And, let's face it, you can't multiply yourself. An overloaded planet cajoles us into overloaded lives but, ultimately, you can't play with all the toys. You can't use all the apps. You can't be at all the parties. You can't do the work of 20 people. You can't be up to speed on all the news. You can't wear all eleven of your coats at once. You can't watch every must-see show. You can't live in two places at once. You can buy more, you can acquire more, you can work more, you can earn more, you can strive more, you can tweet more, you can watch more, you can want more, but as each new buzz diminishes there comes a point where you have to ask yourself: what is all this for?

How much extra happiness am I acquiring? Why am I wanting so much more than I need?

Wouldn't I be happier learning to appreciate what I already have?

Simple ideas for a new beginning

— *Awareness*. Be aware of how much time you are spending on your phone, of how much the news is messing with your mind, of how your attitudes to work are changing, of how many pressures you feel, and how many of them stem from problems of modern life, of being connected into the world's nervous system. Awareness becomes a solution. Just as being aware of your hand on a hot stove means you can take your hand off the stove, being aware of the invisible sharks of modern life helps you to avoid them.

— *Wholeness*. The deficiencies you are made to feel, that society seems to *want* you to feel, you don't have to feel. You were born how you were meant to be, and remain so. You will never be anyone else, so don't try to be. You have no understudy. You are the one who is here to be you. So, don't compare, don't judge yourself on the opinion of people who have never been you.

— *The world is real, but* your *world is subjective*. Changing your perspective changes your planet. It can change your life. One version of multiverse theory states that we create a new universe with every decision we make. You can sometimes enter a better universe simply by not checking your phone for ten minutes.

– *Less is more*. An overloaded planet leads to an overloaded mind. It leads to late nights and light sleep. It leads to worrying about unanswered emails at three in the morning. In extreme cases, it leads to panic attacks in the cereal aisle. It's not 'Mo Money Mo Problems', as the Notorious B.I.G. track once put it. It's more everything, more problems. Simplify your life. Take away what doesn't need to be there.

– *You already know what is significant*. The things that matter are obviously the things you would truly miss deeply if they were gone. These are the things you should spend your time on, when you can. People, places, books, food, experiences, whatever. And sometimes to enjoy these more you have to strip other things back. You need to break free.

The important stuff

A WEEK AGO I went to a charity shop with stuff I'd accumulated and offloaded it. It felt good. Not only charitable, but cleansing. The house is free of a lot of my clutter now. Clothes I never wear, aftershaves I've never sprayed, two chairs no one sits on, old DVDs I'll never watch again, even – gasp – some books I will never read.

'Are you sure you want to get rid of all this?' Andrea had asked, staring at the landscape of bin bags in the hallway. Even she – a natural-born clearer-outer – was taken aback.

'Yeah. Think so.'

The thing is that in the actual process of throwing things out, I ended up valuing the things I had more. For instance, while I was discarding some old DVDs I discovered one I not only wanted to keep, but also re-watch. *It's a Wonderful Life*. And I watched it two nights later.

I definitely don't want to give you a fear of missing out – and it's hardly *of the moment* – but if you have never watched *It's a Wonderful Life* try to. It's not schmaltzy. It's earnest and sentimental, yes, but honestly so. It's raw. It has incredible power. About the big importance of small lives. About why we matter. About the difference a life can make. About why we should stay alive. That film is never a waste of time. It helps you value time.

This is just an example of how removing the mediocre stuff that clogs up your time and living room helps to highlight the good stuff. Similarly, limiting your access to news helps you to prioritise what's important when you do catch up with it. Working fewer hours helps to make those hours more productive. And so on. Declutter. Edit your life.

But, to be honest, the clearing out was actually the easy bit. It's easy to halve the number of clothes in your wardrobe. It's easy to put a better filter on your emails and to turn off your notifications. It's easy to be kinder to people online. It's *relatively* easy to go to bed a bit earlier. It's *relatively* easy to become more aware of your breathing, and to make time for half an hour of yoga a day. It's *relatively* easy to charge your phone overnight *outside* your bedroom. (Okay, that's still a hard one, but I'm doing it.)

The really difficult bit is how to change attitudes inside yourself. How do you edit those?

Those attitudes ingrained in you by society. Attitudes about what you need to do and be to be valued. Attitudes about how you should be working or earning or consuming or watching or living. Attitudes about how your mental health is separate from your physical health. Attitudes about all the things you are encouraged by marketers and politicians to fear. About all the wants and lacks you are supposed to feel in order to keep the economy and social order going.

Yes. Not easy. But acceptance seems to be the key.

Accepting who you are. Accepting the reality of society, but also the reality of yourself, and not feeling like you're incomplete. It's that feeling of lacking that fills our houses and minds with clutter. Try to stay your full self. A complete, whole human being, here for no other purpose than to be you.

'The thing is to free one's self,' wrote Virginia Woolf, struggling with the task. 'To let it find its dimensions, not be impeded.'

By the way, I would be lying if I said I was there already. I am so not there. I am closer, but not even vaguely there. I doubt I will ever be totally there, in that blissful state of nirvana beyond the nervous world of technology and consumerism and distraction. With a mind as clear as a mountain stream. There is no finishing line. It's not about being perfect. In fact, punishing yourself for not being perfect is part of the whole problem. So, accepting where I am – improved and imperfect – is an ongoing task, but a massively rewarding one.

Knowing the things that are unhealthy makes it a lot easier to protect yourself.

It's the same with food and drink. If you know chocolate bars and Coca-Cola are unhealthy then it doesn't mean you are never going to consume them. But it possibly means you might have less of them, and maybe even enjoy them more when you have them, as it becomes more special.

So, instead of block-watching five hours of TV I now just try to watch a single show.

Instead of spending a whole afternoon on social media, I'll spend the occasional ten minutes, always noting the time on the computer when I log on so I can keep track. I try to do kind deeds and good things where I can. Nothing heroic, but the usual – give a bit to charity, talk with the homeless, help people with their mental health, offer up a train seat. Little micro-kindnesses. Not just to be selfless but because doing good things is quite healing. It makes you feel good. A type of psychological decluttering. Because kindness spring-cleans the soul. And maybe makes this nervous planet a little less nervous.

It is an ongoing thing. I try to be okay with myself. To not feel like I have to work or spend or exercise my way into accepting myself. That I don't need to be tough and invulnerable to be a man. That I don't have to worry about what other people think of me. And even when I feel weak, even when I get all those unwanted thoughts and fears, all that *mind spam*, I try to stay calm. I try not to even try. I try just to accept the way I am. I accept what I feel. And then I can understand it, and change the way I interact with the world.

The world is inside you

YOU MAY BE a part of the planet. But, equally, the planet is part of you. And you can choose how you respond to it. You can change the parts that get in. Yes, in one sense, it is easy to see that the planet is exhibiting symptoms similar to an individual with an anxiety disorder, but there is no *one* version of the world. There are seven billion versions of the world. The aim is to find the one that suits you best.

And remember.

Everything special about humans – our capacity for love and art and friendship and stories and all the rest – is not a product of modern life, it is a product of *being a human*. And so, while we can't disentangle ourselves from the transient and frantic stress of modern life, we can place an ear next to our human self (or soul, if you'd rather) and listen to the quiet stillness of being. And realise that we don't need to distract ourselves from ourselves.

Everything we need is right here. Everything we are is enough. We don't need the bigger boat to deal with the invisible sharks around us. We *are* the bigger boat. The brain, as Emily Dickinson put it, is bigger than the sky. And by noticing how modern life makes us feel, by allowing that reality and by being broad-minded enough to change when change is healthy, we can engage with this beautiful world without being worried it will steal who we are.

Beginning

I LOOK AT the clock on my computer.

I do this now to keep track of how long I spend staring at a screen. Simply knowing the amount makes you spend less time at a computer. I suppose that's the key: being aware.

Another awareness. I am aware of the dog, now, beside my feet.

And I am also aware of the view.

The sun is shining outside my window. I can see the sea in the distance. An offshore wind farm on the horizon, little lines of hope. A criss-cross of telegraph wires slicing the scene like lines in an abstract painting. Rooftops and chimneys pointing towards the sky we rarely observe.

I stare at the sea, and it calms me. And I am trying to be in tune with what it is about this world that makes us feel good. This is how we can live in the present. This is how every single moment becomes a beginning. By being aware. By stripping away the stuff we don't need and finding what our self really requires. And from that awareness we can find a way to keep hold of ourselves and still stay in love with this world.

That's the idea. It's hard. It's so bloody hard. But also, it is better than despair. And so long as you make sure it isn't something else you can fail at, once you accept your messy flaws and failures as natural, then it becomes a lot easier.

Later today I will be going to a shopping centre. I don't *enjoy* shopping centres, but I no longer have panic attacks in them. The key to surviving shopping centres and supermarkets and negative online comments or anything else is not to ignore them, or to run from them, or to fight them, but to allow them to be. Accept you don't have any control over them, only over yourself.

'For after all,' wrote the poet Henry Wadsworth Longfellow, 'the best thing one can do when it is raining is let it rain.' Yes. Let it rain. Let the planet be. You have no choice. But also, be aware of your feelings, good and bad. Know what works for you and accept what doesn't. When you know the rain is rain, and not the end of the world, it makes things easier.

But, right now, it isn't raining.

And so, the second after finishing this page, I am going to save this document and close the laptop and head outside.

Into air and sunlight.

Into life.

People I'd like to thank

I WOULD LIKE to thank all the people I have met in real life or online over the last few years who have found the courage to talk about their mental health. The more we talk, the more we encourage others to do the same.

Although books have, ridiculously, only one name on the front they are typically a team effort, and this one more than most. Firstly, I owe infinite and ongoing gratitude to my great, warm, fearless and tireless agent Clare Conville, and everyone who works with her at C+W and Curtis Brown.

I must thank my wonderful and long-suffering editor Francis Bickmore at Canongate, and all the other clever people who read early versions including my brilliant editors across the ocean – my US editor Patrick Nolan at Penguin Random House, and Kate Cassaday at HarperCollins Canada. Also, this book would not be *this* book without the sharp eyes of Alison Rae, Megan Reid, Leila Cruickshank, Jo Dingley, Lorraine McCann, Jenny Fry and Canongate head honcho Jamie Byng. Thanks also to Pete Adlington for his sumptuous work on the cover and all the team at Canongate who have worked so hard on this book and my others, including Andrea Joyce, Caroline Clarke, Jess Neale, Neal Price, Alice Shortland, Lucy Zhou and Vicki Watson.

Thanks to all the social media friends who have allowed me to quote them in this book.

Of course, thanks to Andrea, for being this book's first and most honest reader and for being someone who makes life on this nervous planet less nerve-racking. And apologies to Pearl and Lucas for this book ironically causing me to spend more time staring at a laptop than usual.

And thanks to you for choosing this book out of the near-infinity of books out there. It means a lot.

REASONS TO STAY ALIVE

Matt Haig

'Warm and engaging, and shot through with
humour' *Sunday Times*

CANON GATE

Ruth Hamilton was bo̶ ̶ ̶ ̶ ̶ ̶ ̶ ̶ ̶ ̶ ̶ ̶ ̶ ̶ ̶
her life in Lancashire. ̶ ̶ ̶ ̶ ̶ ̶ ̶ ̶ ̶ ̶ ̶ ̶ ̶
With Love From Ma M ̶ ̶ ̶ ̶ ̶ ̶ ̶ ̶ ̶ ̶ ̶ ̶
Girls, Spinning Jenny, ̶ ̶ ̶ ̶ ̶ ̶ ̶ ̶ ̶ ̶ ̶ ̶
Mile, Paradise Lane, The Bells of Scotland Road, The Dream Sellers, The Corner House, Miss Honoria West and *Mulligan's Yard*, are all published by Corgi Books and she is a national bestseller. She has written a six-part television series and over forty children's programmes for independent television. Ruth Hamilton now lives in Liverpool with her family.

For more information on Ruth Hamilton and her books, see her website at:

www.Ruth-Hamilton.co.uk

A Crooked Mile

Ruth Hamilton

CORGI BOOKS

A CROOKED MILE
A CORGI BOOK : 0 552 14140 2

Originally published in Great Britain by Bantam Press,
a division of Transworld Publishers

PRINTING HISTORY
Bantam Press edition published 1995
Corgi edition published 1995

5 7 9 10 8 6 4

Set in 10/11pt Linotype Plantin by
County Typesetters, Margate, Kent.

Corgi Books are published by Transworld Publishers,
61–63 Uxbridge Road, London W5 5SA,

The Random House Group Limited supports The Forest Stewardship
Council (FSC®), the leading international forest certification organisation.
Our books carrying the FSC label are printed on FSC® certified paper.
FSC is the only forest certification scheme endorsed by the leading
environmental organisations, including Greenpeace. Our
paper procurement policy can be found at
www.randomhouse.co.uk/environment

MIX
Paper from
responsible sources
FSC® C018072

Printed and bound in Great Britain by Clays Ltd, St Ives PLC

For Figaro and Charlie . . .

also
for their lodger, Carol Smith,
who happens to be my agent.

Thanks for all you do for me, Carol.

Thanks to

David and Michael, my sons.
Diane, my editor.
Margaret Mullin, my sanity.
Joe Mullin, my wheels.
Amber, Benny and Scooby, my foot rests.

PART ONE

ONE

He was a tall, spidery man with thin limbs, black clothing and dark, greasy hair. Agitation made him jerk about, as if the arachnid he imitated tried to escape from a web of its own making. 'Can't you keep still?' he roared. 'I've come miles for this and your mams have paid me for the trouble. That lad at the back – yes, you!' He pointed a skeletal finger at the culprit. 'Have you got St Vitas' Dance? You're like a bloody puppet, you are.'

Billy Shipton, who had never kept still in his short life, made an attempt to take in some air. 'I can't breathe,' he managed. 'Me collar's too tight.' He had been the owner of the rigid Eton since his first communion, and he was two years bigger now. Mam had scraped his neck with carbolic and scrubbing brush, and this felony had been compounded by strangulation and two sharp slaps to the ears.

The photographer inserted his plate and glared at the purplish face that belonged to Billy Shipton. There were at least a hundred children in the frame, toddlers squatting on the cobbles, two rows kneeling on uneven stones, their faces twisting with agony. The only decent expressions were the property of those at the back, some seated, some standing on the pavement, the rest balancing on forms borrowed from the Methodist hall. Billy Shipton, on a back row bench, had inserted the tip of a finger between throat and collar. 'You are spoiling the picture,' yelled the impatient stranger. 'Undo the stud for him, somebody.'

The 'somebody', in the shape of Elsie Shipton, leapt across the street and yanked the miscreant to the ground. 'Showing me up,' she wheezed as she removed the offending fastener. 'Again. Always showing me up, you

11

are.' Elsie was a martyr on account of her chest, and the level of her children's sufferings depended on the state of her breathing. As this was a bronchitic day, she clipped the lad once more, the plump hand making his cheek even more colourful. 'Keep still,' she snapped. 'Then your collar will look fastened.'

Billy reclaimed his position, pushing others out of the gap that had closed during his brief absence. The resulting movement had a domino effect, causing three or four subjects to go missing from the ends of the rearmost bench.

The photographer threw up his arms. He couldn't understand why the residents of a slum wanted a picture in the first place. Myrtle Street in Bolton was not a location worth remembering. This particular warren of terraces sported a bouquet of misnomers, Myrtle, Ivy, Holly. There was even a Blossom Place, twin rows of mean houses that had never seen a petal or a blade of grass. Folk hereabout called these the 'Garden Streets', a name that was at odds with the dingy area.

Oh well, it wasn't up to him. It was a job that would pay at least four shillings, so he would just get on with it. 'On the bench, please,' he ordered in a quieter tone. 'And will the little ones try to smile?' The pain in their knees was showing in great round eyes and downturned mouths. 'Just another minute,' he coaxed. 'Then you can get back to your games.'

Megan Duffy, who was seven (eight next time, she kept telling herself) and seated, knew that the smile had frozen on her face. If the wind changed, she would spend the rest of her life grinning. It was cold, very cold for June, but she was going to be brave. Everybody else could look as daft as Billy Shipton, but she was going to come out like a lady. Five more members of the Duffy family were dotted about the group, while the seventh was in the house, too young to be photographed. Megan was clean. She was tired after ironing since five in the morning, but she was polished to perfection, as were her brothers and sisters.

While the spidery man messed about with his wonky tripod, Megan took a furtive look around to check on her brothers and sisters. Annie and Nellie – eleven and ten respectively – were dressed in frocks belonging to Mam. They were in the back row, so overlong skirts and loose waists would not show in the photograph. Megan had a bleached and starched apron over her grey school frock, while the twins, Harold and Albert, had been forced into cruel Eton collars that nipped the skin of their necks. It would soon be over, Megan thought. Then she would be able to free her brothers from the vice-like grip of celluloid. Harold and Albert were special and had to be looked after, because they were the only boys. Little Freda, the next-to-youngest, was at the front in Megan's communion frock. Where was Phyllis? Megan wondered, her head twisting back and forth as she searched for her best friend. Phyllis Entwistle, who lived at number 7, seemed to be missing and—

'What's the matter with you now?' yelled the nasty man. 'You,' he shouted, a bony digit pointing towards Megan.

'I was looking for me brothers,' she mumbled.

'Keep still,' he screamed.

Megan could feel her skin heating up. She had what her dad called a 'paddy', and this temper of hers always started in her cheeks. While roses burned bright on her face, her stomach tickled, as if the words were bubbling behind her ribs. Sometimes, she managed not to speak, but keeping silent often meant several trips down the yard until her stomach stopped tickling. 'You're too slow,' she answered. 'We can't stop here all day, sir.' The 'sir' was added to show that she was polite and well-brought-up.

He almost toppled the precious equipment. Cheeky young madam, she was, with the snow-white frills starched to attention on narrow shoulders. Like the rest of them, she was a thin-boned street urchin, a creature of no importance. And any minute now, the babies would start howling, so he had better hold his tongue, attempt to ignore the brat. He clenched his jaw, bit down hard into the lower lip, squashed his impatience.

He studied the upside-down group in the frame. This was not his forte, not by a long chalk. Studio work was more in his line, engaged couples arranged in front of trees on a painted backcloth, a tasteful pillar in the foreground, perhaps an urn on a plinth. Children came to the studio, of course, but they usually came singly, quietly, in the company of a parent who would shoulder some responsibility. Indoors, he just had to shove his head under a cloth, wave a doll or a toy, capture the smile when it eventually arrived. It did not occur to him that his appearance was daunting, and that most young ones found him ugly to the point of terror or fascination, usually a mixture of the two. Here, he was visible, was not yet hidden in folds of black cloth. 'Don't be rude,' he advised Megan somewhat tardily. 'When everybody is still, I'll take the picture.'

Megan swallowed, knew that she had been naughty – even if she had called him 'sir'. But she was tired, worn out after lighting the fire, making porridge, changing the irons for Nellie and Annie, taking over at the table when the older girls needed a rest. Ironing twelve sheets and clothing for eight people plus one baby was wearying. Mam usually did it, but she was in bed with the newborn Hilda. Hilda was a big disappointment because she was another girl.

When the photograph was finally taken, a corporate sigh of relief came forth from the assembled multitude. Mothers leapt forward to grab offspring dressed in 'Sundays', while a fight broke out among a crowd of lads who had tumbled from a Methodist bench. Elsie Shipton grabbed Billy, separated him from his collar, marched him into the house and slammed her door. The rest of the Shiptons had escaped, had refused point blank to be framed for posterity. So she had paid tuppence towards a photo of just one of her children, and him in an undone collar, too. Well, she would give them all a pasting by bedtime, so she worked to control her breathing, then

14

pushed up her sleeves in order to prepare the ham-like arms for the imminent fray.

Megan led the twin boys into number 13. Harold and Albert were luckier than some of the smaller boys, because they were old enough, at six years of age, to be breeched. Many of the little lads had been photographed in frocks, so that when the devil visited, he would pass them by. The devil wanted boys, not girls. Megan raised her eyes to the ceiling. Mam wanted boys, too. Because she was just another big disappointment, Megan Duffy made herself useful by removing collars, combing hair, changing boots for clogs. 'You can go up now,' she said.

Harold and Albert climbed the stairs, a bit of pushing, pulling and light banter accompanying the ascent. When they had disappeared into Tess Duffy's bedroom, Megan crept up the flight so that she might listen to what she was missing by being a girl. The smile in Mam's voice was audible. 'Eeh, my lovely boys. Come and have a look at your little sister. Don't push like that, Harold. Be nice to your brother, he's just as important as you are.'

Megan nodded sagely to herself. Harold was always the pusher, while poor Albert was often the pushed. Harold wasn't nice. As if agreeing with Megan's thoughts, Hilda, who was three days old, began to wail. On the stairs, the baby's big sister wished she could remember being in a bed with Mam, all warm and snug in a shawl and bonnet. Mam never touched her girls. She was polite to them, reasonably kind to them, but she never showed any love. Albert and Harold got all the attention, all the fussing, while the female members of the Duffy clan just got on with the difficult task of living in near-poverty. The Duffys weren't really poor, though. Megan comforted herself with the knowledge that Dad had a bit put by. And they never went hungry, not like Phyllis.

Still, it was hard work for the Duffy girls. The twins did not go to the shops, never swept, polished, cleaned grates, kneaded bread, got scalded by the 'whites' water. Albert often volunteered, but was excused labour on account of

15

being one of Mam's little soldiers. And when Tess Duffy gave one of her boys the top off Dad's egg, there was sometimes a little bit of yolk left in it. But Megan wasn't jealous, no, she didn't resent the fact that a pair of superior beings had arrived when she was just a year old. Although a bit of yolk would have been nice . . .

Tess Duffy smiled at her sons, gave them the orange. This piece of precious fruit had been presented to her by Joe. Tess's husband always bought her fruit after a confinement. She thought about her life while the orange was peeled, segmented, divided into two exact portions. That rest had been lovely. From 1914 until 1918, she had had no husband. A husband away at war had meant no children and, although she loved Joe dearly, the pattern of yearly childbirth looked as if it might establish itself once more. At the outbreak of the Great War, Tess's children had numbered six. The seventh had just arrived, was yet another girl, and there would probably be a repeat performance within the foreseeable future.

She watched her sons as they devoured the sweet flesh. If this carry-on carried on, she'd be dead inside five years. Each time, the birth got a little harder, a lot more painful. Eventually . . . No! She couldn't die, couldn't leave her boys. Or the girls, she told herself firmly. They were good women in the making, her daughters, folk who would make excellent wives one day. And she'd done it right just once. In 1913, she'd produced not one, but a pair of lovely baby boys.

Tess looked down at the babe in her arms, another screwed-up scrap of blonde, pink-faced humanity, another mouth to feed. Megan was the only Duffy with dark hair, probably a throw-back to Tess's own raven-haired mother who had died many years ago. Tess's mother had died in childbirth . . . She wouldn't think about it, would concentrate on . . . on what? Bug marks on the walls, fungus round the window? No, she could look at her twins.

They had finished eating and were staring at her, Harold's blue eyes expectant, as if he wanted another gift from her. 'There was only the one orange,' she said apologetically.

Harold grinned. Harold was the one with dimples in his fatter face. 'Can we go to the park?' When begging a favour, Harold was always pretty. Albert just kept his eyes fixed on Mam's face, waited for the outcome of Harold's wheedling.

'It's dangerous,' replied Tess. 'You'll have to go with Annie or Nellie.'

Harold looked to Albert for some backing, got no help. He was soft, their Albert, too gentle for his own good. Well, Harold would manage on his own, just as he always did. He studied Mam, estimated her tiredness, waited for the right moment.

Tess found herself wandering again. There'd been a three-year gap between Nellie and Megan, a long wait for another son who hadn't turned up. Perhaps that would happen again. Perhaps she might remain childless from now on, fruitless and free from pain. Still, after Megan, she'd had the twins and . . .

'Mam?'

'What?' Harold was going to be a winner with the girls, she thought.

'Annie and Nellie are doing bread. They got the flour this morning and the yeast, so they'll be stopping in. It's Bolton holidays, we want to go to the park. Can't our Megan come with us?'

Megan. Megan was sensible up to a point, dreamy and distant once she forgot that point. 'She's only seven, only a year older than you two. Megan can't mind you, she's—'

'She's clever and she makes me laugh,' said Albert. The love for his sister shone brightly in his narrow face. 'She's a good looker-afterer.'

Tess was drained. The birthing of Hilda had been a tortuous process, very slow and wearisome. 'Be safe,' she said, her lids drooping towards sleep. 'And tell our Megan to wear an old pinny.' She'd found Megan in a book somewhere, had chosen the name for its sound, like a

17

breath of soft air on a summer evening. Megan. Lovely name, lovely girl. She drifted off on a cloud of exhaustion, the tiny Hilda still nestling in the crook of an arm.

Megan, in the middle of sorting sheets for repair, was accosted by one of her brothers. 'You've to take us,' announced Harold, his dimples deep and charming. 'Mam said.'

Megan was not charmed, not in the least. 'I'm sewing.'

Harold, sure of his ground, chortled. 'No, you're not. You've not started sewing yet. If you don't take us out, I'll tell Mam and that'll be you in trouble again.'

Nellie wandered into the kitchen, sleeves rolled in readiness for pummelling dough. 'Do as you're told, Megan,' she said mildly. Annie and Nellie were Mam's posse, her deputies when it came to organization. Annie and Nellie were already old, tired of a life that promised to be nothing short of drudgery. Annie came in with two bowls and some rising-cloths, bits of muslin that were used as covers for fermenting bread. 'Get gone, Megan,' said Nellie's clone. 'Mam'll be needing her rest for a few days. You know how noisy boys can be.'

Albert placed a hand on Megan's arm. 'You don't need to take us,' he whispered. He wanted to go, needed to get out of the house, yet he couldn't bear to see Megan looking as fraught as the other two girls. Megan was only seven, but she didn't seem to be having a childhood. 'Any road, if you do go with us, you can play with your skipping rope.'

Megan grinned at her favourite person. Albert was keener about the face than his twin, serious, inclined towards generosity. 'We'll go for an hour,' she answered. 'Then when we've had some fresh air, I'll do a bit of mending.' At seven, Megan achieved the finest seams, the neatest darning in Myrtle Street. She even earned the odd penny for 'take-ins', items of mending brought from other houses in the area. Sometimes, she wished she weren't such a good needlewoman, because close work was tedious and hard on the eyes, especially at night under a flickering gas mantle. If she weren't so good at sewing, she might have more free time. 'Come on, then,' she said. 'Back way out, I'll get me rope.'

On their way down Back Myrtle Street, Megan stopped outside the gate of number 7 and begged a favour. 'I just want to call in at Phyllis Entwistle's,' she said. Megan's social sphere was narrow, so she grabbed her chances when they arose. 'You'll have to come in, 'cos Mam doesn't like you left on your own.'

Albert nodded his tacit agreement, waited for Harold to erupt.

'I'm not going in,' announced the larger twin. 'Their house stinks.'

Out of loyalty to Mam, Megan chose not to inform him that the smell in number 13, though different, was just as bad. Everybody's house smelled of something or other. 'You'll do as you're told,' she said firmly. 'Me and Phyllis are down for church cleaning next Saturday, so I've got to make me arrangements.' She smiled, satisfied that she was sounding so grown-up and important. 'Harold, I'm in charge, do as you're told.'

The Entwistle house was less crowded than theirs, though poverty cast its grey shadow in every corner. The fireless grate wanted leading, and the horsehair rocker was ripped in several places. There were only three Entwistle children, and those children had a mam but no dad. Ernie Entwistle was one of the many who never came home, one among thousands buried under foreign soil.

Ida looked up from her darning. She was a tiny woman with thin arms, thin hands, thin hair. Everything about her was sparse, as if she'd been shoved to the back of the queue when bits and pieces were being given out. 'Hello, love,' she said to Megan, the voice as reedy as the rest of her. 'Our Phyllis is in bed, she's not well.'

Megan smiled, took the darning mushroom and the sock, began to mend the small hole. She kept a corner of an eye on Harold, though, because he looked as if he might just dash out of the house at any minute. When the neat weaving was accomplished, Megan begged permission from her pale hostess, then took the twins up the stairs to visit her very best friend. At a paint-starved bedroom door, she turned on Harold. 'Listen, you. Be nice to Phyllis, 'cos she's not well and she's got no dad and—'

'Why?' Harold wore one of the more cherubic of his many beguiling expressions.

'He's dead, is Phyllis's dad and—'

'Why?'

Megan tapped a toe on cracked oilcloth, tried to keep her voice low. 'He died in the war.'

Harold nodded. 'Like our dad got the shrapnel in his leg, and Phyllis's dad got it somewhere else, like in his head or—'

'Yes.' Megan prayed that the lad would shut up. She wasn't fooled by their Harold, not for one minute. Albert was worth ten of Harold, yet—

'Or in his stomach, all blood pouring out.' Harold smiled, well satisfied with himself.

Yet everybody seemed to love Harold, Megan concluded. 'Shut your mouth this minute, Harold Duffy. You're a nasty piece of work, you are. I sometimes wonder how our Albert manages to be so nice when he's your twin. Just behave yourself.' Her arms had crooked themselves into a shape copied from Mam and Nellie and Annie, who often stood with balled fists pressed just below their waists, elbows pointing out sideways. 'One wrong word to Phyllis and I'll set our Nellie on you.'

Harold's eyes narrowed. Nellie was strong and was usually on Megan's side. Nellie knew how to inflict pain without leaving a mark. 'None of you can hurt me,' he said loftily. 'We're not to be hurt, me and him.' He jerked a thumb in the direction of 'him'. ''Cos we're boys.'

Megan inclined her head. 'Our Nellie goes to confession every week. She tells the priests how bad you are. And she tells them about smacking you when Mam doesn't know.' She sniffed, was becoming a professional sniffer, almost as adept as her older sisters. 'And Father O'Riley says you need your hide tanning. So our Nellie's in the clear.' In the

Duffy house, word from beyond the confessional door was law. 'Our Nellie will clobber you,' ended Megan, her tone still soft.

'I'll tell me mam.' He tried to sound defiant, though the words wavered slightly.

'And I'll tell Father O'Riley. So there.' Megan's tongue stuck so far out that the root hurt. She opened Phyllis's door, looked at the three tumbled beds, two empty, one occupied, dragged Harold to Phyllis's bedside. 'He's at it again, Phyllis, trying to rule the roost.' She kept her tone as normal as possible, tried not to let confusion show in her voice. Compared to this child, Ida Entwistle had looked well, even robust. 'Are you poorly?' That was a daft thing to ask, she thought.

Phyllis nodded. 'All over. I ache all over. And . . .' She swallowed, her face crumpling inward against the pain. 'Me neck's sore, me throat. I can't hardly drink nor eat, talking hurts. Sore, I'm sore.'

Megan felt as if she were riveted to the spot. She wanted to run, needed to escape from the pitiful sight of her dear friend, yet she was immobilized by some invisible force that seemed to pierce her body from skull to toes. She cleared her own clogging throat. 'Has the doctor been round?'

Phyllis closed her eyes. 'No. No money.'

Mental arithmetic was not Megan's favourite subject, but her head rattled with the sound of coins stored in a box beneath a certain loosened floorboard. There was a silver thre'pence, four farthings and a couple of ha'pennies and pennies. It was her mending money, the bit she'd kept back from Mam. Not that Mam minded, of course . . . She shouldn't have bought that packet of broken biscuits at the Co-op. Fivepence, she reckoned. No, it might be sevenpence. Would a doctor come for that price?

Galvanized into action, she said a quick 'ta-ra' and followed her round-eyed brothers to the landing. 'I've got to go home,' she explained. 'I need to get some money for the doctor, fetch him up to Phyllis.'

Albert touched his sister's arm. 'Is she going to die, Megan?'

'I hope not.' Megan hoisted the slipping apron up a narrow shoulder where it found poor purchase, slid down again. 'You two stop here. Go round the back and wait for me under the lamp outside number one's gate.' She could sneak into number 13 by the front door and get past Annie and Nellie without their seeing her. They would be up to their eyes in flour anyway, too busy to look for further problems.

Minutes later, she found herself staring breathlessly into an empty box. Harold had found her money again. She kept moving it from one hiding place to another, and he kept finding it. Long fingers curled themselves round cardboard, flattened the box, tossed it back into its useless niche. Sometimes, she almost hated her own brother. With her hands still curled, she descended the stairs, no longer worried about secrecy.

Annie and Nellie turned as their sister entered the kitchen. The story poured from Megan's mouth, while her hands, still white-knuckled, imagined of their own accord how it would feel to strangle their Harold. 'Phyllis'll die,' she sobbed. 'And our Harold will have killed her.'

Annie whipped off her apron and tossed it on to the table. 'I'll come,' she said. 'Our Nellie would flay him alive. He's out of order, is that brother of ours.' After drying Megan's tears, she grabbed her hand and marched down the back street. Albert stood under the lamp, misery etched into the serious face. 'He's gone,' he mumbled. 'Laughing, he was, but I know he's scared.' The tear-brightened eyes fixed themselves on Megan. 'He bought toffees with it, I think. He smelled of mints last night in bed, so I think he's took the money. I asked him if he had, and he just ran off. I didn't know what to do. I didn't know whether to follow him or what.'

Annie squeezed her sister's hand. 'Stop here, Megan. I'll nip down and get the doctor and we'll work out how to pay him.'

Megan breathed a sigh of relief. She was sensible, their Annie, always seemed to know the right thing to do. But the tension did not leave Megan's shoulders, because too many things were wrong. Harold was missing, Mam was in bed, the money had been stolen, Phyllis needed a doctor, Annie had left the bread. Baking for a big family took more than one pair of hands. So above all the big worries in Megan's head sat a bowl of spoiled dough. And it was Harold's fault . . .

After ten or so minutes, Annie returned. 'He's coming. We'd best tell Mrs Entwistle what we've done, then we can go and find our Harold.'

Phyllis's mother was still seated by the cold range oven, her hands occupied yet again by darning. She looked up at the group of three, seemed to stare through them. 'She's poorly,' she whispered.

'Doctor's coming.' Annie spoke in her most common-sensical tone. 'He'll put her right, will Dr Walsh.'

'I can't pay.' The wooden mushroom, clothed in a black sock, fell to the floor. Albert retrieved it, placed it on the table where newspaper tried to play the role of a cloth. A few grains of precious salt lingered in a cracked saucer, and the bread board was empty save for an idle knife that mocked the situation. Annie stared at this implement for a moment or two. 'I've baking on, Mrs Entwistle. I'll fetch you a couple of loaves after, happen a scrape of butter and some dripping.'

Megan no longer managed to worry about spoiled bread, because Mrs Entwistle's panic was suddenly the biggest thing in the room, bigger than the grate and the oven and the torn chair.

'Infantile paralysis,' whispered Ida Entwistle as, mobilized by terror, she rocked back and forth in the ladder-backed chair. 'I've sent the lads to our Vera's.' She paused, ran a pale tongue over paler lips. 'Daughters is special,' she murmured. 'A son is a son till he gets him a wife, but a daughter's a daughter the rest of your life. I can't lose her, I can't.' The grey eyes strayed towards the door. 'I shouldn't have let you go up to her, Megan. But I've only just thought about what's wrong with the lass. It's that infantile, I know it is. My boys came home just a minute ago, and it dawned on me. So I've packed me sons off to safety.'

She swallowed, her eyes wandering over the bare table. 'I've no tea, no milk, can't even offer you a brew. And I can't look at her no more, I can't and she's upstairs all by herself with her dad's coat on her bed and it's only five minutes since I said ta-ra to him and he never came back and now—'

Albert gasped as Annie's hand made sharp contact with Ida's chalky face. 'Stop this,' ordered the tall, thin girl. 'You'll only make yourself ill, then you'll be no good to nobody.' She knelt, took the sobbing woman's hands, tried to rub some life into them. 'Doctor's coming. Our Megan'll pay when she's done some more mending. Stop saying Phyllis has the paralysis. Doctor knows more than we do. Let him do the job he's paid for, don't you go naming what's wrong with Phyllis. And you'll have to go up to her, she's your daughter. It's the same thing as you said before – a mother's a mother the rest of her life, so don't be turning your back.'

They all heard the front door as it swung wide enough to meet the lobby wall. 'I'll go straight up, Mrs Entwistle,' shouted the invisible doctor. The house was silent apart from heavy footfalls on the stairs. Everyone looked up at the ceiling, as if eyes might penetrate the flaking plaster. He crossed the bedroom, stopped, sat on the bed. The four in the kitchen held their breath as a spring twanged beneath the man's weight. Ida's sobs were swallowed, and Annie continued to rub the work-dried hands of this grieving widowed mother.

When he came in, his face was grave. 'I'll have to take her into isolation, Mrs Entwistle. She's got a fever and she needs nursing for a week or two.'

Dim hope, in the form of two spots of pink, sat briefly on Ida's face. 'Will they get her better?'

24

'I don't know,' he answered carefully. 'It's a matter of time, I'm afraid.'

Ida pushed Annie away, leapt from the chair and threw herself at the startled man. 'You've not to let her die – do you hear me? She's me only girl, me only friend. That's my Phyllis you're taking into the fever hospital.' She was pulling on his coat, tearing at the chain of his watch. 'Save her. Do you hear me? You save my Phyllis. Ernie's gone and I can't take no more.'

Annie overcame the frantic Ida by simply lifting her away from Dr Walsh. 'Stop this,' said the eleven-year-old woman. 'Megan, show Dr Walsh out.' While Megan obeyed, Annie dealt with the matter in hand. 'Get her ready,' she ordered. 'Put her in something clean and give her a lick and a promise. If she's going in hospital, let her go decent.'

Ida blinked. 'Water's cold.'

Albert pulled at Annie's sleeve. 'I'll go and fetch some of ours in the bucket. It's only four houses away.'

Annie smiled at him. 'Good lad. And bring that cotton nightie of Mam's – it's on the pulley. She'll not mind when I tell her about the emergency. Go on, son.'

Megan returned up the lobby, passed Albert on his way out, assessed the situation. 'Shall I get Phyllis ready, Annie?'

'No. Stay away, love. We don't know what she's got and we might catch it.'

'But we've . . .' Megan allowed the words to die a natural death. They had already been in the room with Phyllis. Phyllis, being a daughter, was special. Albert and Harold, being sons, were special too. She wouldn't think, mustn't think. Her eyes raked across the room, as if she expected to see the germs marching towards her, an army on the offensive. If anything happened to Harold and Albert, there would be murder done and she, Megan Duffy, would be on the receiving end of it.

When Albert returned, she rushed to the door, relieved him of the nightdress and the white-and-blue enamel bucket, knelt on the remains of a coconut mat in the tiny lobby. 'You're a clever lad, Albert,' she said, the calm in her voice covering a multitude of terrors. 'See, I want you to go and find our Harold. Don't go as far as town or the park, just root about round here, in the back streets and the mill yard. If you find him, take him home. If you don't find him, just take yourself home when the Town Hall strikes four. Can you remember all that?'

''Course I can, Megan.' He touched her face, drew a line along her cheekbone. 'I wish I had black hair,' he said. 'It's more grown-up than blonde hair.' This was his way of expressing love for his sister. He often told her that her eyes were like blue jewels, and she always laughed at him.

'Don't be daft,' she said now. 'Go and do as I said, then with any luck, Mam won't even know about Harold going missing.'

She carried the bucket through to the kitchen. 'Here you are, Mrs Entwistle,' she said. 'For washing Phyllis. I've left Mam's nightie at the bottom of the stairs.'

The two sisters clung together when Ida Entwistle had gone to prepare her daughter. There would be an ambulance in a minute, a black vehicle with a motor and a lot of smoke. 'What do you think, Annie?' asked Megan.

'I don't know what to think,' came the quiet reply. 'I hope our Nellie's managed that batch. It's hard work carrying half a stone of flour on me head in a pillowcase. Waste of money, too, if it's left to spoil. But she'll have to keep an eye on that yeast, she will.' Annie hugged Megan. 'Pray, love. Pray to Our Lady.'

'I will. I'll do five decades tonight.'

They sat together in the old horsehair rocker, each waiting for the clanging of an ambulance bell. 'Whole street'll be out any minute,' commented Annie. 'They'll have their eyes on stalks watching little Phyllis Entwistle getting took away. Dear God, Megan, I hope we don't catch it.'

Megan closed her eyes and screwed up her face while

Phyllis was lifted downstairs and through the front door. She didn't want to catch whatever disease her friend had, but more than that, she didn't want Albert or Harold to catch it. If anything happened to them, she would surely be to blame. The fact that Albert was the better twin was quickly pushed to the back of Megan's mind. Nothing must happen to either of them. No, no, she wasn't telling God that if one had to die it mustn't be Albert. And Mam would create something awful if either of her boys became ill.

Elsie Shipton bustled in, all worries about the photograph forgotten beneath the weight of a neighbour's troubles. She manhandled Ida Entwistle, sat her on the usual chair, cast her eyes over Megan and Annie. 'My lot's gone missing,' she said without preamble. 'There's only our Billy in, and he's about as much use as a rubber knife. So you two can fettle for Mrs Entwistle. I've had our Fred's wages, I can spare a few scraps.' She couldn't spare anything, but this was an emergency . . . 'Go in my house and fetch some tea, sugar and milk. If our Billy's come downstairs, crack him across the head, Annie. There's a bit of bacon in me meatsafe, so fetch two back rashers and an egg. Leave that streaky, it's for bacon and egg pie.' She turned her attention to Megan. 'Run to the butcher's, lass, tell Mr Armstrong we've had a bit of trouble and will he send me some broth bones.'

Ida rocked to and fro, her arms crossed over her chest, as if she were trying to keep her feelings trapped behind the frail cage of ribs. 'You've been a good friend to my girl, Megan Duffy,' she said suddenly. 'I'll never forget you.'

All the strength seemed to dr___ ___ moment. Ida was talking as if Ph___ if she were never coming back ___ steadied herself against the dre___ what was wanted. Broth bones. ___ going for bones.

Outside, she leaned on the hou___

27

took in some deep breaths of oxygen. Harold was right, of course, Mrs Entwistle's house did smell. It smelled because the Entwistles were poor, too poor to afford even the cheapest yellow soap. Mrs Entwistle had gone funny after the war, still wasn't well enough to go back into the mill. Poverty stank, then. She would remember that smell, would try to avoid it when she grew up and got a house of her own.

With broth bones printed firmly on the front of her brain, she began the short walk to Armstrong's butchers. He was nice, was Mr Armstrong. He'd sent nearly a quarter of potted meat and some pork sausages for Mam yesterday, wanted no money. He always gave a present to the mother of a new baby, always had a kind word for the children who visited his shop. Megan nodded, decided to tell Mr Armstrong the tale of Phyllis's illness. That way, she might get more than a couple of broth bones out of this expedition. Oh, she hoped Albert would find Harold soon.

The ambulance that contained Phyllis had stopped at the bottom of the hill. Ambulances were supposed to hurry up, she thought as she rounded the corner on her way to the shop. The driver hadn't even used his bell after loading Phyllis on to the wooden stretcher. People were flapping about, bending down, crying, a woman screamed. Then Megan saw a bundle being lifted, a pile of clothing with arms and legs hanging out of it. The limbs were pale and one of the clogs was missing. When she noticed the blue clog on the floor, Megan sank into a dark abyss where she heard and saw nothing.

But when they revived her, she still knew that Albert had been run over by that ambulance. He was the only boy in the garden streets who wore blue clogs, fashioned by his own father from the very best leather. Megan didn't need close her eyes to achieve a picture of the limp body lifted from the cobbles. That hadn't been a hurt it had been a . . . it had been a lot worse than that. was dead and she, Megan Duffy, had killed him.

28

TWO

Doris Duffy, known by friends and relatives as Deedee because of her initials, towered over her sobbing daughter-in-law. Joe Duffy's mother was a tall woman for one of her generation, seemed even taller now that Tess was slumped in the chair. 'You must pull yourself together, Tessie Nolan-as-was. You've children to feed, a crying baby to see to—'

'I can't. I can't cope no more, not without my Albert.' She had always known deep down that Albert was lovely, so much nicer than his manipulative twin. Not that she didn't love Harold, not that she'd have preferred him to be the dead one. She cleared her throat as guilt overcame her. Would she have been so thoroughly upset had one of her girls died under the wheels of that vehicle? 'There's no way of getting over this, Deedee,' she wailed. 'I feel as if I don't want to live another day.'

Doris took a deep breath, waded in as usual. 'Listen, I lost five. My Joe was the only one I reared to full height. I've seen more little coffins being shifted out of these streets than you've had hot dinners, Tess. You can't just give up and cry about not coping. What's going to become of the rest of your family, eh? What about our Nellie and our Annie, up to their eyebrows in bloody ham and pickle butties? Well? Are you heeding me, madam? What about Harold missing his twin? The lad's not been the same since, because he blames himself for going missing and—'

'He wasn't to blame,' screamed Tess, the words shrill, her tone skirting the edge of hysteria. 'It was Megan.'

Annie left the room and closed the door quietly. The funeral tea was set out in the parlour, but Mam refused point blank to leave the kitchen. After a moment or two, Annie and Nellie, together as always, returned to the small gathering, doled out the sandwiches they'd been making since the crack of dawn. The two older girls kept an eye on their Megan, hoped against hope that the situation in the other room would sort itself out by the end of the day.

Doris was getting nowhere. 'Just you listen to me,' she tried yet again. 'Childer is childer, no matter what they come out as. You're a girl. Were you treated as less than human? Were you? Why are you turning on that poor little lass? She's suffered enough. If Harold hadn't took Megan's savings, then he wouldn't have needed to run off. And if Harold had stopped where he'd been put, our Albert wouldn't have got run over with the ambulance.'

Tess lifted her tear-washed face. 'That ambulance was for Phyllis Entwistle. Our Megan went round to the Entwistles' when she should have been minding my boys. If she'd stuck to what she'd been told, there'd have been no ambulance in the street and—'

'Nay! It's time we both stopped all this iffing, Tess. Are you begrudging help to Ida Entwistle's lot? Ida's not been a full shilling since yon man of hers got killed. Our Megan was nobbut doing her duty, a duty that should have been carried by broader shoulders. Elsie Shipton was only just saying she'd have sorted things out if she'd known about Phyllis being ill. Nobody would have missed the lass at all except for her not turning up to get her photo took.'

Tess sniffed. 'Ida hadn't put into the kitty, so Phyllis wasn't going on the picture anyway.'

Doris stepped back, her hands folded against the urge to batter hell out of Tess's face. She spoke carefully, her voice soft and gentle as she fought the rising anger. 'There was a lot of good little bodies on that photograph that hadn't been paid for. Our Joe's got his own business, so you're the lucky one, aren't you? If you hadn't had the brass, would you have kept your kids in the house that morning? No, you'd have sent them out all the same for the chance of a free photo.' Although she struggled against

30

temptation, one hand broke free, its digits waving under Tess's nose. 'You've not an ounce of charity in you. I don't like having to say these things to you when that little lad's just gone under the sod, but you'll not treat Megan like a sinner. She's a grand lass, our Megan.'

Tess sniffed back the tide of grief. 'I don't care if I never clap eyes on her again, Deedee. She's as good as killed one of my lads.'

'Tess!' The syllable was whispered from the doorway. Joe Duffy closed the door as softly as he had opened it. 'Leave her alone, Mam,' he said. 'She'll come round at the finish.'

'Will she?' Doris challenged her son with her eyes.

'She will.' He dropped a calloused hand to his wife's shoulder. 'Shock does funny things.'

Doris leaned against the table. 'She were like this before, Joe. It's always been "her lads", hasn't it? She wandered round like somebody daft till she got the twins, as if her life depended on producing boys. What for? To inherit their dad's empire? Can you see our Harold sat at a bench in a leather pinny with his gob full of nails?' She shook her head, answered her own question. 'He'll not make a clogger. Cloggers want patience, and Harold has none.'

Joe Duffy stood back and considered his wife. It was one thing having a neighbour four doors down who was soft in the head, but he didn't fancy living with a queer one. It was a shame about their Albert; a terrible pity, but there were six more who wanted looking after, half a dozen kiddies whose mam was absent without leave. He didn't know what to do. If he'd been sitting at his bench, if a customer had come to him with a similar problem, he could have put the world to rights while mending one clog. But this was different. He prided himself on his ability as local mentor, yet his own wife was beyond reach.

Tess shook her head, then buried it in her hands. Doris picked up half a flour cake, plucked off a piece of

31

imaginary dust, bit and chewed absently. 'Not like home-made,' she announced to no-one in particular. 'He used to do a good floury batch, did John Pickavance, but he's skimping on ingredients.' Ordinary things. In her experience, talking about mundane matters usually had a calming effect at times like these.

She swallowed, belched politely behind a hand, fixed her gaze on Joe. He'd been a good lad, a caring son, a loving husband, a kind and generous dad. He'd a bank book, had Joe, savings that Doris added to every week by nipping in her dinner hour to the Bolton Savings Bank with Joe's few bob, the bit he kept back after rent and housekeeping. She performed this small service because the mill she worked in was just a short walk from the bank.

Aye, this was a good man. Three pints a week, Joe drank, always in the same alehouse, always on a Friday. The lad was trying for a house, a place for his family to own, somewhere away from ringworm and lice and filth. Oh, he didn't deserve this. Burying a young one was bad enough, but living with Tess in her present state of mind would be a trial.

He raised eyebrows and hands in a gesture of confusion, then tried once more to make verbal contact with his wife. 'Listen, love. There's no good'll come of you turning on one of your own. Bitterness breeds bitterness, and our Megan's too good a girl to be sent all twisted by what's happened. She's just a child. How can you blame her for the accident? We all make mistakes, and our Megan's biggest one is being too kind, too soft.'

Tess raised her head slowly. 'Time and again I've told them to watch the lads. She let me down, Joe. I'll never trust her again as long as I live.'

Joe limped to the window. There'd be rain later on, he could feel it in the bones of his legs where shrapnel still sat in small clusters that had defied surgery. He gazed outside at the small playground he had made for his brood. There was a painted hopscotch, two hooks in the lavatory doorway from which a baby-swing often hung, a pattern on the scullery wall where the girls could throw a ball, catch it, count their scores. He'd even got some barrels of soil so that flowers might be grown by his children. Joe loved them, all of them. Annie and Nellie were grand, hard-working lasses, Megan was beautiful, imaginative, little Freda was a caution with her missing milk teeth and that funny lisp. Hilda was still a baby, but she was sweet and pretty. Harold. He chewed his lip for a moment. Well, Harold might turn out all right after a few years . . .

Albert. His heart contracted sharply, as if it had been hit by a hammer. Albert would have made a grand clogger. He'd loved folk, had Albert, he'd often sat in the shop listening to his dad's homespun philosophy. It was a tragedy, but life had to go on for the people who remained. The sad fact was that the living were more important than the dead, because they had needs, needs that must be met by their fellow humans.

He placed his hands flat on the low sill, leaned down so heavily that his shoulders came up and almost met his ears. Yet again, he thought about Harold. There was a streak in the lad, a selfishness that Tess had created through over-indulgence. Although another factor had played a part, Joe felt sure. His own father, Stanley Duffy, whose whisky-soaked body had been lowered into the ground years earlier, had been a rotten beggar. May the good Lord forbid, but happen Harold had taken after Stanley Duffy. Deedee still bore one of the scars, a deep, silver line on a forearm where shattered bone had pierced flesh and skin. And Mam had tolerated the man, had even loved him in her own way. 'Mam?'

'Hello?'

He turned, looked at his mother. 'I'm coming home.'

Doris cast a glance in the direction of her daughter-in-law. 'Right,' she said uncertainly.

'I'll fetch our Megan and our Freda with me. Harold can stop with his mam, so can Annie and Nellie – unless they want to follow me, of course. But they're old enough

33

to choose and little Hilda's too young to have a say.'

Tess did not move a muscle. He wouldn't go, couldn't go. If he went, if he left her here with just four of the children, then there wouldn't be any more. She thought about that, considered for the first time a subject other than her own immediate grief. She loved Joe. But if he went, there'd be no more pain, no more struggling to produce babies that seemed to get bigger and louder every year.

'It's up to you, lad,' said Doris. 'Whatever you want, I'll fall in with.'

The woman by the fire still made no move. If he went, she wouldn't be able to replace Albert. If she made a pact with God, if she promised to treat Megan properly, He would surely reward her with another Albert. She was iffing again. Deedee was fed up with all the iffing. 'You're not going,' she muttered eventually. 'I'll pull round, I will.'

Joe considered the words. 'You'll not pull round by taking it out on our Megan, though. I'm not having you making the child's life a misery just because you need somebody to carry the guilt. We're all to blame. I could have took him to the shop – he asked me that morning. You could have made both of them stay in till you were up and about. Me mam should happen have stopped off work to see to the kiddies. It's everybody's fault and it's nobody's fault.' He paused, waited for an answer, got none. 'But if you upset that lass of ours, I'll take her to me mother's and you'll not see either of us again.'

'Right.'

Joe crossed the small room, lifted his wife from the chair. 'Now, you'll stand with me and thank the good people who've come to say ta-ra to our little lad. Even Ida Entwistle's made the effort, and the poor woman's gone that bit further out of her mind worrying about young Phyllis in the hospital. We've to think about others, not just about ourselves and how upset we are.'

She couldn't face it. But she had to. With her face

frozen in neutral, she accompanied her husband, shook some hands, allowed her cheek to be kissed occasionally, noticed Annie and Nellie doing their catering, flicked an eye over Megan who was still as stone near the window.

Harold pulled at Tess's skirt. 'I feel funny,' he said.

Joe nodded. 'Aye, you will, lad. You've been half of a pair so far, now you're one on your own. Be brave.' And Harold was one on his own, thought Joe as he watched Tess beating a retreat towards the kitchen and solitude. Harold Duffy was a bundle of mischief. The word 'mischief', like 'awful', had lost some of its meaning, as if the years had worn away or watered down the severity of such terms. Harold promised to be naughty in the true sense of the word.

'Dad.' The lad was tugging now at Joe's sleeve. 'I'm hot and I feel poorly.'

Joe touched the boy's head, managed not to flinch when his heart did another somersault. The lad was feverish, sweaty, pale except for two unnatural areas of brightness on his cheeks. 'Er . . . go to bed, son.' The man looked round for some help, saw the older girls pouring tea, caught sight of poor little Megan on her own in a corner. 'Come here, lass,' he said. 'Take this fellow upstairs and tuck him in. Don't say anything to your mam for now.' He needed to clear the room, had to send out for a doctor.

When Megan and Harold had gone upstairs, Joe clapped his hands, startled by the sudden quiet. 'I . . . er . . . you know we're grateful for all your help and support, like. Only Tess has took this bad and I think she needs a sleep.' He looked round for his mother, assessed that she was in the kitchen with Tess. 'We just want you all to know that we're thankful . . .' He stared at Ida Entwistle, whose face had suddenly crumpled. 'Ida?'

'It's me!' she screamed. 'If they come near me, they die. Ernie got himself killed, our Phyllis hasn't much of a chance. It's me, I'm bad luck.' She dissolved into floods of tears.

Joe summoned his eldest daughter. 'Annie, get them all

out,' he whispered. 'Go down with Mrs Entwistle and sit with her. But before you do, tell our Nellie to run and get yon doctor. Say nothing to nobody, only Harold's been took bad.'

Annie's pallid face turned chalky-white. She ushered everyone outside, sent Nellie chasing for Dr Walsh, took Mrs Entwistle home and sat with her. When the woman had calmed, Annie abandoned her and rushed home to see what was afoot in her own household.

The doctor was on his way out, Joe at his heels. 'About half an hour, then,' said Dr Walsh. 'And you'll have to tell her, Joe. She'll notice an ambulance, won't she?'

Joe ran a hand through his hair. At the age of thirty-four, he was already turning grey, though the dark blond hid most of the silver in his ample mop. 'She'll go right up the wall, Doc.' If it had been one of the girls, Tess would likely have taken it in her stride, but the remaining boy? Joe shuddered. 'Just do your best,' he begged. 'Oh, and how's Phyllis?'

'Ill.' The doctor strode away towards other families in crisis, some with diphtheria, others with polio or a simple cold that might prove lethal because of bad diet and poor housing. But the Duffys stayed in his mind, because their tragedy seemed the largest on this particular day.

Megan was in the scullery, an ear pinned to the door that fastened the single storey room to the kitchen. She heard Dad coming in, heard him telling Mam that Harold would need to go away to the isolation hospital. Hot tears scalded Megan's face, because this was all her fault. Albert was dead due to her carelessness, now Harold had caught the infantile paralysis from Phyllis.

'NO!' yelled Tess Duffy. 'Not him, not him. If anybody catches that, it's got to be Megan, because she was Phyllis's friend, they were always together. It's not right, Harold's not going, no, no, he's not going to that place. They never come out of there in one piece. Most are in boxes, then there's some in prams like babies, wanting pushing and . . . and . . . Anyway, I'm going up to find

36

my Harold and prove you stupid, Joe Duffy. There's nothing wrong with that lad, he looked lovely this morning, all rosy cheeks and bright eyes.'

'Fever, Tess.' Dad's voice was gruff. 'He's running a high temperature, Dr Walsh said and—'

'When? When did the doctor come?'

Megan bit so hard into her lower lip that she almost cried out against the self-inflicted agony.

'Just now,' said Joe. 'We never told you in case it was something and nothing—'

'Well, it is summat and nowt. That doctor's a quack, get out of me road.'

Megan listened while Mam fled from the room, remained rooted to the spot as footfalls echoed up the stairwell. Dad was quiet, so Megan opened the door and peeped through a slender crack. As he was facing the fire, she could see just his back, and that was shaking. Dad was crying. Megan had gone and made her own dad cry. She closed the door and she knew that she was evil.

After what seemed an endless time, Mam came down the stairs. Because the footsteps were heavy and slow, Megan deduced that her mother was carrying their Harold.

'Tess,' shouted her husband. 'What are you doing? You're not many days out of childbed, and that's a solid lad. Give him here.'

'No. He's stopping with me. Where's the rest of them?'

After a pause, he replied, 'Well, I've sent them upstairs, of course. Germs will have done their job already, only I thought I'd best take no chances. They're in the bedroom till the ambulance has been, then we'll have to disinfect the house.'

Megan crept across the room, steadied her hands on the edge of the slopstone, then heaved down the drain the few crumbs she'd managed to swallow earlier. Vomiting was never a quiet job and, this time, the noise of her discomfort sounded loud enough for all Bolton to hear.

The door swung open. 'Megan,' said her dad. 'What are

you doing in there? Didn't I send you up with our Nellie?'

Megan gasped, fought the sickness. 'Nellie thinks I'm in your room with the baby. I went out the front way and came in the back. Nobody noticed.'

'I'm noticing you now.' Tess's voice came from behind her husband. 'Look what you've started, you bad little bugger. There's our Albert scarcely cold in his grave and our Harold hot enough to fry eggs on his forehead.'

Joe turned. 'Go away, Tess. Take the lad into the parlour and wait for the ambulance.'

But Tess was determined to have her say. 'She wants telling.'

'Get out,' roared the man who never raised his voice. 'Get out of here now, Tess, or I could well do something we might both live to regret.'

The silence was deafening, then Harold began to moan softly, making the small noise of an animal too weak to express its pain fully. He sounded like a puppy, Megan thought irrelevantly. Like a puppy hurt by a cart or a . . . or an ambulance. Had Albert died straight away, as soon as the wheel ran over him? Or did he lie there for a while in great pain, no member of his family to comfort him in his last moments? She hugged herself, tried to squash the images at source.

'Did you hear me, Tess? Go and wait in the front room.'

The woman clutched at her son and took a pace backward. 'This should be you, Megan Duffy,' she mumbled. 'You brought disease in, so you should suffer it.'

Joe Duffy let out a formless roar, a horrible word-free howl. He manhandled his wife out of the small room and slammed the door behind her. 'Megan?' he whispered.

'What?'

He came into the scullery, knelt on the flags and took her small hands in his large and calloused palms. 'It's not your fault. No matter what anybody says – and that includes your mother – none of this is your doing. These things happen.'

She stared hard at him, seemed to be burrowing through his skull in search of true thought, real opinion. 'I shouldn't have took them in Phyllis's, Dad. Only when she never turned up for the photograph, I wondered why. And I took the twins in so I could keep an eye on them.' She gulped some air, prayed that the nausea would pass. 'See, I didn't do what Mam said, did I? And everybody's being punished 'cept me. Mam's right, it should be me in the fever hospital.'

'Your mam's not well, love. She's never on form just after a baby. It'll all blow over, you'll see.'

'No.' She pulled away from him, stood with her back flattened against the outer door. 'I don't want to live here no more, Dad. Our Albert . . . our Albert loved me. I should have minded him and kept him safe.' She fiddled with the pocket in her apron. 'I'm bad, you see. I don't like Harold and I don't like me mam. So I might as well be somewhere else, 'cos I can't bake bread yet, I can only sew and peel spuds.'

'Best at sewing for miles, you are.' What the bloody hell did stitching and mending matter when she was only a baby? Why did Tess make these girls old so soon? 'You're a special child, you are.' The words arrived cracked, broken by many emotions. 'I love you, Megan,' he said. 'Nellie and Annie and Freda love you. Your mam loves all her girls, but she's not worked out how to show it proper, that's all. And our little Hilda's going to need some company while your mother chases about after Harold.' It would have to stop. He must make sure that the young females in his house got some pleasure, some rest from chores. Even when Tess was up and about, she had them stoning steps, blackleading the grate, humping pillowcases full of flour from the Co-op.

She looked up, eyed him steadily. 'They'll not let her in at the fever place.' Her lip quivered for a split second, but she hung on to the edge of control, guided her tongue towards the words she needed. 'If it had been me, or Nellie, Mam wouldn't have worried. I don't think she'd bother even if our Annie got took away, and Annie's bread's great. But because it's a boy that's ill, she'll sleep in a doorway at that hospital. Girls don't count in this house.' She straightened the narrow shoulders. 'So, if it's all right with you, I'll go and stop with Mrs Entwistle. She likes girls and she misses Phyllis something awful. And with her not being well in her mind, she needs somebody.'

Joe rose to his feet, staggered against the wall when disturbed splinters of metal jarred the bone in a leg. 'How old are you?' he asked, though he knew the answer.

'Seven, eight in ten months.'

He inclined his head. 'Seventy, more like. I don't want to lose you, love.'

She nodded, pursed her lips in the manner of a female adult deep in thought. 'You'll not lose me. But Mam's already given me up. She doesn't want to be looking at me. She doesn't want reminding all the while about Albert. And . . . and I don't like being near me mam.' She shivered, wondered whether she was going to come down with the infantile. It didn't matter, did it? 'Mrs Entwistle reckons everything's her fault and I know how she feels. I'll stop with her for a bit.'

'No. You'll not leave my house, Megan. That's an order. Do you understand what an order is?'

She nodded half-heartedly. 'It's a rule.'

'That's right.' He wiped the sweat from his brow, using the cuff of his sleeve as a handkerchief. 'In the war, I had to do a lot of things I didn't like, because I was under orders. See, there's bosses and workers, then there's parents and children. Children have to do as they're told, same as spinners in the mill.'

She shifted from foot to foot. 'Me mother wants me gone. So which order must I listen to? Yours or hers?'

Oh yes, she was seventy if a day, he thought. 'A dad is the biggest boss till you grow up.'

Her eyes lifted until she was staring directly at him. 'She's the boss, Dad. She's here when you're out clogging. How am I going to keep away from her? What if . . . ?'

She ran her nasty-tasting tongue over parched lips. 'What if our Harold dies and all? I'll be blamed for that, too, 'cos I was the one who took him to Phyllis's.'

He thought for a few seconds, listened to the child's quick breathing. 'You can come to the shop with me,' he said eventually. 'While you're off school, you can be my full-time apprentice. And on schooldays, I'll take you in to work with me in a morning, then you can stop with me after school till I shut at night.'

She considered this option. 'Girls don't do clogs. I can't be a clogger's apprentice. There's no girls in that job 'cos the leather-knives is too heavy and sharp.'

Aye, but she was sharper than any knife, he thought. 'Look, lass, there was women doing the putting up during the war. The uppers were cut for them – all they had to do was fasten them to the soles. You can be a putter-up.'

There would be no choice in this matter, Megan knew that. She didn't have enough words for how she felt about Mam, could not quite express how threatened and unloved she felt. It would have been better to live with somebody who didn't care than with somebody who hated her. Megan wasn't Ida Entwistle's daughter, so the two of them might have rubbed along quite well until both lots of trouble blew over. 'Somebody should be with Phyllis's mam,' she insisted. 'She's sent their Jack and their Alec to stop with other folk, so she's on her own all the while. I just thought I'd look after her.'

Joe raked a hand through his hair, leaving the front bit standing up. 'I don't know about that, love. Ida's not a job for a young one, not the road she is these days. Happen I'll think about it.'

Normally, Megan would have laughed aloud at the sight of Dad's rumpled hair, but she couldn't have laughed to save her life at this moment. Suddenly inspired, she latched on to the bits of gossip she'd heard lately. 'Nobody's bothered about Phyllis's mam, or about Phyllis being ill. I've heard them all talking in the street, saying they wish they'd known about the trouble in number seven. But they're all talk. Mrs Shipton says they're all talk.'

'Mrs Shipton's the biggest talker of all, Megan. She's done nowt for nobody.'

She blinked slowly, gave the impression that her patience was stretched. 'Mrs Shipton has a funny chest, Dad, and their Billy's always in bother. At least she made Mrs Entwistle an egg and bacon butty the day Phyllis got took away. All of us should be helping. We should make . . . like a timetable. We've got one of them at school, prayers and religious, then writing and reading, then sums till dinner. We should have made one of them lists and took turns.' She sniffed. 'Mrs Shipton says Ida Entwistle's too far gone for help. Well, I want to see to her.'

He was torn between two urges, one to stay here with this unhappy daughter, the other need pulling him towards the parlour where his son was almost comatose and in the company of Tess. Tess might run from the ambulance men – she was never at her most sensible after a birthing. In fact, even between babies, she was a bit up and down, on the moody side.

'Go and see to Harold,' said Megan.

He raised an eyebrow. 'Do you read minds and all? Happen we should put you on as a turn at the Theatre Royal.'

'I'm not going to laugh, Dad. Me brother got buried today and me other brother's took bad. Me mam doesn't want to see me no more, and Phyllis's mam's worried sick 'cos she loves her daughter. She says a daughter's a daughter the rest of your life. That means girls see to their mams and don't go off fighting Germans. If I stay with Mrs Entwistle, I'll be . . . I'll be appreciated.'

His moustache twitched, but he didn't laugh. Megan was right, this was no day for glee. Why had he never noticed fully how grown-up she was, how sensible? It wasn't a matter of words, had nothing to do with extra letters dropped by mistake into a string of syllables. He rooted round his own mind, searched his own vocabulary

42

as he tried to analyse what was so unusual about his third child. Concepts. Aye, that was the word. Megan knew people, understood motives, feelings, could predict reactions. 'I never realized till today what a clever lass you are, Megan. You'll go a long way, only you're not going as far as Ida Entwistle's.'

She lifted her shoulders, sighed as he patted her head, lingered near the door while he walked away from her. When the ambulance bell clanged, she covered her ears. Albert must have heard that noise, should have kept out of the road even after the bell stopped its racket. Albert. He'd had his life taken away by an ambulance, the very vehicle that had carried Phyllis away, and now Harold was going in one. She could hear her mother screaming, pictured the scene as Harold was torn from Mam's arms. He would be driven now to a place where the only hope was hope itself.

When Megan could contain herself no longer, she wrenched open the back door, noticing that the light outside had begun to dim its way towards night. Running away was daft unless there was some destination to aim for, but she couldn't face Mam, could stay no longer in a house so full of grief and anger. So in spite of Dad's order, she fled, thereby convincing herself that she really was a very bad person.

She turned the corner at the top of Back Myrtle Street, glanced to her right, made sure that no witness lingered at the blind side of number 17, veered left and arrived at the gates of Althorpe Number One. Althorpe's was working in spite of the holiday fortnight. Mr Althorpe, known in these parts as a great boss, had given his workforce a choice – they could take their time off, or they could work for extra money. Over ninety per cent had chosen the latter option.

The mill buzzed its way into the evening shift, the six-till-ten that was worked by Megan's mother between babies. If little Hilda hadn't just been born, Dad would have been the evening parent except for Fridays. On

Fridays he went to King Billy's to drink beer while Annie and Nellie covered for Mam by watching the house for twopence each. That fourpence came from Dad, of course, because Mam never paid any of her children for their labours.

Anyway, Mam wasn't at the mill any more. Mam was yelling and cursing outside the door of number 13, could be heard even above the drone of heavy machinery as she fought to keep hold of Harold.

Megan climbed into a skip outside the carding shop, making sure that she chose one near the wall. If anyone came to collect one of these large, wheeled baskets, he would surely pick one that was more accessible. Cramp became her prime concern as she shifted her weight from side to side in an effort to keep the blood flowing through curled limbs. She'd played in skips before, had enjoyed games of 'house' with Phyllis, who was her best and very sick friend. There'd been no cramp on these occasions, because they'd jumped about a lot, especially when hiding from the supervisors.

Phyllis. Nobody seemed to know what was happening to Phyllis. Would she live, would she die, would she finish up alive but crippled? And did Harold have the same disease? She peered through close-woven wicker, saw nothing but blackness, waited for the shift to come off. She was thirsty, desperately dry. If Phyllis could have been here, they might have made a game of sneaking into the carding shop cloakroom for a sip from somebody's billy-can or lemonade bottle. Mind, she and Phyllis hadn't ever played here in darkness . . .

'No, I'm not bad,' she said quietly, speaking the words in an effort to keep herself company. 'Billy Shipton's bad, with his knock-a-door-and-run and his pinching stuff from shops. I'm not like him, am I?'

'No, Megan,' she answered. 'But you've been careless. It's not just what you did do, it's what you didn't do. She told you to mind the twins, and you didn't. She never told you not to go in Entwistle's, but she would have if she'd known about it. There's sins of thought, word and deed, and you did a deed sin by not doing what she told you.'

A tremendous clap of thunder made her jump. This was the reason for the blackness, then. She had no coat, so the rain drenched her to the skin in seconds. She leapt from her leaking hide, made a dash for the shed, slid past the huge doors and into the cloakroom. A towel hung from a large hook, and she tore it down, rubbed her face and hair until some of the water was absorbed. After a quick look round, she pounced on a white-and-blue billy, lifted off the lid, drank some tea that was sweet, though tepid.

When she heard all the mumbling and laughing, Megan hauled up the lid of the huge first-aid box and folded herself among bandages and gauze, tried not to sneeze when the smells of iodine and camphor climbed into her nostrils. This medicine chest was just another skip, though it had a lid that closed properly with leather straps. She prayed that no-one would fasten the buckles, because if they did, she would be here till somebody had an accident.

They were talking and giggling, changing work slippers for shoes, making jokes about One-Eyed Pete, who was a foreman. 'He's bad enough with just one bloody eye,' said a woman who was invisible to Megan. 'With a pair, he'd have been like God, all-seeing and in two places at once.'

'Excuse me.'

Megan froze when she identified the speaker as her father.

'Have you seen my daughter? She's about so high, dark hair and blue eyes, goes by the name of Megan.'

The 'no' was chorused unevenly.

'Is that Megan Duffy?' asked a woman. 'Sister of the little lad who got buried today?'

'Aye,' answered Joe Duffy.

'We're sorry,' said the woman. Everybody else was sorry, too, and they all said so.

'She's upset, like,' said Joe. 'It's been a big day, what with the funeral and . . . and other problems.'

45

There was a short pause, then another female spoke. 'That was one of Tess Duffy's boys, weren't it? Them little blond twins? Jesus, Tess'll be out of her mind. She sets great store by lads, does that wife of yours. I remember when they were born, she sent Nellie up here to tell her mates she'd had two little lads at last. I'm sorry you've lost one, Mr Duffy. Your name's Joe, isn't it? Joseph Duffy, the clogger? You do my husband's pit irons.'

'Yes.'

Megan pushed a balled hand against her mouth, felt the tears as they scalded her fingers.

'Is there anything we can do?' asked somebody else.

Before Joe could make a reply, the conversation was interrupted by a new arrival. 'Mr Duffy?'

Oh, Megan knew this man's voice. It was Mr Althorpe! She managed, but only just, not to jump out of her skin. Mr Althorpe wasn't frightening, but he was very, very important. He owned the mills, paid everybody's wages, was a well-respected and generous man. And here he was, getting involved in Megan Duffy's naughtiness. Should she come out of her hiding place? No, no, she couldn't find the courage and she didn't want to see Mam, not yet, anyway.

'Half of the shift can be spared,' announced Sidney Althorpe. 'I heard from the corridor that your child is missing. We shall organize a search.'

'No, thanks,' replied Joe. 'She's a good girl and she'll not have gone far. I appreciate the offer, sir.'

'Very well, but make sure you get me if I'm needed,' said the millowner. 'If it's midnight or four in the morning – whenever – you send to Church Road. I am deeply sorry for your family's misfortune.'

Even from the skip, Megan heard her dad's sigh. 'You've all done your whack, ta. It were a lovely wreath you sent. If you see our Megan, stick hold of her and fetch her round to thirteen Myrtle. Don't scold her, she's a bit . . . a bit confused, like.'

Everything went quiet, then Megan realized that her father had left. After a moment or two, Mr Althorpe addressed those who remained. 'Search your yards, please. The Duffys need our help. I'll bid you good evening, then.'

Megan listened to fragments of conversation, fought the sobs that threatened anew when she caught the gist. 'I feel sorry for Tess and her trouble, Ena, but she's never tret them girls right.' Then, 'Anybody'd think the sun shone out of them twins' backsides, and that Harold's a right swine, you know. It were the nice one that died, him with the thinner face. Right thoughtful, he were. But t'other one'll want watching, I can tell you that for nowt.'

She mustn't make a noise, mustn't, couldn't! They carried on, because they didn't know that she was listening. 'Girls is nowt a pound in Tess's house. When she had them twins, I were looking through windows for three wise men and a star, 'cos she acted as if she'd had a miracle or summat. I bet she's sent nobody out looking for t' missing girl, eh?'

A man's voice arrived from the direction of the doorway. 'Shut up, Ena. Second of them twins is down the isolation hospital. Tess Duffy could well have lost both lads come weekend, so we should all watch what we say.'

'Eeh. Are you sure, Tommy?' asked the one called Ena.

'Took him off her at the front door not an hour since. She fair flayed one of the stretcher bearers, near took his eyes out, she did. I never heard a woman scream as loud.'

It was Tommy Wagstaff. Megan knew Tommy Wagstaff because he lived next-door-but-one, on the other side of Billy Shipton. Tommy Wagstaff never went to bed as far as Megan knew. He did the nightwatch here at the mill, then left his post at 5 a.m. to go and act as knocker-up in the terraces everybody called 'the garden streets'. Tuppence per week per house, he charged. He carried a long pole with scratchy wires on the end, and he rattled this against the windows to wake folk for work. And she was going to be sick again in a minute if she didn't get away from these smelly jars of ointment and bottles of medicine.

'Young Megan will have run off to keep away from her mam,' Tommy Wagstaff was saying. Nobody ever called him 'Mr', Megan thought suddenly. Even little kids from the mixed infants called him Tommy Wagstaff.

'I wish I had a gradely lass like Megan,' announced Ena. 'Four boys is enough to put anybody off breeding. She'd have changed her mind, would Tess Duffy, if she'd been lumbered with my crowd, lazy articles, the lot of them. Lads is burdensome, won't get out of bed, won't fetch coal or nothing. I'd have loved a daughter. Poor little lass out in weather like this. I hope she comes to no harm, God love her.'

'Aye, God love her,' repeated Tommy Wagstaff. 'Because her mother doesn't.'

Megan's tears were funded by a bottomless well of self-pity once the room had emptied. She climbed out of the skip, squatted on a bench, waited for . . . for something. Mam didn't love her. Everybody here at Althorpe's Number One knew that Megan Duffy was unloved. The shame of it all burned fiercely in her heart until the Town Hall clock struck midnight. After that, Megan curled up on an old coat and slept fitfully until a hand arrived out of nowhere and shook her to wakefulness.

THREE

She blinked against the light, wondered what might be the source of illumination so intense, so painful. 'Megan? Is that thee?' she heard.

Megan understood that she was Megan but, beyond that, she had no idea about where, why or when. 'What's the matter?' Her eyelids slammed themselves shut once more, because she could not bear the brightness.

A black shape behind the torch moved to one side. 'It's nightwatchman, Tommy Wagstaff from number nine, love. What the heck are you doing curled up like a wet dog on Ena Barlow's old coat? Your dad'll be out of his mind, lass.'

She remembered, sat up, screwed her hands into tight fists and rubbed the sleep from her eyes. 'I've run away,' she said simply. He knew, anyway. He knew that Mam didn't want her and that Dad had been looking for his errant daughter earlier on. 'What time is it?'

'Twoter to quar,' he answered, trying to keep a smile in his voice.

But Megan was used to Tommy Wagstaff's upside-down way of telling the time. 'Quarter to two,' she translated. 'Is that what's called the middle of the night?'

'Just about.' He hauled her to her feet and guided her out of the cloakroom, allowing her time to visit the lavatory on the way. When they reached the cosy cupboard that was his office, he sat her on a high stool and pointed out into the blackness. 'Can you see any bugger in yon yard?' he asked gravely.

She peered sleepily into the thick blanket of night. 'No.'

'Well,' he said as he leaned on his table. 'That may be

49

because there's nobody about, or it may be because you've got the wrong eyes. My eyes is green and I eat me carrots. I can see every crack in the stones, every bit of cotton-fluff, every pool of oil. I can see in the dark.'

'Oh.' Where was this leading? Adults always led somewhere, seldom talked to a child just for the sake of it. She waited, drank the proffered cup of milk, wiped her mouth on a corner of her apron when the cup was empty. The room was warmed by a paraffin lamp in the corner, one with a kind of mantle whose heat was magnified by a large, silver-coloured dish that glowed orange in the centre, behind the ball of heat.

'There's bad folk and dangerous goings-on out there, young Megan. You can't be out and about in the dead of night. Fact is, unless you're related to the cat family, you'll see nowt till it's too late. With eyes as blue as yours, you should be at home in your own bed.'

Everybody in the whole world knew that Tommy Wagstaff was daft. He talked daft, acted daft, dressed daft. According to Mam, he even lived daft, on his own except for half a dozen stray cats, many of them with parts missing – tails, ears, clumps of fur. 'Are you pretending you're related to cats?' She knew that was a stupid question, but things were mostly stupid in the middle of the night, she guessed.

He nodded, his face serious in the dim light afforded by the heater and by a single electric lamp suspended from the ceiling on a length of twisted wire. ''Course I am. Everybody with green eyes has tiger in the blood.'

Sometimes, Tommy Wagstaff was more than daft. He was probably crackers, she thought. People were people, cats were cats, everything had its own place in the scheme of things. 'Nobody is related to cats, Tommy,' she said wearily. ''Cepting for other cats, I s'pose.'

He shook his head sadly in the face of such blasphemy. For Tommy, the world was one big family, all cousins together, some with feathers, some with fur, some baldish and on two legs. The latter category was a source of bewilderment, as its members used weapons, didn't play fair. He blamed a lot of it on monkeys and their intelligence, though he was still researching that particular theory, trying to find out whether or when apes used weapons . . . He cut across this oblique train of thought, considered the problem on hand. 'Megan, your dad's a good man and a hard worker. I bet he's tramping the streets looking for you at this minute. He'll not give up till you go home.'

'I know.' Argument would be a waste of time, she decided. Also, she was hungry, cold and dampish, so she wanted her own bed and her own pillow.

'Shall I take thee home?' He always said 'thee' when he was being extra nice. 'Because I can see in the dark and keep you safe along the way.'

'All right.' She stood up, smoothed dress and apron, ran her hands along twin plaits of hair that hung almost to her waist. 'Take me home, please.'

He cleared his throat. 'I'd . . . er . . . I'd not take too much notice of your mam just now. I don't mean be naughty, it's just that with the new baby and everything . . . well, she's a bit upsy-daisy, like.'

She nodded. If she'd been a boy, Mam would have had this mill scoured by police, would have woken every neighbour for the search. No pebble would have remained unturned had Megan been a lad. But all the same, she had better go home. There was no way out of it, as there was nowhere else for her to go. Really, now that she thought about it, her half-baked stab at escape had been silly, sillier by far than any of Tommy Wagstaff's tricks, dafter than even the worst of Billy Shipton's many carryings-on.

She watched him as he prepared to take her home. Winter and summer alike, he wore a black cap with two greenish feathers stuck on one side and three leather buttons above the neb. His shirt was striped, collarless and extremely dirty. As far as Megan could remember, Tommy had never worn a collar, even on a Sunday. The man's feet sported a pair of special Duffy clogs. Of course, they weren't like anybody else's footwear, weren't sensible, laced, brass-toed and shiny. No, Tommy's feet were encased in navy leather with black metal at the toe. The fastenings were buckles, black again, but with curly bits that reminded Megan of the fancy writing in her missal.

She followed him out to the yard, watched the movement of thin legs inside trousers so wide that they flapped around his ankles. Tommy Wagstaff's trousers were a disgrace. Megan knew they were a disgrace, because everybody said so. They were far too big, big enough – according to Mrs Shipton – to make a four-man tent. Instead of belt or braces, Tommy depended on a length of washing line to save his dignity but, as local folklore had it, Tommy Wagstaff's trousers had never been sponged, pressed or hung out to air. What was it Mrs Shipton was always saying? Something like, 'Yon man's keks are hung on t'line, only t'line should be in t' street, not round 'is bloody middle parts.'

They walked hand-in-hand along the pavement, Tommy's clogs clipping the flags and sending an echo reverberating around the dark and silent houses. Megan carried on thinking about Tommy's clothes, because she didn't want to worry about what was going to happen any minute, needed to keep her mind off Albert, too. And Harold, of course . . .

There was a light in Mam and Dad's bedroom, a dull glow that came from a gas mantle on the wall. Megan heaved a great sigh of resignation, turned the knob, breathed more easily when the door swung inward. It was often left unlocked, yet Megan wouldn't have been surprised if Mam had tried to bolt it tonight while Dad wasn't looking. Because Mam didn't want Megan, didn't care if she never came home again.

Tommy came with her down the short lobby-cum-hallway, past the parlour door and into the kitchen. In the doorway, the two of them froze like statues, their intertwined fingers tightening of their own accord. Tommy wasn't well up on the wiles of women. Cats were easy, but the female version of the human animal was a creature who had defied Tommy's powers of reasoning for several decades. Megan merely stood and waited for the storm to erupt.

Tess Duffy rose to her feet, no expression on her face. 'Come in,' she said tersely. 'Get warm at the fire.'

Tommy hesitated. 'I've left the mill. If anybody pinches owt, I'll be for the high jump come morning.' An angry woman was a thing to be avoided in Tommy Wagstaff's book.

'Right, Tommy,' said Tess. 'Thanks for fetching her home.' She said nothing about this being the middle of the night, carried on as if Megan had been out to the wet fish shop or to the Co-op for five of spuds.

They listened as he clattered out of the house, each avoiding eye contact with the other, each seeming to wait for the other to speak. Tess sat down again, riddled some dead ashes with the poker, cleared her throat. 'Do you want a bit of toast?'

'No. No, thank you.' They'd be wanting a new fire-plate any day, thought Megan. The whole floor was flagged, even the part right in front of grate and oven. A fender in polished brass marked the grate's boundaries, while a sheet of patterned metal covered the slabs contained by this shining kerb. Fire-plates were sold at the ironmonger's, different patterns, different sizes. A blue one might be nice. The old brown plate was showing distinct signs of wear and Megan's stomach was tickling again. Uncomfortable with her mother, she was thinking about fire furniture just to take her mind off things, really . . .

'I think you'd best go to bed, then.'

Megan loitered just outside the kitchen. 'Harold?' she asked tentatively.

Tess stiffened, felt her heart lurch in her throat. 'It . . . it's not your fault. It's not the same as Phyllis.' She shouldn't have blamed the child in the first place . . . 'Your brother's very ill with the diphtheria.'

'Oh.' Megan waited for more information. When none was forthcoming, she asked about her father.

'Out. He's out looking for you. You shouldn't have run off.'

'No.'

Tess wanted to apologize, yet she could imagine no circumstance in which an adult might apologize to a child. The idea of admitting an error seemed foolish, because a parent should never have to explain, should never need to demean herself in front of a daughter. If I could just love her, she thought. If I could only reach out and hold her. But older children didn't suffer cossetting, not in this day and age. Once they started school, all the sloppy business should be over, all the nursing and billing and cooing. 'I hope you've not caught cold,' she managed at last.

'I'll be all right. I just thought you wanted me to go.'

'No. I don't want anybody to go.'

'Will he get better?' Megan hoped with all her heart that diphtheria would be less serious than infantile paralysis. She didn't like Harold, and that fact alone made wanting him to be well so vital, so important. 'Will he, Mam?'

Tess looked her daughter full in the face. 'He's very poorly. They're doing all they can, the doctors.' Her hands twisted the folds of her skirt. 'It's both of them, Megan. First the accident, now—' she cut herself off, lifted a hand to her eyes. 'Dr Walsh gave me something to calm me down. Go to bed.' At least the tranquillizers had stopped the anger, had made her kinder to this poor girl.

Megan followed her instincts. She ran to her mother and put her arms round the shaking woman. 'I love you, Mam. You might not love me, but that makes no difference.' She did love her mam, she did, even though she didn't like being near her some of the time. Before Tess could reply, Megan fled from the room and ran up the stairs. She was a cowardy-custard, she thought as she lay down next to Freda. She had run before Mam could speak one way or the other.

Downstairs, Tess Duffy wept softly, almost passively.

54

Between the silent sobs, she struggled to mouth the right words, 'I think I love you too, Megan. But I can't even say it.'

Joe came in, found his wife in tears. 'Is she back?' He was breathless, panting.

'Aye.' She rubbed at her cheeks, wondered whether her face would ever be truly dry again. 'He'll be lying in that bed, burning up, strangers all round him. They wouldn't let me stay, Joe. They turned me away and—'

'Tess!' He bent over, took hold of her shoulders and shook her gently. 'You'd no right going to the fever place when you've a new baby to feed. Priorities, Tess. Now, just you listen to me. Our Megan ran off. She scarpered because of you. Does that not matter to you? Does Megan not mean anything?'

She lifted her head slowly, as if the movement caused pain. 'I had one brother and he died. Boys is weaker than girls.' She waved a hand towards the upper floor. 'None of them up there would have gone near the ambulance that killed Albert. They're too sensible, girls, they're born knowing things, as if they've been here before. None of the girls has ever suffered much more than a cold. Lads is different. Once they're breeched, the devil knows and he comes for them. If he can't turn them bad, he kills them off.'

He shook her again, squashed the desire to pummel her till she rattled. 'So every grown man is a bad bugger? Every boy that becomes an adult has given his soul to the devil? You're bloody daft, Tess. Do you want to keep all the male kiddies in frocks till they're twenty-one, so the devil will pass them over?'

She didn't know what she meant. 'Boys die,' she said with all the conviction she could muster.

He released his hold, despaired of getting sense from her. 'Where is she?'

'In bed.'

'Did you talk to her, ask her where she'd been?'

Tess shrugged. 'Tommy Wagstaff brought her home.'

He limped as quickly as possible from the house, stood outside the scullery, his eyes raised to a star-sprinkled sky. For several minutes, he lingered in that yard, attempted to knit together the ragged ends of his patience. Sometimes, he wanted to throttle Tess. Sometimes, his wife deserved a thumping.

Still, he told himself inwardly, Tommy Wagstaff was a good man, a bit on the strange side, but not one who would hurt a kiddy. Joe nurtured that thought, hung on to it. He opened the gate, walked up the back entry, turned left into the yard of Althorpe Number One.

After about a minute, Tommy appeared at the door. 'Come in, Joe. I'll make a brew and find you a biscuit.'

They sat on the high stools in Tommy's eyrie, each dipping bits of broken confectionery into thick, stewed tea. When this formality was over, Joe placed his mug on the shaky card table that served as Tommy's dining piece, and looked hard at his host. Joe often marvelled at Lancashire's niceties. He had known that he would have to drink the tea, take the bit of food, sit down and accept what was offered before getting down to business. Only when real trouble was at hand did the Lancashire folk omit the tea ceremony. 'Where was she?'

'Carders' cloakroom.'

'Asleep?'

'Snoozing on an old coat.'

Joe sighed, stared out into the night. 'Harold's been took bad. After Albert, it's all a bit much.'

Tommy dropped his chin, pondered. 'Tess favours lads, doesn't she? There's women like that, a lot of them. They make such a fuss of the boys that they don't notice all the little lasses toiling like cotton-piecers. Shame, that.'

'Aye, you're not wrong there, Tommy. Did our Megan say owt?'

'Not much.' Tommy pulled a crumb from his whiskers, examined it, ate it. 'She's unhappy, I reckon. See, your Annie and Nellie, they're good girls, ordinary lasses, if you get me drift. Now Megan . . .' He chewed on a spent match, then riddled it about in one of his ears. 'Megan's special.' The match was scrutinized, then put to work at the other side of his head. 'Wax,' he muttered. 'I'm a martyr to wax.'

'She's imaginative.' Joe hardly noticed when his companion transferred a blob of something or other from match to coat sleeve. 'She lives in a little world all of her own.'

Tommy coughed. 'They have to.'

'Eh?' Joe stared at the ill-dressed sage, watched blankly while blackened teeth were picked with an implement that had recently mined ear-wax. 'Who has to what?'

'Well, lonely kiddies make their own pleasure. Like they read a lot, or draw pictures. Megan's lonely, wanting love.'

On occasion, Tommy Wagstaff was difficult to fathom, and on other occasions, this so-called daft man hit the nail so hard on the head that it went right home after one blow. Joe felt guilty, uncomfortable, almost defensive. He was supposed to be wise, intelligent. Folk came into the clog shop to air opinions, to seek advice from Joe Duffy. Yet he was fallible, was clutching at straws and making excuses to Tommy Wagstaff. 'She is loved, you know. They're all fed and warm, all dressed as decent as I can afford. There's no neglect in my house.' He sighed, received the silent message that strode mercilessly across the table. 'I know, Tom. It's our Tess. She doesn't carry on all demonstrative to the girls once they're up and about. Whereas she's always had plenty of time for Albert and Harold.'

'I'm nobbut telling thee what tha already knows, Joe. Megan needs a bit of warmth. Dust tha know what I'd do?'

Joe shook his head.

'Put her with your mam. Doris Appleyard-as-was is a good sort. She'll fettle for Megan, keep her cheerful.'

'Tess wouldn't like it.'

Tommy scratched his nose. 'Why? Is she wanting another to train up for when Annie gets wed? Look.' He got down off the stool, leaned against the wall. 'I'll have to do me rounds in a minute.' He fiddled with the wick of a paraffin lantern, groped in a pocket for his box of matches. 'Megan's different. If you keep her in yon house with all that worrying about a dead brother, she'll happen give up whatever dreams she's got. Send her somewhere. Give her to somebody who'll appreciate her.'

Joe rose, clapped the smelly old man on the back. 'Tommy, you're all there with your lemon drops. Why did you never get wed?'

Tommy chortled, coughed, lit his lamp. 'I'm too fast on my feet, Joe. I'm all there like you say, so I've stuck to cats. They spit like women, fight like women, but they don't talk behind your back like women do. Mind, I reckon I might have changed tack if your mother had looked my way. Still, that's history, eh? I'll say ta-ra, then.'

Joe sat awhile and followed Tommy's shadow with his eyes, watched as the vast mill rooms glowed then darkened as Tommy Wagstaff plied his trade. In a couple of hours, the man would be rattling his wires against the windows, 'Come on, Ted Grimshaw, you've a loom waiting, it's sixter to quar,' and 'Wake up, I'll be charging extra, you're wearing me equipment out.' He was wise, old Tommy. He noticed, listened, understood. And Megan must have a life, because she was special, gifted, unusual. Even if she was only a girl.

Joe walked homeward, the damaged legs aching with tiredness, his head buzzing with thoughts, ideas, memories. At the back gate of number 13, he paused, blinked away the water in his eyes. 'You were a good lad, Albert,' he whispered. 'Have a word while you're up there, see if you can get the Boss to save our Harold.' He lifted the latch, paused, sensed that something was wrong.

When a couple of seconds had elapsed, Joe Duffy stepped back on to the cobbles, his eyes straying the length of the short terrace. He knew everybody in this street, some families more thoroughly than others. After raking his vision over number 15, where Mildred Moss, a deaf and cantankerous spinster lived, he turned his attention back to number 13. Tess must have gone to bed, as the house was completely dark. No light showed at Elsie Shipton's windows, and Tommy Wagstaff's place was deserted. At last, he knew what had caught his eye. Ida Entwistle was still up. Although the curtains were closed, a dim yellow glow was stealing through the frail cloth that hung against window panes in Ida's kitchen.

He paused. There was no law about going to bed at a certain time, no curfew to observe. If Ida chose to stay up all night, it was no business of anyone else's. Yet he was uncomfortable, even worried. He sidled down the alley, put himself in mind of a burglar or a sneak-thief. There was a noise in his ears, an internal thumping, as if his heart were keeping time by beating rhythmically on an eardrum. She was a bit off-side, was Ida Entwistle, a slate or two short on her roof. Stress, he reckoned. First her husband was killed, then young Phyllis got put in the fever place. Nerves, he thought, were funny things. Funny, but not laughable.

Her gate swung open, squealed like a cornered rat. He stepped into the yard, sniffed, wondered when the tippler had last been scrubbed with Lanry. Tess was a bugger for bleach, was always dousing everything that didn't move, sometimes splashing things that did move, 'Get out of me road, Freda, I'm Lanrying the yard'.

He pinned his eye to a central crack where the curtains did not meet, saw little beyond a table covered in newspaper. On this surface lay a single chipped cup and some age-curled potato peelings. A terrible silence hung over the place, a quiet that advertised something far more sinister than a mere lack of activity. It would soon be dawn. He should go home, lie down with his wife, stick to a routine that defied recent happenings. Regular habits were the answer to anxiety, he knew that in his bones.

His hand was on the doorknob. 'Ida?' The stage-whisper seemed to echo for miles. He would have to go in.

The noise of his breathing was louder than the daytime clump of the huge steelworks hammer that pounded year after year in the middle of town.

Cautiously, he entered Ida Entwistle's scullery, tried to ignore the crunching sound beneath his feet as he murdered a meeting of cockroaches. Joe was no stranger to vermin, yet he let out an anxious gasp when a small rodent, either a mouse or an immature rat, scuttered across the toe of his clog.

Whatever was wrong hovered in the air like a smell, yet he could pick up no scent that was unfamiliar. Every house in this area stank of bugs, fleas, poverty. The town man had been up not three months earlier, had doused walls with a substance that looked like treacle, reeked of nothing else on earth. Tess had tried powders, potions and sheer willpower, but no compound known to man could rid the 'garden' streets of their million unwelcome residents. He sniffed again, gained no further information via his olfactory system, ventured towards the kitchen. It wasn't a smell, then, wasn't a sound or a sight. Yet his skin crawled, as if some long-forgotten ability had suddenly revived itself. His sixth sense was opening every pore, raising to attention each hair on his body.

Ida Entwistle was suspended from a pulley-hook in front of the grate. She had taken a great deal of care while making her exit, had removed the wooden airer from its ropes, had made from them a noose to end her life. Because the rope was so thin, it had embedded itself deep in her throat, making her face black and ugly. The poor woman's tongue protruded grotesquely from a twisted mouth, while the skeletal, work-scarred hands dangled limply by her sides. She moved slightly in the current of air that Joe had brought in, swung back and forth like an overgrown puppet on unsteady strings. A chair lay on its side to the right of Ida's body. It was plain that she had kicked it away as she launched herself on that final journey into eternity.

Joe fell to the floor, the battle-weakened legs deserting him completely. It seemed that there was a curse on

Myrtle Street, a devil-sent charm that was touching the houses and destroying the tenants. This was a stupid way to think, yet he could not avoid the train of thought that shot through his brain with the speed of a locomotive without brakes. Something terrible was happening here. Phyllis had the infantile, Ida had done for herself, Harold was away with diphtheria, Albert was cold and alone in a grave up Heaton.

'God, I can't get up.' He spoke earnestly to his Maker. 'Get me up. Make me walk out of here, please. Don't let me stop with this poor dead woman.' His head felt strange and light, was beginning to spin.

The Almighty took a moment or two, but He eventually sent the strength Joe needed. In Ida's yard, Joe Duffy gulped great mouthfuls of air, propped himself against the scullery wall, waited for sanity to reclaim its right of residence in his shock-rattled brain. Was Phyllis Entwistle dead? Ida's love for her only daughter had been legendary, easily as powerful as Tess's affection for the lads. Deprived of Phyllis, Ida might well have chosen this terrifying option. So, had that little friend of Megan's shuffled off into the hereafter? And what about Alec and Jack? Who would tell those two lads that they'd lost their mam and their sister as well as their dad?

A sickening thought lodged itself at the front of his consciousness. He heard Megan's voice, remembered the earnestness in her little face. 'Mrs Entwistle shouldn't be on her own, Dad. I'll look after her. She likes girls, but my mam doesn't. I want to go and stay at . . .' No, no! He shook his head violently. How much had Megan sensed? Had that little girl been aware that Ida was nearing the end of her life? Dear God, could Megan have saved the unhappy woman? His body shivered, as if it were trying to shake off the concept. He must not blame himself. Ida might have done this even with Megan in the house, and if Megan had found . . . None of it bore close consideration, so he pulled himself along, made his shock-blinded way back to the mill yet again.

61

Tommy Wagstaff brought Joe into his office for the second time. 'What's up with thee, lad? Can't tha sleep?'

Joe dropped on to the stool while he fought a sudden breathlessness. 'Tommy, Ida's finished herself, she's hanging in the back kitchen. Happen Phyllis is dead, but what about their Jack and their Alec? Somebody's got to fetch a bobby, Ida wants cutting down. She was a good lass, Phyllis. Bonny, too, with that nice red shine to her hair. It always reminded me of Magee's horses, did Phyllis's hair, like a chestnut brown . . .' His chin quivered as he fought the urge to scream. 'Dead, Tommy.'

The knocker-up-cum-nightwatchman studied his neighbour. The blue eyes were ringed with red from lack of sleep, while broad shoulders had slumped forward, turning Joe Duffy into a bundle of grief and despair. 'Look at me, Joe,' he whispered. 'Are you sure they're both dead?'

Joe nodded. 'I'm not daft, you know. I might be a bit rattled over all that's happened, but I'm still all here. Phyllis must be dead, else why would Ida kill herself? And Ida's definitely gone, 'cos I've seen her not ten minutes since.' He swallowed. 'Her face was all . . . all lopsided. I think she went slow, you know. Choked herself to death, she did.'

Tommy gulped audibly. 'Look, I'll run down for Mick Crompton in Holly Street. It's best to get a policeman for this sort of job. Will you wait here, Joe? Can I leave you?'

'Eh?' Joe's face was blank, expressionless. 'Do you think our Tess'll kill herself if Harold doesn't come out of hospital in one piece? I'd never cope, see. I mean, she gets on me nerves with the road she favours boys and changes her moods with the wind, but she's me wife, Tommy and—'

'Joe, I've got to get the bobby.'

'Aye.'

'Will you wait here for me?'

'But she's a good Catholic, is Tess. Suicide's a mortal

sin, isn't it? Eternity's a long time to be stuck in hell. Ida must have gone there. She'll not get buried in the Catholic cemetery, not after taking her own life—'

'Joe!' Tommy waved a hand. 'Will you stop chuntering on about hell and bloody cemeteries. I've got me own opinions about such things, and now's the wrong time to be going into detail. But I will say this much. If there's a God, then He knows the details of Ida's suffering. And unless He's a miserable swine, He'll deal with Ida gentle, like. So sit there, don't move, wait for me.' He rushed off to get help.

Joe looked through a dust-smeared window, watched the sky as it lightened towards morning. Everything was continuing the same, then. The Duffy family had lost one – God forbid that the number should double – while the Entwistle contingent had lessened by three. Poor little Phyllis . . . Yet the sun would rise, birds would sing, Tommy was no doubt preparing to rattle his wires against bedroom windows. Tommy. Where was he? Oh aye, he'd gone down Holly to fetch wotsisface, that young bobby with the cheeky grin. 'You're getting old, Joe,' he whispered into the silence. 'Police used to look like men – they're nobbut lads these days.'

When the shift came on at six, some of its members found Joe Duffy asleep, his head resting on folded arms. The news had spread like wildfire, because Tommy Wagstaff had been late with his calls. Never in the history of man had Tommy Wagstaff been late. Till now. Till poor Ida Entwistle had been found by this crumpled and exhausted clogger. 'Get home, lad,' said One-Eyed Pete. 'Go and see to the missus and the childer, forget the clogs for now.'

Joe stared into the scarred face of Peter Atherton. They'd been together in the mud, together in a canvas hospital while one lost an eye and the other managed to keep his legs. They'd seen and heard things . . . 'Was I right, Pete? Or did I imagine it?'

'You imagined nowt, owld lad. Ida's a goner.'

Joe sat up, pulled on his cap. 'I thought we knew it all, me and you. After that bloody mess . . .' He swept a hand across the small table. 'You think you'll never worry again, don't you? I've seen some corpses in my time—'

'But never a woman. Never a mother.'

Joe nodded. 'She wanted Phyllis back. She loved that kiddy, couldn't bear the thought of life without her.'

One-Eyed Pete ushered a few bystanders out of the nightwatchman's cramped office. 'Phyllis is all right,' he said softly. 'Well, she's alive. Only she's lost the use of her legs. It looks like Ida blamed herself. She'd been saying to Elsie Shipton that Phyllis might never walk again. Seems they told Ida down the hospital that the lass's legs were nigh on useless. And she just couldn't take no more bad news.'

Joe gulped, thirst and dread combining to make his throat so dry that it was almost closed. 'Give us a drop, Pete.'

The foreman opened his billy and poured tea into a blue-ringed cup that served as lid to this enamel container. 'Plenty sugar in that, Joe. Drink it all, your blood'll be tired.'

When the metal cup sat empty on the table, Joe grasped the hand of his lifelong friend. 'Pete, what'll become of Phyllis and them two lads, eh? Somebody might take the boys – Ida's sister, like as not – but who'll want a crippled kiddy? And God Almighty, which one of us is going down town to tell Phyllis about this lot?'

Pete kept his face straight, refused to wince as his fingers stung inside Joe's grip. The clogger was strong, had the ability to cut leather as easily as most folk scraped butter. 'Joe, stop taking other people's problems on your shoulders. It's not five minutes since you buried Albert, and Harold's poorly now—'

'She matters!' cried Joe. 'They all count, whether they're mine or yours or Ida's. We're all responsible for each other. That's what being human means. If we were animals, we'd walk away and leave the lass to die – or we'd finish her off before she slowed us down. They do that, you know. Anything weak or crippled gets killed or left behind. Being human means we stop and carry her.'

Joe walked home at snail's pace. There was activity in the street, people bustling about as if trying to convince themselves that life must continue apace, no matter what. Early step-scrubbers knelt in lobbies, turbaned heads bobbing about while slabs were cleaned and stoned. Some children lingered outside number 7, drawn to disaster like moths to a flame. One of them flew towards him, dark plaits bouncing as she ran. 'Dad!' Megan's face was white with shock. 'Mrs Entwistle. And what about Phyllis? Her mam hanged herself, they say. Where's Phyllis? How can she come home when she's an orphan? Can we have her? Can we? Don't let her go in one of them orphan places, Dad. They have cold porridge and . . . Her legs are no use, Dad. Will they keep her in hospital for ever and ever? Will they? But if we have Phyllis, Mam doesn't like girls as much as boys and . . . and I want to look after me friend.'

Joe heard the fractured sentences, the heart-rending questions. He placed a hand on his daughter's head. There would be no house, no move for the Duffys. His decision was instant and irrevocable, yet he was sure of its rightness. 'Your grandma can leave work and look after Phyllis. You move in with them, love, keep your friend cheerful.'

Megan stopped in her tracks. 'Eh?' She couldn't believe it, couldn't grasp the fact that Phyllis's mam had killed herself, that Phyllis might never walk, that Deedee was somehow involved with a possible solution to Phyllis's homelessness. 'What did you say, Dad?'

He sighed, took Megan's hands in his. 'Your gran's tired, love, worn out with the mill. But she'll soon buck up if she stops at home and minds a couple of lasses.' And Megan might improve too, he thought, might flower once Tess's shadow was removed from the child's sky. 'We'll manage,' he said gruffly, trying to convince himself that a house-move was not the be-all and end-all. For the sake of Phyllis, he was killing his own dream. But he was stopping to give a hand to the weak, was being human. 'We'll have to go round to see Phyllis. I suppose her auntie will have gone down to the hospital.'

'Phyllis will cry,' announced Megan. 'Everybody's dying.'

Joe's heart ached as he studied the serious face of his third child. 'These things happen, my little lass. Sometimes, life looks awful cruel, but there's a reason to everything.'

Megan pondered. 'A reason why Mrs Entwistle did that?' She waved a hand towards the house of death. 'And a reason for Phyllis getting ill and our Albert dying?' She gulped. 'If there's reasons, why can't something good happen for a change? There must be reasons for nice things, too.'

He squatted until his eyes were level with Megan's, tried not to flinch as pain shot its red-hot needles through a knee. 'God knows why these things are happening. He really does know, Megan.' Unless he clung to this belief, this blind faith in his Maker's omniscience, Joe Duffy might well go crazy.

But Megan persisted. 'Mrs Entwistle'll be in hell. Mrs Shipton said that.' Her face was grave.

He moved slightly, tried to give his legs some ease, searched for Tommy's phrases, repeated them. 'God will have mercy. Ida was ill in her mind.'

Megan nodded quickly, agitation fuelling the movement. 'She can't get buried decent, that's what Mrs Shipton says. So, if God has mercy, then our church is wrong.'

Oh, if only Elsie Shipton would learn to keep her gob shut in front of youngsters! The mud was thickening. He'd been up to his ears in France, and he floundered now on a pavement outside his own house. 'Look, just stop worrying, Megan. There's none of us can do anything to help, so—'

'It's not fair.'

It wasn't fair. He knew it wasn't fair, wanted to scream everybody's pain into the street. But nobody had ever guaranteed fairness, so the unmendable had to be accepted. How could he explain this to a little child?

'I'm sorry, Dad. I'm sorry for mithering.'

'Eeh, that's all right, lass. I know how fond you are of young Phyllis.'

She leaned against the wall, one foot lifted to the bricks behind her. 'I'll write to him,' she decided aloud. 'I'll send a letter to the Vaticantic City and ask if Mrs Entwistle can go to heaven.'

Joe shook his head, squashed the weak smile that hovered briefly on his lips. She had a habit of making words longer than they needed to be, and he would miss her little ways. Megan Duffy would always get to the bottom of things, he reckoned. She was clever and determined. It was the latter quality that might well have her in and out of trouble all her life. 'He's a busy man, the pope,' he reminded her gently.

She planted both feet on the pavement, straightened, looked her father full in the face. 'Mrs Entwistle was important,' she announced. 'And so is Phyllis. I can't be having Phyllis thinking her mam's in hell, can I?'

She was so much like him! Hadn't he given Pete a lecture about everybody being vital? 'Write if you like, love.' For Ida's sake, for his daughter's sake, Joe prayed that any reply would be encouraging.

Annie and Nellie came through the door of number 13, their hands still red from scrubbing kitchen flags. 'Oh, there you are,' said Nellie unnecessarily. 'Mam's gone down to the hospital. Doctor came round, said Harold's worse.'

It wasn't over, then. Joe followed his daughters into the house, sat idly by the fire while breakfast was made by female children whose infancy had been shortened because of their gender. She would come screaming through the door at any minute, he thought. The diphtheria had probably won, and Tess would have no son to justify her existence. No, it wasn't over. There was one more death to come, one more funeral – two if he included Ida. And she must be included, he insisted inwardly. No matter what the pope said, Ida Entwistle had been a good woman.

They ate their porridge, tried to bite toast quietly, as if the sounds of living were inappropriate just now. Megan gulped, fought the movement in her stomach, made a dash for the yard when her digestive system refused to co-operate.

Joe sighed, threw down his knife, listened to the clock as it ticked its way towards whatever might happen. 'Go down to the hospital, see to your mam,' he ordered the older girls.

'What about the washing?' asked Annie.

'To hell with the washing,' was his unusually strong response. 'It's folk that matter, not bedding. Is the baby asleep?'

'Aye,' answered Nellie.

'Then get gone and see to Tess. I'll not open the shop today.'

He sat with Megan, their rigid bodies welded together on the horsehair sofa, no space between them as they waited for the next harbinger of doom. The street was definitely cursed, he thought anxiously. As a Catholic, he should not believe in evil spells, should get down on his knees and beg for God's intervention. But his knees were tired and his mind was numb.

'What's diphtheria, Dad?' asked Megan suddenly.

He coughed, cleared the emotion from his tight throat. 'It's a bad disease, Megan.'

Her fingers tightened their grip on her father's hand. 'Will he die? Does everybody have to go and die at the same time? Will we die and all?'

He turned his head, looked at her. She was a bonny lass, their Megan, such a sweet-faced and bright little thing. Not that the others weren't pretty, but this one's dark hair and bright eyes were startling in a family so fair. 'No, we won't all die, lass.' He squashed his own disobedient thoughts. 'It's germs, you see. Some folk shake them off and some don't. As for our Albert . . .' He sniffed back the tears. 'Albert had an accident. Anybody can have an accident.'

A single drop escaped from the corner of a bright blue eye. 'So none of it were my fault?'

Joe all but ground his teeth. She wanted flaying, did Tess. Because the two older girls were compliant, they got no trouble from their mother, while Freda, at five, was still too young to be in Tess's line of fire. But Megan was different inside as well as on the surface. She voiced her thoughts, answered back occasionally, seemed immersed in a search for truth and reason. So she took most of the flak, did poor little Megan. 'You hold up that beautiful head, Megan Duffy. You've never hurt anybody and you never will. I'm that proud of you, I could burst just looking at you.'

Freda ran in from the street, her face burning as a result of hard running. 'Dad! They've cut our Harold's throat, made a hole so he can breathe! Our Nellie's on her way up the street and she told me. It sometimes makes folk better when they cut their throat. Can I have a biscuit?'

The baby started to cry. Joe raised his chin, listened to the sound of young life as it floated down from the ceiling. Harold was breathing, was alive. It was as if the baby Hilda had heard the news and was celebrating her own hold on the world. 'Thank God,' he whispered. 'Go up and see to our babby, Megan. And you can have all the biscuits you can find,' he told Freda.

Much later, when Tess arrived home, Joe brewed tea and listened to his wife's hopeful ravings. 'Drink this.' He pushed a pint mug into her hands. 'You'll need it after all the worrying.'

She drained the cup in two or three gulps. 'Stuck a tube in, they have. I looked at him through a window in the corridor and he seemed contented enough. It's a trache . . . ostomy or something, like another mouth but in his

69

throat. Membrane's covered all his normal breathing, doctor said. He's got . . .' She rummaged in a pocket, brought forth a scrap of paper and struggled with the syllables. 'He's got naso-pharin-geal diphtheria. That's the most dangerous. He's holding his own, but all the germs and the dead cells have blocked his nose and throat. He'd have died but for the hole in his neck.'

Joe said nothing. He'd been to the library, had read up on the subject of diphtheria. It wasn't just the membrane, wasn't just the choking. The bacteria invaded the whole body, shot like wildfire through something called lymph, got into heart muscles, weakened the very core of a child's body.

'Do you think he'll be all right?' she was asking now.

'In God's hands, lass,' he said comfortingly. 'Pray, Tess, for there's nowt else we can do.'

FOUR

Tess fussed about the bedroom, hung over Harold anxiously until his pale eyelids flickered. 'Do you want some broth, love?'

'No.'

'Cocoa? A condensed milk butty?'

'No.' He didn't want anything. Ever since Albert had died, Harold had felt like half a person. There'd been little fun in Albert, little naughtiness, yet Albert had been . . . important. He shifted his head on the pillow, waited for the room to stand still. 'I'm dizzy,' he complained. Any effort, any movement at all seemed to drain him. Sometimes, his eyes were dim, as if blindness threatened to be the next port of call. 'I want Albert,' he whispered.

Tess turned to Megan. She didn't say anything, but the message seemed to shoot out of her eyes like tiny daggers that attached themselves to Megan's soul. If the boys had been minded properly, then Harold might have had his wish.

'Shall I do the shopping?' asked Megan, anxious to be on the move now that her stomach was beginning to play up yet again. She'd noticed lately that Mam was often present when tummy muscles started jumping about and tickling her insides with what felt like red-hot fingers. 'I can go to the Co-op if you want.'

Tess's cold gaze swept the length of her daughter's slim body. She was a good girl, really, was Megan. Yet Tess had to admit to herself that life would be easier in a way without this particular daughter. There was something unusual in the child's eyes, a kind of wisdom that did not sit comfortably on such a young face. 'Five of spuds and two of carrots. And a bit of stewing steak – I'll make some beef tea for Harold.'

Megan ran from the room and clattered her clog-shod way downstairs. She would be out of Mam's way soon, would be moving out of Myrtle Street and into number 6, Holly Street. Deedee was going to leave the mill and set up a little business in the new house. Even Phyllis would be able to help, because a lot of tasks could be performed from the wheelchair. Phyllis's hands had not been affected, though her legs were weak and her mind was scarred by sadness.

'Megan?' Tess, on the top step, towered over her daughter. 'Can't you be quiet? This is still a very sick boy who needs his rest. Have you learned nothing at all? After your pile of mistakes, lady, you should be wiser by now.' She checked herself, listened to the echo of her words. Megan was already sage, too clever for anyone's comfort. 'Learn to think of others a bit more often.' She turned and stalked back into the bedroom.

Outside, Megan leaned on the wall for a moment or two. She could do nothing right. When she was quiet, she was sulking. When she was noisy, she was disturbing Harold. The baby had been farmed out to a woman three streets away, because even the innocent little Hilda cried and upset Tess's son. The house was a mess. Everyone was back at school, so Annie and Nellie could only do so much when they got home. Yet these two older girls were waking up at five o'clock to make bread, to wash and iron, to clean as best they could. Nellie had taken five strokes of Mother Cecilia's strap yesterday for falling asleep during prayers. Mam was doing next to nothing at all, was confining herself to upstairs so that she could watch Harold all the time.

Megan wandered towards the shops, jumped nervously when her name was called. It was Tommy Wagstaff in new trousers and a decent jacket. Because of the new trousers, Megan's jaw dropped.

He smiled broadly, his eyes crinkling at the corners and

72

making lots of happy lines on his face. 'They fell to bits, me other keks. I've gone in for braces now.' He opened the jacket to reveal leather thongs fastened to buttons on his waistband. 'Better than rope, I suppose.' He straightened his jacket, struck a pose, tripped over a paving slab and guffawed loudly. When he had calmed down, he peered closely at the little girl's taut features. She was a lovable lass, too good for the heavy yet invisible burden she seemed to be carrying. 'I hear you're not aiming to be a clogger's apprentice no more, Megan. Starting living at your granny's soon, eh?'

She grinned. You just had to grin at Tommy Wagstaff, because even in new clothes, the man looked like an unmade bed. 'Deedee's taking sewing in,' she replied. 'From big houses where they have a lot of sheets and curtains. And . . .' She paused for effect. 'We might be making clothes for ladies and doing vestments for the churches and altar boys' clothes. Deedee's good at embroidery, see. Mr Althorpe's letting us live in one of his houses. He said it was the least he could do in the . . . circscumsanties.' The word had come out wrong, but Tommy Wagstaff wasn't one to offer a great deal of criticism. In fact, for a grown-up, he was nice, interesting to be with.

He fell in beside her as she began to walk. 'Aye, he's a great man, is Sidney Althorpe. He even has houses out on the moors for people who're not well.'

'Deedee's very grateful. She told him so.'

Tommy had waited years to find Doris Appleyard-as-was in a grateful mood, but he said nothing about that. 'How's young Harold getting on?'

Megan shrugged, tried to shake the worry and guilt from her shoulders. 'Not so good,' she answered. 'Can't get out of bed 'cos he goes dizzy. But he's eating only a little bit, so he will be dizzy, won't he?'

Tommy jangled some coins in a pocket. 'He were a right tearaway, your Harold, couldn't keep hisself out of trouble for more than two minutes at a time, always dragged poor

73

Albert in with him. Plenty of spirit in Harold. Shame if he can't buck up.'

She studied her clogs, clipped a stone flag, regretted yet again that she, as a young lady, was forced to have rubbers rather than irons on the soles. 'He's got a bad heart now.' It was definitely her fault. If she'd watched them, if Phyllis's ambulance hadn't come, if Harold hadn't run off . . . Every day, the same thoughts, the same terrible memories.

'It weren't none of your doing, you know,' he said softly. 'Albert could have had that accident any time, anywhere. And Harold caught diphtheria at school, like as not.'

'I know.' She really did know, but knowing and feeling were two different things. She felt responsible, and emotions were hard to cope with. 'But Mam blames me. She looks at me as if I'm a bad person.'

'Deedee won't do that.' His tone was soft, gentle. 'Deedee's a good woman. If I'd ever got wed, it would have been Doris Appleyard for me. But no. She upped and married Stanley Duffy, and him no better than the rest of us and a lot worse than most.'

Megan, sensing a little romance in the air, slowed her pace and placed a hand on her companion's arm. 'Do you love our Deedee?'

He stopped walking, nodded, his expression suitably solemn and wistful.

'Is that why you let yourself go?'

Tommy frowned. 'Who said owt about me letting meself go? I'm still a fine figure of a man for me age.'

Megan paused, then waded in regardless. 'Mrs Shipton. She says you were very . . . eligibubble. Mrs Shipton's mam carried a torch for you. Was it dark?'

'Eh?'

'Well, you needed a torch. Why did you need a torch and why didn't you carry your own? You carry your own now on the nightwatch, don't you? Was the torch Mrs Shipton's mam carried heavy? Did it take two of you to lift it?'

74

He took off his cap, scratched his head, replaced the old headgear on top of a shock of iron-grey hair. In his experience, life usually got complicated during conversations with folk of the female persuasion. 'What are you on about now, Megan Duffy? I were just trying to remember Elsie Shipton's mam as a young woman. She were very thin, I think. She's still thin. If she stood sideways behind a gaslamp, you'd not notice her. And carrying a torch has nowt to do with carrying a torch. Wait till you're older.' He dragged her along, reminded her about the errands.

'She might like you if you have a bath,' suggested Megan.

'What?' He glanced into the Co-op, saw that no-one was near enough to hear their discussion. 'Elsie Shipton's mam? I've no interest in her, lass. She's nobbut three teeth left, and they're all on the bottom shelf like a row of gravestones.'

Megan sighed impatiently. She shook her head in the manner of an adult trying to be plain but gentle with a child. 'Deedee. If you get clean, my granny might like you.'

He made himself taller, pretended to preen as he stared at his reflection in the shop window. 'I had a bath last month,' he informed her proudly.

'A slipper bath's best,' insisted Megan. 'They've nice, deep tubs at the public baths. You can't get clean in a tin bath, you know.'

He nodded pensively. 'Aye, you might be right. And it has to be a lick and a promise because of the holes. I've no sooner filled it than it's empty.'

She looked him up and down. Even Tommy Wagstaff wasn't daft enough to fetch a leaking bath into the house. In fact, Megan suspected very strongly that Tommy Wagstaff wasn't daft at all. 'You do this on purpose, don't you? Just to make people laugh.' She walked into the shop, turned, came out again. 'I'll call you Mr Wagstaff from now on, Tommy Wagstaff. And you can start getting yourself cleaned up a bit.'

The kind eyes narrowed. 'Can you see right through me?' he asked.

'No. Only partway.'

'Ah, so you are another cat, then. You'll be seeing in the dark next news. By the way.' He sidled closer. 'Does she like cats?'

It was Megan's turn to enjoy a moment of confusion. 'Who?'

'Doris Appleyard-as-was.'

'She likes all animals. Come for tea after we've moved in. And come clean.'

Tommy Wagstaff lingered for a few seconds, watched little Megan Duffy as she made her purchases. There was no need to 'come clean' with this child. She knew. She knew all about him, realized that his eccentricity was a manufactured wall behind which he hid his innermost thoughts and dreams, a barrier between the world and his true self. Perhaps it was time for the defences to be removed. 'Little monkey,' he muttered to himself. Then he carried on to John Pickavance's and bought a crusty cob. 'Tuppence a week for a bath,' he grumbled to the bemused baker. 'You wonder if a woman's worth that much, don't you?' He would have to increase his knocking-up round, because he'd need soap, a flannel and a towel with no holes in it. These were drastic measures, he thought as he walked home. But there again, she did like cats . . .

They were getting the house ready for Phyllis, who would be sleeping on a bed under the stairs in the back kitchen. Megan made sure that her friend would fit into this space by stretching herself out on the new mattress. 'It's nice, Deedee,' she said. 'As long as Phyllis sleeps the right way up. With her head down the narrow end, she'd bump it, wouldn't she?'

Doris Duffy watched while her favourite granddaughter pulled herself out of the triangular space. 'She'll sleep the road she's put, Megan. Phyllis'll not be getting herself out of bed in the middle of the night, will she? There's things we have to know, love, things we'll have to do for her.'

Megan dangled her legs to the floor, took her own weight on her own feet, wondered how Phyllis was going to cope. 'It's a shame,' she said quietly.

Deedee put on her no-nonsense face. 'Never mind about a shame, child. We are going to treat yon lass as if she's family and as if she's normal. Because she is, in her head. It'll be things like baths that'll be difficult. And she'll need a bedpan. Apart from that, she'll sit out in the street when it's fine and she'll work along of me when it rains. In fact, we can both do our stitching in the street when the sun shines. I'll fetch her down to the school for a couple of hours every day, and she can learn along the rest of you. If we start pitying her, she'll be a misery.'

'Right, Deedee.' Deedee was always right. She was one of those people you could depend on, someone who didn't change her mind every time the wind blew. 'Anyway, I'm going to make sure she walks again.'

'Well, I hope it stays fine for you. If you can do what a hospital full of doctors can't manage, then I'll take a dozen caps off to you. Have you scrubbed that hearth in yon parlour?'

'Yes.' They'd been a bit on the posh side, the folk who had moved out of number 6. In the front room, there was a polished wood fire surround and a real cast-iron grate with no oven attached to it. The kitchen had been made bigger by removing the wall between it and the single-storey scullery, and there was a porcelain sink instead of a slopstone. 'It's lovely, this house, Deedee.'

Doris looked at the shining black grate with its oven and copper, cast an eye over a scrubbed table, two easy chairs and four dining chairs. 'He's a good man, is Sidney Althorpe,' she declared. 'Once I get me dresser in, we'll be like bugs in a rug.'

Megan leaned on the table. 'Is this really Mr Althorpe's house, then?' She knew the answer, but Megan loved to hear Deedee talk, could have listened to her forever.

'Oh, he bought several down here some years back, did them up lovely for a few troubled families. The couple who lived here got burnt out at their last place, so Sid Althorpe rented this to them. He's took them up Affetside or somewhere now, because the woman's got consumption and she needs fresh air. Aye, he's a saint, very good to his workers.'

Deedee hadn't worked for Mr Althorpe, thought Megan. 'Why has he given us this house? Didn't you go in a different mill, not one of his?'

Doris nodded. 'He's doing this for Phyllis, love. And he's wanting no rent from us, neither.' Yet this manufactured family would support itself. The mill owner had offered further assistance, but Doris's pride had stood in the way. 'Thank you,' she had said to him. 'But I'll manage.' She was only fifty-nine, she told herself firmly now. There might be many years ahead, and she had no intention of retiring while she remained healthy and alert. 'We shall do very nicely here,' she told her grandchild. And Joe would have his house, thought Doris fiercely. She'd no intention of depriving her one and only of his nest-egg.

Megan thought for a moment. 'I'll have to write again,' she said pensively.

'Write?' Doris busied herself with a duster, began to polish the steel fender. 'What are you writing?'

'To the pope – I told you before. He'll need me new address.'

The duster was folded and placed in the wooden crate that housed all the cleaning materials. The grandmother puffed and panted for a moment, her face reddened by exertion. 'Megan,' she said carefully. 'We can't go digging poor Ida up. She'll be all right where she is.'

'No, she won't. Mrs Shipton says Phyllis's mam is neither fish nor fowl, 'cos she's in unconsecr . . . uncon . . . she's in a grave what's not blessed. She'll have to be moved.'

I could kill Elsie Shipton sometimes, thought Doris. All mouth and no brains, that woman. 'It makes no difference where Ida's remains lie. God will see to her. And I'm not putting Phyllis through a funeral. Leave things alone, Megan.'

Megan hadn't thought about the details, but she realized now that Deedee was right yet again. Phyllis didn't know much about her mother's resting place, so there was no point in making a fuss. Then a thought dropped into Megan's mind. 'What if Phyllis asks to go to the graveyard? Then she'll see that her mother's been put in the wrong part.'

Doris lowered herself into a chair. 'For a seven-year-old, you've the head of a crone, Miss Duffy. Are you planning on pushing yon wheelchair from here to Heaton? How will the child get there if we don't take her? And if we do, there's no notice up to say that Ida's not in church soil. Just shut up and put up, lady.'

Megan held her tongue. But she still wanted the answer. If Pope Benedict was a nice man, he would write and say that Mrs Entwistle could go to heaven. If he wasn't nice . . . Megan didn't want to think about Pope Benedict not being nice. But if he wasn't, she'd be learning no more of her catechism.

After a tap at the front door, a man's voice hailed Doris. 'Are you there, Mrs Duffy?'

'Come in,' she called. 'I've no fire lit, but we can fetch some tea from me son's . . .'

'Don't bother yourself.' He walked into the room, glanced round, studied the arrangements for Phyllis. 'Will it do?' he asked.

Doris smiled. 'It's the best house I've ever been in, Mr Althorpe. By the way, this is Megan, my grand-daughter and Phyllis's friend. She'll be stopping here from tomorrow.'

Sidney Althorpe performed an old-fashioned bow, then ruined the effect completely by winking at the pretty girl-child. 'There'll be a few hearts in pieces ten years from

79

now,' he said. 'You're a nice-looking young woman, Megan. How old are you?'

She watched his face, noticed how alive and mobile it was. 'I'm seven, sir, eight next time.'

He rooted in a pocket. 'There's seven sixpences for you, one for every year.'

'Three and six!' Megan's astonishment showed in her voice. 'That's a lot of money, Mr Althorpe.'

He winked at Doris now. 'And a lot of brain-power in this girl, Mrs Duffy. I've brought some sheets for Phyllis, seconds from Number One. I must have a drunken weaver in there, the number of faults we're turning out. And I've left a parcel of fancies in the lobby, bits and pieces for curtains.' He watched Doris, stepped in before she could object. 'It's not charity. You use them if you can. If you don't want them, pass the parcel.'

'Dad!' The word floated into the house. 'May I come in?'

Sidney Althorpe summoned the invisible speaker. 'You can come in this once, Geoffrey. But after today, the house is spoken for and private.'

A boy of about nine or ten entered the room. He wore good clothes, rather countrified and tweedy, knee-high woollen socks almost meeting the knee-length trousers. He stood still, removed what looked like a deerstalker hat, then blew upward as a fringe of dark hair tumbled into eyes as brown as his father's. 'Good afternoon,' he said to Megan.

She sniffed, awarded him a nod, filed him in the 'daft' category that had recently been vacated by Mr Wagstaff. He looked a proper fool, like a miniature version of his father, all tailored and posh. Though the older Althorpe managed not to look stiff, she admitted to herself. The grown-ups were chatting away like old friends, so she walked past the soft-looking lad and into the parlour. It was lovely, with three gas mantles and a square of decent, green-patterned carpet and that proper fireplace just for keeping warm, not for cooking. With the three shillings and sixpence, she would buy a nice red hearthrug for Deedee. Deedee loved red, said it was warming and cheerful.

'Will you be moving in tomorrow, then?'

She swivelled, faced him. 'That's what your dad said, isn't it?' Was he deaf as well as stupid? 'There'll be me and Deedee and Phyllis. She's me friend and she can't walk.'

'I know.' He wore the air of one who knew just about everything. 'May I visit you sometimes?'

Megan closed her mouth sharply, hoped that the snapping sound had not reached this lad's ears. 'What for?' she managed eventually.

He coloured slightly, glanced at the floor. 'Well, I come to the mills occasionally – they're both on Ivy Street, you know—'

''Course I know. I live round here.' He talked like an old man, she thought. Like a posh old man.

'Oh.' He pulled at his collar, suddenly looked far from posh, put Megan in mind of Billy Shipton on the day of the photograph. 'We live . . . outside Bolton,' he said. 'There are houses around, but not many children. And my sister's such a bore. Do you have sisters?'

She nodded, allowed the boy's embarrassment to continue.

'Most girls I've met are terribly worried about hair ribbons and so on. You seem . . . not to care.'

Megan drew back her shoulders, pulled forward the twin plaits of hair, sighed heavily. 'That's three I've lost this week.'

He laughed. 'And it's not the end of the world, is it?'

'No, it's not.' She tossed away her hair, led the visitor out of the house, decided that he wasn't too bad after all. They sat side by side on the step. 'Me brother died,' she told him. 'Under a motor ambulance that came for Phyllis. And me other brother's got a bad heart after being ill. So there's just girls up and about at our house. He was nice, our Albert.'

They remained silent for a moment or two. 'I was right

about you,' he remarked at last. 'You talk about real things. Fliss worries herself stupid about her complexion. It wouldn't matter who lived or died as long as Fliss got no more freckles and spots. She's so stupid. Fourteen and still stupid.'

Megan glanced sideways. 'You look daft and all,' she informed him. 'Like a shrunk tailor's dummy. And what sort of a name is Fliss? Sounds like a flea or something.'

The laughter that came from him seemed to travel right from the soles of his feet. He laughed like a man, made a noise that was deep and infectious. 'Felicity.' He wiped his streaming eyes. 'That's her real name. It means . . .' He chuckled anew, fought for composure. 'It's taken from the Latin for happiness. She's about as happy as somebody who's lost a shilling and found a bent penny.'

Megan looked at his hands. They were soft and smooth and lightly tanned. He'd never swung from a rope under a gas lamp, had never fought to survive in a streetful of lads. 'Which school do you go to?' she said.

He was instantly sober. 'I'm at a private school at the top of Deane Road – The Manse, it's called. I'm expected to go to Bolton School eventually. My mother sets great store by education, you see. She goes on about it a lot.'

'Oh.' Megan wasn't sure what to say, since no-one within her sphere had ever set great store by anything beyond rent money and new clog-irons. 'Is it nice at your school?'

He shrugged. 'No.'

Megan waited, but he offered no embroidery on the subject. 'I'm at St Mary's. Nuns.' She sniffed again, thought about the black-robed women who haunted the corridors of power in the junior department. 'They cane you if you haven't been to church, cane you if you go in the boys' yard. I wouldn't care – I only climbed over to bash a lad who was hitting our Albert. Our Albert's me dead brother. Me sister Nellie got the strap off the headmistress for falling asleep during rosary. It's horrible at our school.'

He nodded, agreed. 'Same at mine. Well, the same but different. I'm not someone who might be called clever, you see.'

She turned, studied his profile, jumped immediately to his defence. 'You are clever,' she insisted. 'It's like talking to a grown-up. How can you talk like that if you're not clever?'

He looked at her, held her gaze. 'In some ways, I'm bright enough. I like reading and learning about machinery. But it's all this French and Latin they've started teaching us. I'm no academic.'

Megan tutted. Although she wasn't too sure about the word 'academic', she managed to get his drift. 'Take no notice. My dad always says it takes all sorts to make a world.' Her chest hurt when she thought about leaving her dad. But she could almost see the front door of number 13 Myrtle Street from where she sat, and the shop was only a couple of minutes' run from here. 'And you don't have nuns, do you? You don't have to learn all them catechisms and big long prayers. I bet you don't get belted for a dirty neck, either.' She thought about that. 'I bet you've never even had a dirty neck.'

Within seconds, they were pummelling each other and laughing like drunks. 'Of course I've had a dirty neck,' he roared between slaps. 'I'm always falling in the pond.'

She clouted his cheek, though her weight was not behind the stroke. 'What about ringworm?'

'No.'

'Nits?'

'No.'

With every question, she tapped his face. 'Bed-bugs?'

'Never.'

Smiling companionably, they sank back on to the stone step. 'I wish you lived near us, though,' he grumbled. 'I bet you'd fall in the pond.'

Megan mustered her dignity, smoothed her apron and flattened her hair. 'I bet I wouldn't. Unless you pushed me.'

The thought of pushing Megan into the pond was very attractive, though the idea that dominated his mind was the rescue he would perform in such a situation. He would pull her out, take all the green weedy stuff out of her hair, dry that pretty face on his handkerchief and . . .

'You've gone all red,' she accused.

Geoffrey Althorpe didn't want to go home, wouldn't care if he never saw Mother or Fliss again. Dad was all right, though. Geoffrey's love for his father was the only strong emotion he'd ever enjoyed. Till now. Till he'd met this little female urchin with creamy skin and shiny, dark hair. He suddenly felt . . . protective, responsible for her. And that was stupid, since he hardly knew the girl. 'I'm a bit warm,' he admitted. 'Because of these awful clothes.' Mother always made him dress like a gentleman whenever he accompanied his father to the mills. 'Everyone and everything in his or its place, Geoffrey,' she would say sweetly. 'Let them know who you are and what you are, so that they'll be sure of their own place in the scheme of things.' The scheme of things. Mother used that phrase so often . . .

'Never mind.' Megan's tone was soft, comforting. 'When you're older, you'll be able to wear whatever you like.'

Overalls appealed to Geoffrey Althorpe. Overalls, dirty hands and a machine in a million pieces. He liked jigsaws, enjoyed problems that were visible, actual.

A hand fell on his shoulder, and Geoffrey turned to look at his father. Sid Althorpe was a bulky man, tall and broad, brown-haired, brown-eyed, brown-skinned. And there was always laughter in him. 'Come on, Geoff,' he said. 'Before you start people talking. You can't be sitting here with the prettiest girl for miles without causing a scandal.'

Megan knew that her own cheeks were glowing now. She rose, thanked Mr Althorpe for the house and for the money.

'Nay,' said the big man, his voice as broad as any

tackler's. 'Enjoy yourself, Megan. It's not five minutes since I was your age.'

Geoffrey stood to one side, took the silly hat from his father's hand, hid it behind his back. It was too hot for headwear, especially for a stupid-looking hat that would be mocked by the girl from number 6, Holly Street. 'I'll see you again,' he said awkwardly. 'Whenever we come to the mills after school or in the holidays.'

Sid beamed his approval. 'He's taken a shine to you, love,' he joked.

Something stirred in Megan's cluttered memory. 'Is a shine anything to do with a torch, Mr Althorpe? Because I know a man who used to carry Deedee's torch for her.'

Sidney Althorpe's laugh put his son's in the shade. He shook from head to foot, while the noise he made brought neighbours scuttling to their doors.

'Hello, Mr Althorpe,' cried several. 'Somebody tickled your fancy again?' shouted a fat woman from the doorway of number 1.

'Now, Nancy,' scolded the millowner, his words still choked by glee. 'Don't be coarse.'

The plump woman simpered, patted her curlers and went back inside.

'It's the same as a torch,' whispered Sid Althorpe when composure returned. 'It means he likes you. Geoffrey likes you, love.'

Megan ran into the house, her cheeks flaming brightly.

Deedee glanced up from her brass-cleaning. 'What's up?'

'Nothing,' replied Megan. 'I'm . . . I'm going down to see me dad. It's a bit warm in here.' She dashed out by the back door, waited in the alley until she judged the coast to be cleared of Althorpes. A torch. The daft lad who wasn't daft was carrying a torch. The light didn't show, so it must be inside, in his heart with all the other thoughts and dreams.

Megan Duffy walked slowly towards her father's shop, lingered awhile outside the Co-op, looked at her reflection in the window. She was ordinary. Her eyes were a bit big, as was her mouth, but she wasn't ugly and she certainly wasn't beautiful. Above all, she was only seven years old, eight next time. Yet she nursed next to her soul the knowledge that the son of an important man was holding a torch. And Phyllis would be home tomorrow.

Megan leaned against the lamp outside her father's shop, breathed in the mixed scents of wood and leather that betrayed Joe Duffy's trade even to those who could not read. For readers, a vast array of words was appended to the windows but, even so, everything was illustrated for the illiterate. JOE DUFFY'S FAMOUS LANCASHIRE CLOGS, boasted the largest sign. Her dad was famous. Her dad was one of the few who made whole clogs, not just uppers. ALDER SOLES, said another sign next to some drawings of clog bottoms. The legend CLOG IRON, CLASP and TOEPLATE WORKS sat above some pictures of clasps and toeplates. Joseph Duffy, proprietor, was skilled in the handling of no less than three materials. He fashioned soles from wood, uppers from leather, then applied bottom irons, toeplates and clasps of metal. And that, thought his daughter, was the reason why Joe Duffy worked all hours. He refused point blank to buy soles ready-made and ready for uppers.

'Hello, Megan.' It was Billy Shipton from 11 Myrtle Street. He held up a broken clog. 'Me mam's sent me with this'ere. She wouldn't come herself, 'cos she bought a pair of clogs cheap off that chap called Casey, bottom of Chorley Old Road. They were made for a man what died, so they were half price. This one's broke in three weeks.'

Megan took the item, gave it the once-over. 'That's a mining clog,' she said right away. 'Birch sole, good for underground. Whose is it?'

Billy shrugged. 'Our Fred's. He's a spinner now over Doffcocker way, the only one of us what's working proper.'

The little girl nodded sagely. 'See, Billy, alder's best for mill work. It cuts easy whether dry or green and it takes moisture off sweaty feet without cracking.' She could hear her father saying these words, was repeating them by rote. 'Whereas birch is great in the pit. Me dad does some birch soles for pitmen, but he sticks to alder for the mills.'

Billy grinned. 'Aye, we know. Mam wouldn't fetch it to Duffy's on account of your dad's tellings-off. He's warned her before about picking up cheap clogs with wrong wood on the bottoms.'

She nodded again, looked like a teacher instructing a class of infants. 'Yes, and birch has to be dried three months before making. Your Fred's happen got a piece that wasn't ready. Then with the heat in the mill . . . Do you want me to take it in for you? I'll spin him a tale about some poor old man needing a new sole. Only what about the other clog?'

Billy pulled a comical face. 'Nowt to do with us, Megan. If our Fred wants to go and crack his other foot, let him see to the bloody mending hisself.' There was a look in Billy's eyes, something that advertised an emotion akin to desperation. Fred was the breadwinner, and Fred needed his clogs to keep the Shiptons fed and clothed. Poor Billy had a drunken dad who only turned up when the pubs closed or when the police fetched him home.

Megan left Billy and sidled into the shop. Joe looked up and beamed at her, then frowned when he saw the broken clog. 'Is that one of Casey's? I'd know the clasp anywhere. Has he sent birch in a spinning room again, Megan?'

She sighed. It was no use trying to get one over on Dad, no use pretending she'd got the footwear from some old man living on a pension.

Joe studied her face. 'Shiptons?' he asked. 'Has Elsie Shipton sent Fred out in bad clogs again?'

'Yes, Dad.'

He banged home a brass-headed nail, threw down the small hammer, joined his daughter at the counter. 'I'll fix it, I suppose, find the poor lad an alder sole. Then they'll be back with the other foot and nowt to pay with, eh?'

Megan gave him a winning smile. 'They've no money, you know.'

For answer, he blew her a kiss and returned to work on a piece of sycamore. He received green sycamore in January, made his clogs, let the wood dry out on the wearers' feet, took pride in what he called his 'lady-clogs'. Sycamore was for women and children. He held up a tiny clog. 'These are three years old, Megan. They've been passed all down a family, because they were made right. How old is Fred Shipton's clog?'

'Three weeks,' she answered.

'Just shows,' he muttered. 'I'm one of the last proper cloggers. Speaking of lasts, stretch that blue over yonder, love. Just pull it a bit till I can get me lasting pincers to it.' He watched her while she handled the leather. She'd have made a grand clogger if she'd been a lad.

Tommy Wagstaff wandered in. He looked uncomfortably clean and had stuck a red flower next to the feathers in his cap. 'How are you doing, Joe?' he asked. 'I've a fancy for some new clogs, only you know I never want one of your standard blocks. Feel me feet, Joe, make the clogs proper.' Joe Duffy was renowned as an old-fashioned clogger, one who could still do a 'special'. For a 'special', feet were handled, then the clogger's hands travelled from feet to wood, the remembered shape seeming to print itself beneath fingers that forgot nothing. Tommy spotted Megan. 'Hello, lass. Are you taking up footwear after all?'

'I'm just helping,' she replied.

Joe filled his mouth with pegs, released them one at a time and hit them home until all the old nail holes were filled. 'Ready for its rubbers,' he announced proudly. 'A good clog, is that, though I say it as shouldn't.' He turned to Tommy Wagstaff. 'What's that in your hat, owld lad?'

'A poppy.'

'What for?'

Tommy shrugged. 'Decoration.'

Joe chuckled. 'Are you after my mam again? She'll tan

your hide so hard it'll do for my shop. What gets into you at all? You know she's not interested.'

Megan listened, said nothing.

'Where there's life, there's hope,' pronounced Tommy.

'Aye. And where there's my mother, there's a yard-brush to crack you over the ear'ole with. Don't set her off again. There's nothing worse than my mam when you get into one of your courting phases.'

Tommy blew his nose on a pristine handkerchief, flourished the crisp cotton so that it would be noticed. 'I'm altering me ways,' he stated.

'My mam'll alter more than your ways, sunshine. She'll change the shape of your nose if you go sniffing round her back gate again.'

Megan joined the men, thought about being quiet, changed her mind when they both stared at her. 'Deedee likes cats and Mr Wagstaff likes cats,' she told her father. 'So they'll be good friends.'

Joe tried not to laugh. 'Are you matchmaking, our Megan?'

She pondered. What with torches and matches, conversations were getting a bit muddled these days. 'I don't know what you mean,' she replied truthfully. 'But I'm eight in ten months. When I'm eight, I might understand.'

Tommy covered his grin with the handkerchief, then sank on to the bench where the barefooted usually waited for new irons. He put away his hanky, made much of allowing its points to stick out of a breast pocket, bent to remove his old 'specials'. 'I think I'll have an ordinary boot upper this time, Joe. Laces and all.'

Megan's eyes strayed downward, her attention drawn to something that was odd, strange, out of true. In fact, several things were not quite up to scratch, and the articles in question were Mr Wagstaff's socks and toes. The former looked like lacework around the latter, more hole than wool, Megan decided. 'I thought you were changing your ways, Mr Wagstaff.'

'It's his socks he wants to change,' guffawed Joe. 'I

reckon he's worn yon pair since last Preston Guild.'

Tommy nodded at the giggling Duffys. 'Listen, mock me if you must, but I can only do one thing at a time. I've had a slipper bath and bought new towels, I've sorted out me trousers and me hankies. Socks is something I'll get round to in time. I mean, I'm only human. What did you expect, Megan? A magic wand job? I'm working me road round things careful. It's been a shock to my system, all this dressing up. And . . .' He shook a finger at the clogger. 'Never you mind criticizing me, it's time you got some help in here, Joe. You're looking tired out. Get somebody to do the cutting or the putting up.'

Megan looked at her dad. He did look tired, a bit grey under the eyes. Her heart jumped, made her stomach threaten. What if anything happened to Dad? What if he were next on the list? 'I'll help,' she said. 'Deedee won't need me every day.'

Joe placed a hand on Megan's head. 'Calm down. I've a time-served lad from Blackburn coming down next week. He's a good sole-maker, one who can be trusted.' He thought he could feel Megan's panic as his hand dropped to her shoulders. 'Don't fret, lass. Things have got to get better.'

She hoped so. Harold had to improve, had to eat and get out of bed. 'Will our Harold's heart ever be well again, Dad?'

He blinked, dropped a nail, glanced at the nightwatchman. 'We don't know, Megan,' he said carefully.

Dad never dropped nails. Megan sidled round the counter, waved goodbye, went out into the street. He was dropping nails because he was worried, and he was worried because Harold had no chance. Did Mam know? Did she know that her remaining twin would never recover?

Billy joined her. 'What's happening about yon clog?' he asked, the tone deliberately casual.

'He'll fix it.'

'How much?'

She awarded him her full attention. 'Nowt at all, Billy. Me dad knows you've not much coming in. I'll pick it up and fetch it round to your house later on.'

He flushed, looked down at his own bare feet. 'It's a bugger, isn't it?' he asked with the air of one who expects no reply. 'Dry bread in our house, sickness in yours, all that trouble at the Entwistles'. Makes you wonder.'

Megan had never accused Billy Shipton of being sensitive. He was probably just repeating words that had fallen from his mother's lips. But no. She caught sight of his eyes and glimpsed suffering and confusion, realized that he was thinking aloud. 'Don't worry, Billy,' she said softly.

He wiped his nose on the cuff of his tattered jersey. 'I'm hungry, Megan,' he said. 'I'm always bloody hungry.'

She stood still for a moment, wondered what was wrong with Billy Shipton. Harold had been a naughty boy but, compared to Billy, Harold had been an archangel. Billy was a shoplifter. If he wanted something, he took it and took the consequences later. Harold might have stolen in his time, but at least he'd kept his sins inside the house, hadn't spread them all over the Co-op and the green-grocer's shop. 'Billy?' she asked.

He looked her full in the face. 'Well, I'm fed up with it. All that gentle Jesus stuff at school and Mother Cecilia knocking hell out of us. What's bloody gentle about nuns, eh? You've your attendance mark, your mass mark, your spelling mark.' He counted the list on his fingers. 'But the only marks what matter are the ones on your backside when she's let rip with her strap. She picked another lad up with his ears about a month ago. He'd big ears at the start – I reckon you could peg him out to dry now, just fasten his lug'oles to the rope. I think it's all a load of rubbish,' he declared belligerently.

'What is?' she asked.

'Religion, you daft mare. I've got to go to confession and say I stole from the Co-op. Then I've got to pinch from the shops again because it's first up, best fed at our house. So I steal, then I confess again. I've got to steal to bloody well eat.'

He had got the language from his father, guessed Megan. She fiddled about in her apron pocket, brought out a sixpence. She could buy a smaller rug for three shillings, she thought. 'Here. Get yourself some chips and fish, Billy.'

He grabbed the coin, grinned broadly at her. 'I'll marry you when we're grown up,' he announced. 'And we'll always have grub in the house.'

She stood and watched as he scooted off towards the chip shop. It had been an interesting day. Geoffrey Althorpe liked her and Billy Shipton wanted to marry her. They were both carrying torches while she, the match-maker, could strike a light wherever she pleased. Though Deedee would doubtless throw a bucket of water over Mr Wagstaff's feelings if he showed them too clearly.

She walked in the direction of her new home, paused outside number 13 Myrtle Street. An upstairs curtain flickered. She held her breath as Mam's face appeared in the gap. But Mam did not seem to recognize Megan, was looking through and past her. Mam was engrossed, used up by Harold. So Megan carried on towards affection, supper and Deedee.

FIVE

Deedee and Megan had made the best of number 6, Holly Street. They sat together in the front parlour, hutched up close on the sofa as if each sought warmth from the other. Megan bit down on her lower lip, glanced round the room, tried to be grateful and glad. But she couldn't quite manage it. Oh, it was good to have a proper fire, a real fireplace with no oven stuck to it and no fireplate buckling on the flags. There were tiles in the hearth at number 6, real pot tiles set into the floor in a pretty pattern. Mr Althorpe's three shillings had been spent on a fender, a shiny brass kerb that punctuated the edge of the blue-and-white ceramic hearth. Six more vertical tiles, three at each side, slanted inward towards the cast iron grate, and a little hood with a Greek urn pattern hung underneath a mantel of polished wood. So posh, it was.

Deedee sighed. 'Makes you wonder what it's all about,' she muttered, almost to herself. 'Everything seemed to be working out nicely, what with young Phyllis so settled and all. Then we get this.'

Megan gulped painfully, because she didn't want to cry. They had a carpet and a new, low sideboard and some statues under glass domes. They had a proper mirror with a painting of a crinolined lady in a garden round its edge. They had a sofa and two chairs and an occasional table with plants and photos on. And none of it counted, none of it mattered. 'I didn't like our Harold,' she managed to whisper at last.

'Neither did I, and may God forgive me,' answered Deedee. 'But Harold was a human being and he was my grandchild.' It was her daughter-in-law who was the real source of worry. Tess had gone completely odd after Harold's quiet death, had ranted and raved like a madwoman. 'It's diseased round here,' Tess Duffy had screamed in the street. 'Get your lads away from this evil place, get them all out of Bolton.' So wild, she had looked, with the usually soft brown hair standing up in neglected spikes, the mouth gaping, her hazel eyes wild and frantic. 'The devil's got a foot planted in this town and he's coming for your boys.'

Deedee grabbed Megan's hand. 'He'd no chance after that diphtheria, love. Doctor only sent him home to die. It got all through him, did the germ, made his poor heart weak. Even if he had come right this time, he'd have been an invalid for the rest of his days.'

Megan closed her eyes, tried to place her mind on their other downstairs room, that nice kitchen that had been made bigger by breaking through to the scullery. Deedee's dresser was in place now, with all its plates and cups and saucers. A central table always wore a clean cloth, and the curtains were yellow and white, so that every day looked bright and cheerful. But even when she conjured up a vision of the white porcelain sink and the shiny copper, she still couldn't manage to be cheerful. Things. Things had seemed so important just a few days ago. She had been proud of the oilcloth, the shiny grate, the armchairs. She had been glad that Phyllis enjoyed pleasant and warm surroundings. Now, nothing meant anything, nothing was important.

The little girl sighed, glued her gaze to the enormous Sacred Heart painting. The print of the Sacred Heart was hanging by chains from the picture rail, sad eyes raised towards the ceiling. She'd asked Him to spare Harold, had even knelt down and prayed in front of the other picture, the one of Infant Jesus and His Holy Mother. But Harold had still died. 'Prayers don't work,' she announced. 'And Pope Benedict still hasn't wrote back to me from the Vati . . . Vaticantic city.'

Deedee wasn't listening, failed to enjoy the slip of

Megan's tongue. She patted her granddaughter's hand absently. 'Yes, love.' They'd have to go and fetch Phyllis in a minute. Phyllis had been farmed out with Elsie Shipton for the duration of Harold's funeral. Two little boxes had gone under the sod these past few weeks. There was neither rhyme nor reason to what was happening in the garden streets.

'They don't care,' muttered Megan. 'Nuns don't care about hurting us, priests just want money for whisky. Billy Shipton says all the money in the collecting plates goes on drink. I'm not going to church no more.'

'Yes, love.' She should have warned Elsie Shipton to keep her tongue still. Doris Duffy's spine stiffened. If Big Gob had gone on at Phyllis about the location of Ida Entwistle's grave . . . 'What did you say, Megan?'

'I'm not going to mass no more. Or communion, or benediction. It's all wrong.'

Doris shook her head wearily. 'Don't start coming over all contrary-wise. Look, the faith's very hard to understand until you get older.' Even then, she thought, it remained shrouded in mystery for much of the time. 'But you're a Catholic girl. Catholic children go to church schools and to mass on Sundays. You learn your catechism, make your first confession and communion, choose another name and get confirmed. That's life. That's life until you get old enough to pick and choose for yourself.'

Anger bubbled in Megan's chest, simmered, boiled, spilled over. 'It's not fair. I've been to mass, I've been to benediction, I've done a novena. It doesn't work. You can do all that, but your brother still dies and your friend's still crippled. And they don't even bother to let you know whether your friend's mother can get out of hell and into a proper grave. Even when you write letters and ask for help, they take no notice. They don't care.'

Deedee put an arm round the child, patted a trembling shoulder. 'Accepting things is part of the faith, child.'

'Well, I don't care.' Megan dragged herself off the sofa

and stood in front of the posh fireplace. 'I'm going down there now,' she said. 'And I'm going to ask some questions.'

Doris studied the child. She sounded about fifty, looked old, too. Megan had taken up a stance that was immediately recognizable. The arms were folded tight against a pushed-out chest, while the feet were slightly apart, planted to demonstrate determination and to achieve stability. Women looked like this when they stood on doorsteps arguing, when they returned tainted goods to a shop and held their ground until satisfaction was reached. 'Where are you planning on going, Megan?'

'Priest's house.' She blew a tress away from her eyes, no longer seemed old. 'Father O'Riley might be in. He can tell me why the pope didn't write back. Then he can tell me why Phyllis's mother had to get buried at the other side of the railings when it wasn't her fault in the first place.'

Doris sagged backwards, too tired to argue. Phyllis was hard work all day, then the sewing and mending sometimes went on till well past midnight. Her eyes ached. Even the sockets that contained them felt bruised and sore. Now Megan was going all unnecessary, was preparing to start a world war in St Mary's presbytery. Young Father O'Riley was not at his best with children. He seemed to fear them, kept well out of their reach until they metamorphosed into adults. 'I'd not be dashing about and mithering the priest if I were you, love.'

Megan pursed her lips, looked deep in thought. 'Any road,' she said eventually. 'They always tell us to go to them if we're in trouble.' She leaned against the wall, one leg crossed over the other, a toe pointing downward and tapping softly on the carpet. 'There's no problem that can't be dis . . . discussed. That's what Father O'Riley said this morning at Harold's requiem. Now, I wouldn't go to the nuns to ask questions, but I might as well try him.' Once more, she sounded ancient, knowledgeable. 'At least he has no strap fastened to his belt.'

Doris swallowed all her pain, concentrated on the

96

suffering of this poor child. Megan had lost two brothers. She'd never had much of a mother, and her dad was too busy cutting leather and giving lectures in his little shop. Joe was a grand lad, but he would never manage Tess, not in a month of wet Sundays. And now, Doris Duffy, who had buried several children and raised just one son, was expected to be a mother all over again, this time to a girl. 'Megan, try to hang on a couple of days, eh? Give it till tomorrow, see how you feel after a night's sleep.'

'I'm going.'

Doris didn't believe in hard threats and punishment. She had never clouted a child except in fun, and she wasn't going to start now. Kiddies deserved explanations, reasons, help. 'Look, Megan, I can't answer for Tess, but I know our Joe wouldn't want you rattling Father O'Riley's doorknob. I'm only here to see to your everyday needs, lass. So ask your dad what he thinks about your idea.'

'Right.' Megan marched to the door.

'Hang on a minute, lady. You can't go bothering Joe straight after a funeral. He's enough on with Tess and the girls. Stop here. Stay put while I go and fetch Phyllis.'

Megan was not disobedient by nature, but she was still fizzing inside. Although such sensations often preceded digestive problems, the idea of frequent visits to the lavatory was not Megan's current source of worry. No, she was more anxious about calming down. She didn't want to calm down, didn't want to lose her impetus. It was now or never. She was furious about the family's losses, particularly about the death of Albert. He'd been a good little lad, no trouble at all, so why hadn't God picked on him to be minded? That Lazarus man in the Bible – he'd been raised from the dead. Why Lazarus? Why not Albert?

When Deedee had disappeared from sight, Megan dragged on her dark coat and sped out through the back door. As she flew along streets and alleys, she felt little, saw no-one. Deep inside, in the region of the fizzing, she knew that this was an important day, but that knowledge was a part of her, was not something that needed thinking about.

He opened the door, a linen napkin tucked under his chin, some melted butter on the lower lip making him ordinary, approachable. 'Good afternoon, child,' he said. 'And what might I do for you?'

For the first time, Megan realized how young and ordinary he was. Priests were usually old with grey whiskers, but this man was younger than her dad. 'Can I come in, Father?' Her voice was weak, squeaky and scared.

He held the door wide. 'Indeed. Sit down by the fire till I toast you a crumpet.' He picked up a long fork, reminded Megan of the devil. Didn't the devil have a three-pronged fork to jab people with, to push them deep into hell's flames? The fire was fierce, far too hot for Megan. She removed her coat, folded it, placed it on the end of a one-armed sofa, then sat there fiddling with a scab on her knee. What on earth was she doing here? What was she going to say?

Patrick O'Riley spread butter on the crumpet, set it on a plate, handed it to the poor child. Two brothers in a matter of weeks, she had lost. And now her mammy was carrying on demented, screaming and ranting all over the streets. 'Eat that,' he said gently. 'And have a quiet minute till I pour you some tea.' He was not good with children. Many a time, he had sought counsel from the Bishop of Salford, had wondered whether he might not be better placed in a retirement town where folk were older, wiser. But the bishop always laughed at him. 'Away with your bother, Paddy,' the primate usually answered. 'You're not long out of rompers yourself. But take up your burden and follow Christ. It's a long way to the top of Calvary, my son.'

Megan chewed the bits of crumpet, found them rubbery, swallowed as much as she could accommodate, drank her tea. 'Father?' she asked seriously. 'How do we know about God?'

Everything he had dreaded was somehow compressed into this tiny fraction of time. He was a learned man, had spent seven years learning his trade in a famous Lancashire seminary, could argue with the best when it came to doctrine. At twenty-seven, he had been put in charge of a parish, had been given a very large flock to care for. Did he deserve his bishop's praise? 'Few are ready at your tender age,' the good man had said. 'But you are a born shepherd.'

Father O'Riley, the good shepherd, gazed at this child. The little ones bothered him with their simple questions, their virgin minds. It could be so easy to frighten them, to put them off the path forever. And here, out of the mouth of a distressed girl, had come the most basic of all questions. 'God has left us many messages,' he replied carefully. 'He's . . . he's like an architect, our architect. Look around at the simplest things, then you will know that a supreme being must have begun the world. Go out into the countryside, get your daddy to take you to the moors. God planned everything, Megan. The trees and flowers, the birds and animals, the—'

'Cars? Did He plan motor cars?'

He mopped his chin, flung the napkin on to the tray. 'The good Lord gave us the brains to make machines.' A thought began to weave itself at the front of his head, a slender strand of gossamer that suddenly thickened, as if some eight-legged creature had found its sense of direction. He tried to clear his mind, failed. It was the simplicity of children that terrified him, because these young ones had the power to shake his own faith. As children knew so little, their ideas were fresh and pure. And often right? he asked himself. He coughed, hoped that the web in his head would disintegrate soon.

'And to kill Albert.' She picked up the teaspoon, looked at it, decided that Father O'Riley needed a housekeeper who could wash up properly. 'It was a motor that killed my first brother and it was a germ that killed our Harold. Did God make germs too?'

Father O'Riley bent and picked up the poker, gave it an undeserved hard stare before using it to close the damper. 'This coal's a bit frisky, eh, Megan? Yes, God created the lot of it, coal and all, and left us to make the best of a wonderful world. It's hard to understand and impossible to explain, but the Lord put everything here for us, set us down on our feet and made us walk. Then He spoke to some people long ago and gave us the first part of the Bible. Jesus showed us in the New Testament how to be good and He proved to us that God exists.' It was not children he feared. It was himself, his own uncertainties. The web in his subconscious had been growing for some time, was beginning to fasten itself nearer to the forefront of his mind.

'By doing miracles?'

'Partly.' He sensed her direction, tried to head her off. 'The miracles were for non-believers. We don't need them.' But an inner voice told him that a miracle was needed here, because nothing short of magic would pacify this angry and intelligent infant.

Megan looked deep into the priest's blue eyes. 'Mam says you've Irish eyes, Father O'Riley. She says you've a face that tells the truth and shames the devil. So can you please tell me why my brothers had to die? Please?'

He sighed, dropped his chin, looked down at hands that touched the Holy Eucharist every day, that blessed the wine, the living, the dead and the newborn. 'All I can tell you is that your brothers are with God and all his angels. They are happier than we can imagine. God took them into His arms, gave them the special gifts of eternal peace and joy.'

She sniffed, didn't find anything attractive in the concept of an eternity of peace and joy. 'Well, I'd sooner have a miracle like Lazarus. That Martha and Mary got their brother back, so why can't we get our twins back and all? There isn't any miracles no more, is there? They don't get the chance to be raised from the dead, our Albert and our Harold. It's not fair.'

Patrick O'Riley stood with his back to the roaring fire,

accepted the resulting discomfort as part of this impromptu penance. She was a believer, yet she needed a great deal of help, so he would tell her just one of the many strange happenings he had witnessed during priesthood. Perhaps the story might soothe him, too. To calm himself, he allowed an inner voice to chant the beginning of the Credo. He got as far as '*patrem omnipotentem*' before the spider's web cropped up again. Children were near to God. Their newly-created souls brought messages from the Maker, and such messages should be heeded. No, he was not afraid of children, but their godliness disturbed him. He cleared his throat, tried to clear his mind of doubt. 'I'm a truthful man, wouldn't you say?'

'Yes.' She was sure of that, at least.

He dropped his voice, tried to make the tone intimate, secretive. 'There are miracles.' He paused, watched her troubled face. 'One night, there came a knock at my door – the door through which you have just now entered. I answered, and there was no-one there. Again I heard a knocking, again the street was empty. But I was uncomfortable, so I opened up the church and took the Blessed Sacrament from the tabernacle and went outside. There was a shadow. Not a thing to be afraid of, just a misty shape that moved before me. I followed where it led and I came to the house of a dying man. He was a sinner who had lapsed from the church, yet God had seen fit to bring me to that house to offer Extreme Unction. So I have seen a miracle.'

She waited, processed the story, believed every word. 'What did he die of?' she asked.

The priest raised his shoulders. 'I don't know.'

'But he was ill?'

'Of course. He was dying.'

Megan waded in. 'There's all kinds of illnesses. Phyllis's mother had an illness in her head. She didn't know what she was doing, Father O'Riley. The thing what made her kill herself wasn't her fault. So where is she? Is she with our Albert and Harold?'

He tugged at his collar. 'God will have judged. He will have put her on the right track.' Oh yes, this girl had struck a nerve. How often had he pondered about this very subject? Was the visitor from the devil, then? Had Satan sent her here to touch on a matter that already plagued this man's soul? But he looked into her eyes and saw only sadness. 'She's in a better place,' he said.

She would not budge. 'Heaven?'

'Possibly.'

'Purgatory?'

'That's very likely.'

'Then why is she at the wrong side of the railings?' Her voice had pitched itself high, made her sound about three years of age. 'Why didn't she have a proper send-off like other folk? Mrs Shipton's told everybody that Phyllis's mother's in hell. Purgatory's only for a bit of time. But heaven and hell is forever.' She straightened her shoulders. 'God's got to be a nice man. I mean, if He made flowers and all that, He's got to be nice. So why did He let people put Mrs Entwistle on the hell side of the cemetery?'

Suicide. For what seemed like an eternity, Patrick O'Riley had experienced what he called a monkey of a time with this topic. And here sat a child of about eight years, a child with a simple but direct mind. She had not the words to frame her queries properly, yet she wanted and deserved an answer. For one thing, she existed; for another, she was displaying a hunger for knowledge. He stared at her for several seconds, did not manage an immediate reply.

'Can the pope write?' she asked next.

'Well, of course. He's a learned man and—'

'Can he read?'

'Yes, but—'

'He's not wrote back to me. I want Phyllis's mam shifting. All Phyllis's mam's relatives are in the Catholic part. She'll be lonely on her own.'

He drew an unsteady hand across prematurely thinning hair, decided that this Megan Duffy would probably grow

102

up to be something of a nuisance, always questioning. Mentally, he beat his breast for this uncharitable thought. The girl was normal, ordinary, wanted answers to normal and ordinary queries. He gave in with as much grace as he could muster. 'Tell you what, Megan, I'll speak to the bishop. Let's find out what he has to say about the subject. And I'll have a word with Mrs Entwistle's doctor, see can he throw any light on the poor woman's state of mind. Leave it with me.' He was a man of only twenty-eight, yet he felt he had aged past ninety during recent minutes.

Megan awarded him a stiff nod, stood up, pulled on her coat. But before leaving, she decided to have one last say. After all, she'd been cheeky up to now and got away with it. 'Mother Cecilia,' she began warily. 'She . . . she's always belting us. Can God not send a shadow to make her put the strap away? Me mam's been busy, what with the new baby and our Harold's germs, so my big sisters are up early and they're getting strapped for falling asleep at their desks and she picks lads up with their ears and all.' After this marathon of words, she gulped down some air, jerked her chin again, whispered a goodbye and dashed outside.

Father O'Riley stared into the flames for a long time after Megan's departure. His faith was strong because it had been shaken many times. Megan Duffy's might eventually be the same, since she thought a lot, worried too much. He pondered his own childhood, recalled the many occasions on which he had tackled his betters. And his betters had been the real dragons, Christian brothers every man-jack of them, not an ounce of Christian charity in their make-up. He'd been older than Megan, though, had been almost twice her age before the doubts had arrived. But he'd been a fortunate boy, had buried no siblings, had known no suicides.

He stirred the fire, riddled dead ash through the bars. Ida Entwistle. It had been a good family, father, mother, two boys and a girl. And Ida hadn't coped with the loss of her man, hadn't managed to live with the thought of Phyllis's disability. A sick mind, a life dominated by concentrated poison, venom painted on to the unclean barbs that had pierced that woman's heart. Who knew the truth of it? he asked himself as he filled a briar pipe. Who but God had been there in Ida's last pain-filled moments? Did she panic, relent, make that final act of contrition?

For a moment, he was back at school in Dublin. Brother Connor loomed over him with a thin cane, his eyes steely and cruel. 'Because I say so, Patrick O'Riley! Because the church says so, because Jesus Himself decreed it!' And Patrick, just like Megan Duffy, had stood his ground. 'The pope could be ill, Brother Connor. Anybody can be ill, even the pope. So he might be fallible—'

'He's human,' the monk had screamed. 'Except when in communion with God regarding tenets of faith.'

And Patrick O'Riley, priest of St Mary's parish, pastor to thousands of souls, had spoken up yet again. 'If he's human, how does he know the difference between what he thinks and what God wants him to think?'

Absently, the priest rubbed the seat of his trousers, as if he could still feel the cutting edge of that cane. 'Believe,' the mad monk had demanded with every blow. 'Make an act of faith, cleanse your filthy soul.'

Patrick puffed, chewed the pipe's stem, considered his options. There weren't many. Megan was worth fighting for, he was certain of that much. In fact, it was his duty to represent any member of the parish who sought counsel. Yet somehow, this girl-child suddenly represented the whole parish. Her faith might become strong, might desert her altogether if an effort were not made. She had questioned all he fought to believe in, all he struggled to uphold. Questions, answers, more questions. For Megan Duffy and for himself, he might need to speak to bishops, archbishops, cardinals. And if all that failed, he was due a holiday, might enjoy Rome. He grinned, coughed on a puff of smoke. Would the pope grant him an audience?

He sat back, picked up the newspaper, scanned the front page. The spider in his brain had finished its work, had created a whole decision in spite of Paddy's efforts.

Let them all think and do as they pleased, because Paddy O'Riley and Megan Duffy would be going on an outing soon. And on a grave at the wrong side of a low fence, they would place flowers, a cross of palms, some holy water and a spadeful of soil from Ida's family grave. He needed no papal intervention; just a shovel, a prayer and a blessing would do. And after that, the fur would fly.

Megan waited. At last, she heard Dad's irons clattering against flags as he walked down the yard. The shovel scraped, scooped, dropped coal into the scuttle. She pushed open the gate, stared at the stooped figure. 'Dad?'

He seemed startled, jumped to attention the second she spoke. 'Megan? What do you want? Deedee's just been round here looking for you. She's took Phyllis back to number six.' He followed his daughter into the back street. 'What's up, lass?'

She raked her eyes over the dear man's face, saw the pallor, the lines that were etching themselves deeper into his skin. 'Dad, I don't want to make you worry any more, but we'll have to keep an eye on me mam.' A deep breath fuelled her lungs, gave her the strength to push out words that were unpalatable. 'Don't leave her on her own. We've got a pulley line and you know what Phyllis's mam did. Any road, Father O'Riley's going to tell the bishop, but me mam might get put on the wrong side if she does it.'

He blinked, sifted through the clutter till he found a central message. With a deep sigh, he inhaled the young one's fear. It was wrong that his children should carry such burdens. He'd noticed Annie and Nellie, too, had been a witness to their extra-careful vigilance. Ida Entwistle had killed herself after two deaths in her family. Even little Freda knew what was going on, had stood all afternoon like a statue next to Tess's chair. 'Don't be thinking such things, Megan,' he begged. Were they all going to become nervous wrecks because Tess was such a mess? 'Your mam will get better,' he said. 'It just takes time.'

Megan awarded him a single nod before walking up the yard and through the back door. In the scullery, Annie and Nellie were sieving flour. She left them to their work, entered the kitchen, looked at Freda's white face. 'Go to Deedee's,' she told her little sister. 'Let her know I'm here, then ask can you stay for your tea.' She smiled encouragingly. 'There's scones. And you can make Phyllis laugh, cheer her up a bit.'

Freda glanced from her mother to Megan before running out of the house. It was sad at home. Deedee was always jolly, and Deedee's scones were lovely.

Megan sank to the floor and took Tess's hands in hers. 'They're in heaven, Mam. I've seen Father O'Riley and he knows they're in . . .' she struggled to remember. 'In eternal peace and joy. And you've still got us, you know. We might be only girls, but we're here to look after you.'

Tess Duffy raised her head, looked quizzically into the eyes of her third daughter. 'Megan,' she said, her tone dull and rusty. 'Our Megan.'

'Please get well, Mam,' whispered the kneeling child.

Tess looked through and past Megan, saw herself at about the same age, heard her own mother keening. 'My brother died, too,' she muttered. 'And Mam never forgave the world for it.' She couldn't allow herself to sink, she thought suddenly. 'Our house was always miserable after me brother died, Megan. It was as if our mam couldn't be bothered. She never baked again. I did it all.'

'Like Annie and Nellie,' said Megan.

'Yes.' Tess was keenly aware of the gentle pressure on her hands. 'Megan,' she said again.

'Yes, I'm here. We're all here.'

'Joe?'

'Getting coal. And our Annie and our Nellie are in the scullery. The baby's not here, though. You sent her to be minded. And Freda's at Deedee's.'

Tess bit into her bottom lip, stared into the clear azure eyes of this girl, the most beautiful of her daughters. 'I'll

106

try,' she promised huskily. 'I will do me best.' The alternative was too terrifying. If she didn't pull round, somebody might sign a paper and get her put away. Dilys Brindley from the top of Ivy Street had got taken away two years ago, was bundled into a back-to-front coat with long arms and leather fasteners. And she'd never come home since, hadn't Dilys Brindley. 'Will you visit me?'

''Course I will.'

Tess reached deep into her ever-diminishing store of strength, glanced at her husband in the doorway. He'd a scuttle in one hand, a small shovel in the other, pain in his eyes. 'Go and fetch our Hilda after tea,' she told him. 'If we leave her down there much longer, she'll not know where she belongs.'

Joe smiled upon his third child. He didn't know what had been said, but at least Tess seemed to be pulling round a bit. 'You get back to Deedee's, love,' he told Megan. 'Tell Freda she can stop till after tea, then I want everybody here for when our baby comes home. That means Phyllis and all.'

They were a strange procession, thought Patrick O'Riley as he followed the Ford into the cemetery. The doctor's car looked all right, but the vehicle driven by the priest was rather out of place.

He might well lose his parish for this, but he couldn't manage to care. The bishop had been his usual jolly self, had suggested that the matter should be left to cool for a while. Rome's attitude to suicide was rigid, immovable. Ida Entwistle had committed self-murder, had separated a soul from its body. Because of this heinous crime, she could not enter heaven, could not be buried among the good Catholics at the other side of the fence.

Patrick O'Riley lifted Phyllis's wheelchair down from the back of a coal cart. The poor child's aide to mobility was large and unwieldy, would not fit into the car belonging to his friend, Dr Charles Walsh. The contraption was also presenting many difficulties in the life and

107

household of Doris Duffy. But like Doris, Patrick was a never-say-die type, so he had borrowed the horse and cart from a parishioner. Megan, who had ridden beside the priest, jumped down and petted the horse.

Dr Walsh climbed out of his troublesome car, managed to curb the desire to kick hell out of it. A graveyard, he told himself firmly, was not a suitable location for one of his many one-sided arguments with the vehicle. He left the truculent engine to grumble and cough, he didn't need another session with the starting handle. Deedee followed him to the cart, waited while the two men transferred Phyllis from car to chair. 'You've travelled well,' the doctor told his young patient. 'I think we should bring you out again some time, perhaps to the fair or to a cinema.' He nodded at the priest. 'Phyllis is coping marvellously,' he said.

They walked to Ida's unmarked grave, the four who could stand making way for Phyllis, stepping away for a few moments while she mourned her mother's passing. 'She were a good woman, Father,' said the grieving girl. 'She's never hurt nobody, me mam.'

'We know that.' There was a set to the priest's chin, a determination that hid deep turmoil. He was here off his own bat, openly and actively defying the pope and the Bishop of Salford. Oh, one of Benedict's secretaries had written back to Megan, and the letter had been intercepted by Joe Duffy. Benedict XV understood Megan's anguish, would ask God for guidance in this particularly distressing case. But. What a big word that was, thought Patrick O'Riley. But the church's teaching was clear, so Ida Entwistle must stay where she was for the time being.

Phyllis raised tear-filled eyes and looked Father O'Riley full in the face. 'Put me mam in heaven,' she said softly. Ever since Mrs Shipton had told the tale, Phyllis had grieved. Megan's Granny Deedee had torn strips off Elsie Shipton, but Phyllis was glad to know about Mam, because something was being done at last. In a few minutes, the gates of heaven would open and Ida would be guided through by St Peter and the angels.

Patrick O'Riley kissed his stole, hung it round his neck. '*Dominus vobiscum*,' he prayed.

'*Et cum spiritu tuo*,' chorused Megan, Deedee and Phyllis. The doctor, who was not a Catholic, hung back until the priest beckoned him to the graveside. 'All one family, Charlie,' urged the man of God.

He did it all by the book, omitting nothing except the actual burial of a body. When the grave had been blessed and sprinkled with soil borrowed from plots where Ida's family lay, he placed a wooden cross in the centre of this hitherto unsanctified patch. Into the timber, he had burnt Ida's name and date of death, together with the words MAY HER TROUBLED SOUL FIND EVERLASTING PEACE.

Father Patrick O'Riley shivered, seemed to sense even now the wrath that could descend upon his head. Salford had a good bishop, a fine upstanding man of great learning, gentleness, humour. But Rome was a mighty place. In the corridors of power that constituted the Vatican, the name of Patrick O'Riley would surely resound, as this was a sin that must be declared openly.

He tugged at the stiff collar, wondered how much longer he would be able to wear it. More disturbing than that problem was the bigger question – did he want to wear the weeds of a priest? Ida Entwistle was one mere soul, one dead Catholic whose torment had ended in suicide. How many more? he mused. How many good people were there in these unconsecrated patches on the edges of graveyards, on the hems of Christendom?

'It's blessed now,' said Megan. 'Your mam's on her way to heaven.'

Phyllis bowed her head, closed the soft brown eyes. 'Thanks,' she whispered. 'Thanks for doing it, Father O'Riley.'

The priest ran a hand over his head, picked off the stole from the back of his neck, kissed an embroidered cross, placed the sacred item in a small bag. He would need to go to Manchester now, today. No more masses would be said by Father Patrick O'Riley until this matter was resolved. And there was no solution . . . 'No matter what Elsie Shipton says to you now, Phyllis, you'll know that your mammy lies in holy soil. But keep the secret, or others may demand the same treatment. I'll be . . . going away soon, and we don't want every priest in the world having to run round with holy water. Ida was an exception to a rule, so we shall keep today close in our hearts, just the five of us.' The eruption would touch these good people anyway. Yes, they would learn that he had made trouble within the faith. But if everyone kept quiet for a while, the difficulties might be postponed.

The doctor stepped forward. 'Are you all right, Paddy? You've gone a bit pale.'

Patrick nodded, gazed across the cemetery towards another separated plot, a square that contained dozens of plain stone crosses. The nuns lay there in their cheap boxes and cotton shrouds, the vow of poverty obeyed right up to their final exit. Good women? He glanced at Megan, remembered how she felt about such cruel teachers. The harshness of the nuns had been general knowledge for many years, yet this one child's complaint had fastened itself to his soul. Prayers rattled about untidily in his brain, bits of the Pater Noster, some jumbled words from Our Lady's Litany. Did any of it make sense? Even when the phrases were ordered, tidy, were they right? 'How do we know?' little Megan Duffy had asked. How huge that query really was.

'Father?' The doctor sounded anxious.

'I'm fine.' He beckoned, and Dr Walsh joined him, followed him a few paces. 'I'm finished, Charlie,' he whispered. They'd been on good terms for some time, as the doctor often sent for a priest when one of his patients requested a blessing. 'This is the end of my career as a cleric, I'm afraid. But . . .' He looked over his shoulder, glanced at the group by the graveside. 'I'm away to Manchester, then possibly back home to Ireland. I'll beg just one thing of the church. Ida must stay where she is. They'll not remove the blessing, as it isn't a thing that can be washed away. I believed in what I did just now, so it will stand. But I want the bishop to say that I've simply gone away. These children . . .' He lifted a hand, pointed to Megan and Phyllis. 'Their faith is young and fragile. Don't speak about what happened here today, Charlie. Don't let these people know the nature of my argument with the church.'

'I won't. You have my word.' They would know soon enough anyway, the doctor mused. Within days – or even hours – the priest's troubles would become common knowledge. Like disease, gossip travelled swiftly through the slums.

The priest grabbed the hand of his good friend. 'Look after the Duffys and Phyllis. Keep a weather eye on them.'

Charles Walsh felt his eyes pricking. 'Do you have to leave? Just because of a bit of holy water and some prayers?'

Patrick nodded. 'Oh yes. It's nothing to do with water and prayers, son. I've committed a mortal sin—'

'For other folk, though—'

'A sin, nevertheless.' He held up his hand, would brook no further argument. 'I know that God was with me today, Charlie. Yet I've offended His representatives, and my penance will be lifelong.'

Charles Walsh cast an eye over the graveyard, wondered yet again about the meaning of life, of death. 'I see so much pain, Paddy, so much grief and suffering. So do you. How can poor Ida's place of burial matter? What sort of faith is it that will leave a crippled child worrying about her mother's soul? Is there no charity in Catholicism? Is it just a machine?'

Patrick nodded wisely. 'Best not to discuss such things in present company.' Brother Connor appeared in his mind's eye, the cane whipping menacingly, cruelty dripping from the corner of a grim mouth. 'The pope makes

111

no mistakes!' roared the long-dead monk. 'We all interpret things differently,' concluded Patrick.

'Human error,' agreed the doctor. 'There's plenty of that in my line of work, enough to fill ten cemeteries. I suppose we doctors and priests bury our mistakes.'

'We do. Indeed we do.'

They drove back to Bolton, Megan on the cart beside her parish priest, Deedee and Phyllis in the doctor's grumpy black car. 'It doesn't go much faster than the horse,' remarked Megan. 'And there's smoke everywhere.'

There will be smoke, thought Patrick. Etna's vomitings would look calm compared to the misdeeds of a certain ordained Irishman. 'Remember me, Megan,' he said softly.

'I will. Why are you going? Have you got a different job?'

He clicked his tongue at the ambling mare. 'Aye. A different job altogether,' he muttered.

Tess Duffy studied herself in the parlour overmantel. She wasn't a bad person. It was important that she remembered that fact. Mistaken, perhaps, but not a mortal sinner. The answering image looked pale, the skin stretching over cheekbones whose flesh had melted away during recent weeks. First Albert, then Harold. It was some kind of punishment, though understanding why God should take it out on a pair of little boys was difficult.

'I set too much store by them,' she told herself. 'And too little by my daughters. She'll not come home again. And there's another punishment, because if I had to pick and choose, I suppose she's me favourite.'

She walked across the room, dropped into a chair by the window. It was grim out there. Even when the sun shone, there was little true light, as the street was so narrow. The woman across the way at number 10 was cleaning her paintwork, and Tess could hear every clank of the bucket handle as if the woman were here in the same room.

'No, she'll not come home,' she repeated. Megan had often made Tess feel uneasy, scrutinized, criticized, yet Tess didn't like the idea of losing the troublesome child. 'I blamed her,' she whispered softly. 'Just like my mother blamed me.'

She leaned back, closed her eyes, saw herself as a child. They had lived in a street as mean and overcrowded as this one, had endured poverty and near-starvation. Five girls and one boy, the elder Theresa Nolan had birthed during the first eight years of her marriage. Young Tess had brought home the measles, had infected all her siblings until the while lot had suffered spots and runny noses. And, with one exception, everyone had recovered. Kieran Nolan's measles had gone to his head, had inflamed his brain and killed the tiny three-year-old.

'Tess?'

Her eyes flew open. 'What?'

'Are you all right?' Joe's anxious face pushed itself into the room.

'Yes. I'm just . . . working things out in me mind. Leave me a bit, will you?'

She waited until his footfalls marked an adequate distance, then closed her eyes once more. 'It were you!' To this very day, Tess could see her mother standing over her, the dark hair matted and dull, the eyes huge with confusion and anger. 'You fetched the illness into my house. You killed my son!'

'Megan. Oh, Megan,' moaned Tess in the here and now. 'I thought I'd learned from me mam, but I didn't.'

She sat up, watched her neighbour skimming a leather over glass that would be forever dull. 'I know Joe wanted lads,' she muttered. 'For the shop, to carry on his name. And I . . . I'd sooner have lads, but why should this lot suffer through being girls? Deedee's right, as a mother I'm nowt a pound. So I've just got to pull together and make the best.'

She stood, ran a hand through her hair, thought about all the jobs that needed doing. It was time she set to, time to get off her dozy backside and pull her weight. Annie and Nellie, at eleven and ten, were nearing the age when they might go half-time in a mill, so Tess had better get the socks pulled up. She faced herself again, saw the grief that still waited to spill from eyes that had always been huge. 'It were me eyes that attracted Joe,' she said softly. 'Look at the size of them now, Tess Duffy, all black-ringed and bloodshot.'

She was weak, tired from childbed, exhausted by funeral masses and graveside services. She was cold, chilled to the bone without Harold to warm her with his smile, without Albert to cheer her with his cleverness. Cleverness. Tess turned, glanced across the road where Holly and Myrtle joined like a capital T. She was the clever one. Aye, their Megan was the one with the brainbox. Eight next year, she was, so she'd likely finish up doing half-days in four years. 'No,' she said loudly. 'They'll not do that, none of them. They can stop on at school till thirteen or even fourteen, be kiddies for as long as possible.'

Through the lace curtain, she watched her neighbour struggling with a tatty shammy, more holes than leather. Was this their future, then? Was nothing going to get better for Annie, Nellie, Megan, Freda, little Hilda? Christ, what sort of a bloody life was this? She remembered her mother's screams when the last dead baby girl was ripped from her, remembered the flowers, the neighbours visiting with soup and sympathy. 'Oh, Mam,' she whispered. 'I know how you felt, yes, yes, I know now.' Her head nodded rapidly in time with the words. 'But we were both wrong. You shouldn't have blamed me for me brother and I shouldn't have put that burden on our Megan.'

Joe pushed the door open. 'Cup of tea, lass?'

'Yes.' She looked at him. 'I'll be all right, you know. There's no need for you to be hanging about here in case I go hanging about under the pulley. And I've no intention of getting took away, neither. Get back to your clogging, lad, we've a family to feed. And you can pay your mam and all for seeing to Megan and Ida's lass.'

He shuffled into the room. 'She'll not take it off me, Tess. She's doing all that mending and sewing, up all hours.' He sighed, shook his head. 'I've never been able to do owt with me mam,' he muttered.

'Is that what it's about, then?' she asked. 'Do we bring up our children just so they can see to us when we're old? You're not supposed to manage her, Joe. She's stubborn, I'll give you that. And our Megan's took after her.'

He stared at his wife. 'How come you've picked up all of a sudden?'

She tried to smile, knew that the result of her efforts was a pale and watery imitation. 'No choice,' she answered sadly. 'They're dead, they're buried.' Her chest heaved, but she swallowed the sob. 'And life's got to go on.' All the same, it was going to be difficult. Something kept happening to Tess, an event whose regular visits made life extremely burdensome. She could be fine one minute, totally destroyed the next.

It was all connected, she felt, to her monthly cycle. There were the two weeks after the bleeding had stopped, then about forty-eight hours of tearing pain. Dr Walsh had explained at length that this particular discomfort might well be caused by eggs pulling themselves away from an ovary. But worse was always in store. For a week before her 'show', she was rampageous. She argued in shops, wept at the drop of a hat, shouted the odds to anyone who inadvertently hung washing on her line in Back Myrtle Street. And she had even thrown a vase at Joe during one of her monthly tantrums.

And that was not the end of it. When she bled, she bled copiously, suffered pain that almost had her screaming at times. Oh, she couldn't win. Pregnant, she was tired, exhausted by the anxious waiting. Would she get through, would she get a boy, was life going to get easier?

Tess tried to be brave for Joe. This was one of her better times, that brief respite she found somewhere between ovulation and the monthly tantrum. 'I'm not mad,' she told him. 'It's something else, something to do with being a woman.'

'Nobody said you were mad, Tess.'

She shook her head. 'No, but it's all in here.' She pressed a hand to her belly. 'Things happen to my body and I go . . . out of control. When I'm pregnant, I'm fretful—'

'And when you're not, you worry because you're not.'

She averted her gaze. If she hadn't wanted a boy, she would have given it all up here and now, would have told him that she wanted no more babies. But she hoped, so she kept her mouth shut. She would try, in future, to control the swings of moods. But she had tried for endless years, had tried and had failed.

SIX

It was hard work. Every morning, Deedee and Megan gave Phyllis an all-over wash, as she couldn't go with them to the slipper baths for a proper scrub every Friday. After breakfast, Megan dashed off to school, leaving Deedee to do most of the chores. When the house met with Deedee's high standards, the grandmother began the task of making money while Phyllis did a few of the easier jobs like hem-tacking and folding. Megan came home just after twelve, ate her lunch, then wheeled Phyllis down to St Mary's for the afternoon session. At the start, Deedee had taken Phyllis to school, but the days were too short and time was too precious. She worried about Megan and the unwieldy wheelchair, but she had to do her sewing, had to pay the bills.

She was working on some curtains for a doctor's surgery on Derby Street when a knock at the door interrupted the difficult task. The material was a heavy and hideous brocade in a shade that was almost bottle green, hard on hands and eyes. Impatient with the invisible intruder, she marched through the house and flung open the front door. 'Oh, it's you,' she said. 'What do you want? I'm in the middle of me sewing, trying to make a bob or two.'

He grinned. 'Hello, Doris.'

She raked her eyes over him, sniffed the air suspiciously. 'Are you wearing scent, Tommy Wagstaff?'

He was hurt. 'No, I'm not wearing scent. I got some nice soap, that's all, summat a bit different from yellow and carbolic.'

Deedee sniffed again. 'Women's soap, that is. You smell like one of them that looks for work down Bradshawgate on Saturday nights.'

He blushed, shuffled about in his new clogs. 'Doris Appleyard, you are a hard wom—'

'Duffy,' she snapped. 'I'm Doris Duffy, Deedee to me friends and grandchildren. What are you doing stood there like a dog's dinner? I'm in the middle of a pair of curtains, so I—'

'Pull yourself together,' he quipped lamely. Then, feeling even sillier, he added, 'Curtains. Pull yourself together. Get it?'

She glared ominously. 'I got it straight away, and it weren't particularly funny the first time I heard it before the century turned. Why are you here? I've better things to do, you know. And you should be asleep, Tommy Wagstaff. It's no use stopping up all day as well as all night. Get yourself home.'

He'd got himself all wound up and all dressed up for this woman, and she was telling him to shove off. Tommy sighed resignedly. He didn't like to come in an evening when the two young ones were about, didn't want to cause a problem. Courting was a bugger. He'd got it all wrong first time round, and age had not improved his minimal skills. Here he was, trying to look nice, smell nice, talk nice, act nice. And Doris-Appleyard-as-was was making life as complicated as she could manage. And complications were Deedee's forte. 'You never were easy,' he grumbled. 'Always had a smart mouth and something to say on every bloody occasion.'

'Don't swear on my doorstep.'

His face brightened slightly, though even this glimmer of hope was hopeless, short-lived. 'Can I swear in your house, then?'

'No.'

He made an effort to straighten sloping shoulders. 'Fifty-nine and turning sixty, you are. And you've still learned no manners. I've fetched summat for the girls.'

She eyed him with suspicion, refused to listen to a tiny voice at the back of her mind. If she'd married Tommy instead of Stan, she wouldn't have been battered half to death. If she'd married Tommy instead of Stan, she could have made something of this daft knocker-up. If she'd . . . no, she wasn't going to think about all that, not when she'd seven yards of heavy brocade waiting for her inside. 'What have you brought, then?'

He poked a hand into a capacious pocket, pulled out a black-and-white kitten. 'A cat,' he said. She liked cats. Everybody knew how Doris loved animals.

'A cat?' Her eyebrows shot up, all but disappeared into a tumble of iron-grey hair that had broken loose in the course of battle with a difficult seam. 'I do know a cat when I see one, Tommy Wagstaff. That thing's more the size of a mouse.'

'His mother didn't want him, so he's hand-reared.' He puffed out his chest. 'I've a way with cats. And call me Tommy.'

'I'll call you a lunatic, I think. What would I be wanting with a cat? Haven't I got enough with Megan and Phyllis and a living to make for the three of us?'

He tutted. 'He won't eat much.'

'He'll eat nowt in my house, 'cos he's not stopping. We've no room. What with the wheelchair and the bed and me sewing, there's not an inch to spare in that back kitchen. And imagine what a kitten would do with all me bits and pieces. There'd be cotton reels everywhere. Go on. Be off with you and get some sleep.'

The kitten stared at her, its eyes huge and green. 'Mew,' it said quietly.

Doris Duffy was flummoxed. She wasn't often in two minds, because she'd decided long ago to be decisive. But she had a definite soft spot when it came to animals, which was why she'd never kept any. It was cruel, she thought, to shut a cat or a dog in a house while its master worked. But she didn't go out to the mill any more. And it was a bonny little thing, quite dainty and sweet and almost striped like a tiny zebra.

'Are you weakening, Doris Appleyard?' he asked.

'Shut up,' snapped the woman of Tommy's dreams.

'Give it here, we'll have a trial run.' She lifted the little body and placed it in the crook of her arm. 'How many have you got?'

He grinned. 'I'm down to eight, and I've homes promised for four of them. It's quiet at home without a crowd of these little devils.' He stroked the soft fluff, jumped slightly when his hand made accidental contact with the goddess from his youth. She'd been a stunner, had Doris Appleyard. And even now, with her hair turned grey and her figure lean, she was a fine example of womanhood. 'They've all different personalities,' he mumbled.

'I know.'

'Like folk – they vary.'

'I know that and all.'

She had never made life easy. Time and again, he'd gone on the Saturday night trot, the lads on one side of Deansgate, the lasses across the way, everybody looking determinedly casual. It still took place, that strange weekend ritual, the sexes mingling only on the corners. A bit like a cattle market, now he came to think of it. 'You never looked at anybody, so I don't know how you finished up with yon queer feller.'

Doris stared at him as if he had lost his mind. 'Eh?'

'On the Saturday cakewalk. They do it to this day, tha knows. All the boys walk towards Churchgate, while the lasses go the opposite way. They study one another, but they all pretend they're there by accident. I stopped going when you got picked by Stan Duffy.'

She leaned against the door jamb. 'Tommy Wagstaff, if you've a mind to start plaguing the daylights out of me all over again, you can just get yourself back home. I'm near sixty, and I've no intention of pairing off at my time of life. Look.' She tucked the kitten under her chin, held out steady hands. 'Them hands was made for work. I've a young family again, mouths to feed. I can't be dallying on me doorstep with a man that's never grown up.'

'I could help you,' he said hesitantly.

120

'Help me? You'd be more of a hindrance and well you know it. Out all night minding the mill, scratching folks' windows at the crack of dawn, then dozing all the day. You'd be under me feet – so would your cats.' She wagged a finger at him. 'Get off home before I take me yardbrush to you.'

He sighed, saluted, did a quick about-turn. 'Yes, sergeant,' he muttered. 'And look after yon cat.' He marched off smartly, lost his footing for a brief second on an uneven flag, mustered his dignity and strode homeward. She was weakening, and not just about cats. And he'd a secret cache in his house, a tin box containing at least seventy pounds. He could retire, get a little house in the country, put some roses back in Doris Appleyard-as-was's cheeks.

Tommy reached his door, pushed it open, threw himself into his rocker. She was right about one thing – he never went to bed. Lying down was a waste of time. If he sat here, he could doze, watch the kiddies in the street, be a witness to any excitement. Elsie Shipton was the best entertainment for miles, especially when her husband came home the worse for wear. But oh, if Thomas Wagstaff Esquire, bachelor of this parish, could go and live with Doris, if she'd just see sense and marry him, he would change his ways. He nodded, snoozed, smiled to himself. For Doris, he would change the whole world and his socks twice a day. He opened a wary eye. Once a day might be enough . . .

Geoffrey Althorpe walked the length of Myrtle Street twice, passing the odd numbers the first time, the evens on the second occasion. Holly Street started in the gap between numbers 8 and 10, with the blind side of 1, Holly Street on the corner. He crossed the cobbles, stood outside Tommy Wagstaff's house, screwed up brown eyes against a shaft of sunlight that had managed to pierce the gloom. From this vantage point, he could see the door of number 6, was able to study the comings and goings of residents.

The fat woman from number 1 was on her hands and knees in the lobby, her turbaned head bobbing about in time with the scrubbing. Outside number 5, a group of small children played, throwing bits of slate and stone into the road. They were young, far too young for organized games. At least two of them seemed to be male, though all wore dresses.

Geoffrey's eyes slid across to number 6. Nothing. She had to be home from school by this time. Anyway, he didn't even know why he needed to see her. His mother would be furious if she heard about this visit, as it would not fit into her 'scheme of things'. Yet he continued to study the house, waited for signs of life.

'She'll be helping Doris with her sewing,' said a voice behind him.

Geoffrey jumped, turned, saw Dad's nightwatchman. 'Mr Wagstaff,' he said, his voice trembling slightly.

Tommy grinned. It was a change to be called 'Mr Wagstaff'. 'I usually get me full handle, Master Geoffrey. They all call me daft and they all call me Tommy Wagstaff. Is it young Megan you're looking for?' Nothing escaped the notice of the man who seldom slept. Even without much evidence, he could assess a situation and reach a conclusion that was usually correct. 'She's a nice lass, is Megan Duffy.'

Geoffrey swallowed. 'I thought she might . . . come for a walk, play for a while in the mill yard. But if she's busy . . .'

Tommy shook his head. 'Look, just go and knock on yon door, tell them I've sent you to look at the cat.'

The boy allowed a beat of time to pass. 'I beg your pardon?'

'I've give them a cat, a kitten six week old, he is. Say I've asked you to check up on him.'

'But why would I do that? And why would you ask me to do it?'

Tommy scratched his nose. Sometimes, these educated young things made life extremely difficult. 'I don't know.'

He pondered for a moment. 'Aye, happen you're right. It would seem a bit daft. Sithee.' He pulled on the lad's school blazer. 'Come in here and we'll find a reason. No use both of us mooning about like bloody Romeo under that flaming balcony.'

The boy nodded, looked the nightwatchman up and down. 'Is that Shakespeare?' He was going to have to study Shakespeare once he got to Bolton School. The last time he'd taken a peep into *Collected Sonnets*, he had decided that the bard had written in a language that was a long way removed from English. 'Have you read him?' he asked.

''Course. Every Englishman should read a bit of owld Will's work. It's like a duty, same as fighting in wars.'

'Oh.'

The older man heaved the boy into his house and closed the door. 'Cods' heads,' he announced gravely.

Geoffrey didn't like to beg pardon again, as that might indicate either his own stupidity or some criticism of his host's communication skills. He stood between door and dresser, gazed round the room, hoped that his surprise did not show. It was clean, shiny as a new pin. Had Mr Wagstaff changed more than just his trousers, then?

Tommy grinned. 'Same boat as thee, son. Aye, let's hope we're both strong swimmers, for she'd throw the lot of us to the sharks if she felt like it.'

Lost for words, Geoffrey placed himself behind a chair and waited for things to become a little clearer.

'Since I were nobbut seventeen, I've had me eye on Doris Appleyard,' the old man said. 'I'm near me dotage, and I still stand and watch out for her, specially since your dad moved her over yon.' He waved a hand in the general direction of Holly Street. 'I hope your luck's better than mine, lad, or you'll be stood here again in fifty-odd years waiting for a flaming miracle. Still. I think a cod's head'll be your best bet.' He went into the kitchen, returned with an extremely smelly parcel. 'Take that. Tell them you've fetched it for the cat.'

Geoffrey closed his mouth with a snap, fingered the package gingerly before placing it on the table. 'For Megan's kitten?'

'That's right. Say . . .' Tommy groped for words. 'Say you're having fish at home and your mam's cut all the heads off.' Several cats jumped out of a large cardboard box near the fireplace, started sniffing the fish-tainted air.

Agnes Althorpe had never seen a cod's head, had certainly never separated it from the rest of its scaly body, because although Geoffrey's mother enjoyed cooking, she had a strong aversion to fish heads. 'It'd be Mary, I should think. Yes, Mary helps our cook in the kitchen.'

The old man thought for a second. 'Oh aye, I'd forgot as how you'll be all servants and calling cards.' There was no resentment in his tone. People were folk. And folk, like cats, were all different. 'Say Mary gave it you then.'

The boy breathed in through his mouth, tried to avoid the strong perfume that was filling the small room. He could not take this malodorous parcel into Megan Duffy's life. 'Mary doesn't know about Megan's kitten, Mr Wagstaff.'

'Oh.' Tommy sat down, picked up a ginger cat whose mood was verging on hysterical. 'You can wait, Marmalade,' he said. 'Don't start getting wound up in your own tail just because you've had a whiff of cod.'

It was more than a whiff. Geoffrey felt as if the rest of his life would carry this vile aroma, was sure that it had permeated every fibre of his clothing, every pore of his flesh. 'I'll go and find my dad,' he said weakly. 'He'll probably be wondering where I am.'

Tommy jerked his head in agreement, got to his feet, placed the large cat in the centre of a peg rug. 'Now, listen to me, young Althorpe. When it comes to Shakespeare, you come to me. I've had to do summat during the nights, so I've read a lot of books. See, there's a trick to Shakespeare. You've to read it out loud and don't stop at the ends of lines like you would with a poem. He only makes sense if you take a loud run at him.'

124

The lad sighed, nodded resignedly.

'You don't want to go to Bolton School, do you?' asked the nightwatchman.

'No.'

'What are you interested in, then?'

Geoffrey shrugged. 'Machines. Making and mending things.' His eyes twinkled briefly. 'Mother would have a fit if she heard me saying that. It doesn't fit in with the scheme of things, you see.'

Tommy knew Agnes Althorpe, had known her since she'd been apprenticed to the weaving. She'd been a nice lass, but it seemed that marrying well had overwhelmed her. From time to time, Tommy had heard tales of her 'snobbery', though he'd never taken much notice. Still, he reckoned Agnes Catherall-as-was could never be a snob. Life at the rich end had probably terrified her, with the result that she'd worked hard at doing a good job. Her scheme of things was likely a prop to support her flagging confidence.

Tommy followed the unhappy boy to the door. 'I've never fitted,' he said. 'And I've enjoyed me life. Be true to yourself and ignore your mam. If I'd took notice of my old girl, I'd be dripping with goose-grease from September to springtime. She were a bugger for goose-grease, me mam. Ta-ra, now.'

Geoffrey mustered his courage, walked the length of Holly Street, paused outside number 6, heard nothing. He continued to the bottom, turned left into Blossom Place, carried on till he came to Althorpe Number Two. Both mills stood on Ivy Street, one at the top, near Myrtle Street, the other at the bottom, just off Blossom Place. He reached his dad's car, climbed inside and waited.

'Where the hell have you been?' asked Sidney Althorpe when he returned from one of his mills. 'Fish market?'

'I've been feeding Mr Wagstaff's cats,' he lied lamely.

Sidney engaged first gear, rolled down to Blossom Place, drove up Holly Street. 'You didn't see her, then?' There was stifled laughter in his tone.

'Who?'

'Megan Duffy, of course.'

'No.'

The car made its way up Bury Road, seemed to know the route home. 'Your mam'll go a funny colour if she hears you're hanging about after a girl from down there.' Sidney jerked a huge thumb over his shoulder. 'Especially with the Duffys being Catholics. Still, you're only ten—'

'Nearly eleven, Dad.'

'Whatever,' said the senior Althorpe. 'There's no harm in having friends from all over the place, not at your age.' He ground the gears noisily, cursed under his breath. 'One thing, though. Don't be coming home with a pong like that, or your mother will know there's something fishy going on.' Satisfied with this clever pun, he took the poor lad home, home to Agnes.

Agnes Althorpe watched the car as it crunched its smoky and boneshaking way up the pebbled drive. She fingered the pearls at her throat, smoothed her wrinkle-free dress, patted the pale blonde chignon whose shining coils nestled in the nape of a neck that remained cream, young and supple. She'd never had a lot of colour, but she had tried to pretend for years that colour was vulgar and loud, and she made the most of her delicate looks. Her bones were fine and well-shaped, her skin was free from blemish, while her hair had retained a shade of platinum that was almost unbelievable. Powder and paint were applied sparsely, just a hint of pink rouge to emphasize flawless cheekbones, a touch of coral on her lips.

A brief glance in the overmantel mirror verified her prettiness, though she did stop for a moment to place a stray hair back among its sisters. Yes, she was beautiful, and she made much of her looks in an attempt to cover all her other imperfections. Even now, she could scarcely believe that Sidney Althorpe had chosen her. He could easily have had a wealthy wife, someone from an established family. But no, he had picked a mill girl, a slip of a thing from the back streets of Bolton.

She watched while Geoffrey and Sidney walked to the door. Her life could have been so terrifyingly different from this. The swift rise in position had frightened Agnes, was still a source of wonderment. She suspected that she tried too hard, had read too many tomes on etiquette and manners. As she had not been born into affluence, she had concentrated on getting things right. Her concepts of correctness were connected to the positioning of fish knives, the wearing of an appropriate hat, the elimination of dialect from her over-perfected speech. Agnes was not an unusually clever woman, but her instincts were strong. What she lacked in the education department, she made up for in feminine intuition.

Felicity came into the room. 'Mother, might I have a rest from practice? I am so tired of all these scales.'

Agnes stared at her daughter, the girl who had come out all wrong. The once pretty child seemed to have developed a nose whose twin sat in the centre of Sidney Althorpe's face, a feature that looked strong in a man, dreadful on a young woman. Felicity's complexion was at odds with itself, waxy in some parts, glowing with dark red spots around the chin. The thick head of hair had darkened from blonde to a mouse-coloured brown whose texture begged for frequent washing due to greasiness. Only the eyes had survived the cruellest tricks of nature, as these were of a green so clear that they put her mother's in the shade.

'Felicity, push back your shoulders, hold yourself proudly,' chided that mother now. Inwardly, Agnes reprimanded herself, wished she could be nicer. But she worried for her children, was anxious for them to do well. She had not forgotten the taste and smell of poverty; had set her sights on professional accomplishments, even for her daughter. Fliss was female and plain, so she would need to be doubly clever. The mills were there, of course, but even so, Agnes prayed that her offspring would achieve some 'nice' qualifications, diplomas that might allow cotton and all its dirt to become a second string, a distant relative who deserved respect rather than attention.

Felicity, who preferred to be Fliss, straightened her spine and tried not to notice the two bulges in the front of her blouse. Being a little girl had been easy. She'd been Pop's treasure, Mummy's close friend. But lately, life had dealt some hefty blows. For a start, she was ugly. It didn't matter how many times she did her hair, how many times she scrubbed her face, she was still spotty and hideous.

'You'll grow out of all those spots, dear,' said Agnes, her tone intending to be kind.

But Fliss heard the despair that lurked behind her mother's tongue. And she had been such a favoured infant. Then, all of a sudden, her nose had spread out and her skin had started to erupt in nasty pustules that looked like mountains when viewed in a mirror. She wanted to die; if she couldn't die, then she'd like to stay away from school for ever and ever. 'I've done enough piano practice,' she said now. 'So I'll go up and do some homework.'

Agnes disagreed. Even her bridling was understated, just a barely discernible jerk of a shoulder. 'You will stay and eat, Felicity. This is the only time of day when we manage to be a family. Wash your hands, then greet your father.'

After everyone's ablutions, the Althorpes sat down to the evening meal, a repast Agnes had called dinner since reading the books. Sidney, a man who insisted on displaying his origins by tucking the napkin into his collar, always called this afternoon meal his high tea. 'Good day, Fliss?' he asked. He often joked, said he had his low tea at work, two sugars and a dripping butty.

The girl nodded, dipped a spoon in her soup. It had been an awful day. She'd caught three girls whispering and giggling in a corridor, and she knew in her bones that the trio had been mocking Felicity Althorpe's nose, hair, skin. The food stuck in her throat. Even thin soup was hard to swallow, simply because she did not wish to eat. 'May I be excused?' she asked without hope.

'No,' Agnes's tone was not sharp. She was worried about Fliss, so she often treated her badly simply because she did not know how to cope with the girl's behaviour. Felicity had almost stopped taking food altogether. 'You will eat your meal, Felicity.'

While eating, Geoffrey studied his sister covertly. She was a pest in many ways, had recently started making the most awful fuss about her appearance, yet he was beginning to realize that Fliss deserved pity, not derision. She had a strong face, but Mother was disappointed in Fliss's robust looks. In the fourteen-year-old's face, Geoffrey saw something he would come to call character. Fliss hated herself. He choked on a mouthful, excused himself politely, took a sip of water from a crystal glass. His sister hated herself and he hoped that his teasing was not proving a factor in Fliss's suffering.

Mother was going on about Evelyn Grimshaw again. Geoffrey tried to pull his 'Grimshaw' face at Fliss, but Fliss was busy pretending to eat.

'A circular bath, Sidney,' Mother was saying. 'Stuck in the middle of the floor like a big boil. I didn't know where to look.'

Geoffrey felt Fliss's pain when the word 'boil' was mentioned. She did have one or two particularly dreadful facial eruptions at the moment.

'Gold-plated taps.' Agnes dabbed at her mouth with a linen napkin, placed her hands on her knees. 'And Greek urns. Well, she calls them Greek, but they look as if they might have been moulded out of plaster of Paris – probably by an amateur. And bottle green tiles imported from Italy.' She sighed dramatically. 'Some people just don't know how to spend money.'

Sidney made sure his napkin was tucked firmly into his collar. She hated his manners, kept moaning at him about table etiquette. But he had not yet managed to work out how to eat soup without most of it ending up on his waistcoat. 'Money down the drain,' he remarked absently.

Geoffrey choked again, had a vision of notes and coins gurgling through the plug hole in Mrs Grimshaw's round bath.

'Geoffrey, I do wish you would learn some control. You'll have a severe case of indigestion if you're not careful.' She glared at Fliss's full dish, waved at the maid so that the table might be cleared. She didn't want to make a fuss in front of the staff, so she chose not to remark on Felicity's lack of appetite.

When the pork was served, Felicity jumped up with the napkin to her mouth, then fled from the room.

'Sidney,' said Agnes. 'You will have to take her in hand.'

Sid swallowed a drop of water, chased after his daughter. He stood outside the downstairs cloakroom and listened to the sound of Fliss's illness. Every time the children got a bit difficult, he was advised by his wife to take them in hand. Agnes grabbed the credit for their good points, while he was blamed for any flaws in their makeup. Not that they had any flaws, he insisted silently. Though little Fliss was doing a lot of vomiting these days. He tapped on the door. 'Are you all right, sweetheart?'

'Sweetheart' leaned her head against cold tiles, then heaved herself to her feet. She was ill. It was a funny kind of illness, because its main symptom was tiredness, but whatever it was, she couldn't seem to pull out of it. 'Yes,' she managed. 'I'll go up to bed in a minute.'

He waited. Agnes might not be satisfied with a report of this paucity. 'Your mother's worried.'

'I know.' Fliss perched on the lavatory seat, fought for air so that she could think properly. 'It's school. I hate school and it makes me sick.'

Sid pressed his ear to the door. 'That's a good little school, you know. Your mother chose it specially, so that you'd be happy. Ordinary schools are crowded – sometimes fifty children in one class. You're better off than most folk, Fliss.'

'I want to leave. I'm fourteen, so I should leave,' she insisted weakly. Mother wouldn't allow it. She'd have to stay on until she could speak good English and fair French, until she could cobble together a decent piece on the piano and a meaningless rectangle of petit point. She pressed a hand against her heaving stomach, forced herself to breathe deeply, steadily. She would not go back to that school. It was boring, boring and stupid.

'Come out,' he coaxed.

She stood, opened the door, raised her head and studied him with great sad eyes.

'Don't look at me like that, love.' She was breaking his heart. 'There's nothing I can do about school. You know how much store your ma sets by a decent education.'

She breathed in deeply, stood her ground. 'I'm not going any more.'

'What?' It was more than his life was worth – he couldn't go back into the dining room with a bombshell of this magnitude. He loved Agnes with all his heart, had often bled inside while watching her attempts to live up to a station she did not understand. He bowed his head and grunted quietly. The station Agnes fought to achieve did not exist. She'd married an ordinary fellow with money, that was all. There was no need for all the fancy ideas. Agnes was imposing standards on their children, standards born of her own poor education. Had Agnes been tutored in childhood, then she might have realized that happiness was more important than exams. 'Fliss,' he pleaded. 'Please, just try . . .' His words faded as he watched the brown head shaking slowly from side to side. He made another attempt, knew he could not win. There was a lot of Agnes in Fliss, a great deal of determination and bloody-mindedness. 'Only a couple more years, pet—'

'No.' She squared her shoulders as if preparing for battle, fixed her gaze on Sidney Althorpe's worried face. 'I shall come in the mills. Office work to start with, bookkeeping and so on. Then I might attend Miss

131

Dunne's evening classes for shorthand and typing. Her school has a good reputation.'

Sid inserted a finger between collar and throat, decided that the feeling of strangulation was coming not from without, but from inside his chest. Agnes would hit the roof. Agnes might well go into one of her declines. She was famous for her declines, which usually lasted at least three months. And there was nothing false about Agnes Althorpe's periodical weaknesses. He had lifted her out of the slums, and she had become dizzied by the so-called heights of her husband's achievements. The result of that was a recurring discomfort that took the legs from under her. He grunted again, worried about any forthcoming trouble. 'Your mother,' he managed.

Fliss continued to eye him steadily. 'It's time I did something useful, Pop. I can't be a child forever. That awful school is a waste of time and money. Why should anyone need to walk about with a pile of books on her head? And I don't need French and music and needle-work.'

'Learning's never wasted,' he said, gratefully repeating one of Agnes's sayings. 'It sets you up for later life. If you can put your mind to your books, you'll be able to tackle problems more easily. It's not what you learn that matters, it's having the discipline to apply yourself that's important.'

Felicity Althorpe pulled herself together and swept past her father. She didn't see why he should get the blame, couldn't bear the thought of sending Pop in with the message. In the old days, a fetcher of bad news often got killed on the spot . . . When she reached the doorway of the dining room, she paused, gazed upon the scene.

Mother's back was turned towards the door. She always sat in that particular seat so that she might be near to the kitchen. Agnes secretly hated having servants, was at her happiest with her hands stuck in dough and her arms covered in flour. At the least opportunity, the lady of the house would go into the kitchen 'to advise Cook' or 'to have a little word with Mary'.

Geoffrey sat at Mother's right side, while Fliss's empty place was opposite her brother's. Dad's carver was also empty, its arms pointing in the direction of the sideboard.

Agnes moved, giving her daughter the benefit of that perfect profile. 'Felicity?'

The girl strode to the table, her insides churning. 'I've left school,' she said softly. 'I don't care what you say or what you do, I shan't go back.'

Agnes, paler than ever, pushed herself away from the table. 'No,' she muttered.

'Yes,' answered Felicity.

Agnes was screwing up her napkin as if she wanted to strangle it. This was not happening, could not possibly be real. Successful business people did not allow their offspring to neglect the educational side of things. She'd read that in one of the books. Allowing Felicity to leave school at this point would be as bad as having no servants. The Althorpes were business folk, but they were also minor gentry.

Agnes pulled her shoulders back, thought about the consequences of her daughter's rash decision. Evelyn Grimshaw's son was at university, was on his way to being a doctor. Evelyn Grimshaw would be delighted to see the Althorpe girl reduced to working. Agnes lifted her chin high, attempted to make the green eyes cold and hard. 'You will be taken to school. You will be taken inside, if necessary—'

'And I shall walk out again, if necessary.'

Geoffrey swallowed, knew that the others had heard the unattractive gulping sound. Fliss wanted to give up school. He watched the scenario with an interest that touched his soul with red-hot flames, because he, too, would be saying these words in a very few years. He would be eleven within months, so in three years— Would he have the courage? The word 'NO' emblazoned itself in large capitals across his mind. He would never have Fliss's courage. She might go on a bit about spots and hair, might be a bit of a bore at times but, underneath all that, she was a magnificent person. Whereas he would rather run away from home than face Mother.

'You will do exactly as I say,' said Agnes. 'Only the poor from the working class leave school at fourteen.' She blushed slightly, hated herself for seeming to denigrate the very stratum of society out of which she had been lifted. 'We have made plans for you, and you will finish your education.'

'No.'

Geoffrey's opinion of his sister was altering all the time. She was better than magnificent, he decided now. Strong, powerful and right. The rightness lay in the fact that Fliss, like himself, was not bookish. She was a clever girl whose talents were no doubt being wasted at the Carter Academy for Young Ladies. 'Fliss wants to work, Mother,' he whispered. 'We're the same, you see. She wants to be a secretary and I want to be a mech—'

'Quiet!' Agnes never raised her voice. Even now, with confusion staining her cheeks, she clung like a drowning sailor to the tattered life-raft that was her pride. For Agnes Althorpe, dignity was all. She had found that in black and white many years ago. The Lady of the House always merited capital initials in etiquette books. In the scheme of things, a woman of her calibre needed dress sense, skills in home management and, above all, an elegance that should shine throughout the direst of troubles.

Agnes turned up her delicate nose and confronted her daughter. 'You will return to school tomorrow.' Her heart pounded as if trying to escape from its ribcage. What would people say if her daughter left school so early? Would they mutter under their breath about Sidney's parents' attitude to the unlikely match? Would they all labour under the happy delusion that the Althorpes could no longer afford to educate their young? She could not bear this. Slowly, she turned her head and looked across the room.

Sidney stood in the doorway, his jaw still tight as he listened to Fliss's words. 'I shall not be going to school any more, Mother. The subjects taught there will be of no use to me, as I intend to be a secretary in Pop's mills.'

Agnes swivelled and faced her husband. 'My daughter will never set foot inside a mill, Sidney.' She allowed a beat of time to pass. 'Did you know of this plan?' The tone was almost accusatory.

Even from a distance of several paces, Sidney felt his wife's terror. It hung in the room like a dark, wet blanket of fog, and he raised his eyes to see whether the ceiling light had dimmed. Agnes was scared of two things – poverty and what people said about her. He could do nothing to allay her fears. 'She told me not five minutes ago,' he replied lamely. 'It seems to be what she wants, so . . .' The words deserted him. He could grade and card cotton, wind it, spin it and weave it, yet he was incapable of coping with his wife's insecurity. In his opinion, a boss had a duty to master every skill in his factory, right down to sweeping up the rubbish. So why had he never learned the arts a husband needed to comfort a frightened wife? Why had he neglected his family?

'You must take her in hand,' Agnes said now. 'To allow her to work in a mill would be wrong, Sidney. It would not fit into the scheme of things at all. What would people say?'

Sidney nodded, wondered what the scheme was. Did Agnes plan a large wedding for Fliss, a marriage that might feature in the society pages? He saw nothing wrong in the concept of Fliss working for a living. The mill girls worked, he employed females on the clerical staff – there were even a couple of women in the weaving sheds. 'There's nothing wrong with honest work, Agnes,' he said softly. 'Nothing wrong with earning a wage—'

'That is for . . . for people of a different class.' The mistress of the Althorpe household began again to wring her napkin as if it were a wet cleaning cloth. 'Young women in Felicity's position do not need to work. Well – not in that type of job,' she concluded.

'Why?' asked Fliss. 'Why shouldn't I work?'

Agnes shifted her head slowly, removed her gaze from Sidney, glared at this dreadful daughter. 'Your father's family has striven for almost a century so that you might enjoy the life of a lady. You will finish your education, then we shall visit London and buy you a complete wardrobe. There will be parties for you, occasions when young men of your class will be introduced to you. The pick of the crop will come here, and you will receive invitations from other families. That is how it must be, that is the scheme—'

'Scheme of things into which I must fit?' Fliss's cheeks glowed brightly, making the eyes brighter, allowing beauty to pay a brief visit to features that no longer seemed uneven and ill-conceived. 'Who wrote this bible of yours, Mother? Who planned this scheme of things?'

'Society,' replied Agnes smartly. Evelyn Grimshaw would make much of this, she thought yet again.

The maid put her head round the door, disappeared as soon as the mistress's hand waved its signal of dismissal.

Geoffrey rose from his seat. 'Shall I leave the room?' he asked his father.

Sidney shook his head. 'No, lad. It's best that we have all this out here and now.' He walked to the fireplace, opened a wooden box and took out a cigar. When the end was nicked, he lit it, then turned to face the other occupants of the room. 'Sit down, Agnes,' he said kindly.

She sniffed. 'I prefer to stand.'

'Sit,' he ordered, his tone still soft. When his wife was seated, Sidney took up the cudgels on behalf of Felicity and Geoffrey. 'We may as well get this over and done with,' he began. 'There's neither of them wants to be in this scheme you keep talking about, love. She'd rather be a secretary and he needs to be up to his armpits in oil and muck. Mind, I agree with you that he should do accountancy first. All the same, it's time for plain speaking.'

He wandered to the window and gazed out at his kingdom. He was an extremely wealthy man, yet he stayed

136

here in this not quite splendid house on the main road that led to Bolton. There wasn't even room for live-in staff. Only the little maid called Mary stayed here, in a pretty attic with a dormer window and a view he often envied, a landscape that almost touched the Pennine Chain.

The Althorpes could have had a country estate with horses and all kinds of furbelows, but Sidney's feet were firmly planted here. Agnes had wanted to name the house, but it had remained 19 Church Road, would always be just a number. From his dining room bay, Sidney could see the end gable of the next house and, through some trees and bushes, the window of a house across the road. Life, he had decided long ago, was about folk. He knew his neighbours, was on nodding terms with two aldermen, the owner of a bleachworks and a chap who ran a chain of pawnshops.

Sidney inhaled the taste of rich tobacco, turned and looked at his agitated wife. 'I could buy and sell the whole lot of them.' He waved a hand towards the road. 'But I don't want to. We've properties dotted all over the town, two cottages up in Bromley Cross, another over towards Westhoughton. The life you've always wanted has been within my reach for a long time. But think on.' He waved the cigar, leaving a pattern of blue smoke that wreathed about his head before melding into a small cloud. 'Think on about how hard our fathers worked, Agnes. I got here because my dad went short on food, clothes and sleep. Your father spent his youth sawing bars of soap into little blocks to sell from his cart. And, as you well know, that family of yours had to work in the mills when the grocery shop failed. There's nothing wrong with plain hard work.'

She watched him, knew that he was serious. Agnes's strength had always lain in the fact that she understood when to take umbrage, when to resign from battle gracefully. Her cleverest trick had been to lead from behind, to allow him to believe that he was in charge while she ran part of the show with her usual efficiency. But here was a problem that seemed to allow for no compromise. 'I wanted better for my children,' she managed at last. 'Just as our parents improved our lot. For Geoffrey, I imagined a real career – perhaps law. And for Felicity . . .' She cast a glance in the direction of her daughter. 'For her, I foresaw a grounding in the arts.' She swallowed. 'If she leaves the school, I shall be bitterly disappointed.'

'So be it,' he muttered sadly. 'It's not as if we're going to leap from poverty to poverty in three generations, Agnes. They'll always be well-to-do.' He pointed the cigar towards his son. 'He'll probably invent a system for running engines on fresh air and water. And our Fliss is too active to spend her days embroidering hankies and traycloths. You must just be disappointed, love.'

Agnes rose from the table, placing the mangled napkin on a plate. 'As you wish, dear,' she whispered into the heavy silence. 'I must go to bed, as I feel a headache coming on.'

When his wife had left the room, Sidney Althorpe stubbed out his cigar, sat down and attacked his cold meal. 'Never say . . .' He swallowed a mouthful of pork, washed it down with water. 'Never say I do nothing for you, Fliss. Your mother's heart is broken, and there's no use running upstairs and trying to appease her. She wanted you to stay out of the business.' He filled his mouth, chewed, cast his eyes over Fliss. 'And any more of that vomiting will mean hospital for you, young lady. I can't be employing folk too sick to work.'

'I'll be well,' she said with all the conviction she could muster. 'It's school that makes me ill.'

Sidney put down his fork. 'The spots won't disappear overnight, Fliss.' He got up, walked to the sideboard and rooted out the brandy bottle. Agnes would be difficult tonight, all saintly and silent. When coping with a disappointed wife, a chap needed some alcoholic sustenance. 'It's your age, girl. Some get spots, some don't. You're a nice-looking young woman, my dear. But leaving school won't make any difference to your complexion or to your state of health. In fact, a mill can be a place of disease and damnation.'

'I don't care.' She didn't. All she wanted was to be useful. No, that wasn't true. She wanted to be successful to the point of indispensability. One day, when he was old and grey, her father would ask her to take over the running of the Althorpe mills. People would stand aside when she walked through town, would whisper about this being a great woman, a woman of power and—

'Are you listening?' Sidney asked. 'I'm just saying that we're going to be in for some criticism. Girls with your background don't work with their fathers, sometimes don't work at all. You'll stick out like a sore thumb. The mill-hands might resent you, the office girls will be wary in your presence. You see, Agnes is right. What you are planning is definitely not in the proper scheme of things.'

Geoffrey looked from his sister to his father. 'But people should do what they're good at, Dad. And anyway, everybody will like Fliss. She's one of those people who can get on with others.'

'Well, you may be right enough there, son. But what I'm saying is that we'll have to be strong. Can you imagine what your mother's cronies will make of this? They'll be saying we're too poor to have you educated properly, too mean to give you a decent life. Agnes has hit the nail on the head, it should be a Swiss finishing school then marriage. I'm not saying we're wrong, mind, but there'll be a lot of gossip when you turn up for work, Fliss.'

'I don't care.' Her voice was less steady this time. Already, Fliss was becoming concerned about the rashness of her decision, yet she determinedly stood her ground. 'They can talk all they like, Pop.'

When his children had gone to bed, Sid Althorpe sat alone in a chair by the fire, hardly noticing Mary's ghostlike presence. The maid sensed trouble, crept about with the dishes, tried not to jangle cutlery against china.

Mrs Mason was putting on her coat. 'What's up?' she

asked when Mary brought in the last of the dinner. 'No appetites tonight?'

Mary shrugged. 'Miss Felicity never eats much, but the mistress didn't get past her soup, either. Mr Althorpe's ate the pork, only nobody's touched your sherry trifle. It's still on the sideboard with the cheese and crackers.'

Beryl Mason tutted under her breath. Being the Althorpes' cook was a good enough job, what with being allowed to live out and all, only she was getting a bit fed up with folk leaving good food. 'My Harry would love a mouthful of yon trifle,' she muttered. 'Still, mustn't grumble, eh? I've a good little cottage and you're nice and cosy here. But Miss Felicity's getting a bit too picky for my liking.'

Mary placed the tray on a scrubbed table, turned on the hot water tap, threw some flakes into the bowl. 'There's trouble, Mrs M. I can feel it in me bones.'

The cook laughed. 'Bones as young as yours have no feelings, lass. Nay, that's a happy family, is that.' She waved her umbrella in the direction of the kitchen door. 'The missus is bossy with being so nervous, but he's fit for her, you know. He'll not let her step too far out of line, won't Mr Althorpe. And them's good kids. There'll be no arguing in this house, Mary.'

The maid swished the mixture until bubbles formed, then she lowered crystal glasses into the bowl. She'd been 'brung up proper' under Mrs Mason's eagle eye, so she knew the order of play. Glasses, then cutlery, then side plates. If the froth lasted, she could process the rest of the dishes in the same water, but if the bubbles failed, then she had to start again for tureens and pans. 'There's summat up, honest. It's to do with the young miss.'

Beryl Mason skewered the hat to her head with a long pin. 'Vomiting again, is she? It's a decline, is that. I had an auntie went into a real decline. She used to eat all she could lay her hands on, but it all went the same road, down the lavvy. Scalded her throat in the finish, ate nowt but broth up to dying.' She nodded wisely. 'Aye, too much sickness ruins your throat. Mrs Althorpe can't see what's going on under her own nose. She thinks having a decline is just going a bit weak and headachy. Only a proper decline's either eating nowt or eating too much and vomiting.' Having spoken, the oracle peered out at the weather. 'I'll be home before the rain comes. Ta-ra, love.'

Mary rinsed the crystal, held it up to the light. Bright prisms leapt into her eyes, making her blink against such intense prettiness. She dried and polished the glass, counted cutlery, tidied the kitchen. On her way upstairs, she paused outside the young miss's door, heard muffled sobbing. It was a shame, thought Mary. All that money, all those clothes, yet Felicity Althorpe still had more spots than a kiddy with chicken pox. She bit her lip, carried on towards her own room. When her prayers were said, Mary Weston glanced at herself in the mirror. 'I've a lot to be thankful for,' she said to her Maker. 'Not much money, but at least I've no spots.'

SEVEN

It had never happened before. 'This has never happened before, not in all my long years of teaching.' Mother Cecilia tugged at the wide belt encircling her waist, allowed her bony fingers to linger on a leather strap that dangled next to the thick rosary rope. 'I came over from home with hope in my heart, Megan Duffy. That hope has stayed alive until this day.' Frosty eyes wandered over Phyllis, whose position in life had been reduced due to paralysis. Phyllis stared back, would not flinch. 'What have you to say for yourself?' the headmistress asked of the standing child. 'Poor Phyllis has no doubt been dragged into this by you.' She paused. 'Speak!'

'Well,' began Megan, her tongue stiff and dry with terror. 'I'm just not doing it, that's all.'

'And I'm not doing it, too,' echoed Phyllis.

The nun straightened her back and shoulders, looked as if a ramrod had thrust itself the length of her spine and into her skull. 'That is a mortal sin,' she cried, her voice echoing the length and breadth of the main corridor. A classroom door opened, closed again quickly. Mother Cecilia's teachers were not keen on meeting their headmistress in one of her darker moods.

'There is absolutely no choice in this matter. You will learn your catechism and your prayers. If you refuse to obey, then I shall administer the necessary punishment.'

Phyllis nodded. 'Aye. But if you hit her, you'll have to hit me and all. And I might not feel it, anyway. Depends where you belt me, I suppose.' The child drew breath, wondered how she'd found the courage to be so cheeky. It all stemmed from losing her mother and being in a wheelchair, she supposed. The worst had happened – how could anyone hurt her now?

Mother Cecilia coughed, seemed momentarily nonplussed.

Phyllis picked up her thread, carried on with the statement. 'It were my mam and it were my priest. Mrs Shipton says Father O'Riley might even get the sack because he put holy water on me mam's grave. So that's why me and her's not Catholics no more.' She jerked a thumb in Megan's direction. 'We're going to the Methodist church next Sunday. It's near our house and it's got no steps, so the wheelchair goes in easy. And they have a cup of tea and two plain biscuits each after the service in the back of the hall.' She swallowed, gathered courage. 'And nobody gets in trouble for not going to confession and all that, not at the Methodist church.'

The nun breathed. They could tell she was breathing hard because her chest moved up and down a lot, lifted the semi-circle of stiff, white material that sat beneath her chin. 'You cannot be Methodists. You are baptized Catholics.' Because of anger, the words were squeezed past gritted teeth. 'Methodists do not get to heaven. Only Catholics sit at God's right hand.'

From some barely accessible place, Megan latched on to a piece of bravery, translated it, dropped the words in a tone that seemed almost casual. 'Methodists don't have a cane. They don't strap folk and they don't pick lads up with their ears.'

The nun staggered back as if hit by a brick. With one hand, she groped for support, found it in the shape of the black babies' table. This square of polished wood had been placed halfway up the corridor. Children were expected to donate what little money they had to the support of an African infant. For sixpence, a baptismal name could be appended to one of the sweet little faces that lay on the table. Thus far, neither Megan nor Phyllis had managed to save sufficient to choose a name.

A few baby pictures floated to the ground, but Mother

Cecilia seemed not to notice their displacement. 'Punishment is a necessity,' she managed. 'We punish so that you might learn your way up Calvary and into God's arms.'

Phyllis put her head on one side. 'Calvary's in another country,' she said. No way would this nun hit her. She knew in her marrow, even in the too-young bones that had lost most feeling, that this horrible woman would not belt a child in a wheelchair. 'And I can't climb no hills any road, not like this.'

'The statement was metaphorical,' roared the black-clad woman. 'We all have our own Calvary. For you, the suffering has been in the loss of your parents and in your own illness. Only as a Catholic can you travel to heaven.'

Megan bit her lip. There was something a bit magic about nuns. It wasn't nice magic, not like a fairy with a wand and stardust, not like a great big Father Christmas squeezing down a thin chimney, but the sisters had a kind of power that was nothing to do with canes and leather belts. It was invisible, like God. But it was there. She was scared of the stains on her soul, frightened because she'd stopped going to confession, yet her anger was bigger than the fear. 'We want Father O'Riley back,' she mumbled.

'And if he doesn't return?' Sarcasm hung in the air like black thunder clouds.

'We're not coming to church no more,' said Megan. She stared at the headmistress for a long time, waited for something heavy to fall from heaven, an item that would wipe out Megan Duffy and all her sinful ways. When nothing happened, when even the remaining black babies stayed on their table, she took hold of the chair's handles and pushed her friend down the corridor.

'You've not heard the last of this,' shouted Mother Cecilia.

'We've not heard the last of this,' muttered Megan under bated breath. 'We'll be needing tin hats round at Deedee's tonight. Happen we shouldn't have done it, Phyllis. We could have learned the catechism and the prayers. We could have gone to mass and been secret Methodists.'

'Don't talk so daft.' Illness had not affected Phyllis's brain. She was bright enough to make a stand, even if her feet didn't work. And she was loyal enough to make this particular stand for her mam. She blinked away the tears, concentrated on being grateful and angry. The gratitude was for Megan and Deedee, and the anger was on its way to the priest's house. She pictured the dark emissary who would be beating a path to the presbytery at this very minute, black-shod feet stamping over the flags, sombre veil flapping in the breeze, that wide strap slap-slapping against invisible legs. Megan was right. There would be murder tonight.

'We'll not get Father O'Riley back,' said Megan. 'We'll still be stuck with him and his moods.' 'Him and his moods' was Father Kevin Marsh, an Englishman with bad breath and no humour. He was tall and fat with little red veins all over his face, a tracery of damaged tissue that advertised a fondness for whisky and rich foods. 'He's as much fun as a wet Sunday, Deedee says. Do you think Deedee'll understand, Phyllis?'

'No.'

Megan rounded a corner, steeled herself for the last hill. 'You're getting heavier every day, you are. I think we'll have to get a horse to pull you soon. I'll happen see if Magee's Brewery'll lend us one.' She paused, inhaled deeply, threw her weight into the job. 'She might understand.' There was no real hope in her tone.

'She won't. They never do. They just carry on going to church even though Father O'Riley was sacked.'

Megan puffed and panted. 'He wasn't sacked. He just left to go to meetings about it.'

'He left before he was chucked out, that's what Mrs Shipton says. And from what she's heard, Father O'Riley's refused to say sorry. If he said sorry and promised never to bless any more graves without asking, he could come back. Mrs Shipton says the answer's in his own hands and—'

'Mrs Shipton,' croaked Megan breathlessly. 'She knows

everything, does Mrs Shipton. Deedee says Mrs Shipton should rewrite the Bible and all the history books. Take no notice.' But Megan sensed that Mrs Shipton was right in this instance. Father O'Riley had disappeared, had left not even a puff of smoke in his wake. It was that magic again, another spell woven by women in black and by a man in fancy clothes who didn't answer letters. Benedict, he was called. He got carried about in a chair, too, even though he hadn't caught the infantile paralysis. 'Nearly there,' she groaned. And he had loads of money and jewels that could have been sold and used to feed the black babies in the corridor.

They entered number 6, looked for Deedee, called her name. 'She's not here,' said Megan when no answer came from upstairs. 'We'll have to manage.' She prepared what Deedee called the potty chair, lifted the wooden lid, grabbed Phyllis by the waist and swung her round.

'Thanks,' whispered Phyllis as she was lowered into a sitting position. Poor Megan and Deedee had to do so much for her. 'I'm like a great big baby,' she said. But at least she had arms, at least she could manage some things for herself. She bit down on her lip, concentrated on gratitude. 'Megan?'

'What?'

Phyllis struggled to contain her excitement. 'Get off me foot.'

Megan glanced down, saw that Phyllis's soft sandal was trapped beneath a shiny clog. She gulped, looked at her friend's bright eyes. 'Can you feel that?'

'I can. I can feel it, Megan.' Two great tears slid down her cheeks. The moment was made more poignant by the fact that the little girl did not laugh or sob. She simply sat and let the saline find its path down her pretty, careworn face. 'They said, Megan. They told me ages ago it might come back in fits and starts when I'd started doing other things. Doctor said I had to keep me mind off me legs. And I have done, specially today when we told old Cecil what we thought of her. We must have been right, Megan.

146

What we said, what we did – God's sticking up for us –
He's on our side. Happen God's a Methodist after all.'

Megan shivered as a cold thrill of elation touched her
spine. 'We've been sticking pins in you while you weren't
looking. See, when I'm on the floor tacking a seam,
Deedee gives me a nod and I scrape your leg with me
needle or a pin. You never notice, 'cos you're folding or
hemming. Deedee's always said we'd to wait for a sign.'
She swallowed, sniffed back the emotion. 'Phyllis, this is
the sign.' She wondered anew about God and Catholics.
On this very day, Megan Duffy had told Mother Cecilia to
bugger off. Well, she hadn't sworn, but she'd certainly
had her sixpenn'orth. Perhaps Phyllis was right, perhaps
God was a Methodist, then. Perhaps He was pleased about
the girls' plans to join another congregration where
biscuits and cups of tea were served and nobody got
shouted at.

'Get a pin,' begged Phyllis.

'I'll try summat else first.' She heaved Phyllis to her
feet, sorted out the undergarments, closed the commode's
lid, made sure that she took most of her friend's weight.
'Right.' She straightened, made a circle of her arms. 'Can
you feel the floor?'

'I can. Me right foot, it is. Leave go of me, Megan.'

'I daren't.'

'Let me put me hands on your shoulders.'

Cautiously, Megan released her hold, felt the other
child's weight as it began to depend on Megan's shoulders,
which had stiffened in preparation for this momentous
occasion. 'Let it work,' she prayed softly. 'Don't make her
fall.'

Phyllis balanced on her right leg, took a fraction of her
own burden, let out a cry when the knee began to buckle.
Sweat gathered on her brow, started to find a route to her
eyes. 'This is daft,' she muttered. 'I've got a foot and no
leg. How can I have a foot and no leg? Hang on.' She
concentrated, breathed heavily into Megan's ear, swayed
about. 'Pins and needles! I've got pins and needles all

down me right leg. Oh, I can feel it tingling hot and cold.' She dropped back on to the commode. 'I'm going to walk again. I am, I am!'

Mother Cecilia was forgotten for the time being. When Deedee came in from the shops, she sent Megan for her dad. 'Tell him to shut that shop, love. Tell him to get round here immediately if not sooner. And he can fetch them daft-looking contraptions he's been working on.'

The whole of Holly Street and most of Myrtle gathered on the pavement outside Deedee's house. Megan had yelled all over the place, had screamed at the top of her voice that Phyllis was going to get better. She sat on the step after Joe had gone in, told the congregation that Dad had made some irons for Phyllis's legs. 'They're stuck to shoes,' she told the crowd. 'Very special shoes, they are, in real kid leather.'

Phyllis Entwistle was carried out of number 6 by a clogger with a very broad smile. 'It's nobbut one leg,' he told the throng. 'But this little lass'll beat the infantile.' He set her against the wall, propped her with his hands. A corporate sigh of pleasure rose up to the heavens when Phyllis stood alone. Joe kept his palms outstretched in case she tumbled, but the little girl stood with triumph blazing from her eyes. She could feel the whole leg now, as if the blood had only just started flowing back through veins and arteries. The limb was weak, shrivelled and wasted from lack of movement, but it worked, it held her.

Handkerchieves and snot-rags made from shirt tails were passed around as people watched the miracle. 'Eeh, I've never seen nowt like this,' babbled Elsie Shipton. 'If Ida could have known, if she could have hung on . . .' Everyone's thoughts ran on lines similar to Elsie's, though most had the sense not to mention Ida's tragedy on this happier occasion.

'I've made an extension for that chair of yours,' said Joe. 'So you can wear your irons, Phyllis. We'll have you playing hopscotch afore this year's out.'

The crowd began to split, those at the back moving to

148

stand against house walls. Slowly, they made way for some new arrivals, a pair of dark-clad people who seemed to carve their own path as easily as Moses had parted the waves. Priest and nun stood like a couple of crows, feathers slightly ruffled by the unexpectedly large reception. 'A word, Mrs Duffy,' said the female.

Phyllis wobbled, fell into Joe's arms. 'Oh heck,' she muttered. 'I think we're in trouble, Mr Duffy.'

Joe held the child as if she were no heavier than a baby. He sympathized with Phyllis, had worried about her right from the start. His legs weren't up to much. He knew what it was to have pins that were next to useless. Yet he stood firm while Megan fetched the chair. When Phyllis was seated, Joe went into the house and found a stool on which the crippled child's iron-supported legs might rest. 'No bend, you see,' he said to no-one in particular. Then he stooped and spoke to the child. 'But I'll make a bend for you, lass. I'll get some nice, soft leather from Walker's tannery, make you a bit of a kneecap for that right leg. Happen slack springs at the back – or a hinge. I'll think on it, love. Aye, you're coming on a treat.' He stared at the priest. 'Can I help you, Father?'

The priest's mouth hung slack for a moment. 'It's Mother Cecilia who needs to speak,' he said lamely.

The headmistress glanced at a few faces in the crowd before addressing Deedee again. 'Are you in charge of these two girls?'

Deedee nodded. 'I am.'

'Then we must go into the house and pray, because you are rearing a pair of heathens.'

Megan caught her lower lip beneath her teeth, tasted blood, clung like an infant to Deedee's apron. This was awful. The whole street was out – there were even some people from other streets. And Mother Cecilia had come to make a scene. 'Go in, Deedee,' she whispered. 'Take them in the house.'

Doris Duffy looked the nun up and down. Some instinct dictated that she didn't want this woman in her house, didn't like the thought of a drink-soaked priest sitting in one of her chairs. 'Heathens?' she asked tightly.

'Inside,' commanded Mother Cecilia.

Deedee had always considered that her rope was longer than most. She had a temper, but she was also endowed with a great deal of patience. Even so, her tether was suddenly stretched to its limit. She was emotional about Phyllis, she told herself. She was tired after a long day's sewing and shopping, and she had been late coming home to see to Phyllis. Yet she chose not to heed her inner voice. 'I left school nigh on fifty years ago,' she answered. 'So don't be telling me what to do in me own street.'

A deathly hush hung over the houses. Megan shivered, imagined that the world had suddenly come to a halt. Even the smoke from chimneys was almost still, as if it awaited developments. Mother Cecilia's face had gone pale purple. 'They have declared today that they are Methodists,' snapped the nun.

Deedee nodded, though confusion showed in her eyes. 'Well, I've heard nowt about that. They've been brought up Catholic, same as I were, same as me mother and dad were.'

The priest came forward. 'Couldn't we go inside?' he begged.

Deedee breathed in the stench of stale whisky. This was a man of God. This was a man who heard confession and handed out penances, a man who blessed bread and wine each day, who handled the Body and Blood of Jesus Christ. And he was a rotten old drunk. 'We'll stop out here,' she said. 'Air's fresher in the street.'

The nun was running out of what little patience she had. 'Mrs Duffy—'

'You want to watch yourself,' advised Deedee. 'That's a right funny colour you've gone. Folk with that kind of colouring is prone to clots and bleeds in the brain. Any road, I've jobs to do.' She turned, stopped dead in her tracks when a thin hand grabbed her shoulder.

'Don't you care about their souls?'

'Take your hand off me!' The nimble woman spun round, her eyes meeting those of her enemy. Yes, she was an enemy, Deedee decided. There was nothing in the expression, no sensitivity, no humanity. 'Look, Mother whatever your name is—'

'Cecilia.' The tone was trimmed with ice.

'Right.' Deedee nodded, tapped a foot on the pavement. Because of temper, she'd even managed to forget the awful woman's name. She tried to put a bridle on her emotions, but the words spilled out of their own accord. 'Don't come throwing your weight about round here. We go to mass and communion of a Sunday, and the kiddies come to school.' She diverted her attention towards the priest. 'As for you, you've took the place of a sainted man who never touched a drop.'

The crowd was no longer silent. There were many Catholics in the garden streets, and none had ever dared to speak his mind. A man at the back chipped in, his voice barely loud enough to be heard. 'Cruel beggars, the lot of you.' The words reached the visitors, though. Cecilia was plainly disturbed, worried about the size of the mob. 'We shall return when things are quieter,' she announced.

Joe, who was still unclear about the situation, decided it was time to speak up. 'Get it said here and now, sister,' he advised. From the looks of his mother, it would be a cold day in hell before a clerical foot stepped over her door-mat.

Mother Cecilia, who did not appreciate being demoted to 'sister', fixed her pebbly gaze on Joe. 'These two girls have refused to learn catechism and creed,' she barked. 'They intend to go to the Methodist chapel in the future.'

Joe dropped his head, thought for a moment. 'Why?' he asked his daughter.

'Phyllis's mam.' Megan, emboldened by a man at the back who waved his encouragement, spat it all out very quickly. 'It can't be good to send Father O'Riley away. They're not good people, Dad. He put the holy water on Mrs Entwistle because it were a shame. She didn't know

151

what she were doing . . .' The child ran out of steam and courage, allowed her voice to die away.

Phyllis needed to support her good friend by chipping in where Megan had left off. 'Mother, I'm sorry we were rude. But it's funny, see, 'cos I never stood up when I were a Catholic. As soon as I started being a Methodist, I got one of my legs back.'

A woman pushed her way through and stood in front of Phyllis, her head held high as she addressed Mother Cecilia. 'You hit my twins, you did. And they're both dead now.'

Joe took a step forward, placed a hand on his wife's shoulder. 'Tess. Come on, lass.'

'No, I won't,' she snapped firmly. This was one of Tess Duffy's better days. She saw clearly, spoke clearly, had no pain except the one in her heart. 'I've my piece to say, but this isn't the place to start saying it.' She turned and faced the gathering. 'You might as well go home. There's no good will come of you stopping here. What we need is a bit of a meeting about how the school's being run.'

Joe decided to leave her to it. When Tess put her thinking cap on, she was a good organizer. The trouble was, she spent most of her time organizing how to have a son . . .

Tess was amazing even herself, because she seemed to feel so well, so powerful. Still, she wasn't going to start questioning the state of her mind and body, not while she felt so . . . vigorous. And she needed to direct her anger, because it was deep, too deep to be accessed for much of the time. But why should these bloody nuns and priests get away with half-killing children? She squared up to the intruders, placed her hands on her hips, held up her head. 'Time somebody spoke up,' she said, her tone soft. 'When this lot goes home, I'll happen talk then. Better still, I'll come down the presbytery, see you there.'

The priest backed off, worried about such an encounter. Mother Cecilia, who looked near to collapse, was leaning heavily on Father Marsh's arm. Bolts of pure fear shot through her body, causing limbs to weaken and cheeks to glow in a reddish-blueish shade that bore close relationship to magenta. It was the crowd that terrified her. Never had she been among so many people except in church. Would they turn nasty? Was she safe? 'Talk to her, Father,' she said to the priest. 'Explain why these children are misguided. This poor woman is upset, doesn't know what she's saying.'

The crowd broke again, was split by the emergence of Tommy Wagstaff. Tommy Wagstaff plainly meant business, because he was waving his knocking-up stick, an item that made his surname apt. 'He said that,' Tommy cried. 'Jesus on the cross. "Father, forgive them, for they know not what they do." He even forgave his own murderers.' He looked the headmistress up and down. 'Have you learned nowt? Have you not read the good book? Education's nowt to do with punishment. Neither's religion, come to think.'

'Nonsense,' she spat. 'Control is essential.'

Deedee nodded resignedly. The cavalry, in the form of a man who loved her, had arrived late and was in danger of changing the tone of the situation. Nothing was out of hand yet, but if daft Tommy started wagging his stick, murder might ensue. 'Shut up, Tommy,' she said. 'This is no business of yours.'

For once, Tommy ignored the girl of his dreams. 'Jesus would have forgive Ida Entwistle,' yelled Tommy. 'He opened heaven's doors for the bloody thief that hung next to him and no, I'm not apologizing for swearing. You make me sick, the lot of you. There were only ten commandments when Moses kicked off, but there's half a dozen more for us Catholics. Favourite's the one about contributing to the support of our pastors. So we give, and yon feller swills it down his gob every night.'

Tess smiled tightly. 'There's an answer. We've got the answer in our hands.' She stepped nearer to the clerics. 'We'll stop at home. Or we'll go to church in town. As for the kiddies, we'll send them to other schools. There's no need for us to show ourselves up like this,' she told the nun. 'As for you.' Her eyes swept up and down over the priest's bloated face and body. 'I'll see you another time, when there's no audience.'

The ensuing silence was deafening. The march of clogs in another street was plainly audible, the clip-clipping echo of some worker going home for his tea. No-one moved. Joe looked up at the sky, found it empty of birds. This was an uncomfortable moment. He cleared his throat, pressed a hand into Tess's shoulder. 'Come on, love. Let's be getting home to that baby.'

But Tess was dug in. 'I'm stopping here till this lot shifts itself home. I'm not leaving a priest and a nun stood here with all these folk. We are supposed to be charitable.' Her eyes swept over the crowd once more. 'Go home,' she pleaded again. 'You've teas to make and eat, family to see to. We'll have a meeting in our house about half-sixish, decide what to do about church and school.'

'Are you insane?' asked the nun.

Tess dropped her chin, lifted it again. 'If you're really interested, I have been a bit poorly just lately. You see, me twin boys got took, and a neighbour hanged herself. That's the woman Megan were talking about. She never had nothing, Ida Entwistle, not since her man gave his life for a country that didn't give a damn about him and his. Makes you think, eh? We're nobbut talking about things we've a right to talk about, Mother. We'll be doing no harm to nobody. After all, we don't want all our neighbours of other faiths to think we daren't even hold a meeting. That'd make Rome sound like a . . . a dictatorship.'

Joe patted his wife's shoulder, noticed how steady and calm she was. He was pleased in a way, because she was talking some kind of sense. Anger was pulling her out of the deep depression into which she had sunk again of late. He wasn't fooled, not completely. Tess still wanted a son. She accepted her daughters now, listened to them, took more of the household tasks from their shoulders. But deep down, Tess wanted boys. 'We'll go home now,' he insisted gently.

'Hang on a few minutes, Joe,' she begged. 'Let's make sure everybody's all right before we go.' She allowed herself to be moved to one side, but would not leave the scene.

Now that some of the front line had put itself aside, Mother Cecilia decided to concentrate on the minor ranks, though she kept one eye on Deedee as she spoke. 'There was no need for any of this,' she told the crowd. 'Obviously, none of you will go to this meeting of Mrs Duffy's. It would be a grievous sin to take a stance against the church . . .' She paused, saw Tommy Wagstaff's knocking-up stick swaying. 'Well, just follow your consciences.'

'At least we've got consciences,' snapped Deedee. 'And we look after our own. What's the point of sending money for the missions when we can hardly feed the kiddies here? Question of what they call priorities.'

There was no answer, could be no answer. The nun looked at Father Marsh, decided that he was useless. The most disturbing thing was the shame she felt, the guilt she was experiencing in the presence of these parents. It had always been the same in her order. Children were made to obey, were punished for disobedience. There was no room for negotiation, no time for explanation. She and the other nuns were there to educate the young. Above all, their task was to produce strong Catholics who would go forth and produce more Catholics. To allow for any change would be to court disaster. Yet she knew about the unkindnesses, the incidents that left children marked physically and mentally . . .

Deedee burst into these thoughts. 'Right, come on now, you lot. You're making this street look like Bolton football ground with a game starting. We can all talk later on. Go on, go quiet. No need for standing gawping, there's nowt to see.'

The crowd began to disperse, though a handful of

people stood on the opposite pavement, their comments about nuns and priests tailored to be audible by the two visitors.

The priest, afraid of a riot starting, grabbed Mother Cecilia's arm and walked her to the end of the street. Just before they turned left into Myrtle, a few cries reached their ears. They were being called bad buggers, child-beaters, drunks. Father Marsh, a weak man whose opinions were easily swayed, glanced covertly at his companion. 'There may be something in what they say,' he ventured. 'It could be that the school is a little hard on the younger ones.'

Mother Cecilia gritted her teeth. It was just like a man, she decided. Yes, only a man would be swayed by the weight of a mob. 'All schools are the same,' she snapped.

He walked a few paces, had difficulty keeping up with the thin, fleet-footed woman. 'Those with . . . lay staff are perhaps . . . perhaps a little less assiduous in the application of discipline.'

'We have lay teachers,' she replied smartly.

He gulped back a further response, swallowed it so that the awful woman would calm down and walk a little more slowly. His heart pounded in his ears, seemed to be knocking on the frail door that separated him from the afterlife. He was drinking himself to death and it showed. Every member of the congregation seemed to know that Father Marsh was a sot. Because his spirit was diminished, he chose not to remind the nun that all teachers at St Mary's were under her thumb, were too afraid to show compassion to their charges. It was a grim life, he decided. The greyness had forced him to seek solace at the bottom of a glass, yet he found little comfort in the lonely drinking sessions. Priesthood was hard, was made harder by the creature of granite who was forging ahead down the slope to St Mary's. Never mind. He would be home in a minute, and the whisky bottle was still half full.

It hadn't been half full, he decided around eight o'clock. It had been half empty, like his life. He roamed around the sepia-coloured room, had a quick word with the Sacred Heart, then a tender moment with Christ the Infant King. 'It's a mess,' he grumbled to his saviour. 'They liked him, you see. Fourteen came to confession on Wednesday, a miserable dozen plus two. I don't know what to say to them. What am I supposed to tell them when they ask after O'Riley? Do I give them the truth, do I let them know that he's running riot and accosting every bishop and cardinal under the sun? It's turned him, Lord. That poor woman being shoved into the ground like a common criminal has unhinged his mind.' He coughed, broke wind, smiled at the statue. 'Excuse me,' he muttered. 'But there's only the bottle now. Nothing else touches the pain.'

He settled by the fire, cast an eye over the pile of curling sandwiches that had been left by the housekeeper. She lived out now, had packed her bags and left the house shortly after Father O'Riley's dramatic exit. Her sister needed her, she said. Her sister was a strapping great woman who ran a market stall in town, a person who needed no-one. So there was another one living a lie. 'You're not on your own, Kevin,' he said to the mantelpiece. 'We all live a lie to some extent.'

He dozed, wondered in wakeful moments about the great untruth that was usually called life, tried to work out where the next bottle of Scotch would come from. Then the doorbell sounded. Like a terrified rabbit, he jumped up, righted the loosened dog-collar, ran a hand through tousled hair. It might be a death, a request for Extreme Unction. How many hosts had he blessed at the last benediction? Ah, there would be plenty to go round a grieving family, especially since a proportion of the congregation had already deserted St Mary's for St Thomas's.

It was not a death. Tess Duffy strode into the hall, thrust a document into his hand, muttered something about a strike. She left him where he was, proceeded without invitation into the living room. He followed, hoping against hope that his tongue would behave itself. Sometimes, it was uncooperative, particularly after a glass or two. He tasted it, made sure that the fur coat it wore for much of the time had been dissolved by tonight's whisky. The door proved a problem, swinging back on its hinges after he entered the room. He jumped, saved himself from falling, pushed the door home, looked at the woman who stood by his window. 'Mrs . . . er?'

'Duffy.' She stared at him, her face expressionless. 'We've done a petition to get Father O'Riley back,' she stated bluntly. 'It's nowt personal, only he were well thought of round here.'

'Yes. Quite.' She seemed to be swaying about gently, drifting like something under water. 'I'll send it on to the bishop.' Kevin Marsh hoped that O'Riley would come back. These people were unfriendly and judgemental. He wanted to go back to Cheshire, back to a bit of peace and an affluent flock that seemed not to notice when their priest was slightly off-centre. No, she wasn't swaying at all. His eyes were being troublesome again, because the Scotch had been raw and cheap. In Hale, the people had placed enough in the plate for their pastor to enjoy the occasional bottle of pure malt . . . 'Anything else, Mrs er . . . ?'

'Duffy.' She skewered him with her eyes, made him feel as if he were nailed to the oilcloth. 'Also, there's a load of us moving our children to St Thomas's. We're going round there Monday, see if we can get them fitted in. If there's enough of us, yon dragon'll likely get the sack.'

'I . . . er . . . understand how you must be feeling, Mrs . . . er . . . Mrs Duffy.' He straightened, congratulated himself for remembering her name so quickly. 'This is not the way to go about it and—'

'Don't be saying you know how I feel, Father Marsh. I've lost two lads and I've not been a good mother. It's as if I can only let boys in my heart.' She banged a closed fist against her chest. 'It's wrong, it's just me instincts, like.

158

But I can manage me brain even if I can't control me feelings. I'm doing the best I can for me daughters. See, I can save them from old Cecil and her cronies. She's worked her stint any road. Cecilia were teaching when I were a lass – I bet she's going on sixty-five now. I'm not having our Annie and Nellie coming home bent double after she's run riot with her strap. As for Megan – you know how she feels about Catholics. That's a mess we've got to clean up, isn't it? She wants to be a Methodist because they don't have canes and straps.'

He nodded rhythmically, processed the monologue, caught up after a few seconds. 'The Methodists haven't a school.'

'If they had, they wouldn't batter kiddies,' she insisted. 'We're making a stand, Father Marsh. And if you want to help us, if you want our children back at St Mary's, you'd be best doing less of that.' She waved a hand in the direction of his easy chair, where the empty bottle failed to hide behind a cushion. 'Addled, you'll be use to neither man nor beast,' she advised, her tone conversational. 'I'll say goodnight.' She swept past him and out of the house, leaving in her wake a feeling of disgust that was almost tangible.

He sank into the chair, pulled out the bottle, stared at it sadly. 'That's an end to our friendship,' he told the empty vessel. Without drink, he would be ill, more sick than he was on his present diet. He sighed, gazed into the flames. 'I should never have been ordained,' he whispered. 'I can't cope with all this trouble.'

As the flickering coals diminished, he suddenly became sober. No congregation. Oh, there would be some, he thought, those without children, those whose quarrel with Mother Cecilia had been bandaged by the passage of time. He assumed that a few young families might continue to attend, but the garden streets comprised about a fifth of the church's capacity.

He sighed, folded his hands across the mound of his stomach. There would be no more whisky. He grimaced,

159

remembered the last time he'd resorted to sherry and cheap wine. There was no choice but to go teetotal overnight. He needed to dry out and harden, because the dragon lady had to go. A hand reached for the bottle, some automatic pilot seeming to guide its course. But the bottle was as empty as the collection plates threatened to be. The priest closed his eyes, prayed for strength, prepared to set his mind to the organization of letters. Tomorrow, he must write to the order and to the bishop. He belched, muttered an apologetic amen, then dozed till dawn.

St Thomas's RC school was a battle zone. The corridor leading to Miss Shannon's office was narrow, made all the less adequate by Phyllis Entwistle's wheelchair. The child's legs, encased in leather and metal struts, stuck straight out in front of her on an extension made by Joe Duffy. Mothers lined the walls, their facial expressions an improbable cocktail of fear and hope.

'She'll not take us,' announced a thin woman with holes in her shawl. 'They'll all have to go back to St Mary's. This here strike is nobbut a waste of time.'

Tess stiffened, held on to Freda's hand. 'Oh no,' she said clearly. 'If they can't come here, mine'll go to the corporation school. They can still be Catholics. You don't need a good hiding every day to be a Catholic.'

The headmistress came out of her office. Kathleen Shannon was a huge woman in a long skirt, black boots and a white blouse with a stand-to-attention collar of starched lace. The buttons down the front of her chest were straining, as if her body were at war with its wrappings. When she inhaled, the cloth showed the strain, relaxing only when the gigantic chest emptied itself of air. She spoke to Tess. 'Are you the organizer of this fracas?'

Tess didn't know what a fracas was, but she owned up to being its perpetrator.

'Well, this is a mess,' said Miss Shannon. 'Where am I going to put all these children?'

Megan's hand tightened on a handle of the wheelchair.

This great big person looked worse than old Cecilia. She gulped some air, tried to stand firm. She was not going back to St Mary's. Neither was Phyllis.

'They want a change,' answered Tess. 'There's too many beatings at that school. We know kiddies need a bit of putting in their place, only we don't like them coming home with layers of skin missing.'

Kathleen Shannon assessed the ringleader. 'Mrs Duffy?' An eyebrow raised itself. 'Are you the one whose child is on the verge of converting to some kind of non-conformism?'

Tess didn't go in for big words, but she refused to be daunted. 'Yes,' she replied quickly. 'It's on account of Phyllis's mam, Ida Entwistle, who was a poor soul and—'

'Quite.' The second eyebrow joined its twin. 'Father Marsh has given me all the relevant information, thank you.' She cast a glance over the motley throng of shawled mothers and ill-dressed infants. 'I shall take these three.' She pointed to Megan, Phyllis and Freda. 'For the rest . . .' She counted, found eleven further children whose parents seemed to have joined the strike. 'The rest may wait here until the messenger from St Mary's arrives.'

Tess would not budge. 'Take one, take all,' she insisted. 'See yon lad in the corner? He lost a tooth when that old b— . . . when Mother Cecilia threw him in the corner. She told him to pray to the Sacred Heart, only the poor lad were scared and covered in blood. It were the base of the statue that cracked three teeth, and one snapped off at the root. We're talking about real pain here, you know, real pain and criminal damage to kiddies. So we want every child here shifting out of Mother Cecilia's reach, Miss Shannon.'

The headmistress stepped back a fraction. 'Follow me, Mrs Duffy,' she said. 'Leave Freda with her sister.'

Inside the office, the large woman inserted herself between desk and window, forced her corpulence into a space that was barely adequate. 'Sit, please.'

Tess lowered herself into what seemed to be a child's

chair, an item that placed her in a position that was far from advantageous. Was this another bully? she wondered.

As if reading the thought, Kathleen Shannon spoke. 'The usual chair has gone for repair, Mrs Duffy. Our caretaker used it to reach my window.' She smiled briefly, appearing to illuminate the whole room for a fraction of time. 'He went straight through the seat, I'm afraid. So he's in plaster of paris and the chair, too, has been hospitalized for a while.'

'Oh.' This woman probably had a sense of humour, then.

Two hands the size of shovels placed themselves palms down on the desk. 'I shall be plain,' said the owner of the ten thick digits. 'We shall take your daughters and the crippled child because we want no repeats of last week's performance. A young person should not be allowed to blackmail her elders and betters by threatening to turn to Methodism.' The corner of her mouth jerked, but she hung on to her composure. 'As for the rest – they will find some changes when they return to St Mary's.'

Tess's jaw hung for a second. 'There's only one change wanted,' she managed at last.

'Quite.'

Tess didn't know what to do or say. She waited for clarification, but none seemed forthcoming. 'Shall I say . . . what do I tell that lot out there?'

'Nothing.'

'But—'

'If we wait for a moment or two, all will become clear.'

Tess wriggled in the chair, felt like a five-year-old who needed the lavatory. 'They'll think we're favoured,' she said. 'With you taking Megan and Phyllis, they'll think—'

'We've no stairs.' Miss Shannon pointed to the upper floor. 'All the upper rooms are for seniors, so the child in the wheelchair will not need to be carried up and down from one classroom to another. When she reaches the age of eleven, the situation will be reviewed, because at that

162

point, she would go upstairs. At St Mary's, she would need to cope with stairs for Standard Two – next year, that is.'

'I see,' answered Tess. 'It'd be easier for her here.'

'Quite. Then, as Phyllis's friend, Megan will be allowed to attend St Thomas's with Freda, her sibling. It's the best compromise, I'm sure.'

Tess leaned on the chair's low back. Mother Cecilia had been sacked. This woman hadn't said the words, yet it was obvious that the dragon had been removed. 'Where's she gone?' she asked on the spur of the moment.

'Ireland. Back to the main convent. She's tired out, you see. Children are so wearing.'

'I know. I've five girls.' She swallowed. 'I had twin boys, only . . . they've gone.'

'Yes.'

There was something about Miss Shannon, Tess decided. You could tell her just about anything and she'd take it on the chin. 'I blamed Megan for a while. She were in charge when Albert were run over. Then Phyllis got took bad and I thought Megan had let our Harold catch germs. It were a shame.'

Miss Shannon nodded. 'It's so easy to judge a situation by initial appearances, isn't it? Megan seemed to be in charge, seemed to be responsible. But none of us can ever take the full blame or the full credit for life's vagaries.'

It would have been easier without the fancy words. 'How long have I to stop in here?'

The headmistress looked at her watch. It was a fob with a marcasite bow above the hanging face. 'Not long. Your older girls wish to continue at St Mary's, I take it?'

'Aye. They're eleven and ten, settled, I suppose. I told them they could come with us today, but they've friends at St Mary's. And it's just the mothers with younger ones who're here. Any road, if they're having a new headmistress, my big girls'll be pleased enough.'

The two women sat and listened to the announcement. 'Mother Cecilia will no longer be with us,' said a disembodied voice. 'Please return to St Mary's in a decorous fashion, no running in the streets.'

Tess looked at Kathleen Shannon. 'It were women's votes that made this happen,' she said softly. 'My house were full of mothers at the meeting last week.'

Miss Shannon tapped the edge of her desk. 'Some people don't deserve the franchise,' she murmured. 'While others make the best use. We live and learn, don't we?'

'We do that.' Tess nodded, pondered. 'There's one or two things wants changing a bit.'

The large face lit up. 'Mrs Duffy, we've not even started yet. Just wait another fifty years, we'll be running the country. After all, it's too much for men, isn't it?' She rose, pushed the desk forward to ease her passage. 'Come on, let's deal with these three children. Then we'll have a cup of tea and set the world to rights.'

Megan was round-eyed. 'Miss Devine were that nice we couldn't believe it – could we, Phyllis?'

'No.'

'You get stars on a piece of paper what's hung up next to the blackboard. There's everybody's name on it. Three stars means you get your name in the book. Book's on her desk, a big black thing with loads of pages. If your name's in the book twice in one day, you get five minutes extra at playtime. Three times, you can choose what you do in the afternoon. There's painting and drawing and cutting-out for them that gets three times in her book and—'

'And if you know your times tables, Miss Devine says you get an . . . automatic extension . . .' Phyllis struggled for words, excitement making her pink and earnest.

'Exclusion,' prompted Megan proudly. 'Exclusion from arithmetic. If you're exclusioned, you can play shop, weighing things and measuring pints of water that's supposed to be milk—'

'We played shop.' Phyllis's pride shone from her eyes. 'We know some times tables.'

Deedee could not believe what she was hearing. These two actually wanted to go to school, were counting the hours till bedtime. It was plain that some educationalists were folk of vision, then. Children learned best through play, took more in when they were happy. 'Eeh, I'm that pleased.' She hugged her girls in turn. 'Life's too short for folk to be miserable at school. Best years of your life, these are. Aye, you deserve a bit of pleasure.'

Phyllis heaved herself up from the chair, pressed her hands on to the tablecloth. With great effort, she managed to manoeuvre herself into a standing position. 'Three steps in the yard today,' she said. 'All the girls help me and so does Miss Devine.'

'And Miss Shannon,' added Megan. 'Miss Shannon gets you moving every morning after prayers.' She grinned at Deedee. 'Phyllis sits at a proper desk in a proper chair. If she can just get going with the other leg, she'll be able to go to the toilet on her own.'

Deedee watched the courage of Ida Entwistle's little lass, took in the expression on the face, the beads of sweat that gathered on brow and upper lip as she dragged the second limb into position. Any movement on the left side came from the hip, so Phyllis had to muster all her energy and determination to achieve this semblance of mobility. 'Can you still not feel it, love?'

Phyllis smiled broadly. 'It hurts,' she said. 'Round me knee. So it must be coming back if it's hurting.'

Megan tutted like an old woman. 'We were keeping that a secret, Phyllis Entwistle. You were just going to run in here one night and surprise Deedee.'

Doris Duffy sent up a silent prayer to St Thomas, told him that she, too, had been a doubter. It seemed right that these two kiddies should find refuge in a school named after this very human saint. When the girls were seated, she doled out the evening's work. Megan was attaching braid and tassels to curtains while Phyllis, whose skills were minimal, tacked and folded linings for the same set of drapes. Deedee herself was engaged in the mundane task

165

of saving hospital sheets by turning them sides-to-middle with a seam flat enough not to give discomfort to whichever poor soul must lie on the cheap cotton. 'That hospital contract's come through,' she said after snapping a thread between her teeth. 'We shall need to expand. You'll have to carry on sleeping in here, Phyllis, even when you get walking. Megan and me can squeeze into the little back bedroom, then I'll use the front upstairs for our factory. We've two women starting in the morning. And I'm buying a couple of treadles on the weekly.'

Megan gasped. 'Sewing machines? Are we a proper business, then, Deedee?'

'Aye. I'm calling us Fine Seams. Look.' She held up the mended sheet. 'I'd defy anybody to do a better job. We shall have cards printed with my name on, then a list of what we offer.' Yes, Joe would get his house, she thought. No way would she take money from her only son. 'It's time a woman showed that daft lot how to go about trading proper.' She sighed. A member of 'that daft lot' was pressing his nose to her window. 'See?' she remarked to no-one in particular. 'Men. They get everywhere, specially under your feet.'

After Deedee had brought him in from the back yard, Tommy Wagstaff twisted his cap in his hands, watched the kitten for a few minutes, smiled at the girls. 'How did you get on?' he asked.

Deedee tutted. 'Why you have to go hanging about in a person's yard is beyond me, Tommy Wagstaff. Can't you knock on the front door same as gradely folk?'

'No,' he answered smartly. 'I'm fed up with being chased off. So I'm using the servants' entrance.'

Megan and Phyllis told him all about the school, then Phyllis gave him a demonstration of her mobility. The cat, who was called Humbug on account of his stripes, swung from Deedee's sheet, was shooed away, leapt on to the dresser and squatted among Deedee's pots.

'That thing's a menace,' complained Deedee.

'I'll take him back,' offered the visitor.

Deedee's cheeks coloured. 'Leave him,' she snapped. 'He makes me laugh.'

Tommy pondered for a moment. 'I could make you laugh and all. I'm good at making folk laugh. Aren't I, Megan? Aren't I, Phyllis?'

The girls nodded in unison.

Deedee mustered her energies. 'You would make the saints laugh, Tommy Wagstaff.' It occurred to her, not for the first time, that this irritating man, too, was named after her favourite saint. 'Listen, you. I'm not wanting company of your sort. If I wanted a man, I'd advertise in a shop window. Go home, you're nobbut a nuisance.'

He pulled a wry face. 'I'm not giving up on you, Doris Appleyard-as-was. One of these days, you'll be needing me, and happen I'll not come running when you shout.'

Doris nodded. 'It'll be a cold day in the Sahara before I shout for you, mister. Shut that door on your way out.'

When her suitor had left, Deedee turned on the girls. 'Not one word out of either of you. The cheek of him, coming round while the two of you are here.'

Megan wore the most innocent of her many expressions. 'Does he come courting you while we're out, then?'

'No.' Deedee plonked the kitten in his box by the fire. 'And you keep your mouth shut and all,' she told the cat.

'It'd be nice if you married him,' said Megan, deliberately ignoring Phyllis's choking sounds. 'We could have a lot of cats if you married Mr Wagstaff.'

Deedee sniffed, turned down the corners of her mouth. 'Just you listen to me, the pair of you. Don't go encouraging him. From tomorrow, you'll have a bit of freedom, because there'll be less sewing for you to do. Use the time to get walking, Phyllis. As for you . . .' She addressed her granddaughter. 'As for you, less of the cheek and less of the matchmaking.'

Megan shrugged, threaded her needle and sang a few words from 'Early One Morning'.

'Never mind "oh don't deceive me",' cried Deedee. 'Finish your tassels and close your mouth before I sew it shut.' She folded the sheet, took another from the pile, eyed the kitten. 'He thinks he can get in here a bit at a time,' she mused quietly. 'First the cat, then himself in the best cap. It'll be the blinking knocking-up pole next.'

Megan and Phyllis said nothing, while the cat curled up and slept.

'I'd be mad to take him on,' said Deedee to herself. 'He's more of a humbug than this here blinking cat.'

Phyllis composed herself. 'People should be married,' she pronounced after a moment or two.

Doris fixed her lodger with a look of iron. 'Oh yes? And how did you manage to work that out, Phyllis Entwistle?'

'They take up less room,' replied the child. Her knee was hurting again and she was glad of the pain, because discomfort was a feeling, a sign of life. 'Mr Wagstaff has all of that house to himself, so one bedroom's empty. If he was married, a whole family could live at number nine.'

Deedee curled her lip. 'Both bedrooms is empty in yon queer fellow's house,' she snapped. 'He never goes to bed. Nobody could live with a man whose life is back to front and upside down.'

Megan attacked a new length of braid and tassels. 'Oh, never leave me,' she sang with feigned innocence.

'Megan?'

'What?'

Deedee stifled a chuckle. 'Shut up.'

EIGHT

She stood in the doorway, her eyes fixed to the scene. Bales were being heaved about on metal hooks in preparation for breaking at the back of the huge shed. The place reeked of human labour, raw cotton and oil. She did not look at her father, but she guessed that he was waiting for her to change her mind. 'Go now, Pop,' she said softly. 'I'll watch the carding later, then I'll come and visit you upstairs.' He had insisted that she learned the business from start to finish, from breaking to packing. 'You want to know what you're ordering and what you're selling,' he had told her. 'Are you sure about this?' he asked now.

'I'm sure.' He was as worried as Mother, she thought. Her female parent was concerned with how things were going to look to Evelyn Grimshaw with her round bath and gold-plated taps, while Sidney fretted about all the possible accidents that might befall his daughter. 'You want me to understand what goes on, don't you?' she asked. After all, Pop was the one who had set out to put her off by surrounding her with noises and smells. And although her heart seemed to be performing a rain dance, she was determined to make a success of this first day.

'Yes, but—'

'Then leave me to it.'

Sidney Althorpe swallowed all the other things he wanted to say. Agnes was carrying on like a grieving widow, while young Fliss, whose fear-filled eyes were as transparent as crystal, had her head bent like a stubborn horse. 'So be it.' He marched off towards the upper floors and the peace of his private office. There was going to be some sort of explosion at home, he thought. Agnes, for all her airs and graces, had been truly hurt on this occasion. She was terrified of poverty, and she believed that a fuller education would have provided insurance policies for her children in the event of the mills failing. He hummed under his breath, refused to consider the possibility of failure in the cotton trade. His wife was making the mistake of comparing a pair of well-established mills with the corner shop her father had lost. Bolton was cotton and cotton was Bolton. The mills would always be safe.

He sat at his desk, shuffled papers, wondered how his favourite girl was faring. For the time being, Fliss was probably better off here, in Althorpe Number One. It would certainly be more comfortable for her, especially since Agnes had started to ignore the poor girl. And that wouldn't last, he told himself firmly. Agnes was a good woman through and through – she would come round in time, once she'd recovered from Evelyn Grimshaw's reaction to the news. And that was another thing. They all mocked poor Evelyn, but she was another gentle soul.

He rose from his seat, walked round the massive desk, stared through a window, allowed his gaze to travel the length of Back Myrtle Street. Hovels, these houses were. From his present viewpoint, he could see a row of yards with tin baths hanging from nails on walls. The yards were so tiny, seemed to grow smaller as his eyes moved up to the horizon, a line brought closer by dense housing and the chimneys of other mills. 'Aye, we've done a lot for folk hereabouts,' he said aloud. 'We've taken their fields away and put them to work in dripping heat and muck.'

He lit a cigar, leaned back in the leather chair, tried not to feel guilty about being at the upper end of things. 'It's a chain,' he mumbled. 'Like the food chain. We're all links, but I suppose I'm the fastener.' They would have starved without the mills. Mass-production was the thing, everybody busy, each one of them gainfully employed. And he was a philanthropist, he told himself determinedly. He'd folk living rent-free all over the place, women with consumption, men with missing limbs, bronchitis, weak hearts. 'You do your best, Sid,' he muttered. 'Only don't go congratulating yourself, because we could all do more.'

On a whim, the master of the Althorpe mills threw on his coat and went for a wander. This was a sign that something was brewing in his brain, as he usually needed exercise to home in fully on a subject that had not quite reached the balcony seats in his busy, cluttered mind. He stood outside the mill gates, glanced up and down Ivy Street, looked at the size of his domain. The Althorpe empire was one of the few consisting of a double mill. Each factory had six floors and accommodated well in excess of 100,000 spindles. He'd been called an ambitious fool, but he'd survived while lesser mortals, afraid to borrow and speculate, had been left on the sidelines with crumbling, single-storey sheds that had barely outlived the birth of a new century.

'Hello, Mr Althorpe. Have they kicked you out of the works, then?'

Sidney swung round. 'Shouldn't you be getting some rest, Tommy Wagstaff?'

'Happen I should. But it's too nice a day to be stuck indoors. I've another motive, too. One of me cats has gone missing. He's a funny-looking thing with a bent tail and half an ear missing. Clarence, he's called. He comes over yon to Number Two, follows me in the night while I'm watching, so he's happen stuck somewhere inside. I'll look round here first, though.'

They walked up and down the street like old friends, no need for constant conversation. Sidney, in an effort to attract the feline nomad, clicked his tongue from time to time. Tommy, who was used to Clarence's selective deafness, shouted the cat's name every few seconds. 'He'll come home,' he said eventually. 'When his belly rumbles.'

Alone, Sidney stood in the middle of the cobbles and watched the sun as it danced on the Althorpe chimneys, its illumination made intermittent by the quick passage of broken cloud. The job was a good one, he thought. Built in 1902 and 1905, the massive piles of masonry had cost several thousand pounds and the lives of two labourers. Their families were provided for in modest cottages in the middle of town where they handled and sold Althorpe seconds on an open market stall.

He took a step back, ran his gaze over the twin structures. Their scale was immense, while the style was almost flamboyant, especially round the entrances where bright red bricks were ornamented by moulded birds. Sid had wanted to call this pair of factories The Magpie Mills, but Agnes had held him back. 'Scavengers, dear,' she had warned gently. 'You don't want to be thought of as a greedy bird, do you?'

Nevertheless, two large birds had been positioned round each entrance, though few would have deduced that these yellowish extravagances were meant to be magpies. The Althorpe architect was a Manchester man who had borrowed his choice of materials from Oldham's mills. So, in the midst of the 'Nori' or Accrington red brick sat magpies in an improbable shade of butterscotch.

What was he supposed to be thinking of? Should he be concentrating on Fliss, on getting her out of the mills? No, it was something else, something of great importance. His eyes moved of their own accord, caused the rest of him to follow their course and swivel on the spot.

It was the houses, then. He'd spent a fortune on embellishing two places of labour, yet the factory fodder who lived close by were enduring a poverty he had witnessed more than once. Sick beds. Yes, he remembered ailing children, cots brought downstairs, gaslight burning harshly on little flushed faces that begged for peace and darkness. The mantles were lit to keep away vermin, the cockroaches whose tendency to wander over bed covers was famous. Could he kill all those crawling creatures, could he rid the streets of vermin, filth, death?

'Not yet,' he said aloud. 'But you can pretty things up a bit, Sidney Althorpe.' More than that, an inner voice told him. Within ten years, he would reduce these streets to rubble and build them up again with electricity, little patches of garden, perhaps, decent sized rooms with bigger windows. 'That would be grand,' he announced quietly.

Tommy reappeared with a suddenness that was typical of him, a mongrel of a cat with a tattered ear and a question mark tail clutched under one arm. 'Talking to yourself, Mr Sidney? That's best road, that is, 'cos you might get a bit of sense back. He were in a midden down Blossom Place,' he added, his head nodding towards the cat. 'Must have followed me when I went to me other post round two o'clock this morning. Stinks of all sorts, he does.'

'Bins,' announced the boss. 'Free-standing dustbins with close-fitting lids.'

'Eh?' Tommy tried not to flinch when the tightly held cat ran an unsheathed claw across his neck.

'The middens want tidying up. If they were cleaned, they could be used for storing coal.'

Tommy frowned. 'Aye, but what about the outside door? Coal'd get pinched in two shakes. See, they've got to be open to the back street so's the town men can fill their cart. There's just a low brick wall on the insides so we can chuck the muck over, then there's a door to the—'

'I know. We can fill in the outer door and make a little shed – it'll be better than keeping coal under the stairs. Then if everyone has a bin with a lid, the place will be sweeter.' No wonder the yards and houses stank. Rotting refuse was all but connected to the living quarters. 'Go and get that sorted when you've time,' advised Sidney. 'If you want no sleep right this minute, run round these streets and tell me how many bins I need. Then I'll find a brickie and—'

'Cost you a bob or two, that will.'

'Nothing's free, Tommy Wagstaff. We pay with money and we pay with our lives. Health's more important than a few pounds in the bank. Get it sorted.'

'I will. After I've fed Clarence.'

Sidney reached out a wary hand, withdrew it when an

unfriendly paw shot forward, the claws bared in preparation for a strike. 'He's an ungrateful bugger, isn't he?'

Tommy dropped his head, eyed the cat. 'If we expect gratitude from them we help, we'd be best not bothering,' he said carefully, the double-meaning deliberately emphasized.

'I know. But sometimes, we do things just because they need doing.'

The nightwatchman looked directly into his employer's face. 'Aye, we do. Just as long as we know where we stand, eh?' He walked away to feed a creature that treated the world as a debtor, an alleycat whose pride precluded any sentiment for the humans who sustained it. 'They'll only mither,' he told Clarence. 'They'll only want summat else on top.' He placed a third piece of cod in the saucer. 'Like you, men always want more.'

Clarence, who had nothing to say in the matter, licked a paw, cleaned his whiskers, then set about the business of rearranging his battle-scarred fur.

Fliss was exhausted and she knew her cheeks were burning. This overheated sensation owed something to the damp swelter required in the production of cotton, though a proportion of her discomfort was a direct result of all the attention she was receiving. Alone at last, she sat on a stone step near a half-open double door, breathed in some oxygen that felt cool and fresh, laid her head against the wall of green-painted brick. It was her spots. They were probably laughing at her spots, saying how all the money in Althorpe's mills couldn't buy a decent complexion. So pretty, some of the young spinners were, so dainty and light of foot. Though the older ones had looked greyish, worn out.

She pulled herself together, continued with her plan of the mill. Even the paper on which she sketched seemed sweaty, but she was determined to do a thorough job. Her worth must be proved, so that spots and a biggish nose wouldn't matter. She would never get married, as no-one could possibly find her lovable, so she aimed to be unusual, even eccentric. People would say, 'That Miss Althorpe knows all there is to now about the cotton industry.' Bankers would queue up to lend money, men from London would travel hundreds of miles to learn about successful business and—

The door burst inward, had clearly been pushed too hard by someone who had judged it to be closed. 'Bloody hell,' cursed the new arrival as he projected himself towards the seated girl. 'I'll get me marching orders.' He righted himself, saw Fliss, muttered an apology.

'Don't worry about me,' she said. 'You missed me by a mile.'

'Missed the hooter as well, didn't I? My mother's been ill, you see, so I had a bad night. We don't live near my job – there's no knocker-up round our parts, not since Fred Cooperthwaite ran off with Jimmy Chadwick's wife. Who are you?'

'I'm Fliss.'

He looked at her with interest. 'Funny name, that.'

'Short for Felicity.'

He dropped down beside her, removed a flat cap, twirled it absently in hands positioned between his knees. 'Do you think if I walk in backwards at knocking-off time they'll think I've been there all day?'

'No.' He was nice, she decided. Ordinary, sort of brownish, but a decent person. 'What's wrong with your mother?'

He sighed. 'It's her insides, something with a queer-sounding name. She'll not get right this time.'

Even though there was space between them, Fliss imagined that she felt a shiver running through the young man's body. 'My . . . I mean Mr Althorpe will under-stand, Mr . . . er . . . ?'

'Greenwood. I'm Phil Greenwood and I'm eighteen and I'm learning the weaving, ready for my own loom. That's if they'll give me one now. I might just get my marching orders as soon as I show my face. How about you?'

She shrugged, didn't want to tell him the truth, didn't know why she needed to keep him in the dark for a while. 'Just visiting,' she managed. 'Waiting for somebody.'

'Right.' He stopped playing with his cap, turned and looked at her. 'I thought I'd not seen you here before. Do you live near? We could happen meet up some time, go for a walk and a bag of chips.' She looked smart, he thought. Smart and decent, as if she wanted more from life than a giggle and a chat. She was . . . classy, a bit different from most girls of his acquaintance. 'I've my mother to see to, but I can get out for an hour when one of the aunties comes for an evening.'

She bit her lip. 'I'm . . . only fourteen.'

The boy laughed. 'That's all right. I've not asked you to run away with me, have I? Look, I'd best go and face the foreman, but I'll ask you again when I see you, Fliss.'

She waited until he had reached the top of the flight. Without turning she cleared her throat and shouted, 'Tell them you've been showing Miss Felicity Althorpe how the rope race works.'

After a short pause, he found an answer. 'I don't know how it works, do I?'

'That doesn't matter. Just say it.'

The door slammed. Fliss Althorpe suddenly felt chilled and lonely. It was nothing to do with the sweat cooling on her body. It was because he'd liked her, he'd talked to her as if she had a decent complexion. He seemed nice and gentle, not rough at all. Phil Greenwood said 'something' instead of 'summat', and his vowels, though flatter than hers, had not been pressed as flat as Monday's linen.

But how could any man find her attractive? Now that the last of childhood's plumpness had gone, she was almost puny, with limbs that didn't always obey the commands of her brain. She was ugly, stupid, too stupid to stand up to those girls at the academy. How would she cope here? How could she manage among people who were famed for speaking their minds? She was strong in her head, she supposed, was determined to have a go at the

176

job, but what about her stomach? How would she conduct herself if somebody upset her? Was she going to spend the rest of her life heaving in a bathroom each time anyone gave her a dirty look? Still, she'd managed today, hadn't she? People had stared and wondered, but her stomach had remained calm and well-behaved.

A hand lifted itself, investigated the side of her face that had been nearest to him, found that there were blemishes on both sides of her hated nose. 'Perhaps I shan't need to be peculiar after all,' she whispered. Of course, Mother would consider that Phil Greenwood didn't count, that he was only a weaver, from a different and lower level of the scheme of things. But Fliss remembered the tanned skin, the light brown hair, imagined that his eyes, too, had been a palish brown, soft and warm. And Mother was manageable, because she was just a frightened lady who remembered times of want. Fliss almost laughed out loud, because she had almost married herself to a man she had spoken to for about two minutes.

Still, she would hedge her bets. Even when the spots cleared, she would be left with the nose. If she did well in business, then her accomplishment might provide a position into which she could fall if no-one married her. With a hand that trembled with hope, she drew a picture of Phil Greenwood, tore it up, returned to floor plans and spinning bays.

Sid leaned back in the large chair, allowed his slight paunch to relax as far as it could within the restraints of a tailor-made waistcoat. Fliss looked dishevelled and as pale as she did after one of her vomiting episodes. If it hadn't been for those bouts of sickness, perhaps he wouldn't have given in so easily, then Agnes could have had her own way and life at home might have been more comfortable . . .
'Have you been sick again?'
'No, Pop.'
He nodded, waved a hand towards the notebook. 'What's that? Are you starting to write your memoirs?'

She grinned, gave him the benefit of dimples that had become shallower of late. Fliss had been a bonny baby, full-fleshed and brimming with laughter. He sighed, assumed what he hoped was a businesslike expression. 'How many boilers, then?'

'Ten.'

'Right.' He picked up a pen, doodled on a green blotter. 'Not run-of-the-mill boilers, though they do run a mill, eh?'

'Superheaters.' Pleased with herself, she perched on the edge of the desk. 'Twice-heated, twice as efficient.' Fliss dropped her head, determined not to laugh at her father's amazement. 'Ordinary steam passes through pipes and gets reheated by . . .' She scrambled a few pages, found the words. 'By extra flues. The engines are cross-compound and powered by steam. The man down below says there's a transformer house being built so that you can make more electricity. Well, something like that, I think.'

Taken aback by her efficiency, Sid dropped his pen, covered the movement by clicking his tongue. 'You've been busy, then.'

'Yes.' She showed him her drawings. 'There's the main block, engine house, rope race, offices, hoists . . . I think that's supposed to be a dust flue, but my writing went strange in the dark.'

Sidney Althorpe suddenly felt warm. He rose, removed his jacket, stood at the desk with both thumbs hooked into his waistcoat. 'What's the most important thing in a mill, Fliss?'

She looked through him, narrowed her eyes. 'The people, I suppose. Without them, the machines would be no good.'

'Follow that thought,' he said quickly. 'Hold on to it while I get Maggie to make a pot of tea.'

When Sid returned with two steaming mugs, he continued to lecture on the subject of priorities. 'Remember that success brings responsibility. Remember Islington. Do you know about Islington, Fliss?'

She shook her head.

'I've never found out whether it was a cost-cutting matter, or whether it was just a case of poor design, but twenty-one people perished when the floor beams gave way, Fliss. Three floors that machinery went through. Can you imagine how those families must have felt? It's folk first, cotton second, money third and last. And a happy workforce is a productive one.'

'Yes, Pop.'

He eyed her quizzically. 'Don't be agreeing for the sake of it, love. If you're intending coming in with me, I shall want you on the welfare side for some of the time. You can have your own little office where people can come with their problems. Mind, you'll need to be a good five years older before we let you loose on that part of things. So what do you think of your old dad's mills, then?'

Fliss looked down at her notebook. 'Hot and noisy, that's the first impression. But the workers seem happy, especially in the weaving sheds.' She blushed, cleared her throat. 'There was a man who came late, because his mother's ill and—'

'Phil Greenwood. Tall lad, brown hair, a good weaver. He's a head filled to bursting with brains, has Phil, but he got no chance after his father died. His dad was called Phil, too. One of the best master weavers I've ever met. Mrs Greenwood's plagued with stomach problems, can't seem to pull round.'

'She's dying, Pop.'

'I see.' He picked up a small, black-bound book, made a note. 'I'll go round tonight, see what's to be done.' Bessie Greenwood had been dying for ages, but he would visit all the same, because folk like the Greenwood men were few and far between.

Fliss looked at her father with new eyes. There were hundreds of workers in this mill – hundreds more at Number Two – yet Sidney Althorpe could pinpoint a man whose lateness was caused by family illness. 'Do you know them all?'

'Yes. Some better than others, of course. The sick and the poor are the ones to watch. There's a lot of pride, you see. And we must make sure that pride doesn't stop bread and milk reaching a child's empty belly.'

She was beginning to realize the size of the job she proposed to take on. There were acres of rooms, dozens of mules and looms, a million tasks in every day. It threatened to take away her breath, but she hung on, took a draught of oxygen. 'Are all the mills like your two?'

'No,' he answered, his face grave. 'Most are even worse, many are hell-holes where nobody gives a damn. I could be a very rich man, love. I could say "bugger the workers" – excuse my language – but you reap what you sow. There's many a mill round here with no welfare facilities, no sick-bay, not even a bandage. Yes, it's nearly 1920, yet some so-called bosses are riding to hell on the backs of their workforce. Not me, Fliss, not us. The poor sweaty lot downstairs may not show their gratitude, but they're queuing up for jobs here just like they do at Ainsworth's. That means we and the Ainsworths get the best.'

'I'll remember that, Pop.'

He awarded her a smile. 'Yes, I think you will.' It wasn't such a bad day after all. Perhaps his 'little lass' had found her proper niche in life. Well, he might just as well show her another important aspect of mill management. She needed to know about the local baker, who made succulent pasties and fresh sandwiches for those who could afford them. 'Come on,' he said. 'We'll go and get a pie from Pickavance's. Then you can show me round and tell me how my own place works.'

Megan and Phyllis were full of it, bursting with news every time they came home from school. 'She says all women will get the vote in ten years, Deedee. That means picking them men in London that decide everything. She says it's politi . . . political—'

'Cally,' said Phyllis. 'Pole-it-i-cally—'

'Unfair,' finished Megan, her cheeks aglow. 'It's wrong

for less than half the people to be able to choose what happens. Miss Devine tells us things, as if we're real grown-up people. Then we had sums, only it were like a game. Them what got the sums right stood on one leg and hopped about helping them what got them wrong. If somebody put their other foot down, Phyllis banged on her desk and we had to sing God Save the King.'

Deedee wasn't sure she approved of such an unseemly way of learning the national anthem, but she liked the cut of Eileen Devine's gib. The teacher had turned lessons into a game, something to be anticipated, not dreaded. Yet the same woman had the knack of making her students feel important, almost adult. 'Did you get yours right, Megan?'

''Course she did,' answered Phyllis. 'But she's a worse hopper than I am. They don't let me hop, not yet.'

Deedee studied Phyllis's fresher face and straighter gait. 'Still no better, yon left leg?'

The girl grimaced, ready as ever to mock herself. 'You know what the doctors all said, Deedee. This is happen as good as it's going to get. But I can walk, that's the main thing.' With the help of Joe's irons and straps, which had been adjusted by the clogger under Dr Walsh's guidance, Phyllis was able to get about by taking small steps. But the left leg gave her pain sometimes, so she relegated herself back to the wheelchair when life got too uncomfortable. 'How's the factory?'

Deedee pulled a face, walked to the bottom of the stairs, returned after a few seconds. 'They're still sewing. I think they're talking to one another now, but you could have cut the air with a knife yesterday. Bertha Strong walks in with her own machine and that daft lad of hers. You'd have thought they were fetching the Crown Jewels past me doorstep. "Be careful," she kept saying to him. "That's a family heirloom," she says. And Minnie Hattersley's sat there in the bedroom with a face like a stopped clock. "I'm not working with her," she says.'

Megan sat down, her eyes fixed to Deedee's face, as

eager as ever to hear one of her grandmother's anecdotes. 'Why weren't they friends?' she asked guilessly.

'Megan Duffy,' laughed Deedee. 'They've never spoke since Adam were a lad and well you know it. It were over the credit.' She lowered herself into the chair opposite Megan's while Phyllis settled herself in what she called her pram. 'See, Singer started all this credit business, so folk here and in America could pay for the machines out of what they earned out of finished garments.'

'And Bertha Strong were a credit agent,' added Megan.

'Who's telling this tale?' asked Deedee. 'Minnie Hattersley gets herself a Singer way back – ooh, near twenty year since – just before the queen died. Well, she couldn't sew for toffee. So she earned nowt and Bertha Strong repossessed the machine. It were nearing pistols at dawn down Blossom Place. There were them as talked to Bertha and them as talked to Minnie. It got like cowboys and Indians – they even used different shops. And here I am stuck with the pair of them.'

Megan got up, sauntered to the bottom of the stairs, listened to the whirr of treadle-driven wheels. 'How did she learn with no machine?' she whispered.

'I taught her and well you know it, Megan. She used to come to my house under cover of darkness for a whole winter. Then, after my machine got broke, she took a job in Crompton's tailors, worked on one of their machines. I bet it were her as finished my owld Singer off, but I never said nowt. Only she still blames Bertha for taking that other Singer off her.'

Megan laughed, covered the sound with both hands. 'They'll both be trying to be better than one another. So they'll work fast and make loads of clothes, then we'll all be rich.'

Deedee smiled. 'You didn't come down in the last shower, did you? Brains like yours'll have you in and out of mischief till doomsday, our Megan. Speaking of brains – show me that belt again.'

The seven-year-old skipped merrily to Phyllis's bed,

pulled out a box of scraps. 'They're easy, them machines,' she said. 'But I didn't use Mrs Strong's—'

'Better not,' said Doris quickly. 'She'd have you in front of a magistrate before you could say "knife". If you're going to practise, use one of my Singers.' Determinedly, she wiped a worried frown from her brow. She'd two machines upstairs, both on credit, one for herself and the other for Minnie Hattersley. Happen she shouldn't have allowed herself a new one . . . What if the gentry didn't come? What if nobody answered her advert in the paper, 'SEAMSTRESSES AND DRESSMAKERS, COMPETITIVE PRICES, FREE FITTINGS. REPAIR SERVICE FOR ALL HOUSEHOLD LINENS'? Oh heck. But her eyes brightened with interest when the child lifted her creation from the box. 'My,' she breathed. 'If this is what you can do at seven, what—?'

'Eight next time.' Megan liked to make sure that people understood and appreciated her true status. 'It'd be better all one colour, though. But that leather needle goes straight through, never sticks.' She held up the item, allowed it to twist in the air. 'It were in a book, a magazine, only the ones in the drawings were made of cloth. You just make three thin tubes of leather, then plait them. And I put a fringe on the ends, see? If the leather's soft, it'll tie easy like cotton. And I could use cardboard and make proper belts too. Me dad can give me all the leftovers.'

Phyllis reached out and touched the belt. 'That's lovely, Megan.'

'You have it.' Megan loved Phyllis, would have given her just about anything. But she really wanted Phyllis to have proper legs so that they could run and play together again. She covered her emotions by prattling on. 'Me dad's made a gun, Deedee.'

Doris Duffy eyed her granddaughter quizzically. She had learned over the years to allow Megan's balder statements to collect a little embroidery. 'And?'

The child laughed. 'Not a gun like in the pictures.'

'Go on,' begged Phyllis.

'It shoots brass tacks,' said Megan when her laughter had died. 'Little ones for clogs. He's going to make a bigger one, see if he can do me mam's dining chairs in leather. They'll be posh at number thirteen with proper leather seats.'

Deedee sat back, her head nodding rhythmically. Since she had learned to walk, Megan had loved the feel of hide, the smell of it. She'd even been to Walker's Tannery with Joe, had stood there among scents that would scald the nose off a grown man, yet her interest in leather had stood the test. 'You'll work at Walker's,' she prophesied. 'I've always known you'd finish up in the tannery.'

Megan's eyebrows shot upward, almost disappearing into the heavy, dark fringe. 'I won't,' she answered. 'No, I'll not get the stuff ready. But I want to make things with it. Gloves and belts and seats for chairs. Purses and bags and—'

'What about saddles?' asked Phyllis.

Megan. serious now, shook her head slowly. 'No, that's too hard. Things for wearing and things for houses. That's what I'll make.' She placed a hand on her stomach. 'Is there anything to eat, Deedee?'

'Back to normal,' grumbled Deedee, though her tone was gentle. At least they were eating, at least they were healthy. Phyllis needed building up, so she could have two eggs. Doris stood up, smoothed her pinny, glanced at the clock. 'Megan, find yon cat. That daft Tommy Wagstaff's coming for his tea.' She turned glowing cheeks towards the sink. 'He's been down the fishmarket, went late to get bargains and he's fetching us whatever he's managed to lay hands on. For the cat, not for us. First thing he'll ask after is the flaming cat.' She turned the tap. 'Not a word, Megan Duffy.'

'I wasn't going to say anything, was I, Phyllis?'

'No, she wasn't going to say anything.'

Megan winked at Phyllis. 'I know a place where they make frocks, wedding dresses, too. They put an advert in the *Bolton Evening News*, I think they do free fittings.'

Doris swivelled, a large spoon in her hand. 'Shut up, before I clock you with me ladle. I've already told you – not that it's any business of yours – Tommy Wagstaff's coming for tea because he's fetching that fish he gets cheap on the market. Least I can do is give him a butty and a brew.'

'Yes, Deedee,' chorused the girls.

'And anyway, while he's here, I know where he is. If I keep an eye on him, he'll not keep popping up all over the place.'

'Yes, Deedee.'

'And I'm not forced to account for meself to you two or to anyone else, for that matter.'

'No, Deedee.'

Doris Duffy rattled pots and pans, waited for her face to cool. He was a good man. A lot of good men were fools, and a lot of fools were good people. His heart was in the right place, that was the main thing. She was thinking about marrying him. Thinking, no more than that . . .

His head was aching and his legs felt as if even more shrapnel had managed to invade bone and tissue. He'd been on his feet all day stretching and cutting leather, keeping an eye on the lad who'd taken over the making of soles. And even now, he was getting no rest. 'Tess,' he moaned. 'I'm worn out, lass.'

'We're married,' she whispered. 'There's nowt wrong with what we're doing.'

He stared up at the ceiling, tried to avoid catching a glimpse of the white face that hovered over him. The light was meagre but, when he looked at her, he could still make out the set of her jaw, the small, frantic movements of her eyes. She had become insatiable of late, had insisted on lovemaking every night, even while Little Hilda was screaming in her cot. Young Freda had come into the bedroom one night, had voiced her concern about the neglected baby. Freda was only five, so it was far too early for her to start wondering about folk bouncing up and down in beds.

'Tess, stop carrying on like this,' he begged. Other men would laugh at him if they knew, he thought. Most had to beg for favours, had to wait for Saturday night, needed to buy small gifts for wives whose interest in the physical side of marriage was intermittent. But they weren't being used as studs, were they?

'Come on, Joe,' she urged, her tone bordering on desperation.

He eased her away, placed her on her own pillow. 'Tess, this is no good,' he said softly. 'It's nowt to do with love, and well you know it.' She was worrying him halfway to death. Gone was the Tess who had determined to alter the course of her daughters' lives. All she wanted was another pregnancy. Sometimes, he wondered whether she might be as crackers as poor Ida must have been when she hanged herself . . .

She made a noise that was half sob, half cough. 'Remember when you've wanted to and I haven't? Remember how I always gave in because I'm your wife?'

Joe sat up, leaned against the bed-head. 'Look, you're the one who goes on about too many children. You're the one who ran to Old Mother Hubbard for advice about sponges and vinegar. What the heck's changed your mind?' He knew the answer, though he needed her to be honest. Old Mother Hubbard, whose real name was Nancy Unsworth, had been consulted more than once by Tess Duffy. 'You wanted no more,' he added.

'Well, I do now. I've changed me mind.'

Joe rose from the bed, dragged on the old army greatcoat that served as footwarmer on cold nights, as dressing gown when he needed to go down the yard. 'I think I'll make some cocoa. Shall I fetch you a cup?'

'No. I want a husband, not a hot drink.'

Downstairs, he coaxed the fire to life, dropped the grill across the coals, warmed milk in an old pan. He had married a shy girl, a youngster whose early encounters with sex had been difficult. It had taken three – no – four nights of gentle persuasion before the marriage had been consummated. As he blended cocoa and cold milk to a sludge in the bottom of a cup, he thought back to the first couple of years, remembered days when she could hardly look at him, when blushes had stained her cheeks and brightened her eyes. He coughed, swallowed a lump of regret. She had loved him, had gone out of her way to please him, to cook special meals on a low income, to keep herself pretty in washed-out and shabby dresses. For the man in her life, Tess had tried so hard.

Joe sat at the table, cast an eye over the local paper. A woman from Vernon Street had done herself in by drinking a cocktail of rat poison and Lanry bleach. The cocoa seared his throat, made him gag as he imagined how it must have felt to die like that, with the system burnt by noxious fluids. He tried to push the paper away, but he couldn't quite manage it, so he walked about the room for awhile, blew into the cup, sipped the drink.

But some undeniable force made him return to his seat, and his eyes devoured the written word, loitered among the columns devoted to the latest suicide. '*Mrs Holmes was charged with kidnapping in 1917, though her sentence was minimal in view of the fact that she was grieving for a dead child. She was found guilty in that year of taking a baby from its perambulator in Deansgate while the child's mother was inside a butcher's shop. Mrs Holmes, whose husband was killed in the Great War, had no other children. John, who was her only son, died of inflammation of the brain after a mystery illness, possibly a strain of influenza. She is mourned by her sisters and brothers.*'

Joe Duffy finished his cocoa. The death of a child could do strange things to a woman. After all, it was the female who incubated the baby, who felt it grow and kick, who endured the pain of giving life to a new human being. Tess was off her head, but only a little bit. If he didn't humour her, she might go off her rocker completely, might dash away in search of somebody else's boy-child, might steal it, get put away, get hold of bleach, poison, a rope.

'I want another baby, Joe.' She stood behind him, a hand on his shoulder.

'I feel like a horse put to service a mare,' he told her without moving his head. 'And I know what it's all about, love. When we had Albert and Harold, you wanted no more kiddies. But with only girls, you want to try again.' The pain in his head suddenly raged, pounded at the front of his mind. 'We could go on forever having girls. What would you do if we finished up with ten lasses and no lads?'

'I'll take me chances,' she replied softly.

At last, he faced her, screwing up his eyes against the glow of an overhead mantle. 'I don't want any more, Tess. We need to get out of here and find a new start, a decent place—'

'No. We're stopping here.'

He grasped her hands, held them firmly. 'We'd be best off opening up that front bedroom for Annie and Nellie. It's no good having the four of them stuck like that in two double beds and no space to walk about.'

'Three,' she said. 'There's only three now.'

He nodded. 'Aye, since Megan went. And you drove her off, didn't you? Blaming her like that for the accident and for Harold's illness.' Was she fit to be a mother? he wondered fleetingly. The answer came to him just as quickly. No. Tess would be all right if and when she had a son, though it was likely that she would treat all her female children distantly, coldly, fairly. 'You made sure she copped it just like you did when your brother died.'

She bit her lip. 'I know. But me and Megan's put all that behind us now—'

'As long as she keeps her distance.' He felt like biting out his tongue for sounding so sharp. The last thing he wanted was to drive Tess toward a pulley line or a bottle . . . 'Tess, we've enough to feed. Folk are buying a lot of shoes instead of clogs these days.'

She pondered for a moment. 'Where there's mills and pits, there'll always be clogs.'

Joe decided to return to the subject of that empty room. 'No use keeping it as a shrine, you know.' All the lads' clothes were folded on the bed, while their bits and pieces of toys and games had been laid out in a line beneath the window. 'We should let the big girls go in there.'

She wandered away, stood at the curtained window, one hand at her throat, the other pressed against a belly that felt empty and starved. 'That room's for my son,' she said softly. 'It's done in blue distemper and the girls' room's done in peach.'

He cleared a throat that seemed clogged by milk and sugar. 'Lasses can lie in a blue room, love. And we're not so poor that we can't run to a tin of paint.'

'Humour me for now, lad. You don't know what I'm going through.' She turned, moved her hands so that they made a knot near her heart. 'He had spots, just a few. Not as many as me, so we thought there were nowt up with him. He were dark, our Kieran, like me mam and like our Megan.' She gulped, looked through and past him. 'A baby, he were. She said it were my fault, said I shouldn't have gone near him. I know she were in the wrong, Joe, just the same as I've been wrong with our Megan. But it's . . . it's in me, inside in a place I can't touch. I've told meself that I'm unreasonable, only I can't argue with feelings.'

He nodded. 'So you want to keep trying for a lad, eh? Don't you think I've noticed how hard a birthing is for you? Don't you know what I go through, how I blame meself for getting you pregnant in the first place? Tess, you might have three or four more babies, all girls, or you could have a boy and not live to see him.'

'I know.' She walked to the door. 'I'm going back up. Are you coming?'

He shook his head.

'It's all right, I'll leave you alone.' A rim of sarcasm

clung to the words. 'You needn't fear me, Joe Duffy.' She left the room, clomped slowly up the stairs.

Joe Duffy, clogger, husband and father, pressed five knuckles against each eye, rubbed hard to thwart the threat of tears. There were times when there seemed no sense to life. How the heck was he going to manage Tess? He felt sick, old and tired. When the bedsprings creaked, he pulled the army coat across his shoulders and walked through the back door. There was one man who wouldn't laugh at him, and Joe needed to lighten the burden that clung to his cold soul.

'Two kippers, she give me, with bread and butter and three cups of tea.' He stirred sugar into the blue-rimmed mug, banged it down in front of Joe. The man was doing a lot of walking about in the night, looked as if he could do with a friendly ear. But for now, Tommy Wagstaff observed the niceties. 'Two Marie biscuits, son. One for thee and one for me. Dip it if you want.'

Joe dipped, chewed absently.

'I might be in with a chance, eh?'

'You what?'

'Your mam. She cooked me a pair of kippers and give me a scone with strawberry jam. The girls thought it were all a big joke, kept nudging one another and giggling. And Doris had a new pinny on – not a made one – a bought one – it still had the price-tag stuck to the pocket. Now, a man's got to feel encouraged when a woman wears a new pinny.'

'Aye.'

Tommy swallowed the last dregs of tea, chewed on a few leaves, picked some off his front teeth. 'Do you think I'm too old for it, Joe?'

Joe shook his head. 'Nay, it's never too late. Mind, I didn't think she'd take you on, but you can't tell with women, 'cos they change their minds every five minutes.'

'But not their pinnies.'

'No, not their pinnies.'

'Except on special occasions.' Tommy leaned back, twanged his new braces. 'So I've got your blessing, then?'

'Good luck to you,' replied Joe. 'At least me mam's past child-bearing.'

Tommy waited, studied the greyish face of his prospective son-in-law. Mind, she hadn't said yes yet . . . The lad looked weary, worn out to the bones. 'Trouble at home, then?'

Joe shrugged. 'She wants another lad. It's like living with a stranger, Tommy. I mean, she went through a good phase, started doing more and leaving less jobs to the girls. I even thought she were getting to know them and love them. Only now, she's got this wild look in her eyes, as if she's losing her mind. I don't think she's crazy, only she . . . well . . . she's wanting to try all the time, thinks of nowt else. I'm bloody worn out.'

Tommy didn't find this funny. He felt flattered, realized that a grown man could talk to very few people about this kind of stuff. 'So you're having to be a bit of a stallion, eh?'

Joe tried to grin, failed. 'I suppose I know how a woman feels when the chap's at her all the time. Only the boot's on another foot this time. Clog, I should say, not boot.' He glanced down at his carpet slippers. 'Not even clogs, eh, Tommy?'

The older man wiped his brow with a handkerchief that was shockingly clean. 'I'm not right well up on such things with never being wed, but it seems wrong to me that one person should use another just to get what he or she wants. Far as I can work out, it's usually the woman what does all the complaining, because most men aren't after babies when it comes to manking about. I suppose you get a bit mad when she wants you just to get a baby.'

Joe dropped his chin. 'Aye, that's the truth of it. See, I'm worried in case she starts with depression, Tom. But she's gone strange, as if the only thing that matters is getting a son.'

'Do you love her, lad?'

'Oh aye,' answered Joe immediately. 'She's been the only girl for me ever since I first met her at school. We've had a good marriage. Even when she treated the lads different, things were all right. I thought she loved me, you see. But now, I'm wondering whether she just wants me till she gets her son.'

Tommy sighed, placed a hand on his companion's arm. 'Does it matter? Does it really make any difference? It's a child of yours she's after, Joe. All them kiddies are a little piece of you, and she happen wants a boy so that she can bring him up to be a fine man like his dad.'

Joe put his head on one side. 'I'll try to believe that, Tommy. But there's another thing. Remember what I said when young Phyllis got orphaned? We're all responsible for one another. Pete Atherton were stood right here when I said it. He knew what I meant, because we got one another through hell in the war.'

Tommy shook his head. 'I've heard yon tale, lad. You had to sing to stop yoursen from screaming, 'cos the morphine were a bit thin on the ground.'

Joe's chin dropped. 'That's the truth of it. We held one another's hands like babies going to school for the first time.' He shook his head to rid himself of such reminiscences. 'See, there's a lot of people in the world, too many. The place is getting that full, we'll have to be pushing some more off the edge. We do that by having wars. With animals, it's called a cull, but with people, it has to be warfare.'

'And you don't want any more responsibility.'

Joe looked up. 'Kiddies belong to everybody, not just to their mams and dads. We die and get sick, so others have to step in. When you have a child, you give the world an extra burden.'

Tommy nodded thoughtfully. 'Aye, but as well as that, you give the world an extra pair of hands. Are you really saying life's not worth living?'

Joe Duffy didn't know what he was thinking or saying. It was all mixed up in his head, though he remained sure that Tess wanted to carry on breeding for the wrong reasons. 'Her argument's wrong,' he said eventually. 'Well, she's no case to put, just says she wants to carry on till we get a lad. What for? So he can end up with one eye or smashed legs?'

They stayed together all through the night, each expounding theory and questioning the other's beliefs. Althorpe Number Two was neglected, because Tommy was unwilling to leave this good man to his nightmare. When morning came, the nightwatchman stared through his window, watched the clogger walking home in slippers and an old khaki coat. 'Life's a bugger,' he muttered to Clarence. 'Come on, let's wake the bloody world up.'

NINE

Geoffrey Althorpe peered out from behind the huge sliding door of the carding shed. She was here. He knew she was here because he'd heard her voice, had listened intently to the words, 'You'll not catch me, Billy Shipton.' He looked left, right, then across the yard to the mill gate. Megan was with somebody called Billy Shipton, so there was a rival. Billy Shipton was probably versed in all the proper arts, like marbles, hopscotch, jacks and bobbers, because Billy Shipton didn't go to The Manse, wasn't closeted all day with Trojan Wars and simple Latin verbs and elementary biology.

Geoffrey stepped outside and began to beat the toe of his leather boot against the flags. There was nothing simple about *amo*, *amas*, *amat* anyway, it was a load of tripe in a dead language. According to Mr Sidney Althorpe, Latin should have been given a decent funeral centuries ago, should have been laid to rest like all the other dinosaurs. But Mrs Agnes Althorpe believed that learning was precious, so her son spent over a hundred minutes each week with his nose in a book that began *'Julia ad oram ambulavit'*, beyond which short phrase he had little hope of achieving sensible translation. Also, he had never played marbles . . .

When he finally saw her, he seemed to freeze under her gaze. She was . . . she was like a dark daisy with shiny black petals and a sun-soaked face. He choked, pulled at the stiff collar, coaxed some air into restricted lungs. This was all very silly. His feelings for Megan embraced a multitude of elements, like the desire to protect her, stare at her, listen while she talked. If he'd been a decent boy, he would have invested this store of emotion in his sister, in poor Fliss who wanted to be loved and cherished.

Megan Duffy ran to him, pushed him hard against the shed door. 'You've not seen me,' she muttered breathlessly before dashing into the bowels of Althorpe Number One.

Geoffrey stepped forward, scanned the area, managed not to flinch as a figure appeared from behind the general office. A boy with basin-cut mouse-coloured hair and pale eyes shunted to a halt, stood so close that Geoffrey could smell his breath. 'Have you seen Megan Duffy?' asked the panting lad.

'No. At least, I don't think so.' Geoffrey wondered why he'd watered down the lie. 'What does she look like?' he asked before his conscience could take a front seat.

'Black hair, dark eyes.' Billy lifted his head. 'I'll get you, Megan,' he roared.

Geoffrey took a step back, needed to find some cleaner air. Billy Shipton was not exactly dirty, not exactly clean. The real problem lay in the fact that his mouth seemed not to have become acquainted with toothbrush and dentifrice. 'I'll tell you if I see her.'

Billy Shipton frowned. 'You Althorpe's lad?'

'Er . . . yes. My name's Geoffrey.'

The ruffian nodded wisely. 'That's a daft name, is that. Cut it down to Geoff. Geoffrey sounds like a mother's boy.' He pushed his hands deep into the pockets of knee-length trousers. 'They called me bloody William. Can you imagine running about as a bloody William? Soon as I started school, I told me mam I were Billy. It took her a while, like, but she calls me Billy now.'

It was difficult to know what to say to someone like Billy Shipton. He was street-wise, alert, ready to damn a person from the so-called upper classes. Geoffrey was old enough to realize that his family name was not written in the annals of true gentry, yet his own position was tenuous and confusing. Mother tried her best to act superior, while Dad set a lot of store by those who laboured for him. But

Agnes Althorpe's separateness from the lower orders had made communication almost impossible. 'She's just a maid,' she often chided when one of her offspring admitted to mingling with those in the kitchen. 'And Mrs Mason is the cook.' Conversely, Agnes was happiest when seated in her kitchen with a pile of potatoes and a peeling knife. 'Just helping out,' was her usual excuse. But the fact was that both senior Althorpes were truly working class. Yet Mother's scheme of things allowed for few visas when it came to her children's crossings of boundaries. 'Which school do you go to?' asked the uncomfortable boy.

'St Mary's. It's gone a bit better since Megan's mam made all the trouble.' He grinned, displaying teeth that were strong, though discoloured. 'Megan and Freda go to St Thomas's with Phyllis now. Phyllis is Megan's mate what got lame with the infantile. She can walk, like, only she limps and has to keep having a rest in a chair with wheels on. We've had some good races with that. It's like a mix between a big basket and a go-cart, really old. It belonged to a cripple up Blackburn way, then Mr Duffy bought it for Phyllis with her being an orphan. It's got bits for your legs – if you put them on, you can go right fast. Our Fred says it's summat to do with . . . with airy dominoes.'

'I think you mean aerodynamics.'

'Do I? Anyroad, it gets some speed up.' The pale eyes gleamed wetly as they fixed themselves on Geoffrey's custom-made attire.

The heir to the Althorpe mills reddened, felt the heat in his cheeks. He responded poorly to close scrutiny, was always pink-faced when someone stared hard. 'Don't you like school? I hate mine.'

'They don't pick us up with our ears no more.'

His own discomfort was forgotten immediately. 'I beg your pardon?'

Billy howled with laughter. 'You sound like a bloody teacher, you do, all posh and old. The nuns, Geoff. The

196

nuns used to pick us up with our ears or our jerseys, anything they could lay their hands on. They've all got waxy hands, me mam says. As if their fingers are made out of church candles. But they're cruel women.'

'Nuns?'

Billy nodded. 'They're supposed to be good, like, allers bowing and scraping in front of statues and saying prayers out of a little book. Only they shout a lot and give you the strap or the cane. It'll happen again, same as before. They're going on the careful side because of the strike. Megan's mam dragged everybody round to St Thomas's, so our teachers are having to be nice. But they'll forget. It'll be back to sore bums and red ears any minute.'

Geoffrey took a moment or two to absorb the dreadful concept. 'Our vicar shouts a lot.' He searched his memory, tried to come up with an experience that matched Billy's sorry tale. 'And we have to do Latin at the Manse. We have to stand up for half an hour if we've not learned our verbs.'

Billy kicked a pebble, sent it scuttering across to a pile of skips. 'We do Latin and all,' he said. '*Et cum spiritu tuo*, and *credo in unum Deum*, all stuff like that. It's in case we get made altar boys. Mind, I make sure I say nowt when they start with all that rubbish. There's no way I'm wearing a black frock under a white pinny with lace on, not bloody likely. They have to keep bobbing up and down, like, me-mawing about all over the altar steps. It's no good if you've got scabs.' He lifted the rim of a trouser leg, displayed a large area of pink tissue around the kneecap. 'That were the best scab I've ever had, only I picked it off in bed last night. Altar boys is always bleeding with splitting their scabs. So I'm not doing no bloody Latin.'

Geoffrey approved. Billy's reason for avoiding the language of ancient Rome was a valid one. 'I've never had a big scab,' he admitted reluctantly. 'But I still hate Latin. We've one boy who gets it right every time and—'

'And everybody hates him.' Billy, having chipped in so

accurately, peered into the shed. 'There's a girl some-where in yon,' he yelled.

A man approached, his hand raised. 'Bugger off out of it, Billy Shipton,' he roared. 'Mill yards is no place for young folk. How many times do you need telling . . . ?' His voice faded to nothing. 'Oh,' he managed eventually. 'Master Geoffrey.'

'Billy is my guest,' said Geoffrey.

The man all but touched his forelock before retreating into the depths of the shed. Billy whistled under his breath. 'Hey, that were good. Can you take us in some time? Only we could pinch some tubes for the fire, save buying bundles or chopping owld chairs and stuff.'

Geoffrey, who had decided to be Geoff from now on, pondered awhile about poverty. There were always roaring fires in the grates at 19, Church Road. He'd never given a thought to where the makings were found, had not dwelt on the concept of mining coal and splitting wood. He'd seen the wire-bound bundles just inside the coal-shed, ready-made kindling bought by Mary from the mobile chandler whose horse and cart visited the area. Who cut the sticks? How much were those bundles and did the sale of such items bring profit to those who laboured to furnish fires? As for the digging of coal in the centre of the earth – he could hardly bear to consider such a claustrophobic prospect.

'Are you deaf or daft or what?'

'Sorry.'

'I said will you take us in for some tubes?'

Geoff frowned. 'There'd be trouble if we got caught. Though I suppose I'll be the boss here one day, so they might turn a blind eye. Will you work in a mill when you leave school?'

Billy frowned so deeply that his eyebrows almost joined in a single line of hair. 'Well, I'd sooner go in for an apprentice – like summat to do with the steelworks or making machines for mills. Our Fred says I've a technical turn of mind. I think that means I'll be good at making

198

things. I can fix taps and drains and I can mend window frames and all that. Well, I nearly can. When I'm about ten, I'll be able to do things proper.'

Geoff added the name Billy Shipton to his brief list of friends. 'I do know her,' he mumbled. 'And I've seen her, but she told me not to say anything.'

Billy shrugged. 'A promise is a promise. Is she in yon shed?'

'Yes.'

'She'll not get through to spinning from there, not without being seen. Only she can't come out till she's got tubes, it's part of the game.'

Geoff inclined his head. 'Right, then. You stand here while I go and find her. If anybody else tells you to . . . to bugger off, say you're with Master Geoffrey.' The swearword gave him confidence, made him feel about six feet tall. If swearing was all it took to attain a degree of self-assurance, then the language he would practise in future would owe nothing to Cicero. 'I'll be back with Megan and some tubes.'

Before the young master could step into the mill, two figures emerged from the carding shed. One was Fliss, though she looked very strange, while the second was Megan Duffy. Megan Duffy bore little resemblance to humanity. She was covered from head to foot in small bundles of cotton waste, some of which were beginning to detach themselves and float airily towards the ground. She looked like a victim of tar and feathers, all oily and fluffy. 'Oh dear,' managed Geoff while Billy Shipton, who was guffawing like a wild animal, transferred himself to the other side of the yard to avoid Megan's flailing fists.

'She's had an accident,' said Fliss.

This understatement had a strange effect on Geoff, though he managed to hang on to the bubble of hysteria that grew in his throat. Fliss was filthy. It was plain that she, too, had been involved in Megan's misfortune, as her face and blouse were streaked with dirt, while something akin to axle grease was daubed on the backs of her hands.

'Don't you dare laugh, Geoffrey,' warned Fliss. 'Or I'll push you into a skip and fasten the straps.' She glared at Billy, who was rolling around on the floor, the sheer agony of glee having removed any bones he might have had in his body. 'Boy,' she yelled with some authority. 'Get out of this yard before I fetch someone to remove you.'

Billy recovered straight away, clambering to his feet and staggering dramatically through the gates.

'Well,' said Fliss, trying to avoid eye contact with her brother. 'This is a mess.'

Geoffrey coughed, wondered how many more trite comments might come from Fliss's lips. The cough hid his laughter, allowed him to compose himself. 'You must get . . . cleaned up,' he managed finally.

Megan glared at him as if the whole matter were his fault. 'We'll go to my house,' she said, trying to ignore the bits of cotton that adhered to her face. This was a very undignified moment, yet Megan clung to her manners. 'I fell,' she said by way of explanation. 'I upset a can of oil and slipped, then I went head first into a bundle of waste.' If he so much as grinned, she would kill him.

Geoff's expression remained serene. But the rhythm of his heart increased as he realized that Megan Duffy was capable of being naughty. For the first time in ages, she was vulnerable, accessible. 'Right. Shall we go to Myrtle Street or to Holly Street?'

'To Deedee's,' she replied. 'I live with her now.'

'I know.' Even in this dreadful state, she was still beautiful, still breathtaking. He resurrected his manners, spoke to his sister. 'I'm sure Mrs Duffy will let you clean yourself, Fliss.'

A very dishevelled Miss Felicity Althorpe squared her shoulders. 'I've no wish to disturb anyone at home, but . . .' But she didn't like the idea of walking through the sheds. To get to a rest area, she would need to pass hundreds of workers. There'd been smirks on quite a few faces the first time, so she didn't fancy going back through the mill. On the way out, she'd had the child, had been able to hold Megan between herself and the world. If the little girl left, Fliss would have no excuse for her state of disarray. 'Very well,' she conceded. 'We'll take this dirty miss home.'

Deedee's face was a picture. 'Glory be,' she muttered when Megan and Fliss stood before her. 'I've seen cleaner clothes on the rag-and-bone cart. They'd give no donkey-stone for you, Megan Duffy, not in that condition.' She looked at Fliss. 'Did she drag you into trouble and all, lass?'

Geoff cleared his throat. 'It's my sister, Mrs Duffy. She's called Felicity, but she'd rather be Fliss.' While the going was good, he added, 'And I'd rather be Geoff.'

The trainee second-in-command of a cotton empire fixed her brother with a steely look. 'I can account for myself, thank you.' She turned to Deedee. 'This child was running about in the mill. Children are not allowed in there, because they could cause accidents.' She glanced at Megan. 'This is a very small mishap, but she might have been killed by machinery.'

Deedee looked Fliss up and down. She was her father's daughter, all right. Yet she wasn't much more than a child herself. 'We'd heard as how you'd started working for your dad. Sit yourself down while I sort some hot water out.' She shook a finger at her granddaughter. 'Stop all this messing about at Althorpe's, Megan. You've been told before. You're getting a bit too frisky for a woman at my time of life to keep up with.' She turned to Fliss. 'One minute she's as good as gold then, next news, she's doing ninety miles an hour down View Street in Phyllis's wheelchair.'

'Sorry,' mumbled the filthy child.

'You know the mill's a dangerous place, lass. I suppose Phyllis would have been there and all if the doctor hadn't took her to the grave. She can hardly walk, but she still gets in mischief.' Determined not to laugh, she busied herself at the sink. Secretly, she was delighted about Megan's naughtiness. The child had been too serious for a long time. Aye, she deserved some fun.

201

Fliss spread some newspaper on a chair, balanced herself on the edge of the seat. 'May I use your bathroom?' The words were out before she could check herself. Her cheeks blazed. 'Sorry, I wasn't thinking.'

'Never bother,' answered Deedee. 'If you need the lav, it's down the yard, but if it's a wash you're after, hang on a bit. When I've tidied Megan up, these two can make themselves scarce in the back street. We'll have you sorted, Miss Felicity.'

'Call me Fliss.'

Deedee dragged Megan across the room, held on to the child tightly, just as she hung on to her sense of fun. Oh, she'd better not crack off giggling! But Megan looked like an exploded pillow . . . 'Get over here, lady, and stand still for once. There's as much movement in you as there was in that daft Shipton lad the day the picture got took. Slippery as an eel, you are.' She looked over her shoulder, glanced at the photograph on her mantelpiece, latched on to a change of subject. 'And the other daft beggar couldn't even keep out of that, could he?' she asked of no-one in particular. 'Look at him, stood in his doorway. He must have been on tiptoe, because them at the back were all on the bench.'

'He were on a chair, Deedee,' said Megan. 'Mr Wagstaff were balanced on a wooden chair with no back. And stop pulling me hair, Deedee, it hurts.'

Doris sighed resignedly. 'Trust Tommy Wagstaff to get where he's not wanted – on a photo, in a back yard, everywhere except where he should be.' Keeping her face as straight as possible, she scrutinized Megan's clothes. Everything would have to come off, apron, frock, possibly undergarments, too. 'Master Geoffrey – all right, then, Geoff – go and sit in the parlour, please. I shall have to strip this one down to the necessities and start from scratch.'

While she cleaned her granddaughter, Deedee treated her small audience to a list of Tommy Wagstaff's vagaries. 'He never paid, you know. It were the kids' day, tuppence each, but Tommy Wagstaff had to be there. No show without Punch? It's a punch he needs. Keep still, child.'

Fliss watched the woman with the girl, felt somewhat cold and excluded as she maintained her fireside vigil. Agnes Althorpe had never washed her son or her daughter, had always hired a nanny or a nursemaid. What must it be like to enjoy a mother's touch, a grandmother's caress? Both Agnes and Sidney had lost their parents, but Fliss could remember, just about, the voice of a kind lady who used to visit sometimes. Granny Althorpe. Granny Althorpe's hair had been the colour of smoke, and Fliss had sat on that woman's knee, was able to recall a hand stroking her cheek, then a frail shoulder on which she had leaned . . .

'Miss?'

She jumped. 'Sorry, I was daydreaming. Please don't call me miss. You see, I'd be Miss Fliss, because I hate Felicity.'

Megan and Deedee squealed with laughter, the latter relieved to let go of the glee she had been suppressing since opening her door. 'Eeh, stop it.' The tears were streaming down Deedee's face. 'Last time I saw owt as funny as you two were when yon Tommy Wagstaff started dressing up in all his fancy shirts.'

Megan, whose head was in the sink, allowed a few words to bubble up. 'She's always talking about Mr Wagstaff and—' The rest of Megan's comment was literally drowned.

Deedee allowed her favourite grandchild to lift her head out of the water. After all, oxygen was a prerequisite of life, though Megan deserved choking sometimes . . . 'I am not allers talking about Tommy Wagstaff, Miss . . . Fliss. Aye, you're right, that does sound daft. He plagues the daylights out of me, keeps coming round with fish for that cat.' She glared at the fat feline. 'Best fed creature in Christendom, is yon Humbug. Megan, whatever this is in your hair won't come out. I'll have to cut it.'

Megan heaved up her head, yanked herself away from

her grandmother, stood dripping on the coconut matting. 'No. I'm keeping my hair on.'

'Well, that'll be a change, Miss Temper.' She winked at Fliss. 'I'm always telling her to keep her hair on.'

Megan sloshed her way to the mirror, peered at herself. 'I like long hair.'

'So does my brother.' Fliss squashed a smile. 'Especially yours, Megan. Geoffrey is very fond of you, he's always talking about you.' Not in front of Mother, of course. But Geoffrey, who wanted to be called Geoff, had taken to spending time with his older sister, was even allowing her to share secrets that were close to his heart. Geoff was a baby, yet his love for Megan Duffy seemed so true, so real. 'Yes, my brother likes you, Megan.'

Megan chose to ignore these comments, though her face in the mirror wore a little smile that sat somewhat smugly between cheeks that were reddening. 'You're not to cut my hair, Deedee.'

'I know. Don't worry, lass, I were nobbut joking.'

While Megan took clean clothes from the airer, Deedee studied the visitor. 'That blouse'll not come clean, not without a good possing in me dolly tub.' She paused, a hand to her lips as she pondered. 'Hang on a mo while I see to me workers. I were supposed to be making them a brew, but I got sidetracked by your bit of trouble.' She moved to the bottom of the stairs. 'Minnie? Fetch that white blouse, the one you were making for me.'

Megan, who was struggling with her frock, cocked an ear. 'Is it for your wedding?' she asked with an innocence that was transparent.

For answer, Deedee clipped the offending girl with a towel.

Minnie Hattersley, closely followed by Bertha Strong, entered the kitchen. They beamed upon the visitor, beamed upon each other, encompassed Megan and Deedee in this broad show of warmth and kinship. 'Here you are,' said Bertha. 'Minnie cut it out—'

'Bertha tacked it,' interrupted Minnie.

'Then she machined it—'

'Only Bertha did the pin-tucks—'

'Then Minnie finished off.'

'Not the button-holes, Bertha. You did them. Bertha's the best button-holer—'

'And Minnie's a great ironer.'

Deedee straightened her face, hoping not to burst into another fit of laughter. Bertha and Minnie were like a double act from the music halls, one fat, one thin, each feeding the other's ego, each acting as foil to her partner. Their timing was excellent, mused Deedee. 'Aye, it's a grand job, girls. Go on up and I'll fetch you a brew in a bit. And I've made some parkin and fruit loaf—'

'Minnie likes fruit loaf—'

'And Bertha likes parkin.' They went upstairs, leaving behind an atmosphere of unexploded hysteria.

Megan fastened the last button. 'I thought they hated one another, Deedee,' she said, her words crippled by suppressed giddiness. She looked at Fliss. 'They fought like cat and dog, Mr Wagstaff says. He saw them years ago with their hands in each other's hair, scrapping like a couple of cats, he says.'

'They've made it up,' muttered Deedee. 'It were pistols at dawn, then they started working here and it's hearts and blinking flowers and praises sung from morning till night. If they carry on being so nice, I'll burst me corsets.'

'You don't wear corsets no more, Deedee,' exclaimed Megan. 'You said they were killing you.'

A terrible noise came from the visitor. Megan, who was light on her feet, dragged Miss Felicity Althorpe into the back yard. Deedee followed them, a handkerchief to her mouth. Fliss burst into gales of laughter while Megan held tightly to the older girl's hand.

Deedee eyed the scene and managed not to laugh. Fliss looked as if she needed to let go. Aye, she wanted relaxation and three good meals a day, raw-boned, she was. And she'd been as plump as a puppy till a few years back. This was a nervy lass, one who might benefit from a

bit of praise now and again. 'See, get back in here, Fliss.'
It was awkward, calling an Althorpe by a nickname and
without a 'miss' or a 'mister', yet 'Miss Fliss' was, indeed,
unthinkable. 'Get thissen inside and we'll give you a quick
rub down with a damp cloth.'

Megan went into the house, set the kettle to boil, then
watched while Deedee began the transformation of Fliss.
An afterthought struck. 'I'd best send your brother back.'
She nodded her head towards the parlour. 'I'll send him to
go to the mill. Happen his dad's looking for him.'

Fliss tut-tutted. 'Don't you go breaking my little
brother's heart, Miss Duffy. Sit with him, talk to him.'

When the blushing Megan had left the room, Deedee
placed the visitor in a chair, stood behind the girl and let
down the heavy mop of hair. 'Your head's all right, clean
enough. I'll just comb it through.' She arranged the thick
locks in a style that provided a gentle frame for the face.
'There's strength in your features, Fliss.'

'I don't like my nose.'

'You'll grow into it,' said Deedee. 'Bits of folk grow
fast, other bits grow slow.' She walked round, studied her
handiwork. 'With your hair done like that, you're pretty.'

'Not with spots.'

Deedee sighed. 'You young girls – never satisfied.' She
bent down and rooted about in a brass box next to the
grate. 'Here. Wash your face with this morning and night.
It's made from fruit stones ground into powder. This'll
shift anything smaller than Everest. Don't use them fancy
soaps that smell. If you must put soap on your face, make
sure it's plain.' She thrust the package into Fliss's hands.
'And now, you can stop and have a cuppa and some cake.
You want filling up and filling out, you do. If we stood you
sideways at the back of a lamp post, nobody'd notice
you.'

Fliss grinned, then rose to stand in front of the mirror.
The blouse was beautiful, made from pure white lawn
with fine pleats from shoulder to waist, then a collar that
framed the wearer's neck in creamy lace, an adornment

that was echoed at the cuffs. The sleeves were generous, billowing out to the elbows, then narrowing near the wrists. 'This is the loveliest blouse I've ever worn, Mrs Duffy.'

'Less of that, if you don't mind. If you're stuck with Fliss, then I'll stay landed with Deedee. Don't you look a bonny picture?'

Fliss had to agree, though she kept her counsel. The Lancashire interpretation of the word 'bonny' bore little relation to its wider use. If 'bonny' meant plump, then Fliss Althorpe was as fat as a stripped sparrow. But she did look nice. She touched her hair, followed the path of folds created by Deedee, tried to work out how she might repeat the style.

'Rinse your mop in beer,' said Deedee as she cut shives from a fruit loaf. 'Just put a tablespoon of cheap ale in the water, then soak your hair right through. You've a bit of chestnut in there and it should be brought out.'

'I'll smell like a brewery.'

Deedee lifted her face, grinned widely. 'Get some of my lanolin and rose-water out of yon box. That'll fix the beer fumes. And you look so good in that blouse – you can have it for half-price.'

Fliss found the bottle, turned and gave Deedee a hard look. 'I'll pay the full price, if you don't mind. And I'm sure I can get you some customers. I was good at art when I was at school, so I'll make a few posters, put them in shops. And some leaflets. We can get those printed down Mealhouse Lane. My mother might like you to come and make something for her.'

'She'd have to come here,' answered Deedee.

'Oh.'

The older woman poured tea, set out some plates, stuck a spoon in the bowl of sugar. 'Happen she wouldn't like our end of town, Fliss.' Doris remembered Agnes as a shy young lass with lovely blonde hair and green eyes. When Sidney Althorpe had chosen his sweetheart, his parents had tried their best to guide him to richer pastures. And

Agnes had been terrified, had seemed to doubt herself. It was her terror that kept her away from her roots, thought Doris. Mrs Althorpe had probably buried her head in the sand so that she might forget her impoverished background. Doris understood Agnes only too well. 'Aye, she'd not like it here,' she repeated.

'Well, I like it,' announced Fliss. She liked Deedee, loved the house, the people in it, the soft whirr of machinery and the hum of muted conversation that filtered through floorboards and plaster. 'I'll come again,' she said.

'Be sure you do.' Deedee carried tea and cakes to her workforce of two, her mind's eye filled by an image of a sad girl, a poor thing who didn't love herself. 'Aye, you'd better come,' she whispered as she came down the stairs. 'Time somebody took you in hand, girl.'

Dr Charles Walsh had learned, over the years, how to cope with emotion. He had tended the old, the young and the dying of all ages for so long that he had been forced to build a shutter in his mind, an automatic door that closed itself whenever the going got tough. Today, the mechanism had stuck, as if it wanted oil, so he dipped into a pocket and pulled out the best lubricant he knew. The silver-plated flask gave off darts of sunshine, reminding him that a graveyard was not the place for alcohol. Nevertheless, he took a sip, rolled the Scotch round his tongue, hoped that it would anaesthetize his brain as quickly as it numbed tongue and gums.

'She's all right here, now, isn't she?' asked the girl.

'Yes, she's blessed, Phyllis.' The limp didn't show when she stood still. When she stood still, she was a child who promised great beauty. Her hair was of a deep auburn shade that fared well in sunshine, while eyebrows and lashes were dark, almost black. The eyes were huge and brown, with whites so clear that they might have been soaked in Dolly-Blue to bring out the best. When she did not move, she was a painting. Best of all, she was managing without the chair sometimes. Which was just as well, because he'd never have got the thing into his car.

'Why did they both have to die?' she asked.

His stomach lurched. No, the discomfort had nothing to do with his digestive system. As a doctor, he should surely be able to locate the source of his own distress? There were heartstrings, then. Heartstrings were not just bits of poetry, lines from maudlin songs. Something in his chest moved and hurt, seemed to be tugging at the very core of his soul. He was angry, furious with a God who could watch while war created two million widows and five million semi-orphans. 'I don't know, Phyllis.'

'We all die.' Her tone was soft, almost too quiet to be heard.

He heard it. 'Yes, everybody dies at some time.' But not everybody became crippled by polio . . . 'You are doing so well,' he told her. 'Don't you use your chariot much these days?'

She shrugged. 'My pram? No, an ordinary chair will do. But I can't walk all the way to school, so Megan still pushes me some of the way—'

'And the boys race along in the wheelchair while you stand about laughing. I've seen, Phyllis, I've watched the games.'

Her face fell. 'Have I to tell them to stop?'

'No. Take your fun where you can find it.' Too many children became old before their time. 'Shall we go back now?'

Phyllis frowned, looked beyond the doctor. 'Isn't that Father O'Riley?'

He swivelled, caught sight of a brown-clad figure bending low over a grave. 'It doesn't look like Patrick,' he muttered. 'Though I suppose I'm used to seeing him in black. Wait here,' he said to Phyllis. 'I'll wander across and see who it is.'

While the doctor approached, the man mumbled something under his breath, the eyes still downcast, almost closed.

209

'Father? Is that my old friend Patrick O'Riley? What are you up to?'

The priest raised his hand, screwed the top onto a bottle of clear liquid, dragged a length of green-and-gold material from his shoulders. Charles hesitated for a split second, watched while his friend waved the narrow scarf that proclaimed a status that could soon be lost. The priest, too, had something to hide – a bottle, a headful of secrets told not in a surgery, but in a confessional box. 'Hello, Paddy.'

'They've not unfrocked me yet, Charles.' He stuffed the glass container of holy water into his shirt. 'And I stole a stole.' He giggled, making a sound that was uncomfortably close to hysterical laughter. 'The stole is the most important item in a priest's garb, you know. I still have it. So I'm blessing them all, every last man and woman. Catholic, Protestant, Methodist or Jew, they're all being sent into the hereafter on a Catholic ticket, first-class travel, no steerage, holy water from Ireland.'

Charles Walsh stood with his arms folded, stared at the man. He bore little resemblance to the priest he had known, that fine cleric who had worked like a dog on behalf of his church and its parishioners. The shoulders were stooped, weighted by care, while the fine, sandy hair seemed to have increased its rate of retreat towards the back of Patrick O'Riley's head. 'I told you you'd go bald if you kept wearing that biretta, Paddy.'

A hand strayed upward, came to rest on the forehead. 'I have no biretta, just a stole. Went home to Ireland for a while, but it didn't work out. So here I am. They're looking for me, you know. There'll be a meeting, a few lectures, then I'll be asked to repent and to promise never to bless another so-called unworthy grave. And I'll not repent and I'll not promise. So that's me out on my ear, just like this little lot.' He swept a hand across the few graves that sat in the unconsecrated part of the cemetery. 'The only difference between me and them is that their

210

suffering is over, because I've released them. Releasing myself would be difficult.'

'Stop this talk. When did you last eat? You look like a man who's been sleeping under the stars.'

'Astute, you are,' said Patrick. He folded the shabby green material, spat on his thumb, ground some of the dirt deeper into the fibres. 'I went to a wake in Sligo, my Uncle Martin's. He was there as large as life and not as ugly as he used to be, sort of ironed out by the hand of death.' His eyes seemed to focus temporarily on the face of his comrade. 'Did you see an Irish wake ever?'

'No.'

'Well, it's all very hospitable. Mind, there's some who don't have the corpse home any more – those who've gone a bit grand. But the family had the guest of honour in pride of place, in his coffin, at the party. Three fiddles and a melodian, there were, and Michael Murphy did a few turns on the Jew's harp. I stood at the window and listened, it was all very jolly. And wouldn't you say that's a nice cosmopolitan touch? We'd a Jew's harp at a Christian wake. Anyway, I went in to say goodbye to the old man. He was in the best suit, because Auntie Eilish doesn't like shrouds, thinks they're depressing.' He gazed at the ground, seemed to have lost the thread of his story.

'What happened?'

'Eh? Oh, Charlie. I was telling you . . . Well, they threw me out. I landed in all the muck and my stole came off, got thoroughly filthy. I washed it in a stream, but it's not come good. They said I'd no right to wear it. You see, I made a stand for these poor tormented souls, so my family wants none of me.'

'You made a stand for the mentally ill. I'm proud of you. But what's going to become of you? What the hell are you going to do?'

Patrick sighed, nodded his head jerkily. 'First, I'll eat. You can take me home and feed me. Then I'll go off and set the world to rights. There's a Christian mission in Manchester . . . it's a non-denominational thing. So I'll probably go to work with those who've been in prison.'

The doctor turned, waved to Phyllis, then spoke to the good man who stood dejectedly by a row of unmarked graves. 'Phyllis is with me. You'll have to crowbar yourself into the back seat with all my pills and potions. She needs to sit in front—'

'But she's walking.' Patrick O'Riley grinned broadly at the girl he remembered so well, the child whose mother had moved him to break with tradition and with his church. 'Well done,' he shouted. 'It's great to see you up and about.' A frown creased his forehead as he watched the child moving towards the doctor's car. 'Is that as good as she's going to get, Charlie?'

'Hard to say. The muscles will strengthen with use, but there was damage done. She'll always limp, perhaps not as badly as she does today.'

'God love her.' The priest took the doctor's arm. 'Ham and eggs with bread and butter and some thick, sweet tea. Would you have the ingredients of such a prescription, Charlie?'

'Yes.'

'Then all's well with creation.'

Charles Walsh walked towards the car, his head buzzing with all the things that were definitely wrong in his sphere. He'd sick folk to visit, a tramp-like ex-priest to feed, a surgery to attend. Above all these items sat his worry about Patrick O'Riley. They would find him now. They would find him, come for him, strip him of dignity, status and stole. And Dr Charles Walsh would be left with the pieces.

Agnes Althorpe had been reading again and, this time, the literature contained in the Family section of her house-keeping monthly had raised her spirits considerably. She quoted now from the very article that had encouraged her to make a stand against the Evelyn Grimshaws of this world. 'They become our enemies if we cross them, Evelyn,' she said. 'There is a great deal of animosity

212

between mothers and daughters, so one must be supportive. This is a new age. Parents no longer depend on their grown children. We live longer, are active right through to our seventies and beyond, so why should we need to fasten our daughters to our apron strings?'

Evelyn glared at her friend, wondered, rather sulkily, when Agnes Althorpe had last worn an apron. Evelyn was unaware of Agnes's close relationship with the kitchen and its inhabitants. 'Is this just for girls, then? Or are we supposed to allow our sons to leave school at fourteen? Jeremy is doing so well at the university because we forced him to stay at school for all the certificates.'

Agnes nodded, careful not to disturb her perfect coiffure. She bared her teeth in a cold smile, shrugged, wished she had the courage to send this stupid woman home. One day, she told herself. One day, she would have the strength to be just exactly who she was, poor background and all. 'Of course, Jeremy would not wish to follow in his father's footsteps, would he?' she asked carefully. 'Butchering is perhaps not everyone's cup of tea.'

Evelyn sat bolt upright, forced her spine into a rigid line that pushed out the enormous chest till it looked like a well-upholstered bolster. 'Luke's not just a butcher, Agnes. Luke is an artist. his black puddings are selling even in the south, you know. He's won prizes for his sausages.'

'Yes, I know, dear. But that isn't the point. What I'm trying to say is that young women are beginning to run their own lives. Of course, we shall want Geoffrey to do something academic, but Felicity needs to be occupied usefully until a suitable man comes along.' She held up the magazine, quoted. 'After the nurturing period is over, many women are seen by their daughters as obstacles rather than as friends. Win the respect of your female youngster by allowing her to explore the world in which she, too, must eventually raise a family.' With a flourish that fell just short of triumphant, Agnes turned the page, scanned a few lines. 'You see? I knew all along that this was the right thing for Felicity. Of course, we are fortunate, since she can work with her father.'

Evelyn Grimshaw glowered over the rim of her teacup. Evelyn Grimshaw had not read the books on etiquette, so she forgot to dab at her lips with a napkin and, when she spilled tea into her saucer, she simply poured it back into the cup before leaning over for another cake. She was a wealthy woman, but was inferior to Agnes because Sidney killed no pigs and sorted no cotton. Sidney was a cousin once removed from his industry, but Luke got his hands dirty every single day. 'Nice cakes, dear,' she muttered through a mouthful.

Agnes inhaled deeply, then took the plunge. 'In modern parlance, we all have to get stuck in, Evelyn. So I went down to the mill yesterday, just to check on Felicity's progress, then I visited a rather quaint woman called Doris Duffy. She is running a business called "Fine Seams" from one of our houses. You would not believe what she can produce for five shillings. So I ordered several blouses and a dress.' She took a sip of tepid tea, dabbed at her lips, placed the cup and saucer on the table. 'The woman is wonderfully talented. You must visit her, because I'm sure she could do something for you.' It would probably take more than a good seamstress to disguise Evelyn's bumps and bulges.

Evelyn sucked in her lips, causing them to almost disappear in surrounding blubber. Do something for her, indeed! Evelyn's dad had been succesful in greengrocery, so she had automatically married a suitable match. But the woman who sat at the other side of the fancy wheeled tea-table had come from nowhere. Where and how on earth had Agnes Althorpe acquired all these airs and graces? 'So you went back to your old haunts?' As soon as the words were out, Evelyn's skin coloured. It was an unspoken law that Agnes's beginnings should never be mentioned. And friends were hard to find these days, especially for a clumsy great woman with three chins and no waist. She lowered her eyes, expected a storm. Luke had told her years ago that Agnes was ashamed of her roots.

But the storm did not arrive. 'Yes,' said Agnes deliberately. 'Yes, I went home, I suppose.' Her heart raced as all the old fears paid a brief visit to her mind. She remembered an empty grate, an empty stomach, an empty look in her mother's eyes. No, no, those times would never come back, she told herself. And the latter part of her mother's life had been improved immeasurably because of Sidney's kindness. 'Our house is still there,' she said softly. 'With the same door. I almost saw my mother standing there in that long white apron and the dark shawl.' She raised her chin. 'I'm glad I went back. The people are so interesting, so alive. There's an orphan girl living with Mrs Duffy, a sweet child with a limp. We had such fun.'

Evelyn's chin dropped. She had never realized that Agnes Althorpe was on nodding terms with fun. 'I'll . . . come with you next time,' she ventured cautiously.

'That would be wonderful,' replied Agnes.

When Evelyn had gone to the bathroom, Mrs Agnes Althorpe sat and read right through the article again. This would be her bible from now on, because she was going modern. She'd already gone slightly modern, had purchased new clothes, a cigarette holder and some literature about suffrage. Smoking was horrible, but she intended to persevere in the fashion stakes. And visiting the old places had not been without its pleasures. Also, there was no going back to the way things had been in this house. Felicity was already ensconced at the factory, so the lady of the detached residence whose address was 19, Church Road, had decided to allow herself to be carried along in the current created by her daughter and by an article in her monthly magazine.

Evelyn Grimshaw returned, described her new bathroom for the umpteenth time, settled gingerly on the rim of a frail-looking chair and studied her hostess. There was something different about Agnes. In fact, quite a few things had changed over the past weeks. 'Are you wearing rouge?' she asked.

'Just a little.' Agnes snapped open a silver case, extracted a cigarette, screwed it into the ebony and mother-of-pearl holder. She hated tobacco, yet it served her purpose, made her look daring and provocative. She breathed, choked, blew out smoke that was still blue. Inhaling was impossible. Having the wretched dirt in her mouth was bad enough, so she had given up on trying to take it into her lungs.

'I didn't know you smoked.'

'Everyone does.' Agnes's voice was pitched rather high, the vocal cords seeming to rebel against the onslaught of best Virginia. 'It keeps a person slim and agile.'

'Oh.' Evelyn Grimshaw continued to sit precariously on the edge of her seat and on the edge of gentility. 'We're buying another shop,' announced the visitor, her tone trimmed with defiance.

'I know. You told me about that last week.'

'Did I tell you how big it is?'

'Yes.'

'Did I tell you that the mayor gets his meat delivered from Luke's store?'

'Yes.' Agnes took the half-smoked article from its holder, punished it to death in an onyx ashtray. 'Things are changing so rapidly.' She composed herself, stroked a rope of pearls that hung down the front of her dress. 'Divisions in class are a thing of the past. I'm even planning to have all my clothes made by that woman in Holly Street.' She rooted about in her brain, located some words she'd come across a few weeks ago. 'Gifted primitives are all the rage now. Some of these people are so talented. And I think it's up to us to support them.'

'Oh.' Evelyn had little to say, since most of her ideas came second-hand from the woman seated opposite. Agnes's skirt was new. It showed slim ankles clad in best silk, had been cut to cling to the contours of its wearer's body. The blouse was beautiful, in a fine blue cotton with pintucks down the front and cream lace at collar and cuffs. Evelyn had no chance when it came to competition in the

216

field of fashion. She had a strong liking for Luke's black puddings and a fondness for fatty lamb. The deposits from these delicacies sat in clumps of lard all over her solid frame, so she was forced to wear black and navy, colours that might minimize her bodily bulk. 'You look very nice,' she managed.

'Thank you.' The hostess examined her nails, which were perfectly shaped, beautifully manicured.

Evelyn balled her hands into fists, tried to keep them out of sight. She was lucky to have a friend like Agnes, and she didn't want to test her good fortune by advertising too frequently the fact that she did some of her own chores. The Grimshaws had help, but Evelyn could not cope with servants, was a failure when it came to delegation. Pulses beat in the ends of her fingers, reminding their owner that her nails were broken and softened by water and soap, that the digits of her hands were reddened by scrubbing. Agnes had two servants, one to cook, the other to clean. So Evelyn, who was a mere mortal who employed a mere daily, felt blessed each time Agnes allowed her to come for coffee and cake. 'Are the shoes new?' she asked.

Agnes glanced briefly at her leather-shod feet. 'These old things? Goodness, I must have had them for ages.' She pulled a book from behind an ample cushion. 'This was compiled by a Bolton woman called Sarah Fishwick. She's dead now, unfortunately. It seems that she developed blood poisoning after her third prison term.'

Evelyn wondered briefly whether Agnes might open a library. And it was all right to go modern, but the tolerance of criminals was taking things too far. 'Really?' squeaked the large woman.

Agnes nodded, opened the book. 'It's an account of the lives and deaths of women who have fought for the Great Cause.' She emphasized the last two words, made sure that her listener would award them the high case initials they deserved. 'Women's suffrage, Evelyn. When I had finished reading this, I decided that my daughter should leave school and equip herself for the battles to come.'

Silence was the best option, decided the uncomfortable guest. It seemed that Agnes was determined to get educated, and Evelyn was too aware of her own short-comings to try a meaningful reply. As far as she knew, it was the men who went out to fight while women knitted scarves and rolled bandages, but she waited for her guru to continue.

'It's my opinion that they punctured her stomach.'

Evelyn, feeling lost, simply nodded.

But the perfect hostess took account of her guest's confusion. 'Sarah Fishwick was force-fed in a Manchester jail. It's been one of our weapons, you know, the refusal of food. The poor woman died after a particularly brutal attempt at tube-feeding. But when she was well, before she ever went to prison, she wrote down some accounts of the lives of women who fought for the cause. You should read it. And you must spread the word, make sure that everyone understands that we want parity with men.'

After wondering briefly about the meaning of 'parity', Evelyn accepted the slim volume and pushed it into her bag. 'Luke might not like it,' she ventured.

Agnes made a noise that sounded like 'Pshaw,' then continued to lecture her unfortunate audience of one. 'He's not important, not in this instance. I am fortunate, of course, because my husband is a man of vision, but your reply is typical of today's married woman. The Women's Social and Political Union has a slogan which reads "Deeds not Words". Christabel Pankhurst smashed wide open a political meeting in Manchester – oh – more than fifteen years ago. She stood there demanding votes for women. Her set marched on Parliament, only to be attacked by the police. Sarah Fishwick once served twenty-one days for vomiting into a policeman's helmet.' She searched her memory, found little else. 'That is why my daughter is no longer pampered at school. She will vote. One day, she will go with her brother to elect a government.'

Evelyn fidgeted, listened to the growling of her stomach.

Food was always sparse at one of Agnes's tête-à-têtes. She'd rushed her breakfast in order to be here at the required time, and she seldom came out of the house before having a good cooked meal. Her mouth watered as she remembered the kidneys and bacon that lay waiting for her on a marble slab in the pantry. She would have two eggs and a bit of crispy fried bread and—

'Evelyn?'

'Sorry.'

'Sometimes, my dear, you are so vague. I was saying that we need more young women in the field.'

Evelyn bit her lip. 'Which field?' She didn't like grass, found it rather damp and slippery—

'In the field of women's suffrage.'

'Oh. Well, I'll read it, then.'

Agnes tapped her fingers on the arm of the sofa. 'Don't just read – think. Sarah Fishwick was a spinner from Bolton. She left home and went all over the country preaching the ideas of—'

'I can't leave home. How would Luke manage? And when Jeremy comes down from Edinburgh . . .' Evelyn swallowed, cursed herself for trampling on one of Agnes's nerves. Going on about the bathroom had been bad enough, but here she was, boasting and bragging about her son who was at medical school. 'I can't get involved, Agnes.'

Agnes had no intention of getting involved, either. But this had seemed a suitable ploy, a reason valid enough to explain Felicity's departure from the ranks of academia. 'My dear, you are right,' she said soberly. 'We shall watch the movement with interest and we shall pray for the well-being of its members. My daughter will make us proud, Evelyn. She will be there at the forefront when women take the helm.' She beamed upon the visitor. 'More tea? And I could get some sandwiches sent in if you like.'

Evelyn smiled. It was nice to be in the company of a modern free-thinker. Especially when sandwiches were promised.

Joe Duffy stood on the dark landing, listened to the breathing of his daughters. They slept at the back of the house in two double beds that were crammed into a space barely big enough for one. Until recently, Annie and Nellie had shared one bed, Megan and Freda the other. But Megan lived in Holly Street now, so Annie, who was the oldest, enjoyed the comfort of a bed to herself while Nellie shared with the five-year-old Freda.

He pushed open the door, gazed down upon three blonde heads. The moon illuminated the scene, making the girls' hair a silvery-white. Megan was dark. Megan was beautiful, and she had settled well into his mother's house. He missed her, missed the chatter, the questions, that heartbreaking smile.

When the door was closed, he crept across the landing and looked into the empty front bedroom. The twins' bed was still there, as were the toys and clothes. He should shift them. He should come in when she was shopping and clear the room completely, separate her from this unhealthy fixation. Tess would not let them rest in their tiny coffins. She talked to them, visited them often in this room, sang the songs they had enjoyed during their brief stay on earth.

He cocked an ear towards the bedroom he shared with his wife and Baby Hilda. The woman he had married would be waiting for him. Tess still pounced on him regularly, insisted that they made love whether or not they felt like it. The only respite he got was during the few days of each month when she kept to herself of necessity. There was no affection, no warmth. Although Joe still loved his wife, he felt no returning affection, got nothing from her. When her monthly cycle gave him peace, she never hugged him, never kissed him good night. He was here to serve her, to provide her with male offspring. Aye, Megan was best out of it.

He shut off the sight of his dead sons' possessions, steeled himself to face Tess. Tonight, he would speak to her again. Tonight, he would put his foot down, tell her once more that he felt like a dog or a horse on some breeding spree, a mere animal whose sole function was to impregnate a female in the hope of producing something worthy. Sweat made his hands slick, so he dried them on the front of his shirt before turning the doorknob.

She hadn't heard him. She was standing near the window, her figure outlined by moonbeams that shone through the fine fabric of her nightgown. A crooning sound came from her as she rocked slowly from side to side. Sometimes, he knew that she was crazy.

Tess cradled the lower part of her body, wrapping her arms about the newly-planted seed. This was to be her son, the little boy who would silence Tess's own mother. When she slept, she often saw Kieran's face, heard the harsh sound of scolding. 'You brought disease into this house, Theresa Nolan. You killed my son.' Tess stared at the moon. 'Shall I call him Kieran, Mam? Would that please you?'

'No,' said Joe. 'Our children will have their own names, Tess.'

She turned slowly, looked at him. 'I didn't hear you coming in,' she whispered.

'Another baby?' he asked unnecessarily.

'Yes. This will be a boy, Joe. And you're right, we'll call him Joseph.'

Joe walked to the bed, dragged off his clothes. He would sleep tonight. She'd got what she wanted, so he had served his purpose. 'What if it's a girl?' he mumbled. 'Do we call her Josephine?' He expected no answer, got none. Gratefully, he fell asleep in the knowledge that he could claim eight full hours each night for several months. Yet his heart lurched when she climbed into bed and turned away from him. A kiss, a hug and a sweet word would have been nice but, like his daughters, he was learning to expect nothing.

TEN

By 1923, the front bedroom was, of necessity, occupied. Annie and Nellie shared their cramped, rear-facing quarters with the nine-year-old Freda and the three-year-old Hilda. Harriet, at twenty-three months, was a sweet and affectionate baby who had been renamed Hattie. Because of overcrowding and Joe's dogged insistence, this sixth female infant slept in the room that had belonged to Harold and Albert. The lastborn, a mite of just under one year, had been baptized Sarah. She, too, had been placed in the twins' bedroom. Sarah was a noisy, charming and active child with a penchant for centre-stage. Although she cried infrequently, she was often awake through the night. The delightful young imp chattered incessantly in a language all her own, and she needed to be away from her parents so that they might grab some rest. Hattie, who could have slept through earthquakes and world wars, was never disturbed by the monologues of her vivacious sibling.

Tess had become a shadow of herself, a pale painting of the woman she used to be. Gone were the mood-swings that had plagued her life. Since giving birth to two more girls, Tess's depression had become permanent, a part of her make-up. Annie and Nellie, who both worked, were no longer available to help in the house, as mill hours were long and tiring, so Tess's lethargy was causing her home to fall into a state of neglect that alarmed every member of the crumbling household.

She lolled by the fire one Saturday morning, waited numbly for her two older daughters to come off their half-day shift. She was pregnant again, was hanging on to the

222

saying 'Third time lucky'. It couldn't happen again, could it? This third attempt after the deaths of Harold and Albert would surely produce a son?

In spite of her proximity to the fire, she shivered. Hattie and Sarah had been male until the last minute. No, this time, she was carrying a boy. Wasn't she? She fiddled with the edge of her dirty apron, stared at the clock, willed it to move through seconds, days, months. Soon, soon, she would have her wish.

Joe kept the shop open on Saturdays, so Tess was left in the company of the four youngest. Freda was saying something, but the mother of the family was not listening. She sometimes failed to hear their words, hardly ever instigated conversation. She answered questions, did what she considered to be her duty, but she tended not to become involved. When she did consider her children, she realized that she had produced six clones, half a dozen female children who all looked alike except that their sizes were graded.

Megan was different, she mused. Megan, who didn't live here any more, was dark and interesting, quick and beautiful. The other girls were pretty in a bland way, but Tess missed Megan, often felt the urge to drag her home. However, the third daughter of this marriage was a loyal and determined child. No way would Megan be persuaded to leave her Granny Deedee and that girl of Ida Entwistle's.

She prodded the fire, cocked an unwilling ear in the direction of Freda. 'Well, clean it up, then.'

Freda looked at the item that had been deposited on the floor by Hattie. The latter's stabs at potty training were more miss than hit, as Hattie did not enjoy perching on a piece of cold pottery. At least Sarah was still in nappies, thought Freda as she went into the scullery for newspapers and a mop. She was tired, fed up with watching her mother just sitting by the fire day in, day out, no movement, no effort to clean the house. She pushed steeping whites further down into the bucket of Dolly-Blue, then began the task of cleaning up Hattie's mess.

Freda was only nine. She wanted to play with her friends, wanted air, space, a bit of freedom. Yet she was forced by circumstances beyond her control to be minder and mother to Hilda, Hattie and Sarah.

The door from the lobby was pushed open as Freda scrubbed away at the stained floor. Doris Duffy marched in, her face as grim as a month of wet Sundays. Joe had indulged his selfish wife for too long. Joe, who worked like a slave in his shop, was coming home to no tea, no order, no love. So Deedee waded in, grabbed Freda's mop, finished the job. 'Take them all upstairs, lass,' she said tersely. 'I want a word with your mam.' She awarded Tess a glance that spoke volumes, a look that conveyed pity, near-contempt, impatience. 'And you can come down yonder for your tea, after,' she yelled at the disappearing Freda.

Deedee closed the door, threw the mop into its bucket, placed herself in a chair that faced her daughter-in-law's. She would wash her hands in a minute, because she wanted to strike now, while her dander was up. 'When did you last go out, Tess?'

The figure stirred, raised a head that had not seen comb or brush that day. 'Eh?'

'I asked you when were you last on your feet in the fresh air?'

'Er . . .' Tess gazed round the room, her eyes heavy-lidded, as if she had just woken from long hibernation. 'I don't know. I can't go out with all this lot, can I?'

'Course you can,' came the quick answer. 'Freda and Hilda can both walk, then you can put the baby at one end of the pram and our Hattie at the bottom end.'

'I don't feel like it.'

Deedee gripped the edge of the rocker's arms. The house was a mile and a half of mess, a bloody tip – and that was swearing – even if the word hadn't reached her tongue. 'Look at them good chairs, Tess. Look what our Megan did for you. How many folk in these streets have leather seats to their dining chairs, eh? That child could

224

teach you a thing or two, lady. She's making belts and bags and glasses cases by the dozen in her spare time. And you sit there like one of them Buddhas waiting for Christmas.' She paused, pondered. 'Nay, they wouldn't wait for Christmas, being heathens, but you know what I mean.'

Tess fixed her eyes on Deedee. What was she going on about? What the hell had heathens got to do with waiting for a son to be born? 'I'm carrying,' she said simply. 'It can't be another girl. Nobody has eight girls.'

'They do. I know folk who've had ten of one kind and none of the other sort. You get what God sends and just hope they're healthy and in one piece.' Where was the young woman who had brought a strike to the people hereabouts? Where was the Tess who had cared enough to stand up against the beating of her daughters? 'You're going to end up in hospital, you are. There's more movement in a lamp post than in you. So . . .' She rolled up her sleeves. 'I'll start, then Tommy can come up tomorrow and finish off what I leave.'

'Go away,' said Tess.

Deedee's rope shortened so quickly that it seemed to be made of elastic. 'No, I'll not go away. These kiddies are my flesh and blood, they belong to my only son. I'm not standing here like cheese marked tuppence while this place goes to rack and ruin. When did that grate see leading? Has that fire-plate ever been cleaned?' She waved a hand towards the sheet of metal that fronted the hearth. 'It's that black, it's forgot what pattern it were in the first place. Tommy'll see to them jobs. I'll get stuck in to the washing while you move some of this junk.' Her thumb jerked in the direction of the table where breakfast dishes mingled unhappily with last night's plates and cups. 'He brought fish and chips again, didn't he? That lad of mine is having to put in a full day at the cobbling, then another day here seeing to his children's teas.' She rose. 'You're nowt a pound these days, Tess Duffy.'

Between scullery and back yard, Doris Duffy complained

none too quietly while she carried washing from slopstone and bucket to the outside mangle. 'They want a good possing,' she yelled. 'And ten minutes on the washboard.' There was no point in seeking hot water. To achieve hot water, Doris would have needed to shift Tess. In her present mood, she would probably have tipped her son's wife head first into the fireside copper. 'Lazy mare,' she spat as she turned the mangle. 'If I'd room at home, I'd fetch the lot to live with me.'

When a row of almost clean sheets billowed in the back street, Doris steeled herself and re-entered the kitchen. Tess had not moved, save to slump further down the chair. Her head rested on a cushion, while her fingers formed a latticed gate over the rounded dome of her belly.

Doris whipped away the headrest, tried not to flinch as Tess's head made sharp contact with bare wood. 'Get up,' screamed the visitor. 'Get out of that chair, or I'll fetch the town in to you. They'll take yon kiddies, you know. They'll put them in a sanatorium or some such place till homes can be found.'

Tess blinked rapidly, the confusion in her eyes doing a series of vanishing tricks, reappearing briefly each time the lids lifted. 'Why?' She stirred herself, shuffled towards the edge of the seat. 'Joe won't let you do that,' she said, confidence swelling her voice. 'Anyway, I need our Freda. She can run for the midwife when I start.'

'Not when she's at school.'

Tess patted her tangled mop of greasy hair. 'I shall keep her off when I get near. Somebody'll have to see to the others when the pains come.'

Deedee balled her fists, clamped her lips tight shut and walked out of the room. In the lobby, she listened to the sound of a nine-year-old trying to keep the peace, trying to play Mother when she'd never even been a child herself. 'God help me, I'll swing for yon Tess, I will that,' she muttered under her breath. She should have let Tommy buy that bigger house. Instead of moving on, the newly-wed Wagstaffs had taken a shop in town, a couple of rooms where ladies came for fittings, where dresses and coats were put together by the proficient team that was Bertha Strong, Minnie Hattersley and Doris Wagstaff – who was still called Deedee.

She wandered into the front room, tutted when she saw the state of what she termed the parlour. There were clothes everywhere, bits of food, torn newspapers, a doll's torso, its limbs scattered to the four corners. Through the filthy window, she could still make out the shapes of folk going about their daily business. Life. It was for living, not for wasting while children grew up neglected, while a home fell apart. There were mouse-droppings near a skirting. She swallowed what tasted like bile, leaned against a wall, considered the situation.

The best thing she'd ever done was to marry that great stupid lad. She grinned, mocked herself for calling Tommy a lad when he was a man who had reached the wrong side of sixty. Yes, he was a good husband now that she'd cleaned up his act properly. He'd relinquished the nightwatching and the knocking-up, went to work every morning, opened the shop, settled the girls in their sewing room, bowed and scraped to the clients. It was strange, but Tommy Wagstaff was a boon in an area that was exclusively female. He'd installed a green velvet chaise longue and a low table where customers could take tea and little cakes. He spent hours discussing the weather, children, the terrible price of fish and meat, a new shade of blue. 'Aye, that job's a good 'un,' whispered Deedee now. 'God bless him, he's made me a happy woman.'

Her head turned of its own accord. She couldn't be at ease – let alone happy – while all this was going on. Or rather, while nothing was going on. The house stank of neglect, the smell of dirt overpowering the aromas of bugs and rodents. She would have to bring Tommy into it. Whenever she thought of him, she smiled. He waited every morning until she arrived at the shop after doing her household chores, stood at the door while the tram clanged along the road. Then he would help her down the vehicle's step, bring her inside, give her a kiss and a cup of tea. Only when she was at her machine did he go off to buy materials or to sell Megan's bits of magic. Aye, that was another blessing – she was a good leather worker, was their Megan.

She would fetch Tommy tonight. Meanwhile, having left Tommy in charge of the shop, she intended to collect these four little girls from upstairs, then take them home, clean them, feed them, send them back with Megan and Phyllis. It was a rum do, she thought as she collected the noisy quartet. If the next was a lad, there'd be even less hope for this little lot.

She was flattered. Phil Greenwood waited for her almost every lunchtime, spoke to her, followed her with his eyes as she made her way to one of the local shops. Since her promotion to a position of great responsibility, Fliss had taken to eating with her father, usually a pasty or sandwiches made from flour cakes and fresh boiled ham. During such simple meals, they talked not as father and daughter, but as a pair of colleagues who respected one another.

Fliss's need to reject her food had disappeared with the passing of adolescence, and the resulting weight gain sat well on her frame and face, minimizing a nose that had once seemed as huge as Cyrano de Bergerac's. She was content, happy in her work, settled at home. Since Mother's conversion to twentieth-century philosophy, life, though unexciting, had become bearable. Thanks to the Pankhursts, Agnes's pride remained intact, because she had sent forth her daughter to take over the world in the name of womankind.

When the weather was fine, the lad usually stayed at the gate, assumed an attitude of careful indifference as he ate his bread and cheese. Fliss knew that he would always be there, that he would stand at that gate until she was ready. It was nothing to do with money, nothing to do with power. Phil had liked her from the start, would have liked her no matter what.

'How is your mother?' she would ask, her clear green eyes twinkling at him. She could look at people now, was able to show them a face that was free of spots.

He usually answered with a shrug that failed to hide his concern. 'She could go on for years.' He told her about the treatments, the foul-tasting powders that Mrs Greenwood was forced to take, kept Fliss informed when his mother was feeling better. 'She says she's going to do the front step. That'll save me a job.'

She really liked this boy. Many young men in their twenties would be afraid to have neighbours watch them doing a woman's chores, but Phil simply carried on with the tasks that were beyond his mother. In recent weeks, he had washed, ironed, dusted and swept. Each job had brought its own disaster, and he had been regaling Fliss with tales of his stupidity. 'Well, I didn't know I had to wait for the water to cool. Anyway, she's not bothered, because all her underwear was in with the red cushion cover, so she's gone a bit pink, says it makes her feel girlish again.'

Fliss sat at an upstairs window, looked down upon the man who had picked her out.

'Your mother won't be best pleased.'

She turned, blushed, laughed at her father. 'Pop, he's just a friend.'

'That's what all the filmstars have started saying. "We're just good friends", they say, then they get married three days later.'

'I'm not eighteen yet, not quite.'

He studied the girl who had become an invaluable asset to the firm during the past four years. She had taken complete charge of personnel matters and, although he continued to maintain a close interest in his workers, he now felt easy about their welfare. For the folk in Althorpe One and Two, Fliss did more than enough. 'People marry at sixteen,' he said.

'Not me.' She shook her head vigorously, causing the bun at the nape to dislodge itself. She fiddled with pins

229

and net, trapped the wayward tresses. Mrs Duffy, who was now Mrs Wagstaff, had been right about the beer because, after years of treatment, Fliss's hair gave off a new sheen, was more golden in the sun. 'I'm going to work for a long time.'

He nodded wisely. 'Yes, and Mrs Greenwood could linger for years. They do, with her illness. So when she's dead and you're a woman, there'll be a wedding, eh?'

Fliss shrugged, hoped that she looked nonchalant. 'I don't know about that.'

'Your mother will fly through the roof.'

'She's gone all modern,' answered Fliss. 'She even has some of her clothes made by Mrs Wagstaff.'

'Frocks and marriage are two entirely different things, love.'

She opened wide those large, green eyes. 'Not if the frock in question's a wedding gown.'

Sidney guffawed, sank into his chair. 'The very part of you that's going to challenge Agnes is the gift you got from her. Like your mother, you're determined, nearly bloody-minded. So there'll be one hell of a collision up Church Road, just mark my words.' He paused, thought for a moment. 'Whereas Geoffrey's gentle. We could all walk over him and he'd apologize for getting under our feet.'

Fliss, who had grown closer to the 'brat' of late, shook her head. 'No. Geoffrey will simply go.'

Sidney's head jerked itself up. 'What did you say?'

She bit her lip, hoped that she hadn't betrayed her brother. 'Oh, it's just one of my stupid ideas, probably a load of rubbish. I can't see him hurting Mother by leaving home. On the other hand, he won't want to be conjugating Latin for ever and ever.'

'So you believe he'll just be up and away?'

'No.' She injected some firmness into her tone. 'That would hurt everybody.' Geoffrey was a nice lad, but he was probably cowardly. He might very well just leave, but not yet. It would be unfortunate if the parents started watching him like hawks at this stage. 'He's still very young,' she added.

'And he's no accountant. Ah well.' He cleared his throat, began to shuffle some papers. 'This isn't getting the baby bathed, is it? Find me those statements, the maintenance charges from Rochdale. Then nip out and get the same from Number Two.'

Fliss, who didn't want to think about Phil or Geoffrey, got on with her job. For now, it was best to leave not-so-well alone.

'So I don't know what to do. It's a waste of time and money. I keep telling my parents, but my father's too busy and my mother just won't listen. They should have guessed I was useless when I failed the entrance exam the first time. But no, they had me crammed to the brim for the second shot.'

Megan broke a thread with her strong front teeth, glanced outside at the people who were shopping along Bradshawgate. After a day at school, she enjoyed coming here, looked forward to a bit of sewing. Deedee had her eye on the property next door, too, was planning to turn it into DUFFY'S LEATHER WORKS when Megan finished school completely. It would be wonderful to have the shop attached to Deedee's FINE SEAMS.

She dragged her thoughts back into the here and now. Geoff Althorpe was turning up three or four times a week, was distracting her with his mithering. She liked him, she liked him in smaller doses. Still, once the extension was complete, she'd be able to go up to the next floor and hide in a cupboard.

Minnie and Bertha had gone upstairs for a brew, were chatting with Deedee about the opening of their extended premises. The downstairs was to become a bigger shop with fitting rooms at the rear, while the factory was moving to the first floor. The Singers were paid for, as was the shop, so Deedee had decided to take on more workers. 'Just say you're not going to that school any more.' Megan got fed up with Geoff sometimes. She preferred Fliss, because Fliss was brave and strong. 'Or go to school and do nothing. At the finish, the headmaster will throw you out for failing tests and things. Then you can get your wish and be a mechanic.'

She was eleven now. When he looked at her, his cheeks became uncomfortably hot and his hands got sweaty. Thirteen, almost fourteen was a strange age for a boy, he thought. During recreation, his schoolfellows came out with some crude stories and a few lewd expressions. He would smile at them, force a laugh, pretend to enjoy the bawdiness. But the things they mocked were . . . He turned away from the sewing table, displayed an interest in some leather belts. Those awkward moments at school were connected in some odd way with Megan. He wanted to grow up, wanted to marry her and live with her, away from Mother, away from—'

'Pass me the big scissors,' she said.

He complied, enjoyed the painful pleasure of her hand brushing against his. 'I'm going to Australia one day,' he said.

'Very nice.' She tucked a piece of kid under the needle, guided the foot expertly along a straight seam. 'That's where all the thieves got sent,' she added after a moment or two.

'It's a big country, Megan. Loads of space, lots of farms wanting tractors. They need cars, too. They need buses and charabancs to get across from one town to the next—'

'So they'll want people who are interested in engines.'

'Yes.'

She pulled out the stitched bag, placed it on a pile of three or four. They would be taken to Dad's clog shop for finishing. Dad was good at fixing on the frames with their brass clasps. 'I've two belts to make,' she said thoughtfully. 'Special orders, one grey and one tan.'

He leaned on her table, spreading his hands wide apart. 'Will you come with me?'

'Where?'

'Australia.'

She stared at him with great seriousness. 'What for?'

Geoff knew that his face was going puce. He loosened his hated school tie, opened the top button of his shirt. 'Well, I shan't want to go alone. It's better if you do things in pairs.'

'Why? Why would I want to go traipsing off to Australia? It's all sheep and rabbits and criminals, isn't it?'

He swallowed, cursed his mouth for being so dry. Every time he got near Megan, his tongue seemed to cry out for moisture. It was nerves. He knew it was nerves, because the same thing happened in Latin and geography and . . . and during most lessons. Only science was vaguely interesting, and even that got a bit dull when the formulae had to be copied down. 'It's a new place, that's all,' he managed. 'Somewhere for a fresh start.'

She looked round, realized that she was exactly where she wanted to be. 'I don't need a fresh start, Geoff. I've got Deedee, Phyllis, my sisters and my dad.' By the time she remembered her mother, she was prattling again. 'I've got friends at school and Uncle Tommy who married Deedee. There's a tannery here. I get some good leather cheap and . . . and I'm happy.'

'I'm not happy, Megan.'

'Oh.' She waited, found the silence uncomfortable. 'I'm sorry if you're not happy.'

'We could be happy in another place. I'd make you happy. We could go and see kangaroos and koalas and wallabies. They have birds that make a noise like laughing. Nobody could be sad in Australia.'

She awarded him a hard look. 'It's you that's unhappy, not me. I don't need to go anywhere. I don't want to. Will you look in that box, see if there's any grey leather?'

His shoulders sagged as he rooted about for what she needed. He loved her. Because he loved her, he made a mistake, picked out some pieces of brown. 'Sorry.' The look on her face seemed to be printed at the front of his mind. As he rummaged for grey bits, his eyes blinked against the sight of her scorn. 'There you are.'

'Ta.' She fiddled with the scraps, wrapped the longest round a piece of cardboard, smeared glue along the joints. Her hands were supple and tanned. With quick movements, she completed the task, set the item aside until the glue dried sufficiently for stitching. 'I made a leather picture frame yesterday,' she said proudly. 'Me dad's putting brass corners on it, then we'll set it in the window. At this rate, I'll be rich before I'm fifteen.'

She was terrifyingly capable. Megan Duffy was a child from a poor home, a girl whose education had been basic. At the age of eleven, she was producing and selling items of merchandise that were well-made from scraps whose destination would normally have been a rubbish bin. More than that, she was extending her repertoire, inventing and designing new products all the time. He felt small, unimportant, defeated. In spite of his father's money and position, Geoff knew in his heart that he would not come up to scratch, could never be good enough for a girl as vibrant as this one. 'I'm in the way,' he mumbled.

'No.' Megan's natural politeness bubbled to the surface, only to be squashed by a need to be truthful. 'Well, it'd be easier if you just came to the house. You could have your tea on a Sunday.'

Miserably, he shook his head. 'Mother likes us all to sit around reading on Sundays. It's a day of rest.'

'Oh well,' she muttered dismissively. 'I'll see you some time, then.'

He picked up his satchel, crammed the stupid black-and-gold cap on his stupid head, walked outside. She didn't care about him, wasn't interested. At snail's pace, he walked through the town towards his father's mills. He could do his homework there, in an office, could put off seeing his mother for a couple of hours. Evelyn Grimshaw's son was getting on Mother's nerves. Evelyn Grimshaw's son was served up like gravy every night, because Evelyn Grimshaw's son was going to be a doctor very soon. Boys had to do things like that, it seemed, were expected to go off and get university degrees and letters behind their names. How he envied Fliss. Mother had decided to back her daughter, had even taken to visiting the mills she had avoided for years. Dad had met Mother in Number One, long before the refurbishment, long before the building of Number Two.

Outside the Bolton Savings Bank, Geoff paused. If he were to leave school and turn up for work at his father's factories, Mother would have a fit. Fliss could do as she liked, but Geoff would be forced to carry on at his books for ever and ever. He stared at the heavy door behind which his savings lay. At thirteen, nearly fourteen, he was almost old enough to empty his account and book a one-way passage. Almost, but not quite. He gazed at the pavement, counted the months. By this time next year, he might be gone. Would Megan miss him . . . ?

Megan stood at the top of the stairs, pushed a lock of hair out of her eyes. The bedrooms had wanted scrubbing. It hadn't been an easy job, because little water could be used on floorboards, but she'd persevered until the worst of the muck had gone. 'Uncle Tommy?' she yelled.

'That's me.' He appeared in the hallway, a flowered pinafore tied round his thinning frame, a feather duster held out like a sword. 'Avast ye blackguards!' he shouted. 'What do you wish, fair maiden?'

'I'm not fair, I'm dark.' She laughed at him. Every day without fail, Deedee's husband had Megan in pleats. 'Whose pinny is that?' she asked.

'Mine.' He climbed a couple of steps. 'See, really, I'm a woman. Only when me hair started thinning, I thought I'd best start pretending to be a man.' He posed, the feather duster sticking up behind his head, the free hand limp. 'I'm called Esmerelda. What's your excuse, young lady?'

'I've done the floors,' she said, forcing herself to be serious. 'I got a big spile down one of my nails, but I've pulled it out.'

'Iodine,' he suggested.

'No,' she begged. 'Anything but that, Esmerelda. Will you fetch the rugs in? And the beds need spannering back together.'

Deedee arrived at the foot of the stairs. 'Tommy Wagstaff, get a move on. These brasses need more than a spit, then I want yon kitchen turning inside out.' She came closer, edged up the flight. 'Tess is mending curtains,' she mouthed. 'Looks like we've shamed her into doing summat.'

Tommy nodded. 'She doesn't look right to me, love. She seems all swelled up. Not with the baby . . . just . . . all swollen.'

Deedee placed a finger on her lips, went down, closed a couple of doors. When she returned, she sat halfway up the stairs. 'I know what you mean, lad. It's all her joints, isn't it? Her ankles and her wrists. And her face looks grey. This one's not going to come out easy.' She twisted her head round, noticed Megan trying her best to be invisible. 'That's a good girl, Megan. Go in the parlour now, help Phyllis with the polishing. Then we'll fetch that big pan of tater hash from our house.'

She smiled when Megan passed Tommy on the stairs. He clouted the girl with the feather duster, received a quick swipe from the floorcloth in Megan's hand. 'She's fit for you any day, Tommy,' laughed his wife. 'You'll not best our Megan, not in a month of Sundays.'

They sat together on the stairs, talked through the things that still needed to be done. Joe had taken Hilda and Hattie to the park, while Sarah was giving Phyllis the benefit of one of her incomprehensible lectures, goo-ing and da-ing in the parlour. 'I've got a bad feeling about this lot,' said Deedee. 'She's had near misses in the past, has Tess, and she's worn herself down wanting a lad. I've never seen her so ill. And the doctor's not pleased, you know. He came round last week with Father O'Riley, told her that she shouldn't be having babies at this rate.'

'Father O'Riley-as-was, you mean. Fancy him stopping so long at Dr Walsh's – good job they get on, them two.'

He stroked his chin, decided that he needed to strop his razor. 'So Charlie Walsh thinks Tess is in for a bad time?'

Deedee nodded. 'She'll pull through, I suppose, just like she always does. But if we get another lass, what'll she do? Carry on like this till she's middle-aged? We can't get through to her at all. Joe's tried, I've tried, the doctor's had a go. Even Father O'Riley told her to slow the production line down a bit. Oh well. This isn't getting the house done. Look at us working on a Sunday.' She rose, straightened joints that had started to creak very slightly of late. 'Is that my new pinny, Tommy Wagstaff? The one I ran up last week?'

He studied his apron. 'D'you know, I think it is. Well, what a terrible thing I've done.'

Deedee clipped him lightly round the ear. 'Listen, don't push your luck, sunshine. I've enough with all them cats of yours. You'll be out on the street, the lot of you, if you don't behave.'

He shook his head. 'And I love you, too, Doris Appleyard.'

She left him to it, had a look at Tess, carried on with the cleaning. She scrubbed, polished, set mousetraps, cleaned windows. And all the time, she could visualize Tess's grim face. Deedee's mind was troubled, so she worked to ease the pain. Yet when all was complete, when the family sat down in a tidy house to potato hash and red cabbage, Deedee found no solace. Tess ate little, said less. And everyone else could only watch and wait.

The screams were terrible. Joe ran next door, alerted Elsie Shipton. 'Take the children,' he begged. 'Leave Annie and Nellie, they're downstairs boiling water and brewing tea.'

'No bother, Joe.' Elsie had been awake for several minutes, had woken to what sounded like an animal in pain. 'Is that Tess shouting?'

'Aye.' He left Elsie in charge, dashed away to get Nancy Unsworth, the woman who was usually called Old Mother

Hubbard. Old Mother Hubbard was midwife, layer-out and unqualified doctor to folk in the flower streets. She always dressed in black, a long skirt that swept the floor, a voluminous shawl that covered her from head to toe. Nancy Unsworth had told Joe to make sure that Tess had no more babies, but she seemed to understand the situation when she finally opened the door. 'Two minutes, lad,' she whispered through a crack. 'I'll just find me bag of tricks and get dressed. I knew it. I knew she'd carry on for a lad, soft beggar.'

Joe waited, hopped from foot to foot, tried to arrange his thoughts. There was bright blood in the bed. Fresh blood meant that the baby's bag had broken, that his son or daughter was already beginning to separate itself from the womb's nourishment. 'I'm going for the doctor,' he yelled at Old Mother Hubbard's window. 'I'll see you at home.'

Charlie Walsh sent Joe downstairs, then struggled for more than an hour, sweat pouring from his brow as he tried to help the writhing woman. He was no Catholic, no believer in the sacrifice of a mother for the sake of an unborn baby. It was Tess's life he strove to save, yet he knew almost from the start that he was going to lose the battle. It had been an unequal war, anyway, because this woman was not built for prolific breeding. 'Ambulance,' he snapped at Nancy Unsworth. It was unlikely that any medic could save the patient, but he was going by the book. 'Send Joe to my house, tell him to phone the hospital. We need blood – they must have a donor standing by. And get Paddy,' he yelled over his shoulder.

A small baby boy was born at ten minutes to midnight. Just as help arrived in the street below, Charles Walsh placed the infant in the arms of the dying mother. 'It's a boy, Tess,' he whispered. The little one was breathing rhythmically in spite of the difficult birth. The doctor prayed inwardly, hoped that the new arrival was healthy enough to hang on until Tess's inevitable exit. Sometimes, these bad confinements produced children that didn't last for many minutes after being so cruelly starved of oxygen.

She opened her eyes, smiled down at the tiny, bloodied child that lay across her chest, 'Joseph,' she breathed. 'Is he all right?'

The doctor nodded. 'He's grand, love.' With a wave of his hand, he summoned the disgraced priest to the bedside.

Without hesitation, Paddy dragged the worn stole from his pocket, blessed the semi-conscious mother, held her hand until soul and body were divided. 'Sweet Jesus, have mercy on this mother and child,' he muttered thickly. He released the chilled hand, walked to the bedroom door, put his arm across Joe's shoulders. 'I'd no unction, but I did what I could,' he told the white-faced man. 'And I'll baptize the baby.' He didn't need to be a priest to perform this second ceremony. Anyone could baptize in an emergency, even without holy water. He returned to the bed, dipped his fingers into a cup by the bed, wet the child's head, asked for a name.

'Joseph,' answered the doctor. 'She told me he'd to be named Joseph.'

Joe staggered across the room and sank on to the edge of the mattress, touched his wife's face. 'Tess?'

'Sorry,' said Charles Walsh. 'I did my best.' He left a scene he had witnessed only too often in the garden streets, sent the ambulance away. The baby was small, but he was taking air steadily and beginning to cry. Given the situation in this house, it might be as well to allow nature to take its own course. If Joseph lived, he would be a treasure. If he died, there would be no more burdens for the widower to carry.

The doctor, knowing that Mother Hubbard would tend the baby, decided to stay downstairs. He entered the kitchen, looked from Annie to Nellie. They were so patient, so placid. She had made them like this, had turned them into second-class citizens who simply sat, waited for marriage, for childbirth, for death. They needed some relaxation, a break from this depressing house. He smiled a greeting, took a cup of tea, sat in a chair by the fire.

'How's Mam?' asked one of them.

They even sounded alike, he thought. 'Your dad will be down shortly,' he said.

'She's dead, isn't she?'

He closed his eyes, leaned back, curled his fingers round the cup. 'I'm sorry.'

They reached for each other and cried softly, as if even their tears were rationed. When the doctor opened his eyes, he saw two little girls, both blonde, both tired, both appearing to grieve. Their working lives had already begun. Tomorrow, they would get out of bed at the crack of dawn, would go along to the mill. Come rain, shine or a death in the family, these young people would still tend mule or loom until the hooter sounded. They were good, honest folk who would toil till the day they dropped.

'What about the baby?' asked Annie. Annie was the taller, the older of the two.

'He's alive.'

Each girl gripped the other's hands. 'It's a boy,' said Nellie.

'And Mam doesn't know.'

'She does.' Charles Walsh rose, came to the table. 'She saw him, called him Joseph.'

They dried their tears, cleared the table, set it again with porridge bowls and spoons. He watched them closely, noticed how serene they were. They would probably cry again at Tess's funeral, then they would place their mother in small compartments at the back of their minds. She hadn't loved them and she had, perhaps, done them a favour, because they appeared relatively unmoved by her untimely passing.

'Get the book,' said one. Together, they pored over dates and payments, assessed how much the insurance would be. 'It's enough,' said Nellie. 'That'll do the funeral and coats for all of us.'

Charles sat again, gazed into the dying fire while Tess

Duffy's daughters discussed undertakers and coffins. When that subject had exhausted itself, the girls went through a list of nursing mothers, argued quietly about who was best qualified to suckle Joseph. Annie opened a drawer, took out a layette, placed baby clothes in a pile on the sofa. 'Good night,' they said in unison before leaving the room.

He waited until Joe came down, sat for a while with the new widower. Nancy Unsworth appeared with the baby, announced her intention to take him to a decent woman on Ivy Street. Joe nodded his permission, sat silently while his son was removed from the house. 'She got her lad, Doctor Walsh.'

'Yes.'

'And she paid the price. I should have left her alone, I should have made sure she had no more kiddies, but she—'

'Don't torture yourself. You've a hard task in front of you now, Joe.'

'Aye.' Tears coursed down his face. 'She were hard on the girls, but she were all right underneath, you know.'

Patrick O'Riley joined them, placed himself at the table. 'Shall I go next door for the little ones?' he asked.

Joe shook his head. 'Nay, leave it a bit. I'll have to tell them.' He glanced at the doctor. 'Annie and Nellie already know, don't they?'

'They guessed.'

'Have they took it bad?'

The doctor didn't know what to say. Annie and Nellie had gone to bed, would not allow for any distractions. From the age of six or seven, their lives had had a pattern, and it was too late now to divert the course on which they had embarked. 'They . . . took it rather well. A few tears, you know, but they're all right.'

Joe Duffy fixed his gaze on a sepia-coloured photograph that hung above the dresser. It had faded over the years, this picture of a young couple preparing to make vows. A veil of lace surrounded Tess's face, its edges scalloped in

241

accordance with the fashion of those times. What year was it? he wondered, trying to fix his mind on something other than funerals. 1909. They'd been twenty-three years of age, just three months between them.

He closed his eyes. Her gown had been long, tight at the waist, narrow in the sleeves. A hundred buttons down the back, that dress had owned. Well, it had seemed like a hundred later on, when they'd been together that first time. Tess had been so shy, so timid. They'd been the proud owners of a table, two chairs and a bed the day they got married. He remembered working long hours to buy curtains, towels, dishes. There were flowers in her hair. If he opened his eyes, he would see the coronet on her head, a circle of blooms that were destined to fade just as she had.

'Joe?'

Satin shoes. They were upstairs in a bedding box, had gone a bit yellowish over the years. Tess's wedding frock was in the same container, the material wrapped in tissue paper, the veil preserved in its own carton. There was a white missal, a pearl rosary and two holy pictures. The priest had presented each of them with a picture. Joe's, which portrayed his namesake, showed the good man teaching Jesus the art of carpentry. Tess's gift from the priest was an impression of St Theresa carrying flowers.

'Joe?'

He opened his eyes, needed an act of will to separate each pair of red-rimmed lids. 'No shroud,' he mumbled. 'I don't want her going under in a shroud. I'll put her in her wedding dress. I often wondered why she saved it. She can have her satin shoes and her prayer book and her picture of St Theresa. Oh, Tess.' Water poured again from his eyes. 'I don't know how I'll carry on without her.'

Patrick O'Riley came to Joe's side, placed a companionable hand on trembling shoulders. 'Shall I move in for a while, Joe? I'm of no fixed abode, so it would be no problem for me.'

The man by the fire shook his head. 'Nay. This has to be faced, Father.'

242

'Paddy. Remember, I'm Paddy.'

'Right.' Joe wiped his eyes on a towel that hung from the oven door. 'She were her own mother all over again. Lost a brother, did Tess, got the blame for it. She went for Megan after the lads died. I told her, I said, "Don't be carrying on like your mam, Tess." But it were like . . . like something burning in her. It weren't natural, this need for a boy. Took over all her waking moments, it did.' He lifted his haggard face. 'Father Paddy, what the hell am I going to do? I've eight kiddies. How can I raise them on me own?'

Paddy kept his counsel. For the duration of this latest pregnancy, Joe and the children had looked after themselves. 'It'll get sorted out,' answered Paddy. 'Perhaps your mother might help?'

Joe's head shook slowly. 'No. She's enough on with Megan and Phyllis. And there's the shop, the dressmaking business.' He pondered for a moment. 'Anyway, that's not what's bothering me. I loved her. I loved Tess. For all her faults, she was the only woman for me. I can't . . . can't imagine . . .' His voice faded away, was dissolved by more tears.

'The strength will come,' whispered Paddy. 'He'll see your need and He will provide.'

Joe gulped, tried to sniff away his grief. 'I've that shop to run, clogs to make and mend. I can't be minding a new baby, can I? Nellie and Annie are both working, then our Megan's still at school. Oh, Tess. Oh, my poor lass. She's not cold, yet here I am worrying about ordinary things.' He drew in a deep breath, allowed it to escape from lungs that shuddered, coughed to clear his airway. 'We'll not stop here, that's for sure. Two lads and a wife I've lost in this house. And three doors down, poor Ida . . . did that to herself.' He stared at the priest. 'This street's done you no favours, either.'

Paddy dropped his chin. 'The stand I made on behalf of suicides would have come about anyway. A street can't be blamed for a chain of events.'

Joe blinked slowly, shook his head. 'I believe in the devil. Jesus believed in him too. Remember Satan offering Jesus powers? He's still around, Old Nick. He's here, in this house, in this street. We are getting out of Myrtle Street, Father – Paddy, I mean. I can't look at that empty chair . . .' He fixed his gaze on the seat that had been occupied by Tess throughout the latter part of her pregnancy. 'No, I'm not carrying on here.'

The doctor opened his bag, placed two small pills on the table. 'I'll get the undertaker on my way home, Joe. Take these. Sleep on the sofa tonight.' He turned to his companion. 'Stay and help him with the children.'

It was a long night. When Joe finally slept, Paddy went next door, asked Elsie Shipton to keep the young ones. The woman wept when she heard the bad news, reassured Paddy O'Riley, told him that the children had found space in her beds. Paddy watched the birth of morning, prayed on the beads he had owned since childhood. But the decades of the rosary did not soothe him. Once again, he could find no solace for those who remained in this vale of tears.

ELEVEN

The Church of St Mary was packed solid with a crowd of near-motionless people. The congregation responded when necessary, slid tongues and lips around Latin phrases whose meaning was suddenly coming home to those who could translate them. Life ended. For Tess's older children, the cold solemnity of the Requiem hammered home the concept of transience, the knowledge that Tess had gone forever.

Joe sat in the pew nearest to his wife's coffin. He was past reasoning with himself, wondered how he was managing not to tear the lid off. She was inside, was wearing her wedding dress and her satin slippers. Tess had worn those clothes on this very spot many years ago, had made solemn vows to a new husband and to an old priest. Father . . . what was his name? Flynn, he thought. Father Flynn and Tess Duffy were both dead, but Joe was alive and in many kinds of pain. It was over. It was finished, but she was still in that lovely dress, was lying in the place where she had once blushed when the band of gold was pushed on to a slender finger.

Megan didn't cry. She had sat, knelt, stood in her new coat of navy wool, had helped Phyllis when the changing of position became difficult. She and Phyllis were like twins, matching coats and hats, matching shoes. Phyllis's shoes were proving difficult, the insubstantial kid lending too little support to weakened limbs. But Megan was glad about the shoes, as she knew that Phyllis hated to be seen in the sturdy boots prescribed by Dr Walsh.

The service was over. No-one budged an inch when Tess Duffy's coffin was borne out of the church. Joe, his head bowed by an emotion similar to shame, was guilty of the inability to support his beloved wife on her last journey. In the house of God, he cursed the shrapnel in his legs, glancing up briefly to apologize to the Blessed Virgin's statue. At mass, even an unspoken swearword must surely be a mortal sin?

The rest of the people began to shuffle slightly, wondered what to do. They couldn't go outside until the family had left. Those with food in their ovens worried about burnt pie-crusts; those with cotton on mule or loom thought about piece rates. The workers from Althorpe's were here with permission, so they scarcely shifted their feet. The boss, who was standing at the back of the church with his hat in his hands, was paying them work or play, though a funeral fitted neither category. One or two of them looked quickly over their shoulders. If Joe Duffy didn't get a move on soon, Sidney Althorpe might have to take charge.

Sidney's gaze was fixed on the back of Joe Duffy's head. Man and boy, Joe had worked ceaselessly at his bench, had made good, sturdy footwear for a whole community. And now the clogger seemed to have petrified at the front of St Mary's church, was plainly so shocked as to be completely immobilized. The owner of two huge mills and one saddened heart swallowed tears and misgivings, walked the length of the aisle, his gaze drifting over Deedee Wagstaff, Tommy, Phyllis, Megan, then another clutch of Duffy girls whose sizes were assorted. He would get them out of here. Not only now, not just out of the church. Sidney Althorpe was due a few favours, and he intended to call in the debts very soon. Joe needed a rest, a change from clogging. The poor kiddies, too, would benefit from an alteration in lifestyle.

Joe looked up. 'Mr Althorpe?' The man's hand placed itself on Joe's shoulder, was the nearest thing to a caress that could ever occur between two men.

'Come on, lad.' The confusion in the widower's eyes attached itself to Sidney's soul, seemed to cut him inside. 'We've got to get her buried, Joe.'

'Aye.' Joe turned, allowed his eyes to stray over the gathering. It seemed that every house in the garden streets had sent at least one representative. He spoke to Sidney. 'That's a terrible place we live in, you know. Our Albert, Harold, poor Ida Entwistle. Phyllis and all – the infantile, she got. And now . . .' He stared at the structure on which Tess's coffin had recently sat. 'Tess said Myrtle Street were cursed and I agreed with her, though I said nowt.' The furrows on his brow deepened. 'She's gone, Mr Althorpe.'

Was the man meaning that his wife was dead or that the box containing her remains had disappeared? 'She's outside.'

'Aye.' Joe straightened, pulled at Annie's sleeve, swivelled again to face the aisle. While Sidney Althorpe remained at the foot of the altar steps, Joe Duffy led the mourners into the street.

The plumed horses champed and snorted, tapped impatient hooves on cobbles. This was a grand pair of black geldings, tails trimmed and oiled, flanks glistening after careful grooming. Behind them, a glass cage displayed flowers, ribbons, a coffin of dark, shiny wood. Joe walked to where Father Kevin Marsh stood with a white-faced altar boy. It was Billy Shipton. The clogger nodded at the son of his next-door neighbour, wondered briefly how the lad was managing to behave himself sufficiently to merit this sudden elevation in status. And hadn't Billy always sworn he'd never wear a frock on the altar steps? Happen Elsie had pushed the lad into it, then. Aye, she was like that, Elsie. 'Thanks,' said Joe to Father Marsh. 'We'll not be needing you now.'

The priest frowned. 'I beg your pardon?'

Joe Duffy shrugged, tried to shift his brain to work out why he was dismissing the cleric. Then he saw a possible reason, lifted a hand towards Paddy O'Riley. The young ex-priest was nearly bald, thought Joe, worrying simultaneously why he was standing here musing about Paddy's hair and about Billy Shipton being an altar boy. And why did Father Marsh have to go away? Joe nodded, answered himself. Kevin Marsh was a drinker and Tess hadn't approved of drinkers. Furthermore, Tess had thought a lot of Paddy. 'She'll be put under by her own priest,' he said softly.

'But . . .' The cleric blushed, placed a hand over his mouth. The flask in his pocket seemed to burn through the cassock, a monumental sin that was visible, on show for all the congregation to see. 'I'm . . . I'm the parish priest now, Mr Duffy.' He had fought the demon drink, but the battle had been lost, because the devil's elixir had a powerfully strong hold.

Joe, who seldom quarrelled with anyone, was in no mood for small talk. 'She didn't like you,' he said, little sentiment in his tone. 'She liked Paddy. Even the kiddies liked him, though he always said he were no good with young ones.' He breathed in the whisky fumes, watched the priest's uncertain stance. 'You've sent her soul to heaven, Father Marsh. Let Paddy see to our Tess's earthly remains.'

'The graveside blessing should be performed by me.' He was losing face. Every week, the church got emptier. Twice he had opened up the confessional only to sit with his own sins, no penitent at the other side of the grille, no sinner to take his mind off his own shortcomings. 'I shall come to the cemetery,' he said.

Joe's eyes strayed over Kevin Marsh's corpulence, came to rest on the network of veins on nose and face. 'Please yourself. But Paddy will be doing the honours.'

Patrick O'Riley strode forward, pushed aside a small crowd whose members were listening intently to the quiet altercation. 'I'm no longer a priest, Joe,' he said softly.

Joe nodded thoughtfully. 'You're nearer to God than any of us, because you stood up for what you believe in. Tess would want you to bury her.'

Paddy searched his head for ideas. 'I've no purple stole.'

'Green'll do,' came the swift response. 'She weren't that keen on purple, always said it's a miserable colour.'

Kevin Marsh removed the biretta, passed a hand through his hair. 'What shall I do?' It was so humiliating, so undignified. But dignity often eluded him, so perhaps the lack of self-esteem was the cross he would have to bear. So here he was, standing on a cracked pavement, asking an unfrocked priest for advice.

Joe coughed. 'Look,' he said. 'She only stood up once, my Tess. But she did stick to what were right, what she thought were right.' He closed his eyes for a moment, saw Tess marching through the streets at the front of a small procession. Tess had led the revolution, had guided the church's hand. Because of the little lady in the coffin, Mother Cecilia had been banished from the town. His eyelids flickered, raised themselves. 'Catholic nuns can be cruel,' he whispered. 'My wife got rid of yon Cecilia. She hunted that nun out of yon school and out of England. As for Paddy, we're all proud of what he did. Jesus would have done the same thing. Even Rome must know that the living Jesus was of a forgiving nature.'

Paddy O'Riley placed a hand on Kevin Marsh's forearm. 'We'll do it together, Kevin. Half each.'

The shepherd of St Mary's looked at his flock of black sheep. The people stood about in sombre clothes, missals and rosaries clutched in their hands. Paddy was one of the flock. Kevin Marsh stared into the eyes of the layman whose confessions he heard. There were few stains of sin on the soul of Patrick O'Riley. In fact, this was a remarkable man, one who knew his Maker. 'Right, we'll do that.'

The gathering assembled itself in rows of four behind Joe, followed the cortège through the streets. Curtains and paper blinds covered almost every window along their route, while those householders who had been unable to attend the service stood in silent lines along the kerbstones. Catholics blessed themselves in response to their priest's raised hand, Protestant men removed their caps, women bowed their heads. Even the children were quiet, some stopping their games when the procession arrived, others clinging to mothers' aprons, baby-eyes round, thumbs stuffed into small mouths.

In the cemetery, Joe cleared a parched throat, planted boot-clad feet in a position that eased the discomfort in his knees. The twins' stone had been removed, was at the mason's yard. A clay-lined maw had opened itself to the sky, seemed to be waiting to swallow Tess Duffy. Tess's name would be etched now into the space beneath 'HAROLD, TWIN BROTHER OF THE ABOVE'. The 'ABOVE' was Albert.

The widower screwed up his face, refused to cry here in the open. He had to pull himself together, must get on with the business of living for Annie and Nellie, for Freda, Hilda, Hattie, Sarah and Joseph. Megan stood opposite him and he smiled at her. He hadn't forgotten Megan. It was just that he trusted his mother to look after the third-born of his children. Doris Wagstaff was leaning on her dark-haired granddaughter. Little Phyllis Entwistle was being held straight by Tommy who used to be the knocker-up. Tommy was now Joe's stepfather.

When the coffin was lowered into the ground, Paddy stood next to Joe, a hand cupped beneath the clogger's right elbow. Joe shook so hard that the ague transmitted itself into Paddy's body, causing both of them to tremble.

'She didn't like the cold,' said Joe.

'It's not cold in heaven,' came the reply.

'Hotter still down below.' Joe checked himself. 'We know she's not gone yonder, eh? Wanting a lad weren't a sin, were it?'

'No.'

'And she loved the girls in her way.'

'She was what life made of her, Joe.'

'Aye.'

While Joe shook the hands of mourners, Paddy gathered the family together. Annie and Nellie each carried a baby girl, and Freda held the hand of the three-year-old Hilda. Megan stood with Deedee, Phyllis and Tommy. 'You'll all have to be as good as possible,' said

Paddy. 'Because your father has a lot on his mind.'

Hattie frowned while Sarah gabbled some of her nonsense.

'There's the shop to run, so the rest of you must take turns doing chores in the house.'

Annie cleared her throat. 'Will I stop going to work?'

Paddy was in no position to answer this question. 'Something will be sorted soon,' he said. 'For now, one of you must stay at home and mind the babies.'

'Excuse me.'

Paddy and Joe turned simultaneously to find Sidney Althorpe and his daughter standing with their backs to a gravestone in the next row. 'Oh. Hello, Mr Althorpe,' said Joe. 'I saw you in church. Thanks for taking the time.' This was a good man, thought Joe. Never missed a funeral, always sent fruit to a sickbed. 'You needn't have traipsed all this way, – and thanks for helping me out of church.'

'I've come in the motor.' Sidney removed his hat, stared down at Tess's coffin. 'She spun a few miles of cotton for me, did Mrs Duffy.' His eyes fastened themselves to Joe's face. 'That's become an unhappy street.'

Joe dropped his chin. 'Aye, you can say that again.'

Fliss Althorpe stepped forward, shook Joe's tired hand. 'My father and I would like to visit you later this week, Mr Duffy. We may be able to help you in some way.'

'Not charity.' Even now, when his strength had ebbed to zero, the clogger clung to his pride. 'I've a thriving business, Miss Althorpe. I do make a living, you know. And I've a bit saved, enough for us to flit to another part of town.'

'A move would be a good idea,' said Sidney. 'Anyway, this is not the right place for a chat. We came, my daughter and I, to pay our respects to your wife and to offer our condolences. You will lose nothing by allowing me to visit you.' He replaced his hat, smiled at the children, walked away.

Fliss lingered, her eyes fastened to the face of little

Megan Duffy. She knew Megan well, often visited the Wagstaff house and the dressmaking shop. Megan was an interesting child. Although she was only eleven years of age, she had made new blotter frames for the Althorpe offices, had re-covered chairs and the seat of a bench. Dad's plan had to work. Megan and all these other little girls must surely be taken away from streets that had seen so much tragedy. 'I'm very sorry,' she said to Joe before following her father to the cemetery gate.

'A lovely girl, that,' announced Doris. 'Right.' She grabbed Megan's arm, pulled Tommy to attention. 'Come on,' she said grimly. 'Before the butties curl up.'

Sidney stood his ground at one end of the dining table while his wife, at the opposite end, finished her apple pie. 'Now, you can go into one of your declines if you like, Agnes, but my mind is made up. We are buying Hall i' th' Vale.' He loosened his collar, swallowed, hoped with all his soul that she wouldn't guess the truth. The truth was that he already owned the house, had bought it cheap from a man who owed several favours to Sidney Althorpe Esquire. 'Look, love, you're not going to wake up one morning and find yourself back to square one in the middle of Bolton.' Although she hid what he called her silly terrors, Sidney knew his wife well. All the trappings, all the manners were a direct result of Agnes's lack of confidence. Even when she growled, she was only expressing pain. 'The sensible half of you has always wanted a grand house, so this is your chance at last.'

Agnes put down her coffee cup, allowed it to shiver against its saucer for a fraction of time. 'It's a pigsty,' she declared, her voice ominously quiet. Deep inside herself, she was shaking, terrified of change. Yes, a big house would be nice, but she was used to Church Road, had settled. Because of her insecurities, she was digging in her heels. It was stupidity again, she told herself. In her heart, she was still too poor for this man.

Sidney groaned, lowered himself into his carver. 'That

is a beautiful place and well you know it. There's part of it dates back to Queen Elizabeth—'

'And it shows!' Agnes, who had upset herself by interrupting so rudely, dabbed at her lips with a square of lace-bordered cotton. As a modern woman, she had given up declines and she believed in having her say. But she was still a lady, had worked hard at becoming refined. Ladies, even in this day and age, did not interrupt their husbands. 'Sidney, I don't want to live in a hut.'

'And there I was, thinking you'd gone all modern. Aren't you the one who wants changes? Aren't you among those who scream for all women to have the vote?'

She winced against his tone. 'Sidney, it's not like you to shout. What, pray, has suffrage to do with living in a black-and-white nightmare of a house?'

He had lost his thread. She was right, of course – he could find no sense in his argument. But he would find sense in a minute . . . While struggling for something to say, he blundered about, selecting, nipping, then lighting a cigar. 'Agnes, my dear,' he began as he paced about wreathed in a mist of blue smoke. 'I am talking about modernity, about daring to be different. Look how you stood up for young Felicity – look how right you were.' Agnes had opposed Felicity's choice, but Sidney took a safe route by pretending that his daughter's career in the mills had been Agnes's idea. 'Fliss belongs in the workplace, and well you knew it. So now, I ask you to support me in this venture.'

Agnes looked at her polished nails, drew in a deep breath that was meant to hide her tremblings and express how stretched her patience was becoming. 'The Hall has been unoccupied for centuries, Sidney.'

'Nonsense. It was let to tenants for a long time, then some damned fool put a stone extension on the back. In spite of that, it's still a beautiful building. Can you imagine how it will look when restored? Have you seen the spiked finials?'

Agnes, knowing nothing at all about finials, took another breath.

253

Sidney, who had only just read about Hall i' th' Vale's architecture, attempted to blind her completely with a science that was new to him. 'That round-headed entrance archway is a triumph.'

'Like Napoleon's in Paris?' she asked, an uncertain edge to her semi-sweet tone.

He frowned for a second. 'No, dear, not like the Arc de Triomphe. This is the porch – here.' He walked the length of the table, slapped down a picture of the house. 'And what you call black-and-white is a series of moulded string courses.' In response to her unwavering gaze, he floundered. 'Or so I was led to believe,' he added, his tone somewhat lame.

She nodded slowly. 'What exactly is a moulded string course, Sidney?'

He jabbed a finger at the photograph. 'The black-and-white stuff.'

'Exactly.' Agnes rose from her seat. 'Call it what you will, it's still just a big shed painted black and white.'

He gritted his teeth. 'We'll not be living there for ages. It'll take at least . . . oh, five years to bring it up to scratch.' In five years, Joe Duffy's new baby would be starting school. Young Joseph would be robust, as would all the other Duffys, because their dad was going to be caretaker at Hall i' th' Vale, ten bedrooms, acres of land, fresh air and freedom . . . Sidney's brow was furrowed for a moment. This was all very well, but what if Joe wanted to stick to his clogging? 'Then I'm bequeathing it as a museum,' he told his discomfited wife. 'I'm leaving it to the people of Bolton. The name of Althorpe will be written in the annals of philanthropy. We shall chart the progress of cotton from cottage to mill. I intend to fill the attics with memorabilia that can be displayed in the rooms when the time comes.'

Agnes reclaimed her seat, poured herself a glass of water, sipped delicately, placed the crystal on the table-cloth. 'Shouldn't your money go to Geoffrey and Felicity?' Always, always, she worried about penury.

'There's enough,' he answered gruffly. 'We can make our mark, create something that will last forever.' He returned to his carver, perched on its edge while waiting for the storm to pass.

She lifted her shoulders slightly. 'As long as I don't have to live in it.'

Sidney drew deeply on the fat, hand-rolled Havana. It was all planned. The road that led up to Hall i' th' Vale had two cottages, one at each side of a pair of tall, age-wearied gates. He owned the cottages, too, would be able to shelter a couple of stricken families. Anyway, he longed to live in that neglected mansion. 'We shall move in eventually. Once it's ready, you'll love it.' The house wanted occupying, needed light and movement. 'There's a spit in the kitchen,' he announced unnecessarily.

'Good. I hope you find some strong servants to turn the fatted calf above the fire.'

'Agnes, you will be the envy of every woman in this town. I have bought an Elizabethan mansion. Well, some of it dates back to Queen Bess . . . how many of your friends can say that their house is truly different and . . . and superior?'

'And draughty, no doubt.' She folded her arms, raised her chin. 'So you already own it?'

Sidney cursed inwardly. 'Yes.'

'Without saying a word?'

'It was a chance. It was too good to miss. I got it for a song.'

'Right.' she dabbed at her lips once more, rang the little brass bell, stared into space while Mary Weston cleared the table. Fliss and Geoffrey were in their rooms and anyway, there was no point in seeking support from her children. If she made a fuss, called them down, they would only heap more coals on her head. She could imagine the pair of them viewing the purchase as a romantic and meaningful gesture. A museum. They were all going to live in a huge, cold hut with string courses, spiked something or other and few conveniences.

'It will be years,' he reminded her again when they were alone once more.

'Bathroom?' she asked.

'Not yet. There's a lavatory outside, of course.'

'I'm not budging an inch till there's at least one bathroom.'

He attempted a smile. 'Just you wait, Agnes. We'll have chandeliers in the dining hall, great big beauties carved from oak. When you entertain, you will be the envy of everyone.'

She pondered for a moment or two. 'So. What we are really about is the saving of a piece of history.'

'Exactly.' He leaned back into the chair, satisfied now that he could see a chink in her armour.

Agnes pursed her lips. 'Tapestries, of course.'

'Of course.'

'Thick-weave curtains too. They had those very low chairs. The backs were high, but the seats were low, padded and covered with faded material. Studs around the edges of the seats. Of course, the tables would need to correspond in height.' She rose, paced about. 'You will have to keep the spit for posterity, but I want gas and electricity. I wonder where we'll find those great big beds?'

'We'll find them.' She was taking the bait. He held back a smile of triumph.

'I must be consulted at all times, Sidney.'

'Naturally.'

She patted her hair, stood by the window. 'Evelyn Grimshaw will be furious, you know.'

'Yes.'

'She'll be running about with her husband's cheque book until she finds a mansion. Especially since her beloved son got sent down from the university.' Agnes squashed a bubble of unseemly glee. 'And we can stay here until the Hall is ready.' She turned on her heel and faced him squarely. 'Sometimes, Sidney, you seem to do the right thing quite by accident. Shall I pour you a drink?'

Sidney Althorpe basked in the twin glows of wifely approval and Napoleon brandy. Now, all that remained was the job of shifting a large family to Bromley Cross. Compared to what had occurred in recent minutes, the next task would be easy.

'I love you.' He looked up the street, down the street, seemed to be worried about eavesdroppers. 'They'd all think I was after money, but I'm not. I liked you before I knew who you were. I liked you when I first bumped into you on the steps.'

Fliss held her breath. Phil Greenwood loved her. She had a big nose and big bones, yet this young man was pressing her against the wall and towards commitment. She swallowed. 'I think I love you, too.'

He raised an eyebrow. 'You only think?'

'Well, I've never loved anybody before. With the exception of my parents, that is. And I suppose I love Geoffrey now that he's almost stopped being an ass.'

Phil's hands trembled as he gathered the girl close to him. She smelled of flowers and new bread. Her hair was thick and shining and, for endless months, he had wanted to feel its texture. 'Of course, I can't get married while my mother's so ill.'

'I know that.'

He cleared his throat, blinked against blurring vision. Fliss was a wonderful girl, a good woman. Would she wait for him? Mam kept rallying, was up one minute, down the next. The doctor had pronounced the death sentence years ago, yet the old girl battled on regardless. 'When she dies—'

She cut off his words by covering his mouth with her left hand. 'Don't talk about your mother dying, Phil. I don't mind waiting. Eighteen's a bit young, and I'm going nowhere.'

He kissed her, held her so tightly that both of them were breathless after the embrace. 'Waiting will be difficult,' he whispered. 'I want you now, Fliss.'

She deliberately side-stepped his meaning, didn't want to think too closely about giving herself to him. 'We can't be married right away. We have to wait.'

He stroked her hair, threaded his fingers in the silken mass. 'You know what I mean. You know what I want, because you want it too.'

She shouldn't have told Phil where she was going this evening. Dad was in number 13, Myrtle Street, had sent Fliss to fetch Mrs Wagstaff. And now, here she was in Back Holly Street with a man who was being familiar. She suppressed a giggle, told herself firmly that Phil wasn't just any man – he was hers. 'This has to stop,' she said with a firmness that denied her excitement. 'I can't be seen in an alley with you, Phil.' Her mother would scream blue murder, thought Fliss. 'And please don't pull my hair down. I must look . . . tidy, you know.'

He stepped back, pushed his hands deep into pockets. 'Right. I've no hands now, so go about your business.'

She hovered for a moment. 'You're not cross with me?'

Phil smiled sadly. 'No. I'll never be cross with you, love.'

Fliss moved away, smoothed her hair, then bolted to the top of the entry. Had anyone seen? Would the folk hereabout call her a loose woman? She ran down Holly Street, opened Deedee's door, stepped inside. As a frequent visitor, she had been ordered not to knock. 'You're like one of me own,' Doris Wagstaff had often told her.

'You look a bit flushed,' said Doris.

'I ran.'

The older woman tutted. 'Running is not ladylike, Miss Althorpe. Whatever would your mam say if she knew you were dashing about like a young pup?' She swept a couple of kittens from a chair, told Fliss to sit down. 'I'll just do me hair.'

Fliss watched the cats, counted five, thought there were more. 'How many?' she asked.

'Cats?' Deedee jabbed a couple of hairpins into her plaited bun. 'Depends what day it is. Yon feller keeps fetching more in, looks after some while folk are out. Tuesdays, he has Mrs Nuttall's Lucifer. He were named after a fallen angel, rightly so. That cat's din could curdle paint – we've never heard owt to match it. Likes coming here, does Lucifer. They all like coming here, because my daft husband feeds them up with fish and liver.' She dashed across the room, poked her head towards the stairs. 'Tommy? Get a move on. And tell them girls to come down here and all.' She turned to Fliss. 'Since Phyllis started getting upstairs, she's never been on the ground floor. Course, they can share a room these days. It's a grand little home now without Phyllis's bed taking up space.' She glanced round the room, was clearly proud of what she had achieved in the house.

Fliss crossed her fingers, hoped that Pop's plan would work. He wanted to move them all out of Bolton to Bromley Cross. It wasn't far, just a few miles up the moors, but it was fresh and green. 'My father's bought another house,' she announced cheerfully.

'Really?' Deedee pinched her cheeks for colour, dabbed a bit of powder on her nose. 'Another house? That's nice,' she said absently. 'Tommy,' she yelled. 'Get a move on. There's a mill boss waiting up yonder for us.' She lowered her tone. 'Why does he want to see us?'

Fliss shrugged. 'I don't know.'

'You do. You know, but you're not saying.'

'That's right – I do know, but I'm not saying.'

'Cheeky madam.' Doris grinned at the girl who called her 'Deedee', the young woman who treated Doris like a grandmother. 'I were upstairs a minute since,' she said meaningfully.

'Oh?'

'And I hope nobody else were looking out of their windows and all.'

Fliss swallowed. Her second 'oh' was little more than a squeak.

259

'He's a nice enough lad, is Phil, but . . .' Her words tailed off while she searched for the best way to convey what she needed to say.

'But what?'

Doris shrugged. 'Well, his mother.'

'I know his mother's ill, Deedee.'

'Aye.'

'Well?' Fliss glared at the older woman.

'Well, it's like this.' Doris sat down, folded her arms. 'She's very ill. But she weren't always ill, love. Yon lad's not free to marry, because he's already wed. To his mam.'

'I said nothing about marriage.' Fliss's tone was defensive. 'I'm not thinking of marrying anybody at the moment.'

'But you like him?'

Fliss shrugged, tried to lighten the moment. 'I suppose so.'

'And he likes you?'

'Yes.'

'In that case, lovey, you just watch your step. He's a normal man with normal needs, but he'll not be free till yon Bessie Greenwood kicks the bucket. She's got gout, stomach ulcers, varicose veins and a bad heart. To top the lot, her liver's on the blink and there's some who say she's started with cancer. She's also got a fierce hold on life and a stranglehold on her son. Bessie could still be here come 1940, you know.'

Fliss nodded. 'He's done the right thing. He's looking after his mother because she's got nobody else.'

Doris laughed, though the sound was hollow. 'Course she's got other relatives. It's just that they all escaped while the going were good. Phil's her youngest, that's all. The others are scattered about in England and America, but she's sisters nearby. Listen, I've known her for years. The Greenwoods used to live round here near her sisters, but she flitted off to the other side of town because she couldn't get on with nobody. And when she'd moved, she depended on Phil even more. Oh aye, she wants

260

everybody to think Phil's all she's got. Truth is, Phil's the only one who'll put up with the miserable old b— . . . woman.'

Fliss's chin was set. 'Well, it just goes to show how kind and considerate he is.'

'Or how daft. Look, lass. He's got his eye on you. When they get their eyes on you, they want to get their hands and all sorts of other bodily parts on you. Now, he's in no position to make an honest woman of nobody, not while Bessie's doing her dying duck act. And if I'm any judge of folk, he'll be wanting to jump the gun next news.' She held up her hand when Fliss opened her mouth to interrupt. 'And then your dad could be the one with the gun, eh? A bloody shotgun at the altar rails – excuse my language.' The latter part of the sentence was directed not at Fliss, but towards a statue of the Virgin. Then Doris, who was not easily distracted, continued to address Fliss after making the small penance. 'It would break Sidney Althorpe's heart if you got in any trouble.'

Fliss sighed deeply. All this had come from one kiss. 'We are not close, Deedee. There's nothing like that—'

'Yet. Just you heed me, girl. And what would your mam say if she knew you were walking out with a weaver?'

'I don't know. And we're not walking out.'

Doris wagged her finger. 'No, you're leaning on walls in back streets, lady. So you just think on it. You like him and he likes you and you're both young and healthy. I'm saying nowt about him, 'cos he seems all right, but if things ever come to a head, I reckon he'll be forced to choose his mother.'

'The situation won't arise.'

'I hope not. We all hope situations won't arise, but they do. Look at my son, now. He's lost twin boys and his wife.' She closed her eyes against a mind-picture of Joe's grief-stricken face, but the image was printed inside her eyelids too. 'Ida Entwistle's situation arose. And Phyllis's. It's called life, Fliss. Sometimes, I think I've seen enough to last me through this century and the next. But we keep

261

going, don't we? The only thing we can do is warn one another. I'm old. I've been on this earth a long time. So I can use what I've learnt, tell it all to you and hope you'll heed me. Watch him, he's lonely. If he wants to escape from his mam, don't be offering him no help. If he wants to get married, then let him leave her once and for all. There's others who'll take over and care for her. Bessie's sisters will have to rally round and fettle. But watch your step.'

Fliss was relieved when Tommy blundered into the room, because the flak was suddenly directed towards him. 'What are you doing with them brown boots on, Tommy Wagstaff?' asked his wife.

'Me black ones want heeling.'

'Aye, and so do you. Have you got a hanky?'

He pulled a wry face. 'I've not got a cold, so I don't need one.'

She bustled about, opened drawers, slammed cupboards, stuffed a clean handkerchief into his breast pocket. 'A navy suit and brown boots. Whatever will Mr Althorpe think?'

Tommy puffed out his chest. 'He'll think he wished I were still on night duty. He'll think I were a grand guard and a good knocker-up. He'll not see the likes of me again.'

'You're right there,' came the swift reply. 'Especially in them boots.'

Joe stared into the fire. 'Well, I don't know what to think.' He hadn't been thinking, not really, had gone about in a daze since the funeral. 'We need a change, but I don't know that we want to be traipsing off to Bromley Cross.'

Doris's eyes strayed to the door through which Sidney and Felicity Althorpe had just left. 'Well, he's always doing summat for somebody, is Sidney Althorpe. Happen he's trying to help us like he's helped others. The man's one in a million.'

Annie and Nellie sat side by side on the horsehair sofa,

each with her hands folded on her knee, each wearing a calm expression and a grey frock. Throughout the meeting they had remained silent, even when their opinion had been sought. Joe sought it now. 'What do you think, Annie?'

Annie looked sideways at her sister. 'It depends what Nellie wants.'

'Nellie?' asked Joe.

The next-to-eldest Duffy girl shrugged. 'I'll do what Annie wants to do,' she replied.

Doris folded her arms. 'No point asking them, Joe, not till they've had a secret conflab in a corner somewhere.' They were like Siamese twins, yet their grandmother did not mock them. She was pleased that they had one another, had always been glad about their closeness, especially as Tess hadn't been much of a mother . . . She made a little act of contrition, asked God and Tess to forgive her for such uncharitable thoughts. 'Megan?' she asked.

'I'm stopping with you, Deedee.'

'Right, so that's you sorted.' Doris and Tommy Wagstaff had decided almost immediately that they would remain in Holly Street. It was handy for the tram to town, and while their business was expanding, they preferred to be on the spot. 'So it's all down to you, Joe. Mind, I wouldn't go making too many decisions yet, lad. It's a big change, going up yon, and you want to have a good look at it first. But Mr Althorpe's right in his way. A rest from clogging would do you no harm.'

'What about the shop?' asked Joe. 'I can't just pike off and leave it, can I?'

Tommy nodded vigorously. 'Aye, but you could let it. There's that lad you've took on – he can buy the soles ready made, just do the uppers. As long as he makes enough to pay his own wages and a bit of rent, there's nowt lost.'

'I don't want the shop losing any goodwill,' said Joe, amazed because he was thinking and talking about something other than recent tragedies.

263

Megan, who had listened carefully, decided to make her contribution. 'Mills are smelly and noisy,' she declared firmly. 'Annie and Nellie can work on that farm Mr Althorpe mentioned. And Dad – I know you've got money saved, 'cos we've heard Deedee talking about it. You could use that money to pay . . . like a nurse. The nurse could mind our Joseph and the others while you do your taking care.'

'Caretaking,' prompted Doris.

'Yes.' Megan, who did not allow herself to be distracted by the childish mistake, remained in full flood. 'I don't think you should worry about the shop, Dad. Everybody will remember you when you come back in five years. Like Mr Althorpe said, they've got to drain the land round the big house first because all the water from the moors comes down to the garden. So you might have five whole years in Bromley Cross. Hilda and Freda can go black-berrying. It's safer in the country, too.'

Joe leaned back in his chair, closed his eyes against the sight of Deedee sitting in Tess's rocker. But he would take that chair with him. Was he going, then? He nodded to himself. Yes, he was going from here, but to what? 'I'll have to think on this for a few weeks, sort out about schools and things. I mean, we don't want to be stuck miles from everything, do we?'

'There's a Catholic school not too far away,' said Tommy. 'And it would do you all good to live in the country for a while. He only wants you to supervise the workings, Joe. It's cost him a couple of thousand, has that place, so he'll be wanting somebody trustworthy to look after it.'

Joe opened his eyes. 'I'll think about it.' He would have to talk to all his children, too, would need to find out the opinions of those who had reached the age of reason. Even then, they'd be needing to visit Hall i' th' Vale a few times, get familiarized with the lie of the land. 'We can't go on a journey till we know a bit more about what's at the end of it.'

'There speaks a wise man,' said Deedee. 'Although if

you think about it proper, life's one of them journeys, isn't it? We're all on a road without signposts.' She pulled herself together, told herself not to go all philosophical on an empty stomach. 'Now, I've some broken biscuits somewhere.' She delved into her capacious bag. 'Come on, Nellie, get that kettle singing, me tongue's as dry as paper.'

Joe remained seated, watched while life continued around him. 'I went to see Joseph today,' he told Deedee. 'Coming on a treat, he is. We can't go till he's weaned. Whether we go to another house in Bolton or to Bromley Cross, we all go together.'

His mother smiled. 'That's right, lad. That's the way it should be. We can't choose every inch of our path, but we get to pick some of our company along the way.' She was getting whimsical again. With a flourish, she produced the bounty. 'Who wants a digestive?'

Megan fixed her eyes on Granny Deedee and thanked her lucky stars, because Doris Wagstaff was a woman of great wisdom.

TWELVE

Joe Duffy glanced down at the sheet of paper in his hand. Getting here hadn't been too difficult, because the tram terminus was quite nearby. In fact, Joe had enjoyed the walk across from the Harwood road, had seen more trees and grass in half an hour than he'd glimpsed in his whole life. Tess would have liked it up here. She'd always relished seeing things clean and fresh. He paused, leaned on a rickety fence. Tess had enjoyed seeing things neat until she'd become truly obsessed with the idea of having a son. Those last months had been . . . untidy. Worse than that. He remembered the house being filthy, yet he knew he'd have swapped all the countryside in Christendom just to live for one more year in squalor with Tess. But he wasn't going to think about that, because he was going to move on for the children's sake.

Oh, Tess. He breathed in the clear air, inhaling so deeply that the draught seemed to reach his legs, making him stronger, capable of walking the rest of the way. At the end of the narrow track, he consulted the directions again, found Dog Leg Lane on the map, discovered that it was just a few paces away.

Twin gates hung loosely from broken hinges, the wrought iron pitted and corroded with age and neglect. At each side of the lane, a few feet from the broken gates, stood a stone cottage with boarded windows and patched roof-slates. Mr Althorpe already owned this pair of houses, but he had moved the tenants on in order to start some renovations.

If Joe stayed to the right, he could see part of the big house, but he did not catch sight of the whole building

until he met the sharp bend after which the lane had been
so aptly named. Like the joint on a dog's rear limb, the
road was angled sharply just before the halfway mark.

When he finally came upon Hall i' th' Vale, he sagged
against a dead tree-trunk, a huge thing that seemed to have
been shattered by lightning. He touched the burnt wood,
smoothed it as if seeking to offer comfort to the murdered
timber. It was fat for an elm, but it definitely was elm. Joe
loved wood and leather, read the textures of both with his
fingers, assessed them by feel rather than by sight. 'I'm
getting fanciful,' he said quietly. 'But I hope you didn't
suffer. I hope the lightning were quick, quicker than for
. . .' Tess. He did not say the name aloud.

The Hall was awesome. It's real name was, of course,
Hall in the Vale, but like so many locations hereabouts, its
name had been affected by the local dialect. The Bottom of
the Moor had become Bottom o' th' Moor – there was even
a thoroughfare somewhere called Stitch-mi-Lane. Funny
how things' titles got corrupted, he thought. Yet Hall i' th'
Vale seemed right in this instance, as quite a few of these
Elizabethan piles had been absorbed quite beautifully and
naturally into Lancashire's verdant moors.

For a long time, he lingered near the stump, followed
with his eyes the pattern of the mansion. A timber house.
A home that had been hewn from solid oak. The gable end
had a shallow window tucked into the eaves, then a huge
bay hung out, its courses jagged, spoilt slightly by
movement in the land. But the spoiling was at least a part,
if not all of its charm. He smiled sadly, chided himself
once more for acting fey. Yet it was as if this place were
alive and breathing, because no line was straight, no
pattern was true. 'You'd not measure up to a set-square,'
he told Hall i' th' Vale.

The black-and-white designs seemed haphazard, sometimes curling, sometimes making a stab at imitating
straight lines. There were crosses, curves, diagonals,
rectangles. No shape matched its neighbour; each white
section appeared to alter every time he looked back at it.

He walked, found a side entrance-gate, another gable end. At the rear, a stone extension had been added, its texture rough, undoctored. Atop the masonry sat metal spikes, about a dozen sharp spears which pointed skyward. These were all true, so the more modern part of the house was apparently stable. His feet itched, ached to take him inside. He remembered history lessons at school, all those dates, lists of noblemen who had pleased Queen Elizabeth, lists of those who had quarrelled with that tiresome, self-engrossed monarch. History had been dull, yet this place was wonderful.

Joe paused, savoured the moment. He was going to tread where men in silly, puffed-out shorts had walked. An ordinary working man in a flat cap was about to encroach on territory where hats had been plumed and made of velvet. He shivered. Did Anne Boleyn really walk with her head under her arm? Was she the one who had given birth to Queen Bess? Yes. Six fingers on one hand. Some had believed her to be a witch who had produced another witch. Still. Anne Boleyn and Elizabeth Tudor were not likely to be haunting a place in Bromley Cross.

Joe touched the gate, realized that he had not considered Tess for at least ten minutes. The house gripped him, would not let him go. It was love at first sight. How could anyone love a house? he asked himself. It was just a place where folk had lived – he'd seen pictures of another Elizabethan mansion, another hall. He rooted about in his head, remembered a similar house called Hall i' th' Wood. Yes, Samuel Crompton's mam had rented that, and Sam had invented the spinning mule while living in a place very similar to this. Hall i' th' Wood and Hall i' th' Vale – had these been built by the same crew, were they designed by one architect?

He found himself smiling. The sun shone and birds twittered about their daily business. This was proof of life after death, was a reason for continuing. He was going to live here. His children were going to grow here. The inside might be like a shippon, but nothing would stop him from minding this house while the necessary surgery was performed.

'It's grand, isn't it?'

Joe looked over his shoulder, saluted Sidney Althorpe. 'I was supposed to come on me own,' he said.

'I couldn't resist seeing your reaction. A man who has worked with wood must surely be fascinated by a house like this.'

'It's . . . well, I can't describe it.'

'Nor can I.' Sidney led the way through the porch, waited while Joe extracted from his pocket a huge iron key that was at least six inches long. 'I wonder if this is as old as the house?'

'I don't know. The original Hall was probably just the bit to the right of us. It was built for some businessman, possibly a chap in the cotton trade, a fulling miller, he'd be. Mind you, if the Hall's as old as we think, he might have had trouble, because I remember reading about a time when cotton was banned. That could well be down to our favourite neighbours.' He waved a hand in the direction of the Pennine foothills. 'Everybody had to wear wool, by all accounts. Yorkshire folk have never been keen on competition.'

'Born with their pockets sewn up and no sense of humour, that's what my mother always says.'

Sidney laughed. 'Yes, she's a character, is Deedee. Pity she doesn't want to move out here with you. There's plenty of room.'

Joe pushed the door inward. 'I've not said I'm coming yet, Mr Althorpe.'

Sidney watched Joe closely and knew that the clogger was tempted. They paced through a flag-floored kitchen whose area was probably twice as big as Joe's whole house. The fireplace was large enough for a man to stand in, and it contained a spit that was governed by ropes slung through pulleys to the ceiling. 'There's another kitchen,' said Sidney. 'Somebody put in a coal range and a couple of cupboards.' He guided Joe into a smaller area which held the familiar black fireplace with its oven and hinged hob. 'You can use this. And I'm getting the gas fitted, so there'll be a couple of rings soon.'

They walked through the original hall, a room whose proportions were baronial. Tiny windows let in mere chinks of light in which the dust of centuries was suspended. 'Dark,' remarked Joe. 'And there's nowt you can do about it, Mr Althorpe, not without ruining the . . . the proportions.' His voice hit the walls, bounced, returned to him after a split second.

Sidney nodded. 'I know. But the other rooms are smaller. This one won't be used very often – just for functions. So I'm putting a couple of dozen chandeliers in.'

'Proper ones?'

'Oh, yes. We'll get pulleys made to lift the fittings down for cleaning and to replace candles. My wife insists on electricity, and I agree with her. But in this room, there'll be just the coal grates and candlelight.'

Joe turned about, glanced from one end to the other. 'There must be sixty feet or more between them two fireplaces,' he said. 'It'll get a bit cold.'

'And it'll stay that way.'

Joe understood. He pictured how it must have been in this banqueting room – woven hangings on the walls, straw on the floor, perhaps a bit of matting. The man of the house probably sat at the head of the table with the more important guests next to him. There would have been pigs' heads on silver platters, chicken-bones thrown down for dogs, fruit heaped in great piles in the centre of a long table. The candles were probably thick and yellowish, made of tallow. Rich folk ate well and drank heartily in those days. 'I bet they had pewter tankards,' he said quietly.

'And the poker would have been in the fire all night to warm ale and mull wine,' added Sidney.

'Well, I hope they've all gone.' This was the nearest stab at a joke that Joe had managed since the funeral. 'I don't want blokes in tights waking me up to ask if I've polished their swords and rinsed their codpieces.'

Sidney laughed, though he kept the sound quiet. 'Wait till you see upstairs. Tell your children not to play marbles up there, because there isn't a single flat floor.' He walked to a window, used his handkerchief to make a clean circle in the filth. 'The place will be lighter once the windows are washed.' He beckoned Joe, asked him to look through the peephole. 'And there around us are the culprits,' he muttered. 'The moors, Joe. This is truly Hall i' th' Vale, because we're getting all their rain second-hand, then our own rain adds to the problem. The drainage comes first. We've to direct all that water past the Hall and into the streams.'

'You know I'm interested, don't you?' Joe removed himself from the window, faced the boss. 'I don't need to look upstairs. As long as there's a couple of fireplaces for the worst nights, as long as they'll be warm in their beds.'

'Yes, there are some cast-iron grates.'

Joe inclined his head thoughtfully. 'I shall want a wage even though there'll be no rent to pay. It's going to be a responsibility when the workmen arrive. And my savings is spoke for, 'cos I'll need help with the little lad.'

'Right.'

'And where's the farm for our Annie and our Nellie? Is it near? Are they decent folk, the farmers?'

Sidney pointed to the clean bit of glass. 'Two minutes that way, and you're on Eagle Top land. The farmhouse is further up the hill, but your daughters are young and healthy. The Fosters own Eagle Top. They're an old family who can trace their ancestors back to Adam. About three hundred years, they've been there, though the surname has changed once or twice when no sons were born.'

Joe swallowed. 'All for a lad, Mr Althorpe. She put herself through pain and torture till she got a boy. And he killed her.'

'The birth killed her, Joe. It wasn't the child's fault.'

Inwardly, he cursed himself for reminding Joe of the recent past.

The clogger gazed through the window again. 'It's all right, you know. I don't want you or anybody else having to be careful what they say. There's reminders everywhere, especially when I see our Megan. Tess weren't dark, but her hair were nearer in colour to Megan's than to anybody else's. Nay, you can't go about treading on eggshells just in case I get upset.' He faced his soon-to-be-employer. 'Where's the school?'

'At the bottom of Dog Leg Lane, turn left till you get to Eagle Top's first field, then turn right for the village. There's a little Catholic school that's shared by everyone from miles around. Your children will have one of the shortest journeys.'

'Good.'

Sidney Althorpe walked across the room, poked his head inside a chimney. 'Dark as hell', came the muted voice. 'Blocked, probably birds' nests.' He reappeared, his face blackened by soot. 'You'll have to get the sweep in, Joe.'

'Looks as if I already have. You're as mucky as the ragman.'

The mill owner laughed, rubbed at his face with a handkerchief that was less than clean. 'Bit of advice, Joe.'

'Yes?'

'Well, you've told me to speak my mind, so I shall. Don't put any blame on that baby.'

Joe swallowed. 'Aye.' He waited until the other man's perfunctory ablutions were completed. 'Tess got the blame when her brother died, you know. Her mam handled her bad ever after. Then when our twins were took, Tess carried on for a while just like her own mother, blamed our Megan. Mind, I think she managed to get over it, though she never treated the girls like she treated Albert and Harold. So it's up to me to break the mould.'

Together, they left the house, locked doors and gates,

walked down the lane until they reached the car. 'Two grand little cottages here,' said Joe. 'They want a bit doing, but they look sound enough for all that.'

Sidney turned the handle, started the engine. 'I own them, too. There'll be southerners coming to help with the big house, because there are firms down there with the right experience when it comes to Elizabethan work. Some of the workmen will stay in the cottages. But perhaps you might want one when the Hall is back to rights.'

They climbed aboard, sat and waited until the engine stopped coughing. While the vehicle shivered, Joe replaced his hat, found his thinking-cap at the same time. He hadn't been capable of thinking properly, but now, finally, he forced himself to arrange the future. It was daft, really, because half of Bolton had taken advice from the clogger. He had been mending hearts as well as footwear for many years, yet solutions to his own problems were not arriving easily. For a man of supposed wisdom, he was very slow.

'Are you all right?' asked Sidney.

Joe cleared his throat. 'I'll let the shop. But I don't know what I'll do in the long-term. For the time being, I just want to look after my family.'

'So be it.' Well satisfied with his caretaker, Sidney began the drive back to Bolton.

It was an awful dream. He was in an endless, dark corridor with doors along each side. In his right hand, he held the longest of his leather-knives, and he was wearing the hide apron, its many pockets jangling with nails and brass studs. Sweat was pouring into his eyes, so he was forced to blink in order to see the doors. Above each knocker, a weak light flickered, the puny flame illuminating a name rather than a number. The names were those of his children – Freda, Hilda, Hattie, Sarah, Annie, Nellie. There were no doors for Megan and Joseph.

A voice whispered to him. 'Megan and Joseph aren't here, Joe.'

He struggled to see, cursed the salt water that flooded his vision. 'Tess?' he croaked.

'I'm here. Open your eyes, I'm at the end of the corridor.'

Joe forced his eyelids upwards, looked up the narrow aisle. 'Tess?' he called, his tone stronger. In spite of the sweat, he could see now, was floating past the children's doors. His heart pounded when he saw the flames. She was wearing her wedding dress, had fresh flowers in her hair and in her hands. 'Are you in hell?' he asked.

She smiled. Her teeth were perfect in the dream, though in life, one of the upper incisors had been chipped when she had fallen over in ice some years earlier. It was only a dream, he told himself. In a minute, he would wake to hear Sarah chattering in the next room. 'Your tooth's mended,' he told Tess.

'The white flame of eternal love mends everything,' came the reply.

She was in heaven, he thought. Or perhaps the flames of purgatory would be pale like these. Whatever, this was not the red heat of Satan. Transfixed by her beauty, he searched for some purchase, an item to which he might cling and stop himself from floating towards her. Joe's time was not up, and he refused to go forward into eternity.

He stopped, held on to the walls by pressing his palms flat against them. 'I don't want to come yet, Tess. I've got to look after the children.'

'Follow me, Joe,' she begged. 'Joseph is safe.'

'What about the rest of them?' he asked, his tone frantic.

Tess raised an arm, tossed wedding-petals towards the doors. 'They're locked in,' she whispered. 'Locked in, Joe. Our son is asleep in his little bed. Megan's head is resting, too, and she is safe. Our other daughters are asleep forever. Let go of the walls. Don't hang on, because your heart will be broken. Come on, follow me, you must . . .' She disappeared into white-hot fire, but her voice continued to coax him. 'I'm here. Find me. Come into the flame of eternal love.' In her wake, she left the scent of roses, yet the stench of fire overcame the aroma, filled his lungs until he thought he might choke at any minute.

'NO!' He sat up, coughed, shook himself to wakefulness. But the coughing would not stop, because his bedroom was filled by smoke. For a few beats of time, he hovered in that place between sleep and consciousness, then he leapt from the bed, took a pillow with him, held the flock-stuffed bag against his face.

When he opened the door to the landing, a wall of real flame faced him, its greedy tentacles reaching out to embrace him. Instinctively, Joe threw himself into the small front bedroom and snatched the two smallest girls from their bed. Through fierce heat and dense smoke, he carried Hattie and Sarah into his room, closed the door, threw open the window.

A rush of air claimed him, sent him staggering back as if he had been hit, but he persevered, pushed his head into the street, was immediately petrified by the sight outside. The house at each side of his was ablaze. A bell clanged, men ran about shouting, screaming. Someone saw him, opened a blanket, yelled for help. When each corner of the blanket was held, Joe tossed Hattie into the street. A few moments later, he threw out the second child. It was only then that he remembered how still they had been. 'They're dead,' he said aloud. 'The smoke's killed them.'

Joe Duffy fell to his knees, prayed briefly for all his children, then bowed to the untender mercies of fate. 'I told you it were cursed, that street,' said Tess clearly as her husband tried to remain conscious.

'Freda, Hilda, Annie, Nellie . . .' His voice was cracking in the heat. Flames began to eat the door, were helped in their task by the draught from Joe's window.

'Lie down,' begged Tess. 'Lie on the bed. You'll be with me in a minute.'

Joe didn't want to go. He heaved himself up, climbed on to the sill, swayed about because the smoke had drugged him.

'Jump,' shouted a man.

The exhausted clogger glanced down, saw the real firemen holding a white circle. He launched himself into the air, lost all feeling on the way down.

When Joe came to, he was in a hospital bed between Billy Shipton and a man he didn't recognize. 'Annie!' he shouted, though the word was never born. 'Nellie!' The second name, too, stuck in his throat.

A nurse bent over him. She pushed a sliver of ice between his cracked lips. 'You'll be fine,' she said comfortingly.

'My girls?' he managed, though the words were rusty.

'The police and the firemen will let you know,' she answered.

He drifted away again, fell into a sleep that was mercifully dreamless. His mother came. Through thickened eyelids, Joe looked into the troubled face of Doris Wagstaff, knew that all his children were dead. No, not all. Megan and Joseph lived, because they had been away from the ill-fated street.

'I'm here, Joe,' his mother said repeatedly. 'Hang on, lad, you've a lot to live for.'

Night became day, became night again. A policeman visited, held Joe's hand tightly, answered the croaked questions and confirmed what was already known. Four girls had died in the inferno; two female babies, those whose little bodies had been thrown through a window by their father, had perished from the after-effects of oxygen starvation. Joe stared straight ahead, said nothing. Should he have listened to Tess, should he have gone with her into that brilliant whiteness?

Another day followed, and Joe sat up in his bed, pushed food down his scalded throat, nodded when the nurses told him that eyebrows and eyelashes often grew again after being burnt. 'How long have I been here?' he whispered, each word seeming to cut itself from the singed mouth.

'Five days,' answered the woman in green.

He turned, felt no pain in his neck, looked at the still form in the next bed. 'Is that Billy Shipton?'

'Yes,' she said. 'He's lost everybody, Mr Duffy. You've still got your mother and two children.'

Joe nodded. 'Was he hurt?'

'No.' She bustled about straightening bed covers. 'The poor boy's in shock. It seems there's nobody will have him. There are relatives, but we can't persuade any of them to visit. So he'll have to go into the orphanage.' She marched away purposefully, her apron almost crackling with starch.

Joe looked at the occupant of the other bed that flanked his.

The man winked. 'I caught you', he said. 'Then, a bit later on, I fell off the ladder. I'm a fireman,' he explained. 'A fireman with a broken leg.'

'What happened?' The words were clearer, because Joe's need for an answer was stronger than the pain.

'That spinster woman next door to you – she left the gas on, we think. Anyway, the whole side of the street has to come down. Everybody else escaped in time, well before the fire got to their houses. But number seventeen's gone – thank goodness it was empty. Then the spinster's, yours and the Shiptons'.'

'I lost six daughters.'

The fireman nodded. 'I'm sorry.'

Joe sank back on to the hard pillows, thought briefly about Mildred Moss. She'd lived at number 15 for donkey's years, never talked to anyone, always kept her house sparkling. Miss Moss had shopped in town, had refused to open her door to anyone. Those who had dared to look through her window had declared that the house was posh, a bit la-de-dah. Her carelessness had killed Annie, Nellie, Freda, Hilda, Hattie and Sarah.

The tears welled up, but they did not flow. Joe Duffy was beyond tears. There'd been an article in the paper a few years back, a story about a man in Kirk Street whose family had been destroyed by a German bomb. That man died, threw himself under a train at Trinity Street.

But Joe had not lost everyone. Somewhere, he had a little lad who thrived on the milk of a kind woman. In Holly Street, he had a daughter, a mother, a stepfather and a child called Phyllis who was not his. In the next bed, there lay a lad who had served at Tess's funeral. Joe would take him in, too. He would go to Hall i' th' Vale, would bring Joseph to the great house when the weaning process had been accomplished. And Billy could come along as well. They were all children of the one God.

Although he got no response, Joe talked for hours to Billy Shipton, forcing his damaged vocal cords to work towards the lad's recovery. He told him about the Hall, the woods, the moors. He told him about the little school along the road, the farm from which fresh milk, butter, cream and eggs could be bought.

When he had done his utmost for Billy, Joe rested as best he could in a bed that felt like stone, made his plans for the future. But he had left no space for his own shock, had failed to cater for the grief he would experience.

Months would pass before Joe Duffy could take up any kind of work.

'Sit down, Joe,' ordered the clogger's companion.

That was all he heard these days, 'sit down, come for a walk, eat this, drink that'. Sometimes, he didn't hear anything except Tess's voice telling him that he should have followed her.

'There's a brass band on this afternoon. Shall we go?'

Joe looked at the man who occupied the other armchair. 'I'm all right, Mr Althorpe.'

'Sid. I've told you to call me Sid.'

Joe sighed. 'Look, go back to the mill. You shouldn't be here. Neither should I. When are we going home?'

Sidney Althorpe lit a cigar. 'Listen, lad. We're both here in Blackpool, having a nice rest in my nice new bungalow. Why do you want to leave?'

278

'I've children. You've a business to run.'

'It runs itself,' said Sidney. 'And Fliss can take care of any problems.'

Joe rested his head, tried to put his brain into gear. There'd been another place before Blackpool, a nursing home where he had screamed and ranted for an endless time. It was, he thought, a private sanatorium, a dumping ground for surplus ageing relatives of the rich. An old man. Yes, he remembered an old man with hair like a monk's tonsure, just a grey circle with a shiny pate above it. 'Josh,' he said aloud.

'I beg your pardon?'

'I shared a room with a man called Josh. He were forever wetting the bed and singing 'Pack up your Troubles'. Did I go crackers, Mr Althorpe?'

Sidney thought for a moment, decided on the truth. 'You went a bit off-key, I suppose.'

'How long? What year is it?'

'1924.'

Joe pondered. 'What year was . . . the fire?'

'1923. You've been ill for almost six months.'

He was coming out of it. He was in Blackpool, was staying in a house with big windows and no stairs. There was a bit of a girl who came in every day, a little blonde thing called Mabel. Mabel made him beef tea, tripe and onions, rice pudding. 'And how long have you and I been here, Sid?'

The bulky man shrugged, puffed at his cigar, sent up a lot of blue smoke. 'About four weeks. Do you fancy a stroll to the pub later on?' He kept the excitement from his tone, dared not sound too hopeful. During recent months, Joe had been up and down, and Sidney was learning not to believe in Joe's clearer patches.

'Four weeks? What the blazes is going on? What about our Megan and our Joseph? What about Billy Shipton and—?'

'Young Billy's sleeping on your mother's sofa. Joseph's weaned on to cow's milk and slops, and his cot is in the

Wagstaffs' bedroom. Megan and Phyllis are doing well at school—'

'I should see them.'

Sidney picked up the poker, riddled the fire to life. 'Cold for April,' he said. 'And they'll come for a holiday when you're good and ready.'

Joe felt a bubble of panic in his chest. 'Ready? What do you mean by that? I'm Megan's dad, Joseph's dad. And I'm as near to a dad as Phyllis and Billy will ever get. It's nowt to do with whether I'm ready or not.'

Sidney Althorpe eyed the man who had seemed beyond saving. Joe Duffy had ranted for weeks on end about a bright light, about Tess throwing petals at doors. Sedatives had been used from time to time, and the Wagstaffs had waged a war with the infirmary's intention to have Joe certified. Sidney had whisked the clogger away from the hospital, had paid dearly to have the man cared for in a costly nursing home. He listened to the clock's ticking, waited for some evidence that might prove the sanity of his guest.

'You think I want locking up, don't you?'

'No. If I'd believed that, you wouldn't be here. I've more sense than to share a house with a lunatic.' And Agnes had come up trumps, had been working like a lunatic. She was never away from the Wagstaffs' house, had scrubbed floors, cleaned windows. He brushed a hand across his eyes, caressed a picture of his Agnes on her hands and knees with donkeystone and scrubber, his Agnes chatting to neighbours as if this chore were an everyday event. Yes, Agnes Althorpe was made of strong stuff.

Joe jumped up, found his legs to be weaker than ever, sat down again. 'What the heck do I have to do? How can I make you bring my children to me?'

Sidney threw the rest of his cigar into the grate. 'You can tell me again about that bloody light and the flowers and doors with names on. But this time, I want to hear it without your screaming.'

Joe dropped his chin, pondered for a second or two.

'I've not yelled for days. When I did shout, there were no bugger taking notice.' He sniffed. 'Pardon the language.'

'Go on.'

The thinner and older version of Joe Duffy raised his head and looked straight at Sidney Althorpe. 'In case you haven't noticed, Mr Althorpe – I mean Sid – my home got burnt to cinders. I'd six lasses in there with me. I got out and they didn't.'

'Yes.' He did not elaborate.

'I feel guilty. See, they were young, just at the beginning of their lives. It should have been me.'

'No, Joe. It wasn't your time. If it had been your turn, you'd have died.'

Joe breathed deeply, faced the nightmare. 'I had a dream. Tess weren't long gone, and I heard her talking to me, asking me to lie down and die. Look, I didn't see a ghost. The dream was about fire, so it must have come from the smell of burning. I know I've not been right. But . . .' He clasped his hands together in an effort to stop the shaking that plagued him. 'But I had ten children and eight of them are dead.' He separated his hands, chanted the names, counted along the digits. 'Annie, Nellie, Megan, Harold, Albert, Freda, Hilda, Hattie, Sarah and Joseph.' Joe swallowed, tried to ease the dryness in his throat. 'Ten. And there's just two left. I had a wife . . .' He bit hard on his lower lip, tasted blood. 'I survived.'

Sidney nodded. 'And that made you guilty, and the guilt made you break down.'

'Aye. I'd have laid down my life for any one of them. It's knocked me sideways. But please don't keep Megan and Joseph away from me.'

It had never been Sidney Althorpe's intention to deprive the clogger of his children, though he had decided not to expose Megan to the vision of a father who was not intact. Even now, he could not trust Joe's stability. As recently as last week, the man had been clawing at windows, had roared at invisible people who were commanded to save Hattie and Sarah.

281

'That's a bad street, Sid.'

'It's gone. Well, your side has.'

'Good.' He tightened his hands till the knuckles were white. 'I am better. Honest, I'm a lot better. It's just my legs. Mind, they've been on the blink since 1917.'

'Exercise will get you strong again. Shall we go to the brass band concert? It'll be chilly, but we can wrap up. Then a little drop of brandy in the pub, eh? Come on, I'll help you to walk. The sooner you make a move, the sooner you'll be back home.'

'I have no home.'

'You've Hall i' th' Vale, man. Do you think I've been idle during your illness? You've gas mantles, some electricity from a generator in a shed. You've a great big kitchen table, dishes, pots and pans. My wife came to the fore when she heard of your plight. She's got curtains made, put beds in. You know, I never thought I'd see the day when Agnes would actually scrub alongside her servants. But she's trapped mice, washed windows, cleaned a floor or two.' He didn't mention the work she'd done in Holly Street, didn't tell Joe that 19 Church Road had been enlivened by the Wagstaffs' frequent visits. 'There's a crowd of us on your side.'

A single tear made its way down Joe's haggard cheek. 'You've done a lot for me. I do remember some of it. Especially the day you got me out of the hospital. And just lately, you've had to chase me round Blackpool, haven't you?' Yes, this man had dragged him in from the street, had literally sat on him until the tablets took effect. 'Did I get as far as the beach once?'

Sidney grinned. 'You did. There were ladies out there in a terrible flap because a man in a nightshirt was running wild at the better end of the sands.'

'Thanks.'

Sidney rose, placed a hand on Joe's shoulder. 'It was nothing, son.' He noticed that Joe did not dash away that tear. It took a real man to cry without shame, he thought. 'We'll get fish and chips on the way home.'

'Can I have a steak pudding instead of fish?'

A weight seemed to tumble from the older man's shoulders. Somehow, the request for steak pudding proved something. There might be a way to go yet, but Joe Duffy was definitely on the mend.

Bessie Greenwood didn't like Fliss. She had decided from the start not to like her, had fought her son even before the girl had presented herself at the front door. 'She's not one of us,' she repeated stubbornly now. 'All them fancy airs and graces.'

Phil dried a cup, placed it on the table. 'Mam, Fliss has no airs at all and well you know it.'

Bessie sniffed, angled her face so that Phil got the profile. The chin was high and set, the mouth grim. 'Nothing but trouble will come of this,' she said.

'Why? Why does there have to be trouble? Mam, I love her and I'm going to marry her. Even her dad has an idea that we're walking out.'

'What about her mother?'

Phil shrugged, tossed the tea-cloth into the washbasket. 'Fliss doesn't say much about Mrs Althorpe, but from what I've heard, the woman's all right. She's been dashing about the market haggling for bits and pieces to give the Duffys in their new home.'

'Charity,' spat the woman in the bed. 'I don't want their bloody handouts.'

The young man walked out of the kitchen, closing the door none too softly in his wake. Years and years ago, the doctor had said that Bessie Greenwood was on borrowed time. Well, her credit must be good, because she was continuing to extend her overdraft.

He shut himself in the lavatory shed, lit a cigarette, blew smoke through the star-shaped hole in the top of the door. Smoking inside the house was forbidden. It irritated Bessie's tubes, so Phil was forced to indulge this one bad habit in privacy and in the cold. He shivered, wondered what time it was. Fliss would arrive soon, and Mam wouldn't get up to open the door. She'd done a fair bit of walking today, had Mam, but her legs would surely go on strike as soon as Fliss used the door-knocker. Fliss didn't come to the house very often, as their relationship was still somewhat secretive, but the poor girl tried so hard to get on with Mam.

Life was getting no easier. Bessie had seen off her sisters one by one, would have no-one to sit with her while Phil went out. Leaving his mother alone was difficult; leaving her in the company of a house-sitter invited trouble that sometimes verged on riot.

What the hell was he going to do? He'd popped the question, had received the reply he wanted. But how? How was he going to get married when Mam couldn't take to the woman he loved? He opened the door, gazed up at the darkening sky, tried to count the sprinkling of stars. Fliss couldn't live here in Dobson Street. They had a scullery that was too small, so everything happened in the back kitchen. The front room was dingy, about ten by ten, no privacy at all. And the kitchen itself had been made smaller these past two years by Mam's bed.

He stepped into the yard, looked up at the window of his bedroom. If Fliss had been an ordinary mill girl, they might have lived up there most of the time. That little front bedroom could be made into a parlour, then they could have slept at the back of the house. The kitchen would have been shared, and the tin bath would have been used in front of the fire on Fridays, but an ordinary girl might have coped with all that. Fliss was not ordinary. For a moment, he wished with all his heart that Fliss could be just another young woman who wanted a man to take her out of the weaving shed. But no, it was the difference that fascinated him.

Phil bolted the back gate, shut the midden door. Was he after her money? Mr Althorpe would likely buy a house for his daughter, a nice place with a garden and a built-in bath. Yet that would solve nothing, because he would still be forced to take Mam with him. Nobody else would have her. And no, he didn't want the Althorpe money.

Another thought occurred to him. What would he do after he and Fliss were wed? Would he continue with the weaving? What about the other folk in the mill? He already felt some glances that lingered for a fraction or two longer than normal. He already knew what it was for conversations to stop when he approached. That never happened in the shed, because the work was noisy, but he'd heard a few 'shush' noises on the way home. Dear God, what was he going into?

The woman next door peeped out, beckoned him in a stage-whisper. 'Phil?'

'What?'

She stepped outside, propped her arms on the thin slab of wall that separated the yards. 'Yer auntie come up again today, but your ma sent 'er off wi' a few fleas in 'er ear. Tell you what, fer a sick woman, Bessie Greenwood can't 'alf shift. Chased yer Auntie Ethel all the way to the bottom lamp, she did. Fetched 'er a good wallop with t' walking stick and all, she did. Yer auntie could well be in th' infirmary by now wi' concussion.'

'Oh. Thanks for keeping an eye on her.' Even in the gloom, Phil was able to read the pity that softened the neighbour's expression. 'Thanks a lot,' he repeated lamely.

'Yer want ter sling yer 'ook, lad. That one in there'll see us all out, like as not. She makes enough noise while you're at work, tha knows. I sometimes wonder if she's shiftin' t' bloody furniture, all t' racket she makes. Aye.' She patted her curlers, smoothed the straps of her pinny. 'Get gone an' enjoy yersen, lad. I reckon yer mother'll last through three or more Preston Guilds.'

Phil's heart was in his boots as he watched the woman creeping back into her kitchen. How ill was his mam? She'd a list of disorders as long as any man's arm, yet she was capable of mustering enough energy to make trouble whenever possible. For the first time ever, Phil Greenwood found himself wishing that his mother would die. In the past, he'd sometimes prayed for her release, but never before had he wished her gone for his own sake. He shivered again, went back inside.

She was glaring at him. 'I've not had the seven o'clock medicine,' she grumbled.

He counted the pills, took a cup of water to the bed. 'Why didn't you tell me Auntie Ethel had been?'

Bessie managed not to choke on her tablets. 'Has that bitch next door been talking again? What business is it of hers who comes to see me? And why do you want to know?'

Although the kitchen was warm, Phil shuddered once more. 'I pay the rent, Mam. I should know who comes and goes.'

'Oh yes?' she screamed. 'Who fettled for you when you were a lad, eh? Who washed and cooked and ironed and mended day in and day out? Are you going to turn out like the rest, no thought for me once you're wed?'

His hands curled themselves of their own accord, became stiff knots of tension that seemed to seek an outlet for his anger. He imagined that he could feel her stringy neck, that he was squeezing the life out of her. Within seconds, he ran from the house and stood under the lamp waiting for Fliss. Fliss was teaching him how to drive. He needed to calm down so that he might be fit to steer, steady enough to deal with all that double declutching.

Phil shook not with cold, but with something akin to terror. His mam had always been dominant and difficult. But he had never thought of hurting her . . . It would pass, he thought. Then he saw the black car bouncing along the cobbles, heard the phut-phut of its engine. She always left the car well away from the house, always wore a headscarf whenever she came into the street. No-one ever mentioned his relationship with Fliss, because he had done his best to keep the secret. He wanted Fliss. And the only thing that stood in his way was lying in a bed in his house. He swallowed. The feeling would definitely pass, he told himself.

* * *

Agnes perched prettily on the edge of Doris Wagstaff's kitchen sofa. 'This house is a credit to you,' she beamed. 'And not one of my friends goes to Manchester for clothes these days. Even poor Evelyn Grimshaw is beginning to look decent. So clever, the way you draped that suit of hers. You've managed to hide a multitude of sins.'

Doris Wagstaff grinned. The war between Agnes Althorpe and Evelyn Grimshaw was becoming a legend in its own lifetime. But Agnes was made more human by this flaw in her character, thought Doris. 'I want to thank you for all you've done for us, Mrs Althorpe.'

'It was nothing.' With a small sweeping movement, she shrugged away the fact that she had scrubbed, polished, haggled for items in order to furnish Hall i' th' Vale. She had even helped here, in Holly Street, because Deedee had three young ones now. 'Just look at that.' She pointed to a small square of silk that sat on the table. 'You've found the exact shade. It will go very well with my blouse, but the skirt must be made by Friday. Which is why I've taken the unusual step of visiting on a Sunday.'

'It'll be done,' promised Doris.

'And it's very good of you to give up your home for Mr Duffy's sake. I hope you'll all be happy in that big barn of a house.'

Doris gazed round the room. 'Well, it's going to a grand young couple, is this home of mine. They moved into Ida Entwistle's after . . . after she died, you know.' She breathed slowly, deeply. Just two grandchildren left. But she was going to be strong for their sake and for Joe. Joe would be home soon, would be wanting moral support. The last thing Joe needed at the moment was a moaning, blubbering mother. So she'd given up crying. And she'd few regrets about leaving the area, because so many bad things had happened here. It would be good to walk outside without seeing the very spot on which those lovely girls had died . . . She tightened her mouth, held back a sigh. The business would not suffer, she told herself

287

firmly. Fliss Althorpe would drive Doris and Tommy to town each morning, would pick them up in the evenings.

'Ida's daughter will be coming with you?'

Doris, whose daydreaming had been interrupted, jumped slightly. 'What? Oh, I beg your pardon. Yes, she'll be with us. And Elsie Shipton's lad, God love him. He's improved, thank goodness. He used to have a lot of room for improvement, did young Billy.' She poured the tea, smiled at her guest. 'They're all out for a walk, Tommy, too. I never expected to see you on a Sunday, Mrs Althorpe.'

Agnes fidgeted as she prepared to raise a delicate subject. The matching of materials had been an excuse. Really she wanted to talk. What was she doing, at all? It was a long way to come for a friendly ear, yet who else could she talk to? Sidney was messing about in Blackpool, Geoffrey was too young. And Evelyn Grimshaw would have made a dog's dinner of the whole affair, would have spread it from Bury to Manchester by weekend. Anyway, this woman was a decent body, the sort who knew how to keep a secret. It was strange, she thought suddenly, how women confided in those who dressed them or styled their hair. It was as if necessary bodily contact decreed that such relationships had to be close right from the start. 'Mrs Wagstaff, my daughter dropped me here before going to visit a family at the other side of town. Their name is Greenwood.'

Doris looked at the clock, wondered how much time would pass before the children returned. She'd already said her piece, had already warned Fliss about Bessie Greenwood and her son. Oh heck. She pottered about, offered a small cake, poured a second cup of tea for her visitor, glanced through the window. 'Weather's picked up,' she commented. 'And not before time. Tommy were beginning to talk about building an ark for us and his blessed cats.'

'Yes.'

The ensuing small silence was very loud. Doris heard a

clock that ticked too fiercely, a squabble between some starlings and the heavy beating of her own heart. 'They're good friends, Fliss and Phil. They met in the mill.' She cleared her throat in order to gain a couple of seconds' thinking time. 'His mother took badly some years since, wasn't expected to last. But she's like one of them creaking gates that go on forever. Mr Althorpe's always took a close interest in any family trouble. Only now, with him being away and with Fliss being in charge of personnel and all that, she must have took it on herself to make a visit.'

'Nonsense.'

Startled by this comment, Doris felt the heat in her cheeks. 'Mrs Althorpe, it's not for me to talk about your daughter. I mean, I don't know anything worth saying.'

'But you do.' Agnes nibbled at the edge of an iced bun, chewed, swallowed, took a sip of tea. 'I would wager a tidy sum that you know most things about those who work in my husband's mills. Come on, Mrs Wagstaff. I think I know the answer, but I need a bit of proof. Felicity is acting very coyly, refuses to discuss the subject. But I do know that Philip Greenwood is a weaver from Althorpe Number One.'

'That's right.'

'I also know that my daughter is spending many evenings visiting the sick and needy.'

'Oh.'

'And she doesn't walk any more, Mrs Wagstaff. Felicity floats along on a cloud, sings, washes her hair far too frequently, picks flowers in the garden. Every daffodil and narcissus finished up in the house this spring. She has taken little notice of nature's bounties until recently. Would you not agree that such symptoms are indicative of a woman in love?'

Doris lifted a shoulder. 'Happen they are. You see, Mrs Althorpe, Phil Greenwood lives over towards Bury Road, so I never see him or his mam.'

'They used to live in Blossom Place.'

Doris nodded.

'Then they moved.'

Doris nodded again.

'Why did they move away from a place that was so
convenient for the boy's work? Why did she need to get
away from the rest of her family?' Agnes held up a hand.
'Now, I've done a little of my homework, Mrs Wagstaff. I
found out from our coal merchant that Bessie Greenwood
quarrelled with her sisters. Come on, tell me the rest of it.'

Doris, sensing that her back was almost touching the
wall, gave in as gracefully as possible. When her tale
reached its end, she settled back in her chair, exhausted by
Agnes Althorpe's fixed stare.

'So. Not only did Felicity refuse to finish her education.
Not only did she insist on going to work in a factory. She
has also taken up with a man who sounds highly un-
suitable.'

'Phil's all right,' said Doris. 'A bit on the weakish side,
you might say, but . . . but all right.'

'But his mother is not.'

'Aye.'

Agnes sat quietly for more than a minute, her eyes fixed
now to the window. 'Mrs Wagstaff, I am not a snob. I
work very hard at not taking advantage of anyone's
situation. It is true that I have money, but I cannot be
blamed for that. Nor can I be blamed for wanting my
daughter to marry well.'

Doris, who agreed totally, simply inclined her head.

'What am I to do? I suppose my husband already knows
about this alliance. If it has gone on in and around the
mill, he must be aware of it. So, what am I to do?'

'I don't know.'

Agnes got up, paced about the room. 'And if his mother
is so dreadful, why is my daughter continuing to visit her?'

'It's Phil she goes to see, Mrs Althorpe. We can't do
much about our feelings. I mean, there's been kings
who've loved commoners—'

'They didn't marry them.' She blushed, reminded
herself that Doris Wagstaff remembered a certain young

mill-owner who had married a certain apprentice weaver.

'No. And young Fliss hasn't married Phil.'

Agnes stopped pacing, stood in the doorway. 'Years ago, when she was still at school, Felicity gave up food until she got her own way. Sidney supported her, of course, gave in to her right away. My daughter is a clever girl who knows her own mind. And if her mind is set on this Philip Greenwood, she will do all in her power to have him as her husband.'

'It's her heart, not her mind.'

Agnes crossed the room, stood over her host. 'She's confided in you, hasn't she?'

'Not much. But I know she likes him.'

'Likes? Loves?' hissed Agnes. 'What about life? What does she do after that first flush of excitement has died down? Marriage is a business partnership, Mrs Wagstaff. There has to be some common ground on which its members can step from time to time. That's far more important than . . . than fleshly needs.' She pulled at her jacket, as if trying to close in her secret thoughts and fears. 'Can you imagine how such a marriage would survive? Each would have to step out of a familiar environment in the search for middle ground.'

'They might not get married—'

'How long has the relationship survived? Years?'

Doris shrugged, found no ready reply.

'Years.' The visitor provided her own answer. 'And the class difference will be what attracted each to the other. Felicity has all sorts of romantic notions about a classless society. The boy will be fascinated by my daughter's status.'

Doris took a noisy gulp of tea to slake her thirst. 'He didn't know who she were at first. He's always said it wouldn't have made any difference. In fact, Fliss says he sometimes wishes she were an ordinary worker.'

Agnes tried not to glower. It was plain that Felicity had confided in the dressmaker. 'So the boy already realizes that the two of them are ill-matched.'

Doris, who knew she had said enough, tightened her

lips so that no more words could spill out.

Agnes rested her hands on the table's edge, hunched her shoulders. 'I'm weary, Mrs Wagstaff. How must it seem when I come here to burden you with my problems? After all you've been through—'

'Nay, don't be talking like that, Mrs Althorpe. You're better coming to somebody who's suffered a bit. I mean, we all learn from life, don't we? And you can be sure of one thing – what you say here goes no further than these walls. I'll not be rattling about the Town Hall steps tomorrow telling your business to the world and his wife.'

Agnes nodded, sank into a dining chair. 'It seems so . . . so stupid, this problem of mine. At least Felicity's alive, Mrs Wagstaff.'

They sat in companionable silence for a few moments, each thinking about all the dead children. 'I pray for them,' said Agnes. 'I'm not a Catholic, but I pray for those children.'

Doris smiled, though her eyes remained sad. 'The months go by. Time's the best medicine.'

'I'm glad that Mr Wagstaff and the children are out,' said Agnes Althorpe. 'I wanted to talk to you. There's no hurry for the skirt.'

'I know.'

'What are we here for?' asked the visitor.

'We're having a cup of tea and a natter.'

Agnes shook her head. 'That's not what I mean. Take Sidney. He has lived and breathed cotton for as long as I can remember. He looks as if he'll last forever, but he won't live to a ripe old age, because he's too bowed down with exhaustion. Then there's your son. From all accounts, Mr Duffy has slaved in the shop for many years. For what? Sometimes, I feel like telling my husband to sell everything. We could buy a wonderful place on some foreign island, all sea and sand and—'

'You'd hate it,' said Doris.

'Would I?' The perfect eyebrows were arched. 'Why should I hate it?'

Doris laughed. 'Because you'd never see the finished picture. You've two children, so you want to be around to know what happens. There'll be grandchildren, parties, weddings, christenings. You'd be sitting under a palm tree when your grandson said his first word. You'd have nobody to quarrel with. If Evelyn Grimshaw carries on getting hefty, you want to see my clever drapery, don't you?'

Agnes tapped her fingernails on the table. 'You are a very clever woman, Mrs Wagstaff.' She looked at the clock, stood up, rummaged in her bag. When her nose was powdered, she grinned at her seated hostess. 'Yes. We have to hang around to see how it all comes out. Don't we?'

PART TWO

ONE

If anyone in the vale had cared to glance up at Blacktop Moor on a certain June evening in 1926, he would have seen a group of figures outlined against a darkening summer sky. But the villagers of Bromley Cross probably went about their business, while farmhands, at the end of a fourteen-hour day, would have been too interested in sleep to cast an eye towards the far horizon.

Atop the flat-crowned hillock, Joe Duffy looked down on patch-patterned countryside and wondered how he and Tess had managed for so many years in town. Bolton lay to the south in its bowl, houses and factories almost deleted by the exhausts of several thousand chimneys. The bigger offenders poked their red brick nostrils towards the sky, spat fumes and smoke into a firmament whose natural colour was stained by soot and grime. Domestic fires added to the fog, their pall hanging lower, almost sitting on the roofs.

'It's dirty, Dad,' said Megan.

'Aye.' He placed the little lad on the ground, told him not to wander. Would Tess have been healthier up here? Would she have thrived on fresh eggs and cream, might she have survived? He turned, looked towards Hall i' th' Vale. It was a grand house, a wonderful place for children. The gardens had responded well to draining, lawns and hedges almost glowing, as if they boasted of their importance. Joe had discovered a fondness for plants, so his position as caretaker and gardener was assured.

A long time ago, Joseph Duffy Senior had been a clogger, yet he felt no urge to return to his earlier calling. The shop was sold, anyway, so the family he had cobbled together from the remains of three households would remain here in a world that constantly renewed itself. He nodded pensively. Like Mother Nature, the Duffys had made the best of whatever was available. Soon, they would have their own houses at the bottom of Dog Leg Lane. He, Megan and Joseph were to occupy the gatehouse, while Deedee, Tommy, Phyllis and Billy would move into the other cottage, a strange piece of architecture named Twisted Stacks.

'Dad?'

'Yes, love?' His mind was wandering, circling a point. Deliberately, he gave his attention to his one remaining daughter.

'I'm glad we're here.'

'So am I, lass.' So were Billy and Phyllis and Joseph. This youngest Duffy had grown to the age of three, had known no other home. Joe's heart leapt, then seemed to miss a beat. His consciousness had found the pivot on which half-formed thoughts had hung, was homing in. It didn't hurt quite so fiercely now. He stood at the top of the world and knew that he could think about Tess and all his beautiful girls without feeling any great agony.

Billy, awkward at almost fifteen, slipped a hand into Joseph's. He had appointed himself big brother to the Duffy children, had decided from the start that no harm would ever come to little Joseph Duffy, not while Billy Shipton was around. As for Megan – well – Megan was just special, so she occupied a huge corner of his heart. He didn't wish anything for Megan, seemed not to use his head while contemplating her. With Megan, everything came from his soul.

Whenever Billy spoke in whispers to Deedee about his adoptive sister, the old woman became sage and lyrical. 'A dream is a wish from the heart, not from the mind,' she had told him. Deedee understood. Deedee knew how Billy felt about Megan. 'That's where we used to live,' he whispered into Joseph's ear. 'Me and me mam and all our lot . . .' Fred's clog. He remembered the day when Megan

298

had taken the clog for a new sole. He cleared his throat. 'Your Megan and your dad and your mam lived yonder, too. And all . . . and some other people.' He set his chin firmly towards the future, turned his back on death and studied Megan.

Megan smiled at Billy. She was fourteen and he was turning fifteen and they were working together. A whole lifetime of purpose and adventure stretched in front of her, and Billy was going to be a part of it. She loved him. Being only fourteen didn't mean anything, because they were going to get married anyway, no matter what. The leather shop was starting up full-time any day, and it would be a success, especially with Dad acting as unofficial consultant. 'It'll be great,' she told him. There was no need for any explanation. Each always seemed to know what the other meant.

'Oh, aye,' replied Billy. 'The Leather Works'll come on a treat. Doesn't matter that we live all this way out, eh? Fliss and Mr Althorpe will take the lot of us down to work every morning. Till I get me own van.' Deedee had two shops in the middle of town now, one for fabrics and the other for hides. The best part was that these two materials could be used together in repairing furniture. 'Mind,' he whispered. 'We'll have to behave with Deedee next door.'

Megan laughed. 'Leave her to me,' she said. 'I can manage her.' She couldn't, but she liked to pretend.

Phyllis was quiet. Even Megan wasn't aware of Phyllis's secret, because the words were too hard to say. Megan wouldn't have laughed, though. Phyllis Entwistle sensed that her friend would never mock or criticize. But all the same, the situation was weird. And it wasn't her imagination, couldn't be. Nothing in life so far had predisposed Phyllis to stupid romanticism. Nevertheless, the young girl found herself wondering repeatedly whether she might be misreading signals, whether she was being an almighty fool. But he was nice to her. He was nice to everybody, and he was particularly gentle with Phyllis.

'That's Mr Althorpe's chimney,' announced Joseph, a chubby finger pointing towards the town.

'Aye.' Billy put the child down. 'He's a good man, is Mr Althorpe. They queue miles for a job with him.'

Joe Duffy glanced at Billy, saw the seriousness that had etched itself into features that were already mature. Because he'd lost everything and everyone, Billy was a watcher, a guard. His life seemed to consist of looking after all who came within reach. Joe remembered the urchin who had plagued the residents of the garden streets, that dreaded lad with the basin-cut hair, ragged clothes, worn-out clogs. The altar boy situation hadn't lasted, though. Once he'd come out of the worst of his shock, Billy had shown some of the old spirit by refusing point blank to dress like a girl and mee-maw in Latin. Of course, poor Elsie hadn't been around to chase her son to church . . .

Phyllis stood to one side, her mind five or six miles away in the Ecumenical Mission on Flash Street. Inside a decaying house lived a man with very thin ginger hair and a lovely smile. A number of smelly people slept there too, tramps, down-and-outs who were easily courted by a bowl of pea soup and a couple of spare ribs. They didn't mind a bit of preaching and hymn singing once their bellies were filled. She had helped to collect blankets, dishes, food and money from the residents and tradesmen of Bolton, had jangled her collecting tin on Deansgate and Bradshawgate.

'Are you all right, Phyllis?'

Megan's best friend shivered. 'It's gone a bit cold.'

Billy, vigilant as ever, stepped forward, pulled off his jersey and handed it to Phyllis.

'Ta.' She wrapped it round her shoulders, tied the arms at the front. Billy was good to everybody. Billy was an ordinary lad from the garden streets, so nobody would say much if he and Megan settled down together. Whereas—

'You look worried,' said Megan.

Whereas Phyllis was hankering after an older man with very little hair and a dirty green stole that he'd saved from when he used to be a priest.

'Is your leg sore?'

Phyllis shook her head. She was proud of her stance, could be taken for a normal person unless she walked too far. Except loving a priest wasn't normal. 'I'm fine, Megan.'

'Liar.' Megan's tone fell short of accusatory, though not a little hurt showed on her face. She and Phyllis had shared everything for donkey's years, but Phyllis had been holding something back for a long time. In four weeks, a part of their lives would be finished forever, because both would leave Our Lady of Sorrows senior department for the very last time next month. 'Are you worrying about leaving school?' It had been a happy place for both girls, because they had been taught by fine people in proper clothes. Like St Thomas's in Bolton, the Bromley Cross school was a cheerful place. Mind, the name was a bit miserable. One of the funniest things Megan had seen in years was a poster at the bottom of Dog Leg Lane, 'ENJOY YOURSELF – THIS WAY TO OUR LADY OF SORROWS SOCIAL CLUB'.

Billy guffawed. 'Is she heck as like bothered about finishing her schooling, Megan.' He'd been working for months, was employed as a general assistant at Fine Seams. When he wasn't generally assisting, he bore the task of preparing and finishing Megan's work in the leather room. Soon, the shop next door to Deedee's would open, then he and Megan would start to build their empire. Not for one moment did he doubt Megan's ability to make a success of her life. As for himself, he was a worker who would gladly turn a hand to anything. 'Phyllis is looking forward to coming full time in the shop, aren't you?'

Phyllis, whose relationship with needle and thread was not a happy one, made no reply. She wasn't intending to go in the shop. With her fingers crossed beneath Billy's sleeves, she sent up a prayer to her mother. Mam must talk to the saints and keep Phyllis out of dressmaking. Because Phyllis wanted to work within a stone's throw of Paddy O'Riley.

301

'You hate sewing, don't you?' asked Megan.

'Yes. I'm sorry, but—'

'No need to be sorry,' said Megan quickly. 'If we were all made the same, there'd be nothing done in the world. So, what are you going in for? Weaving? Spinning?'

Phyllis shrugged, attempted to make the gesture careless. 'I'd not be able to stand all day. But I'll do something. I'll not expect Deedee and Tommy to keep me forever. Perhaps I'll go in a shop.' In town. She had to be in town, because Paddy was there. 'There's that little wool place near the market. She knows us, does Mrs Spencer, and she's looking for a girl to help out. There's a chair behind the counter, so I could sit down in between serving. Then your dad could pick me up in the van when he gets the rest of you from Fine Seams.' And she could get a lift with Fliss like everyone else in the mornings, she thought. Though really, she wanted lifts in neither direction, because she would like to live nearer to Paddy. She would miss the fields, but . . .

Megan nodded thoughtfully. 'If you want to sell wool, do it in Deedee's shop. She's been thinking about branching out.'

Phyllis swallowed. Mrs Spencer's shop was only a stride from Flash Street, whereas Fine Seams stood at the other end of the town. Even in her dinner hour, Phyllis might not make it there and back, especially in rain. She was the owner of a weather-leg, an item that was often in demand. 'Will we get rain tomorrow?' Tommy would ask. On fine days, she had little pain, but dampness made her knee ache. 'I've promised Mrs Spencer,' she said softly.

Megan closed her mouth and held back the words. Phyllis was one of the family. The family was sticking together, because each and every member had lost so much. But Phyllis Entwistle was showing signs of breaking away. Megan ordered her thoughts, shunted something positive to the front of her mind. 'Still, as long as you're happy – that's the main thing.'

Phyllis drew in her lower lip, tried to stop a sob that

threatened to spill into an evening that was too beautiful for sadness. She took a couple of breaths, then pulled Megan to her side. 'Please don't think I'm ungrateful. But for your dad, I don't know what would have happened to me. See, I've got to start making my own way.'

'Are you leaving us?' whispered Megan.

Phyllis shook the copper-coloured ringlets until they threatened to tumble. 'No. It's . . . well, it's daft. But . . .' She glanced at Billy, waited till he moved away. 'It's the mission.'

Megan dragged her friend towards the path. 'We'll see you at home,' she yelled over her shoulder. When the two girls had walked several paces, Megan slowed in order to match Phyllis's uncertain movements. She was all right on flat ground or on an upward slope, but a downward path interfered with her balance.

'Right,' said Megan. 'Let's hear it.'

Phyllis looked sideways at her companion, noticed for the umpteenth time how beautiful she was. Hair that was almost raven-black flowed back from a flawless complexion of peaches and cream, and the startling blue eyes were framed by thick, sooty lashes. Phyllis sighed, because she hated being a redhead. 'I wish I had black hair,' she moaned.

Megan ground to a halt, pulled at Phyllis's sleeve. 'Hang on, you,' she said. 'Never mind changing the subject. And anyway, your hair's more interesting than mine. So tell me what's going on, Miss Entwistle.'

Phyllis sniffed, cleared her throat, stared into space. 'I want to be near him. Spencer's Wool Shop's just round the corner, so I can call in sometimes and help with soup and stuff.'

'You what?' Sometimes, Phyllis failed to make complete sense.

'Paddy. Mr O'Riley. I . . . I like him.'

'So do I. Everybody likes him.'

'And he likes everybody.'

Megan nodded. 'Well, he did used to be a priest, so he's

supposed to be charitable and friendly. And what's all this got to do with soup?'

Phyllis hung her head. 'I love him, Megan,' she whispered.

Megan snorted. 'You're only fourteen.'

'Same as you.'

'What do you mean by that?'

'You and Billy,' said Phyllis. 'You're only fourteen and fifteen.'

It was different. Megan didn't know how to express the difference, but she clung to it fiercely. 'Phyllis, I've known Billy Shipton all my life, grew up next door to him. He's . . . well, he's just Billy.'

Phyllis, who had known Paddy O'Riley forever, tried to muster a retort. 'And what about Geoff Althorpe?' asked Phyllis archly. 'You've known him ages and he's after you.'

Megan snorted. 'Stop trying to distract me.' She couldn't be doing with Geoff Althorpe. Geoff Althorpe was a big, soft going on seventeen-year-old baby who wanted all his own way and no responsibilities. 'Look, Billy and I are a pair. But Paddy O'Riley's old enough to be your grandad and—'

'He's not. He's only about thirty-four.'

'About thirty-four?' Megan grabbed Phyllis's arm, forced the girl to turn and face the music. 'Look, you can't go chasing after him. He used to be a priest. All he cares about is scruffy old men pinching blankets. He won't get married.'

Phyllis wished with all her heart that she could stop blushing. Her face burned so fiercely that she stuck out her lower lip and sent a puff of air to her heated forehead. 'He wants children,' she whispered. 'He told me he wants to get married and be a dad, but whoever he marries will have to live in his rooms at the mission. He means me, you know. That's why he told me. He says he'll wait for the right girl. Any road, I am the right girl, 'cos it was me he spoke to. And he's waiting till I'm old enough. So.' She straightened her shoulders, retrieved her arm from Megan's grip. 'That's why I'll be working for Mrs Spencer.'

Megan stood and watched while Phyllis stumbled down the path towards home. Had she been able to see herself, Megan might have noticed that her expression was straight out of Deedee's book, thin lips, narrowed eyes, furrowed brow. Like Deedee, she would get to the bottom of things. Whatever trouble might be involved, the bull's horns would be grabbed within days. She blinked once or twice, because this particular bull had been a priest. However, she intended to discover his intentions before Phyllis made a fool of herself.

'Megan?'

She looked over her shoulder, grinned at Billy. 'Race you home,' she yelled.

They reached the Hall in a breathless state, kissed the lady who awaited their return.

'Hang on,' said Deedee. 'Before you go bouncing about inside, Mrs Althorpe's here. There's trouble. So get washed and meet us in the Lancashire kitchen.'

Billy whistled under his breath. 'We've not broken anything,' he muttered.

Deedee reached up and stroked the lad's hair out of his eyes. 'It's Agnes's heart that's broke, love,' she said softly. 'Just questions, that's all. She only wants to talk to you.'

When Billy and Megan had gone inside, Deedee waited for her son to come home. As he came into view, she swallowed her tears and strode forward to meet him. He was precious, was her Joe. He and his children were the most important factors in her life. And Tommy, of course. But there could be nothing worse than losing a son, and her heart went out to the woman whose husband owned Hall i' th' Vale.

Agnes stared blankly into the near distance, her face white with shock. She was seated in an alcove next to an ancient

305

fireplace, her hands folded in her lap. He had gone. Geoffrey had disappeared without a word, no note, no fond words of farewell for his parents.

Doris Duffy stood in front of a shelf piled with copper and brass, ancient cooking utensils that had been culled from Hall i' th' Vale's cellars and from other ageing houses in Lancashire and Cheshire. Only this morning, she had cleaned them all in preparation for the Althorpes' imminent move. 'His dad might find him, Agnes,' she said.

The woman on the spindle-backed chair shook her head slowly, then glanced up at the dear lady who had become a real friend. 'Doris, it's hopeless. Geoffrey was supposed to be staying with Bernard Healey for two weeks. When Sidney spoke to Bernard's father, it became plain that the arrangement had been for one week only.' She swallowed painfully. 'He's had five days. A young man can go a long way in five days.'

Megan, Phyllis, and Billy stood in a huddle by the door, while Joseph Junior wandered about looking for something to do in this roomful of gloomy adults. His father, tired after the walk, eased his body into a chair at one end of a long table whose surface still showed the crude finish of medieval workmanship. 'Try not to worry, Mrs Althorpe.' He had never been able to call his employers by their Christian names, even though his mother was on closer terms. 'He'll turn up. They always turn up, you know.'

Agnes looked the man straight in the eye. 'Do they?' she asked softly.

Joe lowered his gaze, recognized that Agnes had just referred to his own dead children. 'Don't be thinking like that,' he mumbled. 'You know how he hates school. Geoff told me he didn't want to do the Higher Certificate. He'll have got himself a job in some motor car factory, like as not, then he'll be—'

'No.' The single syllable pierced the air, provided ample interruption to Joe's flow of words. Megan made herself look Mrs Althorpe straight in the face. 'Australia,' she said clearly. 'I never thought he'd do it, not really.' She turned slightly so that Billy could not see her face. 'He said he'd not go without me, Mrs Althorpe. And I told him time and time again that I'd be stopping here.' Poor Megan stood trembling in a kitchen that formed the basis of a museum planned by Sidney Althorpe, felt as useless as the ducking stool and the large box mangle. It couldn't be happening. He wouldn't leave, not without telling somebody.

Agnes fixed her attention on the girl, her eyes seeming to devour Megan's face. 'He loves you,' she whispered. Oh, if only he'd stayed! Agnes had changed so much, so radically. Gone was the woman who had needed to do things right. Gone was the woman who had been grateful to her husband for pulling her out of poverty. The love for Sidney still burned brightly, but she had become a settled wife, a person who knew and liked herself.

'Happen Megan's wrong,' said Joe.

The lady of the house forced herself to sit upright. 'All his clothes have gone,' she managed. 'And some books. He must have waited until we were all out, including Cook and Mary. This has been planned.' Megan Duffy had rejected the Althorpe heir. Only a few years earlier, Agnes Althorpe would have been mortified by the possibility of such a liaison. But she knew better now.

'Try and not fret,' said Deedee. 'If you get ill, it'll not fetch him back any quicker.' She hoped with all her heart that Agnes would not suffer a set-back. It had taken ages for Deedee to get the woman to open up her heart, but the job had been a good one so far. Evelyn Grimshaw had grown up too, was a regular visitor at Church Road and at Hall i' th' Vale. Each of these wealthy-by-marriage wives was becoming herself, was no longer ashamed to be seen holding a cloth or even a paintbrush. 'Keep calm,' she added. 'I bet he'll be back inside a week.'

Megan's face was a picture of misery. 'I should have told you,' she whispered into the huge, flag-floored area. The low ceiling seemed to drop even further until it threatened to cut off her ability to breathe. She pulled at her collar, hoped for some distraction. Joseph, who was playing with the spools on a small spinning wheel, raised his head. 'Megan not cry,' he ordered with all the conviction of a bright three-year-old. 'I not crying.'

His older sister, grateful for the interruption, walked across the room, the soles of her leather shoes clipping time-smoothed rectangles of stone. 'I'm not crying either, Joseph.' She took a duster from a drawer, passed it to the child who was so like Albert, little Albert who had died beneath the wheels of Phyllis's ambulance. 'Here, you polish Mrs Althorpe's bellows and trivets.' When Joseph was busy, Megan inhaled deeply, then walked to Agnes's side. 'I am so sorry,' she said. 'But he's been talking like this for years, you see. I mean, it could have been a dream, couldn't it? People are always saying they'll do things, then they never do them. But if I'd said—'

'If you'd said, he would still have gone,' interrupted Deedee. 'The lad's well turned sixteen, so he can do as he pleases.' She looked keenly at Agnes. 'Have his papers gone? Birth certificates and all that stuff?'

The reply came from the doorway. 'He'll not need them.'

Everyone's attention was focused on the new arrival. Sidney Althorpe removed his hat, tossed it onto the table, pushed his hands into the pockets of the dark grey Burberry. 'Any healthy lad can get a ship. There's enough sailing out of English ports, and many of the crew will be runaways. Papers are the last thing he'll need. And when he gets wherever he's going, the sailors will show him how to get an identity.'

'You'll have to go to Australia and fetch him home.' There was a hysterical edge to Agnes's tone.

Sidney shook his head. 'Look, dear, he might not have gone to Australia. Even if he has, he'll be stopping off all over the place to see the world.'

'He'll be using all kinds of public facilities!' Agnes leapt from the chair, ran to her husband. 'Foreigners are notorious for bad hygiene. He'll be ill! You must go and fetch him at once.' Her teeth chattered and her hands fluttered like overgrown and very pale butterflies.

Sidney looked at Deedee, nodded almost imperceptibly. Deedee slid a greenish bottle from her purse, passed it to Sidney without saying a word. He took his hands from the pockets, tipped out a tablet, accepted water from Phyllis. 'Come on, now,' he urged. 'Get this down you.' The nerve tablets hadn't been needed for ages, and Sidney cursed his son inwardly as Agnes swallowed her medicine. The stuff was addictive. He kept some here with Doris Wagstaff; stored the rest in his safe on Church Road. Only in the direst circumstances did any of them resort to the use of such powerful sedatives. Agnes no longer suffered from declines, as those were Victorian, and she was a modern woman. But she reacted strangely to stress, was capable of becoming hysterical if not kept busy. 'Thanks,' he mouthed at Doris Wagstaff. Doris had succeeded where he had failed, because this fine lady had drawn Agnes out to a point where 'the scheme of things' was seldom mentioned. 'Go upstairs,' he advised his wife gently.

Agnes Althorpe did as she was told, allowing Megan to lead her from the room and through the panelled hallway. 'His room's ready,' muttered Agnes. 'All antique furniture and a lovely four-poster. Your grandmother and I made all the drapes.' She paused, placed a hand on Megan's arm. 'Don't blame yourself, my dear. Geoffrey is not for you.' As the drug loosened mind and tongue, she spoke the unfortunate truth. 'I spoiled him. He is not strong enough for you.' Was he strong enough for any young woman of today? she wondered as Megan guided her to the master bedroom. 'I didn't know . . . who to be. But I tried to make them into . . . I tried to turn them into the children Sidney might have had if . . .'

'Lie down.'

Agnes stared at the ceiling, then allowed her eyes to wander round a room whose furnishings reflected the styles and patterns of several centuries. A pair of Cromwellian chairs squatted beneath the latticed window, while a bed-wagon, newly-polished with beeswax, stood opposite the bed as if waiting to be filled with the coals that had warmed Elizabethan linens. A well-bottomed wardrobe filled a space next to the open grate, while newer and more elegant furniture punctuated dark-panelled walls. 'My fault, not yours,' she moaned, fighting to keep her eyes open. 'I didn't know who I was, till . . . Doris showed me how to be me. Why has he gone, Megan? Why?'

Megan pulled a blanket from a carved chest, placed it over Agnes's legs. The bed was not yet made up, but she found a cushion to serve as pillow. 'Go to sleep now,' she urged. 'I'll fetch you some tea and biscuits in a couple of hours.'

'Good girl.' The voice was reedy, transparent. 'You would have done . . . very well . . . for Geoffrey . . .'

Megan blinked back the tears, closed the heavy curtains, sat for a while on a chair which had been made at a time when England had no king. She'd done Oliver Cromwell at school, had learned how Bolton had backed the Roundheads. The chair was as uncomfortable as those silly tin helmets must have been. Mrs Althorpe's mouth was open, allowing small snores to emerge. Geoff. How he had begged, how strongly he had put his case. A new life, a new world, space, greenery and freedom. And Megan had said no, because she hadn't wanted that kind of liberty.

She closed her eyes, leaned back against expensive tapestry. What Geoff had felt for her had not been love, not real love. Love was knowing somebody and being with him. Love was trying hard to get inside someone's head and heart, trying to become a part of his soul. Geoff hadn't known about love, but Megan had been well taught by Deedee. According to that self-appointed family sage, love was two people trying to become one before trying to become several more. And if Megan were to have babies, she would choose Billy to be their father.

Footsteps crunched on gravel, and she peered outside, saw Billy with Joseph. Billy was going to be a wonderful dad. There had been little affection in Billy Shipton's life, because his father had been a drunk, while his mother had laboured under the weight of poverty and overcrowding. Yet Billy was love. The need to care for folk poured from him, spilled out in his laughter, in his words. She would be safe with him. With Billy, she could share her darkest secrets and her wildest imaginings. He didn't look like a hero, but he was a brave, kind lad who loved her.

She rose from the chair, had a look at the sleeping woman, went down to face the music. For years, Billy had been saying the same thing. 'Don't hurt him, Meggy. Don't make fun of him, but don't egg him on.' And she had told a lie, because she'd said that Geoff Althorpe had lost interest in her.

'Why?' asked Billy. There was no need for him to utter more than this one word.

'I thought it would be easier. I didn't want you to be jealous.'

His eyebrows lifted themselves almost to the hairline. 'I trust you,' he said. 'And if you'd wanted him, I would have known.'

'Sorry,' she mumbled.

He lifted her chin with a brown finger, tut-tutted when he saw the frown. 'I'll never be jealous,' he said. 'Because I'll never need to be.'

She gulped back a piece of emotion too mixed to bear a label. 'Billy, I wish we were older.'

He shook his head, wagged a finger under her nose. 'Don't go wishing your life away.'

'You sound like Deedee,' she complained with a grin.

He laughed. 'So do you, madam. All the time.'

'Do you mind?'

He bent down, separated Joseph from one of Tommy's many cats. 'No. Because I love you both.'

Content with that, Megan took his hand and walked along the crooked mile to find her stepgrandfather.

'Just keep still a minute.' Tommy Wagstaff hung from the

roof of a low shed, gnarled fingers curled around the apex, legs bent at the knees as he tried to achieve a degree of stability. A stringy grey cat twitched its thin tail, walked further away from the man who imagined himself to be its master. 'I'll bloody see to you one of these days,' cursed the old man. 'It'll be the vet if you don't shape. You've had nowt but good grub and a comfortable bed. What the hell are you doing up here? Good job you've nine bloody lives, eh?'

Megan hoped with all her heart that 'Uncle' Tommy had more than one life, because Deedee would surely clout him with the yardbrush if she heard him swearing.

Billy ran to the shed, grabbed Tommy's ankles. 'You're worse than Joseph,' he said. 'You need watching all the while, Uncle Tommy.'

'Bloody hell,' yelled the would-be acrobat. 'I near had a heart attack. Why did you creep up on me?' He clambered down, uttered a few more assorted oaths when his shins scraped against the wood. With no sign of gratitude in his expression, he turned on Megan and Billy. 'I very near had him,' he shouted. 'He's wild, is yon Montmerency, and he takes some flaming catching.' He rolled up a sleeve, displayed raw scratches. 'Them's me war wounds,' he muttered. 'And that there mouser is the blinking Kaiser. I should get compensation from the government, I should.'

Billy pursed his lips for a second. 'Isn't that what you get inside the windows when it's cold?'

Tommy studied his adopted nephew. 'Eh?'

'Compensation. Inside the house in cold weather—'

'Don't talk so daft, lad. That's condensation.'

Megan gazed skyward while young Joseph's head moved from one to another, as if he were watching a tennis match. Billy knew what condensation was, because Billy was always reading about that kind of stuff. But the lad had become adept in the art of confusing Tommy. Though it was more likely that each of these protagonists was playing a game whose rules changed with the wind direction. 'Nice day,' she announced, her voice high and silly. 'Nice day for getting stuck up a shed with a mangy old cat.'

Tommy drew himself to full height. Even when his spine was extended, he measured several inches less than his tall wife. 'Where is she?' he asked now.

'Up at the Hall,' answered Megan. 'Geoff's done a bunk.'

'You what?' Cats and sheds were forgotten immediately. 'Eeh, I don't know,' exclaimed the old man, his attempts at dignity forgotten. His shoulders drooped as he thought about Agnes Althorpe. She was a good sort, a girl from Bolton who had recently remembered her roots, a woman who was learning how to enjoy herself after many years of uncertainty. 'She'll go straight up the pole,' he muttered under his breath. 'She'll need them flaming tablets again like she did when she had—' He cut himself short, because he didn't want to talk to these young folk about Agnes's middle-aged female troubles. 'Montmerency will have nowt on her,' he said, ''cos poor Agnes'll be meeting herself coming back if the lad's fled.' He rubbed a hand across his sandpaper chin. 'Where's he gone to?'

Billy shrugged. 'Might be Australia. He's been telling Megan for years he'd be going there once he was old enough. Mrs Althorpe's all for sending her husband on a wild goose chase to the other side of the world. Only it's a big country, is Australia and—'

'Opals,' exclaimed Tommy.

It was Billy's turn to be nonplussed. 'Eh?'

'A book. I had it in the kitchen up yonder . . .' He waved an arm towards the large house in which they had all lived. 'Me and Doris were getting ready for moving into this queer place.' He cast his glance over the uneven chimneys after which Twisted Stacks had been named. 'And he kept reading it every time he visited. I even joked with him about it, asked if he were thinking of opening up a mine down under. I bet he's took that with him. I bet he's gone off to make his fortune.'

'We'd best tell his dad,' said Billy.

Tommy, deep in thought, studied his old boots, as if he sought an answer in their polish-starved uppers. 'Nay,' he said eventually. 'It might not be Australia. They've found black opals in other countries – America, New Zealand and Mexico. I think Japan were mentioned and all. See, he'll be looking for a quick killing, will young Geoffrey. Like his mam used to be, he is, allers trying to please the wrong folk. There were no way Geoff could get himself educated in books. Even his dad wanted him to sit some exams for an accountant. So he didn't know which way to turn, poor lad. If only he'd talked to his mam and dad. If only he'd stuck to his guns like Fliss did.'

Megan touched Tommy's arm. 'Is it my fault?'

The grey head moved from side to side. 'Nay, lass. It were none of your doing, this lot. He's not right for you, not the sort you'll be needing. Poor boy's a coward, can't face up to things proper. I'm just glad you didn't let him talk you into it, Megan. Trouble with Geoff is he'll flit about to suit himself.'

Megan blushed. 'I wouldn't leave you and Deedee or Dad and Joseph.'

Tommy sighed. 'Aye, and you'd not leave Billy, either. Would you?'

'No, Uncle Tommy,' she said softly.

Billy blushed, picked up little Joseph and hid his embarrassment behind the child's head. 'Come on,' he said gruffly. 'Let's go and get Deedee.'

Fliss waited at the bottom of Rowland Street, her stance deliberately casual. She hadn't been to the Greenwoods' house for a while, because Bessie's behaviour during visits had deteriorated to the point of embarrassment. She didn't like Fliss; couldn't take to her at all. It was the many illnesses, of course, that made Phil's mother so unpredictable.

She stepped forward, glanced up to where Back Rowland Street butted against the yards of Back Dobson Street. If Phil didn't turn up soon, she would simply give up and go home. The houses cast long shadows as the sun slipped away, but it was too early for the lamplighter.

Fliss paced about, pulled impatiently at the square of silk that covered her head, thought yet again how silly all this secrecy was. Things would improve soon, she told herself firmly. Things would improve because she had made up her mind about telling Mother. Pop already knew about Phil – well – he had an idea that Phil Greenwood was on Fliss's agenda for the future. Mother might just manage to accept the situation now, because Mother had dragged herself into the twentieth century at last. But strangely, it was Phil who was holding back. He seemed to need to keep their relationship in a back pocket of his mind, as if he dared not do anything to upset the terminally ill Bessie.

In spite of the weather, Fliss shivered. Sometimes, she found part of her mind wishing that Bessie Greenwood could just die. She comforted herself occasionally by insisting that she merely hoped that the woman's discomfort might soon be over, but Fliss's natural candour prevented her from believing this legend.

'Fliss?'

She swivelled, gave him a smile. 'Hello, Phil.'

He dragged her along, glancing about furtively as if he were a spy from some alien power. 'I've had a terrible time,' he said when they reached the yard of an empty house. 'Come in here where we'll not get disturbed.'

She waited until he had pressed his nose against scullery and kitchen windows. When he seemed sure of their privacy, she approached him. 'What's going on, Phil?'

'Murder,' he snapped. 'Sorry, love. It's not quite murder, but it's on the same lines. Your dad came to the house.'

'Oh?'

He nodded quickly. 'Asked where you were.' He couldn't disclose the whole story because, after Sidney Althorpe's departure, Bessie Greenwood had yelled a lot of nonsense about Phil spending all his time with Fliss when

315

he ought to have been minding a very sick woman. 'Your brother's gone.'

Fliss swallowed. 'Gone?'

'Yes. He's left home, taken every stitch of clothing with him. Mr Althorpe mentioned Tommy Wagstaff and some book about opals. Anyway, I'd best get back, because my mother's had one of her turns.'

Fliss needed him, wanted him to come with her on the trams and buses back to Bromley Cross and the Hall. Her little car had gone in to be repaired, and she didn't want to travel alone on public transport. Yet she dared not ask, because that would have seemed unfeeling, uncaring. 'I hope she'll be better soon, Phil,' she said.

He almost ground his teeth. Often, he felt like a carcass that was being dragged about in the teeth of two female hunters, although Fliss left very few teeth marks. It wasn't Fliss's fault, he reminded himself for the hundredth time. And it wasn't really Mam's, either, because Mam suffered a lot of discomfort. He dismissed from recent memory the picture of a woman who screamed at him, who demanded, this, that, fetch me, carry me. There were times when his female parent seemed to be endowed with great energy. He had even found her walking in the yard, her gait suspiciously stable until she had caught sight of her son.

'It's not fair, Phil.' Fliss seldom complained and, even now, her tone was gentle. 'If Geoff's done as he threatened, my mother will be terribly hurt. At times like this, we all need our loved ones. But I have to face this without your support.'

He pushed her against the wall, removed her scarf, placed his hands palms down against bricks at each side of her head. Fliss had lovely, thick hair and startling eyes, but her nose let her down a bit. He kissed the tip of this offending item, told himself firmly that the nose was the only flaw in this wonderfully strong and affectionate girl. 'Fliss, she's getting on. It can't go on forever like this, can it? I mean, she's got so much wrong with her that she's sure to die soon. Then I won't have to feel guilty about having neglected her.'

Fliss nodded. 'I know. But at a time like this, I need you. There'll be a search, I suppose. They'll have to look around Bolton first. I'm always alone. This is almost as bad as having a married lover, I should think. Always, I have to wait for you to contact me at the mill. I can't visit you and—'

'Well, I've not been welcomed with open arms, have I?' His tone was petulant, childlike.

She sighed deeply. 'Mother has changed. When I've suggested that you come for tea, you've refused.' Quickly, she ducked under his left arm and went to the gate. 'I'm going now, because my family needs me. The difference is, of course, that I would never allow myself to be monopolized.' Hating herself for these mean words, she broke into a run, tears threatening to blur her vision. Geoff. That thoughtless brat had abandoned Mother – and just when she was doing so well, too.

Phil started after her, stopped dead in his tracks when she turned a corner. Life was a mess. If only Mam would die, then Phil's horizons would widen considerably. Fliss Althorpe had strength, goodness and money.

As he trudged homeward, he concentrated on the many possibilities, though he tried to forget about the money, because he would have loved Fliss anyway. Wouldn't he . . . ?

It was all so wrong. Patrick O'Riley pushed a hand through the few sandy hairs that had managed to linger on his head. Outside, a group of ill-clad children fought, the subject of argument seeming to be a hopscotch grid chalked on the flags. Rules. They were coming to blows because they could not reach agreement about a sliver of blue slate whose edge had touched a line.

Lines. Barriers. Rules. He sat at a scratched table, rubbed at a circular stain left by a cup. It wouldn't come off. Even if he were to find polish and rag, the mark would remain. It was obeying regulations. Even this scarred table was following a code that dictated the need for order in the form of a french polisher.

'All right, Paddy?' The creased, sun-withered face of a regular peeped round the door. 'Any baccy?'

Paddy shook his head. 'No, Eddie. I don't smoke any more, and—'

'Can I just look in the dormitories? I'll not take anything from a cupboard, but there might be a few dockers on the floor.'

Dockers were cigarette stubs and cigarette stubs were power. Many of the mission's residents spent a full day scouring Bolton's pavements, heads downcast as they searched for tiny scraps of Woodbine or Gold Flake. A man with a couple of recycled cigarettes could enjoy a smoke, or he might barter for another's dinner. 'Eddie, I don't allow anyone into the bedrooms during the day. You should know the regulations by now.' Paddy felt the redness in his cheeks, because he was having his own trouble with the laws of society and the commandments of God.

'Can I have a drink?'

Paddy waved a hand at the intruder. 'One cup, Eddie. Brew it in the mug and go easy on milk and sugar.' The ex-priest settled back in his wooden chair, though his muscles remained as rigid as iron. '*Mea culpa*,' he muttered beneath his breath. So far, he had made negative progress through life. He had been a priest, then a homeless layman, then a failed missionary. His lack of success in the third category resided in the fact that visitors to Flash Street literally sang for their suppers and only for their suppers. And now, Patrick O'Riley was the worst kind of sinner, because he had encouraged a child to fall in love with him. If he were to write a list of his shortcomings next to an account of his good points, then the former would outstrip the latter by a mile.

He'd been invited back into the church. The bishop had sent for him, had pleaded anew. 'Come on, Patrick, you only have to do penance for that one mistake.' And the

318

answer had been in the negative again. He could do no penance, could make no promise about altering his views. And now . . . and now, there was Phyllis Entwistle.

She was a beautiful girl. He cast his mind back to that day in the graveyard when the doctor had found him. How many suicides' graves had he blessed before the bishop caught up with him? A hundred, a thousand? Paddy had not confined his makeshift funeral services to Bolton. Cemeteries in Ireland, Manchester, Wigan and Bury had all accommodated the shabby man with his dirty stole and his bottles of holy water.

Phyllis had stood that day next to Charlie Walsh, her weight depending on the more stable side of her body. If he closed his eyes, Paddy could see her now, pale, drawn, the lovely auburn hair made more vibrant by the lack of colour in her face. The day had become confusing due to lack of food, though the picture of Phyllis Entwistle had remained clear forever. She had looked like a very young Madonna from some ancient Italian painting, smooth-featured, serene but sad.

He lifted his head, cocked an ear towards the kitchen. 'Eddie?'

A sudden stillness was punctured by a high-pitched 'Yes?'

'Get your hand out of that currant jar.'

'I'm nowhere near it.'

'Biscuit jar, then.'

When the rattling had stopped, Paddy rose and walked to the window. His feelings for little Phyllis were confused to the point of pain. Long ago, as a priest, he had feared children simply because their questions had been so simple, so complicated. Then he had met Megan Duffy. Megan had changed him so radically that his calling had deserted him. No. He shook his head, unwilling to place such a huge parcel at the feet of an innocent. Before the Ida Entwistle business, his faith had been shaky. Ida's committal to unconsecrated ground had been a catalyst, no more than that.

A lad in the street had grabbed a girl by the hair, was dragging her towards a lamp post. Other boys arrived with washing line, were preparing to tie up the poor child. Paddy threw up the window, stuck his head through the gap. 'Oy,' he yelled. 'Let her go, or I'll set Eddie on you.' The boys melted away like snow in summer. They were terrified of Eddie, because Eddie growled at them. The old man had learned to growl in his youth when travelling with a circus.

'D'yer want me to go after them, boss?' Eddie stood to one side, a steaming cup in his hand.

'Crumbs in your beard,' said Paddy.

'Sorry.' The man who had earned his living by sticking his head into the maw of a lion suddenly looked sheepish after stealing a biscuit. 'Worse than Oscar, you are,' grumbled the tramp. 'And he had a bite like Satan.' Proudly, and for the umpteenth time, Eddie displayed the Oscar-marks on his neck. 'Not many could survive that, Paddy,' he boasted.

'Most of us would have the sense to stay away from the beast in the first place.'

Eddie Marchant grinned, displaying teeth whose colour ranged from yellow to tobacco brown. 'We all have an Oscar in our lives,' he said. 'Mine had a mane and big teeth, but at least I could see him, hear him. I could even touch the bugger. Pardon.' He took a noisy slurp of tea. 'It's the invisible sods you've got to watch, and them that have two legs. I'd face up to a lion again before tackling some folk, I can tell you.'

'Yes,' mumbled Paddy. He watched the wise old man as he ambled out of the office, tea spilling from an unsteady cup. 'I've met my Oscar,' whispered Paddy into the empty room. His Oscar was not Phyllis. His Oscar was the situation that had arisen out of the existence of a fourteen-year-old girl. He didn't even know what human love was, yet he must have encouraged the naked adoration that shone from the girl's face every time she saw him. Questions. So many questions. Would he ever get married, would he want children, would he wait for the right person to come along? He had replied in the affirmative. And now, Megan Duffy had arrived again with a questionnaire for him to tackle.

After Megan had left, Paddy had sat in this very room, hands clasped in prayer. Part of the answer had come to him. For years, he had known that he must take responsibility for Ida Entwistle's daughter. Blessing a grave had not been enough. The dead were dead and the living were now, here, a set of God-given facts with faces, souls, needs. Megan Duffy wanted her own life. Already, she was committed to Billy Shipton. Doris 'Deedee' Wagstaff would not last forever, nor would her husband. Phyllis's brothers had followed their aunt and uncle to work in the Midlands. And Phyllis was going to be alone.

He sighed, pulled the rosary from a pocket, twisted the worn beads in his fingers. Phyllis had altered the truth, but forgiving her was unnecessary, because she was not yet fifteen. He closed his eyes, saw Megan's face, heard her voice. 'She says you're going to wait for her and you want to get married. She says you want to marry her.'

The tide of life. He was being swept along, was allowing himself to be moved like a piece of driftwood caught in seaweed. Suddenly, his eyes flew open. He remembered the child in the street, the little girl who would have been tied to a lamp post had he not intervened. Nothing like that must ever happen to Phyllis. She was unsure on her legs, had days when walking was a chore, when even the act of eating tired her. He nodded to himself, arrived at the complete answer. Patrick O'Riley had been put into the world to make the path for others, to save people from pain and damnation. And Phyllis somehow represented all that he must do during his remaining time.

'I'll look after her,' he said to the Sacred Heart in the broken frame. He must get little Megan to make one of those kid-covered frames. Yes, he would tidy up the holy picture, tidy up the mission. In a couple of years, Phyllis would live here with him. And after his death, she would have children who would give her comfort.

Perhaps, in spite of himself, he had found his true vocation.

PART THREE

ONE

On 1 May 1930, Megan Duffy attained the age of eighteen. When she woke that morning, a great bubble of excitement sat in her breast. She was on the brink of something wonderful. After today, she would never be the same. Yet after today, her life would follow a path that was not really new, because so many familiar things and people were going to continue to fill her days. But the order of things and people was going to change forever.

From her window, she looked along the crooked mile to where Hall i' th' Vale peeped round the corner, just one small and secretive window throwing out light in many directions. The glass was old, warped and flawed, which was why it was so beautiful. She remembered Mrs Althorpe complaining in the early days, 'Sidney, everything looks wrong out there'. And Mr Althorpe's reply had been memorable, too. 'The windows are not rose-coloured, my dear, but they do provide a different view of life.' He had refused point blank to replace the faulty panes.

Megan stretched, rubbed her eyes, remembered that in spite of her happiness, all was not well with the world. In the next few days, National Cotton Week would begin. This attempt to boost trade had been nicknamed by Boltonians 'petticoat politics', though the title had nothing at all to do with suffrage. The fact was that short skirts had hit the industry hard. In Victorian times, a woman's clothing had often incorporated ten yards of good calico, whereas the modern style demanded only a fraction of that amount.

Then there was that poor man who wore a nappy that he

325

had spun and woven himself – he was going into prison soon for picking up a bit of salt near the sea. Mr Gandhi was getting very thin, and Megan's patience with the British government and its representatives was thinning. As far as Megan and most of her friends were concerned, India should belong to the Indians. 'England is not as great as we were told,' she announced to her reflection. Dad made fun of her – when he felt jolly, which wasn't very often. The terrible pain in Joe Duffy's eyes had lost its edge, but he had become a quiet, reflective man. He said that Megan's philosophy was 'too idealistic'. She laughed, put out her tongue, reached for her dressing gown. Having dressing gowns was wonderful. Mrs Althorpe bought one every other year for Megan as a Christmas present.

As she washed in the new bathroom, whose cramped area had been stolen from the main bedroom, she found herself thinking about Mr Althorpe. He'd been so good to the Duffys. Joseph, who was six, had a bicycle. Megan dropped her toothbrush, felt the tears building up. Annie and Nellie, Freda and Hilda, Hattie and Sarah. They'd never had a bicycle, had never lived in the country where the air was so fresh it brought you wide awake each dawn. Mam. She rubbed Gibb's Dentifrice on her teeth, picked up the brush and riddled it about. Mam would have loved Joseph.

When her grooming was completed, Megan poked her head through the window on the landing, stared at the house that sat opposite hers. Billy Shipton, Phyllis Entwistle, Grandma Deedee and Uncle Tommy Wagstaff lived there, in the cottage called Twisted Stacks. Letters addressed to them always looked funny, because they usually bore the name 'Wagstaff', followed by 'Twisted Stacks' and 'Dog Leg Lane'. So the minds of those who posted the mail must have carried a picture of a man waving a stick at some strange chimneys on a bent road. Although, according to Joe Duffy, not everyone was cursed/blessed with Megan's imagination.

The house in which Megan, her father and Joseph lived was smaller than Twisted Stacks. Its name, The Gate House, was plain in comparison, but the little cottage had a charm all its own. Some of the windows were arched like those in a church, while all doors and windows were set in lovely greyish-green stone borders against which the red brickwork looked wonderful. The Gate House boasted just two ground floor rooms – a live-in kitchen across the back, and a parlour at the front. Upstairs, the rear bedroom had been divided down the middle to create two small rooms, one for herself, the second for Joseph. Today, Megan would claim Dad's bedroom for herself and her husband.

The chimneys across the lane were strange. Not for the first time, Megan wondered how they managed to remain in position, because they looked as if they might have been built by a small child, each block resting not quite squarely on its base. Yet the stacks had survived storm, heavy snow and fierce winds, so she managed, just about, not to worry about the safety of folk who passed by in weathers fair and foul.

It was going to be a lovely day. The sun shone, the birds were fussing merrily and Megan Duffy was to be married in Our Lady of Sorrows church in just a few short hours. When she saw a figure in a window of Twisted Stacks, she backed away. If Billy saw her before the ceremony, they would have bad luck. As a good Catholic girl, she uncrossed her fingers and blessed herself quickly, then touched wood just in case the old sayings had any truth in them. Laughing at herself, she returned to her little room and looked for the umpteenth time at her wedding gown. It was not what the flappers would call stylish, but it was all her own doing. Well, Deedee, Minnie Hattersley and Bertha Strong had done most of the actual sewing, but the creation adhered strictly to Megan's original design. It was a long, full-skirted dress with emphasis on the narrow waist. There were no beads, no fringes, no baubles. Silk as fine as this wanted little help.

Again, she mouthed her thanks to the Althorpes, particularly to Mrs, who had brought the material back from London. Megan's brow furrowed for a second or two as she remembered the reason for the Althorpes' many visits to the south. Geoffrey. Or Geoff, as he had insisted, was missing, had been missing for years. His parents had tracked down a man whose son owned three sheep farms in Australia, had used this contact to spread the message throughout that huge country. No word yet, no letter from Geoff. That annoying boy must have changed his name, because his parents had chased after him right from the start, could have been no more than a few days behind him. Mrs Althorpe would be glad for Megan and Billy today. She would smile and eat and drink, yet those who cared to look might notice the terrible emptiness in her eyes.

Megan sat at her little dressing table, pulled a brush through the tangle of dark curls that was her crowning glory. Her bright blue eyes shone back at her, excitement seeming to glow in the irises. Everyone said that Megan was pretty but, however hard she looked, she couldn't see it. She had black hair, blue eyes and rosy cheeks. There was nothing remarkable in the mirror, nothing to write home about. The brush slowed. With all her heart, she prayed that Geoff Althorpe would stop sulking and send a letter to his mother. He had something worth writing home about. Just 'hello, I'm alive and safe' would brighten the careworn face of Agnes Althorpe.

'Megan?'

She turned, smiled at her little brother. 'Hello, pest. What do you want?'

'I don't want to be a pageboy.'

The bride poked a finger towards the intruder. 'It's only for once and it's for me. You said you'd do it for me. I bought you a quarter of toffees and a puncture kit.'

Joseph leaned on the door frame. 'Velvet trousers is daft. And a frill. I'm six, and I shouldn't wear frills.'

'You promised.'

'I crossed my fingers behind my back, so it doesn't count.'

Megan shrugged, picked up her comb. 'All right. You stay here while the rest of us have a nice party in the church hall. Mary from the big house will look after you. I'm sure we'll find some other boy who'll wear your clothes and eat all the jelly.'

He sidled into the room, stuffed a hand into each of his pockets, tried to look nonchalant. 'What colour is the jelly?'

Megan thought for a moment. 'There's strawberry, raspberry – they'll both be red. Then there's a dark red one called blackcurrant. Lemon, orange, lime. Mr Althorpe's got Manfredi's coming up with some ice cream. And you won't be on the photographs. When I'm old, I'll tell my children that their Uncle Joseph was too frightened to be a pageboy.'

Joseph sat on the edge of the bed, bounced a few times, but his heart wasn't in the movements. 'I'll do it,' he said very softly.

'And your children will ask why you didn't come to your only sister's wedding. Dad will be upset if you stay at home—'

'I'll do it—'

'Deedee will never forgive you. And Uncle Tommy Wagstaff won't take you down to the fair next month.'

'I'LL DO IT!'

She swivelled on the stool, grinned at him. 'Did you say something?'

The child frowned. 'I don't want to move, either. I want to stop here with you. This is my house, you know. Why do me and Dad have to go and live at Deedee's? And why does Billy have to come and live here with you?'

Megan rubbed cream into her hands. Leather work was tough, had thickened her skin. While her hands were not ugly, they were not things of beauty, either. 'All this has been explained to you, Joseph. Billy and I will be a family. After today, my name will be Megan Shipton. When two

329

people get married, they sometimes have a house all to themselves. There's plenty of room at Twisted Stacks. You'll sleep in Billy's room, Phyllis will stay where she is just for now . . .' She hugged Phyllis's secret, was pleased about being the only one who knew the truth. 'Dad's having Deedee and Uncle Tommy's room. They're getting older, you see, and Deedee's started with the rheumatics, so they'll be sleeping in that little room off the kitchen.'

He glanced round his sister's bedroom. 'Who'll be in here?'

'Nobody.'

'And in my room?'

'Nobody.'

'Then why can't I live with you and Billy?'

'Because you can't. It's not as if you're moving miles, Joseph. You'll be just across the lane. If we were sending you to India to help Mr Gandhi, or to Australia to look for Geoff Althorpe, then I could understand you being upset. But you're going ten strides across the lane.' She screwed the lid on the cream pot, wondered when Fliss would arrive to do her hair. 'Is Dad up?'

Joseph giggled, stood up, pushed a sticky package onto her knee. 'I was kidding,' he managed, almost doubled over with glee. 'That's your birthday present. I've only ate two, and they were broke.'

She grabbed him, kissed him, clouted him gently. 'Aniseed balls?'

'Yes.'

'My favourites,' she yelled. 'Aniseed balls for breakfast. Yummy.'

Joe found his two remaining children sitting side by side dividing the sweets between them. 'Happy birthday, Megan,' he said gruffly. 'I got you the shoes.' He handed over a tissue-wrapped package. 'They were as near as I could find.'

She looked at the slippers, smiled up at her father. 'Just like on the photo. I still remember that picture.' After the fire, Joe had often told the story of his and Tess's wedding day. The shoes had been important, because Tess had saved for two months in order to afford them. Every last photograph had gone up in smoke, so Joe had often described items from 13, Myrtle Street. 'They're exactly what I wanted, Dad,' said Megan.

She was still a child, thought Joe. Yet he wouldn't have stopped this wedding for the world. They were right for one another, Megan and Billy. Their love had grown over the years, its foundation firm and strong because it was rooted in friendship. 'You'll be all right,' he told her now. 'He's a good lad.'

'I know.'

'And you're a good girl.'

'She knows,' said Joseph. 'And I know I'm a good lad, because I'm going to wear stupid pants and a frill. If anybody from school sees me, I'm going to say I was tortured downstairs in Hall i' th' Vale till I said yes. Still, it's better than a kilt and something called a sporran. Michael O'Gara was a page at his auntie's wedding, and he had to wear a skirt. All the girls were chasing him to see his underclothes.'

Megan nodded wisely. 'Do him good. It'll show him what girls have to put up with all the time.'

Joseph wore an air of deep shock. 'Boys don't pull girls' skirts up. Not at our school.'

'And I'm the Queen of Sheba,' said Megan. 'Dad, have you seen Fliss? Only she's supposed to be putting my hair up.'

'She'll be along,' answered Joe. 'It's only half past seven, so there's no panic. Come on, Joseph, let's make her last breakfast as a single woman. Leave her on her own a bit. Women get emotional on wedding days.'

Megan, who had seen the water in her father's eyes, made no remark as the two left her room. She moved to the bed, stretched herself out for a few moments. On the wall opposite sat the photograph of all the Myrtle Street gang. This picture had been given to Joe by one of the garden streets' neighbours. 'You need it more than I do, lad,' Mrs Batty had said. 'My kiddies is still with me, but this is all you've got.'

Megan allowed her eyes to stray over the features of her dead sisters. Would Annie and Nellie have been married by now? Would they have changed, looked different from one another with the passage of time? No tears, she told herself firmly. Billy was on the back row with two front teeth gone and his collar stud missing. He had good teeth, had hung on to his first lot for ages. His adult teeth were beautifully white, strong and straight. She loved him. He made her laugh, made her comfortable, made her hot when he stroked her cheek. 'Soon, Megan,' he kept telling her. Billy was the one who had made her wait . . .

She closed her eyes, warned herself to stay awake. Megan had a wonderful capacity for sleep, could slip into a catnap at the drop of a hat. Even when life was exciting, she sometimes dozed through the best bits. Her thoughts were becoming muddled, and she knew that she was in danger of nodding off. But it didn't matter, because Dad and Joseph were making her breakfast. They would pull her round, make her eat, tell her to get dressed and . . . and find her rosary . . . and . . . Fliss was bringing the bouquet . . .

'Come to Australia with me,' said Geoffrey Althorpe.

She stood in the smaller of Hall i' th' Vale's two kitchens. 'I can't. I'm helping Mr Cornwell and he's showing me how to cover furniture.'

Geoffrey frowned. 'Let old Eli Cornwell find somebody else to mend his chairs. He only took you on because your father invented those guns for the studs.'

'I'm sorry. I'm staying here. And if you're thinking of going anywhere, you should tell your mam and dad.'

He coloured, stared guiltily at the floor. 'Without you, I'm going nowhere. You're fourteen now, old enough to come abroad. And I've plenty saved, so I can pay your passage.'

'No.'

His teeth were suddenly bared. They weren't as white as

Billy's had become, weren't straight and strong. 'It's that Billy Shipton, isn't it? You and he have been as thick as thieves according to Fliss. Are you going to marry him?'

She stood her ground, felt the heat in her face. 'I've told you before, I'm marrying no-one. He's . . . he's like a brother. Remember me and Billy lost a lot of people in that fire. So we look after one another, that's all. Any road, it's none of your business, Geoffrey Althorpe.'

'Geoff.'

'Call yourself what you like,' she replied softly. 'But it doesn't change what you are. You're a great big soft lad who wants all his own way. Well, I'm stopping here for the rest of my life, so you can just shut up about the whole thing.'

He grabbed her shoulder, pushed her against the gas cooker. She could feel the knob on the oven door as it tried to bore through the back of a shin. She moved her legs, flinched as he shook her. 'You've no imagination, Megan Duffy. You'll stay here for the rest of your life, you'll marry a boring Bolton man and have hordes of boring Bolton children—'

'I've loads of imagination! My dad's always telling me I'm a dreamer. How do you think I make all the leather things? Also, in case you haven't noticed, there's nothing boring about here!' she screamed into his face. He was too close, was always getting too close. 'You're the boring one, forever going on about what you don't want to do. Stand up to your mother. Fliss did. Aren't you as brave as your sister? And the only reason why Mrs Althorpe's . . . like she is is because she's frightened. Deedee says "Agnes Althorpe doesn't understand her position in life". So you should talk to her, explain that you don't fit into what she used to call her scheme of things. Oh, one more on the list. Bolton's a very important town, what with all the mills, foundries, tanneries, farming, market—'

'You've no idea, Megan. I can't . . . I don't want to be without you. You're forcing me to stay here. It's no use. Mother wants me to go into accountancy. I keep failing the exams. There has to be a fresh start away from Mother.'

Megan, who had understood Agnes since Deedee had said a few things, almost growled her next words. 'Your mam is a good woman. She's nervous, that's all. I mean, look at the decline in cotton. People don't buy as much as they did, so your mam wants you to have a grounding in something else. She only wants you to take advantage of Mr Althorpe's money while it's there. They've spent a fortune on your education. Will you take your hands off me?' She waited until he had taken a step back. 'Mrs Althorpe is good and kind. She's hard on you because she worries.'

He sneered. 'What about Fliss and her weaver?'

Megan shrugged. 'That's all been accepted. They'd have been married but for his mother lingering.' Bessie Greenwood had survived against all odds. Deedee had been heard to say – under her breath, of course – that Bessie Greenwood was too bad to die. According to Doris Wagstaff, God didn't want Phil's mother, and the devil was back at school learning how to cope with such a special case. Deedee was so funny—

'You're not even listening to me. Ever since we were children, I've wanted to be with you.'

'Why?'

'Because . . .' He hesitated. 'I don't know, I just need you to come with me.'

Megan nodded thoughtfully. 'It's because I'm ordinary, from an ordinary family, from an ordinary street. You'd be too daft to manage the sort of girl your mother would line up for you. See, she wanted you both to marry well, to marry money so that you'd be safe. Fliss got out of school because she needed to make a success of her life. So she walked towards something. Whereas you're running away. Running away's no good. It's not what I want to do. I'm like Fliss – I want to make something of myself.'

His upper lip curled. 'You are not like Fliss,' he hissed. 'Fliss is the ordinary one. She went into the business because she thought no-one would ever marry her. We talked about it once, ages ago. With her nose and her spots, Fliss was ugly. So she decided to be unusual.'

Megan bridled, felt her spine stretching as she pulled herself to full height. With the exception of Billy and members of her own family, Fliss Althorpe was Megan Duffy's favourite person. 'Your sister has lovely eyes and a kind face. Your sister has more sense and courage in her little finger than you have in your whole body. I don't love you, Geoffrey Althorpe. I wouldn't run away with you even if I did, because my dad has lost too much already. So just go wherever you're heading for and leave me alone. I don't care if I never see you again.'

He left that same night, went to stay with a friend. A week later, the Duffys, the Wagstaffs, Phyllis and Billy were summoned to Agnes Althorpe's presence. And Megan broke down. 'He said he wouldn't go without me.'

'Where?' asked the missing boy's mother.

'Australia. He asked me to run away with him. I'm sorry, I should have told you. I'm sorry, sorry, sorry . . .'

'What are you sorry for?'

Megan opened her eyes, saw Fliss with a breakfast tray. 'I was dreaming.'

'About Geoff? I heard you muttering "Australia". Come on, forget all the nonsense. This is your special day. No time for regrets on a morning like this, Megan Duffy. Oh, look at those shoes.' She picked up Joe's gift to Megan, stroked the soft, shining satin. 'They'll go so well with your dress. The bouquet's downstairs in the sink where it'll stay cool. We don't want the heads dropping off your flowers halfway up the aisle, do we?'

Megan, who had come to know Fliss quite well, put her head on one side and studied the older girl's pale face. 'What's the matter?' she asked. 'Are you worrying about something?'

Fliss tutted, picked up the brush, started to make some sense of the bride's unruly curls. 'Eat the toast and drink that tea. I'm a bit tired, that's all. Dad's been under the weather lately, so I've had extra work to do.'

Megan, who was wise for her years, stared at their reflections in the glass. She had lost her real sisters and, if she had been able to choose someone to bear the title 'sister', then she would have plumped wholeheartedly for Miss Felicity Althorpe. 'That woman's getting on your nerves again. I can tell just by looking at you that Phil's having trouble with his mother.'

'No. It's not that.'

Megan took a bite of toast and marmalade, flinched slightly when her hair was pulled. 'Leave a couple of curls on my head, will you? I don't want the veil slipping off my bald scalp.'

'Sorry.'

When her cup was empty, Megan picked up where she had left off. 'Years you've waited for Phil. I mean, he seems a nice man, but you've never been out with anyone else, have you?'

Fliss said nothing, because her teeth were clenched round half a dozen hairpins.

'See, according to Deedee, Mrs Greenwood should go and stay with one of her sisters. Even though they don't like her – well, nobody likes her except for Phil – they've said they'll look after her so that you can get married.'

When the hair was coiled, the bridesmaid pulled a face, began to use pins to hold the huge chignon in place. Megan had enough hair for two, she thought, trying to keep her mind occupied. The truth was that Phil's mother, having survived one overdose of painkillers, had threatened to do the job properly if Phil left home. Fliss's lover was caught in a web from which there seemed but one escape route. Bessie Greenwood would have to die before Phil's prison cell could be unlocked.

'You should just get married,' advised Megan. 'Just do it and leave her with one of Phil's aunties.'

'Nobody understands.' The freed mouth moved listlessly to frame these words in a voice that was almost inaudible. Phil wasn't coming to Megan's wedding. Although the senior Althorpes had accepted him as their daughter's fiancé, Bessie Greenwood had made it plain that Phil would be needed at home. 'Me legs is bad,' she had told Fliss during a rare visit. 'In the week, I manage, but it's nice to have a rest Saturdays and Sundays.'

'You're twenty-five,' announced Megan.

'I do know that.'

'Old enough to be a mother.'

'Yes.'

'And you're still waiting for him to get a bit of sense.'

Fliss puffed out her cheeks, blew noisily, then made a face at Megan. 'Shut up. Don't go all clever and annoying on me just because you're getting married.'

'But he's older than you. He ought to be a man, get on with his life.'

Fliss dropped her chin, remembered that those very words had come from her own mouth just days ago. 'We should get on with it,' she had said to him.

'No. You don't understand,' had been the answer. 'If we get married, she'll find some reason why we have to go and live with her. Believe me, my mother will throw herself downstairs and break her neck to get me home. We have to wait. She would destroy our marriage, Fliss, believe me.' Then he had kissed her. For the past couple of years, their relationship had come a long way past mere kisses, yet the tiniest peck from his lips could still make her weak at the knees.

'Find somebody else,' said Megan. 'That'll make him sit up and take notice.'

Fliss prodded her victim, then got to work on pinning the thick wings of hair that threatened to tumble down the sides of Megan's face. 'You've only walked out with Billy. I've never known you to look for anyone else.'

'That's because I knew he was the right one.'

'Exactly,' answered Fliss smartly. 'And that, my dear young friend, is the end of our discussion. The subject is closed. Right?'

'Right.' But while she prepared for her big day, the concern about Fliss remained in Megan's mind. There was

337

something wrong, something extra. It wasn't just Bessie Greenwood and her spineless son that worried the bridesmaid. Even so, there was a wedding to go to, a party to attend. The conversation needed to be resumed, but at a later date.

The church of Our Lady of Sorrows was a mere hut, green-painted and with a metal roof that made a terrible noise during falls of rain. As rain was a frequent visitor to Bromley Cross, Father Blunt, a jovial and kindly man, had given up sermons on wet days. 'Let God send his angels to dance above our heads,' he had been heard to shout above the din. 'And we'll provide the music. Very loud music, please.'

Many among his flock had become hoarse during hymns, though children always enjoyed Father Blunt's wet days. 'It's raining,' they would whisper along the pews when the first drops pinged on corrugated metal. During inclement mass times, several hymns were murdered with impunity, because the Infants and Juniors of Our Lady of Sorrows RC School were wont to express their own special versions of the holy songs. Neither was the Latin service allowed the respect it deserved. Gregorian chant was delivered by selected pupils from the senior school, whose desecration of the Gloria and the Kyrie was of a highly professional standard. But the party piece of these older boys and girls was born of the fact that the 'lady of the manor' was called Agnes. Instead of '*Agnus Dei qui tollis peccata mundi, miserere nobis*', it was often 'Agnes Althorpe, she goes to Hall i' th' Vale on Mondays, eats a lot of Hovis'. Father Blunt knew all about it, but he didn't mind. The young folk were coming to the Lord's house, and that was good enough.

Ian Blunt sat in his vestry with Paddy O'Riley. The latter, though an unfrocked priest, was a welcome visitor at many a presbytery. The less cautious servants of the See of Salford had even invited Paddy to serve at the altar, but Ian Blunt was the only cleric who allowed Paddy to preach. When it wasn't raining, of course. Paddy was to deliver a short sermon during today's wedding. 'The place will be packed,' said Father Blunt. 'They're a well-loved pair, favourites of many.'

The visitor smiled, drank his tea. 'Has Kevin Marsh returned from hospital yet?' he asked. Paddy was a good man, yet he was only human. The pastor who had replaced him at St Mary's was an alcoholic of note. Several times a year, the poor man was scraped from pavement or, worse still, from altar steps by members of his congregation. To the people from the garden streets, their priest had become just another irritation like mice and cockroaches. They scattered poison, set traps, put their priest away for drying out. Fortunately, a junior cleric of sober habits had joined the parish in recent months.

Father Blunt guffawed, stifled his unseemly mirth in a giant white handkerchief. 'He's been sobered up again, or so I'm told. They should let him go once and for all, because he's costing that parish a fortune. There's the whisky and then there's the treatment. They ought to let the poor fellow retire, preferably to a place where Scotch grows on trees or flows in rivers. It's a cause of great concern to me that men like Kevin go on and on, while men of your calibre are cast out into the cold.'

'I'm not cold. Mrs Flanagan keeps all her lodgers warm.' While the top floor of the Flash Street Mission was being renovated, Paddy was living in digs. Eddie the lion man had proved an invaluable asset, as he ruled the mission with a rod of iron while Paddy was 'living out'.

Ian Blunt's eyebrows almost disappeared into the rim of his biretta. 'Does she indeed?'

'Shut up, Ian,' came the swift response. 'Mrs Flanagan has a face like a farrier's anvil, a backside like the number ten tram and a voice that could shame a ship's horn.'

'Aye.' Ian Blunt removed his hat, set it on the table, then stared at it for a long time, wore the air of a mystic who sought answers in a crystal ball. 'How old is she, Paddy?'

'Fifty-seven.'

'Not her, you clown, not Holy-Josephine-Flanagan. You know well who I mean.'

'Eighteen.'

'Exactly.'

'Eighteen and a few weeks if you must have it exactly.'

'And you?'

Paddy lifted a shoulder. 'I'm thirty-eight. If you want it exactly, I'll be thirty-nine in September.'

'Quite.' Father Blunt placed an elbow on the table, rested his chin on the hand. 'You know what everybody will say, don't you? That you're a dirty old man. Worse than that – you're a dirty old man who defied the church's laws. Heavens above, what are you thinking of?'

'I'm in love,' answered Paddy. The wonderful truth was that he did love Phyllis. He hadn't even needed to work at it, because Phyllis was a marvellous girl. 'It's a wonderful feeling and a terrible curse. She loves me and she's going to need looking after. What will become of her when Doris and Tommy Wagstaff die?'

'Away with your bother, man. You know full well that Megan Duffy will always see to Phyllis. And Phyllis manages, doesn't she? Isn't she working part time now in the Bromley Cross Post Office since the wool shop in town closed? Doesn't she stand up for hours on end and never a complaint? Don't fool yourself, Paddy. It's you who needs her, not the other way round.'

Paddy thought about this accusation, decided that he did need Phyllis, that she needed him, that whatever the whys and wherefores, they loved one another. 'We're getting married in two months. Will you be doing the honours or not? By the way, we've been offered the chance of the Bromley Cross Post Office when the current people retire. We're working that one out, because I've committed myself to the mission. But if she really wants the shop, we'll take it. So. Will you marry us or what?'

'You know I'll do it. I just want to make sure that you're sure. It isn't every day I conduct a wedding between two people with twenty years' difference in their ages.'

Paddy glanced at the clock, straightened his tie. 'Funny old world,' he commented, almost to himself. 'Megan Duffy marrying Billy Shipton. I remember when Billy was in and out of trouble like a shuttle through the loom. He was a dab hand with bottles. He would climb over the wall at the back of the shop and pick up the empties that had already been returned. The lad could make one lemonade container pay for a week at the Tivoli cinema. The greengrocer used to send his wife to stand at the door when Billy was shopping. That lad's been turned upside down more often than an egg-timer. Plums, cherries, grapes running out of his pockets.' He shook his head. 'And he's captured the heart of Megan.'

Ian Blunt poured another cup of tea, settled back for a few minutes. 'And you've made your mind up about little Phyllis Entwistle. Yes, I agree, it's a rum world. Never mind your anecdotes about Billy, because young Phyllis is the one who'll be marrying an oddity. It's a rare girl who can say that her fiancé was a priest who defied Rome. A halfpenny on a bottle is small change compared to your history.' He laughed, slurped a mouthful of tea, lit a cigarette.

'I know,' said Paddy, his expression serious. 'She may want to stay round here. She has so many friends in Bromley Cross. Yet I worry about her being pointed at because of me. Bad enough having a limp without being the butt of dirty gossip.' He pondered for a second or two. 'Whatever, she feels safe up here. I might just take the post office for her and work part time there, the rest of the week at the mission. Oh, life's complicated.'

The priest leaned across the table, covered Paddy's hand with his. 'In your heart, you know that the marriage is right. God knows how hard I've tried to dissuade you. You've withstood all my nonsense, so God bless you.' He rose, pulled off his jacket and began to arrange the wedding vestments. An afterthought caused him to turn and look at his guest. 'Have you brought your rotten old stole?' Paddy O'Riley's stole had become a legend in these parts.

'I have.'

Relief showed in the features of Our Lady of Sorrows' parish priest. 'Of course, I don't believe in luck. But don't lose that thing, Paddy O'Riley. It's your flag of freedom. You must wave it at every opportunity, so that we who are too weak to be defiant can say in all honesty that we knew a man who left the priesthood and lived to tell the tale.'

They washed their hands, combed their hair, then went outside to walk the few paces to the little wooden church where Megan Duffy would shortly become Mrs William Shipton.

Billy's legs were a law unto themselves. Normally, he boasted a fine, steady pair of lower limbs that had scored many a goal for Our Lady of Sorrows' Parents' and Friends' Amateur Club, yet today, he felt as if he were blessed with knees made of jelly. He breathed in deeply, tried to look unconcerned.

'Are you nervous?' asked Tommy.

Billy, who had lived with the Wagstaffs for many years, knew that lying would be pointless. 'I'm all right,' he said. 'But my legs don't know I'm all right, so they're playing up.'

'Doris?' yelled Tommy.

She appeared in the doorway, her hat askew. 'What?'

'Shall I give him a brandy?'

Doris Wagstaff stared at Billy for a second or two. 'A teaspoonful, no more. And lock them blessed cats up, Tommy Wagstaff. I'm not having them yowling up the lane after us.'

'Your hat's crooked,' yelled her husband as she disappeared.

'I know,' came the answer. 'But I can straighten my hat, can't I? Pity you can't straighten that face of yours. If you make anybody laugh while our Megan's getting married, I'll put in for a divorce.'

Tommy shrugged, winked at Billy, poured out a hefty slug of brandy. 'She keeps promising this divorce, but nowt happens. See. Get yourself outside of that, son. If it doesn't sort your legs out, it'll put you in a frame where you don't care. Hurry up, me and Deedee'll have to be off in a minute.'

The young man took the glass, drained it in one gulp, then went out through the back door. He had promised to wait until his best man came before leaving the house. Megan didn't want to see Billy, didn't want him to see her. His legs were better, but his heart was racing and breathing seemed difficult. He lowered himself gingerly onto the wooden bench that sat beneath the kitchen window. It was nearly time to go.

Billy Shipton concentrated on his breathing. Because this was a special day, he indulged in a good old think about his family. Their Fred had been his favourite. Like Megan, Billy had lost six people in total, including his parents, Fred and three younger siblings. He recalled the day of the photograph, remembered Mam's anger when everyone except Billy escaped. It was as if that horrible, black-clad man had brought the devil with him. Billy shivered, told himself not to be so stupid. Other people who hadn't been photographed had lived. And some who were on the picture had died . . .

Only Megan understood. Only Megan knew how he had grieved. Boys weren't supposed to cry, yet he had wept bitter tears for a long time. In the big house, he and Megan had found a hidey-hole behind some panelling, a place where priests or royalists and suchlike might have hidden during various periods of persecution. In the darkness, he had wept. And Megan had just sat and waited for his tears to finish.

He was so lucky. She was beautiful and talented, she had forged a career for both of them, she loved him. That last bit was the funny part. Geoff Althorpe had gone all out to get Megan. Geoff Althorpe would inherit money, had journeyed forth into an exciting new world. But Megan,

343

who had imagination and ambition to spare, had stayed here on the crooked mile, was going to marry somebody who was completely unexciting.

How often had he asked her, 'Why do you love me?' Her answer was always the same. 'Because you're Billy'. He'd never have been anyone or anything but for Joe Duffy. Joe had sat for days beside that hospital bed. 'I'm nearly better, lad. Me body's all right, but me mind wants a rest. Mr Althorpe's taking me to a nursing home, then happen to Blackpool for a holiday. We're all going to live in a great big house that wants mending. You can come and live with us, lad. If you want to, anyway. Then Megan and Joseph will be your sister and brother.'

Even then, he hadn't wanted Megan for a sister. Phyllis had become a sister, though. Billy had lost count of the number of children he had bashed for laughing at Phyllis's limp. He grinned now, remembered Megan getting stuck in as well. 'Don't you dare!' she had screamed at them. He could hear her now. 'Don't say anything about her, or I'll rip your eyes out.' She'd always been feisty, had Megan.

A hand touched his shoulder. 'Billy?'

He turned his head, saw Joe. 'She's ready, lad,' said Hall i' th' Vale's resident caretaker. 'She's sat in yon, cool as a cucumber, with both her bridesmaids. Phyllis and Fliss are more nervous than she is. That mate of yours is just coming up the lane. You'd best get to the church.'

Billy swallowed. 'Thanks.'

'You don't know what to call me, do you?'

'No.'

Joe smiled, though the eyes remained sad. 'You call me Dad after the show's over. Aye, I've stopped being your Uncle Joe now. Uncle Joes are just mint toffees in future.'

'You've been good to me,' mumbled the bridegroom.

Joe sighed heavily. 'No way could I have let you go in an orphanage. A long time ago, I decided that children were everybody's responsibility. When Ida died, Phyllis became ours. Same when Elsie went. Elsie Shipton were our neighbour, so—'

344

'And nobody else wanted me because I was a nuisance.'

Joe almost laughed. 'That's the truth. You were that much of a pest, folk were praying on their hands and knees in case they got asked to take you in. But I've no regrets.'

Billy stood up, checked the creases down the fronts of his trousers. 'She could have married somebody rich, you know.'

'Aye. She could likely have had Geoffrey Althorpe if she'd played her cards right, only the lad weren't good enough. Stop doing yourself down, Billy. You're getting a good wife and a business you've both worked for. How many couples your age make furniture, eh? How many folk have people coming all the way from Cheshire just to get their chairs covered?'

'That were all Megan, not me.'

Joe wagged a finger. 'Nay, you're wrong there, Billy Shipton. You're the one who learned driving. Without you, our Megan would have been forced to stick to local trade. It were you that spread her wings, Billy. And who is it that goes round with the calling cards drumming up business? You do. You're the front man, the advance guard. It's your way with folk that's made WAGSTAFFS' what it is today. Must be renting nearly half of Bradshawgate now, what with the frocks and the furniture. A lot of that's your doing. So get gone up to that church and make an honest woman of my daughter before I lose patience.' He patted Billy's shoulder, then went to give away his little girl.

Billy sniffed, hoped his nose wasn't red. He loved Joe Duffy. Joe Duffy was the only real dad he'd ever known. Oh, he remembered the drunk who was married to his mother, remembered the beatings, the fights when there were no coppers to spend on ale. It was a terrible thought, yet Billy Shipton knew that his life would have been a lot worse had his parents survived the fire.

Megan. He marched through the house, said ta-ra to a couple of cats, met his best man on Dog Leg Lane, began the walk to church. His eyes remained lowered until The Gate House was out of sight.

'You all right?' asked his companion.

'Aye.' Billy's legs were strong again. Like the rest of him, they knew that the future would be bright. Any day with Megan in it was cheerful. 'I think I might just get through the wedding,' he said.

'You'd better,' advised Eric Shackleton. Eric was the team's goalkeeper. 'We've a match Wednesday night.'

Billy Shipton grinned from ear to ear. 'I'll be there. If the wife'll let me out.'

Joseph Duffy was in heaven. He had eaten three plates of jelly, four scoops of vanilla ice-cream and seven chocolate biscuits. Because of his tendency to plumpness, such luxuries were usually rationed by Megan. Mind, he wouldn't be living with Megan any more. He eyed Deedee, who was to be his new provider. Deedee's cakes and scones were legendary. Would Deedee go easy on him, would he be allowed to eat nice food?

Joe Senior kept a wary eye on his son. He was a right little glutton, was a bit like Harold when it came to indulging himself. Something pricked his heart. It was always like this when the family came together. He would be doing well, holding his end up, then that tiny, hot dagger would burn him inside. Aye, young Joseph was a little Harold in some respects, but he had some of Albert's traits, too. And like Megan, Joseph was dark-haired.

'All right, lad?' Deedee asked her son.

Joe looked at his mother, wondered where she'd got such a terrible hat. 'Yes. How are you?'

'Fairish to middling.' She leaned over, whispered in his ear, 'I'll be a damned sight better when I can loosen me corsets. I've never wore the blessed things for years, and I'll not be putting them on again after today. Me insides is all squashed.' She straightened, set the feathered hat more squarely on her head. 'Doesn't our Megan look a picture?'

'She does.' He hoped his mother would keep still. She

was tall for a woman, and the hat made her even taller. Each time she moved, he got slapped across the face by the purple-dyed plumes. 'I hope they'll be happy.'

Doris tutted at him. 'Joe, try and see the bright side for once, eh? Life can get better all the time. I mean, it's no use standing there waiting for the next bad thing to happen. And you've had your chances, could have got yourself a decent wife. There's no law on earth that says you've to be faithful to a memory. There's many a chap gets himself remarried after the first wife dies, and many a woman who—'

'Mam. Will you shut up about Maureen Wright? As far as I'm concerned, she's Maureen Wrong. You know damned well I had a job getting rid of her. I'm happy as I am, so stop mithering on about it.'

'Then smile. I don't know. If you had to put up with these corsets, I'd understand. But you should be enjoying yourself.' Sometimes, she lost patience with him, though she appreciated his grief. He had loved Tess with all his heart, had loved every one of his children. But, by now, he should have been making the best of those that remained. She remembered her own time as a young woman, had long ago given up counting the number of stillbirths and miscarriages she had suffered. Joe was all she had, all she wanted. She placed a hand on his shoulder. 'You're a good son. But cheer up, else I'll go home for me rolling pin and give you the walloping you've always deserved.'

A movement outside the window caught Joe's eye, and before he could check himself, Maureen Wright was waving at him. 'Coo-ee,' the lips said, though the sound did not travel through the glass. He groaned. 'Mam, she's back.'

Doris Wagstaff had a job to stop herself laughing. When Joe, Megan and the baby had first come to live in the Hall, Maureen Wright had been employed to mind Joseph. Maureen Wright, a widow whose husband had died in the Great War, had set her cap at Joe. In fact, she had set her heart and soul on marrying the father of little

347

Joseph. 'Be nice,' muttered Doris, her face set in a smile as she returned Maureen's wave.

'I'm off,' he said. 'I'll go and talk to me daughter.'

Doris pulled at a corset bone while no-one was looking, then sat down to watch the show. Her son had taken himself across to where Megan and Billy stood with friends. Maureen Wright, who had not been invited to the wedding, hovered in the doorway. 'Any minute now,' Doris muttered under her breath.

Tommy arrived, a glass of beer in his hand. 'Hey, have you seen who's turned up? Like a bad penny, she is.'

'I know. He'll fly up that road like a rocket in a minute. Mind, he saw her off last time. Remember how he got rid as soon as our Joseph could walk?'

'Aye. That little lad were the youngest assistant care-taker in the world. Mind, that did no harm, 'cos they're close, Joe and Joseph. Look, she's making a beeline.'

'I can't watch,' said Doris. 'Give me a running commentary.' She turned her chair until she faced the back of the hall.

Tommy took a swig of beer. 'She's got him. No, no, he's walked off to talk to Eric Shackleton. Hang on, she's behind him. Her underskirt's hanging down a bit at the back. Pink, it is.'

'Tommy Wagstaff,' muttered his wife. 'Take your mind and your eyes off folks' underclothes. What's happening?'

'She's pinned him to the wall.'

'Brazen hussy.'

Tommy's jaw dropped. 'He's following her outside. Doris, I think she's hooked him.'

'Never!' Doris jumped to her feet, was just in time to see her son disappearing in the company of Maureen Wright. 'Well.' Her face was a picture of incredulity. 'I'll go to the foot of our stairs,' she said.

Tommy laughed, spilled some beer down his shirt. 'Good job you didn't say you'd eat your hat, Doris. Even a goat wouldn't touch that thing.'

She clouted him with her handbag, marched through

the hall, found Joe fiddling with the chain on Maureen Wright's shabby bicycle. Doris would have wagered a small fortune that the woman had deliberately pulled the chain off its cogs. But when she saw the state of her son, whose hands were covered in oil and grime, she reassured herself that the incident must have been accidental, because Maureen Wright's hands were spotless. 'Look at you,' she called. 'I've me husband in there covered in beer, then you out here all oily. Get cleaned up this minute.'

Joe fixed the chain, came inside and rushed off in the direction of the toilets. Just as Doris was about to go in, a small child appeared from behind a clump of bushes. His hands and face were oil-streaked, while Maureen Wright's cheeks had gone bright pink. 'Thanks fer the shillin', Missus,' yelled the urchin.

Doris flew inside and closed the door, laughter bubbling up inside corsets that were far too tight for merriment.

'Deedee?'

She looked into the lovely eyes of her granddaughter, pushed a hand against the pain of glee that had to be suppressed. 'Some women,' she managed, 'will do just about anything to get a man.' She staggered off, left the bride and groom gaping. 'Billy,' said Megan. 'I think you've married into a very strange family. Do you think the insanity will show in our children?'

Billy threw back his head and chuckled loudly. 'Megan, if they're all as daft as your Grandma Deedee, they'll do for me.'

She knew what he meant. There was no-one in the whole wide world who could compare to Deedee.

Tommy stood near a door, one hand mopping the shirt front with a handkerchief. Minnie Hattersley and Bertha Strong were seated at the long table, each congratulating the other about the quality of Megan's wedding gown, about the fine stitching on the bridesmaids' dresses. Phyllis gazed into Paddy O'Riley's eyes, while he shifted from foot to foot, embarrassed because he had not yet

349

learned how to accept her love in public. Megan was content. So many friends had come to celebrate the wedding.

'Billy?' said Megan.

'That's me.'

'I'm Mrs Shipton now.'

'I know.' The grin threatened to split his face. 'You'd best behave from now on,' he said.

'And if I don't?'

'I'll tan your behind.'

Megan Shipton looked round once more at all the happy people. 'Promises,' she joked.

'Just you wait.' Billy's attempt at seriousness was a total failure.

She laughed, stepped away from him. 'Like I said, you're all promises and empty threats.' She turned to run, was held by a hand of iron. He was young, strong, full of life and love. The whole room was full of love and she was happy, so happy that she thought she might burst. 'Let me go,' she pretended to beg.

'Never,' he answered.

And the answer was the one she wanted.

TWO

'She has definitely gone strange, Billy.' Megan shot a few brass studs along the leather she was using to cover the back and arm of a chaise. 'You can go next door after, tell Deedee we're ready for her to do the seat in that brocade.' She waved the gun about. 'We can have this finished by morning.'

Billy, who was stretching and shaping hide, decided to have a rest. 'I'm putting the kettle on, love. Shall I ask the others if they want a break?' The others were two boys and a girl who had been culled by Billy and Megan from a Manchester furniture maker.

'In a bit.' Megan perched on a stool, wiped her brow. It was hot for June, and the sweat was pouring into her eyes, was making it difficult to see what she was doing. 'I'll have lemonade, Billy. Then I want to talk to you.'

They sat side by side on the chaise, were nearer than normal to the ground because the padded seating had been removed so that Deedee could re-cover it. 'Last night, when she came down from the Hall with that butter from Mrs Althorpe, she was as jumpy as a cat on hot slates. Fliss isn't like that. She's steady, you know. Very level-headed and sensible.'

'I do understand what you mean Megan. I've known her a fair few years myself now. But she seemed all right to me.'

Megan sighed, pushed a damp curl from her forehead. Men. Even the best of them didn't notice much. As long as you weren't screaming, tearing your hair out and scratching paint off the walls, you were all right. 'Billy, her eyes were all over the place and she was twitching. Fliss

Althorpe has never been a twitcher. And she didn't answer any of my questions.'

Billy took a mouthful of lemonade. 'Well, I must say you'd have made a good lawyer. You ask more questions than the desk sergeant at the police station.'

'And you would know all about that – NO! Don't tickle me! See, I've lost half my lemonade.' She jumped up, flicked the wetness from her clothes. 'You're still a pest, Billy Shipton.'

He grinned broadly. Megan would never allow herself to be seen outside in her working garb. She wore men's things, an all-in-one overall made from brown cotton, its trousers held up by bib and braces. In bib and braces, Billy's wife was almost edible. 'Even in them daft things, you're a picture.'

She tried to glower, burst out laughing. 'Behave yourself or you'll get the jugful poured over you.' Was it right that any two people should be so happy? Yes. She mustn't start thinking like her dad, mustn't let her life be spoilt by past events. Joe Duffy had turned his back on the chance to marry a nice woman called Maureen. Megan had always liked Maureen, because she was cheerful in spite of having lost a husband, was always telling jokes and singing.

And that was the way it should be, thought Megan now. As far as she was concerned, the dead of Myrtle Street would never be forgotten, yet the surviving witnesses should forge ahead and make a new life. 'I knew we were right for one another, Billy,' she said, her tone lowered so that employees would not hear. 'But we're even righter than I thought.'

'Aye,' he said. 'The job's a good 'un. Mind, I'm a bit fed up with being clocked round the ear'ole with a rolling pin when I come home late. And you pinch all the bed covers. Then there's the cooking. Good job I've a strong stomach. And . . .' He pondered for a few seconds. 'Megan?'

'What?'

'She had sugar in her tea. I've only just remembered.

352

You and Fliss were sat at the table, and I made you both a drink. Now, with me being a creature of habit, I put two sugars in one cup, one and a half in the other – as if I were making the tea for you and me. She drank it, never a word.'

'You sure?'

'Positive. I realized what I'd done, so I was just about to offer her another brew, but you were talking. Then Joseph came to the door and I went to replace that broken spoke on his back wheel. Did she ask you for another cup after I'd gone outside?'

Megan pondered. 'No, she drank it as if she were really thirsty, said she didn't want a second cup. She mustn't have even tasted it, Billy. You know how she hates sweet tea. I told you. I said there was something up with her.'

'You're not wrong, either. Tell you what. You knock off now, then I'll carry on till six. I'll drive the crew home . . .' He wagged a thumb in the direction of the next room, 'Then I'll take Deedee home. Go to the mills, see what's the matter. Fliss'll have her motor, so she'll drop you off at our house later on. Don't worry, I'll have our tea ready.'

Megan cast her eye round the room, calculated how much needed doing. 'Them chairs for that solicitor won't be needed till next week – he's got decorators in. This sofa can be finished by tomorrow dinner. When's your next pick-up?'

'Thursday, Macclesfield. A three-piece suite and two rockers.'

'Right.' She undid the bib, smacked his hand when he reached for her. 'No messing, Billy Shipton.'

He saluted, drained his glass, went back to work. 'I hope she's all right, love.'

Megan, who was changing behind a screen, knew that Fliss wasn't all right. She hadn't even been happy at the wedding a few weeks ago. After kissing her husband, Megan ran next door, told the staff to have a break. She intended to get to the bottom of Fliss Althorpe's problem as quickly as possible. When she stepped into the street, a sudden bout of giddiness forced her to lean for support against the outer door. Well, this was a right carry-on. Although she'd been married for just a short time, Mrs Megan Shipton was almost certain of her pregnancy. 'Stop where you are for at least a year,' she whispered, a hand on her belly. ''Cos if you come early, me and your dad'll be branded.' Yes, this promised to be a pickle and no mistake . . .

Fliss was at her desk when Megan arrived. 'Hello,' she said. 'What are you doing here?'

Megan parked herself in a chair opposite Fliss's. 'Visiting a few old neighbours,' she lied. 'So I thought I'd call in here, see what you're up to. Is your dad in?'

Fliss shook her head. 'He's at the doctor's. Mother dragged him along because he keeps falling asleep in his soup. If she saw how hard he works inventing fancies, she'd understand his tiredness.'

Megan fixed her gaze on the window, though all her attention was directed across the desk. 'Well, it's the only way for cotton now that the petticoats have gone. He should do well if he starts up with curtaining and nice bedding. Tell him to have a word with our Deedee. Between them, they can re-design the inside of every house on Chorley New Road.'

Fliss was tapping nervously on the blotter. 'You look well, Megan.'

'I'm more than well. I'm more than me. I think there's two of us.' She smiled at the older girl's puzzled look. 'It looks like I'm going to have a baby. Don't say anything, not until it's confirmed. It must have happened right away, perhaps on our wedding night. I hope it doesn't come premature, else folk will talk.'

Fliss Althorpe's face was now expressionless. 'Congratulations.'

Megan shook her head. 'Don't say a word to anybody, please,' she begged again. 'I've not even talked to Billy,

354

because it would seem daft after such a short time. But I keep going a bit dizzy, a bit weak in the head. Course, I could be wrong. But I'm not one for dizzy spells and a funny stomach, not since I grew up.' They had been so alike, Megan and Fliss, because each had suffered from what Deedee called the collywobbles when upset. Till now, Megan's stomach had improved, but was Fliss still under-eating when thwarted? She leaned back, gave the older girl the once over, took in the pallor, the pinched mouth, twin semi-circles of darkness that sat beneath eyes of an impossible green. 'Fliss, I know I'm a lot younger than you, but I—'

'Seven years.'

'What? Oh, yes. But I can see there's something wrong. Won't you tell me what it is?'

The woman behind the desk shrugged. 'Nothing, really. Except that I've known Phil for ten years and there's been no progress. We're no nearer to marriage than were were in 1920. His mother's had another operation – the fifth in three years. And she shows no sign of making room for me.'

Megan tutted her impatience. 'You should just do it, get on with it. There's other folk who'd take her in.'

'Really?' A book on the desk was closed sharply, the slapping sound lending an air of finality to the accompanying 'No.' Fliss got up, walked to a cabinet and filed away some papers.

'Fliss, it's just that—'

'Bessie Greenwood is capable of almost anything. She's taken pills before now, massive overdoses. Of course, she banged on the wall and told the neighbour so that help might be made available. But she won't let Phil leave her. She's one of those powerful women you read about, doting mothers who keep a steely grip on their children. Except that most of Bessie's family has escaped. Phil's the only one who's ever shown her any tolerance.'

The younger girl remained still, waited for more. When the silence continued, she jumped up and perched on the edge of the desk. 'Get married. Leave the town and—'

'How can we?' There was emotion in the face now, an expression that spoke of deep anger. 'Megan, it's all very well and good for you to talk. It's been so easy for you and Billy. But I had to persuade my mother that Phil was right for me, and Phil's been trying for years to get Bessie to listen. I cannot live with that woman. That woman refuses to live without Phil. Now, if we took off, how would our marriage survive if his mother killed herself? Can you imagine how awful that would be?'

Megan nodded. 'Yes, I suppose so.' Phyllis's mother had killed herself, and that final act had caused so many to feel guilty. Yet Ida Entwistle had been a good woman, a woman for whom a priest had relinquished his calling. Megan paused for a moment, her mind elsewhere. As the sole recipient of Phyllis's secret, she wondered for a split second whether Paddy O'Riley might be marrying the girl out of pity, or guilt, or both. No, they loved one another . . . She pulled herself up, returned to the business in hand. 'But she's so cruel. How can she turn against you? How can she be so mean?'

Fliss smiled, though her eyes remained clouded. 'Yes, you are a lot younger than I am, Megan. You like most people, don't you? You don't judge them or turn on them. Not everyone is like you. Mrs Greenwood is a nasty, selfish woman. Unfortunately she's also a very sick person, so we can't fight her. If he leaves her, she will die. And that is the whole thing in a nutshell.'

Megan remained unsatisfied. This explanation was one she'd heard a thousand times. Nothing new had been said, yet something new was troubling Fliss. 'Is that all?'

Fliss swivelled on the spot. 'Of course. Why? How much more do I need?'

'Sorry. It's just that . . . I got the idea that you were extra worried and fed up.'

'I'm feeling no worse than usual, thank you. Sorry if I've been a bit sharp, but with Pop being off-colour . . .' She made a stab at smiling. 'Come on, we'll sneak out early and go to Brownlow's Tea Rooms. She does a lovely scone with fresh cream.' As she picked her coat from a hook on the door, Felicity Althorpe closed her eyes and prayed inwardly for some strength, some acting ability. This guest might be young and inexperienced, but she had an eye for people and a nose for trouble. 'Ready?'

Megan smoothed her skirt. 'I wish I could remember to hang things up at work. Every time I get changed to go home, I look like a tramp.'

'You look lovely.' It was true. Little Megan Duffy had grown into a beautiful young woman. She was possibly carrying her first child, was happy, fulfilled, settled. Fliss hoped that the feeling in her heart was not jealousy, because she loved Megan Shipton like a sister. So she went forth bravely for tea and scones, tried to bury the pain in her soul.

'You can't be sure.' His eyes darted from side to side, put Fliss in mind of an animal in a trap. 'And what the hell are we going to do if you are right? She's not recovered from having her intestine shortened. I mean, she needs everything doing for her. And when I say "everything", that's exactly the size of it. Fliss, I have to clean her, wash her, change her.' He ran a hand over his thick, brown hair. 'This couldn't have happened at a worse time.'

She stepped back, waited for some people to walk past. 'Get into the car,' she snapped abruptly. 'I can't be seen or heard discussing my possible pregnancy in the middle of Churchgate.'

Inside the vehicle, he repeated his words about poor timing.

'When was there a good time, Phil?' she asked. If only he were stronger, better at organizing, more positive. 'I have offered to pay one of your aunts to move into the house. If you had arranged care for her, we could have been married years ago.'

He dropped his head. 'I don't want you paying my way.'

Fliss tightened her mouth, decided against stooping to

tell him about the suit he was wearing, the shirts she had bought. On his wrist, he wore a watch that he removed before entering his house. She'd seen him several times, had lingered further down Dobson Street in the car until he had gone inside. Always, always, he protected his mother. 'You're afraid of her,' she said.

'She's old—'

'She's been old for ten bloody years, Phil.'

He had never known her to swear before. 'She can't go on much longer. They've taken enough pieces out of her to fill the shelves in the hospital lab.'

Fliss stared through the windscreen at Trinity Church. As a child, she'd always imagined being married there, because it was so beautiful. Of course, she would probably be married in a church nearer home . . . If she ever got married at all, that was. 'I know I'm having a baby,' she whispered. 'Your baby, our baby. For a long time, I have waited for you to become available. If a child of ours doesn't prompt you to make the break, then you will be stuck in Dobson Street until your mother dies.' Deedee Wagstaff's voice echoed in Fliss's head. 'Only the good die young,' Deedee always said.

He wound the watch, pulled at the sleeves of his shirt. 'I'll tell her when I get in,' he said.

'Tell her what?'

'About the baby, of course.'

She turned her head and looked at him. He had a weak chin. It struck her as strange that she had never noticed before. When he lowered his head an inch or so, a roll of skin formed where the jawbone should have been. 'And what will she say when you inform her of my condition?'

'Well . . .' He was tugging at his tie now.

'Phil!' she shouted. 'Will you stop messing about with your clothes? This is a serious business. How do you think my parents will react when they find out? This isn't something I can hide for a long time, you know. In a couple of months, everyone will be able to tell. I can't go to work indefinitely, can I? I'm there to help with their problems. Many's the time I've counselled a girl whose fiancé was asking for a fuller relationship. And I always tell these females to wait for a wedding ring. Ha ha.' This pale imitation of laughter only served to bring tears into her eyes. 'For God's sake, Phil, make a decision. For once in your life, be a man and do something.'

'I will.' He placed his arm across the back of her seat. 'You're trembling.'

'I'm sorry.' She dashed the moisture from her cheeks. 'I'm sorry to make such a fuss about nothing. After all, I've only disgraced myself and my whole family. Have you never thought about Mother and Pop? Geoff left without a word, hasn't been heard of in years. Now I'm pregnant and unmarried. Think of them, not just of your own mother.'

He closed his eyes and leaned back in the seat. Fliss didn't understand. More than anything, he wanted to be married, yet he couldn't just walk out on Mam.

'Phil?'

'What?'

'Do you love your mother?'

He pondered for a few seconds. His mother had a hold on him, but he wasn't sure about loving her. The only certainty in his mind was that he was opposed to trouble in any shape. At this point in time, he would have to get married. If he didn't, the shame would be too much for him, too much for Fliss. But . . . oh, God. 'No. I don't think I love her. It's more like I owe her something. I was a sickly child and she protected me, made me well. She sat with me day and night through scarlet fever, mumps, measles. Every time, I was sicker than all the other kiddies. So I felt I had to stick with her, especially when the doctors said she was on her way out.' He sighed. 'But she's a long time dying.'

'Yes.'

He patted her shoulder. 'I suppose we could get married in secret, just go tomorrow and get it sorted out. That would give us a bit of time. When you start to show, we can just tell people that we were married all along and—'

'Why?'

He looked at her, an expression of surprise on his face. 'To give me a month or so. I don't need to leave her right away, do I? As long as we're married, then everything will be all right. She may be dead inside a fortnight. The nurses told me they didn't know how she was managing to hang on.'

Fliss stared hard at him, lifted a hand, slapped him hard across the face. 'Get out of the car,' she muttered.

'What?' He released his hold on her shoulder, put a hand against his stinging cheek. 'Why did you do that?'

'Get out.' Her tone was cold and clear now. 'Go. I've had enough.'

'But what about—?'

Her hands curled themselves into fists, though she managed to tighten the rein on her temper. 'I do not want to be married in secret. I do not want to protect your precious mother from the facts of life. We do this thing properly, or we don't do it at all. Right?'

He nodded dumbly.

'Tomorrow night, at half past seven, I shall sit here in the car. If you are not here by twenty minutes to eight, I'll go home. The next morning, I shall leave Bolton and you won't see me ever again.' She couldn't do that, she told herself. She couldn't do what her brother had done to Mother and Pop. 'It is up to you. Come tomorrow to plan a wedding, or stay away and lose me.' Inwardly, she shook with rage. Why had she never seen him as he really was? Or was her view of him suddenly distorted by her condition? How had she managed not to notice his weaknesses? Perhaps she was imagining these faults. After all, she had known him for a long time . . . 'Go now.'

He opened the door, heaved himself out of the car, bent down to speak to her. But she was hammering away at the starter button and the vehicle began to cough its protest about such ill-treatment. Phil stood back as she pulled away in a cloud of fumes and temper. Her driving, which was usually careful, was jumpy and erratic. He leaned against the window of Ye Olde Pastie Shoppe, his face still glowing after that hefty slap. The watershed was here and now. He would have to go home and tell his mother that he was leaving her, leaving Dobson Street. Fliss could wait no longer.

Phil Greenwood lingered beneath a lamp standard at the end of Dobson Street. He would go in soon. Getting out to meet Fliss these days was extra difficult, because Bessie Greenwood plainly believed that her youngest child should be at her beck and call twenty-four hours a day. She accepted the fact that he must work, as his was the only income, though she had pressed him for years about his place of employment. 'Go to Ainsworths',' she had said repeatedly. 'Good bosses, the Ainsworths, a decent family firm.'

He knew all about the Ainsworths, was fully aware that he would be well-treated in their employ, but Fliss was at the Althorpe mills. He sighed deeply, looked up to heaven as if seeking help from an invisible hand. A man torn in two, he was. A man with a sick old mother who needed him, with an unhappy young lover who needed him. Oh God.

Lights were coming on in the houses, small, newborn circles of incandescent yellow. He watched his own window, noticed the brightness as Bessie lit her mantles. She had just had stitches removed from her abdomen, was helpless and at the mercy of her son, yet she was able reach up and light the room. Had Phil been at home, his mother would have been too weak for any such labours. 'Turn the gas down, lad, my eyes are hurting,' she often said. 'Fetch me the paper, make me a brew, nip out for a drop of stout.'

He kicked the base of the lamp, stood aside when the gas man arrived with his ladder. 'Has it gone again?'

'Aye,' said the man as he climbed the rungs. 'Twice this week. They keep chucking stones up and breaking the glass.' He came down, took a small hammer from his bag. 'I've to get all the broken bits out, then the boss will come with a new pane later on. No point lighting it till the glass is in.'

There was no point in anything, Phil told himself. Once he saw Mam getting into one of her states, he would be totally incapable of doing anything for Fliss. Yet he had to. He had to stick by Fliss now, in her hour of real need. He was going to be a dad. At twenty-nine, he was old enough, mature enough to cope with fatherhood. And it promised to be a good life, too, because Mr Althorpe would certainly look after his daughter. Electric lights, a plumbed-in bath, a strip of garden outside the back door. Roses, honeysuckle, a plot where he might grow his own potatoes and carrots. Perhaps a greenhouse for tomatoes. Yes, that would be nice, a little glass house with a paraffin stove, somewhere he could sit alone for a while. He made his goodbyes to the lamp man, trudged at snail's pace towards his own house.

Halfway there, he stopped again, sagged against a wall. He could talk to Mr Althorpe, ask him to come down and sort Mam out. The idea poked its head into the various corridors of his mind, was kicked out within a split second. Mr Althorpe might be – would surely be angry about Fliss's condition. Phil wasn't scared, oh no, not that. He just didn't like trouble. Fliss knew her father, understood him. She must be the one to tell him.

Mam was ironing. As soon as Phil entered the house, she flopped against the table. 'Been hard work, this has. What with carrying the irons to and from the fire, then standing here doing your shirts, I'm worn out.'

She was not supposed to do housework. She was not supposed to do anything at all, because she ought not to have been here. The death sentence, which had been passed a decade ago, had not been acted upon. Phil sighed, felt in his marrow that Bessie would never die, that she would linger to the turn of the century and finish up famous for reaching a hundred plus the normal span.

Without a word, he guided his mother to her bed, sat her on the edge, removed her slippers and lifted the thin legs onto the mattress. When she was settled, he lowered the grill over the coals, set the kettle to boil, changed the irons, took off his jacket and began to work on the pile of clothing.

'Where've you been?'

'With Fliss.'

'Oh aye?' The air almost crackled with the old woman's disgust. 'I'm nowt a pound, me, eh? Just out of the infirmary with half me insides gone, a bag attached to me belly, and me son's dashing round in some flighty woman's car. Nice, isn't it?'

He turned a shirt, smoothed cuffs, folded the collar. 'She's not flighty. I'm the only man she's ever walked out with.'

Bessie sniffed loudly. 'Not much walking, though. Oh no, you're always in that motor, up to no good, like as not. Does her father know how she spends her spare time?'

He lowered the pulley line, hung some pressed clothes along its slats. 'Her father and I have talked, and well you know it. She's a good girl from a good family. I don't know why you can't just accept her.'

'Hmmph. I can tell the road she looks at me that she can't stand the sight. It's not my fault I'm lingering. It's not my fault that I'm old and weary and on me own. There's not a one of them would take me in.' The 'them' to which she referred were members of her family. 'Our Ada's all mouth. "Ooh, I'll look after you, Bessie," she says. But she wouldn't. She'd be off like a shot as soon as one of her grandkiddies had a runny nose or a bit of a cough.' She paused, shook her head wearily, as if the weight of her worry-crammed skull were too much for her. 'You're all I've got, Phil. Without you, I'd have to see myself off.'

Phil ironed some handkerchiefs, placed them on the dresser.

'Are you listening?' she barked, her voice unnaturally powerful for such a sick woman.

'Yes.'

'Will you stop with me?'

He tested the iron by touching its base with a forefinger, began the task of pressing Bessie Greenwood's underwear.

'Do them proper,' she ordered. 'They don't want to be dampish while I'm so poorly. Nothing's aired till it's had a good ironing.' She waited for a moment or two. 'I said will you stay with me?'

'I can't.'

Her jaw dropped. 'What?' She pressed her left hand on her chest. 'Ooh, me heart's jumping all over the place.'

She had no heart. Phil knew that. If she'd had a heart, then she would have loved Fliss. 'I'm twenty-nine,' he mumbled. 'It's time I was married.'

'And I'm sixty-five,' she yelled. 'I've been ill since before I turned fifty. Can't you hang on till I've gone?'

'No.'

She heaved a great, shuddering sigh, fell back against the mound of pillows. 'Get me heart tablets,' she gasped. 'I can't breathe, I can't get me . . . Phil! I need me tablets.'

Slowly, he replaced the iron on its stand in the hearth, picked up a biscuit tin and rooted about for the tiny pills. 'Here,' he said. 'That should put you right.' Without even looking at her, he marched out of the room and into the tiny scullery. His legs were shaking and his hands trembled so violently that he trapped them in his pockets. Would she have died without that little pill? If she died, there would be no trouble, no angry parents to face. He already knew how Mr Althorpe would react. The man was not likely to lose his temper, but the boss's face would wear the hurt look that arrived when something nasty happened in the mill. Like when that woman had a heart attack at her mule some years back. Yes, Mr Althorpe could become so grief-stricken.

He pushed the backs of his legs against the slopstone, waited for her to start. Any minute now, she would wade in. 'Why are you leaving me?' and 'don't get married just yet, wait till I'm better or till I'm not here.' Not here. He liked the idea of that, because it would solve every problem in one fell swoop.

'Phil?'

His head dropped and he screwed up his face against the sound of his mother's tone.

'Phil? Are you there?'

'Yes.'

'I've had a bit of an accident with this here stupid bag. If you'll get me a bowl and some water, I'll see to myself. There's a clean pair of knickers here, so I'll manage. Only I don't want to be too much trouble.'

Phil pulled his hands from their hiding places, picked up the white enamel bowl. In the kitchen, he opened the tap on the copper, caught the flow, placed the bowl next to her bed. 'Anything else?'

She stared at him, her lower lip working as if preparing for tears. 'I'll have to manage, won't I? If you're going off with that girl, I'll have no choice—'

'Shut up.' He towered over her, his head buzzing with temper. Fliss was pregnant and he didn't know what to do. If he walked out of here tomorrow, this nasty old woman would surely send for him, plead with him, break up the marriage before it even started. 'Shut up,' he repeated.

Bessie recoiled, a look of puzzlement on her face. The mouth stilled itself, because she knew that tears would not work at this time. He was not one for tantrums, had never turned on her. Yet she was frightened, terrified of the expression in his eyes. 'You . . . you hate me, don't you?' she whispered.

'No. Just shut your mouth, Mam. Listen for a change. I'm nearly thirty and I'm still stuck here with your bring-me-fetch-me-carry-me. I know you're ill, but I've had enough. Can you understand that? Fifteen years I've worked at Althorpe's. And every bloody day has been the same, hurry up and get home, see to what she needs, what she wants. I'm past coping with it, Mam. I want a life. The lad next door's younger than me, but he's married with three children. That's what I want, an ordinary life.'

She waited until his breathing steadied. 'You'll get no ordinary life with yon Althorpe girl. That dad of hers will buy every stick you sit on, every stitch you wear. You'll be owned by the bloody Althorpe family. She's not right for you. You want a girl from round here, somebody who'll—'

'Somebody who'll be here to mop your mess up? Do you want me to find a nice, quiet lass who'll jump every time you say "boo"? Mam, I wouldn't want any wife of mine living here.'

'You could rent a house in the street, though, then you'd be handy. Only Miss La-de-da'll not want to live in Dobson Street, will she?'

His hands were opening and closing of their own accord. He stuffed the left one into a pocket, used the right to open the door. When it slammed behind him, he ran to the broken lamp and stood in the darkness, his knees threatening to collapse. He didn't know where to go. His aunties would be pleased to see him, as would a couple of his brothers, but none of them had an answer. They had no answer because there was no answer. It was up to him to find a solution.

A couple of lads from a nearby mill walked past, then turned back to scrutinize the figure under the lamp. 'That you, Phil?'

'Yes. Just having a breather. Nice night, isn't it?'

'Come on,' said one. 'They'll be shut in under an hour. Tony Quirke's having a bit of a party in The Three Bells – he's getting wed on Saturday. A drink'll do you good, lad.'

Phil was not a drinker, simply because alcohol did not suit him. Under the influence, he became vague and clumsy, unable to walk or talk in a sensible fashion. But he threw caution to the winds on this occasion. He was going to show Mam. She wasn't going to carry on running his life for him. Bessie Greenwood's love of black beer was one thing, but she hated public houses, had often told her son to stay out of them. Defiantly, he jangled coins in his pockets en route to The Three Bells. She wouldn't like it, and that was half the attraction.

He managed the road all right, but got a bit muddled when it came to negotiating the knots of narrow streets. It was as if somebody had deliberately moved all the houses in an attempt to confuse him. 'That's Mary Foley's place,' he said to himself as he passed an alley. 'So this must be Theresa Cooper's.' But Theresa Cooper had a paper blind, while the house outside whose window he was leaning sported curtains that were still open. He pressed his nose against the glass, giggled when a woman screamed.

He turned left, though working out which was left and which was right took a second or two. Maisie Makin lived in Harrison Street. Maisie Makin was the one who'd just screamed. So, if he carried on across the ends of two back streets, he should arrive home. For some incomprehensible reason, everything was very funny. When he fell over a discarded go-cart, he exploded with laughter while extracting himself from a jangle of pram wheels. At night, sound echoed, bounced around and multiplied itself. Never mind, he would be home in a few minutes.

The lamp continued unlit, so somebody's boss must have forgotten to bring a pane of glass. 'Naughty.' He wagged a finger at the guilty party. 'You should shine your light on the righteous.' The lamp swayed, so he ordered it to keep still, then carried on up Dobson Street. Some windows were lit, others were in darkness. Bessie's was still illuminated. He laughed again, pictured his mother's face. He was drunk and it didn't matter. He was going to be a dad and that was wonderful, a cause for rejoicing. There were some details to be worked out, but everything was going to turn out great. Everything in the garden would be lovely. The garden with the greenhouse and the vegetable plot.

The door swung inward, and Phil paused on the brink of an important moment. He wasn't quite sure what was going to happen, but life was marvellous, was going to continue good. He staggered to the kitchen, kicked this inner door slightly ajar.

'I can smell you from here,' she yelled.

'Not my fault, Mam.' He entered the room, a grin plastered across his features. 'Eric spilled his beer on me.' He had lost count of the number of drinks he had swallowed, but he remembered the accident. Fliss had given him this jacket, so he would have to sponge the beer out, then hang the item in the back yard till the smell disappeared. He belched, smiled broadly, then gulped back the bile that was collecting in his throat.

'Disgraceful,' said Bessie. 'What the hell have you been up to?'

'I've been celebr . . . cele . . . I'm getting married, so we all had a drink. Ever . . . body had a drink. Ever-body.' The word wasn't quite right, but it was near enough.

She stared up at him. 'Married? When?'

Phil thought for a moment. 'Before the baby.'

With an agility he might have admired in different circumstances, Bessie leapt from her sickbed. 'Baby? Has she trapped you that way? You've no bloody sense, you. What have I told you about keeping yourself to yourself?' She grabbed his wrists, pushed her face nearer to him. 'You have to think about me, lad. Wherever you go, I'm coming with you. She'll happen get a gradely house off her dad, so you could find a little upstairs room for me.'

He looked into her eyes. 'No. I'm going to have . . . a greenhouse. To . . . matoes. You can't come. You're bad, you don't like Fliss.' He shook his head until dizziness overcame him, then he pushed his mother onto her bed. 'You can't come. Pills. Take the pills.'

Bessie's jaw dropped. 'Are you saying what I think you're saying? Are you telling me to do away with meself?'

'Yes.'

She gulped audibly, her face as white as the sheet on which she sat. 'You don't mean it.'

368

'I do. Oh, but I do.' He picked up the biscuit tin, had some trouble with the lid. At last, the container opened, its load scattering across the flagged floor. Bottles cracked open, spilled their multicoloured liquid contents all over oil-cloth and rug. Boxes of tablets tried to hide under the table and the dresser, but Phil was too quick for them. He retrieved several, poured pills into his hand, picked up his mother's glass of water. 'It's what you want,' he said. 'I'm only . . . I'm trying to help you.'

She fought like a tigress while he started to cram her mouth with a variety of medicines. When he turned away for a moment, she spat, then screamed.

'Shut up,' he said mildly. 'Take your tablets. Doctor said . . . said they're good for you.' He pushed another half dozen into her gaping mouth, tried to administer water, was thwarted by her movements.

Bessie lashed out with her arms, spat, yelled, spat again. Noises off had begun to arrive as Phil hit her. He forced her to lie flat, took a pillow, held it over her nose and mouth. There were people at the door. Where the curtains failed to meet, a face appeared. Phil remembered somebody shouting when he'd pushed his face against a window. Maisie Makin. That was right. The face would be Maisie Makin trying to get her own back on him. Mam's legs had stopped moving, but her hands flailed weakly against the pillow. This was like a dream, he told himself. Lately, he often had nightmares about killing his mother.

Bessie's hands went still, but he kept the pillow in place. It wasn't a dream, he'd finally done something. What was all the noise? The door caved in. A man lay full-length on the floor, but he jumped up quickly, grabbed the pillow, looked at Bessie. 'You've done for her,' he told Phil.

'Three children.' Phil lifted a hand, pointed accusingly at his neighbour. 'Younger than me. Three children.' The contents of his stomach chose that moment to deposit themselves on the peg rug. He stumbled, coughed, cleared the mess from his throat, had a sip of water from Bessie's glass. 'She took all the pills,' he muttered. This was definitely no dream, because a policeman had arrived. In his sleep, Phil killed his mother, but didn't get caught.

'You young bugger,' snapped the copper. 'Harry?'

Harry, who seemed to be another policeman, stepped into the house, the pointed blue helmet tucked under an arm. 'Right, Sarge.'

'See if you can bring her round,' ordered the man with stripes on his sleeve. 'And I'll take this one down to the cells.'

Phil looked over his shoulder, saw that his mother was being hit. 'What . . . what are you doing?'

'He's trying to get her heart started,' said the sergeant. 'Now get in the van. I must warn you now that you are under arrest. Speak if you like, but we'll use anything you say in court.'

There was something about these words that cut through to Phil's mind, making him sober in an instant. 'She swallowed all her pills,' he shouted. 'I was trying to make her sick.'

The young man from next door shook his head. 'No, you suffocated her. I saw you from the window. So did Jack Ashby from across the street. He went for the police.'

Phil sagged against the table. 'That's a lie. It was Maisie Makin at the window. She was paying me back because I startled her on my way home.'

The younger of the two policemen got off his knees, picked the helmet off the table. 'She choked, I think,' he announced. 'And she's well gone.'

Phil panicked. He was completely sober, though his ears rang and his vision had not returned to normal. 'You don't know what I've been going through,' he said. 'She keeps moaning and asking for this, that, asking for me to tie myself down to this house. I was only trying to stop her.'

'Well, you've stopped her, all right,' said the sergeant. 'She'll moan no more. Come with me.'

Phil was dragged into the street. It seemed that every

door had opened and spilled people on to the pavement. Children cried, women drew old shawls over nightdresses, men stood outside in pyjamas and army greatcoats. 'Done fer 'er at last, 'ave yer?' yelled a voice. 'Yer'd no right ter do that, Phil.'

He stood at the back of the van while the younger policeman unlocked its doors. Things were moving so fast, too fast. They didn't understand. He was going to marry Fliss, was going to live in a nice house with switch-on lights and a garden. A baby was coming. The child would need a father. He clamped his lips tightly, tried not to flinch as he was pushed into the Black Maria. Inside, he perched on a wooden seat, breathed in the scent of fear, the smell of others who had been forced to occupy this small space.

With his head in his hands, he travelled the road to town. He was a murderer. He was a weak man, and he had performed the ultimate act of a person with no strength of character. 'I should have just left her,' he said to the floor. 'I should have gone and never come back.'

He was pulled from the van and thrown into a tiny room with some rough timber boards for a bed. A thin, stained mattress lay on these slats of wood next to a bucket with a lid. His mother was dead. He lay down, listened as footsteps faded along the corridor. Alone. Because of Mam, he was completely isolated.

Later, he was formally charged and issued with a navy overall with no straps. Getting into this one-piece item was difficult. 'So you can't hang yourself,' announced the constable by way of explanation. The laces had been removed from his shoes. 'Same reason,' said the uniformed man when questioned.

Phil lay on the bed again. He had been charged with the murder of Elizabeth Greenwood. Would Fliss rescue him? Did her father have enough influence? Tears collected, poured silently down his face. He was a failure. A real man would have made arrangements for his mother, would have walked away no matter how severe the pressure. A real man would have married Fliss years ago, long before the conception of a baby.

A dim light hung from the ceiling, its outer edges just licking the bucket. Next to this makeshift latrine sat a metal jug and bowl in which he was supposed to wash. He stirred himself to stand, picked up the jug, studied the lip, emptied the water into the tin bowl. It took a long time, but he managed to hone the edge of this protrusion by rubbing it against the stone wall. Moving round the cell, he found several suitable surfaces, even congratulated himself on solving the problem.

But even when sharpened, the edge was dull. He had to work hard on his wrists, and the agony almost defeated him. But he would be brave this once. As his life-blood ebbed, he saw Fliss's face and knew that he had never been good enough. He remembered, too, how distressed she had been when discussing Ida Entwistle, how she had all but wept for the orphaned Phyllis. Fliss feared suicides.

At four o'clock that morning, a constable named Pickering had looked into Phil's cell. The remanded prisoner had been asleep. One hour later, the same officer opened the small grille, saw a body on the floor in pools of blood. He sounded his whistle, turned the key and stepped into the gory scene. There would be trouble, because orders stated clearly that inmates should be checked twice an hour. He knelt in the blood, picked up a wrist to look for a pulse, stifled a scream when the skin parted like a thin, ragged mouth. Both wrists had been cut, the left more thoroughly than the right. He scrambled to his feet, fell backwards into the arms of the desk sergeant.

'Is he dead?'

'I don't know,' said the one who had found the body. 'But he was asleep just over half an hour since.'

'You sure?'

The young man thought about his family, two young boys, another baby due within weeks. No way could he afford to lose his job. 'Yes, I'm sure. He was on the mattress, flat out and snoring his head off.'

'Pretending,' said the sergeant. 'It must have taken him a couple of hours to sharpen that jug.' He waved a hand towards the item. 'We can't give them pots in case they smash them and use the pieces to cut themselves. We take their braces and their shoelaces. And now, we've a clever bugger who sharpens the bloody jug. This means no water in the block from now on.' He sighed, led the constable into the corridor. 'Don't worry, lad, it's not your fault. Just get on your bike and fetch the doctor.'

The policeman rode into the darkness. It was all right because he wasn't going to get the sack. All the same, he wondered what had driven Phil Greenwood to matricide and suicide within the space of a few hours. Had he been a praying man, he would have sought God's clemency for the dead prisoner. But he was just a policeman on an errand, so he got on with the job.

He woke in a hospital bed, saw a dark-haired woman towering above him. She wore a blue frock and a stiff white cap. There was pain in his wrists, pain in his head. 'Why?' he mouthed.

'Why not?' came the reply. 'Were we meant to let you die?'

'Yes.' He moved his head, looked at the policeman who sat in a chair next to the bed. 'I should be dead,' he whispered.

'Not in our cells.' The officer flicked through a newspaper, displayed a marked lack of interest in his prisoner.

Phil closed his eyes, wondered how the hell he'd managed to get into this mess. He couldn't even kill himself properly. Though he'd managed to kill his mother . . . A dart of pure fear shot through him, making his body stiff and still. They had got him. As soon as he recovered, he would be forced to go back to prison. And it wasn't likely to be a local jail, either. He would be taken to a place where many criminals were housed. After the court case, he would probably be hanged.

The blue-clad woman touched his neck, measured the pulse. 'You only lost a couple of pints, I'd say. We've put a bit back into you, and you'll make the rest up yourself. Drink plenty.'

Drink. That was it – he'd been drunk. All the lads from the Claybank mill would verify that he'd had a skinful. Could that be a proper defence? He turned his attention to the constable. 'I want a solicitor,' he said feebly.

Another page was turned. 'I'll talk to the sergeant when I get back to the station. You'll get a lawyer, but I'd wait a day or two if I were you. There's not a lot you can do while you're so weak.'

Yes, 'weak' was the word. He'd allowed his mother her own way for so long that a confrontation had become impossible. He knew even now that he could not have walked out. If he'd gone, Bessie would have dragged him back by fair means or foul. She would have made such a stink that he and Fliss would have been forced to take her in, or to split the marriage until after a funeral whose date could not have been foreseen. So he'd killed her. For Fliss, for himself, for the babe, he had committed murder. He cried, allowed the tears to flow freely, sobbed aloud, could not manage to care about what people would think of him.

'No use crying for your mam,' said the bobby. 'It's too late for tears. You should have thought about the outcome before you killed her.'

'I'm not crying for her,' moaned Phil. 'She's better off. And I would have been, too, if you hadn't come. You don't know. She made me pay because she'd nursed me when I was young. I thought she'd be gone years ago, but she hung on.' He coughed, sniffed back the flood. 'I want to get married.'

'There'll be no wedding for you, lad. As soon as you're standing, you'll be in front of the magistrates for committal. This is a judge and jury case. Cut and dried, too.'

'I was drunk.'

'Tell that to your solicitor.' He folded the paper, stood

up. 'Anyway, I'm off for a brew. Looks like you'll be going nowhere.'

'Hang on.' Phil stemmed the tears. 'How long have I been in here?'

'Night before last.'

The patient swallowed audibly. 'Was it in the papers?'

'Oh, yes.' The man tapped at his folded *Evening News*. 'In the nationals this morning. The *Evening News* has been interviewing your neighbours. They all said what a good lad you used to be and that your mam was a bit tetchy. But none of that will count in the criminal court, I'm afraid.'

'But I was drunk.'

The policeman put his head on one side. 'I've been that way meself, but I never killed anybody. You've no chance. See you later.'

Alone, Phil raised his head from the pillows, looked around. The ward was crammed to bursting with old men, one of whom seemed to be at death's door. As Phil watched, nurses ran about, pulled curtains round a bed. Utensils clattered in bowls, somebody shouted, 'Pulse. It's weak, but he's still with us.' Why were they bothering?

His own heartbeat picked up as he realized the implications of this distraction. The bobby was in the nurses' office drinking tea. All members of staff seemed to be engaged in the fight for the old boy's life. He lifted himself up, swung his legs from beneath the covers, ignored sharp pains in mutilated wrists.

Softly and slowly, he padded past the bed of death and through double doors. In the corridor, he found another door with a key in its lock. 'STAFF ONLY TOILETS' said the legend on an appended ticket. He pushed, listened, heard nothing. Inside the small room, there was a washbasin and a row of hooks from which coats dangled. Further in, he found another small room that contained a lavatory and the ward cleaners' garb – several aprons for women, a blue cotton bib-and-brace overall for a man.

He tore off the nightshirt, pulled on the overalls, a coat and some shoes that were rather small. But this was not a

375

shop, so there was no choice. With his hands and feet crippled by pain, he fled out of the room, down the corridor and into a maze that promised to have no end. Left, right, left – he turned back on himself, realized his mistake, carried on running.

It was evening, so the hospital was quieter than it might have been during the day. Stolidly, he carried on in spite of light-headedness. He had to get out, had to find Fliss, explain himself, persuade her to conceal him. At last, he found a room whose door gaped open. Behind a desk and chair, there was a sash window that lifted easily as soon as its catch was released. He climbed out, stood on a metal platform, then negotiated his slow way down the fire escape.

A bell clanged. Two black cars and a van of the same colour entered the grounds. He leapt into the bushes, rested for a moment, then made his way to the park. Railings presented a problem, but he had come too far, must not give up.

He dropped on to the bowling green, smiled at a man who pushed a roller. 'Late for work,' mumbled Phil. 'Short cut.'

'Be off with you,' shouted the keeper.

Phil needed no second telling. He mustered the last of his energy and began the long trek to Hall i' th' Vale.

THREE

Fliss Althorpe was refusing food again. Her mother had ascended the steep stairs more times than she cared to think about, because she was nursing two invalids. Sidney, whose heart had begun to flag more than slightly after a lifetime of work, was confined to bed on a diet of bread, milk, clear soups and digitalis. He would have to adjust to the drug, the doctor had said. He would also need to lose weight. And without his cigar, the master was what Mary Weston called 'mortallious'. Mary was happy to work for the Althorpes, but she did wish he'd take up smoking again. The maid had voiced this opinion to Agnes, who was taking most of the flak from Sidney. Now, with the servants off duty, it was up to the mistress of Hall i' th' Vale to deprive one patient of nourishment while trying to force-feed the other.

Agnes stood in the doorway of Fliss's room. It was an under-the-eaves bedroom at the front of the hall, a low-ceilinged area with beams, uneven floorboards and a four-panelled latticed window. 'Fliss, you must eat. How can you expect to become strong enough for work if you are starving yourself?'

Fliss, who had little real hope of returning for any length of time to her job at the Althorpe mills, made no reply.

Agnes took a step into the room, bent to straighten a rug. 'It may have been an accident, dear.'

'No.'

'Look, take no notice of newspapers. They exaggerate everything and make up what they don't know.' She bit her tongue against her real feelings, because she had known for some time that Philip Greenwood was not good enough for Fliss. It was nothing to do with breeding or education. The lad was weak. She knew all about weak boys, because she'd birthed one, a young man who, to avoid facing his parents, had apparently disappeared off the edge of Christendom. Geoffrey's exit had been made out of cowardice. She drew breath slowly, fought to hold back tears that still threatened each time she considered her son. But at least he hadn't murdered anybody . . . 'Do try a little of this clear soup, Felicity.'

'Later.'

Agnes came closer to her daughter, perched on the edge of the bed. 'Your father can't work yet, you know. It will be weeks before he returns to the mills. Even then, he will possibly need to work on a part-time basis until the doctor is satisfied with the dosage. Sidney is distraught about this business with Philip. I tried to keep the papers out of our room, but he made Mary fetch them. The shock has done him no good at all. So you must step into the breach, darling.' Like a child, she crossed fingers behind her back and waited for her daughter's response.

Fliss couldn't. She couldn't answer her mother and she couldn't go back to work because she was pregnant, unmarried and worried halfway to death. Worse than that, she was carrying the child of a man charged with murder. Fliss looked at her mother, knew that Agnes's heart would be broken all over again by her daughter's plight. No word from Geoffrey had arrived. Everyone felt fairly sure that he had changed his name in order to gain his so-called freedom. 'I'm sorry, Mother.'

Agnes patted the limp hand that lay on the quilt. 'None of this is your fault. Unfortunately, your name has been linked – albeit loosely – with Philip's for some time, but I told the reporter that he was a friend whose mother you visited as part of your work.'

'Which reporter?'

'One of a pair who were camped on our doorstep. They've been removed by the police, but not before they had become tiresome. They wanted to speak to your father, really, because he has employed Philip Greenwood. However, the *Evening News* has printed what I said, so you must not worry too much.' She prayed inwardly that the prisoner would say nothing. If he were to speak up, then Fliss's reputation could be irreparably damaged. But Agnes continued in hopeful vein, 'As for your feelings for the man, we can only hope that time will heal. You will meet someone else, Felicity. Meanwhile, do not be afraid of questions. If you verify what I said, I am sure no-one will guess that you intended to marry him. Please, please try to get better, my dear.'

Fliss nodded. Phil had always played down the relationship because he hadn't wanted to be teased. He was silly and spoilt and she should have realized that he was no good for her. 'He's still alive, then?' She had loved the man, yet now, after the death of Bessie Greenwood, Fliss's feelings were mixed. Deep inside her mind, there was a place that knew all about Phil. Quickly, she shut off the thoughts as they began to surface. No, she must not believe that he had killed his mother. No, she would blank out the suspicion that he was sufficiently evil to perform that despicable act. She marshalled her brain towards other thoughts. Yet a small voice persisted, continued to say, 'If he lives, you cannot love him. If he dies, he will be out of his misery, but you won't escape this torment.'

'He's alive,' repeated Agnes, aware that the girl had not listened the first time. 'He's in the infirmary under police guard. I expect he'll be out soon.'

'Out?'

'Of hospital.'

'Oh.' But not out of prison. She clutched her mother's hand tightly, began to worry about Agnes's pale face. She was fair-skinned, but the new pallor was almost deathly white. 'Stop fretting, Mother. This lack of appetite is something to do with my being unhappy, I think. But if I try to eat, the result is the same as it used to be. There's no point in taking food until I can digest it. When I'm better,

I'll eat. When I'm eating, I'll be up and about. Pop has a lot of good foremen down in the town. They know what to do. The mills won't suffer.'

Agnes Althorpe walked to the window and closed the curtains. If Fliss wouldn't eat, then sleep might be the next best thing. She turned, walked to the bed, bent over, kissed her daughter and held her close. The hugging had finished years earlier, so both were shocked by this renewed contact. But the older woman's heart was bleeding for her daughter's suffering, while Agnes's own mind reeled from recent shocks. Sidney, that solid man who should live forever, was suddenly ill. Geoffrey had taken off into God knew what, while Felicity, though in her mid-twenties, looked like a frightened baby animal, all huge eyes and stillness.

Fliss hung on to her mother. 'I'm so scared,' she said at last. 'I didn't know he actually hated her. I still don't know what to think. At first, he made fun of himself, laughed because he had to do housework after running a loom all day. He's a good weaver. Pop was thinking of promoting him to foreman.' She gulped back the hysteria. 'His mother didn't like me. When she turned against me, Phil was angry. Not the sort of angry that shouts and tears hair out. No, it was worse than that. A lot worse. It was . . . cold. He became very quiet, stopped talking about home, stopped making jokes. Bessie Greenwood was a very powerful and unpleasant woman, but . . .' Her words faded. He had even tried suicide. None of it bore close inspection, yet she could not keep the thoughts and ideas under control, not completely.

'He might not have done it, Fliss.'

Even now, the girl in the bed noticed her mother's words. 'You've never called me Fliss before.'

'Well, perhaps I shall in future. And please try to look on the better side. The man could be innocent.'

'Yes.' Those concepts were surfacing again, were attaching themselves to feelings of doubt whose roots had taken hold long before the current troubles. She trembled, shook violently. 'She talked all the time, I think. He could not tolerate what she said. He was unable to walk away because of her hold over him. Now, her mouth has been silenced forever.'

'Don't. Just stop tormenting yourself. British justice is famously fair. Let him face a jury, let a lawyer plead for him.'

Fliss's hold on her mother tightened. 'Even then, even if he is acquitted, I don't know . . . I won't be sure . . .'

'Yes, my dear girl. I do understand what you are trying to say.'

The embrace lasted for a few more moments, each woman clinging to the other at a time of terrible need. The mother smoothed bed covers, then left her daughter to sleep and gain strength. On the dark corridor that was the landing, Agnes heard her husband's roar. When she entered the bedroom, he was replacing the telephone on a side table. In spite of a heart complaint, he had to be on top of things. 'Yes?' she asked breathlessly.

'Police. He's out, escaped from the hospital about an hour ago.'

Agnes gripped the door handle tightly. 'Do they think he might come here?'

Sidney shook his head. 'No. You seem to have convinced them that Fliss was only caring for his mother. That statement will suffice as long as no-one at the mill knows too much about the relationship. Even if the workers do suspect anything, they'll keep quiet. They're loyal to me and they love our daughter.'

She closed the door quietly. 'Fliss says there was a bit of talk at the beginning, but because Phil's father worked at Number One till he died, people probably believe that you and she were caring for the widow. Everyone recognizes that you look after your workers and their families. Since she got the car, Fliss has been meeting him all over the place. When she dropped him off, it was always at the bottom of the streets where he lived. We can count ourselves fortunate that the Greenwoods' house was well away from your mills. So the police surely don't expect him to come here looking for Fliss?'

He shook his head. 'No. They were asking me about his friends at the mill, also warning me that a search of all the sheds will be made. Damn it!' He flung back the covers. 'I'm going down to the garden streets, then into work.'

She surprised both of them by flinging herself at him. 'No. I will not allow that, Sidney.'

Baffled by the unusual tone, he stilled his movements. 'What?' he asked eventually.

She drew herself away from him, stood beside the bed. 'How would you feel if I told you how to run your business?'

Sidney stared at her for a second or two. 'I would probably put you in your place.'

'Exactly.'

'And what do you mean by that?'

Agnes swept an arm across the room. 'This is my place of work, dear. Over the years, I have become an expert in household matters. I would be derelict in my duty if I allowed you out of bed. You see, the end product would be substandard. Would you let poor fents be sold as good? No. By the same token, I must do my job properly. The mills are your domain and this is mine. So, stay where you are, Sidney, or I shall send for the doctor and have you forcibly restrained. Don't doubt my seriousness, not for one moment. For once, you will do exactly as I say.'

He could not take his eyes off her. The pallor had disappeared and she was fiery, enlivened and beautiful. She had stopped caring about what people said, what they thought. His wife was a piece of magnificence that seemed to have escaped his notice until now.

'Will you heed me?'

'Yes, Mother.' He pulled a wry face, lay flat on his back. 'But he'll come, Agnes. Oh yes, that boy will come for Fliss.'

Her jaw dropped, and she closed her mouth sharply. 'Surely not. Surely he will not come all this way?'

'He will. Perhaps not tonight, but he will come. You see, he's disposed of one mother, so he needs a new female to attend to his needs.' He nodded wisely. 'I always thought he was a sound enough lad, but he's kept poor Fliss hanging about for so long – well – there has to be something wrong with him. Some men can't cope without a strong woman. And some of us don't know we've got a strong one till she takes advantage of our weaknesses. Look at you, telling me what to do. It's all right, I'm staying where I am. But you must try to watch our girl.'

'Our girl' removed her ear from the door, crept back to bed. Walking was not easy. She had not the fuel for movement, had taken no sustenance for too many hours. The soup. It was cold, but she managed two gulps. Like a greedy child, she tore the bread roll from a folded napkin, chewed, rinsed the mass down with water, chewed another lump. She needed strength. She needed clothes, because she intended to get out tonight. When guilt overwhelmed her, she told herself that she was not a prisoner bent on escape. At twenty-five, she ought to come and go as she pleased.

But she was not pleased. Why was she doing this? she asked herself a hundred times. Because he would come, she replied inwardly. Because there were things she wanted to say to him, questions that needed answers. Above all, she wanted to keep Phil Greenwood away from this house, away from her sick father and her exhausted mother.

When Agnes peeped into the room, Fliss, who was fully dressed beneath the linen, feigned sleep. Her stomach churned its desire to get rid of its load, but she breathed through her mouth, followed a technique that had been taught by the family doctor years earlier. She must hang on, must be ready. A chilled finger seemed to crawl up her spine when the bedroom door closed. For once, she needed her mother. But Mother was not available for consultation because Mother must be protected for a while.

There was a moon. Silvery fingers reached down from the sky, touched a farmhouse, stroked the trees. Fliss had always loved the moon. He sobbed when something sharp bit into his foot, staggered to the edge of the lane while he removed a piece of metal. Inky blood flowed from the instep, matched for lack of colour some new stains on bandaged wrists. Uneven light seemed to render the scene monochrome, bleaching anything that was pale, darkening the greys and browns.

He had carried the shoes for a while, but he could not have borne the pain of them again, so they lay in some ditch now. He was nearly there. With his eyes screwed up against many agonies, he followed his instincts towards Fliss. She would be waiting at her window under the eaves. Everyone must surely know by now that the mother-killer had escaped. But Fliss would be his comfort and his mentor, would surely lead him out of the suffering and into a place of safety. She was the one who could protect him now.

A shrivelled tree-stump sat by the hedge, and he perched on its unevenness, felt the bark as it tried to pierce through the hospital janitor's overall. The cleaner probably wore this garment over his clothes, but Phil was naked beneath the scratchy cloth. His head swam, made his vision poor. Drink, the nurse had said, though he had found no water along the route. A pounding in his chest grew louder, and he shivered, worried briefly that he might die of exposure. For some odd reason, he found the concept funny, started to giggle until the tears flowed. Mam was dead. She had looked after him, had nurtured him and saved his life. And he had killed her. He had failed to finish himself off, yet here he sat at about three in the morning, his mind plagued by worries about his health.

The journey had been fraught with anxiety. It had been impossible to avoid town completely, so he had dodged about among factories, shops, yards, terraces. He had seen the cars, had heard the police running, shouting, searching. They had been so near to him on one occasion that he had listened to a man coughing, had almost petrified as a match stroked the side of a box when a bobby lit a cigarette.

Crippled by the shoes, he had travelled barefoot most of the time, but his feet were sore and swollen from many bumps and bruises. The light-headedness continued and he felt as if he were imagining the whole thing. A coldness in the moon's rays added to the atmosphere of unreality, but the pain was here and now, was reminding him of the sins he had perpetrated in a matter of days. Where were they now, the people who had pitied him? How often he had heard them in the street, 'No use asking her if she wants help – she just tells you to bugger off,' and 'Poor lad has all to do when he comes home, but she's strength enough to scream at my kids'. Where was their sympathy when he needed it?

With an angry movement, he swept a dewdrop from his nose, struggled to stand, cursed the earth for its austerity, the moon for distorting the view. She loved the moon. 'Will you marry me?' How many years ago had he asked the question? Five, six? And he had passed the test, had survived her mother's scrutiny. But no-one could have passed Bessie Greenwood's exam, because there had been no questions, no solutions. Bessie had simply hated Fliss, not for who she was, but because Fliss had been a threat. And all the time, the biggest danger had shared Mam's house in Dobson Street, had broken daily bread with her.

His sense of direction was deserting him. By morning, he could be dead and now, he wanted to live until . . . until what? Oh yes, he needed Fliss to forgive him. He had to see her so that she would understand what he had done. What had he done? The moon had gone out – perhaps God had turned the gas down. No, no, the moon was a satellite that simply reflected yesterday's sun. Or was it tomorrow's? He was slipping, sliding, going down and down . . . Going where? To Fliss. So dark, so cold, so . . . so quiet.

'Get his legs, Megan.'

'Billy, is he breathing?'

'He's freezing to death. Where's that blanket?'

He heard their voices, felt their arms, enjoyed the caress of warm wool against his neck. It was still dark. No slipping now. He was being carried along. Someone strong was holding him beneath the shoulders, but his legs were carried by two people. 'Drink?' he begged.

'In a minute,' said the man. 'Let's get you inside first.'

He was laid flat on something soft, probably a sofa. Water dripped into his mouth, and he guzzled noisily, could not get enough. 'Don't put the lights on,' said the voice he remembered so well. She was here, she had come for him. 'Fliss? Fliss, is that you?' he asked.

'Yes.'

His feet were being cleaned and dressed. 'Megan,' he said. 'The girl with black hair. Didn't you marry Billy?'

'Of course. Billy, make some tea and do a bit of bacon, love. He's frozen stiff. Fliss?'

'I'm here.'

'What are we going to do?'

She made no answer. He lay in semi-darkness, drifted in and out of consciousness, knew that Fliss had not achieved a solution to his plight. She loved him. She would protect him. He brushed aside a few lingering doubts, convinced himself that his sweetheart was simply working out the details. Tea and a bacon sandwich made him stronger, while his eyes were adjusting at last, allowing him to take in this darker view of life. 'Fliss?'

'Yes?' She spoke softly, as if afraid of being over-heard.

'Hide me,' he begged. 'Don't let them find me.'

Billy cleared his throat. 'I'll be off to bed if you don't need me, Megan. There's a Manchester delivery tomorrow, then a collection from Altrincham.' He took a couple of steps towards the stairs, turned on his heel. 'Megan? Go careful now. Remember you're sheltering a wanted man. If you need me, just yell. Mind, the state of him, I doubt you'll get much trouble.' He climbed the stairs, his heart weighted by fear for the woman he loved. 'Don't do it, Meggy,' he mouthed. 'Because he's not bloody worth it.' Poor Fliss. He lay sleepless, waited for a call from downstairs, waited for police at the door.

In the parlour, Megan approached the invalid. 'I'm stopping in this room, Phil. It may work out that Fliss needs a witness, and we're like sisters, me and her. See, I lost my sisters and she never had one. My sisters died in the fire – remember?' She bit her tongue, stopped short of accusing him. The Duffy family had been bereft because of accident. But he had deliberately . . . hadn't he? She must make room in her head, must invent a place where doubt might live, because she was acting as judge and jury in a case that had not even come to court.

Fliss picked up a straight-backed chair, carried it slowly to the couch, sat near his feet. She did not want to touch him, did not want him to touch her. Seconds passed, each beat of time measured by the sound of his breathing, fast and shallow, terrified.

'Come closer,' he begged. Megan would hear everything. He needed to whisper into Fliss's ear, wanted some privacy. 'More tea?' he asked Megan.

The hostess dumped a tumbler of water on an old wine table, brought the table to him. 'I'm staying. You can have another hot drink when you've both said what you have to say.'

Fliss picked at her cashmere shawl, took several deep draughts of air through her mouth. Even now, the cold soup sat like acid in her throat, burning, threatening to make her ill. She lifted her head. 'Why?' There was no need to ask whether, because she knew, had known since the news had first arrived that this young man had murdered his mother. 'Why?' she asked again, her voice stronger.

'There was no other way,' he answered. 'Megan won't tell, will she? Has Billy gone for the police?'

'Billy's in bed,' snapped the witness. 'When we found

you, he wasn't best pleased, but Fliss had knocked us up and asked for our help. Fliss knew you'd turn up, all right.' She gulped back some words about bad pennies, drew breath. 'So say your piece, because I'll only do what Fliss tells me to do.' She set her mouth in a tight line, reminded herself of Grandma Deedee. Deedee's lips went narrow when she was thinking hard. 'And you'd best hurry up – it's near morning.'

He rested for a moment, waited for Fliss to speak. But no words reached him. 'There was no other way,' he repeated. 'She would have done for us, Fliss, so I . . . well, I did for her first.'

The young woman rose, walked to the window, saw a moon made feebler by the threat of dawn. 'You're weak,' she said softly. 'Had you been a whole person, you would have provided cover for your mother, a place where she could have lived out her days. But no, the task was beyond you. Your false pride prevented me from helping to get a home for her. We were going to be married, Phil. That should have been your prime concern, especially . . .' No, she told herself grimly. As far as he was concerned, there was nothing special about now, because she was going to insist that there was no baby. Her pregnancy must be denied, because all links with Phil needed to be severed now, tonight.

They were waiting for her to continue. She must be strong, must be prepared to ignore the cluster of cells in her womb. Like a mantra, she used the words 'no baby', kept them at the front of her thoughts where they could be readily available.

He struggled into a sitting position. 'But you—'

'Yes, your first duty was to me, and your second duty was to see that Mrs Greenwood was comfortably settled. Murder is an abomination, Phil. I never want to see you again.'

The silence was dreadful. It hung like a huge black cloud over the dim room. It was always darkest before the dawn, he told himself, though he gained no comfort from

388

the trite saying. 'Fliss, help me. Please help me to get away.' The desperation showed in his tone, seemed to linger in the sullen atmosphere after he had finished speaking.

She walked to the sofa. 'No. I played no part in your plan, and I will not endanger myself now by being involved as accessory. When the sun comes up, you are going away from this place. The Gate House is Megan's home and my father's property. You are not welcome here.'

The man on the couch fell back against a cushion. 'I didn't know you could be so heartless,' he said.

'And I have never considered you to be capable of cold-blooded murder. This was no way to achieve peace and silence. The saddest part is that you plainly recognized your own lack of character. You knew that you could not leave home. You knew that, Phil. If we had married, she could have forced you to go back to Dobson Street. Why? How could she do that?'

'I don't know.'

She nodded just once, then bent over him and spat words into his face. 'You are spineless. Your will was bent so easily that Mrs Greenwood had no difficulty in dominating you. So you found what you considered to be another strong woman. Me.' She thumped her chest with a closed fist. 'I will not take over where your mother left off. I will not be your second mother, Phil. After all, you might discard me in the same way if I became annoying. Killing is easy.' She paused fractionally, then waded in once more. 'Suicide, in your case, was another soft option. Living with people – staying alive and allowing others to live – takes a strength you do not have.' She staggered slightly, grabbed for Megan, held her close.

'What about the baby?' he asked.

Megan felt the tremors as they passed through Fliss's body. She clung tightly to the older girl, tried to lend her some extra power.

But the shaking stopped as suddenly as it had started

and Fliss needed no assistance. 'A mistake,' she said smoothly. 'A small hiccup in my body's mechanism, no more than that.' It was strange, but she was not protecting herself alone. There was another person involved, a being to whom she had given no thought until this moment. The child. Inside her body, that small tenant seemed to have reached upward until it touched her heartstrings. Its father was stretched out before her, feet and wrists bound and bloodied, face crumpled by self-pity, fingers clawing at a blanket. But for Phil, she felt no sympathy.

She gasped, fought to still a threatening stomach. Contempt for him bubbled in her throat, burned hotter than the undigested food, spilled its load into her tone. 'Thank God you will never be a father, Phil Greenwood. A child of yours might suffer from the same physical defect – an absence of backbone.' Mutely, she apologized to the barely-formed occupant of her womb. This would be her child, hers alone. She would perhaps release him or her for adoption, but whatever happened, the little soul would surely be separated from this awful man.

He wept mutely. Fliss was not expecting his baby after all. The hope he had nourished so far was now translated into words that crept silently across his consciousness. He had hoped, even anticipated that she would take him away, release him not just from prison, but also from the weight of his sins. Had Fliss absolved him, he would have needed no further forgiveness.

She tossed a small canvas purse on to the sofa. 'Take that. Go where you will – I'm sure Megan can find you some old boots and a coat. She and Billy may be trusted to keep my confidence. At eight o'clock, I shall telephone the police and inform them that a man was seen lurking in the vicinity. After all, you might have come to break into the house – all the people at the mills know of my father's money.'

She planted her feet apart, swayed in the manner of a barrister who is summing up for a jury. Her hold on Megan was slight, now, as she seemed to need no support while anger sustained her. 'And I want you to listen very carefully, Phil, because what I have to say now is important. If you mention my name when you are caught – and you will be caught eventually – then I shall speak up. You have not been here, have received no help from me, from Billy, from Megan. As things stand, you might perhaps plead manslaughter caused by temporary insanity. But if I came forward and testified, the case would not go in your favour. If you mention me, my family or Megan's people, then I shall get up in court as a witness for the prosecution.'

His tears dried in the heavy silence that followed. 'What could you say?' he asked eventually.

She pulled away from Megan, shrugged. 'That you have wished your mother dead. That you told me she was a burden when I visited on behalf of my father. I can say that I was worried, but that I hoped common sense and filial duty would prevail. Never speak my name, Phil Greenwood, or I shall make your noose with my own hands. Believe me, any rope I twist will be as sturdy as anything from the Bolton ropewalk, too strong to break when it tests your weight.'

Megan stood in silent wonder, her eyes wide as she absorbed the sight of Fliss's dignity. Even so, there was a frailty about the woman, a sadness in her posture. 'I'll put the kettle on, Fliss,' she said.

'No. Stay here and watch him. I shall make the tea.'

Megan sat down, shared the grey, pre-dawn shades with a murderer, forced herself to look at the man who had committed the foulest of crimes. When the tea was made, the girls stood side by side until he had emptied the cup. Megan rooted under the stairs, found a jacket, some old shoes and socks, a flat cap. Without a word, she handed him the clothing.

He struggled with buttons and laces, gasped when leather pushed against heels that still suffered from raw, punctured blisters. At last, he rose, stood swaying by the sofa. 'Goodbye, then,' he stammered. He gazed at Fliss's face, knew that she hated him. 'I didn't want to lose you,' he said quietly. 'And I have loved you. I still love you. There was . . .' He lifted a hand, dropped it in a gesture of misery. 'There was nothing I could do. She . . . she would have ruined your life.' And what had he done? Precisely that, he thought. He could not take his eyes off her, didn't want to go, was forbidden to stay. He had nothing, no-one, belonged nowhere.

Fliss did not speak. Megan brushed past him, held the door wide. 'You'd best get gone,' she advised. 'It's coming light over yonder.'

He stood in the doorway, looked at the woman on whom he had sought to depend. 'Fliss, I just want to tell you . . .' The words faded to nothing, were frozen in his throat by the coldness of her stare.

'Get gone.' Megan jerked a thumb over her shoulder. 'You've a couple of hours, no more.'

'I don't know where to go,' he said lamely.

'Go to hell,' said Fliss. 'You should find yourself in suitable company there.'

He left the house and Megan closed the door. 'Fliss?' she called. The unmistakeable sound of vomiting came from the kitchen. She grabbed the blanket from the sofa, relegated it to the cupboard beneath the staircase. If Fliss didn't come out of the kitchen soon, she would go and fetch her. Some instinct told Megan that Fliss needed a bit of time to herself.

After a minute or two, the white-faced visitor entered the room. 'I'm sorry you were dragged into this,' she whispered. 'And I'll have to get back to the Hall, because Mother and Pop know about the escape from the hospital. For all I know, my bedroom has already been checked. Though I did stuff some pillows under the covers. From the doorway, it looks as if I'm asleep.'

Megan nodded, sighed. 'No use going back to bed, not for me. I've to be up at seven, in town by half past. I've been commissioned to do some couches at the Town Hall.' Even now, she did not quite manage to keep the pride from her tone. After all, how many girls her age were in a proper business with real profits? But this was no time for self-congratulation. 'Sit down, you look weary.'

Fliss lowered herself into a chair. 'I am pregnant, Megan.'

'Yes. So am I, as you already know.'

Fliss narrowed her eyes, looked at the dim shape of her friend. 'What am I going to do?'

Megan's heart felt ready to break in two. Here she was, with a lovely husband, while poor Fliss had no-one. Worse than that, the baby's father was on the run. 'You'll have to talk to your mam, Fliss. You can't just do nothing about it. I knew you'd told him a lie when you said there was no baby. But you'll want help, Fliss. I'm only eighteen – I don't know the first thing about expecting and giving birth. The doctor gave me tablets – ferrous sulphate, I think they are – you can have some, they're iron.'

Fliss's chin dropped to her chest. 'I'm so tired I can hardly move.' She paused. 'I wonder where he is?'

'Does it matter?' asked Megan. 'Haven't you enough to think about without worrying over Phil Greenwood?' She tempered her tone to fit the occasion, lowered voice and head. 'Do you still love him, Fliss?'

'No.' There was no hesitation, no doubt. 'When I first met him, I suppose I was grateful because of my spots. He didn't seem to mind my complexion. Then he became a habit, a part of my life. But when I realized how weak he was, I wondered . . . Yet I still gave in and let him make me pregnant, so I was weak, too. My mother will die. As for Pop – you know how tired he's been. Imagine how it would be if I told him this. What if he suffered a heart attack? My timing could not have been worse.'

Megan picked up the glass from which Phil had been drinking. 'You've not done this on purpose. Getting pregnant was an accident. We'll have to think about it, decide what's best. Try not to worry. If you worry, you'll never keep food down.'

Fliss closed her eyes, leaned back in her seat. 'Thanks, Megan.'

'What for?'

'Just for being here and for being you.'

He watched the cows as they jostled, impatient to be relieved of milk. They lowed, butted one another on their way to the shippons. A rusty glow to the east forewarned of the sun's imminent arrival, yet he was tired, beyond running. Billy Shipton's old boots were a good fit, but although his feet were easier, he could find no energy, no will to shift himself. Around his wrists, spots on the bandages were turning brown, and there had been no bleeding for some time.

At the top of the moor, he turned to draw breath, looked down into the vale after which Fliss's home had been named. The Hall nestled at the bottom, its gardens neat and orderly after years of drainage and careful tending. It was a beautiful place, a credit to the man who had bought it and restored it to a glory that spanned five centuries. Although as far as Phil Greenwood was concerned, Hall i' th' Vale was now just another place where another woman had betrayed him. Mam had been a burden; Fliss Althorpe was uncaring, had not tried to understand.

He flopped down, uncertain of his immediate aims. Staying alive seemed to be important, though he had little to live for. But he was clearly meant to survive, or he would have bled to death that first night. After killing his mother. Gooseflesh crept along his limbs, made all the tiny hairs stand to attention. He had killed his own mother, the person in whose belly he had developed.

The land attached to Hall i' th' Vale was a sizeable acreage, and Sidney Althorpe had let it out to local farmers. Fliss's expectations were spread beneath him like velvet cloth in many hues, the greens ranging through moss and yellowish to flamboyant emerald. All this would belong one day to Felicity Althorpe, as her brother had disappeared without trace. And he, Philip George Greenwood, had thrown the lot away because of one mistake.

With his head resting on his knees, Phil wept bitterly. Mam hadn't been a nice woman. Everybody in Dobson Street used to talk about her, moan about her. The whole of mankind pitied offspring like Phil, young folk who were left to tidy up the remains of a previous generation. One or two had even said, 'Try greasing the stairs, lad,' or 'Have you no rat poison?' But those same individuals had stood in the street and condemned him on the night of the murder. Could they have lived with it? Could any one of them have gone to work after a night of tea-making and earache brought on by all the moaning?

'Get on with it,' said a small voice in his head. Mam's voice. Even now, she was telling him what to do.

'Shut up,' he said.

She didn't speak again. He was not experiencing a visitation, he told himself. What he had heard was an echo from the past, something whose familiarity had eaten its way into flesh and bone. For well over twenty years, her voice had been his first sensory experience each morning. Now, no-one told him to stir the fire to life, brew the tea, make porridge. No-one would tell him what to do.

He lifted his head, tried to absorb the feeling of aloneness. Peace. No talking, no orders, no machine groaning and creaking, no shuttle to kiss. He'd lost a tooth while kissing the shuttle. His tongue poked around, found the gap, while a finger traced the dent in his face, a small pit that had been mistaken for a dimple on many occasions. Oh, what was he thinking of? Fliss. Being alone. Being . . . nobody.

When the sky's colour brightened to turquoise, he picked himself up, stuffed the purse in a pocket, looked down on Hall i' th' Vale. Would she get the police? he wondered. Could she really do that to a man who loved her? There was no fear, but the absence of terror brought small comfort. His calm was born of the fact that he cared little about what happened to him. Alive was enough for now.

He had been Bessie's son, Fliss's young man – though

few had been aware of that fact – and a weaver at Althorpe's. Now, he was a man in old boots, an overall and a flat cap. Everything he owned was in a drawstring bag, and he had not the strength for counting.

North. He would make for Preston, perhaps. That was a big enough town, somewhere to hide. At a chemist's, he could buy henna. A woman in Dobson Street used that to redden her hair. All the lads called her gingernut. Mam used to make those, crisp biscuits that soaked up tea and tasted like a piece of heaven. Mam. Fliss. He was on his own now, and solitude was not something he comprehended. If he got far enough away, he might find someone who would . . . who would what? Talk to him, understand his position? No, he needed more than that. He needed someone who might guide him, give him a nudge, help him rebuild his life. Not everybody would recognize him, surely?

Phil Greenwood set forth, weariness in his body, a dull glimmer of hope in his heart. If he searched wisely, he would find someone to replace the woman he had killed.

Deedee looked at her granddaughter, wondered what she was up to this time. For Doris Wagstaff, Megan's face was an open book. Each time she stepped out of the fabric shop and into the leather store, Doris needed no more than a couple of seconds to assess the young woman's state of mind and health. 'I've some more of that blue and silver-grey brocade,' she announced, an edge to her tone. 'And straighten your face before the bobbies come for you. A face like that should have a number under it – wanted dead or alive.' Megan was worried. The fretfulness showed in pinched cheeks and a narrow mouth.

Megan threaded her needle. 'Deedee, I've a lot on my mind.'

'A lot on your mind? Well, doesn't that take the broken biscuit. Listen, you've a better life than most, Megan Duffy—'

'Shipton.'

'Aye, I forgot for the minute. Where was I? Oh, and that chap from Mornington Road wants you to look at his love-seat. I don't know why they call them love seats when folk had to sit back to back on the daft things.' She sniffed, paced about a bit. 'I can't see why you're fretting, any road. You've got a lovely home and a baby coming, plenty to eat and a face that would stop the horses.'

'Phil's going to have a number across his chest,' said Megan. 'I'm thinking about poor Fliss, that's all.'

Doris tutted, put her head on one side. 'Look, if he killed Bessie Greenwood, then a number's what he deserves. That were a terrible shock to poor Fliss, but things have to be got over. I mean, none of us liked Mrs G, but we never expected owt like this. It's not your problem, girl. Fliss is back at work, isn't she? Mrs Althorpe said as how the girl's eating again. Well, she didn't put it that road, but she thinks Fliss is on the mend. So what's up?'

Megan rattled her machine along a seam, turned the soft kid, rattled again. 'I'm busy,' she said in a small silence. She carried on, guided the leather, kept her head down. Deedee was a pest and no mistake. She could smell trouble. If somebody within a radius of five miles was in bother, Deedee Wagstaff would home in like a thieving magpie. When the chair cover was finished, she needed to make more noise, so she clattered across the floor in her workday clogs, put her head through the door. 'Billy? Come and help me fit this on the frame, will you?'

'I'm changing a wheel,' came the reply from off-stage. 'Ten minutes.'

Megan sighed. Ten minutes with Deedee could be like a week with the Spanish Inquisition. She straightened her spine, tried to look tall and important, re-entered the workshop. 'That stuff you mentioned should go well with grey leather, Deedee. Shall I make a cuppa? I've a few biscuits in the tin and—'

'Sit.' Doris pointed a bony finger at the chair. 'Get your bum on that, immediately if not sooner. You'll be meeting yourself coming back, you will. Like watching greased blinking lightning. And remember, it's not just yourself you've to think of. Folk having babies need their rest.'

Apart from the odd bout of morning sickness, Megan had never felt better in her life. But she sat, did as she was told. 'I don't want to talk about it.' There was a stubborn sound to her words. 'I can't talk about it.'

'Course you can, I'm your grandma.'

'No.'

'I'm your dad's mother, so—'

'I didn't mean you're not my grandma. I meant my lips are sealed.'

Doris tutted again. 'Well, that'll make a nice change. You've done nowt only prattle since before you could walk. Tess used to wonder if you'd ever shut up.' Her expression softened. 'Eeh, I wish they were all here now. I wish they could see how you've got on. Me and all. Fancy me having me own shop with a parlour for ladies to sit in while they get their frocks made. And our little Megan an upholsterer. Tess would have been so proud, love. We've very near cornered the market in made-to-measure fashions and furniture restoring.'

Megan kept her counsel. If it hadn't been for the fire, Mr Althorpe might not have taken pity on the Duffys, might not have moved the remaining family out to Hall i' th' Vale. Though the good man had said that his decision to move the whole Duffy clan had been made at Mam's funeral. But Dad would possibly have stayed in the clog shop had his girls not died. Opportunities had arrived because of Dad selling the shop and changing his job to estate manager. Yet she would surely give everything away just to have Annie and Nellie and all the others here.

'Sorry, lass.'

'It's all right. I do think about them, you know. The little girls – I hardly knew them. I wonder what they would have been like. And Nellie and Annie could have been mothers two or three times over by now. I'd have been an auntie.'

'And me a great-gran. Great-Granny Deedee – what a title.'

Megan trusted Deedee. The burden of knowledge about Fliss's situation sat heavily in the young girl's heart. Time was passing. Soon, Fliss's bulge would start to show. Megan patted her own rounding belly, wondered how many weeks there would be between the births of a new Shipton and an unwanted Althorpe. Fliss wasn't saying much. Megan had a feeling that something awful was going to happen. She kept picturing the scene – Mrs Althorpe running round like a screw-necked chicken all over again. It had been terrible when Geoff had taken off. 'I felt guilty about that,' she said aloud, surprising herself and Deedee.

'Eh?' The old woman's eyebrows all but disappeared into her hair. 'You what?'

'I was just thinking, that's all. When Geoff Althorpe went off – I just remembered how his mam carried on. You know, he'd said for years that he was going. But I took no notice, because I thought he was daft. If it happened again, I'd be ashamed.'

Doris, sensing the advent of confidences, sat down and waited. Sometimes, it was as well not to interrupt Megan.

'See, I don't know what she'll do. I mean, she's said nothing, not since . . .' She couldn't mention that night, because she had made a promise. But it was so clear in her mind, the blood, the bandages, the near-craziness in his eyes when Fliss told him to go to hell. 'Since the bother over Phil's disappearance, she's been a bit quiet. Something's brewing, Deedee. When Mr Althorpe gets back to work, that'll be the start. Whatever she's going to do . . .' She checked herself, knew she had said far too much. But who could she talk to, where could she go for advice?

The grandmother kept her curiosity on a low flame, held her tongue while Megan sorted her thoughts.

'You'll not tell, will you, Deedee?'

'Depends.' At last, it was time to speak. 'You've told me enough already, Megan. From what I can work out, you're thinking Fliss Althorpe's going to do a bunk, same as her brother did.'

'I never said that.'

Deedee nodded wisely. 'You said enough. So let's have the rest of it.'

An idea shot into Megan's head with the speed of forked lightning. 'I'm going out,' she announced.

Deedee jumped up as quickly as arthritic knees would allow. 'What? Are you leaving me dangling, Megan Shipton?'

Megan smiled. 'Sorry, Deedee. I'll have to go. Don't be worrying, it'll only take half an hour.' She threw off the clogs, pushed her feet into a pair of shoes, dashed to the back door. 'Billy?'

'Hello?'

'I'm going out a minute. See you later.' She turned, found that Deedee had been actually breathing down her neck. 'Don't say anything. Don't ask me anything till I come back.'

Doris shouted after her disappearing granddaughter. 'Don't talk so daft. How can I ask you owt if you're not here?' But her words fell on tramlines, because Megan was already round the corner. The owner of Wagstaff's Fashions and Soft Furnishings for the Home stepped out of the leather shop and into her own domain. 'She wants keeping an eye on,' she said to Tommy.

Tommy screwed up his own eyes over the appointments book. 'That friend of Mrs Althorpe's is on her way.'

Doris clapped a hand to her head. 'Evelyn Grimshaw,' she sighed. 'All I need on top of our Megan acting contrary-wise is an afternoon trying to make Evelyn Grimshaw's bum look normal. Eeh, I wish I were an alcoholic. I could get legless and lambasted and tell Mrs Grimshaw the truth. Which is that she's wasting her money, 'cos she's always going to look like the side of a tram.'

Tommy, who had given up trying to follow his wife's trains of thought, went to put the kettle on. Sometimes, women worked in mysterious ways. With that knowledge

400

in mind, he allowed himself an extra spoonful of sugar before counting out Mrs Grimshaw's fondant fancies.

The Flash Street Mission was two houses knocked together, great high-roofed things with huge chimneys, barred windows and steep steps up to the front doors. Megan heard a man shouting the score, poked her head down towards the cellar. 'Is Paddy there?' she shouted.

'Nay,' came the reply. 'When you see him, tell him we want new arrers and a proper dart board. This 'ere's like a bloody sponge, more holes than owt else.'

Megan grinned. Paddy was going to bring Phyllis to live here for a short time, until she took over the post office in Bromley Cross. After that, Paddy intended to commute, so the good man would have one foot in pea soup and the other in postage stamps. Nothing on earth would ever convince the O'Rileys to turn their backs on the mission. There would be fun, thought Megan, because Eddie the lion man promised to be an interesting second-in-command. Megan walked through the public rooms, mingled with an assortment of men who had wandered in off the streets.

'Hello, love,' yelled a ragged creature in a badly-dented bowler hat. 'He's adding up. I'd not go near him while he's adding up.'

Megan, who knew how thinly the money was spread, pulled a ten shilling note from her purse before entering Paddy's study. 'Study' was a very posh name for a cupboard, she thought. He sat under a new electric lamp, the rays illuminating his head like a halo. He was nearly bald, but he remained an attractive man, mostly because his eyes lit up all by themselves. 'I've brought a donation,' she said. 'So don't be saying we do nothing for you.' Even now, she had a job not to call him Father.

Paddy picked up the money, grinned naughtily, pushed it into his brown wooden box. 'The Mayor's fund is running out again,' he said. 'But with the Lord's help, we'll survive.'

She perched on the edge of a chair, anxious not to disturb the many files that lay piled behind her. 'With the Lord, the Mayor and daft folk like me, you mean.'

'Ah, yes.' He removed a pair of half-moon glasses, looked her up and down. 'Waiting to be a mother suits you, Megan. Did you want Phyllis? She's in the men's kitchen making soup.'

'No, it's you I want.' She placed her bag on the table, sat bolt upright. 'I've a question for you,' she said.

'Fire away.'

She spent a few moments organizing her words. 'Can I still trust you like in confession?'

He considered this. 'I think so. I'm not one for breaking confidences. So get on with it.'

She told him everything, piled a proportion of the worries on to shoulders that were broad and firm. 'And I don't know what to do,' she said when the tale was ended. 'See, if I tell her mam, then her mam might go straight out of her mind. Then there's Mr Althorpe and his pills. He's not likely to get better when he knows this lot, is he? But there again, if Fliss does a disappearing act like Geoff did, then I'm still going to be in the wrong. Whatever I do or don't do, I'm in a pickle.'

'Yes, I can see that.' He stood up and wandered about, though his pacing was limited by piles of documents, magazines, pillows and bedcovers. Each morning, after the men had risen from their mattresses, Paddy had to go round and pick up anything portable. His charges had been known to sell sheets, blankets, cups and saucers, all of which had been smuggled out under coats or through the lavatory window. He stopped near a filing cabinet, banged the drawer shut. 'Mrs Althorpe must be informed immediately,' he proclaimed.

Megan swallowed because she didn't fancy the job.

'Not by you, of course.'

Her shoulders relaxed slightly. 'Who, then?'

'Someone older.' He sat down again, ran his hands through the few strands of hair that remained.

'You've pulled it all out with worrying,' she told him.

'I beg your pardon?'

'Leave your hair alone, Father.'

'Paddy.' This response was automatic. His hands tapped on the table now. 'Let your grandmother do it. Whoever does the telling must be mature. And Fliss will know that you have broken her confidence, but the alternative does not bear consideration. She needs support, help and advice. And the problem will show itself very soon. So get Deedee to do the honours.'

Phyllis came in, the limp disguised by a carefully learned mode of walking. If she took small steps, the damage was less noticeable. 'Megan,' she beamed. 'Is your suit ready?' All Phyllis could think of was her imminent marriage to the man at the desk. 'It's a good job the wedding's soon, or your new outfit would be too small.'

Megan's eyes travelled from one to the other. Any bystander would judge this match to be a crazy one, yet those close to Phyllis and Paddy knew how right it was. He loved her, but he was older, gentler than a callow suitor might have been. And she simply adored him, had worshipped him since childhood. 'I'll be off,' sighed the visitor resignedly. 'I'm on an errand of mercy.'

Before anyone could ask more questions, Megan shot through the house and down the stone steps. She stood in Flash Street, watched the world go by, waited till she got her breath back. There was going to be trouble. No matter what was done or left undone, there would be a right carry-on. Positive steps needed taking, then. Because if Fliss ran away, there would be no help for her.

FOUR

The untidy fairytale cottage known as Twisted Stacks sat at the bottom of Dog Leg Lane, its back door opened wide to the elements. Mother Nature, who was wont to deposit her store of grief on Lancashire's green and pleasant acres, had dried her tears. The sky, tinted by hues that ranged from sapphire to aquamarine, had allowed a few cotton wool clouds to linger on its brilliance. These white patches of fluff made no movement, because the winds had been ordered out of a court over which the sun presided in vivid splendour.

The inside of Twisted Stacks was not untidy. Bottles and jars stood in regimented order along shelves whose surfaces were covered in clean paper. The edges of the paper bore small, evenly-spaced points, each one matching perfectly all its clones. A kettle simmered on a gas cooker with bow-legs, pans with copper bottoms polished like red-gold mirrors hung from sturdy oak beams.

Doris Wagstaff removed a lattice pie from the oven, carried it to the open window for cooling. He was there again, the cheeky little beggar. The blackbird sat on the shed roof, one beady eye fixed on the steaming confection.

'They'll have you, Blackie,' warned Doris Deedee Wagstaff. She recognized him from a droopy wing, though the disability seemed not to hamper him unduly. 'Who broke your feathers in the first place, eh? Was it blinking Montmerency? I'm telling you now, these cats'll make mincemeat out of you.' She'd put collars and bells on all of them. Even the wild and infamous Monty jangled like a biblical leper each time he moved. And that scenario, she recalled, had taken some organizing, though her scars were beginning to heal.

He cocked his head, gave her a throaty warble.

'All right,' she smiled. 'I'll fetch you a bit of something, then you leave my pie alone – understood?'

He jerked his head, appeared to agree.

Doris brought scraps, stood with her breath held while he approached. She had not reckoned herself to be a St Francis of Assisi, had never expected to make any kind of relationship with creatures. But she loved this bird, waited for him morning and evening, shooed away the cats, told her troubles to a yellow-beaked gannet. Sometimes, the bird's missus came along, but the dun-coloured female was shy, intelligent and wary.

He pecked crumbs from the sill, did not flinch when she reached out and touched the frail wing. Her eyes brimmed with a kind of joy as she considered the wonder of it all. Beyond the hedge, field after field rose up towards Blacktop Moor. This beauty had been here forever. When a child called Doris Appleyard had toiled half-time in the mills, when her whole life had been bed, table and work, heaven had been no more than a few short miles away. In the country, the smells were good, clean and wholesome. Even the mechanical tractors seemed to spew out fumes less noxious than vehicles in town, probably because there were so few machines yet. They would doubtless arrive, she thought. Deedee often enjoyed the sight of a pair of horses furrowing a field, felt privileged to be a witness. 'Well.' She lowered her hand, spoke to the bird. 'It's going to be a hard job tonight, Blackie. Think about that when you and your good lady settle for a snooze.'

The bird preened, shook himself, flew back to his perch on the shed's low roof. He knew about the cats, could recognize those bells from yards away. And the two-legged wingless creature in the large brick nest fed him regularly, so he refused to find new quarters while life was going so well.

Deedee walked to the front of the house and stood in the

tiny porch facing the Gate House. She had sent Joe, Joseph and Tommy to keep Billy company while his wife visited Twisted Stacks. Megan and Deedee had planned a ladies' evening, and all males were banned from their places of rest until nine o'clock. It was now almost seven. In a few minutes, Megan and Fliss would arrive. At half past seven, Agnes Althorpe, who was doing the flowers in the Anglican church, would drop in on her way back to the Hall. Deedee fiddled with the jangle of pins in her hair, touched a brooch at her throat, smoothed the crease-free skirt. Agnes was going to drop in, all right. Up to her neck, poor woman.

She set out the cups, was suddenly glad that poor Phyllis wasn't going to be here. Phyllis was spending the night in town, had been given a bed by that Spencer woman who used to have the wool shop. She'd taken a fancy to Phyllis, had Mrs Spencer, was only too happy to have the girl as company now that the shop was closed. Soon, Ida Entwistle's little lass would be gone for good, as she planned to room with Mrs Spencer until her wedding – or until the job and accommodation of postmistress became available. It would be great to go into the post office and buy stamps from Phyllis. Deedee polished a saucer, rubbed a teaspoon on her apron. A priest getting wed was not something she wanted to think about too closely. Once a priest, always a priest. She could not imagine that Paddy O'Riley would have the first notion about being a husband.

Megan stepped through the back doorway. 'Is Fliss here?'

The old woman pretended to look under the table, into a drawer, tried to lighten the tension that had visited her bones. 'I can't see her. Wasn't she coming with you?'

'No. I didn't want to make a fuss in case she cottoned on to us. If she doesn't come soon, I'll nip up to the Hall for her.' She perched on a chair. 'Do you know what you're going to say, Deedee?'

Doris Wagstaff, who had been practising her lines for

twenty-four hours, raised an eyebrow. 'This isn't something that can be planned, love. It'll have to be played by ear.' She offered up a silent prayer as payment for the lie. She didn't know where to begin, and that was the problem. How, though? How would she tell a woman like Agnes that her daughter was carrying the child of an escaped convict?

Megan seemed to read her grandmother's mind. 'You may not have to do it, Deedee. When Fliss comes, tell her what's going to happen. Then she might tell her mother.'

Engrossed in thought, they did not notice Fliss standing in the doorway. She had entered Twisted Stacks from the garden, through a side gate that led directly to Hall i' th' Vale's largest shrubbery. 'Why?' she asked, her voice so quiet that no-one appeared to hear. She repeated the question, and both women turned on their heels and faced her.

Deedee cleared her throat. 'Fliss, you made us jump.'

'Not surprised.' She took a few steps into the kitchen. 'In view of the fact that you're both guilty.' Her eyes raked Megan's face. Apart from her parents, Megan was the dearest person in the world. And now, Megan had let her down, had betrayed her. 'Megan, you can't run my life for me. This was our secret. I'm not a child. I don't need nursing through this. Can't you let me make my own decisions?' She shifted her attention to Deedee. 'Is twenty-five too young? Am I incapable of sorting out my own problems?'

The cuckoo in one of the kitchen clocks chose this moment to announce the hour, seven silly noises performed by a wooden bird on a few pieces of metal.

Megan moved her weight from foot to foot, didn't want to be here, shouldn't have told Deedee about Fliss's baby. And that daft clock seemed to be laughing at its view of the room, as if the scene were something out of a comedy film. To add to the commotion, an old timepiece on the mantelshelf began to throw out a strangled version of Whittington's chimes. Deedee's collection of homeless clocks was almost as unpredictable as Patrick O'Riley's motley group of residents. Megan attempted to find her thread. 'I . . . er . . . well, with your măm upset about your dad—'

'And remembering how bad she took Geoff going off,' interrupted Deedee. 'We were frightened of you just disappearing into thin air. Agnes couldn't cope with that, not a second time. You can't marry him, because you can't find him. Nobody's clapped eyes on him since he ran away from the hospital.'

Megan avoided Fliss's hard look. Surely Fliss didn't think Deedee knew about that as well? No way would she have told about the night when Phil Greenwood had been found in the lane . . . She felt her cheeks burning as she considered the web of deceit into which she, Fliss and Billy had allowed themselves to be dragged. What the three of them had done on that awful night was an offence that was punishable by law . . .

Doris Wagstaff was in full flood. 'And even if you could find him, there'd be no wedding, would there? While he's on the run, nobody'll marry the pair of you, not even the registry. You need birth certificates to get wed, and he'll have none. Then, after he's caught, he'll be in no position to—'

'Stop it!' screamed the white-faced visitor. 'Stop talking to me as if I've just moved up from the mixed infants. Do you think I've no brain at all? Do you seriously believe that I've just been sitting there gazing into space?' She walked closer to Doris. 'I'll have you know, Mrs Wagstaff, that I run two mills single-handedly at present. My father . . .' She swallowed the terrors, planted her feet firmly apart. 'My Pop is a sick man. No shocks, the doctors say. I couldn't protect him from finding out about . . . about Phil Greenwood and his mother. But I can save him for a little longer from . . .' Her voice died.

Doris, who had noticed when Fliss had called her by the full name, placed a hand on the girl's shoulder. 'I'm Deedee, love. Doris if you prefer. But I'm not Mrs

408

Wagstaff, not to you, any road. Look, Fliss, you'll start showing in the next four or five weeks. Have you worked out when it's due?'

Megan answered the query. 'February, same as me,' she said.

Deedee lifted the singing kettle, brewed tea, laid supper on the table. 'Happen you think not eating will solve your problem, eh? Well, it won't. Bad enough playing that game when life's ticking over normal, like. But if you carry on like this with a passenger on board, you'll be finishing your journey in a hearse.' She slammed the teapot on to its wrought iron stand. 'That baby is taking every bit of your nourishment, Fliss. If you eat what's in front of you at every meal, you'll be all right. But if you carry on picking like yon blackbird, you'll die, 'cos the baby needs good grub and nature will give the unborn first pickings.'

Fliss stood completely still, her face expressionless.

'Are you listening to me?'

The girl nodded. 'Oh yes, I'm hearing you. If I died, the problem would no longer exist.'

'If you died, your dad would be riding tandem with you, two carts, two coffins and your mother's shroud on order from the funeral parlour.' Deedee lowered aching bones into a chair. She was tired, too tired for this. 'Do you think me and our Megan can just stand by and watch all this? What sort of a friend would I be to your mother if I didn't try to get some sense from you? And don't blame Megan, 'cos the load was too heavy for her. She's her own carrying to do. Now.' She poured tea, added milk. After a sip, she eyed Fliss, ran her gaze over the girl's body. 'You're disappearing to nowt, lass. Megan's scared for you.'

Megan lifted a cup, offered it to Fliss, flinched slightly when the drink was refused. 'Your mam went crackers when Geoff left home,' she said, her tone gentled by affection for Fliss. 'It took ages for her to come round. If you do the same as Geoff, who'll look after her? Who'll look after your dad if your mam gets taken away poorly? You've got

409

to do something now, Fliss. No good putting it off till you show.' She smoothed a hand over her own belly. 'Look, I'm an early shower, Deedee says. Even if you're a late shower, it's going to happen.'

'Shut up,' whispered Fliss. 'Just shut up and mind your own business.' Without another word, Fliss turned and walked out of the house.

Deedee put her head in her hands. 'You can have all the money in the world, Megan, and it means nowt.' She lifted her face, looked at her beautiful granddaughter. 'What can we do for Agnes now, love? Whatever can we do?'

Megan made no reply, because there was no answer.

Fliss flung herself through the garden of Twisted Stacks, became breathless as soon as the gate was closed. She leaned against the wall, her lungs pleading for air, her heart thumping in its effort to distribute oxygen to heavy limbs. The starved, ill-nourished body could go no further. Had she wanted to move, she would have needed to crawl like a snail. At the front of her mind sat the picture she had glimpsed in mirrors for the last few weeks. She was gaunt, hollow-eyed, exhausted.

She sank into a space behind the hedge, knelt in grass-clippings and garden waste, waited for her tears to start. But none came, because she was too dry, too shrivelled for weeping. In Twisted Stacks, at the other side of a seven-foot wall, Megan and Deedee were deciding her fate. It was too late now, too late to stop things happening. Her hands shook, and she folded them in her lap, tried not to think, prayed for forgetfulness before lying full length in the sweet-smelling dry grasses.

It had happened in a barn, she thought. They had travelled out of Bolton towards Blackburn, had parked the car in the yard of a deserted farmhouse. That hadn't been the first time, but would definitely turn out to be the last. His hands on her body had always been careful, almost tender. With the same hands, he had deliberately snuffed out the life of an old woman. Phil Greenwood had wiped out one piece of humanity shortly after creating another.

Her gorge rose and threatened, but there was no energy in this involuntary movement. The empty stomach, recognizing the futility of its efforts, was half-hearted in these frequent attempts at evacuation. Pain crowded her chest, stung her throat, stained her mouth with acid. She would die soon. Unless she could force herself to actually sit at a table and eat a full meal, she would surely perish.

'I love you,' he said.

She lifted her arms, pulled him close, received him gladly. His teeth were bared as he looked down on her. 'I've killed her,' he whispered. 'She's dead and she can't hurt us any more.' This was a dream, surely?

The pleasure he gave was suddenly turned to agony, was a knife twisting in her belly. No scream came from her mouth, though she tried to make him hear. He had to stop, had to go away into prison. Blood dripped from his wrists, spread its gory wetness on her skin. Mother was there, her expression grim. Pop called out, 'Fliss? Where are you?'

Dry lips framed an answer, though no voice arrived. It must stop. Mother was here, was watching. Mother knew everything. 'Stop,' said Fliss, and he heeded her this time.

'You'll come with me,' he told her. 'We can run away together. You're strong, so you can protect me.'

'NO!' She woke, inhaled the smell of flowers, tasted bile. The sky had darkened and she needed to go home. Home? She lifted her head, peered through a gap in the bushes. Across the shrubbery, she saw Hall i' th' Vale, its aged windows reflecting shards of twilight in many directions. Few panes were true, many were original. That was home. Home was going to be a museum in years to come, a celebration of all those who had worked in cotton. Pop was in there, was resting among antiquities, was fighting a battle to stay alive. And here lay his daughter who prayed for death.

'Come home, my dear.'

She shook her head, waited for wakefulness. But the

voice came again, and this was no longer a dream. 'How long have you been here?' Agnes's tone was soft, not angry.

Fliss stared up at her mother. 'I don't know.'

'We didn't think of searching here. Megan went up to the house, then we looked up and down the lane for you.'

The young woman swallowed, narrowed her eyes. 'Aren't you angry with me?'

'No.'

'But—'

'You're here. You haven't run away to another country without saying goodbye. If you had run away, I'd have died within a week. So would your father.'

Fliss concentrated on breathing, in, out, in, out, tried to still her stomach. 'I am so sorry,' she said eventually.

Agnes raised a shoulder. 'Why should you apologize?'

They hadn't told her. Suddenly, Fliss knew that a part of herself had depended on Deedee and Megan, that she had wanted them to do the telling. Well, it needed to be done, and she would have to get it over now, this minute, before she had time to think. 'I'm going to have a baby.'

'Yes.'

Fliss knew this couldn't be right. Mother had progressed, was neglecting her earlier mission to do the right things, to be seen with the right people, to be a perfect wife to a man she had not deserved. But this? No-one within Fliss's sphere of knowledge accepted the birth of a bastard. Little girls in the mill had been forced into wedlock, had developed the bulge first, the wedding band second. Even down there, where life was raw, real and painful, shotgun weddings were carefully arranged for careless girls.

'Mother, I don't understand. The disgrace, the—'

'Stop this.' The older woman's tone was firm. 'What's done is done. We must be strong, Fliss. This situation must be dealt with by you and me. Sidney is still not strong. Now, I don't want you to worry, because the doctor is hopeful. Soon, your father will be pottering

412

about in the garden. Joseph Duffy might have a fit, because Sidney is to gardening what the iceberg was to the *Titanic*. But we are all hopeful. Your father has suffered a small hiccup, no more. However, we can allow him no distress.'

Fliss shut her mouth with a snap, got up, studied this strange woman who was supposed to be her mother.

'This will be dealt with properly and in secret.' There was a tilt to Agnes's chin, an attitude that bordered on ferocity.

'I can't . . .' Fliss's mouth was as dry as sandpaper. She thought of lemons, tried to bring saliva to her tongue. 'No operation. I can't have . . .'

Agnes nodded. 'You will, I trust, give birth to a live and healthy child.' She cast an eye over the emaciated frame, pleaded with God to make this young woman eat. 'There are people all over the country who want to adopt, wealthy couples who can't produce their own. A place will be found.' She hadn't thought that far, really, hadn't had the time. Though Doris Wagstaff had waxed lyrical, as usual, some story about an order of nuns . . .

'The father is a criminal.'

Agnes brushed this statement aside with a wave of a hand. 'The nuns won't know that. There's a convent outside Chester. They take in unwanted babies and put them up for adoption.' Deedee had told her that just minutes ago.

'What do I do till then, Mother?'

'Ah, now there's a question.'

Fliss dropped her chin, indulged herself in shame. 'I did love him. Sometimes, I knew he wasn't strong, but I blamed his mother for keeping us apart. No.' She lifted her head slowly. 'No, I didn't blame his mother, because she was ill. He should have left her, should have found the backbone to begin a life with me. He is . . . he is a very weak man.'

Agnes touched her daughter's arm. 'Most murderers are spineless. Because of a lack of character, Phil simply

413

removed the woman who gave him confusion. Self-destruction is an easy option when life gets difficult, though there are circumstances, of course.' She thought for a couple of seconds about little Phyllis Entwistle's mother. 'It's sad, really. I'm sure Phil loved his mother. And, of course, we must remember that parents reap what they sow.' She coughed delicately, raised a hand to her lips. 'I placed too great a burden on Geoffrey. Like Philip Greenwood, he ran. As for you – well – I have not been a demonstrative mother.'

'Please don't blame yourself, because—'

'Oh, but I do. You looked for love and found disaster. Now, we must help one another to reap what we have sown.'

Fliss threw herself at her mother, found the tears at last. 'Mother, what about Pop? It can't be hidden, can it?' The words were fractured by loud, ugly sobs.

'Shush, now. Listen to me. Look, stop the tears, Fliss. There isn't the time, you know. A man called Charles Walsh is to be sent for – he's a doctor from somewhere near the mills. Doris trusts him implicitly. Then there's the chap who used to be a priest – isn't he going to marry little Phyllis? Anyway, Doris is fetching these people so that a plan can be made.' She hugged her daughter, patted the trembling shoulders. 'Child, you must eat. Your only duty from now on will be to take nourishment.'

Fliss dried her face. 'What about the mills?'

Agnes shrugged. 'I've run a household, so I suppose I can manage simple things like mules and manpower.'

'You?'

'Why not? Are you suggesting that I'm not capable? Fliss, I used to be a weaver. I know cotton and I know people. What else is there? Won't the men see to the machinery? Of course they will,' she answered herself. 'I can sit at a desk and seem authoritative. I am capable of being quite bossy, you know.'

Fliss managed a watery smile. 'I have noticed.'

'And it's time I put my talents to use, dear. Sidney will

always need help from now on. And . . . well, we don't know when you'll be available, so leave it all to me.'

They walked through the shrubbery and into a rose garden where the air was filled with the heady scent of mature blooms. 'What about the baby?' asked Fliss. 'What about Pop? When he sees, when he finds out, how shall we save him from illness?'

Agnes chewed her lip for a second. 'That's why the doctor and the ex-priest are to come.' She almost smiled. 'They seem strange candidates, yet the two of them will make up our lies. There is nothing on earth that can't be managed by women. We'll allow the men to draw the map, but we shall navigate the waters ourselves.'

Fliss realized yet again that she had never known her mother, that none of them had recognized her strengths. The pale and simpering Agnes had been replaced by a woman of great self-assurance and dignity, and Fliss was sure that Agnes's powers had been born in the garden streets. The lady was a worker who had accidentally become a queen bee.

Agnes paced along at her daughter's side, knowing full well that Doris Wagstaff and Megan Shipton would keep her secret. The truth was that Agnes had disgraced herself this evening, had cried and moaned like a Saturday night drunk who had lost his way home. 'Be strong,' Doris had advised. 'I'm not sure how you'll do it, only you've to be stronger than you really are.'

For Fliss, Agnes would find the energy.

'Are you marrying her out of pity?' Charles Walsh steered the car through a maze of streets, waved occasionally at children who played on the cobbles.

'No.' Paddy settled back in his seat, refused to admit that motor travel terrified him. He was all right on trams and trolley buses, but when it came to cars, his opinion was that a passenger sat far too close to death. The vehicle's black bonnet was all that separated him from the road, so he clung to his seat and gritted his teeth.

'Because that would be wrong.'

'Yes.'

Charlie sighed, hurtled round a corner. 'Blood from a stone,' he muttered.

'Pardon?'

'What the devil's up with you, Paddy? You're as talkative as Cyril Corcoran, and he's been in a coma for seven weeks. I'm making enquiries about your future, old son.'

'I love Phyllis.'

'Right.' Charlie hung on to his laughter. Paddy O'Riley sat as rigid as stone, looked like a man on his way to the gallows. He squashed the concept, could not allow thoughts of a hanging to enter his mind. Fliss's baby's father might be awarded capital punishment. If he ever got caught. 'As long as you're sure. Marriage is a serious step—'

'For goodness sake, haven't I preached on that theme for years? I must admit that I did question myself for a long time. Was I being a fatalist, was I looking after Phyllis as part and parcel of the stand I made for her dead mother? But that's all over. I know she's young in years, but life has given her early maturity. We shall do very well, Phyllis and I.'

The doctor swerved to avoid a dog.

'Do you have to drive so fast?'

Charlie shrugged. 'We're needed and we're late—'

'We'll be more than late – we'll be the late – the dear departed. Slow down.'

The car almost stopped, continued at snail's pace.

'One extreme to the other,' cursed the passenger. 'Just do what you have to do. Just get us there. And pray to God that we come up with a decent solution.'

The rest of the journey was completed in near-silence. They left the car outside the gatehouse, walked up Twisted Stacks' short path, were admitted by Doris Wagstaff. When the usual greetings were over, the two men separated and sat one at each side of the room. Fliss, thin and pale-faced, had folded herself into a chair by the fire, seemed to be trying to make herself as small as possible.

Tommy Wagstaff entered, nodded a quick hello, announced his intention to take Billy for a pint.

'Make sure it's not a gallon,' advised his wife. 'Or you'll be sleeping in the shed.'

A huddle of cats on the rug came apart, each feline collecting and stretching limbs and tail before making for the door. Little bells tinkled on leather collars made by Megan. 'How many?' asked Paddy.

'Too many,' snapped the lady of the house. 'Seven including Monty. He's the one with the biggest bell. I should have bought Big Ben for him – that'd slow him down a bit.'

The feral cat seemed to know he was being discussed. He twitched tail and whiskers, cast a look of utter contempt at these examples of humankind, then stalked out of the room.

'He's a menace,' said Deedee

Agnes Althorpe was near the window, hands folded in her lap, her face serene. She presented a picture of relaxation, but Dr Charles Walsh, who had seen suffering in its many guises, was not fooled. A slight tic at the corner of her mouth gave away the truth, as did a whitening of the knuckles. The woman was sitting on a powder keg of emotion, so the plan would need to be explained very carefully. He cleared his throat, glanced at Paddy. 'Well, we had a good enough journey, though the ex-Reverend seemed a bit ruffled.'

Paddy grinned sheepishly. 'Not at all. You're an excellent driver, Dr Walsh. Mind, I'd have been more pleased if you'd kept all four wheels on the ground, but I'm not complaining.'

There followed an awkward silence, everybody seeming to wait for words from other members of the meeting. Paddy leaned forward in his chair, rubbed the palms of his hands together. 'Are you well, Fliss?'

She nodded, said nothing.

'Eating's a problem.' Agnes dropped the words into the room. 'She must try harder with food, or she'll be ill.'

Charles Walsh gave his attention to the girl. 'You have to eat. Have you seen your doctor?'

Fliss shook her head.

'We thought you might look after her, Dr Walsh.' Twin spots of colour showed on Agnes's cheeks. 'The fewer who know about this, the better.'

'Quite.' He smiled encouragingly at Fliss. 'When this . . .' He failed to find a suitable noun to describe the sombre gathering. 'Later, I'll get the box of tricks and give you the once-over. All right?' He wore an expression that had courted the affection of many timid people. Sometimes, he wished he were married. Had he been married, he might have understood the workings of the female mind. But he had never met a suitable woman, and this was hardly the occasion for regrets on his own part. 'Don't worry,' he said.

'How do I stop?' asked Fliss.

'You lean on your mother, on me, on Mrs Wagstaff—'

'Deedee,' interrupted the hostess.

'And on Paddy. Whenever you need support, contact one of us.' He swallowed, looked at his close friend. 'We've tried to work something out. There may be a better idea soon, but this is what Paddy and I have come up with.' He raised his eyebrows in silent signal, sat down, waited for Paddy to begin.

The ex-priest ran a hand over his head, cursed himself yet again when he reaped a couple of hairs. He'd be bald soon. He would stand at the altar with a glowing bride and a glowing pate . . . 'Fliss,' he began. 'Several things have to be taken into consideration. Firstly, you are going to have a baby. Secondly, we need to find a way of protecting your father from shock and distress. Thirdly, arrangements must be made for the child's future.'

Fliss nodded, unclasped her hands, folded them again. He was a lovely man. They were both nice men, trustworthy, commonsensical. 'Not an easy set of tasks, is it?' The light tone belied inner turmoil.

'No, it won't be easy,' replied Paddy. 'But we can all work together to make as good a job as possible.'

Agnes decided to speak up. 'Where will she go?' The thought of losing Fliss, even for a short time, cut through her heart like a thin blade of steel. 'Because Sidney will soon be up and about.'

Charles Walsh held up a hand. 'One thing at a time, Mrs Althorpe. Go on, Paddy.'

Paddy paced about for a few seconds before coming to rest with his back to the fireplace. 'Initially, we can do nothing until your health improves. Dr Walsh will see to your needs, while Mrs Althorpe can try to get you eating again. As for my role – I am the architect of the plan, so I suppose I hold the post of professional liar.' He held up a hand against Agnes's sharp intake of air. 'Don't worry about this side of it. Jesus Himself would have needed to be a bit frugal with the truth if faced by this sort of thing. Because while we have to protect Fliss, we must also ensure that Mr Althorpe is not disturbed.'

Fliss nodded, was showing signs of involvement at last. 'Pop is the most important one. This heart condition could be made worse if he started worrying about me.'

Paddy cast an eye over the woman by the window, the person who was going to carry the worst of the weight. Fliss's burden would be physical and mental, but Agnes's promised to be the most troublesome. 'For as long as possible, you will stay at home, Fliss,' he said. 'Charlie here is going to become your doctor. The change can be explained quite easily, because his practice is close to the mills. You can say that you've consulted him while you were at work. He'll find a bit of anaemia, a need for tonics and so on. When the . . . the pregnancy starts to become self-evident, you will have to go away until the birth.'

Agnes coughed, wriggled in her chair. 'Where? How will I look after her if she leaves the house? Who'll be there when the time comes?' Already, she was leaving Fliss and

Sidney to the tender mercies of Mary, Cook and a couple of dailies. Agnes had been into the mill four times, had been distressed at first by a level of noise whose intensity she had forgotten, had been accosted by people asking questions about Fliss's health. 'Of course, I'm running the mills, too.' Sidney was amused by his wife's new status, but she would carry on grimly, especially now. Anyway, the mill folk were becoming helpful.

Paddy picked up his thread. 'I take it that Mr Althorpe is already aware of his daughter's absence from work?'

'Yes,' replied Agnes. 'He thinks she's suffering from a minor ailment.' He also believed that his wife was crackers, but that did not need repeating in present company. She tightened her lips, had made up her mind that she would keep going no matter what. Let Sidney laugh, let them all laugh, but she would show a profit at the end of the quarter even if she worked twenty-four hours a day. 'He's not worrying about her at the moment.'

'You will go to Switzerland,' Paddy told Fliss. 'Charlie is going to recommend a cold but dry climate for you this winter. A nun will collect you from the Hall, and your real destination is to be a small convent near Chester. I shall attend the birth, then you'll return home as soon as possible.'

Fliss put her finger on a flaw. 'What if Pop wants to come to Switzerland?'

Charles Walsh shook his head. 'No. You will need total isolation from your family, complete rest.'

For the first time during the discussion, Deedee chipped in. 'She'd not stop long abroad without sending letters and postcards to her dad, would she? I mean, unless she keeps in touch, he'll start worrying.'

'The nuns will cope with all that,' answered Paddy. 'You see, the Catholic church will go to all kinds of trouble to protect the unborn. It's part of our faith, as simple as that. The good women in Chester are used to this sort of business. They look after mothers, keep the babies, then have them adopted. It's their life's work.'

'Do they sell them?' asked Fliss.

Paddy coloured slightly. 'Everything is done legally, but I expect there would be donations to the order from grateful adoptive parents. I'm sorry, this is the best we could muster, Charlie and I.'

The girl looked from one man to the other. She was weak, exhausted, almost bereft of logical deduction. In a few months, she would be a mother, yet she would not be a mother. She felt no affection for the baby's father, yet the slow arrival of some curiosity had outwitted her. Would it be a boy, would it be pretty, would it be lovable? No, no, she must not develop any interest, any affection for the child. 'Will they take it away immediately? As soon as it's born?'

Paddy scratched his head for a moment, remembered the threat of total baldness, shoved the offending digits into a pocket. 'That I don't know. I imagine you'll have only the briefest contact with the newborn.' She was afraid. He could feel her panic, as if it floated in the air like dust motes inside a ray of sun. 'Try not to think too far ahead just yet,' he said gently.

Agnes leaned forward. 'Fliss is the sort who will love children,' she said. 'You must stress the importance of immediate separation.' She did not need to voice her worry about disgrace, about the many tongues that would advertise and condemn an Althorpe bastard. Everyone in the room was fully conversant with the need for total discretion. 'She must not come home with a baby,' she mumbled, her face pink. 'It would finish Sidney.'

The door opened a crack and Megan peeped in. Her cheeks were redder than Agnes's, because she had been guilty of eavesdropping.

'It's all right,' said Fliss. 'Megan knew almost as soon as I did.'

A stream of words poured out of Megan's mouth in a great rush, a jumbled and disorganized message from the tense girl in the doorway. Impatient with herself, Megan pushed her way inside, stood with hands on hips.

'Would you care to repeat that?' asked a bemused Paddy.

'Well.' Megan planted her feet wide, straightened her shoulders. 'They're near enough, any road. Why can't I go and all? I can soon get time off work, 'cos Billy's good with leather – I trained him myself. And if it's only days or weeks between, who's to know? I mean . . . I mean, she might have no more. What if she never gets married? It'd be no trouble and I'd look after it. I mean . . . I mean . . . and she could have it back later on, after all the fuss dies down. Or she can leave it with me. I mean . . .'

Deedee tutted. 'She means. Oh heck, like a bull at a gate, she is. Look, Megan, I'm getting the drift, only these other folk's been learned with the king's English. Start again.'

Megan blew out her cheeks, took a deep breath. 'I'm talking about twins, Fliss. See, babies don't always look like their parents. And twins aren't always the same and it's healthy round here. Rich people are cruel. They send them to boarding school as soon as they can walk and they do French when they're only eight. And Billy won't mind, 'cos . . . 'cos he won't and they'd be treated alike, no favourites and—'

Agnes jumped up. 'No,' she said firmly. 'Fliss needs to leave everything behind – Philip Greenwood and his baby must play no part in her life.'

Fliss sat very still, her gaze welded to Megan's face. 'You would really do that for me?'

''Course I would.'

A pair of tears made slow paths down Fliss's cheeks. 'Thank you, Megan,' she whispered. 'I'll never forget your generosity. Of course, it's not possible. I don't think I'd like to be reminded of . . . of now. But thank you so very much.' In spite of her words, she recognized the weak flame of hope that was beginning to kindle in her breast. Perhaps, after all, she might see the child, might be able to watch him or her grow . . . She would think about this later, would talk through the possibilities with Megan.

The heavily-charged atmosphere was cleared by Deedee. 'Right.' She bustled about a small tea-table, sent Megan to make a brew, took the covers off fresh scones and cakes. 'Get to this table, lady,' she told Fliss with mock-severity. 'You'll eat till you bust, then you'll eat some more.'

Throughout the little party, banter flew between Deedee and Megan, but the two men were watchful. A tiny light had entered Fliss's eyes. And she ate three scones.

FIVE

He'd been on the loose for months, had travelled up and down the country, was lonely, tired and frozen halfway to death. Winter had set in, its chilled fingers numbing his mind, making his body slow and clumsy. But the walled city was filled with people, so he went along with the flow, tried to blend in. He walked past shops almost without seeing them, was vaguely aware of black-and-white frontages and upper galleries where people wandered above street level. Cities and large towns were relatively safe for a fugitive. He had begun to avoid hamlets, as the country bobbies on their sit-up-and-beg bicycles were quick to pick out a strange face.

Money was in short supply. Fliss's purse had emptied itself within weeks, and he had been forced to find labour on farms and in quiet, backwater villages where he had cut grass, mended windows, pruned roses. He was at the end of his tether, would have given himself up weeks ago had it not been for the threat of a hooded man and a very real rope.

After an hour or so, he found himself beside a swollen river. He peered into its green-grey depths, wondered how drowning might feel. The trousers and jacket he had bought in the summer were thin, provided poor protection against frost. A second-hand overcoat hung from his shoulders, might have covered his raw frame twice over with room to spare. When had he last eaten? Today, yesterday? The water would be cold enough to burn the skin from his face. Stealthily, he backed away from death. For some reason that lay well beyond his mind's reach, he had to live on. Soon, soon, he might know why.

A few houses were scattered along the banks, many with moorings and boatsheds attached to gardens. One house in particular stood out, a single-storeyed wooden place with boards over one window. A second window was intact, its dirty lace curtains hanging limp and neglected. No light showed. Most of the other dwellings were illuminated from within, because the dusk of January had spread her early darkness. He walked slowly, carefully towards the wooden cottage, wore the air of a man used to hiding.

At the door, he paused, looked around. No-one could possibly recognize him. Even the mother he had murdered would have been hard pressed to pick him out. Phil Greenwood, master weaver from Bolton, was just another tramp these days. His skin was dark, still tanned from toiling in the baking sun of summer. Lines had etched themselves deep into the skin, and his eyes were smaller, seemed to have shrunk inside folds of skin that had developed through sleepless nights and sun-boiled days. The dye had long since faded from his hair, but the thick, brown thatch was long, unkempt and greasy. In order to look ordinary, he wore a cap into which his wild tresses were tucked.

With marked expertise, he forced the door, then slipped a short crowbar back into his pocket. This piece of iron was as good as any key. Like the thief he had become, he crept into the house, waited until his eyes had adjusted to a gloom that was intensified through being contained. There was a bed. He let out a sigh of relief, pulled a chair from beneath a table, propped it against the outer door. This was his place now. He had battered many of his fellow nomads, refused to share space with other gentlemen of the road. Tonight, he wanted no visitors.

In a cupboard, he found jam and treacle. With a bent spoon, he scraped the jars, almost groaned with pleasure as the sweetness caressed his tongue before plummeting into a stomach that was numb with hunger. He had no bags, carried few possessions on his journey, as luggage might advertise his status. Attention was something he

425

avoided, preferring to steal or to beg for work in order to stay alive.

Blankets folded on a trunk gave birth to a fog of dust as they were wrapped about his body. He sneezed, covered his nose with a hand. Noise was the enemy, and he had practised silence for over six months. When he was forced to speak, the tones were rusty, as if his larynx were threatening to heal over from lack of use. He sat on the flat-topped trunk, shivered his way into relative warmth.

The building was probably the property of some not-quite-wealthy family whose members would use it occasionally for a few days by the Dee. In a second room, he found another bed and some cupboards containing light-weight clothes. A 'captain's' hat hung on a peg, the word SKIPPER announced above the neb. The owners of the hut would hire a boat in clement weather, he thought. The lavatory was outside, a tiny box with a door made from planks. He stared through the window, wondered whether or when he might find the courage to use the facility.

Back in the first room, he found a brass tap on a pipe of bent lead. It was not frozen, and he took a draught of water, using his hand as a cup. A black paraffin stove sat against the wall, fuel in a can by its side. He found a box of tacks, used pieces of blanket to cover windows. Within minutes, he lay in the lap of luxury, his feet toasting near the stove.

He dozed, saw Fliss's face yet again, heard her words as she banned him from her life. The dream jumped about, flitted from Preston to Newcastle, back to Bolton and right into the house on Dobson Street. Mam was fighting him, was pushing him away. She would not die. When the police came, he turned on them, showed them that she was still breathing. Mr Althorpe arrived and waved a big stick, told him to stay out of the mills.

He woke covered in sweat, pulled himself out of the chair and turned down the stove. The stink of paraffin clogged his lungs, causing him to cough convulsively. He found a candle, lit the wick, looked at his stolen watch.

Twenty minutes past three on a cold January morning. He crept out of the house, used the lavatory, went to bed. Tomorrow, he would find work. If he found no work, he would steal. With gritted teeth, he tried to steer his mind towards pleasant thoughts. If he could forget the murder, he might sleep without being plagued by nightmares.

The dark-haired girl passed him a bacon sandwich. 'I never want to see you again,' said Fliss. Inside the dream, he reminded himself that this was not real, that he would wake again soon. When he jumped to wakefulness for the fourth time, he sat by the window, lifted the blanket and waited for dawn. A church clock marked the passage of time. Would they catch him soon, would he hang?

A hand crept to his neck, extended fingers drawing a line against the throat. Everywhere, the police were searching for him. So far, he had outwitted them, had kept several steps ahead. But the law of averages and the law of the land dictated that his time was merely borrowed. He had beaten people, had committed burglaries in houses and shops, had even picked pockets in market places. His victims must surely have reported him.

He took down the blanket, ran his fingers over frost-patterned glass, removed the icy evidence of his own exhalations of breath. A wry smile twisted his features as he considered his own cunning. Even here, in a hut that was separated from the nearest dwelling by at least fifty yards, he guarded himself with unerring instinct. Perhaps, after all, he might defy all rules and remain free forever.

The convent was a large, white house with huge, highly organized gardens and a chapel attached at one side. Residents' rooms were pleasant, high-ceilinged and painted in hopeful pastel shades. Over each bed hung a crucifix of massive proportions, a figure of the tormented Christ picked out in lifelike colours. Fliss often looked at 'her' Jesus, often wished that the blood would fade. Tiny drops coursed down the forehead below His crown of thorns, while the loincloth was stained from the sword of a

427

soldier. 'If you fall off the wall, I'll be very dead,' she informed her saviour. 'So stay where you are, please.'

She gazed out of the window, wondered at her own calm. She'd started feeling better after the fourth month, had become serene, almost bovine. 'I just wait,' she told a robin. 'And I can't manage to worry any more, not properly.' The robin, plainly bored with Fliss's ruminations, flew off.

Sister Mary Joseph put her head round the door. All the nuns were called Mary, but most second names were masculine. 'Are you all right, Fliss?'

'Yes, thank you.'

The nun came in, dug a stick of liquorice from one of her many voluminous pockets. 'It is you, isn't it?' she asked vaguely. 'Or are you pickles and jelly crystals?'

Fliss shuddered. 'No, I'm oranges.'

Sister Mary Joseph flopped on to the bed. 'That's it, I remember now. Aren't you the one who eats the peel?' Without waiting for a reply, she prattled on. 'Even so, you'd be better off than the girl in number six. Coal, she is. Can you imagine that? She's always black, poor soul, and we have to keep filling her scuttle. Three clean nightgowns a day, she has.'

Fliss was very fond of Mary Joseph, who was usually called Joss by the pregnant girls who shared the house with these brides of Christ. Joss was Irish. She had the sort of voice that could lull people to sleep, very soft and gentle, the consonants coated with a velvet brogue. 'Why did you become a nun?' Joss would have made a perfect mother.

'To serve God and mankind at the same time. Did you want another orange?'

'No, thank you.' There had been few official questions, no forms to fill. All the expectant mothers in Nazareth House were in the same predicament. Wealthy families off-loaded their girls here, left them to the mercies of the sisters, returned after weeks or months and retrieved their errant offspring as if nothing unusual had happened. Only yesterday, a mink-draped female had arrived to pick up her daughter. As the family had passed Fliss's door on the way out, the matriarch had been heard to say, 'Well, you look wonderful, darling. A pity you missed Lady Sarah's coming-out ball, but I have you down for two more, and there's a possibility of a third.' The daughter had giggled before asking for a trip round Chester. 'For Northerners, they have some pretty decent clothes, Mummy.'

'You seem a bit glum, Fliss.'

She lifted a shoulder. 'I'm strangely contented, sister. It's as if I've gone into a very unhurried patch.' She turned, placed both hands on the bump. It hadn't shown for ages. When clothes had become too small, Deedee Wagstaff had simply made them larger. Until the sixth month, Fliss had remained at home with her father while Agnes had run the mills. Now, when she looked at her reflection, she saw a slender girl with what looked like a football under her skirt. 'They still haven't caught Phil, you know.'

'So I gather.' The little nun knew the full story, had sat for hours in this room while Fliss poured out her heart willingly, gratefully. 'Ah, they'll get him in time.'

Fliss nodded. 'The baby won't ever know? I mean, will its parents find out about Phil?'

'That'll never happen, I promise. We can say in truth that we know little of the father, but that the mother came from good stock.'

The girl from good stock perched on the edge of a chair, unable to lean back into cushions now that her centre of gravity had been displaced. 'Does anyone ever keep a baby?'

'Well, it's happened once or twice, but not since I've been here. Best not to dwell on it, all the same. Just make yourself comfortable and carry on eating well. God will take care of the rest of it.'

'Will He?' She wanted this baby, didn't want it, wanted Megan to have it, couldn't bear the thought of Megan rearing it in the house at the bottom of Dog Leg Lane, so near, so far. Anyway, no-one seemed to have taken Megan's offer seriously . . . 'Why should God help me, Joss?'

'And why wouldn't He?'

'He couldn't have been there when my baby was made. The father of this child is a murderer, and—'

'Stop it. God is here for everyone, for every single living creature in the world.'

'Even flies?' There was a wry twist to Fliss's mouth.

'Don't be difficult. Flies are here to teach us to be clean. I never did meet a more obstinate girl.' The woman's smile belied her words. She held up the liquorice root, announced her intention to seek out the person who craved this particular confection.

When Joss had left, Fliss opened a drawer and took out her knitting. She was sticking to lemon and white, because pink would have tempted fate. A girl would be nice. She struggled with a dropped stitch, chided herself inwardly for caring. The sex of the infant was of no interest, as she must give him or her away. Girls were stronger, though, more resilient, easier to rear. And . . . the foetus kicked, almost knocked the wool out of its mother's hands. Fliss picked up the stitch, picked up her thought. And a girl would perhaps favour her mother, whereas a boy might turn out to be another Phil, another weak-kneed male.

She followed the pattern, slipped one, purled one, passed the slipped stitch over. Pop was better. She smiled, enjoyed the idea of him being back at his desk. Mother had continued at the mills, was turning out to be a great favourite with the workers. On her last visit, Agnes had gone on at length about her latest scheme – evening classes in reading and arithmetic. Although the folk from the garden streets were astute with their money, several seemed to be lacking in basic skills. So Mother had found her niche at last. In a way, this child had done a lot of good even now, before its birth. Agnes was vibrant when discussing her work, though her worry about Fliss still showed in deepening frown lines whenever she looked closely at her daughter. Still, Mother was keeping herself occupied, so she'd have little time to think about Fliss between visits.

Pop seemed to have swallowed the lie about Switzerland. Fliss had written out several postcards, was supposed to be travelling around from one resort to another during her 'cure'. Foreign nuns on alien soil were compounding the lies by dashing about with trite little messages on picture cards. But as long as his precious girl kept 'moving', Sidney Althorpe would not be tempted to follow her to the Alps.

He was working mornings only. Fliss laid down the half-finished jacket, imagined Pop in his office again. Did he still buy sandwiches for his lunch, did he still insist on stewed tea with two sugars? She closed her eyes, was back in the mill for a few moments. Through Pop's window, she saw the mill gate. Phil Greenwood was standing there, had stood there for months, even years. His house was at the other end of town, and he usually brought a packed lunch, bread, cheese, an apple.

Fliss's eyes flew open. What if he found out about this baby? No, no, he would be far away, possibly abroad. Geoff was abroad. Geoff was another reckless creature, no thought for anyone but himself. But what if . . . What if it really began to matter? What if she gave birth and then refused to give up her son or daughter? Fliss recognized that she was in a strange frame of mind. Her thoughts flitted about like cabbage white butterflies, never settling, never reaching any conclusions. The fact was that she was about to have a baby and . . . and she didn't know how she was going to part with it, didn't know how she was going to keep it.

Joss was sensible. Joss didn't walk about with a face like a wet Sunday, was not like most of her sisters. The veiled woman sat for endless hours with 'her' girls, those in rooms one to ten. There was little communication between residents, so the nun in charge of this particular section was a lifeline who flitted from single room to single room, her mind always open, her smile always real. Joss had forbidden Fliss to think. 'I won't think,' she said aloud. But even as she spoke the words, the cry of a newborn infant reached her ears.

She got up with accustomed difficulty, went back to the window, noticed that the robin had returned. Across the river, near a shack made small by distance, a man stood gazing into the water. Even from far away, his stance seemed sad.

The baby still yelled. It was a rare sound in Nazareth House, as the labour rooms were sealed away by a massive door. Someone had left the door open, then. She heard people running, listened to a man's voice. 'Let me near her, sister.' After a few moments, he shouted again. 'Come on, girl, don't give up.'

Fliss lowered herself on to the bed, looked up at Christ's feet. Down the corridor, a tiny life was screaming. And its mother was in trouble, possibly dying. She thought about Phyllis's losses, about Megan's dead family. A mother was so important.

'Fliss?'

'Oh, hello, sister.'

'Are you all right still?'

Fliss swallowed. 'Who died?'

Joss knew that lying would be futile. 'Number two.'

'Did number two have a name?'

'Of course she did.'

'Tell me her name.'

Joss dropped her head, fingered the huge rope of beads that hung from a belt. 'She was Elizabeth. Pray for her.'

'I will,' replied Fliss. And she did.

Deedee and Agnes were washing dishes in Twisted Stacks. Had a stranger viewed the scene, he would have been forgiven for mistaking these two as relatives – not sisters, not quite – cousins, perhaps, or sisters-in-law. They worked together like a well-oiled machine, the older woman washing, the younger drying and putting away.

432

But had that same stranger looked more closely, he might have noticed pain in both pairs of eyes, might even have guessed that it was shared discomforts that had welded these two so thoroughly together.

'I hate to pile all this on Megan's shoulders,' said Agnes.

'She'll cope. Our Megan's a coper.'

Agnes pushed a pile of crockery into a cupboard. 'When she offered, I dismissed the suggestion out of hand. It would be so difficult for Fliss if Megan took the child to live so close to home. But with Fliss's present frame of mind . . .'

'No option.' Deedee up-ended the enamel bowl, sent the suds down the drain, rinsed bowl and cloth, wiped the draining board. 'When you've no choice, you've no choice. Agnes, we can nobbut wait and see what happens.'

'I know.' Agnes closed the cupboards, sat at the table. 'In a way, I understand Fliss.'

'Aye, so do we all. You can't grow a baby in your belly for nine months without wondering who he is or how she'll turn out.' She placed herself in the chair opposite Agnes's. 'Lass, you'll be worn to nowt. Running mills, making sure Sidney doesn't do too much when he comes to work, worrying over Fliss. Look, if she decides to keep that kiddy, there'll be nowt at all you can do. So stop mithering over summat that's out of your hands.'

Agnes dropped her head. 'So, Megan will have the task of trying to persuade Fliss to give up the baby to person or persons unknown.'

'Aye.'

'Then, if my daughter refuses to do that, Megan will offer again to adopt the baby and to pretend that she has given birth to twins.'

'That's right.' Deedee reached across the table, patted a pale hand. 'Megan knows what to do.'

'What if—?'

'Shut up, Agnes. We can go on what iffing till hell gets froze over, can't we? We've got to face the possibility that

Fliss will decide to bring that child up herself. Now, you've nowt to be ashamed of, and neither has your lovely girl. The only fly in that ointment would be Sidney, and I'm sure he's weathered a few storms in his time.'

Agnes bit her lip, unable to express the biggest of all her fears. He was a sick man. She hadn't told anybody yet, but Sidney Althorpe was living on a knife's edge—

'Cheer up. We're all going visiting, aren't we?'

The visitor nodded, smiled weakly.

Deedee stood up, plonked a hat on the iron curls just as Megan and Billy entered the house. 'We're not going with you,' she told the new arrivals. 'I'd rather get there in one piece,' she declared. 'He rattles my old bones, does Billy, always in a hurry.' She cast an eye over her grand-daughter's rounded frame. 'As for you, lady, you should be riding in Dr Walsh's car while you're in that condition.'

Megan, whose bump was twice the size of Fliss's, put her tongue out. 'Dr Walsh is a terrible driver,' she replied. 'It's just our van that's rattly, not Billy's driving.'

'Stop putting your tongue out. Do you want me to get the carbolic?' asked Deedee. 'That'd soon wipe the cheek out of you.' She turned to Agnes. 'Where does Sidney think you are?'

Agnes arched her eyebrows. 'I'm pretending to go to Manchester to look at reading books. I believe there's a new set out, simple words but interesting content. It seems silly for grown men and women to be reading about cats sitting on mats. Anyway, I've ordered the books by post, but Sidney's not to know that.'

'Well, me and Tommy'll ride with you and Dr Walsh. Phyllis and Paddy can go in the van with these harum-scarums.'

Billy affected an air of hurt. 'I'm a good driver. With a round my size, you've got to be quick. Did you know we've had orders from as far away as York and Harrogate? No use dawdling when there's work to be done.'

Deedee awarded him a hard look. 'Our Megan shouldn't be working. She shouldn't be bending and messing about with leather. Fact is, she'd be working today if she wasn't going into Nazareth House.'

Megan sighed. 'Deedee, stop it. I've never been as well in my life. Anyway, Billy's served his apprenticeship, so he does most of the jobs. And I'll not be working for a while.'

Agnes crossed the room and put her arms around this wonderful girl. 'Inside, you are just like Fliss,' she said. 'Thank you for doing this.'

Megan laughed. 'I'm only going away to have a baby, Mrs Althorpe.'

'But you're going to no ordinary mother and baby home. This is a convent where—'

'Don't remind me or I'll be sick if I think about nuns,' threatened Megan.

'Where girls don't bring their babies home,' continued Agnes. 'If I could have found any other way—'

'I don't mind,' said Megan. 'If she won't let the little one go with the nuns for adoption, I'll have twins. And if she won't allow that, either, then at least I'll be there to let you know.'

Agnes walked away from Megan, spoke to Billy. 'You really won't mind if Megan brings two home?'

'Oh no.' Billy's expression was serious. 'In our family, we open our doors, don't we, love?'

Megan nodded. 'We've lost too many folk between us,' she told Agnes. 'My dad taught me and Billy that family isn't about name. It's about caring.'

Agnes bit her lip. Sometimes, the Duffys, the Wagstaffs and the Shiptons were generous enough to make her cry. 'Megan, please listen.'

'I'm listening.'

'Just do your best. This is a bad time for me to beg a favour, because you have your own delivery to manage. I am so sorry to lay all this at your door.'

Megan gave Agnes a brilliant smile. 'Stop thanking me. I know what I'm doing, I understand what you mean, really I do. I'll say it all again, just so you'll know I'm fit for the job.' She counted the options on her fingers.

'Number one, it might be for the best if Fliss just lets the baby go to a good home, to a woman who can't have children of her own. Failing that, number two, Billy and I are willing, you know we are. Number three, if she goes stubborn, if she decided to keep her baby, I'll be there to keep my eyes open. And that's all there is to it.'

Deedee looked heavenward. 'She makes things sound so easy.'

Megan glanced at Billy. 'I'll have to leave you,' she said.

He grinned, looked every inch the mischievous urchin he once was. Billy had no intention of allowing himself to be separated from his wife and his child, but he simply smiled at her. 'You go, love. They can get in touch with Mrs Althorpe when your time comes.'

Megan bit her lip for a few moments. 'Won't Mr Althorpe wonder where I've gone? He's always dropping in for a little chat with Billy in the evenings. Then there's Dad – there'll be questions, and he doesn't like telling lies. I mean, what if people find out about Fliss not being in Switzerland?'

So many people knew the truth about Fliss. Megan could not imagine any of them giving it away consciously, but she was keen not to tempt fate. With her hands behind her back, she used the digits once more to count off all those who knew the facts. Herself and Billy, Dad, Mrs Althorpe, Deedee and Uncle Tommy, Paddy, Phyllis, Dr Walsh. Nine. 'If any more folk get told what's going on, the truth will come out.'

'It won't,' said Agnes confidently. 'You are going away on doctor's orders for a rest, and that is the whole truth, because Dr Walsh is determined to slow you down. So don't worry.'

'Worry?' Megan squared her shoulders. 'I've told you before, you're the one doing all the worrying.'

'Just one more thing,' said Agnes. 'Nazareth House is expensive, so let me pick up the bill.'

'Right,' agreed Megan. 'I don't suppose we could afford it, not just yet.'

436

Megan allowed her gaze to travel over Billy, Deedee and Agnes, began to absorb the full impact of what was expected of her. She had to go into the convent and make sure that Fliss came out of there alone. And if Fliss balked at an adoption arranged by the nuns, the child would become a Shipton.

Everyone stood still while Sidney Althorpe's car passed the house. He was taking Joe and Joseph to a sale of antiques at a big house outside Chorley. Agnes, who was supposed to have gone to Manchester by train, coloured when the others smiled at her. Lying was not coming easily to any member of this small assembly.

Dr Charles Walsh entered the house, gloved hands clapping together for warmth. 'This weather would freeze the end off your nose,' he complained. 'Who's with me?'

Agnes and Deedee claimed the privilege of riding with the doctor. 'And Tommy,' said Deedee. 'When he shapes.' She strode to the foot of the staircase. 'What are you doing up there?'

'I've lost me collar stud,' came the faint reply.

'Good job your head's stuck tight,' shouted the mistress of Twisted Stacks. 'The studs are in your casket.' She returned to the rest of the group. 'Him and his casket,' she quipped. 'It's an old cigar box that he keeps all his secrets in.' Her face softened. Tommy's secrets were a birth certificate, marriage lines and a sepia photo of his parents. But the biggest secret of all had congregated in her kitchen, each person determined to keep Agnes and Fliss Althorpe's major confidence.

Billy returned with Megan's case. 'I've got all your things in the van,' he said. 'And my case is in the porch.'

'You what?' Deedee's eyebrows all but disappeared into her hair. 'Nay, they can't be catering for expectant fathers and all, Billy. You'd not be at home in a place like that, son. It'll be all big bellies and strange cravings.'

He lifted his chin, stood his ground. 'I'll be stopping in a hotel,' he said firmly. 'That's why I laughed when Megan said she'd be leaving me behind.' He turned to

Deedee. 'Put a notice up in the workshop window, please. Tell folk we're having a holiday. The work's up to date, so nobody'll suffer with us gone.'

Megan grinned. 'You great, soft lad,' she said gently. 'Can't you manage without me?'

'No,' he said. It was the truth.

When everyone had left, Megan and Fliss sat in the visitors' parlour while shadow-like nuns flitted about moving tea things. The convent wasn't used to guests on such a grand scale. Some of the girls' parents would arrive from time to time, though many families chose to ignore their troubled members, presenting themselves only when a childfree resident required taking home.

'It's like living in church,' grumbled Megan. She pointed to a picture of St Thomas placing a finger in one of Christ's wounds. 'That didn't half put me off my sandwiches. And . . .' She swivelled in her chair, pronounced audible judgement on a nun with a hard face. 'She'd pick you up by the ears if she could. I've seen faces like hers before, usually standing behind a strap or a cane.' She patted her belly. 'Hurry up and come out, you. I'm not stopping here long if I can help it.'

'Hush,' whispered Fliss.

Megan blushed. These days, she was often ashamed of herself. A tendency to sarcasm had arrived in recent weeks, and she had fought manfully to squash it. But seeing these black-gowned women made her edgy, as she could not get her mind off the day when Mam had stood up to them. Poor Annie and Nellie, how those hard-working girls had suffered at the hands of so-called goodness.

Fliss, embarrassed because Megan had made no effort to lower her voice, almost squirmed in the chair. 'Joss is nice,' she said defensively.

'Who?'

'The one you saw last time you visited me. She looks after ten rooms. I like it here, but then I'm used to it. It's

438

. . . well . . . even the word peaceful isn't quite good enough. I think it's a holy place.' She nodded, satisfied with her announcement. 'God's here. I mean, I sometimes say funny things, especially when I look at Jesus hanging over my head. He must weigh at least ten pounds, so I worry about him falling. There'll be one over your bed, too. But really, I'm content in Nazareth House.' Sometimes, she could scarcely bear the thought of going home.

'You want your head testing,' said Megan.

Fliss laughed. 'Perhaps I do. But I understand these nuns, Megan. They have a real purpose in life.'

'So do you. Running the mills is a purpose.'

'Is it?' The older girl rose from her chair, beckoned to her companion. 'Come to the chapel. It's lovely in there, beautiful pictures of Christ all round the walls.'

'Stations of the Cross,' Megan informed her. 'All about Jesus carrying His cross up Calvary. A woman wiped His face – Veronica, I think she was called. And the picture of Christ has stayed on the cloth ever since. It's somewhere in Italy. Everything important's in Italy, including more jewels than our king has in London. But Rome's not bothered about folk like you and me, Fliss. Don't be thinking you've stepped into some perfect place, because there's nothing perfect about Roman Catholicism.' She returned a fierce stare that emanated from the hard-faced nun. 'They did nothing for Ida Entwistle, remember that.'

'Come on,' urged Fliss.

Megan stared at her friend. There was a light in Fliss Althorpe's eyes, like dull embers left in a grate at the end of the day. Fliss was calm and collected, but she was . . . Megan didn't want to think about it. If Fliss was on the brink of conversion, then Agnes Althorpe's cup of suffering would run over and there'd be trouble. 'I don't feel like going to chapel, thanks.'

Fliss dropped her hand. 'Aren't you a Catholic?'

'Yes. So's Paddy, and look how he got treated.'

'But he's happy. He and Phyllis are wonderfully suited. I've never seen him so alive.'

Megan cleared her throat. 'Marriage was his second choice. The priesthood was his calling. But he's too good to be another lackey. Look, I know what I believe. I got married in church and this baby will get its name there. I go to mass as often as I can and I make my Easter duties. But sometimes, I think all that's because I got frightened to death as a kid. Don't be sucked in.' The slamming of the door put a full stop to Megan's soliloquy.

'You've upset Sister Mary Peter. Sister Mary Peter never slams doors.'

Megan sniffed. 'My piles bleed for her,' she muttered. 'And no, I haven't got piles, but my heart stopped bleeding for the sisters years ago. Come back and talk to me after your brother's been battered with a strap. Or tell me about how marvellous this religion is when your sister's been thrashed to the last inch for being exhausted during lessons. You're not yourself, Fliss. Everyone's a bit strange carrying a baby. I speak my mind too soon at the moment. You'll get over all this, love. But I'm not going to chapel, so please yourself.'

Fliss, ever the good hostess, showed Megan to her room. Everything had been unpacked and put away. 'If you need anything, pull that rope,' advised Fliss.

Megan giggled. 'At last, I can get the ugly sisters to do as I say. Oh, what a scream.'

Fliss frowned. 'If you pull that rope, one of the nicest people in the world will dash up corridors to find you. Even if she's at mass, Joss will come to help you. It's like saying all Englishmen are bad, isn't it? Don't you think you're grown up enough to give everyone a fair chance?'

'Sorry.' And she was sorry.

'You didn't want to come here, did you?'

For answer, Megan shrugged.

'Go home if you want to.'

'No. I'm stopping here to make sure you won't take the veil while your mam's not looking.'

Fliss perched on the rim of Megan's bed. 'And to make sure I won't take the baby. Isn't that the truth? Hasn't

Mother sent you here to persuade me to get the child adopted?'

Megan tried to turn away, but the young woman's gaze held her, made her freeze like a rabbit in the headlights of an oncoming car. 'That's your business,' she replied. 'I'm here because you need somebody.'

Fliss shook her head slowly. 'No. Actually, I don't need anyone at the moment. I hope you won't mind, but I spend a lot of time in my room, just thinking.' Waiting would have been a better word. This lull before the storm had a reason, and that reason was that Fliss needed to sort out her future. If she kept the child, she could not go home. If she gave away the child, she would not want to go anywhere.

Fliss got up and walked to the door. 'Just one thing,' she said softly.

'What's that?'

'Well . . .' It had stayed with her, the sound of that orphan child screaming while doctors fought to save its mother's life. 'If anything happens to me, will you keep my baby? Will you?'

'Nothing will happen to you, Fliss.'

'But if it did . . . would you?'

'Yes.' They were sisters under the skin, so there was no need for embroidery.

'Thanks.' Fliss returned to her room and carried on waiting.

They walked along the city's walls, looked down on patches where Roman remains had been excavated. 'Central heating,' said Billy excitedly. Billy was devoted to improving his home, was forever painting, decorating and renovating. 'They even had hot pipes warming the rooms, and they built the straightest roads in the world.' One day, he and Megan would have central heating and water warmed by electricity, though they would probably continue to live on the crooked mile . . .

'Aye,' puffed Deedee. 'And if any poor beggar got in the

way of one of your straight Roman roads, he got shifted out of his hut, murdered if he refused. They were cruel, Romans.'

Agnes shuffled along at the back, her mind still filled by thoughts of Fliss. The girl had looked so contented, so . . . so ready for motherhood. Tommy paused, waited for her. 'You all right, Mrs Althorpe?'

She sighed. 'I'm fine, and call me Agnes. Don't worry about me.'

Tommy grinned. 'At least all the shops are shut. My missus would have had a lovely time spending money if it hadn't been so late.'

Paddy and Phyllis, oblivious to the rest, were standing together, arms intertwined. 'Love's young dream,' commented Tommy. 'Mind, he could do with being a bit younger.'

Agnes looked at the couple as if seeing them for the first time. 'They're lovely, Tommy,' she said. 'He's like a child looking at a great new world. And Phyllis is an angel.'

Tommy took her arm. 'Come on, don't be fretting. My Deedee'll set about you if she sees you looking so glum. She's dangerous with a feather duster, is Deedee. We'll just get young Billy settled in his hotel, then I'll drive the van home. Fliss'll be all right.'

Agnes shivered. 'I'm having some terrible thoughts.'

Tommy nodded. 'I know, because they show on your face. You should have told your husband the truth. He's a lot stronger than he was, and this is a terrible bundle for you to carry on your own.'

Agnes Althorpe looked at the rest of the small crowd. She saw Dr Charles Walsh, Paddy and Phyllis O'Riley, Deedee, Tommy and Billy. 'I'm not alone,' she said softly.

'I know that. But your man should be with you. What's up? What have I said?'

Years ago, Agnes would have done anything to avoid showing herself up in public. Yet here she stood in a major northern city, tears streaming down her face. 'I can't tell him, Tommy.' She swallowed a great gulp of pain that

442

threatened to choke her on its way down. 'His heart's bad. Very bad.'

'Oh.' He could not think of a solitary word to say.

'Our doctor told me to let Sidney do as he pleases. There's been damage done, you see, irreparable damage to the muscles of his heart. Oh, I don't understand it completely, but Sidney will simply die. All of us will, I suppose. He could carry on for a great many years, or he could just . . . well.' She straightened her hat, stiffened her shoulders. 'No-one else knows, Tommy.'

'You can trust me.'

'I know.' The tears dried under the heat of her determination. 'We discussed it, the doctor and I, and decided that Sidney should carry on working. If he were forced to stay at home forever, there would be no hope for him.' He could not die, she told herself in an effort to stop the rising tide of panic. She would carry on helping in the mills, would see that he took his tablets. 'We can only do our best,' she muttered.

Tommy nodded. 'Aye, you're right there.' He guided her towards the rest of the group. 'Any time you want to talk—'

'Yes.' She would tell Deedee about Sidney's heart soon anyway. Doris Wagstaff had become a great friend. From Doris and Tommy, she could keep no secrets.

Phil kept well back, pleased because he had no difficulty seeing them. Had this been Saturday afternoon, he might have lost them among shoppers, might have been forced to stay close enough to be recognized. An inch of growth on his chin gave birth to confidence, so he stepped nearer, could hear the voices of Agnes Althorpe and Tommy Wagstaff. He leaned against the parapet, gazed down into diggings. Temper bubbled in his chest, threatened to spill through his throat, so he gulped it back, clenched his fists, breathed deeply. She had betrayed him. Like Mam, she had turned out to be no good after all. How many more women would treat him like dirt? The answer came immediately. None. No female would get the chance to better him, not after all he'd been through.

The other girl's husband was there. He had carried Phil that night, had helped the two girls to get him inside. There was a new air of self-assurance about Billy Shipton. The head was high, the clothes were good, the stride was firm. The woman who called herself Deedee had slowed down. Her thin shoulders were stooped, while the head jutted forward slightly on a neck that seemed to have shrunk back into the spine. Old age had come very suddenly to the female who had helped Fliss to think for herself. He rummaged in the back of his mind, remembered Fliss's words. 'Mrs Duffy says your mother will never let you go, and that she's made a profession out of being your burden.' He sniffed, decided that Doris-Deedee Duffy, now Wagstaff, had played no small part in the murder of Bessie Greenwood.

'Why should I hang on my own?' he asked himself in a low whisper. 'There's others to blame.'

He walked to the opposite side of the city wall, lit a cigarette. Just outside the centre of Chester lay a battered man, his wallet, cigarette case and matches gone. Phil waved the flame until it died, inhaled the smoke born of best Virginia. They had reduced him to this. He was a man of the streets, no permanent address, few clothes, no future. Agnes Althorpe was leaning on Tommy Wagstaff's arm. The chap who had been a priest was all but drooling over that crippled girl, the one who'd been raised with Megan. Phyllis? He thought that was her name. Dr Walsh was talking to Billy, his hand pointing downward. They, no doubt, would be prattling on about the wonders of a city built upon the ruins of another.

Phil Greenwood followed them to a small hotel, stood in a doorway while Wagstaff and Walsh collected van and car. Wagstaff and Walsh – that sounded like a music hall act. It was a pity that he wouldn't get the chance to deal with all these people. But whatever he did, whomever he punished, his trail would become warm again. At the moment, he'd only killed his mother. The police knew about that, were searching for a matricidal man. As for all the robberies – anyone could have perpetrated those petty crimes. Up to now, Phil's retribution had stayed in his own family, so the bobbies weren't likely to be concerned about other people. Mother-killing was special, isolated. If he started working on similar deserving causes, he would become a mass-murderer. They were always found. But his hands itched for some kind of activity . . . Women. They were the true criminals.

He turned, walked towards his little wooden house. There were all kinds of things in the old tin trunk. Bird books, maps, a box of photographs, binoculars. Through the latter, he had found the house on the opposite bank of the Dee. At first, the woman had only looked like Fliss. After Phil had crossed the river, she had become Fliss. And she was carrying his child.

He entered his domain, picked up the field glasses, peered towards Nazareth House. Nuns would be easy. He could get past them, all right, but now there was Megan. Fliss had told him years ago that she and Megan were like sisters. Clever, women were. Devious, imaginative, cruel and selfish. He lowered the binoculars. Nuns were women, weren't they? Did the veil merely cover the same attributes, were they as wicked as all female flesh?

After another quick look, he put down the glasses and lit the stove. With a rusty knife, he shived some bread, wrapped it round cheese, ate with gusto. A baby. The bloody woman was at the other side of a swollen river and she had a swollen belly. His right hand gripped the knife, made stabbing movements into the air. Why should she be allowed to carry on living? She would have company, and he had provided her with that. His child. His son. Her life was going to be comfortable, because she would have someone to fetch and carry for her.

Two cups of hot tea with sugar calmed him. 'You were right, Mam,' he whispered into the darkening room. 'Fliss Althorpe was not for me. I should have listened.'

SIX

'It's a shame,' declared Megan. 'He's having a lovely holiday, is my Billy. I bet he's dug holes in every field between here and Wales. Looking for Romans, he is. I hope he doesn't find any, 'cos they'd be a bit dead by this time.' The backache chose this moment to remind her that she was in labour. 'I know I asked you to be quick,' she told her unborn sitting tenant. 'But I said nothing about lightning. And I never got warned about pain in my back,' she moaned. 'I feel as if I'm splitting in two down the middle of my spine.'

Sister Mary Joseph threaded her needle, winked at Fliss. Megan was one of the lucky ones. Very rarely did the nuns tend a mother-to-be who had a husband, because most 'legitimates' avoided Nazareth House on account of its reputation. 'You'll see nothing till past midnight, Megan,' she prophesied. 'First babies have a habit of staying put for quite some time. Anyway, we'll not be interrupting your husband's pastime until the baby's born. So just be patient till I darn Mother Mary Benedict's stockings. For stockings, she's a woman to be wondered at, for she goes through more pairs than the rest of the convent put together.'

Megan groaned. 'I've changed my mind,' she said. 'I don't think I want a baby after all.'

Joss winked again. 'A bit late in the day for that, isn't it? Relax. When the pain burns, pant like a dog.'

Megan, who had already decided that giving birth would not be a dignified process, was not prepared to breathe like a sweaty canine. She gripped the sheet, ground her teeth, tried to keep the screaming inside her head. 'You shouldn't be here,' she told Fliss. 'It'll put you off.'

Fliss shrugged. 'Put me off if you like, but it's got to happen to me as well. From where I'm sitting, it doesn't look so bad.'

'Huh.' The pain had moved to the front, felt like a steel cage compressing her abdomen. 'From where I am, it's blinking terrible.'

Joss poked the needle through frayed lisle, glanced at Fliss, did a swift double-take that caused her to drop everything. 'Oh no,' she said. 'Not you as well. Haven't I enough on with Megan?' She threw down what was left of the darning, pulled Fliss from the chair. 'Look, your waters have gone.'

Megan, dry as a bone, fixed her eyes on Fliss. 'Trust you to do it backwards way about, eh? Where are you two going?'

'Labour room.' Joss flung the words over her shoulder. 'I'll be back to bring you down in a minute.'

'Can we be together?' asked Fliss. 'And why am I having no pain? Is the baby all right? Why is Megan starting with contractions before . . .?

Megan stared at the ceiling as Fliss's voice faded away along the corridor. Fliss was going to do one of two things. Either she would enter the sisterhood, or she would bring her baby home. Whatever, there promised to be trouble.

They lay side by side in the labour ward, hands joined in the space between the high beds. 'If she tells me to push again, I'll spit at her, I will.' Megan put out her tongue at Mary Francis, the little nun who supervised most births. 'I went to a school run by your lot,' she shouted, pain making her careless of what she said. 'And they were cruel till my mother sorted them out.' She thought about Mam, who had gone through this agony ten times. 'So we were all right then.' After a huge pain, she finished her story. 'Till my mother died and everybody burned to death except me, my dad and our Joseph.'

'God have mercy.' Mary Francis blessed herself.

'And now, here I am with nuns again. Why have all the worst times been with nuns?'

'Perhaps we're sent to help,' answered the good sister.

'No.' Megan pushed, waited, breathed again. 'You were sent to make the problems in the first place. Have you still not got this baby out? How long have we been here, Fliss?'

Fliss, who was determined to make no fuss, felt as if she'd been here for ever. The pain was so huge that it filled her body and her mind, eliminated any possibility of sensible thought. She did everything she was told, kept hold of Megan's hand, fixed her eyes on Joss's face. The clock said ten-thirty, so they had been here for about five hours. Sweat trickled down her face, down her neck, between her breasts. Soon, she would tear wide open. Whatever was happening was going to kill her.

'Fliss?'

'Yes?'

'You're quiet,' said Megan.

'I'm busy.'

'Oh.' Megan screwed together every last vestige of strength, pushed with all her might, almost squashed her friend's fingers. At last, a high-pitched scream reached her ears, and she saw the child hanging in mid-air, all pink and purple and angry. 'Is that mine?' she asked.

'It certainly is,' replied the midwife. She slapped the baby, and the crying increased in volume. 'See?' said Megan. 'The minute you're born, they start on you.'

The nun grinned, looked almost human with her veil pinned back. 'It's a girl,' she said happily. 'With all its fingers and toes. Here.' She placed the infant on its mother's chest. 'What will you call her?'

Megan stared down into a crumpled, crimson face. 'Fred,' she answered absently. 'She's been Fred till now. I think I might call her Helen.' The baby looked more like a Helen than a Freda. One of her sisters had been called Freda, a nice little girl with too much responsibility. But this new old-looking child was definitely a Nellie, though Helen was nicer, posher.

448

Mrs William Shipton swallowed, was suddenly remembering her mother. 'We had a new baby nearly every year, except for during the war. She only wanted boys . . .' She thought about Albert under the wheels of Phyllis's ambulance, saw Harold's face as it became thinner and sadder during those dark days after diphtheria. 'One of my sisters was baptized Helen, only we called her Nellie. The girls were all blonde but for me.' She turned her head, saw Fliss's pain. 'Come on, love,' she whispered. 'If I can do it, you can. Push with the pain, Fliss.'

Five or six minutes later, Fliss's son was born. As she looked at the tiny boy, Megan's grief overwhelmed her. He had no dad. Worse still, the little one's father was the subject of a manhunt that could only end with the hangman's noose. She cried so fiercely that the nuns wheeled her bed into the corridor as soon as the afterbirth had been delivered. 'I'm sorry,' wailed Megan.

Joss nodded. 'I never did think it was a good idea for you to be here. Fliss is a tender soul, and so are you under all that defiance.'

Charles Walsh bustled down the corridor. 'Am I late?' he asked. 'I've been inundated. There's a measles epidemic and the car's gone rheumatic on me—' He stopped, looked at Megan. 'What's wrong? Sorry, I left as soon as I could after Mother Mary Benedict's phone call. What is it?'

Sister Mary Joseph took him on one side, explained about the two births. 'Megan should not have been brought here.'

Charlie nodded. 'She's here at the request of Fliss's mother. May I see Miss Althorpe, please?'

The nun directed the doctor towards his other patient. More footfalls clomped along the mosaic floor. Megan, recognizing the heavy steps, knew who was coming, so she dried her eyes fiercely, rubbing the cuffs of her nightgown over her face. 'It's a girl,' she told him, pulling the shawl well back from her daughter's face. 'Helen, I thought.'

Billy's face seemed to cave inwards. 'Oh, God,' he muttered irreverently. 'We did it, Megan.'

She made herself grin. 'Not so much of the "we", Billy Shipton. I didn't notice you in there when I was doubled up in mortal agony. Where've you been?'

'Have you seen her eyes?'

''Course I have. Where've you been? You were supposed to be coming back during evening visiting.'

At last, he heard her. 'I've been here all the time. They told me you were in labour, asked me if I was a Catholic, then dragged me in for the benediction. Nice singing, but I wanted to be with you. The sisters kept giving me cups of tea and lectures about leaving you in peace to get on with the job. Megan – she is beautiful.'

Megan would not have used that particular adjective, but she knew what he meant. A piece of both of them was lying in her arms, a living, breathing part of their love. 'She's us, yet she's separate.'

'Aye. It's like a miracle, isn't it?'

'I wish . . .' Her voice cracked.

'What, love?'

'I wish our Nellie and our Annie were here. And Freda and Hilda and Sarah—'

'And my mam and our Fred.' He blinked. 'Would you really have called him after our Fred?'

'Yes.'

'I thought you were joking,' he said.

'I never joke, Billy.'

'Eeh, I do love you, Megan Duffy-as-was.'

'No, you don't.'

'I do.'

She smiled. 'It's all right. I was only joking.'

He stopped at the end of the drive, tried to lose himself in the shadows of overhanging trees. She was in there. Billy Shipton was in there, too, but he was official, because he was married to Megan Duffy. The anger swelled up, filled his head, made breathing so difficult that he had to open his mouth and swallow the air. His hands were covered in a slick of icy sweat. Inside Nazareth

House, a woman was carrying his child. Bessie Greenwood had ruined his life, now another woman was cheating him.

'She should have told me,' he muttered softly. The exhalation hung in the air, as if the sentence were leaving its mark in crystals of frost. Lately, the words 'she should have told me' had been chanted over and over in the hut and out on the streets. He had given up beating men, had chosen instead to target women. Women didn't always fight back, and women carried shopping money. Today, as he had laboured over a victim, he had chanted the phrase, had used it as a rhythmic accompaniment to the rise and fall of the crowbar. Had she been breathing at the end? Did it matter? His belly was full and the new scarf and coat were warm. Sometimes, he thought he might be going insane . . .

He stepped back into the bushes as a car came down the drive. It was the doctor's car. Dr . . . Walsh. Dr Walsh was the one who attended most accidents at the Althorpe mills. 'Althorpe,' he said aloud. He fingered the leaves of an evergreen, tried to work out what to do next. Soon, there would be a baby. Had Walsh been a visitor, or had he come to deliver a child? And was the child his, or was it Shipton's?

Lights went out, others came on. Billy Shipton walked down the path, seemed to be floating above the flags. So Billy had become a father. Disappointed with the realization, Phil turned away, followed Billy at a discreet distance. Billy would be doing all right for himself, no doubt. The Duffy girl was talented, had a way with leather. Briefly, he played with the idea of relieving Billy of some cash, but he dismissed the thought. Billy was a man, and men were women's victims. Also, Billy had carried him home that night . . . But so had Fliss.

He loitered near a house, waited until Billy had turned the corner. The difference was that Billy had helped out of decency, but Fliss Althorpe had acted just to save her family name. She had insisted that there was no baby. To protect her parents, she had lied to a man she had pretended to love. She deserved punishment. So, this was why he'd stayed on the loose. God was good after all. The Almighty had decided that Phil Greenwood should see his baby. Seeing the child would not be enough. He must take it away from Fliss, must make sure that it got a proper upbringing. If it turned out to be a girl, he would rear her to respect men. A boy would be easier to bring up, because a lad could be warned about the predators. Life might get complicated, but he didn't mind that. Company. A child would be company for him.

After watching Billy Shipton returning to the hotel, Phil crossed the river and went back to his hut. It was cosy now. The card table sported a red-and-white checked cloth and a vase of stolen flowers. If he padded the inside of the trunk, it would serve as a cradle. Babies cried, though. He would need nappies, milk, bottles, little clothes. And some brandy. Mam had always said that a drop of brandy in the milk made babies sleep.

From a pocket, he pulled matches and a stub of pencil. In the meagre light shed by a single candle, he made out his shopping list, then drew a plan of Nazareth House. The latter was not complete, as he was working from what he'd seen of the comings and goings. But Fliss and Megan were on the ground floor, which fact made things a great deal easier. But first, he had to make sure that his child had been born.

He threw himself into bed, wrapped the blankets tightly around his chilled frame. Tomorrow, he would take the binoculars and watch the convent all day. A convent was run by women, so he could scarcely contain his excitement at the thought of overcoming them. Soon, he would be a dad.

Christopher Althorpe was three days old. 'I can't do it,' his mother said. 'They wanted to take him away as soon as he was born, and I wouldn't let them. This is awful, Megan. I can't do it.'

Fliss had been saying the same things for days. She wasn't going to give up her baby, hadn't an idea where she would live, how she would cope on her own. And Megan had been doing the listening.

'I can't, Megan.'

'I know.'

Fliss patted her son's back, waited for a burp to indicate that the brand new stomach was getting used to holding food. 'I beg your pardon?'

Megan shrugged. 'Well, I've done my best. If you still want to keep him after all I've said, then good luck to you.' She looked down on her own baby's head. 'I tried to put myself in your position, tried to imagine how it must feel. There's nothing in this world that could make me part with our Helen. Anyway, Sister Mary Joseph says your mam's coming today, so happen you can sort something out. He could live with us, you know. I'll be working from home, mostly in the evenings, 'cos this little lass will take some minding. Ouch!' She inhaled against the discomfort of breast-feeding. 'She needs a whole herd of cattle to herself, this one.'

Fliss gritted her teeth against her own pain. Her milk-burdened breasts were bound with bandages, as she had been dissuaded from feeding Christopher. According to Joss, the bond between a mother and a suckling child was almost unbreakable. 'I'm removing this suit of armour,' she announced. 'And I shall feed him myself. They thrive better on mother's milk, don't they?'

'Wait,' begged Megan. 'Let yourself decide from the head as well as from . . . from your instincts. What's best for him, Fliss? I mean, what if your mother won't help? You'd have no money at all, nowhere to live and—'

'I've plenty,' said the older girl rather sharply. 'Every payday, I've banked the cheque, because my parents wanted nothing from me. And money was invested for both of us when we were children.' She paused, gave consideration to her mother's constant unhappiness since Geoff's disappearance. With her son and her daughter fled, what would become of Agnes Althorpe? But the pull between Fliss and this infant boy was stronger than any guilt. He had to come first, for ever. 'So I can get a house and live comfortably for at least five years – possibly ten.'

Megan chose to remain silent. There was the birth certificate to think about for a start. Christopher's father was a hunted man, so Fliss would not put Phil Greenwood's name in the section requiring a father's nomination. Father unknown? Wasn't that worse? And could Mrs Althorpe allow Fliss home with an illegitimate son? It was all very well to talk about buying houses and living somewhere or other for five years, but what about the long-term future?

'I'm going to disappear,' said Fliss softly. 'There's nothing to keep me here—'

'Your mam's coming in a couple of hours.'

Fliss nodded. 'I know. And I'm going to make sure I stick to my guns. This is my son.' She placed the child on Megan's bed, took scissors from a sewing basket, then cut through several layers of bandage. When her upper body was freed, she almost cried, because the discomfort was intense. She put down the gondola-shaped feeding bottle and put the child to a breast. 'See? He's taking the milk gladly now.' Nothing else mattered. Christopher was a large, healthy child with long limbs and a shock of thick, black hair. But he had fretted on bottled milk, and now he would be fine.

'I warned you, Fliss.' The Irish voice was sad and low, held no criticism in its gentle tones. 'So, you will be keeping him.' This was not a question.

'Yes. When I'm stronger, I'll find a place for the two of us.'

Sister Mary Joseph gave Megan a knowing look. 'Will you tell your mother today, Fliss? Isn't she just now on her way?'

Fliss nodded, but kept her eyes fixed on the hungry child. 'I'm going to have a rest,' she said. 'Whatever I say to Mother will need working on.' She covered the feeding child with a shawl, walked to the door, smiled at Joss and

Megan. 'A good sleep for me and Christopher now,' she told them. 'Because we've a hard time in front of us.'

When Agnes Althorpe arrived at Nazareth House, the place was already in uproar. A new mother had gone missing, had taken her baby out into a bone-chilling February afternoon. Megan, in floods of tears, was blaming herself. 'When Geoff told me he was going abroad, I took no notice. And now, even though she said she was leaving, I hadn't the sense to realize she meant now, today.'

Agnes was guided to a chair next to a night light that burned all day beneath a statue of the Sacred Heart. 'I don't believe this,' she kept repeating. 'Not Fliss, no, no. Not both of them. Why, why? I don't believe—'

'Drink this,' ordered the nun.

'What is it?'

'Brandy.'

'I don't want brandy, because I need to be sharp. How long? How far can she have got? Her clothes – did she take them all? Megan, do stop crying, dear. I can't think while you're sobbing like that. But Fliss? Fliss would not do this to me, to her father. What shall I tell him?' She wrung her hands, rocked back and forth in the chair. 'My husband – he's not a well man. All these months I've protected him. How do I explain this to a man with a heart condition?'

Megan's sobs began to subside as she took in the size of Agnes Althorpe's latest problem. It would have been easier if Fliss had told her father the truth right from the start. Now, the poor man would be faced not only with a pregnant daughter, but with a no-longer-pregnant Fliss who had gone missing with an unwanted grandson. She swallowed, hung on to what was left of her composure. 'Sister? Please contact my husband – he's staying at the King's Head. Tell him to get to the train station. Then send the police to the terminus where the trams stop. And there's charas, too, them that go a long way on day trips. She'll not be going to Bolton. Hotels and boarding houses

455

and tea rooms – she'll be needing a sit down and—'

'Hold the horses back awhile,' said Joss. 'Our Mother Superior has already alerted the police. And I'm sure they know their job, Megan.'

Agnes stared ahead, her lips moving as if in silent prayer.

'She's going to buy a house, Mrs Althorpe,' said Megan. 'Last time I saw her, she said she'd enough money for five or ten years. She might rent a place. You can't do that in a day, can you? I mean, she'll have to sleep somewhere tonight. You can't stop out long with a three-day-old baby.' She ran to the door of her room. 'I'm going after her,' she told them. 'Please see to Helen, sister. I'll be back to feed her tonight – ask if one of the other mothers will feed her – or give her a bottle.'

'No,' said Joss, her tone unusually stern. 'Seven more days you will be here. During those days, we are responsible for your welfare.'

'And for Fliss's,' answered Megan cuttingly.

'This is not a prison.' The nun's face was stained with embarrassment. 'She was a free woman.'

'So am I.'

Sister Mary Joseph pulled herself to full height. 'We didn't know about Fliss's intentions. In fact, we are all convinced that she left by climbing through her window, because it was wide open. But I would be at fault if I were to allow you outside.'

'You can't stop me.'

Joss nodded. 'True. But I can send for a man who will stop you. If one of our doctors expresses concern for your condition, then he can force you to stay simply by getting another doctor's signature to his opinion. New mothers are notoriously unbalanced for quite some time after the birth.'

'You wouldn't,' breathed Megan softly.

'Try me,' answered Joss.

Agnes pulled herself back into the here and now. 'She's right. Stay where you are, child. Remember – I am paying for you to be cared for properly. If I can't look after my daughter, I can surely attend to your safety.' She paused, ran her tongue between her lips. 'I take it that Fliss has decided to keep the child?'

'Yes,' chorused the other two.

'Then we must support her,' announced Agnes. 'The shame we might suffer is outweighed by her need for us. She must bring him home.'

In that moment, Megan realized what a wonderful person Agnes Althorpe really was. There were mothers of illegitimate children confined to mental hospitals, erring daughters of rich families who could not bear to live with the stigma. Although Agnes must surely fear the outcome, she was willing to sacrifice all for Fliss. 'You are a real mother, Mrs Althorpe,' she said.

Agnes smiled weakly. 'Megan, go back into your room and look after Helen. We shall find Fliss and the baby without—'

'Christopher,' Megan told her. 'He's called after the saint who carried Jesus over a river.'

'We'll find them,' said Agnes with as much conviction as she could muster.

A door at the end of the corridor burst inward. 'Megan!' yelled Billy. 'Mrs Althorpe!' He pounded along the mosaic floor, his haste seeming to threaten the stability of the building. 'He's outside.'

Megan gave Billy the once-over, noticed how untidy and breathless he was. 'Slow down, Billy. Who's outside?'

'I was.'

They all turned slowly, Megan and Agnes blanching as they recognized the man in the doorway. Megan shivered, hugged herself tightly. Agnes, after an audible gulp, managed to frame a word. 'Sidney.' She jumped from her chair, causing it to rattle against the marble floor.

He walked to his wife's side, placed a bouquet of flowers on a table. 'Hello, Agnes.'

The woman leaned against a wall for support. 'How? Why . . .?'

He smiled. 'You don't think I believed all that

nonsense, surely? I employed a man weeks ago, after Fliss supposedly left for Switzerland. You know, Agnes, it's often the thin ones who give the game away. I know she had her clothes altered to fit, but her bearing gave away the truth. No matter how small the belly, a pregnant woman bears herself differently, shoulders back, stomach forward. Where is she? My man says he thinks the baby has been born.'

'A spy?' Sister Mary Joseph's eyebrows almost disappeared into her veil. 'I've told Mother Mary Benedict about these downstairs rooms needing blinds—' She cut herself off, remembered the seriousness of the situation. 'Sit down, Mr Althorpe.'

He refused. 'I want to see my daughter.'

Agnes seemed to rally. 'I kept it from you. I was so careful of your health—'

'And I was careful with yours,' he replied. 'I didn't want you making yourself ill by worrying about my becoming ill. So I played the game. Now, where is she?'

No-one could lay a tongue on a single word that might have been appropriate. Megan hovered in the doorway of her room, one hand on the brass knob, another covering a heart that seemed ready to jump out of her chest. Sister Mary Joseph kept an eye on Mrs Althorpe, as the poor woman seemed just about ready to throw some kind of fit. Agnes opened and closed her mouth like a goldfish, her face drained of colour, her hands screwed into tight knots.

'Well?' Sidney's concern showed in lines of tension that distorted his face.

Megan bit her lip. 'She's gone,' she said at last. 'A while ago. She's keeping the baby and—'

'Of course,' barked Sidney. 'I've known Fliss long enough to realize that she wouldn't go through with an adoption. I was going to set her up somewhere, make her out to be a widow. Liverpool, I thought. She could have worked on the import side—'

'Shut up!' yelled Agnes. 'As if any of that matters. Where is she?' Agnes had never used the term 'shut up' for as long as Sidney could remember. 'Be quiet, please,' she added by way of apology. 'We must think.'

'My fault,' muttered Sidney. 'I should have told Fliss. I should have said that I knew about her condition.'

Agnes eyed him suspiciously. 'But you didn't want her to bring the child home, did you?'

He coloured. 'No. We are a family of some standing. And, of course, with Phil Greenwood being on the loose, I've been afraid of his turning up to claim paternity before going to the gallows.'

Agnes moved forward and placed her hands on her husband's shoulders. 'God bless you,' she said quietly.

Megan decided it was time she spoke up. 'There is a compromise, you know. I'm still willing to pretend I've had twins. They can both come home and live with me and Billy, and no-one needs to know about it. That way, Fliss could still be with her little boy, but she'd not get treated as a loose woman.'

Sidney swallowed hard. 'You're a good girl, Megan. Let's find her first, sort out the details afterwards.'

Sister Mary Joseph, touched by the scene, dabbed at wet eyes with a handkerchief that looked too starched to be of comfort. 'Jesus will mind them,' she said hopefully.

'Will He?' Megan opened her door, listened to her baby's hungry sobs. Where had Jesus been the night of her sisters' deaths? Where had He been when Phyllis's mam decided to string herself up in the back kitchen? 'Mr Althorpe, get out there and wake the police up, please. I've got . . .' No, she must not mention the awful feeling of dread that sat in her chest. 'I'm worried.'

'We're all worried.' Agnes moved her hands and straightened Sidney's tie, smoothed his beard. 'Come on,' she told him. 'It will be better if we find her, because the police may ask questions. Fliss is a truthful girl, and she may be weak enough to name the baby's father.'

'God forbid.' Sidney looked as if he were grinding his teeth, so tightly did he hold his mouth.

Joss stepped forward, offered food and drink. She, too,

was worried, because there were strange ongoings in the city of Chester. Only a few days earlier, a woman had been battered halfway to death for the contents of her shopping bags.

'No time to eat, thank you,' answered Agnes. 'Of course, it goes without saying that you must not mention the fact that my daughter . . . associated with an escaped criminal.'

The nun bowed her head. 'You have my word, Mrs Althorpe.'

Megan entered her room, picked up her baby, returned to the corridor. The Althorpes looked very small as they walked away to find their missing daughter. 'Is Jesus with them?' she asked, her voice as small as any child's.

'Yes.'

Megan looked Sister Mary Joseph full in the face. 'And the devil knows where Phil is,' she announced. When Sidney and Agnes had disappeared, Megan went in to her room, closed the curtains and fed Helen. There was a chill in Megan's bones and, no matter how many cardigans she piled on top of her nightie, she shivered for over an hour.

Phil threw her on to the bed. 'Don't move,' he growled. He straightened, looked down on the cowering woman. If she would just have a bit of sense, he might be able to allow her to continue alive. His temper simmered gently, because he was hanging on, was deliberately staying calm. She was different from the folk outside, as this was the mother of his child. So he wanted to be careful this time. A robbery was another matter. For a robbery, he needed not to think at all, was forced to jump headlong into a situation before logic could impede his progress. At the moment, he required serenity and silence. 'Don't scream,' he warned. 'Or I'll shut you up. Understand?' When the baby stopped crying, he placed it in the open trunk where a pillow served as mattress. 'What is it?' he asked, his tone menacing. 'Boy or girl?'

'Boy. Christopher.' Fliss stared up at the stranger who was definitely not a stranger, tried to squash the fear that

460

bubbled upward into her throat. He was so unkempt, so wild about the eyes. The candlelight was sparse, and he had covered his face with a scarf while bringing her to this dreadful place. But she knew him, oh yes, she knew—

'Keep still,' he commanded.

If she screamed, he would kill her. Worse than that, he might kill Christopher. She had not expected to see him again except in the form of a photograph on the front page of a newspaper. His clothes hung loosely on the spare frame, and the lank hair reached down to his shoulders once the greasy cap had been removed. 'Why?' she asked softly. 'Why are you doing this to us?'

He lit more candles, turned on her and grinned, displaying teeth that were discoloured and broken. 'I don't remember you as stupid,' he said. 'In fact, you were very clever, much too good for the likes of me. You're selfish, Fliss Althorpe. When I . . . after I'd accidentally killed my mother, you threw me out into the dark, even though my feet and wrists were bleeding. A court would have given me a better hearing. Have you never heard the saying "innocent till proven guilty?"'

She felt as if all her blood had obeyed the law of gravity by seeping through the mattress and on to the floor. There was no strength in her. Even vision and hearing seemed restricted as she took in the seriousness of the situation into which she had walked. 'Why?' she gasped. 'Why are you doing this to us? He's only a baby. None of this is his fault, so why—?'

'Why?' The smile widened, became a laugh. 'I knew I had to stay free,' he said. 'Even when I got so hungry that I'd have given myself up for a slice of bread and dripping.' He nodded vigorously. 'Even then, some part of me made me keep going. This was the reason.' He pointed to the trunk that contained his son. 'You're not having him,' he spat. 'No child of mine is being dragged up by a woman who doesn't care what happens to his father.'

She was weak, had already been drained by the birth. Nobody knew where she was. She had climbed through the window with Christopher in a blanket, had walked down the garden and straight into the path of this horrible man. He was crowing over the trunk, was reaching down with filthy fingernails. 'You know me, don't you?' he said to the baby.

'Leave him alone, please.'

He crossed the poky room in two strides, hit her across the face with the back of a hand. 'Mine,' he snarled. 'My son.' Seeming afraid of what he had done, he backed away from her. 'Don't make me lose my temper.' His voice was quieter, recognizable. This was the man with whom she had made her lovely, vulnerable son. 'When I get mad, things happen, things I can't help. It's my mother's fault, you know.'

He was crazy. Fliss blinked away the stars that had arrived with the blow, tried to muster her resources. Getting out of here was not going to be easy. But Phil would need to go outside at some stage, then she would make a move.

He read her thoughts. 'When I go out, he comes with me. I've got a pram.' He waved a hand towards a second room. 'And milk and feeding bottles. God brought me here.' He walked to the window, lifted the corner of a blanket. 'Months I've been on the run. I've been as far as Newcastle and Leeds, but something led me here. I can see your room from this window. With the field glasses, I can see right inside.'

She lay as still as stone. God hadn't brought Phil here. Some malevolent force had guided his steps. The baby would want feeding soon. Her breasts were heavy and hot, had begun to remind her that Christopher needed nourishment. 'I've begun to feed him,' she managed.

Phil wheeled round. 'Were you going to give him away? I found out about that place – I know it's for unmarried mothers. You didn't care about him, did you?'

'I've run away from there,' she mumbled. 'No-one will make me part from the baby. So I ran off.' Her stomach churned, reminded her of all the years of nervous sickness. 'They won't find us, Phil.'

His eyes narrowed. 'What?'

She coasted along on her instincts, allowed her mouth to lead the way. 'I knew you were nearby. Something told me. We're two of a kind, you and I, Phil.' She had never been a good liar, but motherhood seemed to empower her. 'We can go somewhere, the three of us. For months, I've regretted letting you go, but I was strange during the pregnancy, quite edgy and ill. Look, I've money for a house, for a fresh start. We can all be together.' She remembered now, relived that afternoon when she had looked through her window at a man on the other side of the river. His stance had been sad. She had been staring at Phil Greenwood . . .

He laughed, but there was no merriment in the sound. 'I don't believe you.'

'You must. It's your only chance of a proper life.'

His hands came up and held his head, each palm pressing on an ear. 'No, I'm not listening to Fliss,' he shouted. 'Shut up, will you? You're dead, Mother, so I can't hear you.'

An icy shiver ran the length of Fliss's spine. Although his mother was long gone, he still heeded her. She made herself look into his eyes, saw the desperation and the fear. 'Phil,' she cried. 'Don't take any notice. I'm here now, so I'll look after you. Christopher and I are all you need now. I really will take care of you.' Oh, she would take care, all right. Given a chance, she would hang him herself.

He lowered his arms. 'Will you?'

'Yes.'

'And you'll keep the police away?'

She nodded. 'We'll go to Scotland, live quietly in the wilds.'

'And get married at Gretna Green?'

Her stomach heaved again. 'That would be romantic.'

He wanted to have faith in her, needed to believe. She was his last hope, his only chance. There would never be another woman like Fliss Althorpe. She was intelligent and strong. She would nurture him, would guard him

day and night. 'Feed him,' he said. 'I'll make some tea.'
He lit the black paraffin stove, filled the kettle. 'I've some
biscuits. They're broken, but—'

'Thank you,' she replied. 'It's lovely to see you again,
Phil.' Clever? She would need to be unnaturally astute to
stay one step ahead of this lunatic. 'I'd love a cup of tea.'

She fed Christopher under her coat, could not stand the
thought of this man seeing her body. There was only one
bed, and that was small. Night was coming, and she must
get out of here fast. 'Have you an old towel? He needs
changing.'

He pulled a package from beneath the table, took out a
bundle of terry nappies. 'I got these for you. And some
pins, creams and powder, all for my son.'

She plastered a smile across her stiff features. 'I'm so
glad you thought things out, Phil. I've nothing for
Christopher, you see. The nuns asked me to have him
adopted, so I escaped with very little, because I didn't
want to make them suspicious. But we need to move on
soon. The baby should have warmth, somewhere to have a
bath. And his things will soon want washing.'

'Yes.' He could not afford to trust her, not completely.
He wanted to believe, but months on the road had taught
him not to depend on anyone. 'I've not had a bath since
August,' he said.

'We'll rent a house, a house with a bathroom.'

'In Scotland?'

'Yes.' There was a crowbar on the floor. It wasn't big,
but if she waited till he slept, she might be able to hit him
with it. The concept of lashing out made her shiver.

He passed her an enamel mug filled with tea, took the
baby. 'He's a big lad.'

Fliss sipped, tried not to worry about the germs on his
clothes. The convent had been so clean, so warm. 'He's a
strong boy,' she finally answered. 'But he'll need to be
somewhere better than this. Our son deserves the best of
everything, Phil. When can we go?'

'Tomorrow night,' he said. 'When it's dark, we'll set

out.' A thought struck him. 'Will they be looking for you?'

'I don't know.'

He nodded. 'Night will be best. There are late trains. It doesn't matter where we go at first, as long as we get out of Chester.' He dipped into the trunk, rummaged about beneath the pillow. 'This will help.' He held up a pistol. 'It's loaded and I've more bullets.' He had swapped a silver teapot for this bounty. 'I can get anything we want.' His tone was mild. 'We can look after one another now, Fliss. Will you stay with me for ever?'

She nodded. 'You know I will.'

He stared at her. 'Do you still love me?'

Fliss put down the mug, crossed her fingers under her coat. 'Of course I do,' she said.

The Chester police were busy that day. As well as working to solve the usual petty crimes that plagued the city, they were still hunting a tramp who was attacking people and stealing their belongings. Thus far, six women and two men had been harmed and robbed by one person. Each had given a description, so the force was out on the streets searching. Today, the same shabby man had tied up and beaten a woman who owned a shop. He had emptied the till into a pram before taking boxes of baby clothes. A constable and a sergeant questioned the shopkeeper, took a description, reported back to the station. Most of the other men were out looking for the robber, or for a young mother who had absconded from Nazareth House with her new baby.

Agnes and Sidney sat in the central police station, both exhausted after driving endlessly round the city. Sidney cocked an ear, listened to a conversation that filtered through from the next room. 'Agnes,' he whispered. 'We've reported Fliss and the baby as missing, so what more can we do? We should be out searching again.'

'Let's just wait for a few more minutes. Someone may arrive with news, Sidney.'

He listened again while the officers talked about the day's events. 'Agnes?'

'Yes?'

'Shush.' He put a finger to his lips, lowered head and tone. 'There's a man stolen baby clothes and money.'

She stared at him for a moment. Why on earth was he taking an interest in minor crimes when his daughter was missing?

'It could be Philip Greenwood,' he said.

'Don't be silly, dear. He's . . . he's far away.'

He nodded. 'Exactly. He's on the run, could be anywhere.' The tightness in his chest lifted slightly. 'Agnes, I'm taking you back to the convent, then I'll meet Billy as arranged.'

Agnes frowned. 'I want to stay with you, Sidney.'

'No. Stay with Megan. Wait at Nazareth House in case Fliss goes back there. She may well be regretting her sudden departure. Come along, we'll get you settled for the night.'

She allowed herself to be deposited within the convent walls, fell asleep as soon as her head hit the pillow. Sidney, reassured that his wife was temporarily out of her misery, decided to have a few words with Sister Mary Joseph. 'This man who's been attacking people. May I look at your newspaper?'

She passed it to him, blushed. 'You'll have to excuse the lace effect, Mr Althorpe, but Mother Mary Benedict cuts out anything unseemly.'

He turned to the front page, read a description of the assailant. It could have been Greenwood, could have been anybody. Beneath the legend 'HOLT'S CORSETS', a hole gaped. The Reverend Mother had probably removed a drawing of some whalebone-bound female. 'Here you are, sister.'

She placed the paper on her desk, folded her hands, waited for him to speak.

'Have you noticed anything unusual lately, sister?'

'Well, no.'

'Anybody watching Nazareth House? Any odd movements in surrounding properties or gardens?'

She shook her head, then gave the matter some thought. 'Not on this side of the river.'

Sidney stared at her in silence for a moment. 'The other bank, then?'

'Ah, I'm sure it's nothing. Though I've never known the place to be used in the winter time. It's just a shed, really, but there's a lovely family visits in the summer. One of the men likes birds, because he's always looking through glasses, you know. Still, there are birds in winter, too. Perhaps he came down just to see the ducks. I've very long sight, so although the printed word is difficult, I can see for miles. There's been someone there with the glasses. I've seen him more than once, and I've seen the sun reflected in the binoculars.'

'Was he a tramp?'

The nun smiled. 'The Dee is wide here, Mr Althorpe. I could see a man, but I wouldn't be able to describe him. Even my long sight isn't good enough for detail.'

He walked to the window of the tiny office, peered outside. 'Is it there?' he asked, pointing into the darkness.

She joined him. 'See the tall house with all the windows lit? Then, further down, another big house with just one light?'

He nodded.

'It's between the two of them. You can't see it now, because it's so dark against all the trees. But that's where I noticed a man looking at the birds.'

He thanked her and left the house.

When he opened the car door, Sister Mary Joseph appeared again. 'I'm going with you,' she said. 'I can guide you there.'

'Get back inside,' he said, immediately sorry about his churlishness. 'You don't know what you're going into.'

She smiled at him. 'And neither do you. Open this door immediately, Mr Althorpe. I won't be in the way.'

Resignedly, he helped the nun into the car and sped

round to the police station. Billy was waiting on the pavement, gloved hands beating his body to achieve some warmth.

'Anything?' he asked.

'Perhaps,' answered Sidney. 'Get in.' When Billy was seated behind him, Sidney outlined what Joss had said. 'It's almost opposite Fliss's window,' he said. 'I want to go and look at the place. Sister Mary Joseph is here to keep us on the straight and narrow.'

Billy waved a hand towards the police station. 'Shouldn't we tell them?'

The older man shrugged. 'Could be a wild goose chase, Billy. I've got to do this myself in case it comes to nothing. Let the police carry on with their own searching. If we're wasting our time, at least we're giving them the chance to look elsewhere. Why don't you go back to Megan?'

Billy shook his head. 'Not likely,' he said. 'I'm with you all the way.'

'And so am I,' declared their female companion. 'Come on, Mr Althorpe, don't spare the horses.'

They turned towards the river, drove until Nazareth House was almost opposite the vehicle. Billy peered through the windscreen. 'Is this about right, sister?' he asked.

'Yes, I'll lead the way.'

'Well,' muttered Billy under his breath. 'Coming ready or not.'

She lay on the bed, pretended to be asleep. He had gone through into the other room to lie on a couch. Fliss looked at the door, wished he'd left Christopher with her. The balance of his mind was uncertain, yet the man remained wise enough to defend himself. Had he left the child with Fliss, she would have fled.

There was no moon, and the windows were covered in pieces of thick blanket. With the candles snuffed, she saw very little, shivered on the thin, hard mattress, pulled a smelly eiderdown round her icy shoulders. How had she managed to make such a terrible mess of her life? And it wasn't just her own life any more. Now, there was Christopher to think of, a poor newborn who could not protect himself.

A noise outside startled her. Were there foxes? she wondered. Or burglars? No. This shack would never be targeted. Another sound reached her ears. Was this the cracking of a twig? She sat up slowly, tried to move noiselessly towards the door. Suddenly, she knew she was not alone. 'Phil?' she whispered.

'Keep still.' The whispered order was spat into her ear. 'It'll be a dog.'

She turned, managed to make out the shape of him. Under an arm, he carried a white bundle. The bundle breathed, hiccuped, made sucking noises. 'May I hold him?' she asked.

'No.' He placed Christopher in the open trunk, grabbed Fliss's arm. 'I'm used to the dark,' he mumbled. 'I can see for both of us, so don't worry. And the gun's in my hand.'

The baby began to cry. 'He can sense me,' said Fliss. 'He's hungry.'

Confusion reigned in Phil Greenwood's mind. There was somebody outside, somebody who had come for Fliss. Christopher's howls were travelling towards a crescendo, so whoever was outside would realize by now that the shack was occupied. He could almost smell the person who stood at the other side of the hut's flimsy door. 'Who's there?' he snarled softly.

Fliss ripped herself away from him, hurled her body on to the trunk. If that gun went off, she must save the child from certain death.

The first shot echoed round the room as if it bounced from the walls of a cavernous hole. A second explosion fought with the sound of the door crashing inward, a man's body spread-eagled on its surface. 'Fliss,' said the felled man.

She jumped to her feet, threw herself at Phil Greenwood, her hands tearing at his hair, gouging flesh from his neck and face. The gun was fired again, but she felt nothing except his blood on her hands. A second man came, dragged her outside, but she brought Greenwood with her, both stumbling over the figure on the floor. Nothing on earth could have made her release the hold. After three more shots, she began to feel tired, but she forced herself to fight on for her son's sake.

'Fliss!' screamed Billy.

For answer, Fliss opened her mouth wide and sank her teeth into a filthy hand.

'Let him go!' shouted Billy.

'My baby,' she breathed after spitting out the dirt. 'Mine, not yours.'

Phil Greenwood's hands relinquished their hold on the gun. It must be empty of bullets now, he thought. Why wouldn't she die? He felt sure that she had received at least two bullets, could not understand how she was managing to hang on so strongly. 'You said you'd stay with me,' he snarled, his hands fastening round her throat.

Fliss gulped, tried to breathe. There was pain somewhere, in her chest or her stomach – she couldn't quite pinpoint it. She was tired, very tired.

He squeezed harder. She could smell his breath, could feel his rancid hair as it brushed against her face.

'Die, bitch,' he said. 'For ever, you said. Scotland, you said.' With every word, his grip seemed to tighten.

Billy, who had been frozen by fear for several seconds, came to life, crept up behind Phil Greenwood and picked up the dropped pistol. For a moment, he hesitated, his hand seeming to test the gun's weight. Then he brought its butt down on the man's skull. A crunching of bone made Billy gag, but he repeated the blows until there was only softness left. He inhaled, knew that he had just literally beaten out a man's brains.

Fliss sank beneath the weight of the dead tramp, felt his last shudders, heard moisture gurgling in his throat. A shadow bent over her, placed a hand on her head. 'Joss?' murmured Fliss.

'Yes, it's me.'

Fliss fought the rattling in her chest. Even n̲ pain remained dull, yet she knew she had been s̲ 'Megan. Take the baby to Megan. Twins. Tell her . . . good-bye. Tell her I'm sorry. Tell everybody I'm very sorry.'

Billy turned away and vomited. The gun slid from his hand, fell with a dim thud into the grass. There was blood everywhere. He could smell it, taste it, see its blackness in the miserly light of midnight.

He pulled himself together, turned to talk to Fliss, saw her lying next to what remained of Phil Greenwood. The nun was standing very still, seemed to be praying, her hands clutching the crucifix on the rosary. Billy dropped to his knees, begged Fliss to wake, but she was not moving. Then he touched her, felt her life dripping from a huge wound in her chest. She had been shot before tackling Greenwood, then. Billy got up, ran to the hut, used three matches before managing to light a candle with hands that were almost beyond co-ordination. He stood in the doorway with his legs threatening to buckle, shone the feeble light on the man who lay in a heap on a shattered door.

Sidney Althorpe was spread awkwardly, an arm twisted beneath his upper body. There was no mark on him, yet he, too, seemed lifeless. 'No,' sobbed the young man. 'God bless you, Mr Althorpe.' His heart went out to Agnes in that moment, because the dead were dead and past suffering. Mrs Althorpe had nobody now.

The nun approached him, took his bloody hands in hers. 'Mr Shipton?'

'Yes?'

She squatted down, felt for a pulse in Sidney Althorpe's neck, found nothing but death. 'Fliss's last wish was that the baby should go to Megan.'

Billy nodded. 'I understand.'

'I must take Christopher away from here.' She could hear the baby crying in the trunk. But the condition of this young man forced her to delay leaving the scene. 'We'll try to get you warm,' she muttered. He was going into deep shock, a condition that would be made worse by the searingly cold wind. His teeth chattered loudly, and his eyes were beginning to close.

'Please,' she whispered. 'Come right inside, at least.' She helped him to climb over Sidney Althorpe's body, forced him to lie on the floor, covered him with whatever came to hand. 'Stay conscious if you can.' She lit the stove, set the kettle, peered at Christopher. The child had drifted into sleep, seemed warm enough.

'I killed him!' screamed Billy. 'I hit him and hit him till I'd smashed his brains. Megan! Megan, I killed him!'

Joss ran to Billy's side, rubbed warmth into fingers that had begun to freeze into claws. 'Come on, now,' she said. 'All that will be forgiven. You have saved a child's life.'

'But Fliss?'

'Not your fault,' she replied.

'I should have looked for him. I should have followed him and found him. We helped him to get away. On that night when he escaped from hospital . . . Oh my God,' he moaned. 'His skull was so thin. It was like cracking an eggshell.'

'Please,' she begged. 'Please forgive yourself.' She ran with the baby to the car, hoped that she would remember the little she'd learned about driving a tractor. It was important that she moved fast. While Christopher Althorpe screamed his hunger, Sister Mary Joseph closed her eyes, prayed, then set off into the night.

Billy sat on a stool and waited for the police. When they arrived, a strange calm overcame him. 'I did it,' he said. The shaking had stopped. 'Greenwood kidnapped Miss Felicity Althorpe and a new baby. I killed him.' He waved a hand towards the bloodied corpses. 'He shot Fliss, then I killed him. Mr Althorpe . . . he just died. Nobody killed him.' He shook his head. 'No, that's not true. Greenwood killed him, too, in a way.'

'You'd better come along with us, lad.'

He bowed his head in sorrow and went along with them.

SEVEN

Megan Shipton walked up and down in front of the Town Hall steps, her hands gripping firmly the handle of a twin pram. Billy had gone off to park the van in which they had travelled from Bromley Cross. Deedee, who had left her sewing business in the capable hands of Minnie Hattersley and Bertha Strong, was in the Co-op buying cheese. According to Deedee, the Bolton Co-operative Society sold the best, crumbliest Lancashire cheese in the town.

With her head held deliberately high, Megan crossed the road to look at shops, dawdled next to a window filled with shoes, bought a newspaper from a man on the corner. She imagined that she could feel the looks, was aware that many who passed by might be remembering recent reports in the presses. 'MURDERER FOUND DEAD IN CHESTER', 'FELICITY ALTHORPE KILLED WHILE PROTECTING HER NEWBORN SON.' 'SIDNEY ALTHORPE DIES OF HEART FAILURE.' And, of course, the most riveting of headlines – 'BOLTON MAN REMANDED IN GREENWOOD CASE – "I KILLED HIM," SAYS WILLIAM SHIPTON'.

It had all been so dramatic, so compelling. The only missing link was the identity of Christopher's father. There had been gossip, of course, the usual conjectures. 'Was it Phil Greenwood's baby?' How many times had that question been asked? she wondered. She missed Fliss terribly. Another lovely sister lost, another treasured life snuffed out. But she kept going for the babies, for her own Helen, for Fliss's little Christopher.

'Megan?'

She swivelled, saw a woman from the garden streets. 'Hello, Mrs Banks. How are you?'

Molly Banks bent down, pushed her head into the gap between the pair of hoods on the pram. She emerged after several seconds of 'ooh and diddums', awarded Megan a grin that owed much to the manufacturers of porcelain. 'Grand,' she declared. 'Two little smashers, they are. Do they keep you busy?'

Megan nodded.

'Well, I've allers said as how twins is hard. Used to argue with me sister over it, 'cos she had two with nobbut thirteen months atween them. She reckoned they were more trouble than twins. But let me tell you – my twins had me up the bloody pole and no mistake.'

'They're very good,' said Megan. 'Christopher sleeps a lot, but the young madam wants a lot of attention. Helen likes to be the star turn.'

The woman nodded sagely. 'Course . . .' she dropped her voice, glanced over her shoulder. 'Course, you'll have to do your best and mek sure as they're both treated same road.'

'Yes.'

Molly licked her lips nervously. 'With one of them not being yours, like.' Her hand raised itself to touch Megan's arm. 'I don't mean nothing, love. All of us just wishes you the best. We're proud of you.'

Megan felt her skin heating, managed to remain calm. 'We'll adopt Christopher,' she said. 'Once things have all been sorted out, Mrs Althorpe, Billy and I will get the papers drawn up.'

'Yes, yes. And how's Mrs Althorpe doing these days, love?'

'The same.'

'No better, then?'

'No.' Megan rocked the pram gently, sought a change of subject. 'Why aren't you at work, Mrs Banks?'

The mouth opened wide to allow a loud cackle to be born. 'I've finished, lass. Nay, I'm going on sixty-four,

474

you know. That's no grand age, like, but it were me hands as done for me. They've gone a right funny shape and they hurt summat mortal, specially of a morning.' She held up two sets of digits that bore a strong resemblance to winter trees, all twisted and gnarled. 'I can hardly open a quarter of tea.'

'I'm sorry,' said Megan. She was sorry. It was a shame for folk who worked all their lives only to finish up crippled and dependent. 'How are you managing?'

'Me daughter sees to me.' Again, the little head turned to look for spies. 'We've took a collection,' she said proudly. 'I were in charge, on account of me being what they call trustworthy, see. We thowt a lot of our boss, you know. And his daughter – well – she were just a pearl, poor lass. Any road.' She straightened rounding shoulders. 'We had a meeting down the Dog and Gun.'

'Really?' Megan's eyes searched the street for Deedee, saw no sign. This had been Deedee's idea. 'We'll go to town and do a bit of shopping, let the world and his wife see how proud we are of these babies,' Deedee had announced. And she had disappeared. As per usual.

'It's like a memorial fund.'

Megan gave her full attention to Molly Banks. 'What did you say, Mrs Banks?'

'For what you might call a 'membrance. We've got some photos of Mr Althorpe and the young miss. So we want you to put them in frames, like, them leather ones with brass corners. Then we're having one of them plaques with their names on.' She shook her head, caused the curlers to clank together beneath the headscarf. 'They mun be remembered.'

Megan held her breath for a moment. 'That is a very nice thought,' she said carefully, her eyelids moving to shift the emotion that sprang forth too readily of late.

Molly grinned again, patted her wayward curlers with a twisted hand. 'Our Molly even has to do me hair, you know. I like a few curls when I go for me gill of stout. You never can tell, I might click. I told me daughter I were

475

looking for a man, and she said, "Well, Mam, if you do click, I hope you get one as opens tins and does curlers." She gets a bit past herself, my youngest. On the cheeky side, that one.'

It was then, when the retired mill worker talked about her curlers and her gill of stout, that Megan understood the truth. They didn't care who Christopher's dad was. They didn't care about Phil Greenwood and all the trouble. This little woman was telling Megan and the whole world that the Althorpe spinners and weavers wanted to mark the passing of two wonderful people. 'Thank you, Mrs Banks,' she said.

'Eeh, it's no bother, girl. Mind, there is one thing. When the Missus is better, we want her to come down and see us all. Aye, I said I'd never set foot in yon again, not after fifty years of sweated toil. Only she were a good boss, that Mrs Althorpe. Firm, you know. Firm, but fair. Mek sure she pulls round, will you?'

'I'll do my best.'

Deedee bustled along, a huge bag of shopping dragging an arm downward. As ever, she had been for cheese and bought enough rations for a battalion. 'Molly Banks!' she exclaimed. 'Who's let you out?'

'Meself,' replied Molly. 'I got time off for good behaviour and arthritis.'

Deedee placed her shopping on the floor, declared Molly's hands to be a shame and asked had she tried dog oil. 'How's Martha Dewhurst? Did she get her operation? And Eileen Sharples – what happened about her bunions? Last I saw, she were walking about with big holes cut in her clogs.'

Megan stepped away and allowed the two old friends to indulge in their favourite topic, which seemed to be the many maladies that plagued people of their acquaintance. 'I mean, she just stood there,' said Deedee in her 'confidential' tone. 'We told her to get down to the infirmary and have it seen to quick smart. But would she? Oh, no, not Nancy Cranfield. Next news, we're all stood in a line behind the funeral procession.'

It was being so cheerful that kept them going, Megan thought.

Billy walked down Newport Street, his hands stuffed deep into pockets, head down, shoulders bent. Megan's heart went out to him. At long last, the nightmares were abating. For a while, he had even slept downstairs so that his wife's sleep would be interrupted only by the demands of Helen and Christopher. But early on, after his night with the police and his hour in court, he had relived the killing of Phil Greenwood with a frequency that had terrified Megan.

He lifted his head, saw Mrs Banks.

She hurled herself at him, grabbed his arms. 'God bless you, Billy Shipton. Aye, it's nobbut five minutes since I clattered you about the head with me pot towel. Who'd have known you'd turn out to be such a fine man?' She dabbed at her eyes, but the tears tripped shamelessly down her grinning face. 'Lad, you'd make ten of any other, I can tell thee.'

Billy allowed a faint smile to visit his lips. 'It was so quick,' he mumbled. 'There was nothing else for it.'

Megan felt the tension draining out of her upper body. It was a miracle that she'd retained enough milk for one child, let alone two. She had worried about worrying, had been concerned that her breasts might dry because of her Billy's pain. He was better. Dr Walsh had predicted that Billy would improve once he started talking about the trauma. Mrs Banks was an angel. Heavily disguised, but a saint for all that.

'I've belted him, too, in my time.' Deedee came alongside Billy and Molly. 'A whole apple pie, once, eh?' She lightened the moment by laughing aloud. 'I'd done it all nice, too, brown sugar on the top.'

'It tasted good,' he admitted.

'Cooling on me sill, it were,' added Deedee. 'Till he pinched it.'

The two women fought over Billy's crimes, each wanting to be the one who had suffered most. They went through pea-shooters, tied-up door knockers, broken windows and several dozen cakes and pastries. 'And he once pinched four punnets of strawberries from outside the greengrocer's,' laughed Deedee, determined to have the last word. 'He were sick for three days. And new bread – this lad could smell it a mile off.'

Molly howled with glee. 'It were us what made a man of him,' she roared. ''Cos our good food built him up.'

The noise attracted attention. Within minutes, a small group had gathered to join the fun, many of its members coming forward to congratulate Billy on his bravery, to praise Megan for taking on Fliss's baby.

When they finally escaped, Deedee, relieved by Billy of shopping and one of her worries, walked behind the young couple and counted her many blessings. All she needed now was for Agnes Althorpe to get better. Once that happened, her cup would run over. In fact, she would need a bucket, because no cup could possibly be big enough to contain Deedee's joy.

Charlie Walsh, though far from his dotage, had become a crusty bachelor. Years spent in and around the garden streets had set his mouth and furrowed his brow, so he looked older than his years. He placed the stethoscope in his brown leather bag, walked to the window of Agnes Althorpe's room and gazed down into beds that promised roses, dahlias and lupins. What a wonderful setting. What a lovely place in which to succumb to insanity. He pursed his lips, stuffed a hand into each pocket of his sensible jacket. 'Go mad if you insist,' he said softly. 'I suppose going off your rocker could be one of your options.'

The woman in the bed remained motionless.

'Carry on like that, and we'll send for a taxidermist,' he mumbled.

She turned, stared at the doctor's back. He was the one who was looking after Fliss. But Fliss was . . . no. She would go to sleep in a minute. Asleep, she felt nothing, didn't even dream.

'Or the undertaker,' he continued. 'He might as well measure you up, make his job easier in a few months' time. Because months is all you'll have, Mrs Althorpe, if you carry on starving yourself and lying in bed.' She was coming back out of the almost catatonic state in which she had existed since the night of the double tragedy. He had to strike now, while the iron was warming up. 'Starvation is a painful death, I'm told.'

Fliss used to starve herself. Whenever she was upset, her stomach would play up. There was someone else like that, too. Ah yes, Megan Duffy, now Shipton, had a ticklish digestive system. So alike, those two girls. She remembered a big house full of statues, nuns in long gowns that swept the floor, but she mustn't think, oh no, she mustn't—

'Fine example you are,' announced the doctor. 'The mills are sitting there waiting for you. Thank goodness you've one or two supervisors with brains and honesty.'

On the dressing table stood the bronze-lidded box in which she kept her jewels. Fliss was to have them, of course. Sidney had bought so many lovely things over the years. Sidney.

'He was a good man, one of the best,' said Charlie Walsh. 'He wouldn't be spread out there in his bed like a thing carved from granite. The longer you stay, the harder it's going to be for you to be up and about again. For one thing, your muscles will start to shrivel. Then your mind will become completely closed. After that, you'll need constant surveillance, probably in a hospital.'

Her knee twitched. Where was Sidney? A desperate unease overcame her, spreading its tentacles through her chest and into her brain. All four limbs began to tremble as this nameless, faceless terror flooded into her whole being. 'No,' she whispered. It was like being in a dark place filled with wild and angry animals, because she could not pinpoint the source of panic. When the panic reached its crescendo, she had become fear itself. It was as if she didn't exist any more. Agnes Althorpe had all but disappeared beneath the weight of something she was too small to contain. 'Help me.' Her tone was as soft as the springtime breeze that stroked the budding plants in Hall i' th' Vale's many gardens.

He walked to the bed, saw the sweat on her brow. 'That's a severe anxiety attack,' he said. 'You have to face life, Mrs Althorpe, or those attacks will become your only companions.'

She shuddered, fought to reach the surface. 'Don't drown me,' she whispered.

'Go into it,' he told her quietly. 'Go into the fear, Agnes. Let it wash over you, because it is no more than a rush of adrenaline. To come out, you must first go in.'

'Dead?' she asked breathlessly. She felt as if she had run at least a mile. Inhaling was difficult and her vision had become cloudy. 'Are they dead?'

'Yes.'

'Buried?'

'Yes.'

She had lain here in stupid isolation while Sidney and Fliss made their last journeys.

'Agnes, this is understandable, explainable. I didn't mean to be harsh, but I needed to shock you out of this stillness. Life does go on, indeed it does. You've a grandchild to think of. Megan's looking after both Helen and Christopher.' He held up a hand. 'Don't worry, the children are doing very well.'

She stared through him, past him and into a future that seemed greyer and colder than death itself. Her heartbeat slowed until it no longer echoed the sound of frenetic drums. Fliss, oh Fliss. She had given herself to that dreadful man, had— 'Is he dead?' she asked. 'Greenwood – is he dead?'

The doctor nodded.

'How?'

Understanding how little Agnes knew of recent weeks, he sat on the bed and held her hand. 'He died at the same time as Fliss and Sidney.'

The huge green eyes were suddenly alight. 'Did Sidney kill him?'

'No.' He squeezed her fingers in an attempt to offer comfort. 'Billy Shipton killed Greenwood. Your husband had a massive heart attack.' He waited for the next question.

'My daughter?'

'She was shot.'

Agnes swallowed audibly. 'So. He killed his own mother, then murdered the mother of his child.' Her words seemed to be sending away all those crashing waves of panic. She must talk, talk. 'He ended lives, so many lives,' she said.

And much more, said a voice in the doctor's head, though he kept quiet. Telling Agnes about Phil Greenwood's other crimes would have achieved nothing, but the fact that this villain had left a trail of disorder and suffering in his wake was common knowledge. 'Take it on board,' he pleaded. 'Then do something for Megan and Billy. Megan needs respite, because two babies are more than twice as difficult as one. And . . .' He paused, coughed. 'And Billy is recovering after the court hearing.'

She gripped his hand fiercely. 'Hearing?' Her tone was shrill. 'But why? What has he done to deserve judgment?'

'He was acquitted, of course, but he had to answer questions about the death of Philip Greenwood.'

Her jaw hung for a couple of seconds. 'That was wrong. He tried to save my daughter, didn't he?'

Charlie nodded. 'He's a brave man.'

'They're both brave. Megan and Billy . . . How's Doris?'

'Deedee is fine. The rheumatism plagues her, but she keeps going.'

'As must I.'

'Quite.'

She clambered out of the bed, swayed on legs that were unsure after weeks of inactivity. What had she been doing? she wondered. How had she rested while injustice hung in the air like a pall of putrefaction?

481

'Be careful,' he warned. 'You can't run on an empty fuel tank.'

'Porridge,' she snapped. 'Porridge and soup – I'm sure I can take liquids. And a tonic. You must write a message for the chemist, then Mary will fetch a bottle. Something with iron in it, something that tastes vile.' She dragged on a dressing gown, tore at her hair with a comb. 'I need something nasty to remind me of what's happened here, doctor.'

He watched her, thought about what she had to face. The Althorpes were a family of note, a moneyed clan with pride and dignity. She would have to swallow more than iron, he thought grimly. There were mills to run. There was an illegitimate child who was in the care of someone else. There was no man to share the burden, no son or daughter who might offer comfort.

She cut into his thoughts. 'I'll get better,' she told him softly. 'But I can't take that baby. He's not just Fliss's son.'

The doctor nodded. 'Whatever he is, none of this is his fault. He's just a tiny innocent.'

'So was his father during infancy.'

As there was no point in pursuing the matter, Charlie picked up his bag and made for the door. 'If you want to visit the cemetery, I'll take you.'

She stopped him in his tracks. 'I shall drive myself, thank you. And my first journey will be to help the living. For the dead, I can do nothing. Nothing at all.'

Alone, she released the tears that had lain dormant for endless days. Like a river whose banks had broken, the water poured from her eyes until several handkerchiefs lay sodden on the dressing table. Then she washed, dressed herself and went out to face an unkind world.

The world was unexpectedly gentle. Well, the portion she found in Hall i' th' Vale was sympathetic. Evelyn Grimshaw threw herself at Agnes, her weight making the embrace almost painful as she squashed the smaller woman to her ample flesh. 'You're not on your own, Agnes. I'm here and Doris Wagstaff's coming over later on. We're your friends and we'll see you through this.'

Agnes extracted herself from the too-close encounter, awarded Evelyn a watery smile. 'Thank you for coming.'

Evelyn wobbled across the room and perched on the edge of a chair that was too low for her bulk. She tortured a scrap of handkerchief, gazed up at the lady she had sought to emulate for so many years. 'These things happen, Agnes.'

'Which things?' Agnes pulled a bellrope, waited for Mary to appear.

'Awful things.' The linen was wound round several fat fingers.

'Really? I haven't noticed anyone else's husband dying just lately.' Determined not to succumb to further tears, she stared through the window, could not look at Sidney's rocking chair. He had sat there every night with his brandy. The trembling had lessened, but the fear of another panic attack was strong.

'I was meaning . . . that poor baby.'

Agnes rested a hand on the window sill, attempted to hide the shivering. When Mary came in, she ordered tea for two, tried not to see the redness in the eyes of the young woman who had served the Althorpes since leaving school.

'The child is well enough, Evelyn,' she said when the two of them were alone once more. 'The truth is that Megan is a suitable person to take him on. She and Billy will make wonderful parents. And Joe Duffy is kindness itself, so Fliss's boy will be cared for.' Agnes suddenly realized that she could trust this woman. No, the realization was not sudden at all. Evelyn had always been a good soul underneath. 'Evelyn, thank you for being here.'

'I've been here days, Agnes. Luke and I decided that I should wait for you to come round.'

'You've slept here?'

'Yes. You're my best friend, Agnes. You're not

frightened of hard work and . . . well, I think you're a very decent sort of woman altogether.'

Agnes felt the need to apologize for her absence. 'I'm sorry, but sleep was probably my medicine and my escape.'

The big woman burst into tears. 'I thought I'd never be able to tell you. But when Jeremy was sent down from the university, it wasn't just because he'd failed his examinations. I am a grandmother, too, you see.' The last words floated uncertainly on a flood of tears.

'Don't cry.' Agnes was surprising herself, because she sounded so calm, so controlled. 'Fliss waited a long time for that dreadful man. I suppose he wore her down in the end.' She turned, tried to keep her gaze averted from the rocking chair. 'Our children never hurt anyone, my dear. If Jeremy does nothing worse than fathering a love child, then you have no worries.'

The visitor dried her eyes, blew her nose noisily. 'See, you've always been so . . . so correct, Agnes. I wanted to be like you, but Luke's only a butcher and—'

'And I was a weaver.' Agnes folded her arms firmly, trapped unsteady fingers out of sight. 'When Sidney asked me to marry him, I walked about in a golden daze for ages. Then I started to worry. How could I cope with the household of a rich man? Which forks, which knives would I need to use?' She bit her lip. 'Life is so stupid, Evelyn. I read all the books on etiquette, and now I realize how unimportant it was. He's gone, you see. So has Fliss. And Geoffrey might just as well be dead, too.'

'Don't say that, Agnes.'

'I've no-one.'

Evelyn threw up her fat arms. 'You've us. There's me and Luke, then there's Doris and Megan. And that little boy's going to need you—'

'No.' Agnes was sure of one thing. Even if she had to spend the rest of her years in solitude, she would never nurture a child belonging to Philip Greenwood. 'Don't say any more. My mind is made up, and I must eat because there's work to be done. The mills need me. The workers need an Althorpe and I'm the last one, the only one.'

Evelyn thought about Christopher, kept her lips closed.

Agnes sat down when Mary fetched the tray. 'Be Mother,' she said to her friend. 'My hands are too shaky.'

Evelyn poured and watched, noted how drawn Agnes's face had become. 'Just take things slowly,' she advised.

Agnes laughed, though the sound was chilled and hollow. 'I've rested enough,' she said. 'And I'll have sugar in my tea, because I need the energy.'

There had been no trouble getting Agnes Althorpe to agree to a Catholic baptism. A crowd of people was squashed into the rear half of the church building, the portion where Megan and Billy had held their wedding reception. This was the social club attached to the church of Our Lady of Sorrows. Had Megan been in lighter mood, she might have laughed all over again at the misnomer.

Christopher and Helen had behaved beautifully throughout the service. Now, in the back half of the hut, the 'twins' were enjoying a huge amount of attention. At ten weeks of age, the babies were beginning to focus their eyes on a world that promised to be interesting.

'She's been here before,' declared Deedee for the umpteenth time as she looked into the eyes of her great-granddaughter. 'I reckon she were that queen everybody got feared to death of.'

'Elizabeth?' asked Megan.

'No, her with the horse and cart.'

Megan tried, without success, to achieve a mental picture of a monarch driving a wagon.

'Boadicea,' said Billy helpfully.

Deedee put her head on one side. 'That's the one. Her name sounds like some kind of skin disease. Where's Phyllis?'

Megan pointed to the other side of the room where

Paddy was engaged in animated conversation with Father Blunt. Next to her husband stood Phyllis, a rounded belly proclaiming that Father Patrick O'Riley-as-was would be a different kind of father within months. 'Doesn't she look well?'

Deedee nodded. 'Aye, she's even walking better. Eeh, remember when we got her, Megan? Bed under the stairs, commode against the wall, wheelchair taking up half the parlour?'

'I remember.'

'Billy and all.' Deedee winked at the 'terrible caution' who had married Megan. 'Not a word to say for himself for months after that fire.' She touched his face, ran a finger along his chin. 'Like sandpaper, that beard of yours. Did you shave?'

''Course I did.'

Deedee smiled at him. He was a lovely chap, a sensitive man who had been dealt some poor cards. 'Billy, I love you like one of me own. So does Joe.' She moved her head, located her son. 'Come here, you,' she ordered. 'Look at him. He's pretending Maureen's turned up by accident, but I'll bet a pound to a penny he asked her.' She put a finger to her lips as Joe approached.

'What do you want now, Mam?' She'd had him ragged since the crack of dawn, had he cleaned his shoes, which tie was he going to wear. If she'd questioned him about washing behind his ears, he would not have been surprised.

'Maureen Wright's looking nice. It suits her, that shade of green.'

Joe pretended to notice for the first time the woman who had hung on to his arm and on to every word for the past hour or so. 'Aye, she looks all right.'

Megan and Billy couldn't take any more. Although she had begun to believe that she'd never laugh again, Megan hastily changed an explosive giggle into a cough which she hid behind a handkerchief. Billy took a sudden and all-consuming interest in a notice board that advertised

486

forthcoming attractions. 'They've a beetle drive next week,' he managed, his tone decidedly shaky. 'And a rummage sale on the last Friday of the month.'

'Have they?' The disobedient laughter was escaping in the form of tears that coursed down Megan's cheeks. She dabbed at them, muttered on about springtime bringing on one of her colds.

Joe was not fooled. 'You don't fool me,' he said. 'I thought I were old enough and ugly enough to make me own mind up about which tie I wear and who I talk to.' This was all addressed to his mother. 'And if you really want to know, Mam, I'll be taking Maureen to the Theatre Royal next week. Balcony seats and a box of chocolates and all. Does that suit?'

Deedee wore the air of an offended angel. 'What's on?' she asked sweetly.

'Variety,' he replied with dignity. 'There's a comedian, two singers, a magician and some performing dogs. If you want to know any more, I'll write a full list and post it to you tomorrow.' He stalked back to Maureen.

Megan mopped her face. 'Deedee, you shouldn't torment him.'

'Me? Any road, why do you think we have kids if it's not to keep us young and give us a bit of pleasure?' She beamed broadly. 'There'll be another wedding come summer, just you mark my words.'

The door that led to the church opened slowly. Megan, who was facing in the wrong direction, saw Deedee's expression change. 'What's up, Deedee?' she asked.

'Nowt. Don't turn round, either of you.'

Megan and Billy froze like a pair of statues. Across the room and towards the rear, two bundles were being passed from hand to hand. These babies were getting ruined, thought Megan ruefully. Helen would carry on something woeful later on, because she loved playing to an audience.

Billy nudged his wife. 'What's going on, Megan?'

She shrugged, glanced at her grandmother. 'Wait a

minute,' she advised. 'If Deedee says stand still, we stand still.'

A hand touched Megan's shoulder. 'For the children,' said a quiet voice.

'Hello, Agnes.' Deedee's face threatened to split in two. 'Are you going to have a bite? We've some nice bits and pieces, scones and tasty sandwiches.'

But Agnes shook her head, directed her words to Megan and Billy. 'I want to thank you,' she said softly. 'For being such good friends to my daughter and to me.' She pushed an envelope into Billy's hand. 'That's for whatever you may need for Helen and . . . and for Christopher.'

Billy muttered a word of thanks.

'Do you want to see the babies?' asked Megan eagerly. 'He has a look of . . . Well, he's a nice looking little thing, very well-behaved.'

'No. I must go now, because I've things to do.' Agnes smiled at Deedee, turned and walked out of the hall.

'Give her time,' advised Deedee. 'She'll come round.'

Billy's hand shook as he read the envelope's contents. 'Five hundred pounds,' he breathed. 'My God, we could buy a house with this.'

Megan took the cheque, pored over it. 'No. This goes straight in the bank for Christopher.'

'It's for both of them,' insisted Deedee.

Megan shook her head. 'No,' she declared firmly. 'This is for Fliss's baby. After all, our Helen's got everything she could want. Christopher's got no mam.'

Deedee shrugged. 'You can't buy a mother, lass.'

'I know,' answered Megan. 'But if he can't have Fliss, this might buy him a chance of something else, like a business or a house to live in. I know you can't buy a mother, Deedee. You've either got one or you haven't.'

Deedee inclined her head. Not all the tea in China could have made Tess Duffy into a proper mother. 'All right, love,' she said. 'Whatever you say.'

Tommy arrived at his wife's side, gave her a prod. 'Hey, was that Agnes Althorpe?' he asked.

Deedee rolled her eyes. 'That's what I've always liked about you, Tommy Wagstaff,' she muttered. 'You're so quick to notice things.' She took his arm. 'Come on,' she told him. 'We've a christening cake to cut.'

Megan held Billy's hand. 'Let's go and rescue the crowd from our children, love.'

Joe Duffy looked at his daughter, watched young Joseph cooing over Christopher and Helen. He was an uncle now, was little Joseph. How strange life was, he thought. A family lost, then a family gained. He turned to his companion. 'Are we ready for a bit of cake, then?'

Maureen nodded. Where Joe Duffy was concerned, she was ready for anything.

EIGHT

The young man strode along Dog Leg Lane, a suitcase in one hand, a canvas sack strapped to his back. He was tall, in his early twenties, broad about the shoulders, dark-haired, erect in stature. When he reached the sharp bend in the rough track, he dropped his luggage and stared ahead, seeming to drink in the sight of Hall i' th' Vale with the thirst of a desert nomad. It was still beautiful, but smaller than he remembered. Everything was smaller. The Town Hall clock, which had seemed enormous, was no longer as impressive as it used to be. Mill chimneys still dominated the sky in town, but they were not the monsters of his dreams.

He picked up his bags, strode forward. Footsteps approached, and he turned to see a man walking towards him. He had mouse-coloured hair, a pale skin and lean but muscular limbs. 'Billy?' he shouted. 'Is that Billy Shipton?'

Billy stopped in his tracks. There were still several yards between the two of them, so none of the visitor's features was clear enough. Whoever this was had enjoyed a lot of sunshine, thought Billy. 'Oh heck,' he said under his breath. It wasn't, it couldn't be. Geoff would have written first, would have told his mother – wouldn't he? After all these years? 'Geoff?'

'That's me,' replied the man jauntily. 'I've come back to face my punishment. Father was furious, I suppose?'

Billy nodded. 'It was your mam suffered the most,' he replied.

Geoff dropped his burdens again, ran down the lane and clapped Billy on the back. 'Good to see you,' said Geoff cheerfully.

Billy's hand was pumped up and down in a vice-like grip of greeting. 'Well . . .' Billy licked his drying lips. 'Is your mother expecting you?' He knew the answer, but occasions demanding small talk were not Billy's favourite events. 'You're looking very well,' he added lamely.

Geoff knew he looked well. The sun of several Australian summers had warmed his skin, while work had tightened muscle and sinew. 'Thank you.'

'So.' Billy won his hand back, wondered if any fingers were broken. 'You've come back, then.' What a stupid thing to say. Hurriedly, he appended, 'for good? Are you stopping?'

Geoff shook his head. 'For a while.' He glanced down the lane. 'Are you still living hereabouts? The parents were just about to move into the Hall when I . . . emigrated.'

Billy jerked a thumb over his right shoulder. 'We live in the Gate House at the other end of the lane.'

'Ah. And is everyone well?'

Billy shrugged. The living were well and the dead were buried. How much did this man know? Had he heard about his father and his sister? No. There was too much levity in the voice, too much courage in the stance. 'All right, I suppose.'

'You came up here with the Wagstaffs, didn't you?' Without waiting for a reply, Geoff continued, 'with that splendid woman they called Deedee. And . . . er . . . and a girl called Megan Duffy.'

'That's right.'

Geoff studied the lad who had chased Megan round Althorpe Number One, the one who had always been close to Megan. Too close. 'Remember that day in the mill yard when you wanted tubes as firelighters? And Megan and Fliss came out tarred and feathered? I'll never know how Megan's grandmother kept a straight face when we arrived in Holly Street.'

'I remember,' said Billy. 'I was doubled up in a corner, because I'd never seen anything so funny, even at the pictures.'

Geoff nodded. 'We ought to have taken photographs.'

After a short silence, Billy asked, 'How's Australia?'

'Wonderful.' Geoff launched into a long lecture about the mining of ores, the development of sheep farms and the need for transport systems. Billy listened, his nervousness increasing. Not once had Geoff asked about the Althorpe family's welfare. Surely he would ask after Fliss and his father soon?

Geoff stared past Billy, fixed his eye on the lane. He had made it. He had managed without Father, without Mother, without Fliss and without education. Like Megan, he had found his gift, and his gift was the mining of opals. Oh, the machines he had built and the sifting systems he had invented. The future promised great things. Already, he had started to reap a little of what he had sown. His name had begun to resound in mining circles, because he knew how to work, how to delegate, how to invest. At least, the name Douglas Mann was famous. But he'd come home to find his papers, to prove his identity and to find the girl he had loved for so many years. Even in Australia, he would need papers to get married. 'Is . . . is Megan well?'

'Yes.'

'Her father, her brother?'

'Champion.'

'Oh. Right.' He would go to visit his parents first, as that was the right thing to do. But really, he ached for Megan Duffy. She wouldn't be married yet, as she was only about nineteen, and that leather business should be out of her system by now. When she heard about the ranch, when she saw the acres he owned and the house he had built for her . . .

'How long have you been back?' asked Billy.

Geoff shrugged. 'In England? Oh, a couple of weeks. We docked in Southampton, so I took the opportunity of seeing London on my way up here. I bought gifts for Mother and Father and Fliss.' For Megan, he had carried from Australia a necklace of rare black opals.

492

Billy staggered against the hedge as if he had been hit by a brick. The man was a weak beggar, but he didn't deserve this. He didn't know. Geoffrey Althorpe had come all the way from Australia, and he had no idea that his father and his sister were dead, that the love of his life was wed and saddled with two babies.

'Are you all right, old man?'

'Fine, ta. No, I ate something yesterday, a bit of fish that tasted off. So I'm a bit below par.'

Geoff nodded quickly. 'Still with Mr and Mrs Wagstaff, are you?'

Billy, for want of ideas, mumbled something akin to assent.

'I thought for a while that Megan might marry you, but—'

'Come and see her,' begged Billy. 'She's in, because the leather shop's closed for a few weeks.' He dug around in his brain. 'Refurbishment.' It would all come better from Megan, he thought. At last, Billy was able to talk about the death of Phil Greenwood, but he always chose his audience carefully.

'Megan's still working, then?'

'Off and on, like.' That, at least, was the truth, as Megan had been too busy with Helen and Christopher. 'Come on, then.'

'I should see my parents first.'

Billy swallowed a sudden surge of moisture in his mouth. 'Er . . . your dad's not there, and your mam might be out and all. But Megan's in.'

He didn't need much persuading. After combing his hair and stashing the luggage beneath a bush, Geoff accompanied Billy to the Gate House. On the way, he regaled Billy with tales of wide expanses of country, kangaroos tame enough to be hand-fed, wallabies that were born comedians. 'I've built a ten-roomed house,' he said proudly. 'It can be expanded, of course, as there's no shortage of land. I live near enough for schools and shops, far enough to be private. I've got several horses,

493

my own sheep and pigs, a few hens. I've . . .'

He didn't half ramble on, thought Billy as they neared their goal. Every sentence began with 'I'; every word sang its praises to a man who had walked out on his family. Not once had he asked after Agnes, Sidney or Fliss. 'I'll leave you here, then,' he said when they reached the gate. 'But first, I want a quick word with Megan. In private, like.' He shot into the house, leaving Geoff Althorpe standing mid-sentence near the gate.

'I couldn't let you face him without a warning,' said Billy to Megan. 'Only talking about it, saying what happened, it's . . . well, I can't do it to him. I'm sorry, love.' He shook his head sadly. 'I can't carry all the bad news Geoff needs to hear. He loved you, Meggy. I think he still does.'

'Never mind,' she said softly. After the passing of a couple of months, Billy was all right, but she wanted him to stay that way. 'Wheel him in, but stop in the garden. Don't leave me and the two kiddies alone with that selfish bugger.' She remembered how Geoff Althorpe had annoyed her in the past, how he had stood for what seemed like hours going on and on about school, what he wanted, what he didn't want . . .

He smiled sadly. 'Language, Meggy.'

'Oh, go away. Deedee Wagstaff,' she chided, the levity of her tone denying inner turmoil.

She arranged herself in a chair by the window, forbade her hands to straighten her hair. What she looked like didn't matter. There was a job to be done, and she could not leave it to poor Mrs Althorpe. Mrs Althorpe was in Southport, anyway, had taken off for a fortnight with Evelyn Grimshaw. Megan couldn't help smilng about that, because Luke and Evelyn had been wonderful these past weeks. It was almost as if Luke had two wives, because he had taken to looking after Agnes, who was wont to say, 'He's brought me black puddings again. Will you have them?' And now, Luke Grimshaw had organized a holiday for his 'two brave lasses', one of whom was probably the wrong side of seventeen stones . . .

'Hello, Megan.'

She looked up, could not stop her jaw from dropping. He was beautiful. Weather had ripened his skin, had given it a sheen that screamed of good health and hard work. He had always been dark, but now he was the colour of creamy coffee. His hair was thick, its sun-lightened brownness cut close to the well-shaped head. 'Hello, Geoff.'

He placed himself in a chair opposite hers. 'It's good to see you again.' She was lovely, lovelier than he remembered. The thick hair was coiled at the nape of her neck, a few black tendrils escaping to frame her perfect face. The mouth had become generous, was eminently kissable. But really, it was her body that made him tremble. Since his return to England, everything had seemed disappointing, small, confined behind walls or covered in the filth of industry. But here sat the exception. She was rounded, ready for picking, mature and yet young, she was—

'Geoff?'

She was married. His eyes were cold as they fastened themselves to the band of gold on her left hand. 'Who?' he asked briskly.

'I beg pardon?'

'Who did you marry?'

'Billy, of course.'

He stiffened, sat bolt upright. 'He said nothing. We walked together down the lane, but he never mentioned being married to you. Why didn't the man speak up?'

'Why didn't you?' she asked softly.

He stared at her quizzically.

'Not one single word from you all these years, Geoff Althorpe. Have you no idea what your mother went through after you disappeared? Did you give no thought to your dad and Fliss? They were the ones who had to look after Mrs Althorpe. You broke her heart. She was on all sorts of pills for a long time. Why didn't you write?' She chided herself inwardly. With so much bad news to convey, she should not have gone for him. 'Sorry,' she muttered quietly.

The colour on his cheeks darkened. 'Because I wanted to become successful first. I wanted to come home when—'

Her apology was forgotten. 'In triumph? You wanted to come home to a brass band and bunting, is that it? I wanted, I wanted, I want. It's like a bloody chorus, isn't it? We should happen set it to music.'

He glowered, his hands clenched into tight fists. 'I changed my name so that I wouldn't be found. My idea was to make a good living, then come home for you.'

The clock sounded the quarter. 'I told you I'd never leave Bolton.'

'You might have changed your mind.'

'No.' She smoothed her cotton print skirt, cocked her head to one side as she listened for the babies to wake for feeding. 'I am very happy here, thank you.'

There was nothing more to be said. He rose slowly from the chair, made for the door.

'Sit down,' she said, the tone rather imperious.

He turned. 'Why? We've nothing to say. You're happily settled with a man who looks as interesting as boiled cabbage, so you won't want to spend time with me, will you?'

'Sit.'

Something in the timbre of her voice slowed his progress, but he had no intention of obeying her completely. Instead, he stood by the sideboard and waited for her to continue.

'Your mother is in Southport with Evelyn Grimshaw.'

He smirked. 'That will be no holiday for Mother. Even on her better days, Evelyn Grimshaw was barely tolerable.'

'Evelyn Grimshaw is still here, Geoff. She didn't dash off. And she and Mrs Althorpe have become the best of friends. People change, you know.' She cast an eye over him. 'Well, most people change, anyway.'

He suddenly felt gawky and schoolboyish, was reminded of the day when he had stood in Tommy Wagstaff's living room with a parcel of fish in his hot hand. She had always done this to him, had always made him awkward. 'Get to the point,' he said.

'I'm sure you should sit down.'

He heard the warning, folded his arms as if protecting himself. He was not afraid of her, could not possibly fear a mere mortal, especially one of the female variety. His conquests over recent years had been many. Women adored him, admired his good looks, his speech, the power he wielded in the workplace. Yes, the Australian girls loved him. Perhaps he should walk out of here now, out of the house, away from Hall i' th' Vale and back to a ship. 'Carry on.' The two words were trimmed with sarcasm, as if he dared her to do her worst.

She cleared her throat, wished she had more time. Geoff was a fool who had often angered her, but she felt no dislike for him. It was a shame that he had never found the courage to talk to his parents, because he might have stayed had some air been cleared. She studied him, tried to take the edge off the bombshell she was about to drop. 'Things have happened,' she began somewhat lamely.

'Things do happen, Megan.'

'Yes.' The babies would wake soon. She stiffened her spine, tried to inject some starch into her brain. 'Mr Althorpe's dead, you see.'

He closed his mouth with a snap. 'When?'

'Just over two months ago.'

'I see.' His legs felt a bit wobbly, as if the area around his knees had turned to jelly.

'And Fliss.' She paused, swallowed, drew breath. 'Fliss is dead, too.'

He groped with his hands, looked like a blind man as he staggered to the chair. 'No, no. Not Fliss.'

'I'm sorry.' And she was sorry. Not just for Fliss, but also for this misguided young man whose long awaited re-entry into England had become a total disaster.

His teeth chattered as he stammered one word, 'How?'

Megan rose from her chair, ordered herself to be charitable, bent down before him and took his hands. 'Geoff, they were both murdered. Well, Fliss was murdered and your dad died trying to save her. Surely this must have been reported in Australia?'

'I . . . I've been travelling for weeks. The ship . . . it takes a while. Murdered?'

She nodded, grasped his fingers tightly.

'Mother?'

'She wasn't involved, wasn't there when it happened.'

He opened his mouth wide, took in greedy gulps of air to still his heaving stomach. Fliss's stomach used to play up. So did Megan's. He looked into her eyes, saw pity and sadness. 'Why can't you love me?' he asked. 'If you could love me, I could bear all this.'

Something in Megan's chest went cold when she heard these words. He hadn't asked how or where or why, hadn't asked whether Sidney and Fliss had suffered. Even now, he was wrapped up in himself, was concerned only with his own pain.

She ran her tongue over her lower lip, told her temper to stay on its lead. 'I love Billy,' she said. 'And the children.'

'Children?' His voice cracked when it hit the second syllable. 'You have children?'

Megan nodded. 'They're like twins, I suppose. Phyllis and I were like twins, you know.' She was patting the backs of his hands as she spoke. 'My children are not real twins, Geoff. Helen is mine, Christopher is Fliss's. They were born on the same day in the same room.'

He frowned. 'Fliss was married, then.'

'No.'

The mantel clock marked another quarter. 'So the baby is . . . who was the father?'

'Phil Greenwood. He was a weaver at Number One. They'd known each other for years, but Phil's mother put

498

a stop to any chance of marriage. Only Phil wanted his own way, you see, and his mother was standing in his way. So he murdered her. I suppose that wouldn't have been in the Australian papers, because Mrs Greenwood had no connection with Australia. But Mr and Mrs Althorpe went to all kinds of trouble trying to find you. I believe the *Daily Herald* contacted the Australian papers in an attempt to have you found in time for your dad's and Fliss's funeral.'

He was looking through her, past her. 'I don't want the mills,' he said faintly. 'I'm going back.'

Megan jumped up, backed away from him. She stood with her feet apart, arms akimbo, cheeks blazing with fury. 'I never mentioned any bloody mills, did I? Your mother can run the mills blindfolded and with both hands tied, so can half the workforce. She did it when your dad was in bed with heart trouble. Don't be thinking you're needed to take over the reins, Geoff Althorpe.' She bit her lip, but failed to stem the tide. 'You're just like Phil Greenwood, you are. There's no trail of corpses, but you have no time for anybody but yourself. You kill people too, Geoff. In here.' She made a fist, beat her breast.

He shook his head in the manner of a person waking after a long sleep. 'A bad heart, you say?'

'Yes. Your dad had been ordered to rest, so your mother wouldn't let him out of the house for ages. She ran the mills for a while, then he started to get better. They were visiting me and Fliss in Chester when . . . when it happened.'

He still didn't understand. 'Who killed Fliss and Dad?'

'Phil Greenwood.'

'After murdering his mother?'

'That's right.'

He stood up, marched up and down the small room. Everything had gone disastrously wrong. He had come back to marry Megan, and the silly girl had fastened herself to that white-faced goon outside. Now Dad and Fliss were dead. He stopped mid-stride as the truth finally hit him. He had loved his dad, had loved his sister. They had both been kind to him. Now, the only one left was a mother who had forced him to attend that hateful school. 'We never got on, Mother and I. She expected the wrong things of me.'

'That was because she expected even more of herself. When your father married her, she never felt good enough. So she spent the following twenty years trying to live a lie. She's changed, too.'

'Oh.' Another thought found its way to his mouth. 'Why wasn't he in prison?'

Megan knew that his mind had reverted to the murderer. Like anyone in shock, he was having trouble sifting through the bad news. 'He cut his wrists in the police cell after being arrested for his mother's murder. They took him to hospital and he escaped.' She gulped, would not tell him the rest of the tale. If she and Billy had gone for the police that night, Fliss would have been alive today.

Geoff straightened. 'Where is he now?'

'Dead.'

He frowned. 'They hanged him rather quickly, didn't they?'

'Billy killed him.'

His eyes closed for a few seconds, then flew open to reveal terrible confusion. 'Billy? Your Billy?'

She nodded just once.

He walked to the fireplace, stood with his back to the grate, stared through the window at a killer who was tending a patch of garden. 'How did Fliss die?' he asked eventually.

'Shot.'

'Dad?'

'He broke down the door of the hut where Phil Greenwood was holding Fliss and the baby. I think his heart gave out under all the strain. But he was murdered, too, because he would have been here today except for Phil Greenwood.'

500

Geoff continued to stare at the man in the garden. He was so pale, so thin.

Megan cut into the visitor's thoughts, knotted them to her own. 'Billy's had a rough time,' she whispered. 'He got arrested, because he beat Phil Greenwood to death with the gun that killed Fliss. He's better than he was, Geoff. He can talk about it sometimes. But after what he's been through, he couldn't tell you all this bad news. Do you understand?'

He nodded dumbly.

A baby cried. Geoff lifted his eyes to the ceiling, stared so hard that he seemed to be trying to bore right through the plaster. 'And Fliss's baby is here.'

'Yes.'

He lowered his gaze, placed his attention on Megan. 'That was all so unnecessary,' he said. 'Phil Greenwood was not right for Fliss. She could have made a good marriage, but she would have her own way.'

'We all want our own way, Geoff.'

'Yes. Yes, I suppose we do. If I'd stayed . . .' If he had stayed, then Fliss would never have got into all that trouble. He could have been her mentor, her champion. He would have driven Phil Greenwood away . . .

'She loved him.'

He was so startled that he almost jumped. 'You always did know what I was thinking, Megan. You are the only woman I've ever felt close to.' He looked through the window again. 'Billy's a hero, then.'

Megan smiled sadly. 'What he did terrified him. Your dad was on the floor, already dead, I suppose. And Greenwood had Fliss by the throat. So Billy put an end to him.'

'And rightly so,' said Geoff Althorpe.

'Killing's never right,' she told him gently. 'But sometimes, it's understandable.'

'Quite.' His mother was alone now, alone and living in a barn of a place that had started life as an Elizabethan hall. What would people think of him if he sloped off to

Australia again while his mother was still grieving? 'How is my mother?'

She shrugged lightly, one ear tuned in to the stirring infants above. 'Better. She never went to the funerals, because she just . . . Well, I suppose she just slept. She wouldn't talk, then the doctor shook her out of it. I think your mother's a very strong woman, stronger than we all thought. And she's a business head on her, too. But she needed this rest, especially after working so hard.'

'Thank you, Megan,' he mumbled. 'I'm glad you're happy.' He wasn't. If she'd only been miserable, he might have persuaded her to go back with him.

'You're welcome. And I'm very, very sorry that I shouted at you.'

'No matter. What I always loved about you was the fact that you could have managed me. You're strong.'

'So was Fliss,' said Megan. 'That was why Phil Greenwood wanted her.' She looked hard at him. 'Have you changed? Is there any chance that you've finally grown up?'

'I suppose so. Australia makes you mature pretty quickly. For a start, there's the weather. In some parts of Queensland, we get a hundred and eighty inches of rain.' He walked to her side. 'Oh God, why did they have to die like that?'

She was pleased that he seemed to have stopped thinking about himself for the moment. 'That's a question we've all been asking God, but He's not seen fit to answer yet.'

'I mean, what am I going to do about Mother?'

Icy steel entered Megan's chest again. 'We'll look after her. There's no need for you to worry about her.'

'That wouldn't be right. She and the child must be cared for. Even if . . . what did you say his name was?'

'Christopher.'

'Even if Christopher is a bas— a love child, he is one of my family.'

She folded her arms. 'Your mother doesn't want him. Billy and I are going to adopt him.'

Geoff smiled with the air of a schoolmaster who has decided to be kind to one of his many wayward charges. 'That won't do, I'm afraid. The boy is an Althorpe.'

'And I'm a Shipton. So I'm not good enough, is that it?'

His head turned of its own accord to glance at Billy.

Megan lifted her head high. 'Ah, so my husband's not good enough. As long as I know where we stand, Mr Althorpe. After all, with your dad dead you're head of the family, aren't you? Or are you? You'll find your mother's tougher than she used to be. If she wants me to have Christopher, then I'll have him. And there won't be a damn thing you can do about it.'

'We'll see,' he muttered.

She breathed a sigh of relief as he left the house. Being loved by a man like Geoff Althorpe was not comfortable. She thanked her lucky stars that she had not loved him in return, then climbed the stairs to feed her children.

The meeting was held in the Lancashire kitchen. It had never been used as a kitchen, as it had been prepared for the days to come when Hall i' th' Vale would be a museum.

Agnes Althorpe sat at the head of the long, rough-hewn table, while her son occupied a seat directly opposite hers. To Agnes's right, Deedee, Tommy and Joe had settled, and Megan and Billy sat to her left with a solicitor, a crusty grey man with a crusty grey beard. He shuffled papers, blew his nose, pulled one end of his moustache out of his mouth. 'Shall we begin?' he asked.

Agnes shook her head. 'There are others to come,' she said.

Everyone looked at the row of chairs in front of the huge grate. Who else could possibly be expected? They sighed, shuffled about, wondered what Agnes was up to this time. She'd become a bit firm lately, especially since Geoff had arrived from the blue. There had been no fatted calf for him. According to Mary Watson, the mistress had kissed him, asked him how he was, then carried on writing a letter of thanks to some newspaper whose editor had sung Billy Shipton's praises after Greenwood's death.

The solicitor cleared his throat, then made much of pulling a gold hunter from his pocket.

'You'll be paid for your time,' said Agnes sweetly.

The man coloured, carried on messing about with the ribbons on a cardboard file.

Mary Weston entered from the smaller kitchen, carrying a tray with tea, cakes and small sandwiches. While these refreshments were consumed, a hum of self-conscious chit-chat flitted about the table. There were discussions on the weather, a show at the Theatre Royal and the fact that Paddy and Phyllis O'Riley had finally taken over the local post office properly. 'He'll still do the mission,' Deedee informed them. 'But he'll have helpers, so he can be at home a bit more.'

Tommy asked whether anyone had seen Geranium, and Megan Shipton had difficulty keeping the relief out of her voice when she answered in the negative. Geranium, a docile-looking tortoiseshell, could strip several layers of paint plus undercoat from any door in thirty seconds.

'She's a farm cat,' said Tommy to no-one in particular. 'Farm cats have ways.'

As no member of the meeting invited further explanation, the subject died a natural death.

'Who are we waiting for, Mother?' asked Geoff at last.

'People who've been good to me,' answered Agnes. 'Those who've been around when I've needed them.'

The young master of the house lowered his glowering face and took a sip of tea.

'The nights are drawing in,' remarked Mr Ponsonby. Mr Ponsonby, of Smith, Smith and Atkinson, was not blessed with an imagination. He had drawn up all the necessary papers, and he wanted to be home before dark.

'Not long now,' said Agnes.

The maid returned with several people behind her. She

waved them in, waited till they were seated by the grate, then exited without a word. In front of the spit and an old copper cauldron sat Phyllis and Paddy O'Riley, then three men whose clothes and shoes had been cleaned for the occasion. Megan smiled at the man with the shiny knees, because his trousers were so old that they glinted as brightly as his boots.

'These are the new managers of the Althorpe mills,' said Agnes by way of introduction. 'As my son has decided to spend his life abroad, I thought I should bring in some help, because I'm not getting any younger. Mr Fisher, Mr Cornwell and Mr Roberts will be taking complete charge of the mills as from Monday of next week. Mr Fisher is going to be the general manager, and Mr Cornwell and Mr Roberts are to take on the running of one mill each.'

No-one could think of a word to say.

Agnes continued. 'Mr and Mrs O'Riley are here about another matter. As they are to take joint charge of the post office, and since I know full well that they are concerned about the mission, I wanted to take this opportunity to reassure them that the work will be funded in part from my own money.'

Paddy rose, his mouth ready to frame his gratitude, but he sat down again when Agnes shook her head. He gripped Phyllis's hand tightly, then waited for further instructions.

'There is no need for you to stay any longer,' Agnes advised the people near the fireplace. 'But I wanted those present to bear witness to my intentions. Mary will serve tea in the library.' When the five newcomers had left, Agnes gave her attention to Mr Ponsonby. 'Your turn, I think,' she said.

He rose to his feet with much scraping of chair legs on the flag floor, adjusted his papers, fixed an aged pince-nez on the bridge of his nose. This was a squat man with a great deal of stomach, and everyone's gaze seemed to be fixed on the buttons of his waistcoat, as this item of clothing was under tremendous stress.

'It'll burst wide open in a minute,' Megan told Billy in a whisper.

Billy, who was cheering up very nicely of late, coughed politely behind a hand.

'Well now.' The solicitor cleared his throat, the action causing further strain on the row of six buttons. 'Sadly, Mr Althorpe passed away some weeks ago. We are all aware of that, and I'm sure that I can offer our joint condolences for the loss of a husband and father. Miss Felicity, too, has passed away, and this second death has a bearing on what is to happen here this afternoon.'

Geoff wore the air of a man who has heard it all before. He leaned back in his chair and studied the ceiling.

Mr Ponsonby carried on, his tone somewhat shrill and breathless due to the tightness of his clothing. 'When Mr Althorpe made his latest will, he knew nothing of the whereabouts of Mr Geoffrey Althorpe. Because of that, he left everything in the hands of his wife.' He beamed at the lady in question. 'And she proposes to dispose of her assets in the following fashion.'

'But you've not died,' interrupted Deedee. 'You can't have your will read while you're still here. It's not right, it's not decent.'

Tommy took his wife's hand. 'Shut up now, Deedee. She can do what she wants.' He nodded at Mr Ponsonby. 'You carry on, lad. Take no notice.'

Mr Ponsonby peered over the pince-nez, received a nod from the lady of the house. 'Hall i' th' Vale is to continue in the care of Mr Joseph Duffy.' He beamed kindly at Joe. 'Your salary is to be increased, and the house known as Twisted Stacks is to be yours without rent. In fact, the deeds of the cottage will be placed in your possession within the week.'

Joe fixed his astonished gaze on Agnes. 'Thank you,' he mouthed.

The fat lawyer opened two buttons, and his waistcoat seemed to breathe a sigh of relief before standing at ease. 'Warm day,' offered the waistcoat's owner by way of explanation. 'Megan and William Shipton are now the owners of the Gate House. They will also adopt the child known as Christopher Althorpe-Shipton.'

Megan could not help herself. The mixed feelings showed in her face as she spoke. 'You don't know him,' she told Agnes. 'When you know him, you'll want him.' Parting from one of her 'twins' would cause great pain, but she would prefer Agnes's decision to be an educated one.

'She knows him,' said Deedee. 'Every time you've gone to the leather works for a couple of hours at the weekend, Agnes has minded him.'

Megan's jaw sagged slightly.

'He needs a young mother,' explained Agnes. 'And a good father. Don't worry, I shall always be his grandmother.'

The solicitor picked up his thread and another sheaf of notes. 'The child Christopher is to continue to be known as Christopher Althorpe-Shipton. At some time in the future, he is to be told of his origins. Christopher Althorpe-Shipton will inherit the mills. The rest of the estate is to be divided between him and any legal heirs born to Geoffrey Althorpe.'

The expression on Geoff's face had changed in recent moments. He had travelled from knowing, to accepting, to disbelieving without ever leaving the table. But now, he jumped to his feet. 'Why are all these people here?' he cried. 'How can you display all the dirty linen in front of people who aren't family?'

'These are all the family I have had,' answered Agnes.

'I am your family,' he roared, one fist beating melodramatically against the broad chest. 'I am your son.'

'You are a stranger,' she replied softly. 'I have missed so many of your years that I am now having to learn you all over again. You went away. You went away because, unlike your sister, you had not the spine to stay and weather the storm. I love you.' She nodded her head, as if trying to convince herself. 'But I don't know you at all.'

'Mother!' The fist made sharp contact with the table.

507

She held up her hand. 'Geoffrey, you have made a good life for yourself. How many here have a house that overlooks the Great Barrier Reef? You have partnerships in so many mines . . .' She counted on her fingers. 'There's lead, copper, silver, zinc, opal – need I go on? And, wisely, you have taken an interest in transporting goods and people all over Queensland so that the outposts will be served and encouraged to grow.' She smiled at him. 'You don't need my bit of money, because you have inherited the finest gift of all. That gift is from your father. You have his eye for business, Geoffrey. Use it and use it well.'

Beneath the tan, he blanched until his skin was several shades paler than it had been at the beginning of the meeting. He pushed back his chair, ignored the clatter when it fell to the floor, then he stalked out of the room.

Agnes bit her lip, closed her eyes.

'Shall I fetch him?' asked Megan.

'No.' I lost him years ago, Agnes told herself firmly. He cares for no-one but himself, and my chances of finding him now are no better than they were years ago and ten thousand miles ago. She opened her eyes, looked at Mr Ponsonby.

'The preparation of Hall i' th' Vale as a museum and park is to begin immediately. Mr Wagstaff and Mr Duffy will be briefed later in this matter, as Mrs Althorpe is concerned that all aspects of cotton in Lancashire should be displayed, from the latest looms and mules to those used by cottagers before the mills.'

Deedee sat bolt upright. 'Nay, you're never going to live in a museum, are you?'

For the first time that day, Agnes smiled broadly. 'I already live in a museum, Doris, except for the fact that it's not finished.' She allowed a few beats of time to pass. 'I'm moving to Southport,' she announced excitedly. 'Evelyn and I found the house during our holiday. We also found a lock-up butcher's shop and a second house just like mine. Luke has been persuaded, so we are all going to live at the seaside.'

508

Megan clapped her hands. 'That's wonderful,' she said, her eyes wet with happiness. It was right that Mrs Althorpe should have something for herself, something new.

'And you'll all come for holidays,' Agnes told them.

Mr Ponsonby, who was a bachelor but not by choice, preened himself and fastened his waistcoat. But he needn't have bothered, because the mistress of Hall i' th' Vale was smiling at everyone except him. He undid a few buttons as a compromise, fixed his eyes on the documents before him. 'That's about all,' he said. 'Except for payments concerning your servants. Yes, yes, our business is concluded.'

'Not quite,' said Agnes. She allowed her smile to die, then rose to her feet. 'I want to thank each and every one of you for your support over the years. Doris – or Deedee – you have made my clothes and made my life interesting. Tommy, thanks for all the cups of tea and for all the stories about your cats.'

Tommy blushed, scraped a hand across his sandpaper chin.

'Did you shave before you came out?' asked his wife.

'Shut up,' grumbled the old man. 'Let me get a bit of praise for a change, besom.'

When the self-conscious laughter had died, Agnes turned her attention to Joe. 'You were a good friend to my husband,' she said softly. 'He trusted you implicitly.'

Joe mumbled his thanks, wished he'd brought a hanky.

'And Megan.' Agnes's expression softened. 'You and your grandmother were so good to my daughter. She told me that you, Megan, had become a sister to her. I know that she would have wanted Christopher to live with you and Billy.'

Billy's turn was next. 'What can I say to you?' asked Agnes. 'In court, you said that you regretted killing Greenwood. Billy, you are a fine young man.'

He looked around the table, saw all the kindness in the

faces. Even Mr Ponsonby looked a bit watery and down in the mouth. 'I am sorry,' said Billy. He hadn't talked in company about that night, not since court, anyway. 'Oh, I have my regrets,' he said now. 'Happen I shouldn't have hit him so hard, because I spent too much time on him. If I'd clouted him a bit less, I might have had the chance to save Fliss from bleeding to death.'

A silence hung over the room as each person remembered Fliss.

'She was . . . powerful,' said Megan at last. 'Without ever being unkind. Fliss was the sort of person who could have changed the whole world through kindness. I never met anyone cleverer than Fliss.'

Agnes stared at the beautiful young woman who had just verbalized everyone's thoughts. 'Look inside yourself, Megan,' she said. 'Because you are the mirror image of my little girl. All that you've just said about Fliss is true, but it applies to you as well. Go and look after my grandson. And when you have a minute to spare, change the world with your goodness.'

When the meeting broke up, there was not a single dry eye in Sidney Althorpe's Lancashire kitchen.

The young woman walked along Dog Leg Lane, a small child clinging to each of her hands. Ahead of her and just around the corner was Hall i' th' Vale museum with its beautiful facade and gardens. Members of the public often travelled up this track to look at prize-winning roses and perfect lawns, were guided round the house by a Mr Duffy who had learned his history well.

Helen stopped to pick buttercups while Christopher clung fiercely to the hand of the only mother he had ever known. At five, he was intelligent, bright enough to have been told that he was different, that Megan had chosen him specially to be her son. He had become fairer than Helen, with nut-brown hair and clear green eyes. Helen was as dark as her mother, with eyes of a startling blue.

'Mum?' said the little boy.

510

'Yes?'

'When I grow up, can I make things from leather?'

'If you want to.'

'I don't have to work at the mills, do I?' A nice lady called Granny Agnes had told him about the mills last week.

'No, you don't have to.'

He smiled, let go of her hand, went to join his sister. Christopher would be going to Australia soon. With mixed feelings, Megan fixed her eyes on this precious son. Yes, she was glad that the rift between Agnes and Geoff had healed. Yes, six weeks in another country would be a wonderful experience for Christopher. Helen, too, had been invited, as had Megan and Billy. But Megan had decided to stand back while Agnes and Geoff enjoyed Fliss's son. And Agnes might change her mind, as might Geoff. The latter could grow tired of Australia, could return and run the mills. Whatever, the Althorpes needed much space and time. In a few weeks, Geoff and Agnes would have chances for discussion.

Megan leaned against a stile, watched her children as they struggled to make a buttercup chain. In a minute, they would start to walk the rest of the crooked mile to find Grandpa Joe. Grandpa Joe and Uncle Joseph were the minders of the great house. And there was a new Granny called Maureen. She had a bike. Everyone made fun of her bike, because she'd chased Grandpa Joe for years. 'Too slow,' Deedee often said to her son. 'You should have got some roller skates, Joe.' Megan laughed to herself, thought back to her wedding day when Maureen had paid a lad to detach her chain. But Maureen was right for Dad. She made him laugh and was beginning to iron a few of the worry lines out of his face.

'Can't see it from here,' remarked Helen after spitting out a length of buttercup stalk.

It was true, thought Megan, true in more ways than one. Along the crooked mile, there was much to see. But once the bend was reached, the view altered beyond compare. The moors were still there in the background, and fields provided a radiant frame for the Hall's splendour. But a newcomer would have been surprised at the change, because his eye would probably home in immediately on unexpected Elizabethan splendour.

Life was a crooked mile, she thought. People got born, learned early on what their setting would be. But many of them would reach a bend in the road and find another view. Billy was all right now. The angle in his road had taken him into fear and horror, but his path had evened itself out with the passage of time. Deedee, a great-grandmother, had endured many changes of direction, yet she still enjoyed her time with Tommy.

Megan blinked. The crookedness of life's miles was sometimes kind. Had her sisters and her mother known that death was just around their corner, they would have known no happiness at all. She liked to imagine that all the Duffy girls had dreamed of days when the garden streets would fade away into the distance, that Tess Duffy had looked forward to having a son, perhaps two. The bends in life's road were essential.

Helen smiled up at her mother and began to say the rhyme.

> 'There was a crooked man
> And he walked a crooked mile
> Found a crooked sixpence
> Upon a crooked stile.'

Megan laughed out loud, gathered up her twins and walked on towards the next bend in her road.